THE BARBOUR COLLECTION OF CONNECTICUT TOWN VITAL RECORDS

THE BARBOUR COLLECTION OF CONNECTICUT TOWN VITAL RECORDS

DURHAM 1708–1852

EASTFORD 1847–1851

EAST HADDAM 1743–1857

Compiled by

Lorraine Cook White

Genealogical Publishing Co., Inc.
Baltimore, Maryland

Library of Congress Catalogue Card Number 94-76197
International Standard Book Number 0-8063-1544-X
Made in the United States of America

INTRODUCTION

As early as 1640 the Connecticut Court of Election ordered all magistrates to keep a record of the marriages they preformed. In 1644 the registration of births and marriages became the official responsibility of town clerks and registrars, with deaths added to their duties in 1650. From 1660 until the close of the Revolutionary War these vital records of birth, marriage, and death were generally well kept, but then for a period of about two generations until the mid-nineteenth century, the faithful recording of vital records declined in some towns.

General Lucius Barnes Barbour was the Connecticut Examiner of Public Records from 1911 to 1934 and in that capacity directed a project in which the vital records kept by the towns up to about 1850 were copied and abstracted. Barbour previously had directed the publication of the Bolton and Vernon vital records for the Connecticut Historical Society. For this new project he hired several individuals who were experienced in copying old records and familiar with the old script.

Barbour presented the completed transcriptions of town vital records to the Connecticut State Library where the information was typed onto printed forms. The form sheets were then cut, producing twelve small slips from each sheet. The slips for most towns were then alphabetized and the information was then typed a second time on large sheets of rag paper, which were subsequently bound into separate volumes for each town. The slips for all towns were then interfiled, forming a statewide alphabetized slip index for most surviving town vital records.

The dates of coverage vary from town to town, and of course the records of some towns are more complete than others. Altogether the entire Barbour Collection--one of the great genealogical manuscript collections and one of the last to be published--covers 137 towns and comprises 14,333 typed pages.

INTRODUCTION

TABLE OF CONTENTS

ABBREVIATIONS

ae.------------age
b. ------------born, both
bd.------------buried
B. G.---------Burying Ground
bp.----------- baptized
d. ------------died, day, or daughter
decd.---------deceased
f.-------------father
h.-------------hour
J. P.-----------Justice of Peace
m.-------------married or month
res.------------resident
s.-------------son
st.-------------stillborn
w. -----------wife
wid.----------widow
wk.-----------week
y. -----------year

THE BARBOUR COLLECTION OF CONNECTICUT TOWN VITAL RECORDS

DURHAM VITAL RECORDS
1708 - 1852

	Page
ADAMS, Joseph, of Cleaveland, O., m. Louisa **CLARKE**, of Middletown, Oct. 17, 1847	442
Margaret, m. Caleb **CARR**, Feb. 11, [1735], by Rev. Elizur Goodrich	327
ADDRES, Elizabeth, d. Thomas, bp. Oct. 5, [1777]	326
AKINS, [see also **ATKINS**], Robert, m. wid. Sarah **LYMAN**, Mar. 23, 1758, by Rev. Elizur Goodrich	327
Sarah, d. Robert & Sarah, bp. Mar. 11, [1759]	308
Sarah, wid., m. Elias **AUSTIN**, Nov. 9, [1772], by Rev. Elizur Goodrich	332
Seth, s. Robert & Sarah, bp. July 25, [1762]	312
ALBY, Calvin, of Saybrook, m. Maria **SCRANTON**, of Durham, Jan. 14, 1836	437
ALFRED, Rachel, d. Thomas, Jr., bp. Apr. 22, 1733	268
ALLEN, Ann, had d. Dolle, b. Feb. 13, 1771	394
Dolle, d. Ann, b. Feb. 13, 1771	394
Gideon, s. Mabel **GLOYDE**, bp. Jan. 22, 1743/4; father Gideon **LEETE**	283
Sarah, d. Feb. 25, 1803	410
ALVORD, ALVERD, ALUORD, [see also **AVERD**], Aaron, m. Mehetabel **STRONG**, Nov. 6, 1739	362
Aaron, s. Aaron & Mehitabel, bp. July 23, 1749	289
Abigail, d. Elisha & Hannah, bp. June 29, 1746	286
Amy, d. Aaron & Mehetabel, bp. May 25, 1755	297
Asahel, bp. Feb. 21, 1741/2	280
Belah, s. Aaron & Mehethabel (Mabel), b. Aug. 31, 1741; bp. Sept. 6, 1741	279,362
Eliphaz, s. Jonathan, bp. Jan. 17, 1741/2	280
Katharine, d. Aaron & Mehitable, bp. Mar. 28, 1747	287
Katharine, d. Aaron & Mabel, bp. Nov. 11, 1750	292
Lucy, d. Aaron & Mehetabel, bp. Apr. 26, 1752	294
Mahethabel, d. Aaron & Mehethabel, b. Oct. 1, 1745; bp. Oct. 6, 1745	285,363
Selah, s. Aaron & Mehethabel, b. Mar. 26, 1743; bp. Mar. 27, 1743	281,362
Thomas Gold, s. Asahel & Mary, bp. Mar. 7, 1741/2	280
ANDREWS, [see also **ANDRUS**], Asahael, s. Joseph & Betsey, b. Dec. 4, 1816	421
Benjamin, s. Joseph & Betsey, b. May 24, 1819	421
Frances E., m. Ezra G. **JOHNSON**, Apr. 19, 1840	439
ANDRUS, [see also **ANDREWS**], Abigail, m. Joel **PARMALEE**, June 30, 1706	354

Page

ANDRUS, (cont.)
Anne, m. Amos **CAMP**, Dec. 18, 1716, by James Wadsworth, J. P. 343
ARNOLD, Charles G., m. Betsey M. **SMITH**, Sept. 19, 1841 439
James, Lieut., m. Tabatha **PARSONS**, b. of Durham, Feb. 21 (27), 1765, by Rev. Elizur Goodrich 329.387
James, s. James & Tabatha, b. Oct. 26, 1782 402
James, Col., d. Aug. 25, 1806 411
James C., m. Abigail **FLAGG**, Mar. 9, 1831 435
Tabitha, d. Col. James & Tabitha, b. Dec. 27, 1776 399
Whiting, s. James & Tabatha, b. Sept. 25, 1785 403
ATKINS, [see also **AKINS**], Adeline, of Middletown, m. William **STEVENS**, of Berlin, Sept. 25, 1843 440
Elihu, m. Ruth **BALDWIN**, Oct. 29, 1772, by Rev. Elizur Goodrich 332
ATWELL, Bishop, s. Jesse & Phebe, b. Dec. 4, 1812 415
Electa, [d. Jesse & Mary], b. Mar. 5, 1776 401
Fanny, [d. Jesse & Mary], b. Aug. 8, 1774; bp. [1774] 324,401
George, s. Jesse & Phebe, b. Oct. 17, 1805 415
Harriet, [d. Jesse & Mary], b. June 25, 1781 401
Henry, s. Jesse & Phebe, b. Dec. 7, 1791 415
Jesse, m. Mary ______, June 16, 1767 401
Jesse, s. Jesse & Marah (Mary), b. Feb. 28, 1770 395,401
Jesse, d. July 11, 1781 401
Molly, d. Jesse & Mary, bp. Mar. 26, [1769] 318
Polly, d. Jesse & Marah (Mary), b. Feb. 16, 1768 395,401
Salle, d. Jesse & Marah (Mary), b. Mar. 17, 1772; bp. Mar. 22, [1772] 321,395,401
William, [s. Jesse & Mary], b. July 2, 1778 401
William, s. Jesse & Phebe, b. Dec. 9, 1809 415
AULIFFE, John M., m. Matilda **ROBINSON**, Aug. 16, 1840 439
AUSTIN, Abigail, d. Jess & Elizabeth, b. Dec. 4, 1758; d. Sept. 12, 1760; bp. Feb. 4, 1759 308,379
Abraham, s. Moses & Hannah, bp. Sept. 29, 1751 293
Archibald, s. Elias & Eunice, bp. Feb. 3, 1754 295
Dorothy, d. Moses & Hannah, bp. Nov. 29, 1747 288
Elias, m. wid. Sarah **AKINS**, Nov. 9, [1772], by Rev. Elizur Goodrich 332
Elijah, s. Elias & Eunice, bp. Feb. 2, 1751/2 293
Elisha, s. Jesse & Elizabeth, bp. Oct. [ ], [1767] 317
Elizabeth, d. Jane **LEWIS**, bp. Jan. 16, [1757] 306
Elizabeth, d. Jesse & Elizabeth, bp. Oct. 8, [1769] 319
Gloriana, d. Elias & Eunice, bp. Feb. 11, 1759 308
Hannah, d. Moses, bp. Oct. 1, [1758] 308
Hophni, twin with Phinehas, child of Elias & Eunice, bp. Apr. 10, [1757] 306
James, s. Jess & Elizabeth, b. Mar. 5, 1763; bp. Mar. 13, [1763] 312,381
Jess, m. Elizabeth **WARD**, Jan. 26, 1758 379
Joel, m. Esther **PARMALEE**, May 12, 1840 439
Martha, d. Elias & Eunice, bp. Aug. 10, 1746 286
Martha, d. Elias & Eunice, bp. Dec. 10, 1749 290

Page

AUSTIN, (cont.)
Moses, of Wallingford, m. Lucy **SEWARD**, of Durham, Mar. 26, [1761], by Rev. Elizur Goodrich 328
Moses, s. Elias & Eunice, bp. Oct. 11, 1761 311
Nabe, d. Jess & Elizabeth, b. Mar. 7, 1761; bp. Mar. 8, [1761] 310,379
Phinehas, twin with Hophni, s. Elias & Eunice, bp. Apr. 10, [1757] 306
Sarah, d. Jess & Elizabeth, bp. July 7, [1765] 315
Stephen, s. Elias & Eunice, bp. Nov. 29, 1747 288
Thaddeus, s. Moses & Hannah, bp. June 16, [1754] 295
Thomas, s. Jesse & Elizabeth, bp. Mar. 12, [1774] 324
----, d. Jess & Elizabeth, bp. May 10, 1772 322
AVERD, AUERED, AVERED, [see also **ALVORD**], Abigail, d. Israel & Abigail, b. Mar. 1, 1733/4 359
Ann, d. Israel & Abigail, b. Jan. 15, 1740/1; bp. Jan. 18, 1740[1] 278,359
Hannah, d. Israel, bp. July 26, 1747 287
Israel, m. Abigail **BEACH**, Aug. 25, 1731, by Rev. Mr. Bliss, of Hebron 359
Mical, s. Israel* & Abigail, b. July 29, 1732; bp. Aug. 21, [1732] (*First written "James" in bp., then changed to "Israel") 267,359
Sarah, d. Samuel & Abigail, bp. May 6, 1744 283
AVERY, Ichabod, m. Martha **POMEROY**, Aug. 13, 1841 439
BABCOCK, Anne, m. Frederick **CRANE**, Jan. 1, 1778 400
BACON, Daniel, of Williamstown, m. Hannah **ROBINSON**, of Durham, Aug. 20, [1767], by Rev. Elizur Goodrich 330
BAILEY, Alelia, m. John **GRAVES**, Dec. 5, 1825 432
Alpha M., m. Augustus **SEWARD**, Feb. 27, 1840 439
Amelia, d. Jabez & Lucretia, b. Dec. 10, 1810 419
Austin, m. Mary R. **BRAINARD**, Oct. 25, 1824 432
Catharine, of Durham, m. Horace **WOODING**, of Hamden, Conn., Oct. 1, 1848 443
Daniel J., s. Jabez & Lucretia, b. June 10, 1817 419
Henry, m. Mary **PARSONS**, Aug. 12, 1837 438
Henry E., m. Martha J. **BROOKS**, Mar. 27, 1842 440
Henry W., s. Jabez & Lucretia, b. Dec. 20, 1812 419
John, m. Ursula **SCRANTON**, Jan. 1, 1839 438
Julia A., d. Jabez & Lucretia, b. Nov. 18, 1820 419
Julia E.,, d. Jabez & Lucretia, b. Nov. 27, 1814; d. Aug. 23, 1815 419
Justus I., m. Eunice E. **LYNN**, b. of Durham, May 4, 1845 441
Lydia, m. Worthington **SCRANTON**, b. of Durham, Mar. 10, 1845 441
Reuben, of Haddam, m. Rhoda **FAIRCHILD**, of Durham, Aug. 27, 1777, by Rev. Elizur Goodrich 333
Stephen, of Durham, m. Nancy **MERRIMAN**, of Wallingford, Oct. 25, 1846 442
William Y., m. Sarah **STEVENS**, Nov. 25, 1830 435
BAKER, Phebe, w. of Samuel, bp. Jan. 22, 1731/2; d. two days after 266
Ruth, bp. Mar. 26, 1732 266
Ruth, m. Joseph **FOWLER**, Apr. 2, 1736, by Rev. Nathaniel Chauncey 356

Page
BALDWIN, Aaron, s. Moses & Abigail, bp. Jan. 25, 1729/30 264
Aaron, s. Abial & Mehitabel, b. Nov. 8, 1770; bp. Nov. 11, 1770 320,393
Abiel, s. Ezra & Ruth, bp. May 3, 1730 264
Abiel, s. Abiel & Mehitabel, b. Aug. 28, 1762; bp. Aug. 29, 1762 312,381
Abiel, m. Mehethabel **JOHNSON**, Apr. 1, 1756 372
Abiel, d. Aug. 11, 1802 409
Abner, s. David & Abigail, b. May 27, 1726; bp. May 28, 1726 261,347
Adah, d. Noah & Mehetabel, bp. Apr. 18, [1773] 323
Amos, s. Ezra & Ruth, bp. Apr. 22, 1744 283
Ann, of Durham, m. Samuel **ROBINSON**, of Madison, Sept. 12, 1827 433
Ann Bates, d. Timothy W. & Ann, b. May 15, 1831 428
Anna, d. Reuben & Mabel, b. Nov. 18, 1787 422
Curtiss, s. Abiel & Mehethabel, b. June 20, 1766 386
David, s. Abial & Mehithabel, b. Nov. 23, 1768; bp. Dec. 4, [1768] 318,389
Eben, s. Ezra & Ruth, bp. Mar. 9, 1734/5 270
Ebenezer, of Granville, m. Lois **WETMORE**, of Middletown, Mar. 5, 1759, by Rev. Elizur Goodrich 327
Ebenezer Gurnsey, s. Timothy W. & Ann, b. Feb. 22, 1825 426
Elnathan, s. Ezra & Ruth, bp. May 25, 1746 286
Eunice, d. Abiel & Mehithabel, b. Aug. 2, 1760; bp. Aug. 10, [1760] 310,376
Eunice, d. Reuben & Mabel, b. June 25, 1785 422
Ezra, twin with ----, s. Ezra & Ruth, bp. May 8, 1737 273
Ezra, Jr., m. Elizabeth **LYMAN**, b. of Durham, May 16, [1764], by Rev. Elizur Goodrich 329
Ezra, s. Reubon & Eunice, bp. Mar. 27, [1774] 324
Hannah, m. Josiah **FOWLER**, June 6, 1723 353
Hannah, d. Noah & Mehethabel, b. Dec. 15, 1762; bp. Dec. 19, 1762; d. Feb. 4, 1763 312,385
Hannah, d. Noah & Mehetabel, bp. Nov. 27, 1774 325
Hezekiah, s. Noah & Mehetabel, bp. Sept. 1, 1771 321
Isaac, m. Alva **MERWIN**, Sept. 17, 1823 431
James, s. Noah & Mehetabel, bp. Dec. 10, [1769] 319
John R., of Menden, Ill., m. Mary Ann **COE**, of Durham, Jan. 23, 1842 439
Jonathan, s. Abiel & Mehethabel, b. June 6, 1758; bp. June 11, [1758] 307,374
Martha, d. David & Abigail, b. Dec. 23, 1728; bp. Dec. 29, [1728] 263,347
Mary, d. David & Abigail, b. Mar. 22, 1723 347
Mary, d. David & Hannah **STEPHENS**, d. of Thomas, bp. Mar. 24, 1723 258
Mehithabel, d. Abiel & Mehithabel, b. May 21, 1764; bp. May 27, 1764 314,384
Noah, s. Ezra & Ruth, bp. Sept. 2, 1739 276
Noah, m. Mehetabel **PARMALEE**, July 30, [1760], by Rev. Elizur Goodrich 327,380
Noah, s. Noah & Mehetabel, bp. Feb. 28, 1768 317
Phebe, d. Ezra & Ruth, bp. Oct. 1, 1732 267
Phebe, m. Elah **CAMP**, May 14, 1760, by Rev. Elizur Goodrich 327,378

Page

BALDWIN, (cont.)
Phebe, d. Noah & Mehitabel, b. June 3, 1761; bp. June 4, [1761]; d. June 4, 1761 311,380
Phebe, d. Noah & Mahethabel, b. Dec. 4, 1763; bp. Dec. 4, [1763]; d. Dec. 31, 1763 313,385
Reuben, s. Ezra & Ruth, b. Apr. 29, 1749; bp. Apr. [ ], 1749 289,421
Reuben, m. Eunice **CAMP**, May 27, 1773, by Rev. Elizur Goodrich 332
Reuben, m. Mabel **JONES**, June 4, 1782 422
Rhoda, d. Abiel & Mehethable, b. Jan. 25, 1757; bp. Feb. 6, [1757]; d. May 30, 1766 306,373,386
Ruth, d. Ezra & Ruth, bp. Oct. 25, 1741 279
Ruth, d. Ezra & Ruth, bp. Mar. 22, 1751/2 294
Ruth, m. Elihu **ATKINS**, Oct. 29, 1772, by Rev. Elizur Goodrich 332
Ruth, d. Abial & Mehitabel, b. Oct. 30, 1772; bp. Nov. 2, [1772] 322,395
Sarah, d. Noah & Mehethabel, b. Nov. 13, 1765; bp. Nov. 17, 1765 315,387
Seth, s. Abial & Mehitabel, b. Apr. 27, 1775; bp. Apr. 30, [1775] 325,398
Smith Samuel, of Martinsburg, N. Y., m. Mary **FAIRCHILD**, of Durham, Oct. 17, 1839 439
Timothy W., of North Guildford, m. Ann **BATES**, of Durham, May 16, 1821 430
William A., m. Betsey **CAMP**, Sept. 22, 1830 435
----, s. Abiel & Mehetabel, bp. June 15, [1766] 315
----, twin with Ezra, child of Ezra & Ruth, st. b. [ ] 273

BALL, Abigail, of Springfield, m. Moses **PARSONS**, s. Joseph, of Northampton, Mass., Jan. 20, 1710. Removed to Durham about 1710 352
Hannah, d. David & Elizabeth, bp. Nov. 10, 1745 285
Humfrey, of Lebanon, m. Ruth **GRISWOLD**, of Durham, Apr. 23, 1766, by Rev. Elizur Goodrich 329
Mary, d. David & Eliz[abeth], bp. Feb. 28, 1747/8 288

BARNES, BARNS, Benjamin, of Granville, m. Mary **COE**, of Durham, May 12, [1763], by Rev. Elizur Goodrich 328
Bethiah, wid., bp. Aug. 26, 1739 276
Daniel, s. John & Bethiah, bp. Nov. 25, 1739 276
John, [s. of wid. Bethiah], bp. Aug. 26, 1739 276
Mehetabel, [d. wid. Bethiah], bp. Aug. 26, 1739 276
Mehetabel, of Middlefield, m. Benjamin **SMITH**, Jan. 29, 1761, by Rev. Elizur Goodrich 328
Moses B., m. Martha J. **GALPIN**, Feb. 1, 1842 440
Patience, m. Daniel **SQUIRE**, Sept. 1, 1730, by John Russell, J. P. 356
Seneca, of Northford, m. Mary **HART**, of Durham, Nov. 1, 1835 437

BARRET, Parsons, s. Richard & Sarah, b. June 7, 1784 403
Polly, d. Richard & Sarah, b. Apr. 9, 1794 406
Richard, d. May 5, 1822 417
Sally, d. Richard & Sarah, b. Dec. 20, 1790; d. Apr. 19, 1794 403,406
Samuel, s. Richard & Sarah, b. June 10, 1781 403
William, s. Richard & Sarah, b. June 10, 1799 409

BARTHOLOMEW, Chauncey, m. Sophronia **PARMALEE**, Aug. 1, 1826 433

	Page
BARTHOLOMEW, (cont.)	
Eliza Emeline, d. Oren & Emeline, b. Oct. 8, 1822	420
Hezekiah, m. Sally **NEAL**, of Wallingford, Nov. 22, 1842	440
Margaret Ann, d. Oren & Emeline, b. Apr. 2, 1820	420
BARTLETT, BARLET, BARTLET, Abigail, d. Samuel, bp. Oct. 12, 1777	326
Abraham, s. Abraham & Submit, b. Apr. 14, 1759; bp. June 3, [1759]	309,375
Anne, d. Isaac, bp. May 16, [1756]	298
Clarissa, d. Samuel & Abigail, bp. Apr. 11, [1773]	322
Clarissa, m. Manoah **CAMP**, Apr. 24, 1794	416
Hannah, m. Gershom **BIRDSEY**, b. of Middletown, Nov. 12, [1772], by Rev. Elizur Goodrich	332
Hannah, d. Samuel, bp. May 29, [1775]	325
Joel, s. Samuel & Abigail, bp. Feb. 17, 1771	320
John Camp, s. Abraham, Jr. & Melinda, b. Dec. 24, 1785	401
Mindwell, d. Abraham & Submit, b. July 6, 1770; bp. July 8, [1770]	319,397
Olive, d. Abraham & Submit, b. June 6, 1766; bp. June 8, [1766]	315,386
Ruth, d. Abraham & Submit, bp. Dec. 26, [1773]	323
Samuel, m. Abigail **INGRAHAM (INGHAM)**, b. of Durham, June 16, [1768], by Rev. Elizur Goodrich	330,392
Samuel, s. Samuel & Abigail, b. Apr. 23, 1769; bp. July 2, 1769	318,392
Submit, d. Abraham & Submit, b. Apr. 10, 1764; bp. Apr. 15, 1764	314,383
BASSET, Lyman, m. Orpha **PARSONS**, June 21, 1824	431
BATES, BATE, Aaron, s. Stephen & Mindwell, bp. Nov. 6, [1757]	307
Abiah Southmayd, d. Samuel, Jr. & Hannah, b. Dec. 15, 1787	404
Abigail, d. Samuel & Abigail, bp. Oct. 18, 1747	288
Abigail, wid. of Haddam, m. Ens. Simeon **PARSONS**, of Durham, Nov. 30, [1772], by Rev. Elizur Goodrich	332
Alvey, d. Curtiss & Clarissa, b. Nov. 24, 1789	404
Ann, d. Stephen & Mindwell, bp. Mar. 2, [1760]	309
Ann, of Durham, m. Timothy W. **BALDWIN**, of North Guilford, May 16, 1821	430
Anna, d. Stephen & Patience, bp. Feb. 8, 1718/19	256
Anna, d. Stephen & Patience, b. Feb. 5, 1719/20	347
Anna, d. Sam[ue]l & Abigail, bp. Nov. 18, 1744	284
Anne, of Haddam, m. Timothy* **WACKLEY**, of Durham, Sept. 17, [1767], by Rev. Elizur Goodrich (*Note says "Jonathan")	330,392
Anne, d. James & Anne, b. May 9, 1780	404
Anne, d. Daniel & Anne, b. Aug. 14, 1799	410
Bela, s. Stephen & Mindwell, bp. July 4, [1762]	312
Clarissa, d. Moses & Martha, bp. Feb. 23, [1772]	321
Clarissa, d. Curtiss & Clarissa, b. Feb. 4, 1792; d. May 10, 1794	404,405
Curtiss, m. Clarissa [ ], Dec. 14, 1776	404
Daniel, s. James & Mary, bp. July 8, 1750	291
Daniel, s. James, Jr. & Anne, bp. Sept. 10, [1769]	319
Daniel, s. James & Anne, b. Sept. 25, 1770	404
Daniel, m. Anne **SMITHSON**, Oct. 24, 1790	404
David, s. John & Elizabeth, bp. Mar. 4, 1749/50	290
Ebenezer, s. James, Jr., bp. Oct. 9, 1774	324

Page

BATES, BATE, (cont.)

Ebenezer, [s. James & Anne], b. Oct. 3, 1775; d. June 6, 1779 404
Ebenezer G., m. Mary Ann **SWATHEL**, Mar. 26, 1823 431
Ebenezer Guernsey, s. Daniel & Anne, b. May 14, 1805 411
Edith, d. John, bp. Mar. 17, 1754 295
Elias, s. Moses & Martha, bp. Aug. 29, 1773 323
Elihu, s. Samuel & Sarah, bp. Mar. 1, [1767] 316
Elizabeth, d. Stephen, 3rd, & Mindwell, b. Aug. 3, 1750; bp. Aug. 5, 1750 291,372
Elizabeth, d. John, bp. Apr. 26, 1752 294
Elizabeth, m. Silas **WILLIAMS**, May 1, 1834 436
Eph[raim], s. Stephen & Patience, bp. Aug. 3, 1729 264
Eunice, d. Samuel & Sarah, bp. Sept. 10, [1769] 319
Gurnesy, [s. James, Jr. & Anne], b. Feb. 1, 1772; bp. Mar. 22, [1772] 321,404
Hannah, d. John & Edith, b. July 28, 1742; bp. Aug. 4, 1742 281,360
Hannah, d. James & Mary, bp. Apr. 6, [1760] 310
Hannah, m. Charles **COE**, Oct. 30, 1784 401
Hannah, d. Samuel & Hannah, b. Feb. 24, 1793; d. Feb. 13, 1794 404.405
Hinsdel, s. Oliver & Lois, b. Dec. 25, 1757; bp. Jan. 1, 1758 307.383
Jacob, s. John, bp. Nov. 2, 1746 286
James, s. James & Abigail, bp. May 22, [1715] 254
James, s. James & Mary, bp. Oct. 19, [1740] 278
James, Jr., of Haddam, m. Anne **GURNSEY**, of Durham, Dec. 24, 1765, (1766), by Rev. Elizur Goodrich 329,404
John, s. James & Abigail, bp. Apr. 7, 1717 255
John, s. John, bp. Nov. 20, 1743 282
John, s. Curtiss & Clarissa, b. Oct. 20, 1787; d. Apr. 22, 1792 404
John, s. Curtiss & Clarissa, b. Aug. 19, 1798 409
Katharine, d. James, Jr. & Anne, bp. Oct. 26, 1766 316
Katharine, d. James & Anne, b. Oct. 26, 1767 404
Keziah, d. Stephen, 3rd, & Mindwell, b. Sept. 6, 1753 372
Lament, d. Lois, b. Jan. 7, 1762 381
Lemuel, s. Stephen, 3rd, & Mindwell, b. Aug. 29, 1755; bp. Aug. 31, [1755] 298,372
Linus, [s. Stephen, Jr. & Lois], b. Sept. 6, 1751], bp. Sept. 8, 1751 292,381
Lois, [d. Stephen, Jr. & Lois], b. Jan, 7, 1754; bp. Jan. 13, 1754 295,381
Lois had d. Lament, b. Jan. 7, 1762; wid. had d. Lament **CRANE**, bp. Apr. 4, [1762] 312,381
Lucy, twin with Stephen, d. Stephen & Patience, bp. Feb. 12, 1720/1 257
Lucy, d. Stephen, bp. Apr. 4, [1724/5] 260
Lucy, d. Oliver & Lois, b. Jan. 25, 1756; bp. Jan. 9, 1757 305,383
Mary, d. Stephen & Patience, b. June 11, 1732; bp. June 11, 1732 267,354
Mary, d. James & Mary, bp. July 28. 1745 285
Mary, d. James & Mary, bp. June 29, 1755 297
Mary Ann, of Durham, m. Horatio N. **FOWLER**, of Middletown,

Page

BATES, BATE, (cont.)
Sept. 12, 1827 433
Meriah, d. Daniel & Ann, b. Apr. 12, 1796 410
Mindwell, w. of Stephen, bp. July 29, 1750 291
Moses, s. Samuel, b. after the death of his father; bp. June 24, 1750 291
Nathaniel, s. John, bp. Mar. 24, 1744/5 284
Oliver, s. Stephen & Patience, b. Aug. 26, 1734; bp. Sept. 1, 1734 269,356
Parsons, s. Moses, bp. July 23, [1775] 325
Patience, d. Stephen & Patience, b. Jan. 11, 1716/17; bp. May 5, 1717 255,347
Phebe, d. Stephen, Jr. & Lois, b. Feb. 4, 1756; bp. Feb. 8, 1756 298,381
Phebe, d. Daniel & Anne, b. Feb. 13, 1792 405
Phillis, negro child of Stephen & Patience **BATES** bp. July 16, 1749 289
Phinehas, [s. Stephen, Jr. & Lois], b. July 26, 1749; bp. July 30, 1749 289,381
Phinehas, m. Esther **CURTISS**, Dec. 5, [1771], by Rev. Elizur Goodrich 331
Rhoda, d. Oliver & Lois, b. Sept. 1, 1760; bp. Oct. 5, [1760] 310,383
Robert, s. James & Mary, bp. Aug. 14, [1757] 306
Samuel, s. James & Abigail, bp. Feb. 2, 1712/13 253
Samuel, s. Samuel & Abigail, bp. Apr. 24, 1743 282
Samuel, m. Sarah **SPELMAN**, b. of Haddam, May 17, [1764], by Rev. Elizur Goodrich 329
Samuel, s. Samuel & Sarah, bp. Mar. 10, 1765 314
Samuel, Jr., m. Hannah **SOUTHMAYD**, Nov. 13, 1786 404
Sarah, d. James & Mary, bp. Mar. 18, 1738/9 276
Sarah, d. James & Mary, bp. May 8, 1743 282
Sarah, of Haddam, m. Ambrose **FIELD**, of Durham, Sept. 17, [1767], by Rev. Elizur Goodrich 330,391
Sarah, d. Samuel & Sarah, bp. June 28, 1772 322
Stephen, m. Patience **SEWARD**, Dec. 29, 1715, by James Wadsworth, J. P. 343
Stephen, twin with Lucy, s. Stephen & Patience, bp. Feb. 12, 1720/1 257
Stephen, s. Stephen & Patience, b. Mar. 20, 1722/3; bp. Mar. 20, 1722/3 258,347
Stephen, 3rd, m. Mindwell **SEWARD**, Mar. [ ], 1749 371
Stephen & Patience had negro child Phillis bp. July 16, 1749 289
Stephen, bp. July 29, 1750 291
Stephen, s. Stephen & Lois, bp. July 29, [1759] 309
Stephen, [s. Stephen, Jr. & Lois], b. July 10, 1762 381
Stephen, s. Stephen & Mindwell, bp. Apr. 14, 1765 314
Stephen, s. Samuel, bp. Nov. 9, 1777 326
William, s. [Samuel, Jr. & Hannah], b. July 9, 1790 404
----, child of Samuel, bp. Jan. 1, 1775 325
BEACH, BEECH, Abel, s. Benjamin & Dinah, b. Feb. 9, 1711/12;

Page

BEACH, BEECH, (cont.)
bp. Feb. 17, 1711/12 252,341
Abigail, d. Richard & Hannah, b. Feb. 15, 1710/11 344
Abigail, d. Richard & Hannah, b. Feb. 15 (5), 1710/11 342,344
Abigail, m. Israel **AUERED**, Aug. 25, 1731, by Rev. Mr. Bliss, of Hebron 359
Alpheus, of Northford, m. Mary **SKINNER**, of Durham, Oct. 21, 1843 440
Benjamin, s. Richard & Hannah, b. May 5, 1720 /1; bp. May 8, [1720] 256,346
Benjamin, s. Abel & Margaret, bp. Oct. 5, 1738 275
Dinah, m. Samuel **NORTON**, May 13, 1713, by Rev. Nath[anie]ll Chauncey 349
Eunice, d. Richard & Hannah, b. Mar. 28, 1716; bp. Mar. 31, 1717 255,346
Hannah, d. Richard & Hannah, b. May 15, 1714; bp. May 16, 1714 253,344
Hannah, d. Joseph & [Exp[erience], bp. July 4, 1736 272
Joseph, s. Benjamin & Dinah, b. Oct. 24, 1710 340
Lydia, d. Azariah & Lydia, bp. Apr. 28 or 29, [1733] 268
Mindwell, d. Azariah & Lydia, bp. Aug. 1, [1731] 265
Miriam, d. Joseph & Exp[erience], bp. Feb. 16, 1734/5 270
Phebe, d. Joseph & Experience, bp. Apr. 2, 1738 275
Sarah, d. Richard, bp. Mar. 8, 1723/4 259
BEARDSLEY, Harriet, of Meriden, m. Albert **WARD**, of Durham, Oct. 7, 1831 435
BEAUMONT, Elijah, m. Sophronia **NETTLETON**, May 27, 1827 433
BEECH, [see under **BEACH**]
BEECHER, Bennet B., of Woodbridge, m. Sarah **BISHOP**, of Durham, Nov. 18, 1832 435
BEERS, Phinehas, m. Mary **CURTISS**, June 25, 1822 430
BEMUS, Fanny, m. Nelson **HOLCOMB**, Feb. 7, 1827 433
Hannah, m. George W. **GORHAM**, Dec. 1, 1826 433
Henry E., m. Hannah **SUL[L]IVAN**, Sept. 28, 1860 443
BENJAMIN, Asher, s. Samuel, bp. Feb. 16, 1751/2 294
Judah, of Milford, m. wid. Rhoda **TRENCH**, of Durham, June 2, 1779, by Rev. Elizur Goodrich 334
Samuel, bp. Feb. 16, 1751/2 294
----, w. of Samuel, bp. Feb. 16, 1751/2 294
BIRDSEY, Gershom, m. Hannah **BAR[T]LETT**, b. of Middletown, Nov. 12, [1772], by Rev. Elizur Goodrich 332
BISHOP, Abigail, d. Abraham & Mehetabel, bp. Mar. 18, [1759] 308
Abraham, s. Abraham & Mehetabel, bp. July 25, [1762] 312
Abraham, m. Mary **THOMAS**, b. of Durham, Oct. 7, 1773, by Rev. Elizur Goodrich 332
Adah, d. William, Jr., bp. June 11, [1775] 325
Ann, d. William & Patience, b. May 29, 1740 372
Ann, m. Abijah **CURTISS**, Aug. 13, 1777 399
Anne, m. Samuel **SQUIER**, Sept. 30, 1756 377
Anne, w. of Reuben, d. Jan. 17. 1765 384
Anne, d. Reuben & Sarah, bp. Nov. 19, [1769] 319
Benjamin, s. Reuben, bp. Nov. 6, [1774] 324

Page

BISHOP, (cont.)

	Page
Benoni, s. W[illia]m, Jr., bp. [1774]	324
Charles, s. William & Patience, b. July 26, 1744; bp. July 29, 1744	283,372
Charles, m. Martha **HICKOX**, Dec. 12, [1768], by Rev. Elizur Goodrich	331
Charles, s. Charles & Martha, bp. Oct. 28, [1770]	320
Clarissa, wid. of Zebulon, d. Sept. 29, 1830	428
Daniel, s. Abraham & Mabel, bp. June 2, 1754	295
Elizabeth, d. Abraham, bp. Jan. 22, [1758]	307
Hannah, d. Timothy, bp. Mar. 9, 1734/5	270
Hannah, m. John **NORTON**, Dec. 21, [1757], by Rev. Elizur Goodrich	327
Harriet, m. Lewis I. **DAVIS**, Aug. 3, 1829	434
Hiram, m. Mariah **LUCASS**, July 11, [1831?]	435
Huldah, d. William & Patience, b. June 24, 1742; bp. June 27, [1742]	280,372
Huldah, m. David **SQUIER**, Feb. 9, 1761	381
Joel, s. Reuben & Anne, b. Oct. 2, 1759; bp. Oct. 7, [1759]	309,384
John, s. Abraham, bp. Feb. 8, 1756	298
Jonas, s. Timothy, bp. June 3, 1734	269
Jonas, m. Phebe **CRANE**, Jan. 19 (20), 1763, by Rev. Elizur Goodrich	328,381
Lucy, d. Tim[othy], bp. May 22, 1737	273
Mary, d. Timothy, bp. June 3, 1734	269
Mary, m. Jared **SEAWARD**, Sept. 12, 1753	369
Mahetabel, d. Abr[aha]m & Mehetabel, bp. Sept. 21, [1760]	310
Nathan, s. Charles & Martha, bp. Feb. 27, [1774]	324
Nathaniel, of Durham, m. Huldah **FRANCIS**, of N. Killingworth, June 29, [1757], by Rev. Elizur Goodrich	327
Prudence, d. William & Patience, b. Mar. 8, 1749	372
Prudence, m. David **CURTISS**, Jr., Dec. 27, 1770, by Rev. Elizur Goodrich	331
Reuben, m. Anne **WRIGHT**, Mar. 9, 1758	384
Reuben, s. Reuben & Anne, b. June 4, 1762; bp. June 6, [1762]	312,384
Reuben, of Durham, m. wid. Sarah **WALKLEY**, of Haddam, Dec. 12, [1768], by Rev. Elizur Goodrich	331
Rhoda, d. William & Patience, b. Mar. 21, 1754; bp. Mar. 24, 1754	295,372
Rosanna, d. William & Patience, b. July 2, 1756; bp. Aug. 15, [1756]	298,373
Sally, d. Charles & Martha, bp. Dec. 22, [1771]	321
Sarah, d. Timothy, bp. May 3, [1740]	279
Sarah, of Guilford, m. Joseph **WRIGHT**, Jr., of Durham, Dec. 17, [1767], by Rev. Elizur Goodrich	330,389
Sarah, of Durham, m. Bennet B. **BEECHER**, of Woodbridge, Nov. 18, 1832	435
Sylvanus, s. William & Patience, b. July 16, 1738; bp. July 22, 1738	275,372
Thalmene, s. Nathaniel & Huldah, bp. Oct. 23, [1757]	307
Timothy, of Guilford, m. wid. Abigail **INGRAHAM**, of Durham, Feb. 15, 1770, by Rev. Elizur Goodrich	331

Page

BISHOP, (cont.)

Tryphena, d. William & Patience, bp. Feb. 1, 1761 310
William, s. William & Patience, b. Aug. 11, 1746 372
----, child of Reuben, bp. May 10, 1772 321
----, d. Abraham, bp. [1774] 324

BLAKEMAN, Guy, m. Anne **CAMP**, Mar. 11, 1821 430

BLAKESLEE, Obier, m. Sarah Ann **MORSE**, Dec. 14, 1836 437

BLATCHLEY, Abraham, of Durham, m. Elizabeth **STONE**, of Guilford, Nov. 16, 1727 348

Joel, of Gulford, m. Margery **ROBINSON**, of Durham, Oct. 10, 1825 432,433
Joel, m. Harriet **HULL**, Aug. 8, 1839 438

BOARDMAN, Sarah, of Weathersfield, John **PARMALEE**, of Durham, Nov. 24, 1730 361

BOLLES, [see also **BOWLES**], Abigail S., of Middletown, m. Brainard **MONTAGUE**, of Sandersfield, Mass., Feb. 11, 1833 435

BOOTH, Anna, m. Nathan **CURTISS**, May 13, 1761 380

BOWLES, [see also **BOLLES**], Betsey, m. Jehial **JOHNSON**, b. of Middletown, Jan. 2, 1834 436

Mary, d. David, bp. June 10, 1744 283

BRADLEY, Ashbel, s. Phebe **CRANE**, bp. May 7, [1758] 307

Harriet, m. Samuel **STEVENS**, May 4, 1836 437

BRAINARD, Alanson, of Durham, m. Ellen **COOK**, of Northford, Aug. 8, 1847 442

Alonzo, of Haddam, m. Diana **PLATT**, of Durham, Dec. 15, 1844 441
Blinn I., m. Catharine H. **FOOTE**, May 1, 1830 434
Fanny M., of Haddam, m. Joseph H. **PADDOCK**, of Middletown, July 10, 1844 441
Margaret, m. Thomas **CANFIELD**, Nov. 26, 1740 359
Mary, m. Huntington **SOUTHMAYD**, Apr. 24, 1834 436
Mary R., m. Austin **BAILEY**, Oct. 25, 1824 432
Sarah M., of Durham, m. Lester **CORNWALL**, of Meriden, Oct. 6, 1846 442

BRAY, Anne, wid., d. June 10, 1823 423

BRISTOL, Calvin, s. Nathan & Hannah, bp. Apr. 16, [1775] 325

Mary, m. Amos **HUBBARD**, June 15, 1758 374
Nathan, m. Hannah **MERWIN**, Jan. [ ], 1773, by Rev. Elizur Goodrich 332

BROOKS, Asa, s. Charles & Mehethabel, b. Nov. 19, 1756; bp. Dec. 5, 1756 305,373

Charles, m. Mehethabel **NORTON**, Oct. 13, 1753 367
Joseph, s. Charles & Mehethabel, b. Jan. 8, 1754; bp. Jan. 13, 1754 295,368
Lucretia, m. Samuel **CURTISS**, Oct. 3, 1810 414
Martha J., m. Henry E. **BAILEY**, Mar. 27, 1842 440
Phebe, d. Charles & Mehethabel, b. July 19, 1755; bp. July 27, 1755 297,372
Phebe, d. Charles, bp. Oct. 29, [1758] 308

Page

BROWN, Charles, of Meriden, m. Juliet **GRIFFING**, of Guilford, May 22, 1832 435
James, m. Peninnah **MEEKER**, Feb. 7, 1766, by Rev. Elizur Goodrich 329
Mary, bp. June 4, [1758] 307
Mary, of Haddam, m. David **WOOD**, of Greenwich, Nov. 1, [1759], by Rev. Elizur Goodrich 327
Mary, bp. Apr. 11, 1766 301
Mehetabel, bp. May 4, [1766] 315
Mehetabel, m. Joseph **INGRAHAM (INGHAM)**, b. of Durham, Aug. 19, [1767], by Rev. Elizur Goodrich 330,388
Penina, w. of James, d. Jan. 4, 1811 412
Sarah, bp. Feb. 4, [1759] 300
Sarah, ae 17, bp. Feb. 11, 1759 308
BRYAN, Lucius P., of Waterbury, m. Jennett **WHITE**, of Durham, Aug. 25, 1836 437
BUCK, Rachel, d. Sarah, b. Mar. 22, 1708 340
Sarah, m. Joseph **FRANCES**, Oct. 2, 1750 372
BUEL, Barbara, of Killingworth, m. Elnathan **CONNER**, of Wallingford, Apr. 21, 1830 434
BULKLEY, Dorcas, m. Saxton **SQUIRE**, Feb. 8, 1779, by Rev. Elizur Goodrich 333
BULL, Hannah, m. James **CURTISS**, Jr., Sept. 12, 1734 380
BURR, Lorinda, of Haddam, m. Phinehas **NETTLETON**, of Killingworth, Nov. 15, 1840 439
Sarah, of Haddam, m. John **SEAWARD**, of Durham, May 10, 1769 391
BURRITT, BURRIT, BURRETT, Ann, d. James, bp. Dec. 8, 1723 259
Ann, d. Dea. [ ] & Sarah, bp. Oct. 16, 1743 282
Charles, s. Dea. Israel & Sarah, bp. Aug. 31, 1746 286
Hannah, d. James & Sarah, bp. May 3, [1740] 279
Hannah, of Durham, m. Titus **FOWLER**, of Granville, Apr. 9, 1765, by Rev. Elizur Goodrich 329
Israel, s. Dea. Israel & Sarah, b. [Aug. 14, 1736]; bp. Aug. 15, 1736 272
Israel, d. May 25, 1806 411
Jared, s. William, bp. May 1, 1774 324
Mary, m. Daniel **MERWIN**, Jr., May 11, 1741, by Rev. Nathaniel Chauncey 360
Sarah, d. Israel & Sarah, b. Nov. 2, [1734]; bp. Nov. 3, 1734 270
Sarah, d. William & Anne, bp. Oct. 18, 1772 322
-----, Dea., had negro Elisha, bp. Aug. 8, 1731 266
-----, Dea., had negro Peter, bp. Dec. 17, 1732 268
-----, Dea., had negro Prudence, d. Reuben & Dinah, bp. May 5, 1734 269
-----, Dea., had negro Prudence, d. Dinah, bp. May 25, 1735 271
-----, Dea., had negro Titan, s. Peter & Dinah, bp. Nov. 13, 1737 274
-----, Dea., had negro Hagar, d. Relor & Dinah, bp. Dec. 2, 1739 277
-----, Dea., had negro Prudence, d. Peter & Dinah, bp. June 9, 1745 284
BURTON, Oliver, s. Simeon & Mary, b. June 9, 1740 359
Oliver, s. Simeon & Hannah, bp. Aug. 3, [1740] 278

	Page
BUTCHER, Margery, m. Asher **ROBINSON**, b. of Durham, June 11, [1761], by Rev. Elizur Goodrich	328,382
BUTLER, Betcy, d. William & Sarah, b. May 20, 1793	405
Charles, s. William & Sarah, b. Mar. 21, 1779	405
Chauncey, s. William & Sarah, b. May 7, 1791	405
Elizur, s. William & Sarah, b. Mar. 3, 1781 (Elijah?)	405
Eliza, m. Timothy **RUSSELL**, Oct. 27, 1822	430
Harriet, d. William & Sarah, b. Aug. 11, 1788	405
Jeremiah, m. Anna **COE**, Sept. 20, 1769	394
Jeremiah, s. Jeremiah, bp. Mar. 17, 1771	320
Jeremiah, s. Jeremiah & Anna, b. May 4, 1771	394
John, s. Jeremiah & Anna, b. Sept. 13, 1772	397
Katharine, d. Jeremiah, bp. Mar. 21, [1779]	326
Lyman, m. Eunice B. **SOUTHMAYD**, May 23, 1823	431
Polly, d. Jeremiah & Anna, b. Mar. 18, 1770; bp. May 13, [1770]	319,394
Rayner, s. Jeremiah & Anna, b. Aug. 15, 1774	397
Sarah, w. of William, b. Feb. 23, 1758	405
Sarah, d. William & Sarah, b. Mar. 7, 1784	405
Stephen, s. Jeremiah & Anne, b. Mar. 26, 1776	398
Timothy, m. Sarah **HULL**, Oct. 5, 1778, by Rev. Elizur Goodrich	333
William, b. Apr. 16, 1752	405
William, m. Sarah **HULL**, Sept. 29, 1778	405
William, s. William & Sarah, b. June 16, 1786	405
-----, d. Jeremiah, bp. [1774]	324
BYINGTON, Christian, d. Joel & Christian, b. Dec. 22, 1779	413
Christian, m. Ozias **CAMP**, Apr. [ ], 1807	413
CALLENDER, Polly, m. Timothy **COE**, Jr., Jan. 10, 1803	415
CAMP, Aaron, [s. Job & Rachel], b. Feb. 18, 1755; bp. Feb. 23, 1755	297,388
Abiathar, s. John (3rd) & Damaris, b. Nov. 16, 1732; bp. Nov. 19, 1732	267,354
Abiel, s. Edward & Mary, b. Aug. 29, 1734; bp. Sept. 1, 1734	269,357
Abiael, d. Jan. 21, 1821	424
Abigail, d. Eleazar, bp. July 26, 1741	279
Abigail, m. John **CRANE**, Apr. 7, 1762	381
Abraham, Capt., had negro Dolphin, of Norfolk, m. Zill, negro of Lieut. David **COE**, of Middletown, May 11, [1764], by Rev. Elizur Goodrich	328-9
Abraham, s. Phinehas & Martha, bp. May 30, [1773]	323
Abraham, m. Mary Ann **COE**, May 28, 1828	434
Adah, d. Nathan & Rhoda, bp. Nov. 25, 1733	269
Adah, m. Benjamin **PICKET**, Dec. 5, [1758], by Rev. Elizur Goodrich	327,394
Adah, d. Ens. Samuel & Phebe, bp. Dec. 1, 1771	321
Adah, m. Stephen **TIBBALS**, Dec. 8, 1822	430
Adah Ann, d. Lyman C. & Emma, b. Mar. 22, 1816	419
Albert, s. Abiael & Lucinda, b. Oct. 1, 1804	423
Alexander, m. Abigail W. **MAYNARD**, of Durham, Feb. 22, 1842	440
Alfred, m. Phebe **PARMALEE**, Apr. 2, 1823	431
Amanda, m. Edmond **ORTON**, Jan. 1, 1821	430

	Page
CAMP, (cont.)	
Amos, m. Anne **ANDRUS**, Dec. 18, 1716, by James Wadsworth, J. P.	343
Amos, s. Amos & Anne, b. Sept. 22, 1717; bp. [Oct. 23, 1717]	255,342
Amos, s. Phineas, bp. Jan. 6, 1771	320
Ann, d. Israel & Ann, b. May 20, 1756	352
Ann, w. of Israel, d. Mar. 18, 1765	385
Ann, m. Israel **GODDARD**, Feb. 3, 1769, by Rev. Elizur Goodrich	331
Anna, d. Elnathan & Eunice, bp. June 28, 1772	322
Anna, see also Hannah	
Anne, d. Israel & Ann, bp. May 20, 1750	291
Anne, d. Elnathan & Eunice, bp. June 2, [1771]	320-1
Anne, d. Heth & Mary, b. July 16, 1776	398
Anne, w. of Charles, d. Feb. 14, 1818	416
Anne, m. Guy **BLAKEMAN**, Mar. 11, 1821	430
Ashael, s. Edward & Mary, bp. Mar. 1, 1740	279
Ashur, [s. Job & Rachel], b. July 29, 1769; bp. July 30, 1769	318,396
Benjamin Benonia, s. Manoah & Charissa, b. Feb. 10, 1795	428
Benoni, [s. Cornet Job & Rachel], b. Sept. 7, 1773; bp. Sept. 19, [1773]	323,396
Benoni, [s. Manoah & Clarissa], b. Feb. 10, 1795	416
Betsey, d. Elias, Jr. & Elisabeth, b. Apr. 4, 1789	405
Betsey, d. Thaddeus & Betsey, b. June 25, 1808	412
Betsey, m. William A. **BALDWIN**, Sept. 22, 1830	435
Betsey B., m. Carlos [**CAMP**], May 9, 1833	435-6
Betsey Byington, d. Ozias & Christian, b. Feb. 5, 1812	413
Betsey Lyman, d. Manoah & Charissa, b. Mar. 11, 1810	428
Betsey Lyman, d. Manoah & Charissa, b. May 5, 1814	428
Carlos, m. Betsey B. **CAMP**, May 9, 1833	435-6
Caroline D., m. Peris **STURTEVANT**, Apr. 28, 1824	431
Cecilia A., of Durham, m. Julius **RICH**, of Chatham, Sept. 12, 1830	435
Charles, s. Ebenezer & Sarah, b. Jan. 16, 1791	416
Charles, m. Anne **MILLER**, Jan. 1, 1817	416
Charles Augustus, s. Ozias, 2d, & Polly, b. May 10, 1822	417
Cornelia, m. Henry E. **NETTLETON**, Sept. 6, 1839	438
Damaris, w. of John, Jr., d. Aug. 25, 1737	379
Damaris, d. Elnathan & Eunice, b. Mar. 4, 1762; d. Mar. 30, 1762; was twin with Talcott and bp. Mar. 7, [1762]	311,382
Damaris, d. Elnathan & Eunice, b. Dec. 21, 1768; bp. Jan. 29, 1769	318.392
Daniel, s. Amos & Ann, bp. Feb. 8, 1718/19	256
Daniel, s. Phinehas & Martha, b. Dec. 4, 1768; bp. Jan. 29, 1769	318,392
David, s. Elnathan & Eunice, bp. Sept. 21, 1766	316
David, s. Elnathan & Eunice, b. Sept. 23, 1766	389,392
David, Ens., of Woodbury, m. wid. Mary **HUBBARD**, of Durham, Dec. 28, [1772], by Rev. Elizur Goodrich	332
David, d. Oct. 13, 1808	411
David N., m. Sarah A. **HOWD**, Nov. 25, 1845	441
David Nelson, s. Elah & Orib, b. Oct. 3, 1820	424
David P., m. Nancy E. **STRONG**, Aug. 11, 1833	436

Page

CAMP. (cont.)

Delight, m. Horace **NEWTON**, May 24, 1826 432

Dennis, s. Elnathan & Eunice, bp. Feb. 19, [1775] 325

Dinah, d. Edward & Mary, bp. Jan. 7, 1738/9 276

Ebenezer, s. Samuel, bp. Oct. 30, [1763] 313

Ebenezer, s. Samuel & Phebe, b. Nov. 28, 1763 383

Ebenezer, s. Capt. Israel & Mary, bp. Nov. 18, 1770 320

Eder, s. Ens. Edward, bp. Aug. 15, 1762 312

Edward, Ens., of Middletown, m. Esther **CRITTENDEN**, of Durham, June 20, 1758, by Rev. Elizur Goodrich 327

Edward, s. Ozias & Christian, b. Jan. 19, 1809 413

Edward P., s. Lemuel & Patty, b. Apr. 12, 1808 427

Edwin Stiles, s. Thaddeus & Betsey, b. Dec. 1, 1803 412

Elah, s. Nathan, bp. May 25, 1729 263

Elah, m. Phebe **BALDWIN**, May 14, 1760, by Rev. Elizur Goodrich 327,378

Elah had negro Sharp, m. Phyllis, Aug. 13, [1767], by Rev. Elizur Goodrich 330

Elah, s. Elah & Phebe, b. Feb. 11, 1768; bp. Feb. 14, 1768 317,389,392

Elah had negro Sharp, bp. Mar. 4, 1770; Cambridge, s. Sharp & Phillis, bp. Mar. 4, 1770 302,319

Elah had negro Dan, s. Sharp & Phyllis, bp. Oct. 13, 1771 321

Elah had negro Peter, bp. May 10, 1772 322

Elah, d. Oct. 17, 1787 403

Elah, s. Nathan O. & Phebe, b. July 22, 1792 403

Elah, m. Orib **LEE**, Dec. 2, 1819 424

Ele[a]nor, [d. Job & Rachel], b. Aug. 28, 1771; bp. Sept. 1, 1771 321,396

Eli, s. Nathan & Rhoda, bp. Apr. 24, 1726 261

Elias, s. Nathan & Rhoda, bp. Feb. 2, 1717/18 255

Elias, s. Elah & Phebe, b. Aug. 28, 1765; bp. Sept. 1, [1765] 315,385

Elias, Jr., m. Elizabeth **SPENCER**, Oct. 17, 1788 405

Elias, s. Luke & Grace, b. Feb. 4, 1794 412

Elijah, see under Elizur

Elize, d. Elias, Jr. & Elizabeth, b. Apr. 20, 1795 405

Elizabeth, d. John, 2d, & Hannah, b. Oct. 20, 1748 369

Elizabeth, of Durham, m. Rev. Samuel **JOHNSON**, of Albany, Feb. 18, 1773, by Rev. Elizur Goodrich 332

Elizabeth Mariah, d. Heth F. & Phebe, b. Sept. 23, 1821 420

Elizur, [s. Manoah & Clarissa], b. Aug. 22, 1804 416,428

Elizur, m. Fanny **CLARKE**, Oct. 1, 1827 433

Elnathan, s. John, Jr. & Damaris, b. Jan. 24, 1834/5; bp. Jan. 26, 1734/5 270,379

Elnathan, m. Eunice **TALCOTT**, May 23, [1759], by Rev. Elizur Goodrich 327,379

Elnathan, d. May 12, 1807 411

Enoch F., m. Mary A. **COE**, b. of Durham, Nov. 4, 1847 442

Enos Spencer, s. Nathan O. & Phebe, b. Dec. 30, 1789 403

Ephraim, s. John & Hannah, bp. July 6, 1729 263

Eunice, d. Abraham & Martha, bp. Oct. 13, 1745 285

Page

CAMP, (cont.)

Eunice, d. Elnathan & Eunice, b. Apr. 25, 1760; bp. Apr. 27, [1760]; d. Mar. 31, 1762 310,379,382
Eunice, d. Elnathan & Eunice, b. June 23, 1764; bp. June 24, [1764] 314,384
Eunice, m. Reuben **BALDWIN**, May 27, 1773, by Rev. Elizur Goodrich 332
Eunice, w. Elnathan, d. Aug. 2, 1804 410
Ezra, s. Elah & Phebe, b. Oct. 31, 1770; bp. Nov. 4, [1770] 320,392
Frances, s. Abiael & Lucinda, b. Sept. 29, 1814 424
Frances A., m. Leander R. **PARSONS**, b. of Durham, Nov. 26, 1846 442
Frederick, [s. Manoah & Clarissa], b. Nov. 21, 1800 416
Frederick, s. Manoah & Clarissa, b. Nov. 21, 1801 428
Frederic Nelson, s. Thaddeus & Betsey, b. Oct. 7, 1811 426
Frederick Nelson, d. July 12, 1825 426
Gad, [s. Job & Rachel], b. Jan. 3, 1757; bp. Jan. 9, 1757 305,388
Gilbert, s. Abiael & Lucinda, b. July 31, 1817 424
Hannah, d. Nathan & Rhoda, bp. Nov. 20, [1720] 257
Hannah, d. John, 2d, & Hannah, b. Feb. 11, 1739/40 363
Hannah, called Anna, d. Sergt. John & Hannah, bp. Feb. 17, 1739/40 277
Hannah, d. Job & Rachel, b. Oct. 15, 1753; bp. Oct. 23, 1753 294,353
Hannah, m. Ozias **CAMP**, Oct. 6, [1757], by Rev. Elizur Goodrich 327
Hannah, m. Lieut, Abraham **SCRANTON**, Jr., Jan. 1, 1772, by Rev. Elizur Goodrich 331,409
Hannah, d. Capt. Samuel, bp. Nov. 9, 1777 326
Hannah, d. Heth & Mary, b. May 17, 1784 400
Harriet, m. George W. **JEWETT**, Sept. 11, 1823 431
Harriet Eliza, d. Guernsey & Cynthia Ann, b. Sept. 18, 1823 426
Harriet Parmalee, d. Lyman C. & Emma, b. Oct. 3, 1817 419
Henry, s. Thaddeus & Betsey, b. Apr. 26, 1802 412
Henry, d. July 15, 1825 426
Henry C., m. Caroline E. **WRIGHT**, Sept. 6, 1829 434
Henry T., s. Lemuel & Patty, b. Aug. 30, 1804 427
Herschal, [s. Manoah & Clarissa], b. Jan. 15, 1798 416,428
Heth, s. Eleazer, bp. Mar. 2, 1734/5 270
Heth, m. Mary **TIBBALS**, Nov. 20, 1766, by Rev. Elizur Goodrich 329
Hezekiah, s. Israel & Ann, b. May 21, 1752 352
Horace, s. Abiael & Lucinda, b. July 14, 1811 424
Huldah, d. Israel & Annie, bp. Mar. 24, 1754 295
Ichabod, s. John, bp. Feb. 20, 1725 261
Ichabod, m. Sally **JOHNSON**, Mar. 31, 1823 431
Israel, s. J-----, bp. Feb. 16, 1723/4 259
Israel, m. Ann **TALCOTT**, Dec. 24, 1747 352
Israel, m. Mary **GURNSEY**, Dec. 24, 1766 388
Israel, s. Ens. Israel & Mary, b. Jan. 29, 1768; bp. Jan. 31, 1768 317,389
Israel, m. Rhoda **SMITHSON**, May 3, 1789 407
Israel, d. Nov. 5, 1807 411
Israel, m. Rachel H. **MAYNARD**, Oct. 1, 1839 438
Israel S., m. Clarissa **DICKINSON**, May 1, 1827 433

Page

CAMP, (cont.)

Jane A., m. Francis M. **FORTES**, Nov. 25, 1845 441
Jennet, m. George W. **JEWETT**, Apr. 30, 1828 434
Jerusha, w. of John, Jr., d. Jan. 22, 1744/5 379
Jerusha, [d. Job & Rachel], b. Mar. 19, 1763; bp. Mar. 20, [1763] 313,388
Job, s. John, bp. May 19, [1728] 263
Job, m. Rachel **TALCOTT**, Dec. 28, 1752 353
Joel, s. Amos, bp. Dec. 26, 1720 257
John, m. Hannah **HICKOX**, June 27, 1728 355
John, Jr., m. Damaris **STRONG**, [ ], 1730 379
John, s. John, 2d, & Hannah, b. Mar. 2, 1738; bp. Mar. 5, 1737/8 274,363
John, Jr., m. Sarah **MERWIN**, July 11, 1739 379
John, Jr., m. Jerusha **PARMALEE**, Mar. 17, 1742 379
John, Jr., m. Abigail **FIELD**, Apr. 13, 1749 379
John, Lieut., had negro Rose, bp. Oct. 16, [1763]; Jenney, d. Rose, bp. Oct. 16, [1763] 301,313
John, 3rd, m. Eunice **COE**, Feb. 29, [1764], by Rev. Elizur Goodrich 328
John, d. Jan. 6, 1767 387
John, Lieut., m. wid. Hannah **MADDOCKS**, Apr. 19, 1770, by Rev. Elizur Goodrich 331
John, s. Capt. Israel & Mary, b. May 18, 1773; bp. May 23, [1773] 323,396
John S., m. Parnel **CAMP**, Oct. 15, 1822 430
John Spencer, s. Elias & Elizabeth, b. July 17, 1797 408
Joseph had negro Caesar m. Candace, Dec. 25, [1771], by Rev. Elizur Goodrich 331
Joseph P., Jr., m. Caroline E. **ROBINSON**, b. of Durham, June 28, 1854 443
Josiah, s. Charles & Anne, b. Jan. 24, 1818 416
Katharine, d. Edward & Mary, bp. July 25, 1736 272
Katherine, d. John, 2d, & Hannah, b. Jan. 16, 1744/5; bp. Jan. 20, 1744/5 284,363
Katharine, of Durham, m. Enoch **COE**, of Granville, Nov. 6, 1768, by Rev. Elizur Goodrich 331
Katharine, d. Heth & Mary, b. Aug. 20, 1770 396
Katharine Louisa, d. Thaddeus & Betsey, b. Nov. 15, 1814 426
Leunora, d. Thaddeus & Betsey, b. Aug. 19, 1805 412
Libbeus, s. Heth & Mary, b. Nov. 20, 1772 (Lebbeus) 396
Lemuel, s. Israel & Mary, b. Nov. 15, 1770 393
Lemuel, s. Abiael & Lucinda, b. Oct. 14, 1808 424
Levi, s. Ab[raha]m, of Middlefield, bp. Mar. 13, [1757] 306
Libbeus, see under Lebbeus
Lois, d. Abraham & Martha, bp. Dec. 25, 1743 282
Lois, d. John & Hannah, bp. Mar. 1, 1746; d. within 16 ds. 287
Lois, d. Ozias & Hannah, bp. Feb. 5, [1758] 307
Louisa Fairchild, d. Urania, bp. Feb. 12, [1758] 307
Lucinda, d. Elias, Jr. & Elisabeth, b. Jan. 28, 1793 405
Lucinda, m. Charles **GAY**, June 1, 1826 432

Page

CAMP, (cont.)

Lucy, m. Wyllys **ELLIOTT**, Feb. 19, 1823 431
Luke, [s. Job & Rachel], b. July 28, 1765; bp. Sept. 8, 1765 315,388
Lyman Coe, s. Lyman C. & Emma, b. July 2, 1820 419
Manoah, [s. Job & Rachel], b. Dec. 31, 1760; bp. Feb. 1, 1761 310,388
Manoah, m. Clarissa **BARTLET**, Apr. 24, 1794 416
Manoah, d. Mar. 5, 1842 429
Mariah, d. Abiael & Lucinda, b. Apr. 13, 1806 424
Mary, d. John, bp. Apr. 5, 1730 264
Mary, d. Eleazar, bp. June 26, 1737 274
Mary, d. David & Mary, bp. Feb. 20, 1742/3 281
Mary, m. Robert **CRANE**, b. of Durham, Oct. 31, 1765, by Rev. Elizur Goodrich 329
Mary, d. Heth & Mary, b. Sept. 26, 1778 399
Mary, d. Ozias & Christian, b. Aug. 23, 1808 413
Mary, m. Phinehas **MEIGS**, Aug. 20, 1833 436
Mary G., d. Lemuel & Patty, b. Aug. 26, 1800 427
Mary J., m. William A. **PARMALEE**, Aug. 13, 1840 439
Melinda, d. John & Eunice, bp. May 12, [1765] 315
Moses, s. Abraham & Martha, bp. Aug. 30, 1747 288
Nathan O., m. Phebe **SPENCER**, May 16, 1787 403
Nathan Ozias, s. Elah & Phebe, b. Feb. 10, 1763; bp. Feb. 27, 1763 312,385
Nathan Ozias, s. Nathan O. & Phebe, b. Jan. 4, 1796 406
Nathaniel, s. David & Margery, bp. Sept. 10, [1758], by Mr. Williams 307
Noyes, s. Luke & Grace, b. Nov. 21, 1797 412
Orren, m. Delight **IVES**, b. of Durham, Nov. 29, 1827 433
Oren J., s. Oren & Delight, b. June 13, 1829 427
Ozias, s. Nathan & Rhoda, bp. Sept. 5, 1731 266
Ozias, m. Hannah **CAMP**, Oct. 6, [1757], by Rev. Elizur Goodrich 327
Ozias, s. Samuel & Phebe, b. Dec. 26, 1758; bp. Dec. 31, [1758] 308,379
Ozias, s. Samuel & Phebe, b. Jan. 28, 1780 413
Ozias, m. Christian **BYINGTON**, Apr. [ ], 1807 413
Parnel, m. John S. **CAMP**, Oct. 15, 1822 430
Pernel, d. Israel & Rhoda, b. Oct. 6, 1799 410
Phebe, d. John, 2d, & Hannah, b. Feb. 3, 1741/2; bp. Feb. 7, 1741//2 280,363
Phebe, d. Israel & Ann, b. Oct. 26, 1748 352
Phebe, m. Timothy **PARSONS**, Jr., Jan. 2, 1772, by Rev. Elizur Goodrich 331
Phebe, s. (sic), Elah & Phebe, bp. Feb. 14, [1773] 322
Phebe, d. Ens. Samuel, bp. Oct. 9, 1774 324
Phebe, d. Ozias & Christian, b. June 24, 1813; d. Jan. 5, 1814 413
Phebe Elizabeth, d. Elah & Orib, b. Sept. 3, 1822 424
Phineas, s. John (Jr.) & Damaris, b. June 15, 1731; bp. Oct. 3, 1731; d. Oct. 7, 1743 266,354,379
Phinehas, s. John, Jr. & Jerusha, b. Jan. 13, 1744/5; bp. Jan. 13. 1744/5 284,379
Phineas. m. Martha **HALL**, b. of Durham, Jan. 8, 1767, by Rev.

	Page
CAMP, (cont.)	
Elizur Goodrich	330,392
Rachel, [d. Job & Rachel], b. Dec. 13, 1758; bp. Dec. 17, [1758]	308,388
Rebeckah, [d. Job & Rachel], b. July 12, 1767; bp. July 19, 1767	316,396
Rebeckah, d. Heth & Mary, b. July 26, 1768; bp. Aug. 21, [1768]	317,390
Rejoice, s. Israel & Ann, b. Oct. 23, 1759; bp. Oct. 28, [1759]	309,385
Rejoice, m. Ruth **PICKET**, Mar. 14, 1779, by Rev. Elizur Goodrich	333
Rhoda, d. Nathan & Rhoda, bp. Jan. 20, 1722/3	258
Rhoda, m. Joel **PARMALEE**, Jan. 6, 1742/3	385
Rhoda, d. Israel, bp. Aug. 15, [1756]	298
Ruth, d. John & Hannah, b. Oct. 9, 1733; bp. Oct. 14, 1733	268,355
Ruth, m. Lemuel **GURNSEY**, Dec. 18, 1755	372
Ruth, d. Elah & Phebe, b. Aug. 8, 1761; bp. Aug. 9, [1761]	311,380
Sally, d. Nathan O. & Phebe, b. Jan. 27, 1788	403
Sally, d. Israel & Rhoda, b. Sept. 5, 1794	407
Sally, m. Elisha **NEWTON**, Dec. 13, 1820	429
Samuel, s. John & Hannah, b. Nov. 11, 1735; bp. Nov. 16, 1735	271,356
Samuel, m. Phebe **COE**, Sept. 3, 1756	379
Samuel, s. Samuel & Phebe, b. June 2, 1761; bp. June 7, [1761]	311,380
Samuel, Col., d. Nov. 3, 1810	412
Samuel, m. Betsey A. **CONE**, Jan. 28, 1827	433
Samuel Guernsey, s. Guernsey & Cynthia Ann, b. Dec. 24, 1825	426
Sarah, m. Thomas **SEWARD**, Mar. 31, 1720, by James Wadsworth	346
Sarah, w. of John, Jr., d. Jan. 14, 1740/1	379
Sarah, m. Brotherton **SEWARD**, Nov. 23, 1748	366
Sarah, d. Israel & Ann, b. Apr. 30, 1763; bp. May 8, [1763]	313,385
Sarah, d. Samuel & Phebe, b. Sept. 26, 1766; bp. Oct. 5, 1766	316,387
Sarah A., d. Oren & Delight, b. Jan. 19, 1831	427
Seth, s. Phinehas & Martha, b. May 31, 1767; bp. June 7, 1767	316,392
Sophronia, d. Lemuel & Patty, b. June 30, 1796	427
Statira, d. Samuel & Phebe, b. Jan. 9, 1757; bp. Jan. 16, [1757]	306,379
Statyra, m. Gideon **CANFIELD**, Jr., Jan. 18, 1775, by Rev. Elizur Goodrich	333
Sylvester, s. Elnathan & Eunice, bp. June 22, 1777	326
Talcott, s. Elnathan & Eunice, b. Mar. 4, 1762; twin with Damaris, bp. Mar. 7, [1762]	311,382
Thaddeus, s. Heth & Mary, b. Nov. 19, 1780	400
Thaddeus, s. Thaddeus & Betsey, b. May 13, 1820	426
Theodore Dwight, s. Thaddeus & Betsey, b. Jan. 24, 1815	426
Thomas C., m. Betsey A. **PARKER**, June 11, 1834	436
Thomas S., m. Almira **COLES**, Dec. 23, 1813	413
Thomas Spencer, s. Elias, Jr. & Elisabeth, b. Jan. 3, 1791	405
Timothy Dwight, m. Mary **PAGE**, b. of Durham, Nov. 4, 1847	442
Urania, d. John, Jr. & Damaris, b. Aug. 14, 1737; bp. Aug. 14, 1737	274,379
Urania, of Durham, m. James **CORNEL**, of Middletown, June 6, [1762], by Rev. Elizur Goodrich	328
William Augustus, s. William S. & Margaret, b. Sept. 22, 1822	419
William Smithson, s. Israel & Rhoda, b. Apr. 23, 1796	407

Page

CAMP, (cont.)
William Smithson, s. Israel & Rhoda, b. Jan. 2, 1790; d. Sept. 20, 1795 407
Zipporah, d. Edward & Mary, bp. Jan. 13, 1744/5 284
Zipporah, m. Giles **ROSE**, b. of Durham, June [ ], 1767, by Rev. Elizur Goodrich 330
----, s. Phineas, bp. Sept. 10, [1775] 325
----, twin s. Israel & Rhoda, b. Jan. 18, 1792 407
CANFIELD, Ann, d. Gideon & Ann, bp. Apr. 6, 1746 285
Ann, m. Ephraim **COE**, Oct. 17, 1754 351
Anna, m. Samuel Bowman **WETMORE**, Nov. 7, 1768, by Rev. Elizur Goodrich 331
Anne, d. Gideon & Anne, b. Mar. 30, 1746 364
Asher, s. Gideon & Ann, bp. Jan. 9, 1757 305
Bethiah, d. John & Bethiah, b. Feb. 4, 1762; bp. Feb. 7, 1762 311,381
Dan, s. Gideon & Ann, b. June 27, 1754; bp. June 30, 1754 295,372
Dan, m. Comfort **NEWTON**, Nov. 22, [1775],by Rev. Elizur Goodrich 333
Edward, m. Eliza **ROBINSON**, Nov. 22, 1842 440
Gideon, m. Anne **ROBINSON**, Oct. 28, 1740 359
Gideon, s. Gideon & Anne, b. Sept. 10, 1750; bp. Sept. 23, 1750 291,366
Gideon, Jr., m. Statyra **CAMP**, Jan. 18, 1775, by Rev. Elizur Goodrich 333
Israel, s. Gideon & Anne, b. Sept. 15, 1741; bp. Sept. 20, [1741] 279,360
Jane E., m. Lyman C. **ROBINSON**, b. of Durham, Jan. 19, 1845 441
Jesse, s. Phineas, bp. Aug. 31, [1777] 326
Job, s. Gideon & Anne, bp. June 24, [1764] 314
John, m. Bethiah **MOSS**, Jan. 19, 1748/9 365
John, s. John & Bethiah, b. Oct. 23, 1751; bp. Oct. 27, 1751 293,350
John had negro Rose, m. Dando, negro of Col. Elihu **CHAUNCEY**, Apr. 30, 1767, by Rev. Elizur Goodrich 330
Katherine, d. Gideon & Ann, b. June 16, 1748 365
Katharine, of Durham, m. Jacob **CLARK**, of Haddam, Oct. 26, [1769], by Rev. Elizur Goodrich 331
Margaret, w. of Thomas, d. Mar. 15, 1757 350,351
Mary, w. of Thomas, d. July 30, 1740 351
Mary, d. Jan. 16, 1761 350
Phinehas, s. John & Bethiah, b. Apr. 10, 1753 367
Phineas, m. Amy (Anne) **NEWTON**, Apr. 1, 1773, by Rev. Elizur Goodrich 332,397
Rebeckah, d. Gideon & Ann, b. Oct. 16, 1743; bp. Oct. 16, 1743 282,363
Rebecca, of Durham, m. John **HAMILTON**, of Granville, Dec. 7, [1762], by Rev. Elizur Goodrich 328
Statyra, d. Phinehas, bp. Dec. 17, [1775] 325
Submit, d. John & Bethiah, b. Jan. 26, 1758; bp. Jan. 26, [1758]; d. Jan. 29, 1758 307,374
Thomas, m. Margaret **BRAINARD**, Nov. 26, 1740 359
Thomas, s. John & Bethiah, b. Feb. 14, 1749/50; bp. Apr. 1, 1750 291,366
Thomas, d. Dec. 1, 1760 351
Thomas, d. Nov. 25, 1770 393

Page

CANFIELD, (cont.)
Thomas, s. Phinehas & Anne, b. Mar. 28, 1774; bp. [1774] 324,397
Timothy, s. Gideon & Anne, bp. Aug. 5, [1759] 309
Titus, s. Gideon & Anne, bp. Jan. 24, 1762 311
CARR, Ann, of Simsbury, m. Elisha **LINES**, of Waterbury, Jan. 8, 1845 441
Caleb, m. Margaret **ADAMS**, Feb. 11, [1735], by Rev. Elizur Goodrich 327
Clement, s. William & Sarah, bp. May 17, 1767 316
Content, d. William & Sarah, bp. Aug. 11, 1771 321
Jemmy, s. William & Sarah, bp. Feb. 28, [1773] 322
Joanna, d. William & Sarah, bp. Aug. 13, 1769 319
Josiah, s. William & Sarah, bp. Nov. 18, [1759] 309
Lewis, s. Caleb & Margaret, bp. Oct. 4, 1761 311
Robert, s. William & Sarah, bp. Oct. 9, [1763] 313
Ruth, d. Caleb & Margaret, bp. Feb. 18, [1759] 308
Sarah, m. Caleb **SEWARD**, Jr., Jan. 21, 1713/14, by Rev. Nath[anie]ll Chauncey 342
Sarah, d. William & Sarah, bp. Nov. 29, [1761] 311
William, s. William & Sarah, bp. Jan. 9, 1757 305
CARRIER, Benj[amin] H., m. Mary A. **STRONG**, May 2, 1842 440
CATLIN, John S., m. Hannah **HALL**, Oct. 28, 1822 430
CHADEAYNE, Deborah Ann, m. Elizur **HALL**, Oct. 30, 1821 430
CHAFFEE, F. P., of Middletown, m. Ellen A. **HULL**, of Durham, Sept. 15, 1851 443
CHALKER, Almira, m. Charles **ROBINSON**, Jr., Nov. 27, 1828 434
Benjamin, m. Polly **PRATT**, Apr. 6, 1828 433
Emily, m. Leonard **HULL**, Mar. 16, 1834 436
Martin M., m. Frances A. **RICHMOND**, July 9, 1849 443
Walter J., m. Hannah Jane **ROBINSON**, July 9, 1849 443
CHAMBERLIN, CHAMBERLAIN, Asa, [s. Asa & Martha], b. Jan. 26, 1779 408
Asa, m. Electa **ROBINSON**, Jan. 17, 1826 432
Clarissa Ann, m. William **THOMAS**, Aug. 26, 1829 434
Elisabeth, [d. Asa & Martha], b. Dec. 4, 1768; bp. Aug. 13, 1769 319,408
Harry, s. Asa & Martha, b. Apr. 9, 1782. Entered Sept. 10, 1799 408
Huldah, [d. Asa & Martha], b. Dec. 15, 1772; bp. Dec. 20, [1772] 322,408
Martha N., m. William R. **REYNOLDS**, Nov. 26, 1846 442
Parmelee, [s. Asa & Martha], b. Nov. 14, 1777 408
Polly, [d. Asa & Martha], b. Aug. 8, 1775; bp. Aug. 13, [1775] 325,408
Rufus, [s. Asa & Martha], b. Aug. 31, 1770; bp. Sept. 9, [1770] 320,408
CHAPMAN, Levi, of Saybrook, m. Elizabeth **HULL**, of Durham, Sept. 15, [1767], by Rev. Elizur Goodrich 330
Mehitabel, m. Eli **CRANE**, Jan. 18, 1768 393
Paul, s. Sylvanus & Elizabeth, bp. Jan. 18, 1740 278
Sarah, d. Sylvanus & Eliz[abeth], bp. Feb. 20, 1742/3 281
CHATFIELD, Elizabeth, m. John **TURNER**, Oct. 18, 1792 408
Lewis, m. Rachel **GRISWOLD**, Apr. 17, 1828 433
CHAUNCEY, Abigail, d. Nathaniel & Sarah, b. Oct. 2, 1717;

	Page
CHAUNCEY, (cont.)	
bp. Oct. 23, 1717	255,341
Catharine, d. Capt. Elihu & Mary, b. Apr. 11, 1741	360
Charles, s. Capt. Elihu & Mary, b. Dec. 28, 1729; bp. Dec. 30, 1739; d. Jan. 13, 1740/1	277,359
Charles, s. Col. Elihu & Mary, b. May 30, 1747; bp. May 31, 1747	287,378
Elihu, s. Nathaniel & Sarah, b. Mar. 24, 1710	340
Elihu, Capt., m. Mary **GRISWOLD**, d. of Samuel, late of Killingworth, Mar. 28, 1739, by Capt. David Buil, J. P., in New London County	358
Elihu, Col., had negro Dando, m. Rose, negro of John **CANFIELD**, Apr. 30, 1767, by Rev. Elizur Goodrich	330
Elihu, Col., d. Apr. 11, 1791	406
Elizabeth, w. of Elnathan, d. Feb. 9, 1791	417
Elnathan, s. Nath[anie]ll & Sarah, b. Sept. 10, 1724; bp. Sept. 13, 1724	260,341
Elnathan, m. Elizabeth **GALE**, Feb. 6, 1760	375
Elnathan, Capt., d. May 4, 1796	406
Elnathan Elihu, s. Capt. Elnathan & Elizabeth, bp. Mar. 22, [1767]	316
Katherine, d. Nathaniel & Sarah, b. Sept. 22, 1714; bp. Sept. 26, [1714]	253,340
Katharine, d. Elihu & Mary, bp. Apr. 12, [1740]	279
Katharine, Mrs., m. Rev. Elizur **GOODRICH**, Feb. 1, 1759	377
Katharine, d. Capt. Elnathan & Elizabeth, bp. Aug. 12, [1764]	314
Mary, wid. of Col. Elihu, d. Mar. 1, 1801	409
Nathaniel, of Durham, m. Mrs. Sarah **JUDSON**, d. of Capt. James **JUDSON**, of Stratford, Oct. 12, 1708, by Rev. Charles Chauncey, of Stratford	342
Nathaniel, s. Nath[anie]ll & Sarah, b. Jan. 21, 1720/1; bp. Jan. 21, 1720/1	257,341
Nathaniel, Rev., had negro Jenny bp. Sept. 20, 1730	265
Nathaniel William, s. Elnathan & Elizabeth, b. Sept. 12, 1761; bp. Sept. 20, [1761]	311,380
Sarah, d. N[athaniel] & Sarah, b. Feb. 24, 1711/12; bp. Mar. 2, 1711/12	252,340
Sarah, d. Major Elihu & Mary, b. Sept. 22, 1742; bp. Dec. 26 1742; d. Aug. 15, 1744	281,360
Sarah, d. Elihu & Mary, b. May 7 (8), [1745]; bp. May 12, 1745	284,378
Worthington Gallup, s. Capt. Elnathan & Eliz[abeth], bp. Apr. 12, 1772	321
CHEDSEY, [see under **CHIDSEY**]	
CHIDSEY, CHEDSEY, CHEDSY, Charles P., m. Sarah **SQUIRES**, June 2, 1840	439
Joseph, of Guilford, m. Polly **COE**, of Durham, Mar. 16, 1809	412
Maria, of Durham, m. John **WADSWORTH**, of New York City, Aug. 21, 1834	436
Zerujah, d. Nov. 24, 1771	396
CHIPMAN, Abigail, m. Cornelius **HULL**, Jan. 1, 1746	390

Page

CHIPMAN, (cont.)
Elizabeth, m. Samuel **PARSONS**, Jan. 21, 1746/7 363
Paul, s. Silvanus & Elizabeth, b. Jan. 16, 1740 360
Paul, d. Sept. 2, 1760 350
Sarah, d. Silvanius & Mary, b. Feb. 17, 1742/3 364
Sarah, m. Jared **WHEADON**, b. of Durham, May 24, [1764], by Rev. Elizur Goodrich 329,384
Silvanus, bp. May 18, 1740 277

CHITTENDEN, Beriah, m. Huldah **NEWTON**, Mar. 15, 1774, by Rev. Elizur Goodrich 332

CHURCH, Edward P., of Middletown, m. Amelia M. **CLARKE**, of Durham, Nov. 29, 1832 435

CLAPP, Mehetabel, of Northampton, m. Simeon **PARSONS**, of Durham, Oct. 12, 1731, by Rev. Jonathan Edwards 356

CLARKE, CLARK, Aaron, s. Hezekiah & Olive, b. June 4, 1815 423
Allen, m. Sally **SWATHEL**, Sept. 22, 1803 411
Alonzo C., of Haddam, m. Freelove M. **SCRANTON**, Nov. 28, 1839 438
Amelia M., of Durham, m. Edward P. **CHURCH**, of Middletown, Nov. 29, 1832 435
Anne, d. Joseph, bp. Feb. 18, 1719/20 256
Betsey, d. Allen & Sally, b. May 14, 1812 414
Betsey, m. John A. **COLLINS**, Mar. 1, 1830 434
Cornelia, d. Hezekiah & Olive, b. June 21, 1813 423
Eliphalet, s. Joseph, bp. Oct. 7, 1722 258
Fanny, d. Allen & Sally, b. June 14, 1807 411
Fanny, m. Elizur **CAMP**, Oct. 1, 1827 433
Hannah, of Durham, m. James **GRIDLEY**, of Farmington, Jan. 12, 1735, by Rev. Elizur Goodrich 327
Hannah Post, d. Hezekiah & Olive, b. Feb. 8, 1822 428
Hezekiah, m. Olive **LEE**, Nov. 3, 1807 423
Hezekiah Post, s. Hezekiah & Olive, b. July 3, 1808 423
Jacob, of Haddam, m. Katharine **CANFIELD**, of Durham, Oct. 26, [1769], by Rev. Elizur Goodrich 331
James, s. Jonathan & Ruth, b. Oct. 23, 1773, in Romney, N. H. 413
James, m. Tamza **STEPHENS**, Nov. 5, 1799 414
John, s. Reuben, bp. July 4, [1762] 312
John Coe, s. Allen & Sally, b. Jan. 23, 1810 414
Lavinia, d. James & Tamza, b. Oct. 10, 1800; d. Feb. 25, 1802 414
Lewis, s. Ens. Jacob, bp. Mar. [ ], 1783 326
Louisa, of Middletown, m. Joseph **ADAMS**, of Cleaveland, O., Oct. 17, 1847 442
Mehetabel, d. W[illia]m & Eliz[abeth], bp. Feb. 27, [1757] 306
Olive, s. William & Elizabeth, b. Sept. 5, 1761; bp. Sept. 6, [1761] 311,380
Olive, d. Jacob & Katharine, bp. Feb. 4, 1770 319
Phebe, d. Jacob & Katharine, bp. Oct. 17, [1773] 323
Reuben, s. Reuben, bp. May 6, 1764 314
Samuel W., m. Eliza P. **RANNEY**, Dec. 6, 1837 438

Page

CLARKE, CLARK, (cont.)
Samuel Wilson, s. Hezekiah & Olive, b. Nov. 9, 1810; d. Sept. 27, 1813 423
Samuel Wilson Lee, s. Hezekiah & Olive, b. July 22, 1819 423
Susan, d. Allen & Sally, b. Mar. 12, 1805 411
Thomas H., of Haddam, m,. Betsey M. **PARSONS**, Oct. 3, 1843 440
William, s. William & Judith, bp. Jan. 25, 1729/30 264
William, s. William & Elizabeth, b. Nov. 8, 1758; bp. Nov. 12, [1758] 308,374
William Allen, s. Allen & Sally, b. May 8, 1818 428
CLYME, James, of New Haven, m. Lusina **REED**, of Durham, Oct. 7, 1821 430
COE, Aaron, s. Ephraim, bp. Feb. 21, 1730/1 265
Aaron, m. Phebe **PARSONS**, Nov. 28, 1754 383
Aaron, s. Aaron & Phebe, bp. Sept. 14, 1766 316
Abel, s. Lieut. Joseph, bp. July 30, [1727] 262
Abel, s. Abel & Prudence, b. July 20, 1768; bp. July 24, [1768] 317,390
Abel, d. Jan. 10, 1798 408
Abel had negro Richard, d. Oct. 31, 1822 417
Abigail, d. Capt. ----, bp. Feb. 20, 1731/2 266
Abigail, d. Joseph, Jr., bp. Jan. 12, 1745/6 285
Alandon, d. Morris & Lucy, b. Aug. 16, 1789 406
Ann, d. Ephraim & Ann, of Middlefield, b. Sept. 5, 1757; bp. Sept. 11, [1757] 306,378
Anna, d. Oliver & Lydia, b. Apr. 11, 1796; d. May 13, 1796 410
Anna, m. Jeremiah **BUTLER**, Sept. 20, 1769 394
Anne, d. Timothy & Anne, bp. May 26, [1771] 320
Ashur, s. Josiah & Sarah, b. Sept. 9, 1757; bp. Sept. 11, [1757] 306,373
Benjamin, s. Ephraim & Hannah, b. Mar. 7, 1741; bp. Mar. 7, 1741/2 280,360
Benjamin, m. Lydia **CURTISS**, Oct. 13, 1823 431
Canfield, s. Ephraim, Jr. & Ann, b. Sept. 26, 1763 383
Catherine, d. John & Ann, bp. Apr. 6, 1755 297
Catharine, m. Henry **LOTHROP**, Nov. 25, 1824 432
Charles, s. Abel & Prudence, b. July 12, 1760; bp. July 13, [1760] 310,376
Charles, m. Hannah **BATES**, Oct. 30, 1784 401
Chester, twin with Lester, s. Joel & Sally, bp. Sept. 13, 1796 408
Daniel, s. Ephraim & Hannah, bp. Dec. 24, 1732 268
Daniel, s. Ephraim, Jr. & Anne, b. Aug. 4, 1755 378
Daniel B., m. Cynthia **ROBINSON**, Sept. 1, 1841 439
David, s. Joseph & Abigail, b. Feb. 18, 1717; bp. Mar. 24, 1716/17 254,347
David, s. David & Hannah, bp. July 26, 1747 287
David, Lieut., of Middletown, had negro Zill, m. Dolphin, negro servant of Capt. Abraham **CAMP**, of Norfolk, May 11, [1764] by Rev. Elizur Goodrich 328-9
Ebenezer, s. Robert & Barbarah, b. Aug. 21, 1715; bp. Aug. 21, 1715 254,344,345
Edwin, m. Cornelia C. **PARMALEE**, Mar. 16, 1826 432
Edwin Thomas, s. Timothy, Jr. & Polly, b. Dec. 4, 1803 415
Elijah, s. Abel & Prudence, bp. Mar. 20, 1757 306

Page

COE, (cont.)

Elizabeth, d. William, bp. Oct. 21, 1774 324
Enoch, s. Ephraim & Hannah, bp. Nov. 14, 1736 273
Enoch, of Granville, m. Katharine **CAMP**, of Durham, Nov. 6, 1768, by Rev. Elizur Goodrich 331
Ephraim, s. Eph[raim] & Hannah, bp. July 26, [1724] 259
Ephraim, bp. Aug. 19, 1744 283
Ephraim, m. Ann **CANFIELD**, Oct. 17, 1754 351
Eph[raim] had negro Susa, bp. Apr. [ ], [1771] 320
Ephraim had negro Zillah, bp. June 2, 1771 302
Eunice, d. John & Hannah, bp. Feb. 27, 1742/3 281
Eunice, d. Simon (Simeon) & Anna, b. Jan. 14, 1762; bp. Feb. 21, [1762] 311,380
Eunice, m. John **CAMP**, 3rd, Feb. 29, [1764], by Rev. Elizur Goodrich 328
Eunice, d. Joel & Sally, b. Apr. 21, 1794 408
Hamlet, s. Morris & Lucy, b. Aug. 22, 1785 406
Hannah, d. Ens. Robert & Barbara, bp. Apr. [ ], 1721 257
Hannah, d. David & Hannah, bp. June 21, 1741 279
Hannah, d. Joseph, bp. June 12, 1743 282
Hannah*, d. John, Jr. & Anna, bp. Apr. 20, 1746 (*Anna) 285
Hannah, d. Josiah & Hannah, b. May 1, 1766; bp. May 11, [1766] 315,390
Hannah A., m. William **PECK**, Oct. 22, 1837 438
Hannah Angeline, d. Abraham & Rebecca, b. May 3, 1809 426
Henry M., m. Betsey **ROBINSON**, b. of Durham, Oct. 12, 1834 436
Henry Moulthrop, s. Timothy, Jr. & Polly, b. Oct. 12, 1811 415
Ithamar, s. Aaron & Phebe, b. Sept. 10, 1755; bp. Sept. 14, 1755 298,383
James, s. Joseph, Jr., bp. Nov. 23, 1740 278
Jerusha, d. Abel & Prudence, bp. Dec. 5, 1762 312
Jesse, s. Davie & Hannah, bp. Nov. 20, 1743 282
Jesse, negro child of Ephraim & Hannah, bp. Aug. 6, [1749] 289
Jesse, s. Morris & Lucy, b. Apr. 2, 1780 406
Joel, s. Ephraim & Anne, b. Aug. 10, 1766; bp. Aug. 10, 1766 316,407
Joel, m. Sally **TALCOTT**, Jan. 31, 1791 408
John, s. John & Hannah, bp. Jan. 11, 1718/19 255
John, s. John & Anna, bp. Oct. 25, 1747 288
John, m. Susannah **SWADDLE**, Dec. 10, 1797 408
Jonathan, s. Robert & Barbarah, b. [ ] 13, 1710 342
Joseph, s. Joseph & Abigail, bp. Sept. 5, [1713] 253
Joseph, s. Joseph & Abigail, b. Sept. 5, 1718 347
Joseph, s. Josiah, bp. Mar. 9, 1748/9 289
Joseph, s. Josiah & Sarah, b. Mar. 18, 1748/9 367
Josiah, d. Feb. 14, 1798 408
Katharine, m. Lemuel **PARSONS**, Jan. 28, 1779, by Rev. Elizur Goodrich 333
Katharine, d. Oliver & Lydia, b. Apr. 5, 1797 411
Lester, twin with Chester, s. Joel & Sally, bp. Sept. 13, 1796 408
Linus, m. Maria **SEWARD**, Sept. 15, 1834 436

	Page
COE, (cont.)	
Lois, d. John & Hannah, bp. Aug. 20, 1732	267
Margaret, m. Joseph **TUTTLE**, Dec. 25, 1820	429
Martha, d. Robert & Barbarah, b. Mar. 21, 1713; bp. Mar. 22, 1712/13	253,345
Mary, d. Robert & Barbarah, b. Apr. 11, 1717; bp. Apr. 14, 1717	255,345
Mary, d. Ephraim & Hannah, bp. Mar. 30, 1740	277
Mary, d. David & Hannah, bp. Oct. 27, 1745	285
Mary, of Durham, m. Benjamin **BARNS**, of Granville, May 12, [1763], by Rev. Elizur Goodrich	328
Mary, d. Ephraim & Ann, bp. Dec. 12, 1768	318
Mary, d. Abel & Prudence, b. Jan. 1, 1774; bp. Jan. 2, 1774	323,397
Mary, d. Oct. 26, 1776	398
Mary A., m. Enoch F. **CAMP**, b. of Durham, Nov. 4, 1847	442
Maryann, d. Timothy, Jr. & Polly, b. Nov. 1, 1809	415
Mary Ann, m. Abraham **CAMP**, May 28, 1828	434
Mary Ann, of Durham, m. John R. **BALDWIN**, of Menden, Ill., Jan. 23, 1842	439
Mercy, d. John & Anna, bp. July 23, 1749	289
Mercy, m. Joseph **PARSONS**, Dec. 7, [1775], by Rev. Elizur Goodrich	333,400
Merick Rejoice, s. Abraham & Rebecca, b. June 27, 1804	426
Miles, s. Josiah & Sarah, b. Sept. 24, 1755; bp. Sept. 28, 1755	298,373
Morris, m. Lucy **ROSSETER**, June 15, 1775, by Rev. Elizur Goodrich	333
Morris, s. Morris & Lucy, b. Mar. 20, 1783	406
Nathan, s. David & Hannah, bp. May 23, 1742	280
Noah, s. Charles & Hannah, b. May 24, 1786	401
Oliver, s. John & Ann, bp. Sept. 15, 1751	292
Oliver, m. Lydia **SWATHEL**, Jan. 1, 1794	410
Oliver Bates, s. Oliver & Lydia, b. Aug. 5, 1798	411
Parsons, s. Charles & Hannah, b. Feb. 4, 1792	403
Phebe, d. John & Hannah, bp. Jan. 25, 1735	272
Phebe, m. Samuel **CAMP**, Sept. 3, 1756	379
Phebe A., m. Samuel C. B. **PRAT[T]**, Sept. 28, 1839	438
Phebe Ann Tabatha, d. Abraham & Rebecca, b. Aug. 13, 1817	426
Phinehas, s. Joseph & Abigail, bp. Oct. [ ], 1718	255
Phinehas, s. Joseph & Hannah, bp. Jan. 8, 1737/8	274
Phinehas, s. Josiah & Sarah, b. June 5, 1753	369
Polly, d. Charles & Hannah, b. Sept. 13, 1788	402
Polly, of Durham, m. Joseph **CHEDSEY**, of Guilford, Mar. 16, 1809	412
Prudence, w. of Abel, d. Nov. 23, 1795	406
Rachel, d. Robert & Barbara, bp. Oct. 22, 1732	267
Rejoice, s. Timothy & Phebe, bp. Nov. 19, [1769]	319
Reuben, s. Robert & Barbara, bp. Dec. 22, 1728	263
Rhoda, d. Josiah & Sarah, b. Feb. 1, 1750/1; bp. Feb. 3, 1750/1	292,367
Rhoda, of Durham, m. Stephen **TUTTLE**, of New Haven, Nov. 19, [1772], by Rev. Elizur Goodrich	332
Robert, s. Ens. Robert & Barbarah, b. June 11, 1719; bp.	

Page

COE, (cont.)
June 14, 1719 256,345
Robert, s. Robert & Barbara, bp. June [ ], 1723 259
Robert, s. Reuben, bp. Aug. 15, 1762 312
Rosannah, d. Simeon & Anna, b. Dec. 22, 1749; bp. Dec. 24, 1749 290,366
Sally, d. Morris & Lucy, b. Mar. 30, 1778 406
Sally, m. Capt. John **HART**, July 15, 1800 413
Sally, d. Oliver & Lydia, b. Apr. 8, 1805 411
Samuel, s. Ephraim & Hannah, bp. Aug. 7, 1727 261
Samuel, s. Morris & Lucy, b. May 4, 1776 406
Sarah, d. John, bp. Dec. 19, 1725 261
Sarah, d. Simeon & Anna, b. Mar. 4, 1757; bp. Apr. 10, [1757] 306,377
Sarah, d. Josiah & Hannah, b. Mar. 5, 1762; bp. Mar. 7, [1762] 311,390
Sarah, m. Samuel W. **LYNN**, Jan. 24, 1829 434
Seth, s. Ephraim, bp. Jan. 5, 1734/5 270
Seth, s. Ephraim & Ann, bp. Oct. 6, 1771 321
Simeon, s. John & Hannah, bp. Mar. 26, 1721 257
Simeon, s. Simeon & Annah, b. Feb. 12, 1755; bp. Feb. 16, 1755 296,371
Simeon, s. Morris & Lucy, b. June 22, 1794 406
Sybylla, d. John, bp. May 5, [1723] 259
Sibel, m. Joseph **HULL**, Jan. 1, 1746 364
Talcott, s. Joel & Sally, b. Dec. 21, 1791 408
Tamar, d. John & Hannah, bp. Oct. 26, 1729 264
Tenta, d. Morris & Lucy, b. July 26, 1791 406
Thomas, s. Robert & Barbara, bp. June 25, 1727 262
Timothy, s. Ephraim, bp. Nov. 24, 1728 263
Timothy, s. Simeon & Anne, b. Oct. 21, 1746; bp. Oct. 26, 1746 286,364
Timothy, s. Ephraim & Ann, b. Sept. 16, 1760; bp. Sept. 16, [1760] 310,378
Timothy, m. Phebe **THOMAS**, b. of Durham, July 29, 1766, by Rev. Elizur Goodrich 329
Timothy, s. Timothy & Phebe, bp. July 25, [1773] 323
Timothy, Jr., m. Polly **CALLENDER**, Jan. 10, 1803 415
Timothy J., m. Ann M. **HULL**, Jan. 3, 1842 440
Timothy Jewett, s. Timothy, Jr. & Polly, b. June 19, 1819 415
William, s. Ens. Robert, bp. June 7, 1730 264
William, s. Oliver & Lydia, b. Apr. 24, 1801 411
William Callender, s. Timothy, Jr. & Polly, b. Jan. 1, 1808 415
Zipporah, d. John & Hannah, bp. Jan. 10, 1741/2 280
----, w. of Ephraim, bp. Aug. 19, 1744 283
----, d. Abel, bp. Jan. 2, 1774 (Note says "Mary") 323
----, [child] of Timothy, bp. June 25, [1775] 325
----, s. Oliver & Lydia, st. b. Sept. 28, 1794 410

COLES, Almira, m. Thomas S. **CAMP**, Dec. 23, 1813 413

COLLINS, John A., m. Betsey **CLARKE**, Mar. 1, 1830 434
Joseph, m. Tabatha **STRONG**, Oct. 19, 1824 432

CONE, Betsey A., m. Samuel **CAMP**, Jan. 28, 1827 433
Hannah S., m. Albert M. **SIZER**, Dec. 24, 1838 438

	Page
CONE, (cont.)	
Noyes, m. Polly A. **LYNN**, Apr. 30, 1837	437
CONNER, Elnathan, of Wallingford, m. Barbara **BUEL**, of Killingworth, Apr. 21, 1830	434
COOK, Abigail, d. Benjamin, of Black Rock, bp. Aug. 10, [1740]	278
Abigail, d. Wilson & Mary, bp. Oct. 26, 1755	298
Content, d. Thomas, bp. Dec. 10, [1775]	325
Delight, d. Jesse & Anne, bp. Mar. 13, [1774]	324
Dinah, d. Thomas & Hannah, bp. July 30, 1769	318
Edmund, s. Jesse & Rhoda, b. Nov. 17, 1767; bp. Nov. 29, [1767]; d. Feb. 17, 1768	317,389
Elisha, s. Thomas, Jr. & Hannah, bp. May 17, [1767]	316
Ellen, of Northford, m. Alanson **BRAINARD**, of Durham, Aug. 8, 1847	442
Hannah, d. Thomas, Jr., bp. Aug. 24, 1755	298
Huldah, d. Thomas, Sr., bp. Aug. 21, [1763]	313
Jesse, of Durham, m. Ruth **FAIRCHILD**, of Haddam, Oct. 21 (22), [1760], by Rev. Elizur Goodrich	327,387
Jesse, m. Rhoda **TALCOT[T]**, Oct. 27, 1766, by Rev. Elizur Goodrich	329,387
Jesse, m. Wid. Anne **GRISWOLD**, Oct. 20, [1771], by Rev. Elizur Goodrich	331,395
Joyie, d. Jesse, bp. Oct. 15, 1775	325
Katharine, d. Samuel Done & Rebecca, bp. July 18, [1773]	323
Mary, w. of Wilson, bp. Nov. 11, 1753	294
Mary, d. Wilson & Mary, bp. Dec. 2, 1753	294
Miles, s. Thomas, Jr., bp. June 16, [1765]	315
Millecent, d. Jesse & Ruth, b. Nov. 19, 1761; bp. Jan. 23, 1763	312,387
Noah, s. Samuel Doan (Done) & Rebeckah, b. Dec. 11, 1767; bp. Jan. 15, 1769	318,389
Phebe, d. Samuel Doan & Rebeckah, b. May 6, 1769; bp. May 7, [1769]	318,393
Rebekah, d. Wilson & Mary, bp. Nov. 30, [1760]	310
Rebekah had d. Phebe **DONE**, bp. May 7, [1769]; father Sam[ue]ll **DONE**	318
Rhoda, w. of Jesse, d. July 29, 1771	395
Rhoda, d. Jesse & Ann, b. July 15, 1772; bp. Aug. 16, [1772]	322,395
Robert, [s. Jesse & Ruth], b. Mar. 11, 1763; bp. Mar. 20, [1763]	313,387
Ruth, w. of Jesse, d. Apr. 5, 1766	387
Ruth, d. Jesse & Rhoda, b. July 27, 1769; bp. Sept. 10, [1769]	319,391
Samuel, s. Samuel Done & Rebecca, bp. July 28, [1771]	321
Samuel Dane, s. John, bp. June 19, 1743	282
Samuel Done, of Durham, m. Rebekah **PICKET**, of Haddam, Dec. 4, 1766, by Rev. Elizur Goodrich	330,389
Sarah, d. [Jesse & Ruth], b. Jan. 17, 1765; bp. Jan. 27, 1765	314,387
Tryon, s. Thomas, Jr. & Hannah, bp. Oct. 27, 1771	321
Wilson, bp. Nov. 11, 1753	294
Wilson, s. Wilson & Mary, bp. Sept. 25, [1757]	307

Page

COOK, (cont.)
-----, d. Thomas, bp. Feb. 27, [1774] 324
-----, child of Jesse, bp. Aug. [ ], [1777] 326
COOLEY, Asahel, of Wallingford, m. Sarah **MERWIN**, of Durham, Jan. 23, 1766, by Rev. Elizur Goodrich 329
COOPER, Seth B., m. Elizabeth **STRONG**, Aug. 6, 1837 438
CORNEL, [see under **CORNWELL**]
CORNWALL, [see also **CORNWELL**], Lester, of Meriden, m. Sarah M. **BRAINARD**, of Durham, Oct. 6, 1846 442
CORNWELL, CORNEL, [see also **CORNWALL**], Charles, m. Eunice Jennett **SHELDON**, Oct. 5, 1823 431
Jacob, s. Jacob & Hannah, b. Apr. 25, 1778 402
James, of Middletown, m. Urania **CAMP**, of Durham, June 6, [1762], by Rev. Elizur Goodrich 328
COTTON, John, s. John, bp. June 14, [1761], at Middletown 311
CRANE, Abiathar, s. Elihu & Mary, b. Jan. 29, 1765; bp. Feb. [ ], 1765 314,384
Abigail, d. Henry & Abigail, bp. June 1, [1712] 252
Abigail, d. Henry & Abigail, b. June 6, 1712 343
Abigail, d. Silas & Marcey, b. Sept. 10, 1730; bp. Sept. 13, 1730 265,343
Abigail, m. Brotherton **SEAWARD**, Nov. 9, 1752 350
Abigail, wid. of Capt. Henry, d. Aug. 31, 1754, in the 78th y. of her age 351
Ann, d. Henry & Mercy, bp. Oct. 12, 1716 286
Ann, d. Henry & Marcey, b. Oct. 8, 1746 364
Ann, m. Daniel **HALL**, Jr., Sept. 21, 1766, by Rev. Elizur Goodrich 329,388
Asa, [s. Frederick & Anne], b. Mar. 12, 1780 400
Ashbel, s. Phebe, b. Dec. 10, 1757 374
Charles, [s. Frederick & Anne], b. Feb. 1, 1782 400
Clarinda, d. Elihu & Mary, b. Nov. 23, 1767; bp. Dec. 6, [1767] 317,388
Clarissa, d. John & Abigail, b. July 31, 1762; bp. Aug. 1, [1762] 312,381
Concurrence, d. Henry & Abigail, b. Mar. 25, 1708 339
Concurrence, m. Nathaniel **SEWARD**, Feb. 2, 1730 355
Concurrence, d. Henry & Marcey (Mercy), b. Nov. 14, 1744; bp. Nov. 18, 1744 284,363
Concurrence, m. John **JOHNSON**, b. of Durham, Jan. 15, 1765, by Rev. Elizur Goodrich 329
Elam, s. John & Abigail, b. July 23, 1768; bp. July 31, [1768] 317,391
Ele[a]nor, d. Silas & Lucretia, b. Sept. 19, 1768; bp. Sept. 25, [1768] 317,389
Eli, s. Silas & Mercey, b. Nov. 27, 1742; bp. Nov. 28, 1742 281,362
Eli, m. Mehitabel **CHAPMAN**, Jan. 18, 1768 393
Eli, s. Eli & Mehitabel, b. July 9, 1770; bp. Aug. 26, [1770]; d. Dec. 3, 1776 320,393,398
Eli, s. Eli & Mehitabel, b. Feb. 24, 1777 398
Eli, d. Oct. 5, 1781 399
Elihu, s. Henry, Jr. & Mercy, b. June 24, 1735; bp. June 29, 1735 271,356
Elihu, m. Mary **FOWLER**, Apr. 26, [1759], by Rev. Elizur Goodrich 327,378

Page

CRANE, (cont.)

Elihu, s. Elihu & Mary, b. Jan. 18, 1763 381
Enos, s. Henry & Mercy, b. Aug. 10, 1751; d. Aug. 28, 1751; bp. Aug. 11, 1751 292,352
Enos, s. Silas, Jr. & Lucretia, b. Feb. 13, 1762; bp. Feb. 14, [1762] 311,380
Eunice, [d. Frederick & Anne], b. Jan. 13, 1784 400
Flood, s. Silas & Mercy, b. Feb. 12, 1734; d. June 2, 1743 356,362
Flood, s. Silas & Marcey, b. Feb. 27, 1744/5; bp. Mar. 3, 1744/5; d. Jan. 6, 1763 284,363
Frederick, s. Silas & Abigail, b. Feb. 24, 1751/2 368
Frederick, s. Sergt. Silas & Mercy, bp. Mar. 1, 1751/2 294
Frederick, m. Anne **BABCOCK**, Jan. 1, 1778 400
Hannah, m. Joseph **SEWARD**, Jr., Apr. 26, 1720, by Rev. Jared Elliot, of Killingworth 342
Hannah, d. Silas, Jr. & Lucretia, b. Apr. 15, 1757; bp. Apr. 17, [1757] 306,373
Henry, s. Henry & Concurrence, b. Oct. 25, 1671 345
Henry, s. Henry & Abigail, b. Mar. 20, 1710 340
Henry, Jr., m. Marcey **FRANCIS**, June 7, 1732 354
Henry, Capt., d. Apr. 11, 1741 351
Henry, s. Sergt. Henry & Mercey, b. Dec. 11, 1748; bp. Dec. 18, 1748 288,365
Henry, d. Feb. 1, 1768 389
Henry, m. Jerusha **PARMALEE**, June 24, 1773, by Rev. Elizur Goodrich 332
Hood, s. Silas & Mercy, bp. Feb. 16, 1734/5 270
Huldah, d. Silas & Mercey, b. Apr. 30, 1747; bp. June 7, 1747 287,364
Huldah, of Durham, m. Gurdon **HULL**, of Killingworth, Nov. 10, 1773, by Rev. Elizur Goodrich 332
James, s. Henry, bp. Dec. 17, [1775] 325
Jerusha, d. Henry, bp. Mar. 28, [1779] 326
Jesse, s. Silas & Mercy, b. June 5, 1732; bp. June 11, 1732 267,354
Jesse, m. wid. Rebekah **SEWARD**, Mar. 3, [1763], by Rev. Elizur Goodrich 328
Jesse, s. Eli & Mehitabel, b. Apr. 28, 1782 399
John, s. Henry, Jr. & Mercey, b. Mar. 27, 1733; bp. Apr. 1, 1733; d. Dec. 12, 1736 268,355,357
John, s. Henry & Mercey (Marcy), b. July 1, 1741; bp. July 5, 1741 279,360
John, m. Abigail **CAMP**, Apr. 7, 1762 381
Lament, d. wid. Lois **BATES**, bp. Apr. 4, [1762] 312
Lucretia, d. Silas & Lucretia, bp. May 10, 1772 322
Lucretia, d. Silas & Lucretia, b. July 19, 1772 394
Lidia, d. Eli & Mehitabel, b. Dec. 14, 1779 399
Mary, d. Henry, Jr. & Marcey, b. Nov. 24, 1739; bp. Nov. 25, 1739 276,358
Mary, d. Silas & Lucretia, b. Nov. 27, 1766 386
Mary, d. Robert & Mary, b. Aug. 7, 1767; bp. Aug. 9, 1767 317,390
Mehitabel, d. Eli (Elah) & Mehitabel, b. Nov. 15, 1768; bp. Dec. 25, 1768 318,393

Page

CRANE, (cont.)
Mercy, wid. of Silas, d. Aug. 29, 1782 400
Miles, s. Elihu & Mary, b. Feb. 18, 1761; bp. Mar. 8, [1761] 310,378
Miranda, d. John & Abigail, b. Jan. 20, 1771; bp. Feb. 3, 1771 320,393
Nathan, s. Sergt. Silas & Mercy, b. Sept. 18, 1754; bp. Sept. 22, 1754 296,370
Nathan, s. Eli & Mehitabel, b. Jan. 14, 1772; bp. Jan. 20, 1772 321,398
Oorondates, s. John & Abigail, b. Nov. 10, 1763; bp. Nov. 13, [1763]; d. May 12, 1766 313,383,386
Phebe, d. Henry & Mercy, bp. Jan. 12, 1737/8 274
Phebe, d. Henry, Jr. & Mercey, b. Feb. 6, 1737/8 357
Phebe had s. Ashbel, b. Dec. 10, 1757 374
Phebe, had s. Ashbel **BRADLEY**, bp. May 7, [1758] 307
Phebe, m. Jonas **BISHOP**, Jan. 19 (20), 1763, by Rev. Elizur Goodrich 328,381
Rachel, d. Henry & Jerusha, bp. Feb. 19, [1775] 325
Rebeckah, [d. Frederick & Anne], b. Aug. 25, 1778 400
Rejoice, s. John & Abigail, b. Oct. 10, 1775; bp. Jan. 14, 1776; d. Feb. 17, 1777 326,398
Rejoice, s. John & Abigail, b. May 31, 1778 399
Robert, s. Silas & Marcey, b. Feb. 18, 1739 359
Robert, m. Mary **CAMP**, b. of Durham, Oct. 31, 1765, by Rev. Elizur Goodrich 329
Robert, s. Robert & Mary, b. Nov. 12, 1768; bp. Dec. 25, [1768] 318,390
Robert G., s. Sergt. Silas & Mary, bp. Feb. 24, 1739/40 277
Ruth, d. Sergt. Silas & Macey (Mercey), b. Dec. 12, 1749; bp. Dec. 17, 1749 290,365
Sarah, d. Silas, Jr. & Lucretia, b. Nov. 7, 1758; bp. Nov. 12, [1758] 308,374
Silas, m. Marcey **GRISWOLD**, Nov. 27, 1729 343
Silas, s. Silas & Mercey, b. Nov. 9, 1737; bp. Nov. 13, 1737 274,358
Silas, d. Jan. 15, 1763 351
Silas, s. Silas & Lucretia, b. Dec. 13, 1763; bp. Dec. 25, [1763] 313,383
Sybil, d. Eli & Mehitabel, b. Apr. 17, 1774; bp. May 1, 1774 324,398
Timothy Botchford (Botsford), s. John & Abigail, b. June 10, 1773; bp. Aug. 8, 1773 323,397
Zeleck, s. John & Abigail, b. Feb. 23, 1766; bp. Mar. [1766] 315,386
----, Capt., had negro Holland bp. Jan. 7, 1727/8 262

CRITTENDEN, CRUTTENDEN, Abraham, s. Abraham & Sarah, b. Aug. 3, 1714; bp. Aug. 5, 1716 254,343
Anna, d. Abraham & Sarah, bp. Dec. 25, 1726 261
Ebenezer, s. Samuel & Sarah, b. Oct. 18, 1757; bp. Oct. 23, [1757] 307,376
Esther, of Durham, m. Ens. Edward **CAMP**, of Middletown, June 20, 1758, by Rev. Elizur Goodrich 327
George, m. Eliza A. **STRONG**, May 19, 1824 431
Immer, s. Samuel & Sarah, b. Mar. 17, 1766; bp. Mar. [ ], [1766] 315,388
John, s. Samuel & Sarah, b. Oct. 27, 1761; bp. Nov. 1, [1761] 311,384
Mary, d. Abraham & Sarah, bp. Sept. 23, 1722 258

Page

CRITTENDEN, CRUTTENDEN, (cont.)
Mary, d. Abraham & Sarah, b. Sept. 27, 1722 346
Medad, s. Samuel & Sarah, b. May 23, 1764; bp. May 27, 1764 314,384
Nath[anie]l, s. Abraham, bp. Apr. 5, 1730 264
Nathaniel, s. Abraham & Sarah*, b. July 21, 1731; bp. July 25, 1731 *(Changed from "Barbara" to "Sarah" in baptism) 265,354
Noah, s. Samuel & Sarah, bp. Aug. 14, [1768] 317
Osee, s. Samuel & Sarah, b. Jan. 18, 1760; bp. Jan. 20, 1760 309,376
Samuel, s. Abraham & Sarah, b. Feb. 7, 1733; bp. Feb. 20, 1733/4 269,356
Samuel, s. Samuel & Sarah, b. Sept. 27, 1755; bp. Sept. 28, 1755 298,376
Sarah, d. Abraham & Sarah, b. May 10, 1715; bp. May 15, [1715] 254,344
Sarah, d. Abraham & Sarah, b. Sept. 12, 1718; bp. Sept. 15, 1718 255,344
Sarah, m. Abner **TIBBALS**, Aug. 26, 1747 368
Susannah, d. Abraham & Sarah, b. Sept. 5, 1720; bp. Sept. 11, [1720] 256,345
CROWELL, Eliza, m. Benjamin **THOMAS**, June 2, 1830 434
Henry, m. Persis **SOUTHWORTH**, July 30, 1821 430
CRUTTENDEN, [see under **CRITTENDEN**]
CURTIS, CURTISS, Aaron, s. James, Jr. & Hannah, b. Sept. 9, 1737; bp. Sept. 11, 1737 274,380
Aaron, of Granville, m. Hannah **GRISWOLD**, of Durham, May 11, 1763, by Rev. Elizur Goodrich 328
Abigail, d. James & Hannah, bp. Sept. 17, 1732 267
Abijah, s. John & Dinah, b. Mar. 2, 1750; bp. Mar. 4, 1749/50 290,353
Abijah, m. Ann **BISHOP**, Aug. 13, 1777 399
Ann, m. Robert **FAIRCHILD**, May 18, 1730 363
Ann, d. Ephraim & Elizabeth, b. Sept. 1, 1740 363
Anna, d. Nathan & Anna, bp. May 13, [1770] 319
Anna, m. Israel **SCRANTON**, Oct. 12, 1800 420
Anna Elizabeth, d. Samuel & Lucretia, b. May 11, 1815 414
Anne, d. Abijah & Ann, b. Dec. 6, 1779 399
Augustus, s. Nathan & Anne, bp. Oct. 12, 1766 316
Augustus, s. Nathan & Anna, bp. Oct. 23, 1774 324
Charles, s. David, Jr. & Prudence, bp. Feb. 16, 1772 321
Clarissa, d. Nathan & Anna, bp. May [ ], [1768] 317
Cynthia, of Durham, m. Henry D. **FOWLER**, of Middletown, Nov. 19, 1840 439
Daniel, s. David & Thankful, b. Oct. 7, 1753 353
David, s. James & Hannah, bp. July 5, [1724] 259
David, m. Thankful **THOMSON**, Jan. 22, 1747 352
David, s. David & Thankful, b. May 19, 1750; bp. May 20, 1750 291,353
David, Jr., m. Prudence **BISHOP**, Dec. 27, 1770, by Rev. Elizur Goodrich 331
David, s. Abijah & Ann, b. Jan. 31, 1795 407
David, s. Samuel & Lucretia, b. July 25, 1823 424
Dinah, d. John & Dinah, b. Jan. 21, 1766; bp. Jan. 26, 1766 315,386
Dinah, d. Abijah & Ann, b. July 23, 1785 407
Dinah, wid. of John, d. Sept. 6, 1800 409

Page

CURTIS, CURTISS, (cont.)

Ebenezer, s. David & Thankful, b. Jan. 17, 1749; bp. Jan. 22 1748/9 289,353
Emeline, m. Aralon W. **RUSSELL**, Oct. 12, 1836 437
Esther, d. James & Hannah, b. Aug. 22, 1715; bp. Aug. 28, [1715] 254,344,345
Esther, d. David & Thankful, b. Nov. 15, 1751 353
Esther, m. Phinehas **BATES**, Dec. 5, [1771], by Rev. Elizur Goodrich 331
Eunice, d. James & Hannah, bp. June 23, 1734 269
Eunice, of Durham, m. Samuel **SUTLIEF**, of Haddam, Mar. 21, [1735], by Rev. Elizur Goodrich 327
Hannah, d. James & Hannah, bp. Oct. 8, 1727 262
Hannah, d. John & Dinah, b. Jan. 8, 1755; bp. Jan. 12, 1755 296,375
Hannah, d. Nathan & Anna, bp. Mar. 1, [1772] 321
Hannah Hall, d. Samuel & Lucretia, b. Aug. 29, 1823 424
Helen, d. David, bp. Nov. 17, 1751 293
Ichabod, s. Abijah & Ann, b. May 17, 1790; d. May 10, 1791 407
Ichabod, s. Abijah & Ann, b. Apr. 3, 1792 407
James, Jr., m. Hannah **BULL**, Sept. 12, 1734 380
James, Sr., had negro Pelu, bp. May 18, 1740 277
James, s. Nathan & Anna, bp. Feb. 14, [1762] 311
James, s. Nathan & Anna, bp. May 22, 1763 313
James, m. Sally **MORROW**, Nov. 2, 1791 403
John, s. James & Hannah, b. Nov. 21, 1721; bp. Nov. 21, 1721 257,346
John, m. Dinah **NORTON**, Nov. 18, 1747 353
John, s. John & Dinah, b. May 5, 1757; bp. May 8, [1757] 306,375
John, Jr., m. Lydia **HALL**, Dec. 29, 1794 408
John, d. July 1, 1800 409
John, m. Ruth **PARMELE**, June 2, 1801 409
John, s. Samuel & Lucretia, b. Nov. 2, 1811 414
Linus, s. David & Prudence, bp. Nov. 21, [1773] 323
Lois, d. John & Dinah, b. July 15, 1760; bp. July 20, [1760] 310,377
Lydia, w. of John, Jr., d. July 6, 1799 409
Lydia, d. John & Ruth, b. Oct. 7, 1802 411
Lydia, m. Benjamin **COE**, Oct. 13, 1823 431
Mary, d. James & Hannah, b. July 4, 1717; bp. July 21, [1717] 255,345
Mary, m. Phinehas **BEERS**, June 25, 1822 430
Nathan, s. James, Jr. & Hannah, b. June 23, 1735; bp. June 29, 1735 271,380
Nathan, m. Anna **BOOTH**, May 13, 1761 380
Olive, d. Abijah & Ann, b. Apr. 24, 1778 399
Phebe, d. James & Hannah, b. Oct. 4, 1719; bp. [Oct.] [1719] 256,345
Phebe, d. John & Dinah, b. June 16, 1752 353
Phebe, d. Abijah & Ann, b. Feb. 27, 1783 407
Phebe, d. Samuel & Lucretia, b. Apr. 12, 1817 414
Phebe Ann, d. Nathan & Anna, bp. Sept. 9, [1764] 314
Phebe Ann, m. Bridgman **GURNSEY**, Feb. 5, 1786 402
Samuel, s. Abijah & Ann, b. July 13, 1787 407

Page

CURTIS, CURTISS, (cont.)
Samuel, m. Lucretia **BROOKS**, Oct. 3, 1810 414
Samuel Brooks, s. Samuel & Lucretia, b. July 13, 1813 414
Sarah, d. James & Hannah, b. Mar. 15, 1712/13; bp. Mar. 22, 1712/13 253,343,345
Sarah, d. David & Thankful, b. May 7, 1755; bp. May 18, 1755 297,373
Sarah, d. John & Dinah, b. Oct. 11, 1762; bp. Oct. 17, 1762 312,381
Sarah, d. Samuel & Lucretia, b. May 31, 1819 414
DAVIS, Amos, s. Amos & Hope, b. Sept. 1, 1788 402
Cynthia E., of S. Killingworth, m. Morgan **DAVIS**, of N. Madison, Sept. 27, 1835 437
Eunice, of Killingworth, m. Evelyn **SCRANTON**, of Madison, Jan. 24, 1836 (Both names of females in book) 437
Lewis I., m. Harriet **BISHOP**, Aug. 3, 1829 434
Louisa E., of Watertown, m. Noble **LEWENRONTH**, of Waterbury, Oct. 15, 1844 441
Luca, d. Amos & Hope, b. Jan. 24, 1787 402
Morgan, of N. Madison, m. Cynthia E. **DAVIS**, of S. Killingworth, Sept. 27, 1835 437
Thorrit, m. Patty **KELSEY**, Sept. 23, 1824 431
DESBURY, Vila, d. Nehemiah, d. Nov. 28, 1822 417
DICKINSON, Clarissa, m. Israel S. **CAMP**, May 1, 1827 433
Lydia, m. Harvey **ROBINSON**, Oct. 29, 1821 430
DIMOCK, DIMOCH, DIMMOCK, Daniel, m. Thankful **MERRIMAN**, May 27, [1762], by Rev. Elizur Goodrich 328,381
Mabel, d. Daniel & Thankful, bp. Sept. 9, [1770] 320
Mary Lyman, d. Daniel, Jr. & Sophia, b. Sept. 1, 1812 423
Patte, d. Daniel & Thankful, b. May 7, 1768; bp. May [ ], [1768] 317,389
Phebe, d. Daniel, bp. Sept. 7, [1777] 326
Sarah, d. Daniel & Thankful, b. May 9, 1766; bp. May [ ], [1766] 315,386
Thankful, d. Daniel & Thankful, b. June 22, 1763; bp. June 26, [1763] 313,383
Thankful, m. James **ROBINSON**, Jr., Mar. 16, 1785 403
-----, s. Daniel, bp. [1774] 324
DONEY, [see under **DOREY**]
DOREY, DONEY, James, s. James & Jane, bp. Apr. 5, 1747 287
John, s. James & Jane, bp. Dec. 9, 1753 294
Louren, s. James & Jane, bp. Dec. 5, 1756 305
Rachel, d. James & Jane, bp. Oct. 28, 1750 292
Seth, s. James & Jane, bp. Dec. 11, 1748 288
DOWD, DOUD, Frederic, of Madison, m. Charlotte **HICKOX**, Feb. 24, 1834 436
Rachel, m. Thomas **TIBBALS**, Dec. 22, 1748 369
DUDLEY, Betty, of Guilford, m. Josiah **SQUIRE**, of Durham, Dec. 5, 1766, by Rev. Elizur Goodrich 330
Mary, m. Abiathar **SQUIER**, Mar. 9, 1763 396
DUNN, DUN, DONE, Daniel, s. Timothy & Mehetabel, bp. Nov. 11,

Page

DUNN, DUN, DONE, (cont.)
[1759] 309
Daniel, s. Tim[othy] & Mabel, bp. July 29, 1771 321
Emily, m. Lewis **NORTON**, Jan. 22, 1826 432
Jon, s. Tim[othy] & Mabel, bp. July 29, 1771 321
John, s. Timothy & Mehetabel, bp. Nov. 13, [1774] 324
Mabel, d. Timothy & Mehetabel, bp. July [ ], [1772] 322
Molly, d. Timothy & Mehetabel, bp. May 17, 1767 316
Phebe, d. Sam[ue]ll **DONE** & Rebekah **COOK**, bp. May 7, [1769]
(Probably Phebe **COOK**) 318
Ruth, d. Timothy & Mehetabel, bp. July 2, 1769 318
Timothy, s. Timo[thy] & Mehetabel, bp. Jan. 9, 1757 305
EDEE, Azubah, bp. Sept. 12, 1742 281
ELLIOTT, Isaac, s. Jared, bp. May 1, [1763], at Killingworth 313
Jenet, d. Timothy & Lydia, b. Mar. 2, 1811 420
Jennett, m. William **ROBINSON**, Aug. 15, 1836 437
Lucius, s. Timothy & Lydia, b. July 9, 1807 420
Lucy R., m. Erastus **JONES**, Feb. 21, 1826 432
Lucy Rose, d. Timothy, b. Aug. 7, 1803 420
Luzerne, s. Timothy & Lydia, b. Mar. 4, 1814 420
Luzerne, m. Hannah **ROBINSON**, Sept. 24, 1839 438
Lydia M., of Durham, m. Jackson **MANN**, of Carlisle, Ky.,
Oct. 6, 1844 441
Lydia Mariah, d. Timothy & Lydia, b. Jan. 16, 1818 420
Wyllys, m. Lucy **CAMP**, Feb. 19, 1823 431
ELY, James S., of Meriden, m. Amelia S. **HARRISON**, Aug. 30, 1846 442
Jerusha, d. Samuel & Jerusha, b. Jan. 3, 1753 369
Phebe, d. Samuel & Jerusha, b. Jan. 24, 1742; d. Jan. 28, 1748/9 365
Samuel, s. Samuel & Jerushah, b. June 21, 1750; bp. June 24,
1750 291,352
Samuel, s. Dr. Samuel & Jerusha, bp. Feb. 23, 1755 297
EVEREST, Abigail, d. Benjamin, bp. May 25, 1729 263
Jared, s. Benjamin, bp. Aug. 6, 1727 262
FAIRCHILD, Abigail, twin with Hannah, d. Thomas & Thankful, bp.
Apr. 29, 1745 284
Abraham, s. Edmund & Mary, bp. Jan. 16, 1736/7 273
Alexander, s. Curtis & Marcey, b. Dec. 14, 1736; bp. Feb.
13, 1736/7 273,362
Ann, d. Thomas & Thankful, bp. Nov. 5, 1738 275
Ann, d. Curtis, bp. Oct. 12, 1740 278
Anne, d. Curtis & Marcey, b. Oct. 1, 1740 362
Asenath, d. Tho[mas] & Thankful, bp. Dec. 5, 1742 281
Benjamin, s. Tho[mas] & Thankful, bp. Nov. 23, 1740 278
Caleb, s. Edmund & Mary, b. Jan. 27, 1737; bp. Jan. 29, 1737 274,357
Catherine, d. Thomas & Thankful, bp. Dec. 17, 1730 265
Dinah, d. Tho[mas] & Thankful, bp. Dec. 26, [1736] 273
Edmund, s. Samuel & Mary, b. Aug. 12, 1714; bp. Aug. 15, 1714 253,342
Edmund, s. Thomas & Thankful, bp. Aug. 9, 1747 287

Page

FAIRCHILD, (cont.)
Edmund, s. Samuel & Phebe, bp. Mar. 22, 1751/2 294
Elisha, s. Samuel & Phebe, bp. May 16, 1736 272
Elizabeth, d. Capt. Robert & Anne, b. June 14, 1743; bp. June 19, 1743 282,363
Elizabeth, d. Sam[ue]l & Phebe, bp. Sept. 22, 1745 285
Enos, s. Thomas & Thankful, bp. Oct. 29, 1732 267
Eunice, d. Edmond & Mary, bp. Sept. 22, 1745 285
George, s. John & Rhoda, bp. May 12, 1754 295
Hamlet, s. John, bp. May 16, [1756] 298
Hannah, twin with Abigail, d. Thomas & Thankful, bp. Apr. 29, 1745 284
Joel, s. Samuel & Phebe, bp. Apr. 13, 1755 297
John, s. Curtis & Mercy, b. Feb. 15, 1728; bp. Feb. 16, 1728/9 263,361
Lewis, s. Curtis & Mercey, b. May 6, 1730; bp. May 9, 1731 265,362
Lois, d. Edmund & Mary, bp. Mar. 20, 1742/3 281
Lucy, d. Samuel & Phebe, bp. Feb. 13, 1742/3 281
Mary, d. Sam[ue]ll, Jr. & Mary, b. July 1, 1712; bp. July 6, [1712] 252,343
Mary, d. Thomas & Thankful, bp. Sept. 1, 1734 270
Mary, of Durham, m. Smith Samuel **BALDWIN**, of Martinsburg, N. Y., Oct. 17, 1839 439
Millecent, d. Jesse & Ruth, b. Nov. 19, 1761 (Note says it should be "Millecent **COOK**") 387
Phebe, d. Samuel & Phebe, bp. May 25, 1740 277
Rachel, d. Edmund & Mary, bp. Dec. 6, [1741] 279
Rachel, d. Sam[ue]l & Phebe, bp. Jan. 31, 1749/50 290
Reuben, s. Curtis & Marcey, b. Dec. 18, 1734; bp. Dec. 22, 1734 270,362
Rhoda, of Durham, m. Reuben **BAILEY**, of Haddam, Aug. 27, 1777, by Rev. Elizur Goodrich 333
Robert, s. Samuel & Mary, b. Nov. 19, 1703 363
Robert, m. Ann **CURTIS**, May 18, 1730 363
Robert, s. Curtis & Marcey (Mercy), b. Jan. 16, 1738; bp. Jan. 7, 1738/9 275,362
Ruth, of Haddam, m. Jesse **COOK**, of Durham, Oct. 21, (22), [1760], by Rev. Elizur Goodrich 327,387
Samuel, s. Samuel & Mary, b. Aug. 10, 1708 341
Samuel, s. Samuel & Phebe, bp. Oct. 18, 1747 288
Sarah, d. Samuel & Phebe, bp. May 21, 1738 275
Silvanus Ashur, s. Samuel & Phebe, bp. June 15, 1735 271
Zipporah, d. Curtis & Mercey, b. Jan. 1, 1732; bp. Jan. 6, 1732/3 268,362
Zipporah, d. Curtis & Marcey (Mercy), b. Nov. 7, 1732/ bp. Nov. 14, 1742 281,362

FENN, FEN, Mary, d. John, bp. Dec. 10, [1732] 268
Mary, m. Samuel **PARSONS**, Jr., Dec. 1, 1758 375
Samuel, s. Sam[ue]l, bp. Dec. 5, 1742 281
Susanna, d. Samuel, bp. Mar. 28, 1737 273

FERGUSON, Eben, s. Sam[ue]l, bp. Dec. 6, 1731 266

Page

FERGUSON, (cont.)
James, s. James & Martha, bp. Dec. 3, [1769] 319
John, s. Sam[ue]l & Isabel, bp. Jan. 11, 1729/30 264
Joseph, s. James & Martha, bp. Oct. 4, 1772 322
Samuel, s. James & Martha, bp. Dec. 3, [1769] 319
FIELD, Abigail, m. John **CAMP**, Jr., Apr. 13, 1749 379
Abigail, d. Ambrose & Sarah, bp. Mar. 15, [1772] 321
Ambrose, of Durham, m. Sarah **BATES**, of Haddam, Sept. 17, [1767], by Rev. Elizur Goodrich 330,391
Charlotte Angeline, m. John **JACKSON**, Aug. 31, 1845 441
Robert, s. Ambrose & Sarah, b. June 10, 1770; bp. June 17, [1770] 319,393
----, [child] of Ambrose, bp. Aug. 13, [1775] 325
FLAGG, Abigail, m. James C. **ARNOLD**, Mar. 9, 1831 435
FOOTE, Catharine H., m. Blinn I. **BRAINARD**, May 1, 1830 434
FORTES, Francis M., m. Jane A. **CAMP**, Nov. 25, 1845 441
FOWLER, Aaron, s. Joseph* & Hannah, bp. Feb. 13, 1736/7 (*Should be "Josiah") 273
Abiathar, s. David & Elizabeth, b. Aug. 31, 1754; bp. Sept. 1, 1754 296,378
Abredgget*, m. Samuel **HART**, Oct. 9, 1759 (*Bridget) 386
Amos, s. David & Elizabeth, b. Aug. 1, 1752 378
Amos, m. Sarah **HINMAN**, Jan. 2, 1777 398
Anne, d. Caleb & Anne, b. Oct. 28, 1761; bp. Nov. 1, [1761] 311,380
Anne, m. Nathaniel **THAYER**, Nov. 6, 1791 407
Betsey, m. Eliakim W. **HULL**, Nov. 19, 1819 435
Bridget, see under Abredgget
Caleb, s. Josiah & Hannah, b. Jan. 7, 1727; bp. Jan. 15, 1726/7 261,353
Caleb, m. Anne **ROSE**, Jan. 10, 1759 380
Caleb had negro Thomas m. Thankful, Jan. 8, 1772, by Rev. Elizur Goodrich 331
Caleb, d. June 21, 1807 411
Charles Augustus, s. Reuben R. & Catharine, b. Apr. 13, 1798 426
David, m. Mary **MILES**, June 15, 1724/5 346
David, s. David & Mary, b. Jan. 21, 1728/9; bp. Jan. 26, 1728/9 263,347
David, m. Elizabeth **HALL**, Apr. 21, 1736, by Theophilus Yale, J. P. 357
Edmund, s. Caleb & Anne, b. Feb. 25, 1770; bp. Mar. 4, 1770 319,397
Elihu, s. Josiah & Hannah, bp. Oct. 22, 1732 267
Elihu, s. Joseph* & Hannah, bp. Mar. 4, 1738/9 (*Josiah) 276
Elihu, s. Elihu & Mary, bp. Feb. 27, 1763 312
Elizabeth, d. Josiah & Hannah, b. Oct. 11, 1728; bp. Oct. 13, 1728 263,353
Elizabeth, d. David & Elizabeth, b. Feb. 27, 1742; bp. Feb. 27, 1742/3 281,363
Elizabeth, of Durham, m. Amos **HARRISON**, of Northford, May 20, [1762], by Rev. Elizur Goodrich 328
Esther, d. David, bp. Sept. 20, 1747 288
Hannah, d. Josiah & Hannah, b. Apr. 12, 1725; bp. Apr. [ ], [1724/5] 260,353
Henry D., of Middletown, m. Cynthia **CURTISS**, of Durham, Nov.

	Page
FOWLER, (cont.)	
19, 1840	439
Horatio N., of Middletown, m. Mary Ann **BATES**, of Durham, Sept. 12, 1827	433
Hosmer, m. Harriet E. **NETTLETON**, Nov. 6, 1826	433
Irene, d. Caleb & Anne, b. Nov. 5, 1764; bp. Nov. [ ], 1764	314,388
Jane A., m. Cyrus **KELSEY**, May 12, 1835	436
John, s. David & Elizabeth, b. May 7, 1740; bp. May 11, 1740	277,363
Jonathan, s. Josiah & Hannah, b. Aug. 20, 1730; bp. Aug. 23, 1730	264,353
Joseph, m. Ruth **BAKER**, Apr. 2, 1736, by Rev. Nathaniel Chauncey	356
Josiah, m. Hannah **BALDWIN**, June 6, 1723	353
Josiah, s. Josiah & Hannah, b. Mar. 31, 1724; bp. Apr. 5, 1724	259,353
Josiah had negro Pelor, s. Judith, bp. Nov. 14, 1736	273
Josiah, d. Sept. 7, 1757	351
Julius, s. Caleb & Anne, b. Apr. [ ], 1768; bp. May 1, [1768]	317,396
Levi, m. Mary L. **MUNSON**, b. of Northford, Oct. 11, 1852	443
Lucretia, d. Caleb & Anne, b. Mar. 10, 1772; bp. May 10, 1772	322,397
Mary, d. David & Mary, b. Feb. 2, 1731; bp. Feb. 14, 1730/1	265,353
Mary, w. of David, d. Dec. 2, 1734	351
Mary, d. Joseph & Ruth, bp. Dec. 21, 1740	278
Mary, m. Elihu **CRANE**, Apr. 26, [1759], by Rev. Elizur Goodrich	327,378
Mary Jane, of Durham, m. Edwin **GATZMER**, of Philadelphia, Pa., Sept. 1, 1853	443
Miles, s. David & Mary, b. Mar. 9, 1726/7; bp. Mar. 12, 1726/7	261,346
Noah, s. Joseph & Ruth, bp. Feb. 5, 1736/7	273
Oliver, s. David & Elizabeth, b. June 2, 1737; bp. June 5, 1737	274,357
Ozias, s. Caleb & Anne, b. July 25, 1766; bp. Aug. 3, [1766]; d. Apr. 14, 1767	316,388
Ozias, s. Caleb, bp. [1774]	324
Phebe, d. Joseph & Ruth, b. Sept. 19, 1735; bp. Sept. 21, 1735	271,356
Reuben Rose, s. Caleb & Anne, b. June 17, 1763; bp. June 19, [1763]	313,388
Ruth, d. Joseph & Ruth, bp. Mar. 25, 1738/9	276
Sarah, d. Sergt. Josiah & Hannah, bp. July 14, 1734	269
Sarah, d. Joseph & Ruth, bp. Sept. 23, 1744	284
Sarah, of Durham, m. Elisha **MILLAR**, of Farmington, Oct. 18, 1764, by Rev. Elizur Goodrich	329
Sarah, m. Moses **SEAWARD**, May 5, 1791	409
Seth, s. David & Elizabeth, b. Jan. 1, 1744; bp. Jan. 6, 1744/5	284,378
Sophronia, of Durham, m. A. M. **GRISWOLD**, of Killingworth, Jan. 23, 1845	441
Titus, s. David & Elizabeth, b. Nov. 29, 1738; bp. Dec. 3, 1738	275,357
Titus, of Granville, m. Hannah **BURRIT**, of Durham, Apr. 9, 1765, by Rev. Elizur Goodrich	329
William, s. Reuben & Catharine, d. June 26, 1792	417
-----, had negro Judith, bp. Oct. 31, 1736	273
FRANCIS, FRANCES, Abigail, d. Joseph & Martha, b. July 3, 1762; bp. July 4, [1762]	312,381

Page

FRANCIS, FRANCES, (cont.)
Charles C., [twin with Lydia J.], s. [Thomas & Lydia D.] b. July 20, 1837 429
Concurrence, d. Joseph & Martha, b. Feb. 17, 1766 386
Dan[ie]l, s. Daniel, bp. Aug. 24, [1729] 264
Daniel, s. Daniel & Elizabeth, bp. May 1, 1737 273
Elizabeth, d. Daniel & Elizabeth, bp. Jan. 10, 1730/1 265
Henrietta G., [d. Thomas & Lydia D.], b. Nov. 22, 1841 429
Hezekiah, s. James, bp. Sept. 22, 1754 296
Huldah, d. Daniel & Elizabeth, bp. Mar. 11, 1732/3 268
Huldah, of N. Killingworth, m. Nathaniel **BISHOP**, of Durham, June 29, [1757], by Rev. Elizur Goodrich 327
Huldah, d. Joseph, bp. June 8, 1777 326
James, s. Daniel & Elizabeth, bp. July 19, 1725 260
James, s. Thomas, bp. May 26, 1754 295
James, twin with Jonathan, s. James & Sarah, bp. July 22, [1759] 309
James, s. Wait C. & Mary, b. Apr. 30, 1806 411
Jonathan, twin with James, s. James & Sarah, bp. July 22, [1759] 309
Joseph, s. Dan & Eliz[abeth], bp. June 14, [1724] 259
Joseph, m. Sarah **BUCK**, Oct. 2, 1750 372
Joseph, m. Martha **PORTER**, Jan. 26, 1758 374
Lucretia, d. Joseph & Martha, b. Apr. 24, 1764 383
Lydia J., [twin with Charles C., d. Thomas & Lydia D.], b. July 20, 1837 429
Maranda, d. Wait C. & Mary, b. Feb. 11, 1796 411
Marcey, m. Henry **CRANE**, Jr., June 7, 1732 354
Mary, d. James, bp. Nov. 12, 1749 290
Mary, d. Wait C. & Mary, b. May 6, 1801 411
Mary, m. Jefferson **IVES**, Jan. 16, 1823 430
Mary, m. Seth R. **PARSONS**, May 5, 1832 435
Mercy, d. Daniel & Elizabeth, bp. Feb. 2, 1734/5 270
Miranda, see under Maranda
Nathan, s. Daniel & Eliz[abeth], bp. June 28, 1741 279
Nathan, s. James & Sarah, bp. Jan. 30, [1757] 306
Phebe, d. Wait C. & Mary, b. Feb. 2, 1799 411
Rachel, d. Joseph & Martha, b. July 2, 1768 389
Rosanna, d. James. bp. Feb. 16, 1751/2 294
Roswel, of Killingworth, m. Anne **HULL**, of Durham, Oct. 15, 1777, by Rev. Elizur Goodrich 333
Sarah, w. of Joseph, d. Oct. 11, 1753 372
Sarah, d. Joseph & Martha, bp. Jan. 28, 1759 308
Stephen, s. Joseph & Martha, bp. July 8, [1770] 319
Thomas, s. Daniel & Elizabeth, bp. Sept. 3, 1727 262
Thomas, m. Lydia D. **THOMPSON**, Nov. 15, 1836 437
Thomas A., [s. Thomas & Lydia D.], b. June 29, 1844 429
Titus, s. Joseph & Martha, b. Aug. 22, 1760; bp. Aug. 24, [1760] 310,376
Wait Cornel, s. Thomas & Susanna, bp. May 30, [1773] 323
William H., [d. Thomas & Lydia D.], b. Dec. 28, 1839 429

Page

FRISBIE, FRISBEE, Dorcas, [d. Jonah & Elizabeth], b. June 10, 1767; bp. July 19, 1767 316,394
Elizabeth, [d. Jonah & Elizabeth], b. Feb. 23, 1761 394
James, s. Jonah & Elizabeth, b. July 31, 1771 392
Jonah, m. Elizabeth **HICKOX**, Sept. 27, 1758 394
Jonah, [s. Jonah & Elizabeth], b. Aug. 25, 1765; bp. Sept. 1, [1765] 315,394
Rachel, [d. Jonah & Elizabeth], b. Aug. 27, 1763 394
Rachel, d. Josiah* & Elizabeth, bp. Sept. 4, [1763] (*Jonah?) 313
Thaddeus Grannice, [s. Jonah & Elizabeth], b. Jan. 5, 1760; bp. July 12, [1761] 311,394
Timothy, [s. Jonah & Elizabeth], b. Apr. 20, 1769; bp. Apr. 23, [1769] 318,394
FULLER, Jonathan I., m. Martha **STEVENS**, Nov. 27, 1828 434
GALE, Elizabeth, m. Elnathan **CHAUNCEY**, Feb. 6, 1760 375
GALPIN, Lavina A., of Durham, m. Lucius **HOLCOMB**, of Granby, June 21, 1830 434
Martha J., m. Moses B. **BARNS**, Feb. 1, 1842 440
GATZMER, Edwin, of Philadelphia, Pa., m. Mary Jane **FOWLER**, of Durham, Sept. 1, 1853 443
GAY, Charles, m. Lucinda **CAMP**, June 1, 1826 432
GAYLORD, GAILORD, GAYLOR, GAYLOUR, David, s. John & Eliz[abeth], bp. Jan. 20, 1716/17 254
Eleazer, s. Joseph & Mary, bp. June 11, 1721 257
John, s. John & Eliza, bp. Nov. 21, [1714] 253
Joseph, b. [ ] 22, 1674; entered June 20, 1706, in his 33rd y. 340
Joseph, Sr., d. Feb. 2, 1711/12 341
Joseph, s. Joseph & Mary, bp. Sept. 9, 1716 254
Lois, d. Joseph & Mary, b. Apr. [ ], 1711 342
Mary, w. of Joseph, b. May 25, 1678; entered Jan. [ ], 1706, in the 29th y. of her age 340
Mary, d. Joseph & Mary, b. Nov. 22, 1700 340
Mary, d. John & Eliz[abeth], bp. Mar. [ ], 1719 256
Mary, d. John & Eliz[abeth], bp. Sept. 25, [1720] 257
Ruth, d. Joseph & Mary, bp. Mar. 7, [1713/14] 253
Samuel, s. Joseph & Mary, b. July 5, 1709 340
Sarah, w. [Joseph, Sr.], d. Feb. 12, [1711/12] 341
Thankful, d. Joseph & Mary, b. Jan. 25, 1703//4 340
Timothy, s. Joseph & Mary, b. Nov. 29, 1706 340
GILLOT, [see also **JELIT**], Abijah, s. Abraham, bp. Apr. 10, 1720 256
Eliphelet, s. Abraham, bp. May 19, 1718 255
Margery, d. Abraham, bp. Feb. 11, 1715/16 254
Rebeckah, d. Abigail* & Mary, bp. Nov. 4, [1722] (*Abraham?) 258
GILLUM, Abigail, d. Benj[ami]n & Elizabeth, b. May 29, 1761; bp. May 31, [1761] 311,380
Ashur, s. Benjamin & Elizabeth, b. Dec. 4, 1763; bp. Dec. 11, [1763]; d. Jan. 4, 1764 313,383
Ashur, s. Benjamin & Elizabeth, b. Apr. 13, 1765; bp. Apr. 28, [1765] 315,384

	Page
GILLUM, (cont.)	
Benjamin, m. Elizabeth **SEWARD**, June 26, 1754	377
Denis, of Durham, m. Mary **ISBILL**, of Killingworth, Aug. 7, 1825	432
Elizabeth, d. Benjamin & Elizabeth, b. May 24, 1757; bp. May 29, [1757]	306,377
Elizabeth, d. Feb. 18, 1827	427
Elizur, s. Benjamin & Elizabeth, b. Feb. 11, 1773; bp. Feb. 14, [1773]; d. Feb. 16, 1773	322,397
Elizur, s. Benjamin & Elizabeth, b. Oct. 4, 1774; bp. Oct. 9, 1774	324,397
Nathan, s. Benj[amin] & Elizabeth, b. Nov. 4, 1767; bp. Nov. 8, [1767]	317,389
Phebe, d. Benjamin & Elizabeth, b. June 19, 1770; bp. July 1, [1770]	319,397
Rachel, d. Benj[amin] & Elizabeth, bp. June 14, 1754	296
Rachel, d. Benjamin & Elizabeth, b. July 12, 1754	377
Rachel, m. Nathan **SEWARD**, May 6, [1772], by Rev. Elizur Goodrich	332,394
Sally, d. Asher & Sally, b. Dec. 24, 1788	425
Sally, m. Seth **TIBBALS**, Mar. 6, 1814	425
Sarah, d. Benjamin & Elizabeth, b. Apr. 24, 1759; May 6, [1759]	309,377
GLAYDE, GLOYDE, Mabel had s. Gideon **ALLEN**, bp. Jan. 22, 1743/4; father Gideon **LEETE**	283
Rachel, d. James & Mabel, bp. July 18, 1740	278
GODDARD, GODARD, Anne, d. Israel & Ann, bp. Oct. 20, 1751	293
Anne, d. Israel & Ann, b. Oct. 16, 1752	382
Erastus, s. Israel & Ann, b. Mar. 27, 1748	382
Israel, s. Israel & Ann, b. Jan. 30, 1750; bp. Feb. 4, 1749/50	290,382
Israel, m. Ann **CAMP**, of Durham, Feb. 3, 1769, by Rev. Elizur Goodrich	331
Phebe, d. Israel & Ann, bp. Sept. 10, [1769]	319
GOODRICH, Charles Augustus, s. Rev. Elizur & Katharine, b. Mar. 2, 1768; bp. Mar. 6, [1768]; d. Jan. 25, 1804	317,389,410
Chauncey, s. Rev. Elizur & Katharine, b. Oct. 20, 1759; bp. Oct. 21, [1759]	309,377
Elihu, s. Rev. Elizur & Katharine, b. Sept. 16, 1764; bp. Sept. 23, [1764]	314,384
Elihu Chauncey, d. Aug. 20, 1802, at Neighigary	410
Elizur, Rev., m. Mrs. Katharine **CHAUNCEY**, Feb. 1, 1759	377
Elizur, s. Rev. Elizur & Katharine, b. Mar. 24, 1761; Mar. 29, [1761]	310,380
Elizur, Rev., d. Nov. 21, 1797, at Norfolk	408
Katharine, d. Rev. Elizur & Katharine, bp. Jan. 14, 1776	326
Nathan, s. Rev. Elizur & Katharine, b. Aug. 1, 1770; bp. Sept. 9, [1770]	320,393
Samuel, s. Rev. Elizur & Katharine, b. Jan. 12, 1763; bp. Jan. 16, 1763	312,381
GOOLTHRAIGHT, Ebenezer, m. Esther **TIBBALS**, Sept. 8, 1828	434

	Page
GORHAM, George W., m. Hannah **BEMUS**, Dec. 1, 1826	433
Mary Ann, m. Stephen L. **NORTON**, May 16, 1831	435
GRAHAM, Chauncey, m. Sarah **MERWIN**, Nov. 11, 1782	401
Chauncey, s. Chauncey & Sarah, b. July 26, 1783	401
Mary, d. Dr. Chauncey & Sarah, b. Apr. 7, 1789	403
Rhoda, m. Richard **HUBBARD**, May 20, 1827	433
Sarah, d. Chauncey & Sarah, b. Sept. 18, 1784	401
Stephen, s. Chauncey & Sarah, b. Dec. 13, 1736	402
William E., m. Eunice **SCRANTON**, Oct. 11, 1840	439
GRAVES, GRAVE, GROVES, Abigail, d. Noahdiah & Sarah, b. Sept. 25, 1725; bp. Sept. [ ], [1725]	260,356
Ann, d. Joseph & Ann, bp. Mar. [ ], 1734	269
Benjamin, s. Samuel, bp. Jan. 1, 1758	307
David, s. Noahdiah & Sarah, b. Oct. 5, 1728; bp. Oct. 6, 1728	263,356
David, bp. Dec. 9, 1753	294
David, bp. Nov. 9, 1755	298
Elizabeth, d. Noahdiah & Sarah, b. June 21, 1723; bp. June 23, [1723]	259,356
Elizabeth, m. Moses **SHELDON**, Apr. 20, 1749	352
Ezra, s. Roswel & Lois, bp. Dec. 26, 1756	305
Frances Amelia, d. John A. & Amelia, b. June 9, 1821	427
Henry, s. John A. & Amelia, b. Feb. 4, 1829	427
John, m. Alelia **BAILEY**, Dec. 5, 1825	432
Joseph, s. Samuel, bp. Apr. 13, 1755	297
Lewis, s. David & Hannah, b. Nov. 7, 1755	372
Mahethabel, m. Cornelius **HULL**, Feb. 1, 1714/15, by Abraham Fowler, Esq.	345
Noahoriah*, s. Noahdiah & Sarah, b. June 20, 1721; bp. June 25, 1721 *(Noadiah)	257,356
Noahdiah had negro Ceazar, bp. June 20, 1742	280
Prudence, m. Joseph **WHEELER**, Apr. 13, 1732	355
Rozwell, s. Noahdiah & Sarah, b. Dec. 5, 1731; bp. Jan. 16, 1731/2	266,356
Roswel[l], s. Roswel[l] & Lois, bp. June 18, 1758	307
Sam[ue]l, s. Samuel, bp. Dec. 1, 1746	286
Sarah, d. Noadiah & Sarah, bp. May 1, 1720	256
Sarah, d. Noahdiah & Sarah, b. Mar. 20, 1720/1	356
Sarah, w. of Noadiah, bp. Apr. 28 or 29, [1733]	268
Sarah, d. Samuel, bp. Dec. 2, 1750	292
Seth, s. Roswel[l] & Lois, of Granville, bp. Sept. 21, [1760]	310
Timothy, s. David, bp. Jan. 13, 1754	295
Timothy, s. David & Hannah, b. Feb. 1, 1754	370
----, w. of David, bp. Dec. 9, 1753	294
GRIDLEY, James, of Farmington, m. Hannah **CLARKE**, of Durham, Jan. 12, 1735, by Rev. Elizur Goodrich	327
GRIFFING, Juliet, of Guilford, m. Charles **BROWN**, of Meriden, May 22, 1832	435
GRISWOLD, A. M., of Killingworth, m. Sophronia **FOWLER**, of Durham, Jan. 23, 1845	441

	Page
GRISWOLD, (cont.)	
Aaron, s. Sam[ue]l, bp. Apr. 6, 1729	263
Aaron, s. Jeremy & Bathsheba, bp. Dec. 18, [1743]	282
Ann, d. Samuel, bp. Oct. 22, [1738]	275
Anne, wid., m. Jesse **COOK**, Oct. 20, [1771], by Rev. Elizur Goodrich	331,395
Deborah, twin with Dorathy, d. Hezekiah, of Black Rock, bp. Mar. 30, 1735	271
Dorathy, twin with Deborah, d. Hezekiah, of Black Rock, bp. Mar. 30, 1735	271
Elizabeth, d. Samuel, bp. Sept. 12, 1736, at Black Rock	272
Hannah, d. Sam[uel] & Hannah, bp. May 23, 1742	280
Hannah, of Durham, m. Aaron **CURTIS**, of Granville, May 11, 1763, by Rev. Elizur Goodrich	328
Jared, s. Moses & Ann, b. Mar. 13, 1769; bp. Mar. 19, [1769]	318,392
Jeremiah had negro Zilpah, d. Jenny, bp. Nov. 5, 1738	275
Jeremiah, s. Jeremiah, bp. Aug. 15, [1756]	298
Joel, s. wid. Sarah, bp. Sept. 28, [1777]	326
John, s. Samuel & Hannah, of Black Rock, bp. Sept. 6, 1747	288
Jonathan, s. Hez[ekiah], bp. July 26, 1741	279
Lydia, d. Jer[emiah] & Bashua, bp. Nov. 5, 1738	275
Lydia, of Durham, m. Reuben **PARMALEE**, of Guilford, Oct. 12, [1763], by Rev. Elizur Goodrich	328
Manus, child of Sam[ue]l, bp. Sept. 10, [1727]	262
Marcey, m. Silas **CRANE**, Nov. 27, 1729	343
Mary, d. Hezekiah, of Black Rock, bp. May 14, 1732	267
Mary, d. Samuel, late of Killingworth, m. Capt. Elihu **CHAUNCEY**, Mar. 28, 1739, by Capt. David Buil, J. P., in New London County	358
Mary, d. Daniel, bp. Apr. 12, 1752	294
Moses, s. Jonathan * & Bashi, bp. Aug. 2, 1741 *(Jeremiah?)	279
Moses, m. Ann **SMITHSON**, b. of Durham, Feb. 3, 1768, by Rev. Elizur Goodrich	390,392
Moses, d. Sept. 30, 1770	392
Notwithstanding, d. Jeremiah, bp. Mar. 4, [1759]; d. Mar. 5, [1759]	308
Notwithstanding, [child of Jeremiah & Sarah], b. Apr. 16, 1764; bp. Apr. 29, 1764	314,395
Phebe, d. Dan, bp. Feb. 19, 1748/9	289
Phebe, d. Jeremy & Bathsheba, bp. Dec. 2, 1753	294
Rachel, m. Lewis **CHATFIELD**, Apr. 17, 1828	433
Rhoda, d. Samuel, of Balck Rock, bp. June 15, 1740	277
Rosamond, [twin with Rosetta], d. [Jeremiah & Sarah], b. Oct. 20, 1766; bp. Oct. 26, 1766	316,395
Rosetta, [twin with Rosamond], d. [Jeremiah & Sarah], b. Oct. 20, 1766; bp. Oct. 26, 1766	316,395
Ruth, d. Jeremiah & Bathsheba, bp. Feb. 10, 1744/5	284
Ruth, of Durham, m. Humfrey **BALL**, of Lebanon, Apr. 23, 1766, by Rev. Elizur Goodrich	329
Samuel, s. Samuel, bp. June 25, 1744	283

	Page
GRISWOLD, (cont.)	
Samuel, [s. Jeremiah & Sarah], b. May 29, 1769; bp. June 4, [1769]	318,395
Sarah, d. Samuel, of Black Rock, bp. June 22, 1731	265
Sarah, w. Jeremiah, bp. Aug. 8, [1762]	312
Sarah, wid. had s. Joel, bp. Sept. 28, [1777]	326
William, s. Daniel, bp. May 20, 1750	291
GULLONY*, Mary, d. John & Abigail, bp. Nov. 23, [1735] (*Should be "**GUTHRIE**")	271
GORDON, James, s. Hope **WHITMORE**, b. Oct. 30, 1779	402
GURNSEY, GUERNSEY, Ann, d. Lieut, Eben & Rhoda, bp. Feb. 6, 1747/8	288
Anne, d. Ebenezer & Rhoda, b. Feb. 3, 1747	365
Anne, of Durham, m. James **BATES**, Jr., of Haddam, Dec. 24, 1765 (1766), by Rev. Elizur Goodrich	329,404
Bridgman, s. Lemuel & Ruth, b. June 11, 1758; bp. June 11, [1758]	307,375
Bridgman, m. Phebe Ann **CURTISS**, Feb. 5, 1786	402
Catharine, d. Eben & Rhoda, bp. Jan. 21, 1732/3	268
Content, d. Lemuel & Ruth, b. Sept. 9, 1756; bp. Dec. 19, 1756	305,373
Ebenezer, d. Eben[eze]r, bp. June 26, [1726]	261
Ebenezer, b.[Feb. 1, 1736], bp. Feb. 1, 1736; d. same day	273
Ebenezer, s. Ebenezer & Rhoda, b. Feb. 26, 1737/8; bp. Feb. 26, 1737/8	274,362
Ebenezer, s. Lemuel & Ruth, b. Feb. 3, 1764; bp. Feb. 5, 1764	313,387
Ebenezer, Capt., m. wid. Anne **LYMAN**, b. of Durham, Feb. 18, [1768], by Rev. Elizur Goodrich	330
Elinour, d. Ebenezer & Rhoda, b. June 22, 1727	349
Katharine, d. Ebenezer & Rhoda, b. Jan. 15, 1732/3	362
Katharine, m. Capt. James **WADSWORTH**, Jan. 13, [1735]*, by Rev. Elizur Goodrich *(1757 on page 351)	327,351
Lemuel, s. Eben & Rhoda, bp. Feb. [ ], 1730/1	265
Lemuel, m. Ruth **CAMP**, Dec. 18, 1755	372
Lemuel, s. Lemuel & Ruth, b. Jan. 8, 1762; bp. Jan. 10, 1762	311,387
Lemuel, d. July 17, 1794	405
Lemuel, d. Sept. 23, 1820	423
Mary, d. Ebenezer & Rhoda, b. Oct. 12, 1734; bp. Oct. 13, 1734	270,362
Mary, m. Israel **CAMP**, Dec. 24, 1766	388
Rhoda, d. Eben & Rhoda, bp. Oct. 20, [1728]	263
Rhoda, d. Ebenezer & Rhoda, b. Oct. 23, 1728	349
Rhoda, d. Lemuel & Ruth, b. Feb. 24, 1760; bp. Mar. 2, [1760]; d. Dec. 4, 1760	309,387
Rhoda, d. Lemuel & Ruth, b. Dec. 6, 1765; bp. Dec. 8, 1765	315,387
Rhoda, w. of Capt. Ebenezer, d. Oct. 14, 1767	389
Sarah, d. Ebenezer & Rhoda, b. May 22, 1742; bp. May 23, 1742	280,362
Sarah, of Durham, m. Thomas **LEWIS**, of Farmington, Dec. 24, 1765, by Rev. Elizur Goodrich	329
Sarah, m. Simeon **PARSONS**, Feb. 19, 1795	406
GUTHRIE, GUTHY, GUTHRY, Abigail, d. John & Abigail, bp. May 3, 1742	280
Abigail, s. (sic) John & Abigail, b. July 21, 1742	360

Page

GUTHRIE, GUTHY, GUTHRY, (cont.)
Ebenezer, s. John & Abigail, bp. July 20, 1740 278
Ebenezer, s. John & Abigail, b. July 29, 1740 359
Ephraim, s. John & Abigail, b. Mar. 1, 1737; bp. Mar. 5, 1737/8 274,359
Mary, d. John & Abigail, bp. Nov. 23, [1735] (Written "Mary **GULLONY**") 271
Mary, d. John & Abigail, b. Dec. 20, 1735 356
HALE, HAIL, Curtis, s. Elisha & Sybil, bp. Sept. 22, 1751 292
Elias, m. Eliza Ann **MILLER**, Sept. 26, 1836 437
Phebe, d. Elisha & Sybel, bp. June* 7, 1754 (*July) 296
Rachel D., of Durham, m. Heman **STONE**, Jr., of Madison, June 5, 1839 438
Sybil, w. of Elisha, bp. July 14, 1751 292
HALL, Betsey, m. Burwell **NEWTON**, Dec. 20, 1814 416
Bristol, s. Timothy & Sarah, bp. Sept. 23, [1764] 314
Daniel, Jr., m. Ann **CRANE**, Sept. 21, 1766, by Rev. Elizur Goodrich 329,388
Daniel, s. Daniel, 2d, & Ann, b. Mar. 16, 1776 398
Daniel, 2d, d. Aug. 17, 1776 398
Day, d. Dec. 19, 1810 412
Deborah, d. Timothy & Sarah, bp. Dec. 20, 1766 316
Ebenezer, s. Timothy & Sarah, bp. Dec. 25, 1757 307
Elizabeth, m. David **FOWLER**, Apr. 21, 1736, by Theophilus Yale, J. P. 357
Elizabeth, d. Daniel, Jr. & Ann, b. Dec. 25, 1768; bp. Jan. 1, 1769 318,390
Elizur, m. Deborah Ann **CHADEAYNE**, Oct. 30, 1821 430
Gad, s. Timothy & Sarah, bp. Feb. 17, [1760] 309
Hannah, m. John S. **CATLIN**, Oct. 28, 1822 430
Harriet, d. Henry & Electa, b. Aug. 31, 1806 413
Harriet, m. Samuel G. **TIBBALS**, Sept. 8, 1828 434
Henry, s. Daniel, Jr. & Ann, b. Dec. 3, 1771; bp. Dec. 8, [1771] 321,395
Jerusha, d. Daniel, 3rd, & Elizabeth, b. Aug. 4, 1772; bp. Aug. 9, [1772] 322,394
John, s. Timothy, bp. Oct. 23, 1753 294
Luther, s. Daniel, Jr. & Ann, b. Feb. 3, 1767; bp. Feb. 8, [1767] 316,388
Lydia, m. John **CURTISS**, Jr., Dec. 29, 1794 408
Malvina, d. Henry & Electa, b. Jan. 20, 1809 413
Martha, m. Phineas **CAMP**, b. of Durham, Jan. 8, 1767, by Rev. Elizur Goodrich 330
Mary, d. Daniel, 3rd & Elizabeth, b. Sept. 7, 1774 397
Mehitabel, m. Hezekiah **PARMALEE**, Apr. 18, 1737 382
Miles, s. Timothy & Deborah, bp. June 27, [1773] 323
Phebe, d. Timothy, Jr. & Deborah, bp. Mar. 10, [1771] 320
Sarah, d. Timothy & Sarah, bp. Mar. 7, [1762] 311
Sarah, m. Abner **NEWTON**, Apr. 29, 1823 431
Timothy, m. Deborah **HULL**, May 2, 1770, by Rev. Elizur Goodrich 331
Timothy, d. July 29, 1771 394
Walker, s. Tim[othy], bp. Feb. 15, [1756] 298
-----, d. Daniel, 3rd, bp. [1774] 324

HALL, (cont.) Page
-----, [child] of Timothy, bp. Jan. 1, 1775 325
HAMILTON, John, of Granville, m. Rebecca **CANFIELD**, of Durham, Dec. 7, [1762], by Rev. Elizur Goodrich 328
HAMLIN, Experience, d. William, bp. Nov. 22, 1761, at Middletown 311
HAND, Abraham, s. Lemuel & Hannah, b. Oct. 17, 1751; bp. Oct. 20, 1751 293,374
Abraham, m. Ruth **SOUTHWORTH**, [1772], by Rev. Elizur Goodrich 332
Esther, d. Lemuel & Hannah, b. Feb. 21, 1754; bp. Feb. 24, 1754 295,374
Hannah, bp. Sept. 22, 1751 293
Jehiel U., m. Eliza **SWATHEL**, May 12, 1829 434
John, s. Abraham & Ruth, bp. Jan. 3, 1773 322
Lemuel, bp. Sept. 22, 1751 293
Mary, d. Lemuel & Hannah, bp. July 13, 1768 317
Nathan, s. Lemuel & Hannah, b. Sept. 10, 1756; bp. Nov. 14, [1756] 298,374
Phebe, d. Lemuel & Hannah, bp. Feb. 17, 1771 320
HANDY, Anne, of Guilford, m. Eliphaz **PARMALEE**, of Middletown, Aug. 3, [1768], by Rev. Elizur Goodrich 330
HARDIN, Peter, m. Esther **JACK**, colored, June 2, 1824 431
HARRISON, Amelia S., m. James S. **ELY**, of Meriden, Aug. 30, 1846 442
Amos, of Northford, m. Elizabeth **FOWLER**, of Durham, May 20, [1762], by Rev. Elizur Goodrich 328
Amos, m. Harriet **HART**, Oct. 12, 1831 435
Linas, m. E. **JONES**, [ ], 1838 438
HART, Daniel, s. Samuel & Bridget, bp. July 13, 1768 317
Edward, [s. Samuel & Patience], b. Jan. 12, 1808 413
Emeline Rebeckah, d. John & Sally, b. Sept. 28, 1802 413
George, [s. Samuel & Patience], b. Apr. 14, 1810 413
Harriet, d. John & Sally, b. June 20, 1811 413
Harriet, m. Amos **HARRISON**, Oct. 12, 1831 435
John, twin with Rebecca, s. Samuel & Bridget, bp. Oct. 25, 1772 322
John, Capt. m. Sally **COE**, July 15, 1800 413
Katherine, d. John & Sally, b. Jan. 25, 1814 414
Leander, s. John & Sally, b. Jan. 30, 1809 413
Lois, d. Samuel & Bridget, bp. Mar. 12, [1775] 325
Mary, d. Samuel & Abredgget (Bridget), b. June 24, 1762; bp. Aug. 8, [1762] 312,386
Mary, of Durham, m. Seneca **BARNES**, of Northford, Nov. 1, 1835 437
Rebecca, twin with John, d. Samuel & Bridget, bp. Oct. 25, 1772 322
Ruth, d. Samuel & Abredgget (Bridget), b. June 8, 1766; bp. June 15, [1766] 315,386
Ruth, d. Daniel & Hannah, b. Aug. 6, 1800 412
Ruth, m. Henry **MALTBY**, Dec. 12, 1821 430
Samuel, m. Abredgget* **FOWLER**, Oct. 9, 1759 (*Bridget) 386
Samuel, s. Samuel & Bridget, bp. Feb. 19, 1764 313
Samuel, s. Samuel & Abredgget, b. Feb. 23, 1764 386
Samuel, s. Samuel & Bridget, bp. July 22, [1770] 320
William, [s. Samuel & Patience], b. Apr. 26, 1806 413

Page

HART, (cont.)
William, m. Sophia **NEWTON**, Sept. 23, 1821 430
HARVEY, Sally, d. Elisha, b. Aug. 7, 1766 415
Sibyl, m. Burwell **NEWTON**, Nov. 19, 1795 416
HAWLEY, HOWLEY, Hannah, d. Jehiel & Hope, bp. Nov. 21, [1725] 261
Hope, d. Jehiel & Hope, bp. July 18, 1719 256
John, s. John, bp. Mar. 25, 1750 291
Lucy, d. Stow, bp. Oct. [ ], 1765 315
Martha, d. John, bp. Jan. 20, 1744/5 284
Mary, d. Jehiel & Hope, bp. Sept. 12, [1714] 253
Matthew, s. Ephraim & Phebe, b. Feb. 1, 1713/14; bp. Feb. 7, 1713/14 253,343
Rebeckah, d. John, bp. May 30, 1712* (*1742?) 280
Samuel Stone, s. Jehiel & Hope, bp. June 10, 1722 258
Sarah, d. John, bp. July 5, 1747 287
HENMAN, [see also **HINMAN**],Aaron, s. Sarah **TORRY**, bp. Aug. 31,1767 317
Enoch, s. Zecariah & Hannah, bp. May 25, 1746 286
Enoch, s. Zechariah, bp. Nov. 5, 1749 290
Mary, twin with Samuel, d. Samuel & Mary, bp. Aug. 1, 1736 272
Nabby, d. Sarah **TORRY**, bp. Oct. 29, [1758] 308
Reuben, s. R[e]uben & Hannah, bp. Apr. 3, 1737 273
Samuel, twin with Mary, s. Samuel & Mary, bp. Aug. 1, 1736 272
Sarah, d. Hazael & Anne, bp. Apr. 24, [1757] 306
Wilkinson, s. Samuel & Abigail, bp. June 10, 1733 268
HICKOX, HAYCOX, HEYCOX, HICCOCK, HICCOX, Ambros, s. Samuel & Hannah, b. Oct. 23, 1742; bp. Oct. 24, 1742 281,360
Asa, s. Lieut, Joseph & Martha, bp. Aug. 1, 1773 323
Ashur, s. Samuel & Hannah, b. June 27, 1756 373
Benjamin, s. Joseph & S------, bp. Aug. 22, 1736 272
Catharine, d. Joseph, bp. May 23, [1727] 262
Charlotte, m. Frederic **DOWD**, of Madison, Feb. 24, 1834 436
Daniel, s. Joseph & Martha, bp. Jan. 10, 1768 317
Darius, [s. Joseph & Martha], b. Mar. 8, 1759; bp. Mar. 11, [1759] 308,376
Darcos, d. Samuel & Hannah, b. July 19, 1747; bp. July 26, 1747 287,364
Eliza, d. Stephen & Ruth, bp. Mar. 25, 1722 258
Eliza Ann, d. James & Hope, b. June 24, 1823 426
Elizabeth, d. Stephen & Ruth, b. Mar. 21, 1722/3; d. Jan. 30, 1723/4 347
Elizabeth, d. Joseph, Jr., bp. May 30, 1725 260
Elizabeth, d. Samuel, bp. Sept. 17, 1738 275
Elizabeth, m. Jonah **FRISBIE**, Sept. 27, 1758 394
Giles, s. Joseph & Martha, bp. Apr. 28, [1765] 315
Hannah, m. John **CAMP**, June 27, 1728 355
Hannah, d. Joseph & Sarah, bp. Aug. 6, 1738 275
Hannah, d. Samuel & Hannah, b. Oct. 17, 1740; bp. Oct. 19, [1740] 278,360
Hannah, d. Samuel & Hannah, b. Oct. 17, 1749; bp. Nov. 5, 1749 290,366
Isaac W., m. Elizabeth **WHITE**, June 6. 1843 440
James, s. Joseph & Sarah, bp. May 20, 1733 268
James, [s. Joseph & Martha], b. Nov. 23, 1751; bp. Dec. 1, 1751 293,376

Page

HICKOX, HAYCOX, HEYCOX, HICCOCK, HICCOX, (cont.)

James, m. Rhoda **PARMALEE**, Dec. [ ], 1774, by Rev. Elizur Goodrich 333
James, s. James & Rhoda, b. June 9, 1788 419
James, m. Hope **SMITH**, Sept. 30, 1815 419
James Lawrence, s. James & Hope, b. Oct. 4, 1820 419
Jerushah, d. Joseph & Sarah, bp. Oct. 27, [1723] 259
John, s. John & Mary, bp. Sept. 4, [1720] 256
Jonathan, s. Stephen, bp. Mar. 14, 1724/5 260
Joseph, s. Joseph, bp. Apr. 6, 1729 263
Joseph, m. Martha **WILLCOKS**, Dec. 8, 1748 376
Joseph, bp. Mar. 25, 1750 291
Joseph, [s. Joseph & Martha], b. July 12, 1757; bp. July 17, [1757], by Mr. Stiles, of N. H. 306,376
Katharine, d. James & Katharine, b. after the death of her father; bp. Aug. [ ], [1725] 260
Katharine, d. Joseph & Martha, bp. June 19, [1763] 313
Leander P., m. Lucy **PARSONS**, May 20, 1832 435
Lois, d. Stephen & Lydia, bp. Feb. 10, 1744/5 284
Martha, [d. Joseph & Martha], b. May 24, 1750; bp. May 27, 1750 291,376
Martha, m. Charles **BISHOP**, Dec. 12, [1768], by Rev. Elizur Goodrich 331
Nathaniel, s. Samuel & Hannah, b. Mar. 21, 1754; bp. Mar. 24, 1754 295,370
Nathaniel, m. Rebeckah **ROSSETER**, of Durham, Oct. 7, 1773, by Rev. Elizur Goodrich 332
Rachel, d. Samuel, bp. Nov. 18, 1744 284
Rachel, d. Samuel & Hannah, b. Nov. 13, 1745 363
Rachel, d. Joseph & Martha, bp. July 13, 1768 317
Reuben, s. Stephen & Lydia, bp. Jan. 18, 1746 287
Reuben, s. Joseph & Martha, bp. Dec. 28, [1760] 310
Reuben, s. Hannah, bp. June 11, [1769] 318
Rhoda, d. Joseph, bp. Sept. [ ], 1755 298
Rhoda, [d. Joseph & Martha], b. Oct. 6, 1755 376
Rhoda, m. William **TRENCH**, Nov. 10, 1773, by Rev. Elizur Goodrich 332
Ruth, d. Stephen & Ruth, b. Aug. 31, 1719; bp. Oct. [ ], [1719] 256,345
Ruth, d. Joseph & Sarah, bp. July 27, 1735 271
Sam[ue]l, s. Stephen & Ruth, bp. July 27, [1712] 252
Samuel, s. Stephen & Ruth, b. Sept. 23, 1712 341
Samuel, s. Samuel & Hannah, b. Apr. 5, 1752; bp. Apr. 12, 1752 294,368
Sarah, d. Stephen & Ruth, b. Apr. 14, 1716; bp. Apr. 15, 1716 254,343
Sarah, d. Joseph, bp. Apr. 18, 1731 265
Sarah, d. Stephen & Lydia, b. Oct. 3, 1743; bp. Oct. 9, 1743 282,363
Stephen, s. Stephen & Ruth, b. July 17, 1714; bp. July 18, [1714] 253,343
Stephen, s. Stephen & Lydia, bp. July 2, 1749 289
Tamson, m. Daniel **SOUTHMAYD**, Dec. 25. 1838 438

Page

HICKOX, HAYCOX, HEYCOX, HICCOCK, HICCOX, (cont.)
Tamzin Mariah, d. James & Hope, b. Dec. 27, 1818 419
Thankful, d. John & Mary, b. Mar. 30, 1723; bp. Mar. [ ], [1723] 259,348
Walter Smith, s. James & Hope, b. Nov. 17, 1816 419
William, [s. Joseph & Martha], b. Aug. 31, 1753 376
-----, w. of Joseph, bp. Mar. 25, 1750 291
HICKS, Samuel, m. Sarah **PARMALEE**, Oct. 8, 1821 430
HIGGINS, Ichabod Lewis, s. Ichabod & Jane, b. Apr. 1, 1771 396
Samuel, s. Capt. -----, mariner from Eastham, bp. Dec. 19, 1742 281
Silas, m. Susan **IVES**, July 31, 1836 437
HILLS, HILL, Aaron, s. Daniel & Leah, bp. June 7, [1731] 265
Ann, [d. Benoni & Hannah], b. June 11, 1743, in Goshen 365
Belah, [s. Benoni & Hannah], b. Aug. 24, 1741, in Goshen 365
Beriah, [s. Benoni & Hannah], b. Aug. 31, 1727; bp. Sept. 3, 1727 262,365
Daniel, s. Daniel & Leah, bp. July 19, 1725 260
Hannah, d. Benony & Hannah, b. Oct. 5, 1724, in Suffield 365
Hephzibah, d. Dan & Leah, bp. May 19, 1734 269
John, [s. Benoni & Hannah], b. Dec. 13, 1732; bp. Dec. 17, 1732 268,365
Leah, bp. Nov. 25, 1722 258
Lois, d. Daniel & Leah, bp. Nov. 7, 1736 273
Mary, d. Benoni, bp. Jan. 3, 1730/1 265
Mary, d. Benoni & H[annah], bp. Sept. 21, 1734 270
Mary, [d. Benoni & Hannah], b. Sept. 25, 1734 365
Medad, [child of Benoni & Hannah], b. Apr. 27, 1729 365
Moses, s. Dan[ie]l & Leah, bp. Jan. 28, 1727/8 262
Ratchel, [d. Benoni & Hannah], b. July 8, 1739; bp. July 15, 1739 276,365
Sarah, d. Leah, bp. Nov. 25, 1722 258
Sarah, of Haddam, m. Clement M. **PARSONS**, of Durham, Mar. 10, 1844 440
Seth, [s. Benoni & Hannah], b. Sept. 13, 1736; bp. Sept. 19, 1736 272,365
Susanna, d. Dan & Leah, bp. Apr. 21, 1723 259
Susannah, of Durham, m. Giles **PORTER**, of Haddam, Feb. 26, 1764, by Rev. Elizur Goodrich 328
Zimry (Zimni), [child of Benoni & Hannah], b. Dec. 16, 1725; bp. Dec. 19, 1725 261,365
HINMAN, [see also **HENMAN**], Aaron, s. Zachariah & Hannah, b. Jan. 6, 1740; bp. Jan. 20, 1739/40 277,384
Aaron, m. Elizabeth **WELLES**, b. of Durham, Oct. 21, 1765, by Rev. Elizur Goodrich 329
Edward, s. Zechariah & Hannah, bp. Aug. 1, 1743 282
Edward Welles, s. James & Abigail, bp. Apr. 4, [1773] 322
Elihu, s. Zachariah & Hannah, bp. Dec. 29, 1744 270
Enoch, s. Hazael & Ann, b. Dec. 30, 1758; bp. Dec. 31, [1758] 308,374
Freelove, d. James & Abigail, bp. Aug. 9, [1772] 322
Hannah, d. Hazael & Ann, b. June 17, 1760; bp. Aug. 24, [1760] 310,380
Hazael, s. Zec. & Hannah, bp. Sept. 10, [1732] 267
Hazael, m. Ann **TORREY**, May 11, 1756 373

Page

HINMAN, (cont.)
Hazard, d. Dec. 14, 1760 351
James, s. James & Abigail, bp. Aug. 9, [1772] 322
James, s. David & Hannah, bp. Oct. 10, 1730 265
Melinda, d. Aaron & Elizabeth, b. Apr. 15, 1766; bp. Dec. 27, 1766 316,390
Rachel, d. James, bp. Oct. 15, 1775 325
Rhoda, d. Elihu & Rhoda, bp. Apr. 28, 1773 323
Sarah, d. Samuel & Abigail, bp. Oct. 3, 1731 266
Sarah, d. Hazael & Ann, b. Apr. 21, 1757 373
Sarah, m. Amos **FOWLER**, Jan. 2, 1777 398
Sarah, d. James, bp. June 22, 1777 326
Sylvia Burroughs, d. James & Abigail, bp. Aug. 9, [1772] 322
William, s. James & Abigail, bp. Aug. 9, [1772] 322

[HITCHCOCK], [see under **HICKOX**]

HOADLEY, Lucinda, m. Chauncey C. **STEVENS**, Mar. 9, 1823 431

HOLCOMB, Lucius, of Granby, m. Lavina A. **GALPIN**, of Durham, June 21, 1830 434
Nelson, m. Fanny **BEMUS**, Feb. 7, 1827 433

HOLT, Benjamin, of Wallingford, m. Anne **MERWIN**, of Durham, May 2, 1770, by Rev. Elizur Goodrich 331

HOPSON, Reuben, of Wallingford, m. Sarah **TIBBLES**, of Durham, Nov. 7, [1771], by Rev. Elizur Goodrich 331

HOTCHKISS, Richard H., m. Anne **NETTLETON**, Aug. 17, 1828 434,443

HOUSE, Sarah, d. Samuel & Rachel, bp. Sept. [ ], [1725] 260

HOUSEMAN, John W., m. Eunice **SPINER**, [ ], 1837 438

HOWD, Catharine Elizabeth, m. W[illia]m S. **POST**, Aug. 1, 1848 442
Horace, s. Augustus & Catharine, b. Aug. 25, 1822 420
Sarah A., m. David N. **CAMP**, Nov. 25, 1845 441
Sarah Adaline, d. Augustus & Catharine, b. Feb. 24, 1820 420

HOWE, Abijah, s. Sumner & Sarah, b. May 14, 1746 (Probably Abijah **STOWE**) 371
Daniel, s. Sumner & Sarah, b. Oct. 9, 1751 (Probably Daniel **STOWE**) 371
Ephraim, s. John & Lydia, bp. May 24, 1730 264
John, s. John & Lydia, of N[ew] Haven, bp. May 8, 1715 254
Noah, s. Nanthaniel & Mary, b. Oct. 13, 1745, in Wallingford 265
Robert, s. Sumner & Sarah, b. Nov. 2, 1748 (Probably Robert **STOWE**) 371

HOWELL, John Z., m. Charlotte Ann **LANISON**, Nov. 14, 1826 433

HUBBARD, Amos, m. Mary **BRISTOL**, June 15, 1758 374
Amos, Dr., d. Nov. 15, 1767 389
Edwin, m. Lucy **STRONG**, Sept. 17, 1825 432
Eli, m. Georgiana **LEACH**, May 20, 1846 442
Mary, wid., of Durham, m. Ens. David **CAMP**, of Woodbury, Dec. 28, [1772], by Rev. Elizur Goodrich 332
Richard, m. Rhoda **GRAHAM**, May 20, 1827 433

HULL, Abigail, [d. Cornelius & Abigail], b. July 26, 1749; bp. July 30, 1749 289,390

Page

HULL, (cont.)

Abigail, m. Samuel **SEAWARD**, May 7, 1760 378

Abigail, of Durham, m. Samuel **WEEKS**, of Woodbury, Feb. 14, 1775, by Rev. Elizur Goodrich 333

Andrew, m. Ann **PARSONS**, b. of Durham, June 5, 1848 442

Ann, [d. Cornelius & Abigail], b. Feb. 3, 1755; bp. Feb. 9, 1755 296,391

Ann M., m. Timothy J. **COE**, Jan. 3, 1842 440

Anne, of Durham, m. Roswel **FRANCIS**, of Killingworth, Oct. 15, 1777, by Rev. Elizur Goodrich 333

Charles, [s. Cornelius & Abigail], b. May 5, 1760; bp. May 11, [1760] 310,391

Cornelius, m. Mahethabel **GRAVE**, Feb. 1, 1714/15, by Abraham Fowler, Esq. 345

Cornelius, s. Cornelius & Mahethabel, b. Oct. 5, 1719; bp. Nov. 8, 1719; d. June last day, 1722 256,345,346

Cornelious, s. Cornelious & Mahethabel, b. Oct. 31, 1723; bp. Nov. 3, 1723 259,347

Cornelius, m. Abigail **CHIPMAN**, Jan. 1, 1746 390

Cornelius, [s. Cornelius & Abigail], b. Mar. 5, 1748 390

David, [s. Joseph & Diana], b. Nov. 26, 1790 410

Deborah, m. Timothy **HALL**, May 2, 1770, by Rev. Elizur Goodrich 331

Diana, [d. Joseph & Diana], b. Aug. 19 (29), 1788 410,424

Diana, m. Seth **TIBBALS**, June 11, 1807 424

Edward C., m. Clarissa **NETTLETON**, Oct. 9, 1839 438

Eliakim, b. Aug. 1, 1752 403

Eliakim, m. Rachel **WELLES**, Mar. 14, 1787 404

Eliakim W., m. Betsey **FOWLER**, Nov. 19, 1819 435

Elizabeth, d. Cornelious & Mahethabel, b. Apr. 25, 1721; bp. Apr. [ ], 1721 257,346

Elizabeth, d. Joseph & Sibel, b. July 1, 1747; bp. July 5, 1747 287,364

Elizabeth, of Durham, m. Levi **CHAPMAN**, of Saybrook, Sept. 15, [1767], by Rev. Elizur Goodrich 330

Elisabeth, [d. Joseph & Diana], b. Aug. 19, 1796 410

Ellen A., of Durham, m. F. P. **CHAFFEE**, of Middletown, Sept. 15, 1851 443

Giles, s. Cornelius & Abigail], b. July 4, 1762; bp. July 11, [1762] 312,391

Gurdon, of Killingworth, m. Huldah **CRANE**, of Durham, Nov. 10, 1773, by Rev. Elizur Goodrich 332

H. Amelia, of Durham, m. Henry **RIGGS**, of New Haven, Mar. 9, 1845 441

Hannah, d. Jehiel & Ruth, b. Jan. 21, 1754; bp. Jan. 27, 1754 295,371

Hannah, d. Joseph & Sybil, b. June 5, 1761; bp. June 7, [1761] 311,382

Harriet, m. Joel **BLATCHLEY**, Aug. 8, 1839 438

Huldah, [d. Cornelius & Abigail], b. Mar. 6, 1758; bp. Mar. 12, [1758] 307,391

Jehiel, s. Cornelious & Mahethabel, b. Feb. 28, 1728/9; bp. Mar. 2, 1728/9 263,347

Page

HULL, (cont.)

Jehiel, m. Ruth **PHELPS**, Nov. 8, 1750 371
Jehiel, s. Eliakim & Rachel, b. July 31, 1789 404
John, s. Cornelius & Mahethable, b. Jan. 14, 1717/18; bp. Mar. 2, 1718 255,345
John, s. Joseph & Sybil, b. Nov. 20, 1756; bp. Nov. 28, 1756 305,373
Joseph, s. Cornelius & Mahethabel, b. Apr. 29, 1716, bp. May 6, 1716 254,345
Joseph, m. Sibel **COE**, Jan. 1, 1746 364
Joseph, s. Joseph & Sibel, b. Dec. 24, 1749; bp. Dec. 24, 1749 290,366
Joseph, [s. Joseph & Diana], b. Oct. 28, 1786 410
Josiah, s. Joseph & Sybil, b. Apr. 4, 1759; bp. Apr. 8, [1759] 308,375
Leonard, m. Emily **CHALKER**, Mar. 16, 1834 436
Louisa, of Durham, m. Charles G. **LYMAN**, of Colebrook, Nov. 29, 1832 435
Mehethabel, d. Cornelious & Mahethabel, b. Sept. 30, 1725; bp. Oct. 3, [1725] 260,347
Mahithabel, d. Joseph & Sibil, b. July 3, 1754; bp. July* 7, 1754 (*First written "June") 295,370
Mehetabel, m. Ithamar **PARSONS**, Jr., May 21, [1772], by Rev. Elizur Goodrich 332
Mehetabel, m. Robert **SMITHSON**, Mar. 25, 1778, by Rev. Elizur Goodrich 333
Phebe, d. Joseph & Sybil, b. Jan. 21, 1769; bp. Jan. 29, 1769 318,391
Phebe, of Durham, m. Abel **SANFORD**, of Middletown, Dec. 29, 1840 439
Phebe Ann, m. Charles **IVES**, [ ] 437
Rachel, b. Sept. 20, 1750 403
Rachel, d. Eliakim, b. Feb. 11, 1783 404
Rebecca, d. Susannah, bp. July 18, 1742 281
Rhoda, d. Timothy, bp. Mar. 21, [1779] 326
Ruth, d. Jehiel & Ruth, b. Feb. 1, 1751; bp. Mar. 17, 1750/1 292,371
Samuel, [s. Cornelius & Abigail], b. Dec. 10, 1752; bp. Jan. 14, 1751/2 293,390
Samuel Roberts, s. Cornelius, bp. Mar. 2, 1728/9 263
Sarah, m. William **BUTLER**, Sept. 29, 1778 405
Sarah, m. Timothy **BUTLER**, Oct. 5, 1778, by Rev. Elizur Goodrich 333
Silas, s. Joseph & Sibil, b. May 26, 1764; bp. May 27, 1764 314,383
Statira, d. Jehiel & Ruth, b. Jan. 25, 1759; bp. Jan. 28, 1759 308,381
Stephen, [s. Joseph & Diana], b. July 19, 1794 410
Sibil, d. Joseph & Sibil, b. Apr. 6, 1752; bp. Apr. 12, 1752 (Sybil) 294,368
Sylvanus, [s. Cornelius & Abigail, b. Oct. 13, 1746; bp. Oct. 19, 1746 286,390
----, s. Cornelius & Mary, bp. [1774] 324
----, child of Gu[r]don, bp. Jan. 3, 1779 326

HYDE, Charlotte M., m. Joseph **WARD**, Sept. 24, 1821 430

	Page
INGHAM, [see also **INGRAHAM**], Abigail, d. Joseph & Abigail, b. May 13, 1745; bp. May 19, 1745	284,375
Abigail, m. Samuel **BARTLETT**, June 16, 1768	392
Benjamin, s. Joseph & Abigail, b. Mar. 29, 1756; bp. May 2, [1756]	298,375
David, s. Joseph & Abigail, b. Sept. 5, 1750	375
David, s. Joseph & Mehetabel, bp. June 19, [1768]	317
Joseph, s. Joseph & Abigail, bp. Nov. 14, 1742	281
Joseph, m. Mehithabel **BROWN**, Aug. 19, 1767	388
Samuel, s. Joseph & Abigail, b. June 7, 1753	375
Sarah, d. Joseph & Abigail, b. Nov. 21, 1747; bp. Nov. 22, 1747	288,375
INGRAHAM, [see also **INGHAM**], Abigail, m. Samuel **BARTLET[T]**, b. of Durham, June 16, [1768], by Rev. Elizur Goodrich	330
Abigail, wid. of Durham, m. Timothy **BISHOP**, of Guilford, Feb. 15, 1770, by Rev. Elizur Goodrich	331
Joseph, m. Mehetabel **BROWN**, b. of Durham, Aug. 19, [1767], by Rev. Elizur Goodrich	330
Joseph, s. Joseph & Mehetabel, bp. Jan. [ ], 1770	319
Sarah, m. Jonathan **SQUIRE**, May 9, 1774, by Rev. Elizur Goodrich	332
ISBILL, ISBIL, Benilla, m. Albin **SHIPMAN**, Sept. 15, 1826	432
Mary, of Killingworth, m. Denis **GILLUM**, of Durham, Aug. 7, 1825	432
Sarah, m. William **SHELLEY**, June 2, 1824	431
IVES, Charles, m. Phebe Ann **HULL**, [ ]	437
Delight, m. Orren **CAMP**, b. of Durham, Nov. 29, 1827	433
Henry Nelson, s. Jefferson & Mary, b. May 6, 1824	426
Jefferson, m. Mary **FRANCES**, Jan. 16, 1823	430
Mary, of Durham, m. Joseph **WINSHIP**, of Hartford, Feb. 10, 1833	435
Palina, m. Sidney **NORTON**, b. of Durham, Oct. 31, 1821	430
Susan, m. Silas **HIGGINS**, July 31, 1836	437
JACK, Esther, m. Peter **HARDIN**, colored, June 2, 1824	431
JACKSON, John, m. Charlotte Angeline **FIELD**, Aug. 31, 1845	441
Mary A., of Durham, m. Samuel S. **SPENCER**, of Middletown, Oct. 1, 1848	442
JELIT, [see also **GILLOT**], Margarret, d. Abraham & Rebecca, b. Feb. 8, 1715/16	344
JEWETT, George W., m. Harriet **CAMP**, Sept. 11, 1823	431
George W., m. Jennet **CAMP**, Apr. 30, 1828	434
JOHNSON, Abigail, d. [John], bp. Oct. 15, 1775	325
Benjamin, s. John & Concurrence, bp. Feb. 5, 1769	318
Concurrence, w. of Dea. John, d. Feb. 24, 1803	410
David, s. David, bp. June 14, 1730	264
David, Jr., m. Jerusha **THOMAS**, Mar. 14, 1751	377
David, Jr., bp. Nov. 17, 1751	293
David, m. Nancy J. **SEWARD**, July 31, 1826	433
Diana, [d. David, Jr. & Jerusha], b. Sept. 24, 1758; bp. Sept. 24, [1758]	308,377
Elisha, of Middletown, m. Mary **SEWARD**, of Durham, July 31, [1760], by Rev. Elizur Goodrich	327

	Page
JOHNSON, (cont.)	
Eunice, d. Benjamin & Eunice, b. Sept. 16, 1733; bp. Sept. 23, 1733	268,358
Eunice, d. [Lemuel], bp. Nov. 9, 1777	326
Ezra G., m. Frances E. **ANDREWS**, Apr. 19, 1840	439
Hannah, d. Joseph, bp. Jan. 28, 1732/3	268
Jacob, 2d, of Middletown, m. Harriet E. **SMITH**, of Durham, June 19, 1844	440
Jehial, m. Betsey **BOWLES**, b. of Middletown, Jan. 2, 1834	436
Jerusha, d. David, bp. Nov. 14, [1756]	298
Jerusha, d. Lemuel, bp. Mar. 21, [1779]	326
John, s. Benjamin & Eunice, b. July 28, 1739; bp. Aug. 5, 1739	276,358
John, s. Benjamin & Eunice, bp. Nov. 8, [1741]	279
John, m. Concurrance **CRANE**, b. of Durham, Jan. 15, 1765, by Rev. Elizur Goodrich	329
Lemuel, of Middletown, m. Jerusha **NORTON**, of Durham, Nov. 11, [1772], by Rev. Elizur Goodrich	332
Lemuel, s. Lemuel, bp. Mar. 23, 1783	326
Lewis, s. Lemuel, bp. Sept. 10, 1775	325
Marcey, d. David & Ruth, b. Mar. 6, 1727/8	342
Mary, d. David & Ruth, bp. Mar. 3, 1733/4	269
Maurice, see under Morris	
Mehetabel, d. Benjamin & Eunice, b. Nov. 23, 1734; bp. Nov. 24, 1734	270,358
Mehethabel, m. Abiel **BALDWIN**, Apr. 1, 1756	372
Mercy, d. David & Ruth, bp. Mar. 3, 1727/8	262
Mercy, [d. John, Jr. & Abigail], b. May 2, 1778	399
Morris, (Maurice), [s. John, Jr. & Abigail], b. Dec. 12, 1773; bp. Mar. 13, [1774]	324,399
Nabbe, [d. John, Jr. & Abigail], b. Oct. 22, 1780	399
Nancy, twin with Sally, d. Capt. [John] & Abigail, bp. Mar. [ ], 1783	326
Rachel, d. John & Concurrence, bp. Dec. 8, 1765	315
Rebecka, [d. David, Jr. & Jerusha], b. Sept. 21, 1756	377
Rhoda, [d. John, Jr & Abigail], b. Oct. 6, 1775	399
Sally, twin with Nancy, d. Capt. [John] & Abigail, bp. Mar. [ ], 1783	326
Sally, m. Ichabod **CAMP**, Mar. 31, 1823	431
Sally, m. Jonathan **MUNSON**, Nov. 27, 1823	431
Samuel, s. Benjamin & Eunice, bp. Sept. 4, 1743	282
Samuel, Rev., of Albany, m. Elizabeth **CAMP**, of Durham, Feb. 18, 1773, by Rev. Elizur Goodrich	332
Samuel C., s. Samuel C. & Phebe, b. Feb. 2, 1820	422
Sarah, of Middletown, m. Hezekiah **TALCOTT**, of Durham, Mar. 28, 1765, by Rev. Elizur Goodrich	329,387
Submit, d. Benjamin & Eunice, b. Sept. 28, 1736; bp. Oct. 3, 1736	272,358
Thankful, d. Benj[amin] & Eunice, bp. May 14, 1738	275
Theodore, s. Samuel C. & Phebe, b. Apr. 13, 1821; d. Aug. 15, 1822	422

	Page
JOHNSON, (cont.)	
Theodore Nelson, s. Samuel & Phebe, b. Oct. 22, 1822	422
Thomas, [s. David, Jr. & Jerusha], b. Dec. 13, 1751; bp. Dec. 15, 1751	293,377
Timothy, s. David, Jr., bp. Nov. 17, [1754]	296
----, w. of David, Jr., bp. Nov. 17, 1751	293
----, s. John & Concurrence, bp. [1774]	324
JONES, JOHNES, E., m. Linas **HARRISON**, [ ], 1838	438
Erastus, m. Lucy R. **ELLIOTT**, Feb. 21, 1826	432
Hannah, d. John, bp. Apr. 20, 1746	285
Hannah, w. [John], d. Dec. 4, 1759	351
Harriet E., of New Haven, m. Charles **PRITCHARD**, of Waterbury, Nov. 13, 1843	440
James, s. John, bp. Nov. 28, 1756	305
James, s. John & Hannah, b. Oct. 16, 1758; bp. Oct. 29, [1758]	308,380
John, d. Nov. 25, 1759	351
John Immanuel, s. John & Esther, bp. Mar. 14, [1773]	322
Mabel, m. Reuben **BALDWIN**, June 4, 1782	422
Mary, d. John, bp. Jan, 22, 1743/4	283
Phinehas, s. John, bp. Dec. 8, 1751	293
Sarah, d. John, bp. Jan. 21, 1749/50	290
Sarah, d. John & Hannah, d. Nov. 28, 1759	351
Sarah, d. John & Esther, bp. Jan. 13, 1771	320
William, s. John & Esther, bp. Mar. 26, [1775]	325
JUDSON, Sarah, Mrs., d. Capt. James **JUDSON**, of Stratford, m. Nathaniel **CHAUNCEY**, of Durham, Oct. 12, 1708, by Rev. Charles Chauncey, of Stratford	342
KELSEY, Cyrus, m. Jane A. **FOWLER**, May 12, 1835	436
Hannah, m. Medad **STRONG**, b. of Durham, Feb. 9, 1775, by Rev. Elizur Goodrich	333
Jane, m. Abel **TIBBALS**, Oct. 7, 1776	399
Patty, m. Thorrit **DAVIS**, Sept. 23, 1824	431
KILBOURN, Abigail, d. Hezekiah, bp. May 7, 1732	266
Elisha, s. Hez[ekiah], bp. Oct. 23, 1726	261
Elizabeth, d. Hezekiah, bp. Apr. 21, 1728	262
Mary, d. Hez[ekiah], bp. Mar. 22, 1729/30	264
KNOWLES, Lucius M., of Durham, m. Elisabeth R. **SHELLEY**, of Madison, June 13, 1852	443
LANE, Elizabeth, Mrs., m. Joseph **TIBBALS**, Oct. [ ], 1752	391
Stephen D., m. Sarah A. **POTTER**, Dec. 4, 1848	443
LANISON, Charlotte Ann, m. John Z. **HOWELL**, Nov. 14, 1826	433
LAS, [see under **LOAS**]	
LATIMER, Ann, d. David & Mary, bp. Mar. 17, 1733/4	269
LAWS, Daniel, s. Jown* & Abigail, b. June 2, 1775 (*John)	398
Hannah, d. John & Abigail, b. May 28, 1772	398
Samuel, s. John & Abigail, b. Jan. 16, 1770	398
LEACH, Georgiana, m. Eli **HUBBARD**, May 20, 1846	442
Leveret Marsden, m. Lydia Maria **THAYER**, b. of Durham, Feb.	

	Page
LEACH, (cont.)	
7, 1844	440
LEAVITT, LEVET, David, s. David, bp. Mar. 25, 1722	258
John, of New Haven, m. Sarah **SKINNER**, of Northford, Apr. 6, 1840	441
LEE, James, of Guilford, m. Ruth **MERWIN**, of Durham, Sept. 28, 1825	432
Olive, m. Hezekiah **CLARKE**, Nov. 3, 1807	423
Orib, m. Elah **CAMP**, Dec. 2, 1819	424
LEEMAN, LEMING, Abigail, d. Jeremiah & Abigail, bp. Nov. 19, [1721]	257
Jeremiah, m. Abigail **TURNER**, July 4, 1716, by Thomas Ward, J. P.	343
Jeromy, s. Jeromy & Abigail, bp. May 12, 1717	255
Mathias, s. Jeromy, bp. June 7, 1719	256
LEETE, LEET, Allen, s. Gideon, bp. Oct. 13, 1728	263
Alvin, s. John & Abigail, b. Oct. 20, 1728	347
Ann, d. John, bp. July 23, 1727	262
Asa, twin with Tamar, s. Benjamin, bp. Sept. 11, 1726	261
C[h]loe, d. John & Eliz[abeth], bp. Jan. 25, 1729/30	264
Daniel, s. Benjamin, bp. Feb. 5, 1720/1	257
David, s. John & Elizabeth, bp. Apr. 21, 1728	262
Elias, s. John, bp. July 23, 1727	262
Elizabeth, m. James **MINOR**, Sept. 1, 1841	439
Ezekiel, s. Ben., bp. Aug. 16, [1724]	260
Gideon, m. Abegail **ROSSETTER**, Sept. 6, 1727, by Rev. Nath[aniel]ll Chauncey	348
Gideon, s. Gideon & Abigail, b. May 5, 1731; bp. May 9, 1731	265,357
Hannah, d. John & Elizabeth, bp. Oct. 28, 1739	276
Levi, s. Benj[amin], bp. May 2, 1731	265
Phillis, d. John & Elizabeth, bp. Oct. 24, 1731	266
Sarah, d. Ben[jamin], bp. May 25, 1735	271
Submit, d. John & Eliz[abeth], bp. Jan. 8, 1737/8	274
Susanna, d. Benj[amin], bp. Apr. 12, 1719	256
Tamar, twin, with Asa, d. Benjamin, bp. Sept. 11, 1726	261
Temperance, d. Benj[amin], bp. May 18, 1729	263
Zeruiah, of Guilford, m. Horace **PARMALEE**, of Durham, Oct. 18, 1832	435
LEWENRONTH, Noble, of Waterbury, m. Louisa E. **DAVIS**, of Watertown, Oct. 15, 1844	441
LEWIS, [see also **LOAS**], David, s. Jane, b. July 10, 1758	377
Elizabeth, d. Jane, b. May 28, 1755	377
Jane had d. Elizabeth **AUSTIN**, b. May 28, 1755; bp. Jan. 16, [1757]	306,377
Jane had s. David **MEEKER**, b. July 10, 1758; bp. Dec. 17, [1758]	308,377
Jane had d. Rachel, b. Dec. 18, 1760	378
Rachel, d. Jane, b. Dec. 18, 1760	378
Thomas, of Farmington, m. Sarah **GURNSEY**, of Durham, Dec. 24, 1765, by Rev. Elizur Goodrich	329
LINES, Elisha, of Waterbury, m. Ann **CARR**, of Simsbury, Jan. 8, 1845	441
LINLEY, Mary, m. Dan **PARMALEE**, Jr., Mar. 27, 1803	416

	Page
LOAS, LAS, [see also **LEWIS**], Benjamin, s. John & Abigail, b. May 4, 1784	400
Daniel, s. John & Abigail, d. Jan. 12, 1788	402
Henry, s. John & Abigail, b. June 9, 1786; d. Sept. 26, 1794	402,406
Joseph, s. John & Abigail, b. Sept. 18, 1780	400
Joseph, s. John & Abigail, b. Sept. 28, 1780	402
Moses, s. John & Abigail, b. Sept. 23, 1777	398
LOTHROP, Henry, m. Catharine **COE**, Nov. 25, 1824	432
LOVELAND, Elijah, of Middletown, m. Sarah **STRONG**, of Durham, June 19, 1843	440
Eunice, m. Anson **MEIGS**, Sept. 26, 1821	430
Harriet, m. Sylvanus **SHELLEY**, June 21, 1824	431
Isaac, d. July 12, 1830	428
Jonathan, s. Jonathan, bp. Dec. [ ], 1777	326
LUCAS, LUCASS, Ahaziah, s. Richard & Sarah, bp. July 8, [1764]	314
Amaziah, s. Richard & Sarah, b. July [ ], 1764	391
Joel, s. William & Tryphena, bp. Aug. 14, [1768]	317
Joel, s. William & Tryphena, bp. July [ ], [1771]	321
Mariah, m. Hiram **BISHOP**, July 11, [1831?]	435
Olive, d. William & Tryphena, bp. May 11, [1766], by Mr. Denison	315
Patience had d. Sarah, bp. Dec. 5, 1742	281
Sally, d. Richard & Sarah, bp. Mar. 1, [1767]	316
Salle, d. Richard & Sarah, b. Mar. 2, 1767	391
Samuel, s. William & Tryphena, bp. Sept. 1, [1765]	315
Sarah, d. Patience **LUCAS**, bp. Dec. 5, 1742	281
Sarah, of Durham, m. David **STONE**, of Haddam, Jan. 29, [1761], by Rev. Elizur Goodrich	328
Stephen, s. Richard & Sarah, bp. Apr. 16, [1769]	318
Timothy, s. William & Tryphena, bp. Sept. 1, [1765]	315
Tryphena, d. William & Tryphena, bp. Sept. 1, [1765]	315
William, s. William & Tryphena, bp. Sept. 1, [1765]	315
LYMAN, Abel, s. Sergt. Thomas & Ann, bp. Feb. 10, 1749/50	290
Abel, [s. Thomas & Anne], b. Feb. 12, 1750	390
Abel, m. Adah **PICKETT**, Mar. 15, 1790	423
Ann, w. of Thomas, bp. Aug. 10, [1740]	278
Anne, [d. Thomas & Anne], b. Jan. 10, 1748; bp. Jan. 24, 1747/8	287,390
Anne, m. David **TALCOT**, b. of Durham, Sept. 16 (17), [1767], by Rev. Elizur Goodrich	330,389
Anne, wid., m. Ebenezer **GURNSEY**, b. of Durham, Feb. 18, [1768], by Rev. Elizur Goodrich	330
Charles G., of Colebrook, m. Louisa **HULL**, of Durham, Nov. 29, 1832	435
Daniel, [s. Thomas & Anne], b. Jan. 27, 1756	390
David, s. John & Hope, bp. Apr. 21, 1746	285
Dwight Alpheus, s. Abel & Adah, b. Jan. 14, 1797	423
Edward Henry, s. George & Sally, b. Jan. 8, 1802	411
Elizabeth, d. Thomas & Elizabeth, bp. Apr. 5, 1713	253

	Page
LYMAN, (cont.)	
Elizabeth, d. Aaron & Rebecca, bp. Nov. 7, 1731	266
Elizabeth, [d. Thomas & Anne], b. Mar. 4, 1744; bp. Mar. 11, 1743/4	283,390
Elizabeth, d. Noah & Sarah, bp. Nov. 5, 1749	290
Elizabeth, m. Ezra **BALDWIN**, Jr., b. of Durham, May 16, [1764], by Rev. Elizur Goodrich	329
Elsa Lavinia, [d. William & Weltha Maria], b. Oct. 7, 1843	429
Eugene Lewellyn, [s. William & Weltha Maria], b. Oct. 21, 1845	429
Frances Amelia, d. Abel & Adah, b. Mar. 4, 1793	423
Frederick, s. George & Sally, b. Oct. 11, 1812	414,426
George, m. Sally **SMITHSON**, Mar. 7, 1801	426
Gilbert Augustus, [s. William & Weltha Maria], b. July 1, 1836	429
Hannah, d. Eben & Exp[erience], bp. June [ ], 1723	259
Hannah, d. John & Hope, bp. June 19, 1743	282
Hannah Mariah, [d. William & Weltha Maria], b. Jan. 18, 1830	429
Henry Allen, [s. William & Weltha Maria], b. July 20, 1825	427,429
James, [s. Thomas & Anne], b. June 10, 1753	390
James, s. Abel & Adah, b. June 28, 1815	423
John, s. John & Hope, bp. May 4, 1740; d. immediately	277
John, s. John & Hope, bp. Jan. 13, 1744/5	284
Jonathan, s. Noah & Elizabeth, bp. Apr. 21, 1717	255
Julia Ann, [d. William & Weltha Maria], b. May 14, 1831	429
Katharine, d. John & Hope, bp. Nov. 8, 1741	279
Loisa Jane, [d. William & Weltha Maria], b. May 16, 1834	429
Mary Charlotte, d. William & Weltha Maria, b. June 15, 1828, at Rochester, Vt.	427,429
Miles, s. Noah & Sarah, bp. Mar. 24, 1744/5	284
Mindwell, d. Eben[eze]r & Exp[erience], bp. Sept. 15, 1718	255
Noah, s. Noah & Eliz[abeth], bp. Jan. 24, 1713/14	253
Noah, s. Noah, bp. June 21, 1747	287
Noah, s. Noah & Eleanor, bp. Dec. 26, [1773]	323
Phinehas, s. Noah & Elizabeth, bp. Mar. 6, [1714/15]	254
Richard Melvin, [s. William & Weltha Maria], b. Feb. 3, 1840	429
Ruth, d. Eben, bp. Nov. 22, 1724	260
Ruth, d. Eben, Jr. & 2nd w. bp. Nov. 30, 1735	271
Sally, w. of George, d. Sept. 28, 1825	426
Sarah, d. Thomas & Ann, bp. May [ ], [1740]	279
Sarah, d. Thomas & Ann, bp. Aug. 14, 1740	278
Sarah, [d. Thomas & Anne], b. May 29, 1741	390
Sarah, wid., m. Robert **AKINS**, Mar. 23, 1758, by Rev. Elizur Goodrich	327
Sophia, d. Abel & Adah, b. Dec. 3, 1790	423
Thomas, s. Thomas & Eliz[abeth], bp. Feb. 13, 1714/15	253
Thomas, bp. Aug. 10, [1740]	278
Thomas, s. Thomas & Ann, bp. Feb. 16, 1745/6	285
Thomas, [s. Thomas & Anne], b. Feb. 14, 1746	390
Thomas, d. Apr. 20, 1761	351,390
Thomas, m. Rachel **SEAWARD**, Jan. 30, 1771, by Rev. Elizur	

Page

LYMAN, (cont.)
Goodrich 331
Thomas William, s George & Sally, b. Apr. 23, 1810 413
Urbane, [s. William & Weltha Maria], b. Mar. 1, 1842 429
William Oliver, [s. William & Weltha Maria], b. Nov. 16, 1832 429
LYNN, Anna, m. Roswel[l] **STEVENS**, June 24, 1829 434
Betsey, m. Arelno **THOMPSON**, Sept. 11, 1842 440
Clarissa, of Durham, m. George S. **MORSE**, of North Haven, Sept. 27, 1846 442
Eunice, E., m. Justus I. **BAILEY**, b. of Durham, May 4, 1845 441
Ezekiel W., m. [ ], Mar. 14, 1837 437
Polly A., m. Noyes **CONE**, Apr. 30, 1837 437
Samuel W., m. Sarah **COE**, Jan. 24, 1829 434
MADDOCKS, Daniel, s. Dan[ie]ll & Hannah, bp. Apr. 12, [1767] 316
Hannah, wid., m. Lieut. John **CAMP**, Apr. 19, 1770, by Rev. Elizur Goodrich 331
MALTBY, Amy, d. William & Rosanna, bp. May 7, [1775] 325
Henry, m. Ruth **HART**, Dec. 12, 1821 430
MANN, Jackson, of Carlisle, Ky., m. Lydia M. **ELLIOTT**, of Durham, Oct. 6, 1844 441
MANNING, Thaddeus, s. Thaddeus & Elisabeth, b. Feb. 23, 1780 400
MARSH, Laura Artelissea, bp. July 31, 1853, by Rev. Mr. Pease 429
MASON, Nathaniel P., m. Orpha M. **SQUIRES**, July 1, 1839 438
MATTOON, Irena, d. Sarah, b. May 31, 1824 428
Sarah had d. Irena, b. May 31, 1824 428
MAYNARD, Abigail W., m. Alexander **CAMP**, Feb. 22, 1842 440
Leonidas, m. Abigail **SCRANTON**, Sept. 28, 1845 441
Rachel H., m. Israel **CAMP**, Oct. 1, 1839 438
MEEKER, MEEKOE, Aaron, s. Sam[ue]l, bp. May 18, 1729 263
Ann, d. Joseph, bp. Jan. 9, [1725] 261
Benjamin, s. Samuel & Mary, bp. Sept. 18, 1720 257
Daniel, twin with David, s. Joseph & Ann, bp. Oct. 27, 1734 270
Daniel, s. Daniel & Mary, bp. July [ ], [1772] 322
David, twin with Daniel, s. Joseph & Ann, bp. Oct. 27, 1734 270
David, s. Jane **LEWIS**, bp. Dec. 17, [1758] 308
Elizabeth, d. Samuel & Mary, bp. June 22, [1718] 255
Jemimah, d. Joseph & Ann, bp. Nov. 28, 1731 266
John, s. Joseph & Ann, bp. May 1, 1738 275
Josiah, s. Samuel & Mary, bp. July 11, 1731 265
Lavinia, of Durham, m. James N. **PHELPS**, of Wallingford, Dec. 27, 1840 439
Mary, d. Samuel & Mary, bp. May 16, 1722 258
Mary, d. Samuel & Mary, bp. Oct. 28, 1733 269
Mary, d. Nathaniel & Tamar, bp. June 25, 1749 289
Mary, m. Beriah **MURRY**, July 21, 1765 336
Nathan, s. Rebecca, since the w. of Timothy **STOW**, bp. May 26, [1771] 320
Nath[anie]ll, s. Samuel & Mary, bp. Oct. 4, [1724] 260

	Page
MEEKER, MEEKOE, (cont.)	
Peninnah, m. James **BROWN**, Feb. 7, 1766, by Rev. Elizur Goodrich	329
Phinehas, s. Joseph, bp. Dec. 8, 1728	263
Rebeckah, d. Joseph & Ann, bp. Dec. 14, [1740]	278
Rebeckah, m. Timothy **STOW**, June 13, 1769	392
Samuel, s. Samuel & Mary, bp. Apr. 28, 1717	255
Sam[uel], s. Daniel & Mary, bp. July 24, [1768]	317
Schuyler, s. Rebecca, since the w. of Timothy **STOW**, bp. May 26, [1771]	320
------, d. Sam[ue]l & Mary, bp. Jan. 15, 1726/7	261
MEIGS, Anson, m. Eunice **LOVELAND**, Sept. 26, 1821	430
Phinehas, m. Mary **CAMP**, Aug. 20, 1833	436
MERRIMAN, Andrew, m. Eliza **PECK**, Aug. 6, 1827	433
Nancy, of Wallingford, m. Stephen **BAILEY**, of Durham, Oct. 25, 1846	442
Thankful, m. Daniel **DIMOCH**, May 27, [1762], by Rev. Elizur Goodrich	328,381
Theoph[ilus] had negro Peggy, bp. Feb. 10, 1774	323
MERWIN, Alva, m. Isaac **BALDWIN**, Sept. 17, 1823	431
Ann, d. Dan[ie]l & Mary, bp. June 21, 1747	287
Anne, of Durham, m. Benjamin **HOLT**, of Wallingford, May 2, 1770, by Rev. Elizur Goodrich	331
Daniel, Jr., of Durham, m. Elizabeth **WELLS**, of Haddam, Dec. 20, 1738, by Henry Brainard, J. P.	358
Daniel, Jr., m. Mary **BURRETT**, May 11, 1741, by Rev. Nathaniel Chauncey	360
Daniel, s. Miles & Mary, b. May 30, 1746	369
Daniel, s. Daniel & Mary, bp. June 1, 1746	286
Daniel, Jr., d. May 15, 1758	385
Daniel, d. Apr. 11, 1766	386
Daniel, m. Rebekah **SEWARD**, b. of Durham, Dec. 14, 1769, by Rev. Elizur Goodrich	331,392
Daniel, s. Daniel & Rebecca, bp. Sept. 9, [1770]	320
Daniel, s. Daniel & Rebeckah, b. Sept. 29, 1770	393
David, s. Miles & Mary, b. Feb. 10, 1763; bp. Mar. 13, [1763]	312,381
Elizabeth, d. Daniel & Sarah (Mary), b. Feb. 14, 1722/3; bp. Feb. 17, 1722/3	258,347
Elizabeth, w. of Daniel, Jr., d. Oct. 29, 1739	359
Elizabeth, d. Daniel & Mary, bp. Feb. 7, 1741/2	280
Elnathan, s. Daniel & Mary, bp. Sept. 1, 1745	285
Eunice, d. Miles, Jr. & Mary, b. Apr. 27, 1770; bp. Apr. 29, [1770]	319,393
Hannah, d. Daniel & Mary, bp. Sept. 22, 1751	292
Hannah, m. Nathan **BRISTOL**, Jan. [ ], 1773, by Rev. Elizur Goodrich	332
Hannah, [d. Miles & Mary], b. Aug. 31, 1787	402
Israel, s. Daniel & Mary, bp. June 4, 1749	289
James, s. Daniel, Jr. & Elizabeth, b. Oct. 19, 1739; bp. Oct. 21, 1739	276,358-9
Jerusha, d. Miles, Jr. & Mary, b. Aug. 27, 1768; bp. Dec. 4, [1768]	318,393

Page

MERWIN, (cont.)

Jesse, [d. Miles, Jr. & Mary], b. Dec. 23, 1782; bp. Mar. [ ], 1783 326,402
Job. s. Miles & Mary, b. Feb. 16, 1749; bp. Feb. 19, 1748/9 289,369
Mary, d. Miles & Mary, b. May 24, 1755; bp. May 25, 1755 297,376
Mary, m. Stephen **NORTON**, Jr., Mar. 23, 1778, by Rev. Elizur Goodrich 333
Mary, [d. Miles & Mary], b. May 14, 1785 402
Mary, w. of Lieut. Miles, d. Jan. 18, 1793 404
Mary, m. Thomas **NOBLE**, Apr. 27, 1824 431
Miles, s. Miles & Mary, b. May 1, 1744; bp. May 6, 1744 283,369
Miles, Jr., m. Mary **PARMALEE**, b. of Durham, Nov. 4, 1767, by Rev. Elizur Goodrich 330,393
Miles, s. Miles & Mary, b. Feb. 2, 1772; bp. Mar. 8, [1772] 321,402
Miles, Lieut., d. Dec. 12, 1786 404
Nancy, [d. Miles & Mary], b. Oct. 25, 1778 402
Nancy, m. Gaylord **NEWTON**, Dec. 5, 1838 438
Noah, s. Miles & Mary, b. Nov. 9, 1752 369
Olive, [d. Miles & Mary], b. Dec. 12, 1773; bp. Feb. 20, 1774 323,402
Phebe C., m. Seymour **WHITE**, Oct. 5, 1836 437
Rachel, d. Daniel & Rebekah, bp. [1774] 324
Rhoda, d. Miles & Mary, b. Aug. 19, 1757; bp. Aug. 21, [1757], by Mr. Clarke 306,376
Rhoda, [d. Miles & Mary], b. Nov. 11, 1780 402
Rhoda, m. Edmund **SAGE**, June 28, 1829 434
Ruth, [d. Miles & Mary], b. June 25, 1776 402
Ruth, of Durham, m. James **LEE**, of Guilford, Sept. 28, 1825 432
Samuel, s. Daniel & Rebekah J., bp. Dec. 6, [1772] 322
Sarah, m. John **CAMP**, Jr., July 11, 1739 379
Sarah, d. Daniel & Mary, bp. Aug. 8, 1743 282
Sarah, d Miles & Mary, b. June 7, 1760; bp. June 8, [1760] 310,376
Sarah, w. of Daniel, d. Sept. 23, 1764 384
Sarah, of Durham, m. Asahel **COOLEY**, of Wallingford, Jan. 23, 1766, by Rev. Elizur Goodrich 329
Sarah, m. Chauncey **GRAHAM**, Nov. 11, 1782 401
------, child of Daniel, bp. Sept. 14, [1777] 326

MILES, Mary, m. David **FOWLER**, June 15, 1724/5 346

MILLER, MILLAR, Amos, Jr., m. Elizabeth **TIBBALS**, of Middlefield, Apr. 7, 1766, by Rev. Elizur Goodrich 329
Anne, d. Caleb, b. [ ], 1791, at Middletown; m. Charles **CAMP**, Jan. 1, 1817 416
Elisha, of Farmington, m. Sarah **FOWLER**, of Durham, Oct. 18, 1764, by Rev. Elizur Goodrich 329
Eliza Ann, m. Elias **HALE**, Sept. 26, 1836 437
Giles, s. Giles, of Middlefield, bp. Apr. 23, [1758] 307
Henry L., m. Mariah **MILLER**, Nov. 30, 1845 442
Hiram, of Middlefield, m. Catharine **SHELLEY**, of Durham, Apr. 8, 1845 441
John W., m. Polly **MILLER**, b. of Middlefield, July 10, 1826 432

Page

MILLER, MILLAR, (cont.)
Mariah, m. Henry L. **MILLER**, Nov. 30, 1845 442
Polly, m. John W. **MILLER**, b. of Middlefield, July 10, 1826 432
Rebecca, m. David **ROBINSON**, Jan. 26, 1719/20 349
MINOR, James, m. Elizabeth **LEETE**, Sept. 1, 1841 439
MITCHEL[L], Abner, [s. Jonathan & Lydia], bp. Apr. 13, 1740 277
Camp, s. Jonathan & Bashua, bp. Nov. 8, [1741] 279
Jonathan, bp. Apr. 13, 1740 277
Lydia, w. of Jonathan, bp. Apr. 13, 1740 277
Lydia, d. Jonathan & Lydia, bp. Nov. 25, 1744 284
Sarah, [d. Jonathan & Lydia], bp. Apr. 13, 1740 277
MOFFET, MOFFAT, Abigail, d. Lemuel & Huldah, bp. June 28, 1767 316
Anne, d. Lemuel & Anne, bp. July 11, [1773] 323
Hannah, d. Lemuel & Huldah, bp. Sept. 10, [1769] 319
Lemuel, m. wid. Huldah **NEWTON**, Oct. 21, [1763], by Rev. Elizur Goodrich 328
Lemuel, s. Lemuel & Huldah, bp. June 2, [1771] 321
Lemuel, s. Lemuel, bp. June 29, 1777 326
Rachel, d. Lemuel & Anna, bp. Nov. 20, [1774] 324
MONGER, [see under **MUNGER**]
MONTAGUE, Brainard, of Sandersfield, Mass., m. Abigail S. **BOLLES**, of Middletown, Feb. 11, 1833 435
MO[O]RE, Lucy, d. Merwin, bp. May 2, [1756] 298
----, d. Marvin Reynold, bp. Dec. 25, 1757 307
MORGAN, Martha, bp. Feb. 7, 1741/2 280
Thomas F., m. Lucinda **STEVENS**, Aug. 6, 1833 436
MORRIS, Adonijah, s. Adonijah & Sarah, b. Oct. 26, 1723; bp. Dec. 29, 1723 259,355
Anna, d. Adonijah & Sarah, b. Feb. 24, 1728; bp. Apr. 7, 1728 262,355
James, s. James, bp. Jan. 21, 1721/2 257
John, s. Adonijah & Sarah, b. Nov. 15, 1725; bp. Dec. 12, 1725 261,355
Timothy, s. Adonijah & Sarah, b. Jan. 27, 1730; bp. Mar. 8, 1729/30 264,355
MORRISON, Margaret, d. Theophilus & Elizabeth, bp. Mar. 16, 1728/9 263
Sarah, twin with Theophilus, d. Theophilus & Elizabeth, bp. June 22, [1725] 260
Sarah, d. Theophilis & Elizabeth, bp. Oct. 22, 1727 262
Theophilus, twin with Sarah, s. Theophilus & Elizabeth, bp. June 22, [1725] 260
Theophilus, s. Theophilus & Elizabeth, bp. July 10, 1726 261
MORROW, Sally, m. James **CURTISS**, Nov. 2, 1791 403
MORSE, [see also **MOSS**], George S., of North Haven, m. Clarissa **LYNN**, of Durham, Sept. 27, 1846 442
Joseph S., of Durham, m. Mary O. **NETTLETON**, of Killingworth, May 4, 1841 439
Sarah Ann, m. Obier **BLAKESLEE**, Dec. 14, 1836 437
MORTON, Elisha, s. Thomas, bp. Nov. 22, 1741 279
MOSS, [see also **MORSE**], Bethiah, m. John **CANFIELD**, Jan. 19, 1748/9 365

Page

MOULTRUP, Rhoda, of Durham, m. Solomon **ROSE**, of Granville, Mar. 25, 1762, by Rev. Elizur Goodrich 328
MUCKET, Amos Manwarren, s. James & Ann, b. Mar. 21, 1822 427
Charles Denison, s. James & Ann, b. Mar. 6, 1824 427
Frances Edgar, s. James & Ann, b. Feb. 2, 1839 429
Martha Ann, d. James & Ann, b. Oct. 24, 1828 427
Mary Temperance, d. James & Ann, b. Apr. 3, 1831 428
Neamiah Murias, s. James & Ann, b. July 21, 1834 428
Olive Smith, d. James & Ann, b. July 9, 1820 427
MUNGER, MONGER, MUNGAR, Dinah, d. John & Deborah, b. Apr. 5, 1712; bp. May 18, 1712 252,343
Lucie, d. John A. & Deborah, b. Sept. 10, 1713; bp. Nov. 1, 1713 253,343
MUNSON, Jonathan, m. Sally **JOHNSON**, Nov. 27, 1823 431
Mary L., m. Levi **FOWLER**, b. of Northford, Oct. 11, 1852 443
Sally, d. Tobe L. & Lucy, b. Mar. 1, 1785 425
Sally, m. Asahel **STRONG**, May 12, 1803 425
MURRAY, MURRY, Beriah, m. Mary **MEEKER**, July 21, 1765 386
Curtiss, s. Beriah & Mary, bp. Jan. 3, 1768 317
Sabra, d. Beriah & Mary, b. Aug. 24, 1765; bp. Feb. 9, 1766 315,386
NEAL, Sally, of Wallingford, m. Hezekiah **BARTHOLOMEW**, Nov. 22, 1842 440
NETTLETON, Anne, m. Richard H. **HOTCHKISS**, Aug. 17, 1828 (1823) 434,443
Clarissa, m. Edward C. **HULL**, Oct. 9, 1839 438
Eliza J., m. Hartwell [**NETTLETON**], Apr. 7, 1838 437
Harriet E., m. Hosmer **FOWLER**, Nov. 6, 1826 433
Hartwell, m. Eliza J. **NETTLETON**, Apr. 7, 1838 437
Henry E., m. Cornelia **CAMP**, Sept. 6, 1839 438
Joseph, s. Eliphaz & Lydia, b. Jan. 10, 1793 407
Lydia, d. Eliphaz, b. Dec. 9, 1798 409
Lydia, of Killingworth, m. Charles **THOMPSON**, of Guilford, Apr. 5, 1810 422
Mary O., of Killingworth, m. Joseph S. **MORSE**, of Durham, May 4, 1841 439
Mimemery, d. Eliphaz & Lydia, b. May 27, 1795 407
Phinehas, of Killingworth, m. Lorinda **BURR**, of Haddam, Nov. 15, 1840 439
Polly, d. Eliphaz, b. Oct. 16, 1801 409
Polly, m. Selden **STEVENS**, Mar. 12, 1826 432
Polly, of Durham, m. Hinchman **ROBERTS**, of Middletown, Mar. 23, 1835 436
Sarah Ann, m. Nathan G. R. **SOUTHWICK**, Sept. 28, 1845 441
Sophronia, m. Elijah **BEAUMONT**, May 27, 1827 433
NEWTON, Abiather, s. Burwell & Eunice, bp. Mar. 10, 1754 295
Abner, s. Abner, bp. Oct. 23, 1726 261
Abner, twin with Roger, s. Burwell & Eunice, bp. Jan. 20, 1765 314
Abner, m. Sarah **HALL**, Apr. 29, 1823 431
Amy, d. Abner & Huldah, bp. Feb. 3, 1754 295
Amy (Anne), m. Phineas **CANFIELD**, Apr. 1, 1773, by Rev. Elizur

Page

NEWTON, (cont.)
Goodrich 332,397
Asher, s. Abner, Jr. & Huldah, bp. June 10, [1759] 309
Burwell, s. Abner, bp. July 20, 1729 263
Burwell, s. Burwell & Eunice, b. Jan. 6, 1757; bp. Jan. 16, [1757] 305,415
Burwell, m. Sibyl **HARVEY**, Nov. 19, 1795 416
Burwell, m. Betsey **HALL**, Dec. 20, 1814 416
Comfort, d. John & Mary, bp. Mar. 30, 1755 297
Comfort, m. Dan **CANFIELD**, Nov. 22, [1775], by Rev. Elizur Goodrich 333
Cyrus, s. Abner, bp. Feb. 8, 1756 298
Elisha, m. Sally **CAMP**, Dec. 13, 1820 429
Elizabeth, d. Lemuel & Huldah, bp. Sept. 23, [1764] 314
Elizabeth, d. John, bp. Oct. 5, [1777] 326
Gaylord, m. Nancy **MERWIN**, Dec. 5, 1838 438
Hannah, d. John & Mary, bp. Apr. [ ], 1766 315
Horace, m. Delight **CAMP**, May 24, 1826 432
Huldah, d. Abner & Huldah, bp. Oct. 27, 1751 293
Huldah, wid., m. Lemuel **MOFFET**, Oct. 21, [1763], by Rev. Elizur Goodrich 328
Huldah, m. Beriah **CHITTENDEN**, Mar. 15, 1774, by Rev. Elizur Goodrich 332
Isaac, s. John & Mary, bp. Feb. 28, 1747/8 288
Isaac, s. Burwell, bp. Dec. [ ], 1770 320
Israel C., s. Elisha & Sally, b. Mar. 23, 1822 419
John, s. Abner, bp. Oct. 23, 1726 261
John, s. John & Mary, bp. July 29, 1750 291
John, s. Burwell & Sibyl, b. Aug. 5, 1798 416
Maria A., of Durham, m. Henry **WARD**, of Middletown, May 13, 1852 443
Martha, d. Abner & Huldah, b. Oct. 16, 1749; bp. Nov. 5, 1749 290,352
Mary, d. Burwell & Eunice, bp. Apr. 15, [1759] 308
Mary, d. John & Mary, bp. May 8, 1763 313
Rhoda, d. John & Mary, bp. July 13, 1760 310
Roger, s. Abner, bp. May 15, 1737 273
Roger, twin with Abner, s. Burwell & Eunice, bp. Jan. 20, 1765 314
Roger, s. Burwell & Eunice, bp. May 29, [1768] 317
Samuel, s. Abner, bp. Nov. 5, 1732 267
Samuel, s. Burwell & Sibyl, b. Dec. 30, 1796 416
Samuel, m. Betsey H. **PARMALEE**, Nov. 23, 1827 433
Sarah, d. John, bp. May 7, [1758] 307
Sophia, d. Burwell & Sibyl, b. Feb. 7, 1810 416
Sophia, m. William **HART**, Sept. 23, 1821 430
Stephen, s. John, bp. Feb. 8, 1756 298
Submit, d. Burwell & Eunice, bp. June 6, [1762] 312
Sibyl, w. of Burwell, d. Apr. 19, 1813 416

NICHOLS, Mary, m. George H. **WELTON**, b. of Waterbury, Jan. 28, 1844 440

NIEF, John, s. Patrick & Lucy, b. Dec. 30, 1764; bp. Apr. 14, 1765 315,384
Patrick, m. Lucy **RICHARDSON**, Aug. 4, 1764 384

	Page
NOBLE, Thomas, m. Mary **MERWIN**, Apr. 27, 1824	431
NORTON, [see also **ORTON**], Aaron, s. Isaac & Mary, b. Mar. 26, 1749; bp. Nov. 5, 1749	290,370
Aaron, s. John, 3rd, & Mary, of Killingworth, b. June 24, 1751; in Durham; bp. June [ ], 1751	292,368
Abel, s. John & Mary, of N. Killingworth, bp. July 4, [1762]	312
Abigail, d. Isaac & Mary, b. Oct. 14, 1736; bp. Oct. 31, 1736	273,361
Abigail, w. of Stephen, bp. June 11, 1749	289
Abigail, d. Stephen & Abigail, bp. June 25, 1754	296
Abigail, d. Stephen & Abigail, b. July 14, 1754	371
Abigail, m. Dan **PARMALEE**, Jan. 11, 1776	398
Abigail Clarissa, d. Lewis & Hannah, b. Jan. 1, 1813	414
Alfred, s. Ozias & Hannah, b. July 16, 1798	412
Amos, s. John & Mary, bp. Nov. [ ], 1764	314
Andrew Talcott, s. Lewis & Hannah, b. Jan. 23, 1809	414
Ann, d. Isaac & Mary, bp. Dec. 23, 1744	284
Ann, d. John, bp. Feb. 3, 1754	295
Ann Elizabeth, d. Stephen L. & Jerusha, b. Feb. 28, 1821, at Cheshire	428
Anne, d. Isaac & Mary, b. Dec. 19, 1743	370
Benjamin, s. John & Eliza, bp. July 11, 1719	256
Benjamin, s. John & Elizabeth, b. July 12, 1719	345
Benjamin, bp. June 29, 1746	286
Benjamin, [s. Benjamin & Elizabeth, of Killingworth], b. July 10, 1746; bp. July 13, 1746	286,375
Charity, [d. Benjamin & Elizabeth, of Killingworth], b. Sept. 24, 1758; bp. Nov. 12, [1758]	308,375
Charles, s. Ephraim & Mary, b. Dec. 8, 1738; bp. Dec. 11, 1748	288,368
Charles, s. Stephen L. & Jerusha, b. July 17, 1824	428
Clarissa, d. Ozias & Hannah, b. Aug. 15, 1794	412
Daniel, s. Joseph & Prudence, bp. Mar. 2, 1734/5	270
Daniel, s. Joseph, Jr. & Prudence, b. Mar. 2, 1735/6	360
David, s. Sam[ue]l & Dinah, bp. Aug. 20, 1721	257
David, s. Sam[ue]l & Dinah, bp. Jan. 30, 1725/6	261
David, s. Samuel & Dinah, b. Feb. [ ], 1726	349
Deborah, d. Joseph, b. Nov. 1, 1707	339
Delia W., d. Lyman & Olive, b. May 28, 1798	410
Dinah, d. Samuel & Dinah, b. Nov. [ ], 1723; bp. Nov. 24, 1723	259,349
Dinah, m. John **CURTISS**, Nov. 18, 1747	353
Ebenezer, s. Samuel & Dinah, b. Dec. 30, 1715; bp. Jan. 1, 1715/16	254,349
Ebenezer, s. Thomas, bp. Oct. 2, 1743	282
Eli, s. John & Mary B. R., bp. May 8, [1757]	306
Elihu, s. Jesse, Jr. & Prudence, b. Jan. 11, 1732	354
Elihu, s. Joseph, Jr., bp. Jan. 16, 1731/2	266
Elisha, s. Thomas & Mary, b. Nov. 21, 1741	360
Elizabeth, d. John & Elizabeth, b. Jan. 15, 1725/6; bp. Jan. 21, 1727/8	262,357
Elizabeth, w. of Benjamin, bp. June 29, 1746	286
Elizabeth, m. Joseph **SEWARD**, Jr., Jan. 14, 1748/9	365

Page

NORTON, (cont.)

Elizabeth, d. Ephraim & Mary, b. June 19, 1751; bp. June 23, 1751 292,368
Elizabeth, [twin with Elnathan, d. Benjamin & Elizabeth, of Killingworth], b. May 10, 1755; b. May 18, 1755 297,375
Elnathan, [twin with Elizabeth], s. Benjamin & Elizabeth, of Killingworth], b. May 10, 1755; bp. May 18, 1755 297,375
Ephraim, s. John & Elizabeth, b. Aug. 21, 1721; bp. Aug. 27, 1721 257,348
Ephraim, bp. Dec. 4, 1748 288
Ephraim, s. Charles, bp. Sept. 3, [1775] 325
Esther, d. Joseph, Jr. & Prudence, b. Dec. 18, 1738; bp. Dec. 24, 1738 275,360
Esther, of Durham, m. Miles **NORTON**, of Goshen, Dec. 14, [1758], by Rev. Elizur Goodrich 327
Eunice, d. Charles & Elizabeth, b. Mar. 6, 1771 395
Experience, d. Noah & Experience, bp. Sept. 23, 1759 309
Hannah, d. Thomas & Mary, b. May 22, 1751; bp. May 26, 1751 292,370
Hannah, [d. Benjamin & Elizabeth, of Killingworth], b. Sept. 17, 1752 375
Hannah, d. John, Jr. & Hannah, b. May 7, 1758; bp. May 14, [1758] 307,385
Hannah, w. of John, d. Dec. 13, 1772 395
Hannah, m. Benjamin **TAINTER**,Jan. 17, 1779,by Rev. Elizur Goodric 333
Isaac, s. Joseph & Deborah, b. Aug. 17, 1712 342
Isaac, m. Mary **ROCKWELL**, of Windsor, Nov. 12, 1735 361
Isaac, s. Isaac & Mary, b. Mar. 23, 1747; bp. Mar. 29, 1747 287,370
Jerusha, of Durham, m. Lemuel **JOHNSON**, of Middletown, Nov. 11, [1772], by Rev. Elizur Goodrich 332
Jerusha, d. Stephen L. & Jerusha, b. June 3, 1828; d. Oct. 27, 1828 428
Jerusha, d. Sept. 13, 1828 428
Joel, s. John, 2d, & Deborah, b. Sept. 20, 1745; bp. Sept. 22, 1745; d. July 2, 1746 285,365
Joel, [s. Benjamin & Elizabeth, of Killingworth], b. Sept. 17, 1750; bp. Sept. 23, 1750 292,275
Joel, s. Isaac & Mary, b. May 13, 1753 370
Joel, s. John & Hannah, bp. Mar. 17, 1771 320
Joel, s. John & Hannah, b. Apr. 24, 1771 395
John, s. John & Elizabeth, b. Feb. 16, 1714/15; bp. Feb. 20, [1714/15] 253,344
John, s. John & Deborah, of Saybrook, bp. June 30, 1734 269
John, bp. Mar. 4, 1743/4 283
John, s. John, 3rd, & Mary, of Killingworth, b. Feb. 23, 1748; bp. Apr. 16, 1749 289,350
John, m. Hannah **BISHOP**, Dec. 21, [1757], by Rev. Elizur Goodrich 327
John, s. John, Jr.* & Hannah, b. June 10, 1763; bp. June 19, [1763] In baptism given as "John, 3rd") 313,385
John, Lieut., d. Nov. 4, 1770 393
John, m. Sarah **TAINTOR**, Mar. 24, 1774 397
Jonathan, s. John & Elizabeth, b. Feb. 18, 1711/12; bp. May 18, 1712 252,341
Jonathan, bp. Feb. 5, 1737/8 274
Jonathan, s. Jonathan & Ruth, bp. Mar. 5, 1737/8 274
Jonathan, s. Jonathan & Ruth, b. Aug. 27, 1745 364

Page

NORTON, (cont.)

Joseph, s. Joseph & Deborah, b. Sept. 2, 1709 341
Joseph, m. Prudence OSBORN, Sept. 16, 1729 353
Joseph, s. Elihu & Dinah, bp. July 29, [1759] 309
Laura, d. Stephen L. & Jerusha, b. June 20, 1826 428
Leverett, s. Ozias & Hannah, b. Nov. 28, 1791 412
Levi, s. Thomas, bp. Sept. 17, [1758] 307
Lewis, s. **Stephen & Abigail, b. Apr. 28, 1766; d. Jan. 8, 1770** 393
Lewis, s. **Stephen & Elizabeth, bp. May 4, [1766]** 315
Lewis, s. Stephen & Mary, b. Oct. 15, 1785 414
Lewis, m. Hannah **SWATHEL**, Dec. 16, 1805 414
Lewis, m. Emily **DUNN**, Jan. 22, 1826 432
Lucy, d. **John, Jr. & Hannah, b. Sept. 27, 1765; bp. Sept. 29, 1765;** d. Nov. 20, 1766 315,385,388
Lydia, d. Isaac & Mary, b. Mar. 5, 1739/40; bp. Mar. 9, 1739 /40 277,361
Lyman, s. Stephen & Abigail, b. June 1, 1763 383
Lyman, Dr., m. Olive **WELD**, June 18, 1795 410
Lyman Lewis, s. Lewis & Hannah, b. July 4, 1810 414
Lyman Warren, s. Stephen L. & Jerusha, b. Nov. 13, 1822 428
Mary, d. Isaac & Mary, b. July 1, 1737; bp. June 3, 1738 275,361
Mary, d. John & Mary, of Killingworth, b. Apr. 13, 1743 350
Mary, w. of John, bp. Mar. 4, 1743/4 283
Mary, d. John & Mary, of Black Rock, bp. Apr. 15, 1744 283
Mary, w. of Ephraim, bp. Dec. 4, 1748 288
Medad, s. Stephen & Abigail, b. June 30, 1749; bp. July 2, 1749 289,352
Medad, d. Dec. 27, 1821 423
Mehetabel, d. Joseph & Prudence, b. July 12, 1730; bp. Aug. 23, 1730 265,353
Mehethabel, m. Charles **BROOKS**, Oct. 13, 1753 367
Miles, of Goshen, m. Esther **NOTON**, of Durham, Dec. 14, [1758], by Rev. Elizur Goodrich 327
Miles, s. Charles & Elizabeth, b. May 30, 1769; bp. Nov. 12, [1769] 319,395
Mindwell, d. Ephraim & Mary, b. Oct. 21, 1756; bp. Nov. 14, [1756] 298,373
Moses, s. John & [Mary], bp. Jan. 4, 1716/17 286
Moses, s. John & Mary, of Killingworth, b. Dec. 28, 1746 350
Nathan, s. Elihu & Dinah, bp. Jan. 16, [1757] 306
Noahdiah, [s. Benjamin & Elizabeth, of Killingworth], b. Aug. 17, 1748 375
Noah, s. Samuel C. & Dinah, b. Jan. 24, 1728/9; bp. Jan. 26, 1728/9 263,348
Noah, m. Experience **STRONG**, Dec. 29, [1757], by Rev. Elizur Goodrich 327
Ozias, s. Stephen & Abigail, b. Dec. 31, 1759; bp. Jan. 6, 1760 309,382,412
Ozias, m. Hannah PARMALEE, Mar. 14, 1790 412
Ozias P., s. Ozias & Hannah, b. Dec. 4, 1800 412
Phebe, d. Jonathan & Ruth, b. May 10, 1750; bp. May 13, 1750 291,366
Phinehas, s. Thomas & Mary, b. Apr. 23, 1748 370
Prudence, d. Joseph, Jr. & Prudence, bp. Aug. 24, 1742 281

Page

NORTON, (cont.)

Rebeckah, d. John, Jr. & Hannah, b. Nov. 20, 1759; bp. Nov. 25, [1759] 309,385

Rosa, d. John & Mary, of Killingworth, b. Aug. 16, 1745 350

Ruth, d. Jonathan & Ruth, b. Aug. 20, 1743; bp. Aug. 20, 1743 282,364

Salle, d. John, Jr. & Hannah, b. Dec. 10, 1767 389

Samuel, m. Dinah **BEACH**, May 13, 1713, by Rev. Nath[anie]ll Chauncey 349

Samuel, s. Samuel & Dinah, b. Mar. 20, 1714; bp. Mar. 20, [1713/14]; d. Mar. 21, 1718 253,342,349

Samuel, s. Samuel & Dinah, b. Mar. 6, 1718; bp. Mar. 9, 1718 255,349

Samuel, d. July 13, 1767 388

Sarah, d. Thomas, bp. Mar. 29, 1746 285

Sarah, d. Jonathan & Ruth, b. Feb. 23, 1747/8; bp. Feb. 28, 1747/8 288,366

Sarah, d. Thomas & Mary, b. Mar. 26, 1756 370

Sarah, d. Charles, bp. Aug. 8, 1773 323

Sarah, d. John, bp. Apr. 30, [1775] 325

Sidney, m. Palina **IVES**, b. of Durham, Oct. 31, 1821 430

Stephen, s. John & Elizabeth, b. June 7, 1724; bp. June 7, [1724] 259,348

Stephen, s. Jonathan & Ruth, b. June 21, 1741; bp. June 28, 1741 279,362

Stephen, bp. June 11, 1749 289

Stephen, s. Stephen & Abigail, b. Jan. 26, 1756 372

Stephen, Jr., m. Mary **MERWIN**, Mar. 23, 1778, by Rev. Elizur Goodrich 333

Stephen, Capt., d. Nov. 13, 1808 411

Stephen L., m. Mary Ann **GORHAM**, May 16, 1831 435

Stephen Lyman, s. Dr. Lyman & Olive, b. Sept. 5, 1799 410

Silvanus, s. Isaac & Mary, b. July 16, 1742; bp. July 18, 1742 (Sylvanus) 281,361

Thomas, s. Thomas* & Deborah, b. May 13, 1715; bp. May 15, [1715] (*Note says "Joseph") 254,344

Thomas, m. Mary **STEDMAN**, Nov. 5, 1740 359

William, s. Ozias & Hannah, b. Apr. 19, 1797; d. same month, 24th day 412

Zipporah, d. Isaac, bp. Oct. 26, 1755 298

-----, w. of Jonathan, bp. Feb. 5, 1737/8 274

NOYES, John, s. John **NOYES** & Esther **WADSWORTH**, bp. Oct. 1, [1758] 308

William, s. John **NOYES** & Esther **WADSWORTH**, bp. July 12, [1761], (See **WADSWORTH**) 311

ORTON, [see also **NORTON**], Edmond, m. Amanda **CAMP**, Jan. 1, 1821 430

OSBORN, Nathan, s. Samuel & Hannah, bp. Sept. 16, 1733 268

Prudence, m. Joseph **NORTON**, Sept. 16, 1729 353

Timothy, s. Samuel & Hannah, bp. Oct. 20, 1734 270

PADDOCK, Joseph H., of Middletown, m. Fanny M. **BRAINARD**,

Page

PADDOCK, (cont.)
of Haddam, July 10, 1844 441

PAGE, Asa, of Wallingford, m. Eunice **PAGE**, of Brandford, May 7, [1759], by Rev. Elizur Goodrich 327
Eunice, of Brandford, m. Asa **PAGE**, of Wallingford, May 7, [1759], by Rev. Elizur Goodrich 327
Mary, m. Timothy Dwight **CAMP**, b. of Durham, Nov. 4, 1847 442
Nathaniel, of Goshen, m. Eleanor **WRIGHT**, of Durham, Nov. 5, 1760, by Rev. Elizur Goodrich 328

PALMER, Joel, of Greenwich, m. Abigail **SQUIRE**, of Durham, Mar. 1, 1779, by Rev. Elizur Goodrich 333

PARDEE, Clarissa, m. Israel **SCRANTON**, Feb. 9, 1813 420
Lucy Alvira, d. David & Althea, b. Jan. 2, 1815, at Southington 423
Stephen Decatur, s. David & Althea, b. Feb. 10, 1822 423

PARK, William, of Haddam, m. Elizabeth **SUTLIF**, of Durham, May 29, 1755 351

PARKER, Betsey A., m. Thomas C. **CAMP**, June 11, 1834 436

PARMALEE, PARMELE, PARMELEE, PAMELY, Aaron, s. Joel & Abigail, bp. Oct. 25, [1723] 259
Aaron, s. John & Sarah, b. Sept. 17, 1736; bp. Sept. 19, 1736 272,361
Abigail, d. Joel & Abigail, b. July 12, 1715; bp. [Aug. 21, 1715] 254,354
Alexander, s. John, bp. Aug. 11, 1745 285
Ann, d. John & Sarah, b. Jan. 6, 1732; bp. Jan. 6, 1732/3 268,361
Betsey, d. Dan & Abigail, b. Oct. 24, 1781 399
Betsey A., d. Dan, Jr. & Mary, b. Dec. 23, 1805 417
Betsey H., m. Samuel **NEWTON**, Nov. 23, 1827 433
Camp, [s. Joel & Rhoda], b. Mar. 17, 1765; bp. Mar. 17, 1765 314,385
Charles, [s. Hezekiah & Mehitabel], b. Sept. 17, 1753; bp. Oct. 30, 1753 294,382
Charles, s. Dan, Jr. & Mary, b. Oct. 5, 1815 417
Clarinda, d. Phineas & Eunice, bp. Nov. 6, [1768] 318
Constant, s. Phineas & Eunice, bp. June 21, [1761] 311
Cornelia C., m. Edwin **COE**, Mar. 16, 1826 432
Dan, [s. Hezekiah & Mehitabel], b. May 15, 1748 382
Dan, m. Abigail **NORTON**, Jan. 11, 1776 398
Dan, s. Dan & Abigail, b. Feb. 3, 1783; bp. Mar. 23, 1783 326,400
Dan, Jr., m. Mary **LINLEY**, Mar. 27, 1803 416
Eli, [s. Eliphaz & Anne], b. Feb. 9, 1781 399
Eliphaz, [s. Joel & Rhoda], b. Dec. 27, 1743; bp. Jan. 1, 1743/4 283,385
Eliphaz, of Middletown, m. Anne **HANDY**, of Guilford, Aug. 3, [1768], by Rev. Elizur Goodrich 330
Elizabeth, d. Horace & Mary, b. Jan. 14, 1821 422
Elizabeth, m. Samuel G. **STEVENS**, June 23, 1841 439
Esther, m. Joel **AUSTIN**, May 12, 1840 439
Eunice, twin with Lois, d. Phinehas & Eunice, bp. Feb. 20, [1773] 322
Eunice, d. Levi & Phebe, b. Apr. 3, 1778 400

Page

PARMALEE, PARMELE, PARMELEE, PAMELY, (cont.)

Hannah, d. Joel & Abigail, b. Aug. 27, 1717; bp. Sept. 1, 1717 255,354
Hannah, [d. Hezekiah & Mehitabel], b. Apr. 14, 1738; bp. Apr. 16, 1738 275,382
Hannah, of Durham, m. Noah **ROBINSON**, of Granville, Nov. 8, [1758], by Rev. Elizur Goodrich 327
Hannah, [d. Joel & Rhoda], b. Sept. 2, 1761; bp. Sept. 6, [1761] 311,385,412
Hannah, d. Dan & Abigail, b. Nov. 1, 1776 398
Hannah, m. Ozias **NORTON**, Mar. 14, 1790 412
Hezekiah, s. Joel & Abigail, b. Jan. 10, 1710/11 (1712) 342,354
Hezekiah, m. Mehitabel **HALL**, Apr. 18, 1737 382
Hezekiah, [s. Hezekiah & Mehitabel], b. June 20, 1745; bp. June 23, 1745 285,382
Hezekiah, m. Mercy **SMITH**, June 10, 1756 382
Hezekiah, s. Dan, Jr. & Mary, b. July 25, 1811 417
Horace, of Durham, m. Zeruiah **LEETE**, of Guilford, Oct. 18, 1832 435
James, s. Hezekiah & Mercy, b. July 15, 1757; bp. July 17, [1757]; d. Nov. 30, 1759 306,382
James, s. Phineas & Eunice, bp. Feb. 27, 1763 312
Jerusha, d. Joel & Abigail, b. Apr. 10, 1721; bp. Apr. 16, 1721 257,354
Jerusha, m. John **CAMP**, Jr., Mar. 17, 1742 379
Jerusha, [d. Joel & Rhoda], b. Aug. 15, 1749, bp. Aug. 20, 1749 290,385
Jerusha, m. Henry **CRANE**, June 24, 1773, by Rev. Elizur Goodrich 332
Joel, m. Abigail **ANDRUS**, June 30, 1706 354
Joel, s. Joel & Abigail, bp. Mar. 15, 1712/13 253
Joel, s. Joel & Abigail, b. Jan. [ ], 1713/14 343
Joel, s. Joel & Abigail, b. Mar. 8, 1714 354
Joel, m. Rhoda **CAMP**, Jan. 6, 1742/3 385
Joel, [s. Joel & Rhoda], b. Aug. 6, 1758; bp. Aug. 13, [1758] 307,385
John, s. Joel & Abigail, b. Oct. 17, 1708 339
John, s. Joel & Abigail, b. Sept. 22, 1709 354
John, of Durham, m. Sarah **BOARDMAN**, of Weathersfield, Nov. 24, 1730 361
John, s. John & Sarah, b. Feb. 18, 1738; bp. Mar. 4, 1738/9 276,361
John, s. Horace & Mary, b. Feb. 5, 1818 422
Levi, [s. Joel & Rhoda], b. June 22, 1745; bp. June 23, 1745 285,385
Lois, twin with Eunice, d. Phinehas & Eunice, bp. Feb. 20 [1773] 322
Lucretia, d. Noah & Ann, b. Feb. 15, 1815 421
Mary, d. Joel, b. [ ] 12, 1706 339
Mary, d. Joel & Abigail, b. Nov. 11, 1707 354
Mary, [d. Joel & Rhoda], b. May 27, 1747; bp. May 31, 1747 287,385
Mary, m. Miles **MERWIN**, Jr., b. of Durham, Nov. 4, 1767, by Rev. Elizur Goodrich 330,393
Mary A., m. Alvin **ROBERTS**, Oct. 1, 1827 433
Mary R., d. Dan, Jr. & Mary, b. July 8, 1809 417
Mehithabel, [d. Hezekeiah & Mehitabel], b. Aug. 31, 1742; bp.

Page

PARMALEE, PARMELE, PARMELEE, PAMELY, (cont.)

Sept. 9, 1742 281,382

Mehithabel, w. of Hezekiah, d. Feb. 14, 1755 382

Mehetabel, m. Noah **BALDWIN**, July 30, [1760], by Rev. Elizur Goodrich 327,380

Mehitable, d. Dan & Abigail, b. Mar. 4, 1785 401

Moses, [s. Hezekiah & Mehitabel], b. Apr. 15, 1751; bp. Apr. 21, 1751 292,382

Nabby, d. Dan & Abigail, b. Jan. 2, 1792 401

Noah, [s. Eliphaz & Anne], b. Nov. 25, 1773; bp. Nov. 28, [1773] 323,399

Ozias, [s. Eliphaz & Anne (Amy), b. Dec. 7, 1771; bp. Dec. 15, [1771] 321,399

Ozias, s. Noah & Ann, b. July 12, 1806 421

Phebe, d. Levi & Phebe, b. Apr. 18, 1782 400

Phebe, m. Alfred **CAMP**, Apr. 2, 1823 431

Phinehas, s. Joel, bp. Sept. 20, [1724] 260

Phinehas, s. John & Sarah, b. Oct. 16, 1734; bp. Oct. 20, 1734 270,361

Phinehas, m. Lucy **ROSE**, May 15, 1777, by Rev. Elizur Goodrich 333

Rachel, [d. Joel & Rhoda], b. Apr. 24, 1756; bp. May 2, [1756] 298,385

Reuben, of Guilford, m. Lydia **GRISWOLD**, of Durham, Oct. 12, [1763], by Rev. Elizur Goodrich 328

Rhoda, [d. Joel & Rhoda], b. Feb. 1, 1752; bp. Feb. 2, 1751/2 293,385

Rhoda, m. James **HICKOX**, Dec. [ ], 1774, by Rev. Elizur Goodrich 333

Rhoda, [d. Eliphaz & Anne], b. Jan. 20, 1778; bp. Jan. 25, 1778 326,399

Rosanna, [d. Joel & Rhoda], b. Mar. 5, 1754; bp. Mar. 17, 1754 295,385

Rosemon, d. John & Sarah, b. Oct. 24, 1731; bp. Oct. [ ], 1731 266,361

Ruth, [d. Eliphaz & Anne], b. Sept. 27, 1769; bp. Aug. 18, 1771 321,399

Ruth, m. John **CURTISS**, June 2, 1801 409

Samuel, s. John & Sarah, b. Oct. 20, 1740; bp. Oct. 26, 1740 278,361

Sarah, d. Joel & Abigail, b. Aug. 28, 1719 354

Sarah, d. John & Sarah, b. June 24, 1742; bp. June 27, [1742] 280,361

Sarah, m. Samuel **HICKS**, Oct. 8, 1821 430

Simeon, [s. Hezekiah & Mehitabel], b. Aug. 3, 1740; bp. Aug. 3, [1740] 278,382

Sophronia, m. Chauncey **BARTHOLOMEW**, Aug. 1, 1826 433

Theodore Nelson, s. Dan, Jr. & Mary, b. Jan. 7, 1804 416

Thomas, m. Zeruiah **PARMALEE**, Sept. 1, 1834 436

William, s. Noah & Ann, b. Jan. 24, 1820 421

William A., m. Mary J. **CAMP**, Aug. 13, 1840 439

Zeruiah, d. Noah & Ann, b. Dec. 24, 1811 421

Zeruiah, m. Thomas **PARMELEE**, Sept. 1, 1834 436

PARRISH, Hannah, d. John & Sarah, bp. Aug. 15, [1720] 256

PARSONS, Aaron, s. Lieut. Samuel & Rhoda, b. Sept. 3, 1711 342

Aaron, s. Aaron & Abigail, bp. June 15, 1735 271

Aaron, s. Ithamar & Sarah, b. Nov. 10, 1758; bp. Nov. 12, [1758] 308,401

Aaron. m. Lucy ----*, Oct. 3, 1782 (***HAWLEY**, dau. Sam Stone **HAWLEY**, b. 1765. Handwritten in margin of original manuscript.) 401

Page

PARSONS, (cont.)

Aaron A., s. Marcus & Orpha, b. Oct. 31, 1819 | 419
Abigail, d. Moses & Abigail, b. Feb. 10, 1712/14*; bp. Feb. 14, 1713/14) (*Probably 1713/14) | 253,341
Abigail, d. Aaron & Abigail, bp. July 20, 1746 | 286
Abigail, d. Moses, bp. June 21, 1747 | 287
Abigail, w. [Moses], d. Dec. 4, 1760 | 350
Amanda, d. Aaron & Lucy, b. July 11, 1799 | 409
Amanda, m. Guernsey **STRONG**, Sept. 7, 1823 | 431
Ann, d. Aaron & Abigail, bp. Oct. 28, 1733 | 269
Ann, d. Aaron & Abigail, b. Nov. 13, 1733 | 355
Ann, m. Andrew **HULL**, b. of Durham, June 5, 1848 | 442
Betsey M., m. Thomas H. **CLARKE**, of Haddam, Oct. 3, 1843 | 440
Calvin Hawley, s. Aaron & Lucy, b. Sept. 20, 1791 | 403
Catharine, d. Samuel, Jr. & Mary, b. Aug. 30, 1757; bp. Sept. 4, [1757] | 306,375
Charles, s. Joseph & Mercy, b. Dec. 7, 1778 | 400
Clement, m. Phebe **SMITH**, Apr. 30, 1828 | 434
Clement M., of Durham, m. Sarah **HILL**, of Haddam, Mar. 10, 1844 | 440
Curtiss, s. Aaron & Lucy, b. Apr. 23, 1783 | 401
David, s. Ithimar & Sarah, bp. June 1, 1735 | 271
David, s. Samuel, Jr. & Mary, b. Oct. 1, 1758; bp. Oct. 7, [1759] | 309,385
Dency, d. Joseph & Marcy, b. May 25, 1786 | 404
Eleanor, d. Samuel Fenn & Martha, bp. Aug. 16, [1772] | 322
Ele[a]nor, d. Dec. 23, 1810 | 412
Eliphaz, s. Moses, bp. Jan. 14, 1738/9 | 276
Eliza A., m. Samuel **WILCOX**, July 20, 1836 | 437
Elizabeth, d. Moses & Abigail, bp. Mar. 17, 1722/3 | 258
Elizabeth, d. Moses, bp. Dec. 25, 1743 | 282
Elizabeth, d. Ens. Samuel & Elizabeth, b. July 14, 1756; bp. July [ ], [1756] | 298,374
Elisabeth, w. of Lieut. Samuel, d. July 6, 1785 | 401
Elizur, s. Ithamar, Jr., bp. Dec. [ ], 1777 | 326
Esther, d. Timothy & Mary, bp. Feb. 22, 1729 | 264
Esther, m. John Noyes **WADSWORTH**, Oct. 27, [1757], by Rev. Elizur Goodrich | 327
Eunice, d. Moses & Elizabeth, bp. Nov. 19, 1732 | 267
Eunice, d. Joseph & Mercy, b. Apr. 26, 1784 | 401
Eunice, w. of Simeon, d. Apr. 12, 1791 | 403
Hannah, d. Timothy & Mary, bp. Sept. 17, 1727 | 262
Hannah, d. Aaron & Lucy, b. Jan. 22, 1785 | 401
Harriet M., d. Marcus & Orpha, b. Oct. 10, 1816 | 419
Henry, m. Jane **WHITE**, Sept. 7, 1834 | 436
Ithamar, s. Ithamar & Sarah, bp. Oct. 28, 1750 | 292
Ithamar, Jr., m. Mehetabel **HULL**, May 21, [1772], by Rev. Elizur Goodrich | 332
Ithamar, d. Jan. 21, 1786 | 401

Page

PARSONS, (cont.)

Jemima, d. Timothy & Mary, bp. Apr. 27, 1735 — 271
Jerusha, d. Aaron, bp. Sept. 24, 1738 — 275
John, s. Moses & Abigail, bp. July 6, [1712] — 252
John, s. Samuel & Mary, b. June 12, 1713; bp. June 28, 1713 — 253,341
John, s. Timothy & Mary, bp. Jan. 1, 1737/8 — 274
Joseph, s. Samuel & Elizabeth, b. Dec. 25, 1747; bp. Jan. 24, 1747/8 — 288,365
Joseph, m. Mercy **COE**, Dec. 7, [1775], by Rev. Elizur Goodrich — 333,400
Josiah, s. Timothy & Mary, bp. Feb. 24, 1739/40 — 277
Josiah, s. Samuel, Jr. & Mary, b. July 20, 1755; bp. July 27, 1755 — 297,375
Katharine, d. Joseph & Mercy, b. Sept. 2, 1781 — 401
Leander R., s. Marcus & Orpha, b. Jan. 23, 1822 — 419
Leander R., m. Frances A. **CAMP**, b. of Durham, Nov. 26, 1846 — 442
Lemuel, s. Samuel & Elizabeth, b. May 2, 1753 — 374
Lemuel, m. Katharine **COE**, Jan. 28, 1779, by Rev. Elizur Goodrich — 333
Lucy, d. Moses, Jr., bp. July 3, 1737 — 274
Lucy, m. Leander P. **HICKOX**, May 20, 1832 — 435
Marcus, s. Aaron & Lucy, b. Feb. 23, 1789 — 402
Martha, d. Moses & Abigail, b. Oct. 5, 1716; bp. Oct. [1716] — 254,344
Mary, d. Samuel, Jr. & Abigail, b. Oct. 23, 1770; bp. Oct. 28, [1770] — 320,393
Mary, m. Henry **BAILEY**, Aug. 12, 1837 — 438
Mary M., d. Marcus & Orpha, b. June 23, 1814 — 419
Mehethabel, d. Samuel & Elizabeth, b. Mar. 5, 1750/1; bp. Mar. 17, 1750/1 — 292,374
Mehitabel, w. Simeon, d. Aug. 9, 1766 — 386
Mercy, d. Moses, Jr., bp. Apr. 6, 1735 — 271
Moses, s. Joseph, b. Jan. 15, 1687, in Northampton, Mass.; m. Abigail **BALL**, of Springfield, Jan. 20, 1710. Removed to Durham about 1710 — 352
Moses, s. Moses & Abigail, b. Oct. 19, 1710 — 340
Moses, d. Sept. 26, 1754 — 350
Naomi, d. Moses, bp. June 7, 1741 — 279
Naomi, d. Sergt. Ithamar & Sarah, bp. Apr. 20, 1755 — 297
Nathan, s. Ithamar & Sarah, bp. Sept. 30, 1744 — 284
Nathan, s. Aaron & Lucy, b. May 9, 1787 — 402
Nathan H., m. Maria W. **STURTEVANT**, b. of Durham, May 14, 1846 — 442
Noah, s. Simeon, bp. Feb. 19, 1737/8 — 274
Noah, d. May [ ], 1774, at Hispaniola — 397
Orpha, m. Lyman **BASSET**, June 21, 1824 — 431
Otis, s. Aaron & Lucy, b. May 4, 1803 — 410
Paul, s. Ens. Samuel & Elizabeth, b. Jan. 17, 1762; bp. Jan. 24, 1762 — 311,383
Phebe, d. Ithamar & Sarah, b. Sept. 13, 1732; bp. Oct. 1, 1732 — 267,355

Page

PARSONS, (cont.)

Phebe, m. Aaron **COE**, Nov. 28, 1754 383
Phebe, d. Thomas, Jr. & Mehetabel, bp. Nov. 20, [1774] 324
Phebe, d. Aaron & Lucy, b. Mar. 8, 1796 407
Phinehas, s. Simeon & Mehetabel, b. Mar. 7, 1733; bp. Mar. 17, 1733/4 269,355
Rachel, d. Aaron & Abigail, bp. Mar. 4, 1743/4 283
Rhoda, d. Ithamar & Sarah, bp. Nov. 27, 1737 274
Rhoda, d. Aaron & Lucy, b. Mar. 13, 1794 405
Samuel, uncle of Moses **PARSONS**, removed from Northampton, Mass., to Durham, about 1710; m. Mary **WHEELER**, of Durham, [Dec. 15], 1711, by Rev. Nath[anie]ll Chauncey 342,352
Samuel, s. Moses & Abigail, b. Mar. 1, 1718/19; bp. same day 256
Samuel, s. Timothy & Mary, bp. July 4, 1725 260
Samuel, s. Timothy & Mary, b. July 1, 1726 347
Samuel, s. John & Esther, bp. Mar. 30, 1735 271
Samuel, m. Elizabeth **CHIPMAN**, Jan. 21, 1746/7 363
Samuel, Jr., m. Mary **FENN**, Dec. 1, 1758 375
Samuel, Ens. had negro Richard, m. Phebe, June 15, [1762], by Rev. Elizur Goodrich 328
Samuel, s. Joseph & Marcy, b. Aug. 29, 1788 404
Samuel Fenn, s. Samuel, Jr. & Mary, b. Jan. 24, 1751; bp. Mar. 17, 1750/1 292,375
Samuel Fenn, m. Martha **PICKET**, Jan. 7, 1771, by Rev. Elizur Goodrich 331
Sarah, d. Ithamar & Sarah, bp. Mar. 15, [1740] 279
Sarah, d. Joseph & Martha, b. Jan. 28, 1759 375
Sarah, w. of Ithamar, d. Apr. 13, 1794 405
Seth, s. David & Rebecca, bp. Sept. 18, [1757] 307
Seth R., m. Mary **FRANCIS**, May 5, 1832 435
Simeon, of Durham, m. Mehetabel **CLAPP**, of Northampton, Oct. 12, 1731, by Rev. Jonathan Edwards 356
Simeon, s. Simeon & Mehetabel, b. Nov. 25, 1732; bp. Nov. 26 1732 267,354
Simeon, Jr., m. Eunice **ROSSETTER**, Mar. 16, 1758 383
Simeon, Ens., had negro Phebe, bp. Apr. 21, 1764 301
Simeon, Ens. had negro Phebe, bp. Apr. 29, 1764; Lydia, dau. Richard & Phebe, bp. Apr. 29, 1764 314
Simeon, Ens. had negro Peter, s. Richard & Phebe, bp. July 8, [1764] 314
Simeon, Ens., had negro Ishmael, s. Richard & Phebe, bp. Apr. [ ], 1766 315
Simeon, Ens., had negro Peg, d. Richard & Phebe, bp. Oct. 29, [1769] 319
Simeon, Ens., of Durham, m. wid. Abigail **BATES**, of Haddam, Nov. 30, [1772], by Rev. Elizur Goodrich 332
Simeon, Ens., d. Jan. 6, 1781 399
Simeon, m. Sarah **GURNSEY**, Feb. 19, 1795 406

Page

PARSONS, (cont.)
Simeon, d. July 12, 1819 414
Tabitha, d. Timothy & Mary, bp. Jan. 20, 1744/5 284
Tabatha, m. Lieut. James **ARNOLD**, b. of Durham, Feb. 21 (27), 1765, by Rev. Elizur Goodrich 329,387
Talcott, m. Betsey M. **SAVAGE**, Oct. 31, 1836 437
Timothy, m. Mary **ROBINSON**, Nov. 30, 1719, by Rev. Mr. N. Chauncey 346
Timothy, s. Timothy & Mary, bp. Jan. 21, 1732/3 268
Timothy, Jr., m. Phebe **CAMP**, Jan. 2, 1772, by Rev. Elizur Goodrich 331
Timothy, d. Mar. 12, 1802 409

PECK, Eliza, m. Andrew **MERRIMAN**, Aug. 6, 1827 433
William, m. Hannah A. **COE**, Oct. 22, 1837 438

PENFIELD, Abigaile, m. Timothy **ROSSETTER**, Feb. 4, 1711, by Rev. Thomas Ruggles 348

PHELPS, James N., of Wallingford, m. Lavinia **MEEKER**, of Durham, Dec. 27, 1840 439
Ruth, m. Jehiel **HULL**, Nov. 8, 1750 371

PHILLIPS, PHILIPS, Clarrissa, m. Henry **SIMONS**, colored, May 5, 1825 432
John, s. Thomas & Tabitha, b. Oct. 6, 1742; bp. Oct. 10, 1742 281,361
Thomas, s. Thomas & Tabatha, b. Oct. 1, 1740; bp. Oct. 5, 1740 278,359

PICKETT, PICKET, Adah, [d. Benjamin & Adah], b. Dec. 22, 1760; bp. Feb. 1, 1761; d. June 29, 1765 310,394
Adah, [d. Benjamin & Adah], b. Sept. 11, 1766 394
Adah, m. Abel **LYMAN**, Mar. 15, 1790 423
Benjamin, m. Adah **CAMP**, Dec. 5, [1758], by Rev. Elizur Goodrich 327,394
Benjamin, [s. Benjamin & Adah], b. July 19, 1765; bp. July 21, [1765] 315,394
Daniel, s. Samuel & Hephzibah, bp. Aug. 6, [1749] 289
Eleanor, wid., of James, m. Abraham **SCRANTON**, May 10, 1757, by Rev. Elizur Goodrich 327
Elizabeth, d. John & Eliz[abeth], bp. July 9, 1749 289
Hannah, [d. Benjamin & Adah], b. Mar. 4, 1764; bp. Apr. 8, 1764 313,394
James, s. Samuel & Hepzibah, bp. Mar. 23, 1755 297
John, s. John & Eliz[abeth], bp. June 25, 1754 296
Joseph, [s. Benjamin & Adah], b. Sept. 13, 1769; bp. Oct. 22, [1769] 319,394
Lucy, d. John & Elizabeth, bp. Sept. 16, [1759] 309
Martha, d. James & Eleanor, bp. Oct. 23, 1753 294
Martha, m. Samuel Fenn **PARSONS**, Jan. 7, 1771, by Rev. Elizur Goodrich 331
Martha, d. Benjamin, bp. Dec. 10, [1775] 325
Mary, d. John & Elizabeth, bp. Feb. 9, 1751/2 293
Ozias, [s. Benjamin & Adah], b. Dec. 7, 1762; bp. Dec. 12, 1772 312,394
Phebe, d. Samuel & Hephzibah, bp. Apr. 26, 1752 294
Phineas, s. Samuel & Hephzibah, bp. Sept. 25, [1757] 307
Phinehas, m. Anne **SQUIRE**, Oct. 4, 1778, by Rev. Elizur Goodrich 333

	Page
PICKETT, PICKET, (cont.)	
Rebeckah, d. Samuel & Mary, bp. Oct. 26, 1735	271
Rebeckah, d. Sam[ue]l & Hephzebah, bp. Mar. 29, 1747	287
Rebekah, of Haddam, m. Samuel Done (Doan) **COOK**, of Durham, Dec. 4, 1766, by Rev. Elizur Goodrich	330,389
Rhoda, m. Joseph **SMITH**, b. of Durham, Sept. 10, [1767], by Rev. Elizur Goodrich	330,395
Rhoda, [d. Benjamin & Adah], b. Sept. 7, 1768	394
Ruth, [d. Benjamin & Adah], b. Nov. 19, 1759; bp. Nov. 25, [1759]	309,394
Ruth, m. Rejoice **CAMP**, Mar. 14, 1779, by Rev. Elizur Goodrich	333
Samuel, s. Samuel & Hephzibah, bp. June 8, [1760]	310
PLATT, Diana, of Durham, m. Alonzo **BRAINARD**, of Haddam, Dec. 15, 1844	441
POMEROY, Martha, m. Ichabod **AVERY**, Aug. 13, 1841	439
PORTER, Giles, of Haddam, m. Susannah **HILL**, of Durham, Feb. 26, 1764, by Rev. Elizur Goodrich	328
Martha, m. Joseph **FRANCIS**, Jan. 26, 1758	374
POST, W[illia]m S., m. Catharine Elizabeth **HOWD**, Aug. 1, 1848	442
POTTER, Sarah A., m. Stephen D. **LANE**, Dec. 4, 1848	443
PRATT, PRAT, Polly, m. Benjamin **CHALKER**, Apr. 6, 1828	433
Samuel C. B., m. Phebe A. **COE**, Sept. 28, 1839	438
PRITCHARD, Charles of Waterbury, m. Harriet E. **JONES**, of New Haven, Nov. 13, 1843	440
PROUT, Ebenezer, s. Harris, bp. Nov. 22, [1761]	311
PUNDERSON, Damaris, m. William **SEWARD**, Sept. 19, 1710, by Abraham Bradley, J. P., of New Haven	343
RANNEY, Eliza P., m. Samuel W. **CLARKE**, Dec. 6, 1837	438
RANSOM, Harriet, m. Timothy **SMITH**, b. of Durham, Aug. 17, 1846	442
REED, Chauncey, s. John & Catharine, b. Mar. 25, 1809	417
Henry, s. John & Catharine, b. Mar. 23, 1807	417
Lusina, of Durham, m. James **CLYME**, of New Haven, Oct. 7, 1821	430
REYNOLDS, William R., m. Martha N. **CHAMBERLAIN**, Nov. 26, 1846	442
RICE, Abraham W., m. Rhoda Ann **WORTHINGTON**, July 30, 1828	434
RICH, Julius, of Chatham, m. Cecillia A. **CAMP**, of Durham, Sept. 12, 1830	435
RICHARDSON, Lucy, bp. Feb. 4, [1759]	300
Lucy, ae 19, bp. Feb. 11, 1759	308
Lucy, m. Patrick **NIEF**, Aug. 4, 1764	384
RICHMOND, Catharine, of Durham, m. Marvin **RILEY**, of Middletown, May 12, 1821	430
Frances A., m. Martin M. **CHALKER**, July 9, 1849	443
Hannah, b. Mar. 6, 1770, in Killingworth; m. James **TIBBALS**, Apr. 21, 1799	415
RIDEL, Rosella, m. Henry **TUCKER**, [ ]	438
RIGGS, Henry, of New Haven, m. H. Amelia **HULL**, of Durham, Mar. 9, 1845	441
RILEY, Marvin, of Middletown, m. Catharine **RICHMOND**, of Durham, May 12, 1821	430

Page

ROBERTS, Alvin, m. Mary A. **PARMALEE**, Oct. 1, 1827 433
Anna, [d. Samuel & Rachel], b. Mar. 16, 1722/3; bp. Mar. 17, 1722/3 258,358,366
Elijah, s. Ebenezer, bp. Nov. 22, [1761] 311
Elijah, s. Simeon, bp. Nov. 22, [1761] 311
Elizabeth, d. Samuel & Rachel, b. Jan. 24, 1717/18 346
Elizabeth, d. Samuel & Rachel, b. Mar. 24, 1717/18 358
Eliz[abeth], [d. Rachel], bp. Oct. 28, 1722 258
Elizabeth, d. Samuel & Eliz[abeth], bp. Feb. 7, 1741/2 280
Elizabeth, w. of Sam[ue]l, bp. Dec. 20, 1741 280
Hinchman, of Middletown, m. Polly **NETTLETON**, of Durham, Mar. 23, 1835 436
Jerusha, w. of John, bp. Dec. 20, 1741 280
Joel, s. Sam[ue]l & Rachel, bp. Oct. 24, 1736 272
Joel, [s. Samuel & Rachel], b. Oct. 27, 1736 358,366
John, [s. Samuel & Rachel], b. July 16, 1734; bp. Aug. 28, 1734 269,358,366
John, bp. Dec. 20, 1741 280
John, s. John & Jerushah, bp. Aug. 19, 1744 283
Mary, [d. Samuel & Rachel], b. Aug. 7, 1731; bp. Aug. 8, 1731 266,358,366
Noah, [s. Samuel & Rachel], b.Oct. 21, 1739; bp. Oct. 21, 1739 276,358,366
Phebe, d. Samuel & Elizabeth, bp. Dec. 5, 1742 281
Rachel, bp. Oct. 28, 1722 258
Rachel, [d. Samuel & Rachel], b. Dec. 7, 1728; bp. Dec. 8, 1728 263,358,366
Samuel, m. Rachel **WEBB**, Mar. 22, 1716/17 (1716), by James Wadsworth, J. P. 345,358
Samuel, s. Samuel & Rachel, b. Mar. 9, 1719/20; bp. Oct. 28, 1722 258,346,358
Sarah, [d. Samuel & Rachel], b. Sept. 26, 1725 358,366
Sarah, d. John & Jerushah, bp. Jan. 17, 1741/2 280

ROBINSON, Abiathar, s. Daniel & Abigail, bp. Nov. 11, 1750 292
Abigail, d. David & Rebecca, b. Mar. 9, 1737/8; bp. Mar. 12, 1737/8 274,364
Amy, d. James & Amy, bp. May 11, [1760] 310
Angelina, d. Richard & Tabathy, b. Oct. 29, 1809 418
Ann Maria, d. Asher & Eunice, b. July 26, 1820 424
Anna, d. David & Rebecca, b. Dec. 5, 1720; bp. Dec. 11, 1720 (Anne) 257,349 359
Anne, m. Gideon **CANFIELD**, Oct. 28, 1740 277,364
Asher, s. David & Rebeccah, b. May 4, 1740; bp. May 11, 1740 328,382
Asher, m. Margery **BUTCHER**, b. of Durham, June 11, [1761], by Rev. Elizur Goodrich 315
Asher, s. Asher & Margery, bp. Nov. 17, 1765 386
Ashur, s. Ashur & Margaret, b. Nov. 21, 1765 411
Asher, d. May 4, 1808
Betsey, d. Charles & Concurrence, b. Mar. 24, 1813 418
Betsey, m. Henry M. **COE**, b. of Durham, Oct. 12, 1834 436
Caroline, d. Richard & Tabathy, b. Sept. 16, 1805 418
Caroline E., m. Joseph P. **CAMP**, Jr., b. of Durham, June 28, 1854 443

Page

ROBINSON, (cont.)

Charles, s. Charles & Concurrence, b. Sept. 30, 1805 418
Charles, Jr., m. Almira **CHALKER**, Nov. 27, 1828 434
Content, d. Charles & Concurrence, b. Jan. 3, 1799 418
Cynthia, d. Richard & Cynthia, b. Dec. 19, 1821 418
Cynthia, m. Daniel B. **COE**, Sept. 1, 1841 439
Dan[iel], s. David & Rebeccah, b. May 2, 1725; bp. May 16, [1724/5] 260,349
David, m. Rebecca **MILLER**, Jan. 26, 1719/20 349
David, s. David & Rebecca, b. Mar. 4, 1720/1; bp. Mar. 4, 1721/2 258,349
Ebenezer, s. James & Amy, bp. Nov. 3, 1754 296
Electa, m. Asa **CHAMBERLAIN**, Jan. 17, 1826 432
Eliza, d. Richard & Tabathy, b. Nov. 16, 1794 418
Eliza, m. Edward **CANFIELD**, Nov. 22, 1842 440
Emma, d. Richard & Cynthia, b. Apr. 26, 1815 418
George, s. Charles & Concurrence, b. Jan. 28, 1808 418
Giles H., m. Emily **WHEELER**, Oct. 13, 1825 432
Hannah, of Durham, m. Daniel **BACON**, of Williamstown, Aug. 20, [1767], by Rev. Elizur Goodrich 330
Hannah, m. Luzerne **ELLIOTT**, Sept. 24, 1839 438
Hannah Jane, m. Walter J. **CHALKER**, July 9, 1849 443
Harriet, d. Charles & Concurrence, b. Oct. 13, 1801 418
Harvey, m. Lydia **DICKINSON**, Oct. 29, 1821 430
Henry, s. James, Jr. & Thankful, b. Oct. 23, 1787 403
Henry, s. Richard & Cynthia, b. Aug. 17, 1819 418
Henry, m. Phebe A. **SOUTHMAYD**, Sept. 2, 1835 436
Henry Parmalee, s. Asher & Eunice, b. Sept. 29, 1822 424
Israel, s. James, Jr. & Thankful, b. Apr. 12, 1789 403
James, s. David & Rebeckah, b. June 10, 1731; bp. June 17, [1731] 265,354
James, s. James & Amy, bp. Nov. 28, 1756 305
James, s. James & Amy, bp. May 8, [1763] 313
James, Jr., m. Thankful **DIMMOCK**, Mar. 16, 1785 403
James, s. James, Jr. & Thankful, b. Nov. 14, 1791 403
James, s. Charles & Concurrence, b. July 13, 1822 418
James, s. Richard & Cynthia, b. June 15, 1829 429
Joel, s. David & Rebeccah, b. Mar. 31, 1733; bp. Apr. 1, 1733 268,364
Joel, m. Hannah **WILCOCKS**, Apr. 3, 1774, by Rev. Elizur Goodrich 332
John, s. David & Rebecca, b. June 25, 1722; bp. June [ ], 1723 259,349
John, s. James & Amy, bp. Dec. 4, [1757] 307
John, s. Charles & Concurrence, b. July 13, 1803 418
John, m. Phebe **SCRANTON**, May 15, 1826 432
Lyman, s. Charles & Concurrence, b. Apr. 20, 1810 418
Lyman C., m. Jane E. **CANFIELD**, b. of Durham, Jan. 19, 1845 441
Margery, of Durham, m. Joel **BLATCHLEY**, of Guilford, Oct. 10, 1825 432,433
Mary, m. Timothy **PARSONS**, Nov. 30, 1719, by Rev. Mr.

Page

ROBINSON, (cont.)
N. Chauncey 346
Mary, d. Timothy & Mary, b. Nov. 3, 1722 346
Mary, d. David & Rebecca, b. Dec. 7, 1734; bp. Dec. 7, 1734 270,364
Mary, w. of David, d. Oct. 17, 1746 351
Matilda, m. John M. **AULIFFE**, Aug. 16, 1840 439
Moses, d. Nov. 14, 1820 425
Moses Austin, s. Moses & Electa, b. Feb. 17, 1821 425
Nathan, s. Ens. James & Amy, bp. Oct. 29, [1769] 319
Noah, s. David & Rebecca, b. May 29, 1736; bp. May 30, 1736 272,364
Noah, of Granville, m. Hannah **PARMALEE**, of Durham, Nov. 8, [1758], by Rev. Elizur Goodrich 327
Orpha, d. Richard & Tabathy, b. July 23, 1796 418
Phinehas, s. David, bp. July 27, 1729 264
Phinehas, s. David & Rebeckah, b. July 24, 1730 349
Phinehas, s. Charles & Concurrence, b. May 22, 1798 418
Rachel, d. Ashur & Margery, b. Apr. 16, 1762; bp. Apr. 18, [1762] 312,382
Rebeckah, d. David & Rebeckah, bp. Dec. 18, 1726 261
Rebecca, d. David & Rebeccah, b. Dec. 5, 1727 349
Rhoda, d. Dan & Abigail, bp. Apr. 13, 1755 297
Richard, s. Ens. James & Anne, bp. Dec. 15, [1771] 321
Richard P., s. Richard & Cynthia, b. Apr. 9, 1817 418
Rosetta E., m. James **WADSWORTH**, Sept. 8, 1845 441
Rosetta F., d. Richard & Cynthia, b. May 26, 1824 429
Rossetta Fayette, d. Richard & Cynthia, b. June [ ], 1824 426
Ruth, d. Phineas & Susanna, b. Aug. 10, 1755; bp. Aug. 17, 1755 297,373
Samuel, s. Asher & Margery, bp. July 29, [1770] 320
Samuel, s. James, Jr. & Thankful, b. Dec. 5, 1785 403
Samuel, of Madison, m. Ann **BALDWIN**, of Durham, Sept. 12, 1827 433
Sarah, d. Phineas & Susanna, bp. Feb. 26, [1758] 307
Sarah Chittenden, d. Asher & Eunice, b. Oct. 30, 1828 427
Seth, s. Asher & Margery, bp. June 28, [1768] 317
Sophronia, d. Richard & Tabathy, b. Oct. 17, 1802 418
Sophronia, m. John **SWATHEL**, Jr., Nov. 3, 1820 416
Statyra, d. Phineas & Susanna, bp. Sept. 30, 1764 314
Stephen, s. Ashur & Margery, b. Jan. 14, 1764; bp. Jan. 15, 1764 313,385
Susanna, d. Phinehas & Susanna, bp. Aug. 24, [1760] 310
Tabathy, d. Richard & Tabathy, b. Jan. 31, 1800 418
Timothy, s. David & Rebeckah, b. Apr. 29, 1728; bp. May [ ], [1728] 262,349
William, s. Charles & Concurrence, b. Aug. 2, 1818 418
William, m. Jennett **ELLIOTT**, Aug. 15, 1836 437
William Augustus, s. Asher & Eunice, b. Oct. 20, 1826 427
ROCKWELL, Aaron, s. Ezra & Jemimah, b. May 20, 1752 370
Daniel, s. Ezra & Jemima, b. Apr. 5, 1750 366
Daniel, s. Ezra & Jemima, b. Dec. 11, 1765 387
David, s. Ezra & Jemima, bp. Apr. 8, 1750 291

	Page
ROCKWELL, (cont.)	
Eunice, d. Ezra & Jemima, b. May 21, 1763; bp. June 19, [1763]	313,382
Jemimah, d. Ezra & Jemimah, b. Aug. 20, 1754; bp. Aug. 20, 1754	296,371
Mary, of Windsor, m. Isaac **NORTON**, Nov. 12, 1735	361
Rachel, d. Ezra & Jemima (Jeremiah), b. Jan. 26, 1747/8; bp. Jan. 29, 1747/8	288,366
Rebekah, d. Ezra & Jemima, bp. Mar. 16, 1760	309
Sam[ue]l, s. Ezra & Jemima, of Scantick, bp. Mar. 22, 1745/6	285
Samuel, s. Ezra & Jemimah, b. Mar. 30, 1745/6	364
Timothy, s. Ezra & Jemima, bp. Aug. 28, [1757]	306
ROSE, Anne, m. Caleb **FOWLER**, Jan. 10, 1759	380
Damaris S., d. Jon[a]th[an] & Abigail, bp. [probably 1721/2]	258
Daniel, s. Jonathan & Abigail, b. Jan. 12, 1716/17; bp. Jan. 13, 1716/17	254,342
David, s. David, bp. Apr. 4, 1736	272
Elisha, s. Jonathan & Abigail, bp. Feb. 8, 1718/19; bp. Mar. 1, 1718/19	256
Elisha, s. Jonathan, bp. June [ ], 1728	263
Elizabeth, d. Jonathan, bp. Feb. 20, 1725	261
Giles, m. Zipporah **CAMP**, b. of Durham, June [ ], 1767, by Rev. Elizur Goodrich	330
Israel, s. Jonathan, bp. Oct. 13, 1734	270
John, s. Jonathan, bp. Feb. 18, 1719/20	256
Justice, s. Jonathan, bp. Mar. 22, 1723/4	259
Katharine, d. David, bp. Dec. 4, 1737	274
Lucy, bp. Oct. 5, 1766	301,316
Lucy, m. Phinehas **PARMALEE**, May 15, 1777, by Rev. Elizur Goodrich	333
Mary, d. Jonathan & [Abigail], bp. Jan. 2, 1736/7	273
Mary, d. Jonathan, bp. July 26, 1741	279
Nathan, s. Jonathan, bp. June 3, 1744	283
Sharon, s. Jonathan, bp. Mar. 21, 1730/1	265
Soloman, s. Jonathan & Mary, bp. Apr. 29, 1739	276
Solomon, of Granville, m. Rhoda **MOULTRUP**, of Durham, Mar. 25, 1762, by Rev. Elizur Goodrich	328
Zebulon, s. Jonathan, bp. Jan. 18, 1746	287
ROSSETTER, ROSSITER, ROSSETER, ROSSEDOR, ROSTER,	
Abegail, m. Gideon **LEETE**, Sept. 6, 1727, by Rev. Nath[anie]ll Chauncey	348
Abigail, d. Bryan & Katharine, bp. Nov. 25, 1744	284
Abigail, d. Bryan & Katharine, b. Dec. 11, 1744	367
Asher, s. Timothy & Abegaile, b. Oct. 16, 1715	348
Bryan, s. Timothy & Abegaile, b. Oct. 22, 1713	348
Bryan, m. Catharine **STRONG**, Sept. 2, 1736	367
Bryan, s. Bryan & Catharine (Kate), b. Aug. 6, 1742; bp. Aug. 8, 1742; d. July 28, 1755	281,367
Bryan, [s. Rowland & Mary], b. Sept. 6, 1760; bp. Sept. 7, [1760]	310,389
Caroline M., of North Guilford, m. David B. **ROSSETER**, Nov. 22,	

Page

ROSSETTER, ROSSITER, ROSSETER, ROSSEDOR, ROSTER, (cont.)
1842 440
Catherine, d. Rowland & Mary, bp. Mar. 13, [1757] 306
Catharine, [d. Rowland & Mary], b. Mar 6, 1767 388
Content, d. Rowland & Mary, bp. Feb. 5, 1769 318
David B., m. Caroline M. **ROSSETER**, of North Guilford, Nov. 22, 1842 440
Eunice, m. Simeon **PARSONS**, Jr., Mar. 16, 1758 383
Eunice, [d. Rowland & Mary], b. Sept. 9, 1764; bp. Sept. 9, [1764] 314,389
James, s. Giles, bp. Oct. 19, 1777 326
Katherine, d. Bryan & Katherine*, b. Nov. 10, 1737; bp. Nov. 13, 1737; d. Mar. 28, 1756 (*Kate in baptism) 274,367
Lucy, d. Rowland & Mary, b. Dec. 8, 1754; bp. Dec. 8, 1754 296,371
Lucy, m. Morris **COE**, June 15, 1775, by Rev. Elizur Goodrich 333
Rebeccah, d. Timothy & Abegaile, b. Jan. 5, 1718/9 348
Rebecca, m. Samuel **SEWARD**, May 17, 1739 378
Rebeckah, d. Rowland & Mary, b. Oct. 23, 1753; bp. Nov. 10, 1754 296,371
Rebeckah, m. Nathaniel **HICKOX**, Oct. 7, 1773, by Rev. Elizur Goodrich 332
Rowland, s. Timothy & Abegaile, b. May 8, 1721; bp. May 21, 1721 257,348
Rowland, m. Mary **STRONG**, Apr. 11, 1753 371
Samuel, s. Giles, bp. Oct. 19, 1777 326
Susanna, d. Bryan & Catharine*, b. Dec. 6, 1739; bp. Dec. 9, 1739; d. Apr. 2, 1753 (*Baptism gives the name as Kate) 277,367
Timothy, s. Josiah, b. June 5, 1683 348
Timothy, m. Abigaile **PENFIELD**, Feb. 4, 1711, by Rev. Thomas Ruggles 348
Timothy, s. Timothy & Abegaile, b. June 10, 1725; bp. June 13, [1725]; b. 4 mos. after death of his father 260,348

RUSSELL, Aralon W., m. Emeline **CURTISS**, Oct. 12, 1836 437
Timothy, m. Eliza **BUTLER**, Oct. 27, 1822 430

RUTTY, ----, m. Abiah **SOUTHMAYD**, Nov. 12, 1826 433

SAGE, Edmund, m. Rhoda **MERWIN**, June 28, 1829 434

SANFORD, Abel, of Middletown, m. Phebe **HULL**, of Durham, Dec. 29, 1840 439
Hannah, d. Joseph & Mary, b. July 23, 1729; bp. July 27, 1729 264,357
Jonah, s. Joseph, bp. Sept. 7, [1735] 271
Jonah, s. Joseph & Mary, b. Aug. 1, 1737 357
Oliver, s. Joseph & Mary, b. Aug. 22, 1732; bp. Sept. 24, 1732 267,357
Sarah, d. Joseph & Mary, b. July 28, 1731; bp. July 30, 1731 265,357

SAVAGE, Betsey M., m. Talcott **PARSONS**, Oct. 31, 1836 437

SCRANTON, Abigail, m. Leonidas **MAYNARD**, Sept. 28, 1845 441
Abraham, s. Abraham & Beulah, b. Dec. 3, 1749; bp. Dec. 3, 1749 290,368
Abraham, m. Eleanor **PICKET**, wid. of James, May 10, 1757, by Rev. Elizur Goodrich 327
Abraham, Jr., Lieut., m. Hannah **CAMP**, Jan. 1, 1772, by Rev. Elizur Goodrich 331,409
Abraham, [s. Abraham & Hannah], b. May 3, 1787 409

	Page
SCRANTON, (cont.)	
Abraham, s. Israel & Clarissa, b. Dec. 14, 1817	421
Alonzo Camp, s. Israel & Clarissa, b. Nov. 20, 1814, at Rochester, N. Y.	420-1
Anna Curtiss, d. Israel & Clarissa, b. Mar. 21, 1816, at Rochester, N. Y.	421
Anne, w. of Israel, d. Dec. 24, 1810	412
Beriah, s. Israel & Anna, b. Dec. 4, 1810	420
Content, [d. Abraham & Hannah], b. Mar. 11, 1783	409
David, s. Abraham & Beulah, b. Oct. 27, 1751; bp. Nov. 3, 1751	368
Emero, s. Israel & Clarissa, b. Dec. 25, 1822	421
Enos. s. Abraham & Beulah, bp. Nov. 25, 1753	294
Eunice, m. William E. **GRAHAM**, Oct. 11, 1840	439
Evelyn, of Madison, m. Eunice **DAVIS**, of Killingworth, Jan. 24, 1836	437
Freelove M., m. Alonzo C. **CLARKE**, of Haddam, Nov. 28, 1839	438
Gurnsey, s. Abraham & Eleanor, bp. Mar. 2, [1760]	309
Hamlet, s. Abrahm, Jr. & Hannah, b. Dec. 1, 1772; bp. May 2, 1773	323,409
Harriet Amanda, d. Israel & Anna, b. July 5, 1803	420
Henry, [s. Abraham, Jr. & Hannah], b. May 10, 1775; bp. June 18, [1775]	325,409
Hiram, s. Israel & Clarissa, b. Sept. 24, 1819	421
Ichabod, s. Abraham & Ele[a]nor, bp. Mar. 12, [1758]	307
Ichabod, s. Abraham & Ele[a]nor, b. Aug. 31, 1762; bp. Sept. 5, 1762	312,381
Israel, [s. Abraham & Hannah], b. Apr. 4, 1778	409
Israel, m. Anna **CURTISS**, Oct. 12, 1800	420
Israel, m. Clarissa **PARDEE**, Feb. 9, 1813	420
Israel, s. Israel & Clarissa, b. Apr. 4, 1813, at Rochester, N. Y.	420
Joy, [d. Abraham & Hannah], b. Mar. 7, 1781	409
Manda, [d. Abraham & Hannah], b. Apr. 13, 1785	409
Maria, of Durham, m. Calvin **ALBY**, of Saybrook, Jan. 14, 1836	437
Mary Aurelia, d. Israel & Anna, b. Feb. 5, 1808, at Camden, S. C.; d. June 3, 1809	420
Mary Aurelia, d. Israel & Anna, b. Oct. 15, 1809, at Camden, S. C.	420
Phebe, m. John **ROBINSON**, May 15, 1826	432
Serina, d. Israel & Clarissa, b. Feb. 7, 1821	421
Talemachus Norman, s. Israel, b. May 12, 1806, at Camden, S. C.	420
Ursula, m. John **BAILEY**, Jan. 1, 1839	438
Worthington, m. Lydia **BAILEY**, b. of Durham, Mar. 10, 1845	441
SEARS, Charles, of Haddam, m. Diana **STEVENS**, of Durham, d. of Thomas, Aug. 19, 1779, by Rev. Elizur Goodrich	334
SEWARD, SEAWARD, Aaron, s. John & Ruth, bp. Feb. 24, 1732/3	268
Abegail, d. John & Ruth, b. Dec. 2, 1720; Dec. 4, 1720	257,348
Abigail, d. Brotherton & Abigail, b. July 28, 1753	350
Abigail, d. Ephraim & Abigail, b. Mar. 8, 1758	394
Abraham, s. Caleb & Sarah, bp. [probably 1721]	257
Abram, s. Moses & Sarah, b. Oct. 11, 1772; bp. Oct. 18, 1772	322,396

Page

SEWARD, SEAWARD, (cont.)

Adah, d. Sam[ue]ll & Abigail, bp. Feb. 6, 1763 312
Amos, s. Thomas & Sarah, bp. Mar. 27, 1726 261
Ann, d. Brotherton & Sarah, b. Mar. 7, 1748; bp. Mar. 9, 1748/9 289,366
Ashur, [s. Samuel & Rebeckah], b. Oct. 14, 1745 378
Asher, s. Samuel, bp. Apr. 19, 1752 294
Augustus, m. Alpha M. **BAILEY**, Feb. 27, 1840 439
Beulah, d. Joseph & Hannah, b. May 8, 1727; bp. May 21, 1727 262,347
Beulah, d. Samuel & Abigail, bp. Mar. 6, [1768] 317
Brotherton, s. Joseph & Hannah, b. July 28, 1724; bp. Aug. 2, [1724] 260,347
Brotherton, m. Sarah **CAMP**, Nov. 23, 1748 366
Brotherton, m. Abigail **CRANE**, Nov. 9, 1752 350
Caleb, s. Caleb & Lydia, b. Jan. 2, 1691 340
Caleb, b. Mar. 14, 1662; settled in Durham May 4, 1699 with his w. Lydia & 4 children 339
Caleb, Jr., m. Sarah **CARR**, Jan. 21, 1713/14, by Rev. Nath[anie]ll Chauncey 342
Caroline, d. Lieut. Joseph & Hannah, b. Aug. 6, 1739; bp. Aug. 12, 1739 276,359
Caroline, d. Samuel & Abigail, bp. Mar. 31, 1765 314
Charles, s. Ephraim & Abigail, b. Sept. 14, 1750; bp. Sept. 23, 1750 291,368,393
C[h]loe, d. Eben & Sarah, bp. Nov. 21, 1731 266
Concurrence, d. Sept. 1, 1776 398
Damaris, d. W. & Damaris, bp. Apr. 15, 1716 254
Damaris, d. Ebenezer & Dorathy, bp. July 20, 1740 278
Daniel, s. Caleb & Lydia, b. Oct. 16, 1687; d. Apr. 28, 1688 339
David, s. William & Damaris, b. June 23, 1714; bp. June [ ], [1714] 253,344
Deborah, d. John & Ruth, b. June 2, 1722; bp. June 3, [1722]; d. June 15, [1722] 258,348
Eben, s. Eben & Dorathy, bp. Mar. 18, 1738/9 276
Ebenezer, s. Caleb & Lydia, b. Jan. 7, 1703 341
Ebenezer, s. Ebenezer & Dorothy, bp. Sept. 23, 1744, after they removed to Bedford 284
Eleanor, d. Joseph & Eleanor, b. Oct. 9, 1714 341
Eleanour, w. of Joseph, Jr., d. Dec. 20, 1714 342
Eliz[abeth], d. Noahdiah, bp. Nov. 22, 1724 260
Elizabeth, d. John & Ruth, bp. Dec. 7, 1734 270
Elizabeth, m. Benjamin **GILLUM**, June 26, 1754 377
Elnathan, s. Jared, bp. Feb. 16, 1755 296
Enos, s. Nathaniel & Concurrence, b. July 14, 1734; bp. Aug. 21, 1734 269,355
Enos, s. Eben & Dorothy, bp. July 13, [1735] 271
Enos, s. Ens. Nathaniel & Concurrence, d. Oct. 5, 1742 361
Enos, d. July 14, 1801 409
Ephraim, s. Caleb & Lydia, b. Aug. 6, 1700; was the first English child, b. in Durham 341

Page

SEWARD, SEAWARD, (cont.)

Ephraim, m. Abigail **WETMORE**, Oct. 19, 1743 363
Esther, d. John & Ruth, bp. June 21, 1730 264
Esther, d. Samuel & Abigail, bp. July 5, [1761] 311
Hannah, d. Joseph & Hannah, b. Feb. 21, 1730/1; bp. Feb. 21, 1730/1 265,355
Hannah, m. Eliakim **STRONG**, June 4, 1751 371
Hannah, d. Jared, bp. June 25, 1758 307
Hannah, d. Apr. 23, 1769 390
Harvey, s. Moses & Sarah, b. Aug. 18, 1792 409
Helena, d. Joseph & Helena, bp. July 17, [1715] 254
Henry, s. Ens. Nathaniel & Concurrence, b. July 7, 1736; bp. July 11, 1736 272,361
Henry, d. May 10, 1764 384
Hephzibah, d. Joseph & Hannah, b. Nov. 27, 1722; bp. Dec. 2, 1722 258,347
Isaac, s. Moses & Sarah, b. June 19, 1776 402
James, s. Ephraim & Abigail, b. Oct. 20, 1744; bp. Oct. 21, 1744 284,363
Jearid, s. Joseph & Hannah, b. Feb. 22, 1727/8; bp. Feb. 23, 1728/9 263,347
Jared, m. Mary **BISHOP**, Sept. 12, 1753 369
Job, s. Ephraim & Abigail, b. Nov. 8, 1746; bp. Nov. 9, 1746 286,364
Joel, s. Eben & Dorothy, bp. Nov. 25, 1733 269
John, s. John & Ruth, b. May 15, 1726; bp. June 19, 1726 261,348
John, s. Lieut. Joseph & Hannah, b. May 11, 1737; bp. May 15,1737 273,359
John, of Durham, m. Sarah **BURR**, of Haddam, May 10, 1769 391
Joseph, m. Ele[a]nour **WHEELER**, Jan. 14, 1713/14, by Rev. Nath[anie]ll Chauncey 343
Joseph, Jr., m. Hannah **CRANE**, Apr. 26, 1720, by Rev. Jared Elliot, of Killingworth 342
Joseph, s. Joseph & Hannah, bp. Apr. 16, 1721 257
Joseph, Jr., m. Elizabeth **NORTON**, Jan. 14, 1748/9 365
Joseph, Lieut., d. Nov. 19, 1764 386
Katharine, d. Tho[mas], bp. Dec. 31, 1727 262
Laurana, d. Noahdiah & M-----, bp. May 5, 1734 269
Lucretia, d. Joseph & Hannah, b. Jan. 15, 1732/3; bp. Jan. 21, 1732/3 268,355
Lucy, d. Nathaniel & Concurrence, b. Nov. 7, 1732; bp. Apr. 28 or 29, [1733] 268,355
Lucy, of Durham, m. Moses **AUSTIN**, of Wallingford, Mar. 26, [1761], by Rev. Elizur Goodrich 328
Lydia, d. Caleb & Lydia, b. May 22, 1689 340
Lydia, w. of Caleb settled in Durham May 4, 1699 "being then about 35 y. old" 339
Lydia, d. Noahdiah & Hannah, b. Jan. 17, 1722/3; bp. Jan. 20, 1722/3 258,346
Lydia, d. Ephraim & Abigail, b. Jan. 18, 1753 393
Lidia, wid. of Caleb, the first settler in Durham, d. Aug. 24, 1753 350
Maria, m. Linus **COE**, Sept. 15, 1834 436

Page

SEWARD, SEAWARD, (cont.)

Martha, d. Caleb & Sarah, bp. Jan. 4, 1723/4 259
Mary, d. William & Damaris, bp. Sept. 22, 1717 255
Mary, d. Caleb, Jr. & Sarah, b. Apr. 8, 1719; bp. Apr. 12, 1719 256,344
Mary, d. John & Ruth, b. Feb. 17, 1725; bp. Feb. 21, [1724] 260,348
Mary, d. Noadiah, bp. Jan. 11, 1735/6 272
Mary, of Durham, m. Elisha **JOHNSON**, of Middletown, July 31, [1760], by Rev. Elizur Goodrich 327
Mehitabel, d. Ephraim & Abigail, bp. Jan. 8, 1748/9 289
Mindwell, d. John & Ruth, bp. Mar. 23, [1728/9] 263
Mindwell, m. Stephen **BATES**, 3rd, Mar. [ ], 1749 371
Moses, s. John & Ruth, b. Nov. 7, 1727; bp. Nov. [ ], 1727 262,348
Moses, m. Sarah **THOMAS**, b. of Durham, Apr. 9, 1761, by Rev. Elizur Goodrich 328,380
Moses, s. Moses & Sarah, b. Jan. 11, 1764; bp. Jan. 15, 1764 313,387
Moses, m. Sarah **FOWLER**, May 5, 1791 409
Moses, d. Oct. 17, 1799 409
Moses, s. Harvey, b. Feb. 3, 1815 424
Nancy J., m. David **JOHNSON**, July 31, 1826 433
Nathan, s. Thomas, bp. June 14, 1730 264
Nathan, s. Nathaniel & Currence, bp. Oct. 22, [1738] 275
Nathan, m. Rachel **GILLUM**, May 6, [1772], by Rev. Elizur Goodrich 332,394
Nathaniel, m. Concurrence **CRANE**, Feb. 2, 1730 355
Nathaniel, s. Ens. Nathaniel & Concurrence, b. Oct. 16, 1738 361
Nathaniel, Lieut., d. Apr. 2, 1770 392
Nathaniel, s. John & Sarah, b. May 21, 1770; bp. May 27, [1770] 319,392
Nathaniel, s. Nathan & Rachel, bp. Apr. 24, [1774] 324
Nathaniel, d. Dec. 28, 1801 409
Noahdiah, m. Hannah **SMITH**, Oct. 19, 1721, by Rev. Phinehas Fisk, of Haddam 346
Noahdiah, s. Eben & Dorothy, bp. Feb. 21, 1741/2 280
Patience, m. Stephen **BATE**, Dec. 29, 1715, by James Wadsworth, J. P. 343
Phebe, d. Thomas & Sarah, bp. Feb. 9, 1723/4 259
Phebe, m. Thomas **STRONG**, Jan. 16, 1746 361
Polly, d. Moses & Sarah, b. Mar. 8, 1795 409
Rachel, [d. Samuel & Rebeckah], b. July 11, 1750; bp. Apr. 19 1752 294,378
Rachel, m. Thomas **LYMAN**, Jan. 30, 1771, by Rev. Elizur Goodrich 331
Rachel, m. Abraham **STOW**, Feb. 25, 1779, by Rev. Elizur Goodrich 333
Rebecca, [d. Samuel & Rebeckah], b. Oct. 2, 1743; bp. Apr. 19, 1752 294,378
Rebekah, wid., m. Jesse **CRANE**, Mar. 3, [1763], by Rev. Elizur Goodrich 328
Rebekah, m. Daniel **MERWIN**, b. of Durham, Dec. 14, 1769, by Rev. Elizur Goodrich 331,392
Ruth, d. John & Ruth, b. June 1, 1719; bp. June 7, 1719 256,348
Ruthamah, d. Noahdiah & Mary, bp. Jan. 1, 1737/8 274

Page

SEWARD, SEAWARD, (cont.)

Salmon, s. Thomas & Sarah, bp. Jan. 21, [1720/1] 257
Samuel, s. Lieut. Joseph & Hannah, b. Jan. 30, 1734/5; bp. Feb. 2, 1734/5 270,359
Samuel, m. Rebecca **ROSSETTER**, May 17, 1739 378
Samuel, [s. Samuel & Rebecca], b. Apr. 1, 1740 378
Samuel, d. Dec. 19, 1751 350
Samuel, s. Samuel, bp. Apr. 19, 1752 294
Samuel, m. Abigail **HULL**, May 7, 1760 378
Sarah, d. Caleb, Jr. & Sarah, b. Jan. 8, 1714/15; bp. Jan. 9, 1714/15 253,344
Sarah, m. Sumner **STOW**, Dec. 1, 1736 359
Sarah, w. of Caleb, d. May 7, 1746 351
Sarah, d. Brotherton & Abigail, b. Aug. 8, 1757; bp. Aug. 14, [1757] 306,374
Sarah, d. Moses & Sarah, b. June 3, 1769; bp. June 4, [1769] 318,391,396
Sarah, of Durham, m. Pruda* **STEVENS**, of Kensington, Aug. 4, 1773, by Rev. Elizur Goodrich (*Written "Peruda") 332
Seth, s. Moses & Sarah, b. Apr. 15, 1766; bp. Apr. [ ], 1766 315,387
Silas, s. Brotherton & Abigail, b. Feb. 4, 1760; bp. Feb. 10, [1760] 309,378
Solomon, s. Thomas & Sarah, b. Jan. 19, 1720/1 346
Stephen, s. Brotherton & Abigail, b. Apr. 19, 1755; bp. Apr. 20, 1755 297,371
Submit, d. John & Ruth, bp. Aug. 22, [1731] 266
Submit, m. Ebenezer **TIBBALS**, May 23, 1754 391
Sutlief, s. Moses & Sarah, b. Mar. 25, 1762; bp. Mar. 28, [1762] 312,387
Sylvanus, s. Noadiah, bp. Sept. 4, [1726] 261
Thomas, s. Caleb & Lydia, b. Dec. 19, [ ] 340
Thomas, m. Sarah **CAMP**, Mar. 31, 1720, by James Wadsworth 346
Timothy, [s. Samuel & Rebeckah], b. Aug. 30, 1741; bp. Apr. 19, 1752; d. Aug. 2, 1759 294,378
William, m. Damaris **PUNDERSON**, Sept. 19, 1710, by Abraham Bradley, J. P., of New Haven 343
William, s. William & Damaris, b. July 27, 1712; bp. July 27, [1712] 252,344
William, s. Samuel & Abigail, bp. June 11, [1769] 318
----, s. Moses & Sarah, bp. Oct. 18, 1772 (Note gives the name as "Abraham") 322
----, s. Samuel, bp. [1774] 324

SHELDON, SHELDEN, Eunice Jennett, m. Charles **CORNWELL**, Oct. 5, 1823 431
Ezra, s. Moses & Elizabeth, b. Nov. 7, 1750; bp. Nov. 11, 1750 292,352
Mary, d. Moses & Elizabeth, bp. Oct. 23, 1753 294
Moses, m. Elizabeth **GRAVE**, Apr. 20, 1749 352
Moses, s. Moses & Eliz[abeth], bp. Apr. 12, 1752 294

SHELLEY, Catharine, of Durham, m. Hiram **MILLER**, of Middlefield, Apr. 8, 1845 441

Page

SHELLEY, (cont.)
Elisabeth R., of Madison, m. Lucius M. **KNOWLES**, of Durham, June 13, 1852 443
Jerome, m. Jennette S. **WARD**, Aug. 22, 1844 441
Jerome, m. Betsey Ann **THOMAS**, b. of Durham, Jan. 9, 1848 442
Sylvanus, m. Harriet **LOVELAND**, June 21, 1824 431
William, m. Sarah **ISBIL**, June 2, 1824 431
SHIPMAN, Albin, m. Benilla **ISBIL**, Sept. 15, 1826 432
SIMMONS, Henry L., s. Elisha & Jerusha, b. Jan. 10, 1810 427
SIMONS, Henry, m. Clarrissa **PHILLIPS**, colored, May 5, 1825 432
Sally, m. Allen **WAY**, Oct. 7, 1831 435
SIZER, Albert M., m. Hannah S. **CONE**, Dec. 24, 1838 438
SKINNER, Mary, of Durham, m. Alpheus **BEACH**, of Northford, Oct. 21, 1843 440
Sarah, of Northford, m. John **LEAVITT**, of New Haven, Apr. 6, 1840 441
SMITH, Aaron, s. Steph[en], bp. Apr. 16, 1738 275
Abigail, d. Stephen, bp. Dec. 11, 1743 282
Ann, d. Stephen, bp. Dec. 23, 1739 277
Benjamin, m. Mehetabel **BARNES**, of Middlefield, Jan. 29, 1761, by Rev. Elizur Goodrich 328
Benjamin Young, s. Daniel, bp. Apr. 3, 1743 282
Betsey M., m. Charles G. **ARNOLD**, Sept. 19, 1841 439
Betsey Marsh, d. Rev. David & Catharine, b. May 20, 1806 417
Catharine Chauncey, d. Rev. David & Catharine, b. Aug. 27, 1800 417
Chauncey Goodrich, s. Rev. David & Catharine, b. Oct. 19, 1807 417
Daniel, s. William, bp. Feb. 22, 1735 272
Daniel, s. Daniel, bp. Dec. 8, 1754 296
David, s. Stephen, of Haddam, bp. Apr. 7, 1734 269
David, "ordained over the Church and Congregation of Durham, Aug. 15, 1799" 408
Desire, d. Stephen, Jr., bp. Aug. 2, 1741 279
Elizabeth, d. John, bp. Sept. [1731] 266
Elizabeth, d. Joseph & Rhoda, b. Apr. 23, 1771; bp. May [1771]; d. May 9, 1773 320,395
Elizur Goodrich, s. Rev. David & Catharine, b. May 30, 1802 417
Franklin S., of Middletown, m. Lucy A. **THOMPSON**, of Durham, Sept. 27, 1846 442
Gustavus Walter, s. Rev. David & Catharine, b. June 16, 1815 417
Hamlet, s. Joseph & Rhoda, b. June 29, 1773; bp. Aug. 1, 1773 323,396
Hannah, m. Noahdiah **SEWARD**, Oct. 19, 1721, by Rev. Phinehas Fisk, of Haddam 346
Harriet E., of Durham, m. Jacob **JOHNSON**, 2d, of Middletown, June 19, 1844 440
Henry W., m. Harriet M. **WAMSLEY**, Apr. 25, 1842 440
Hope, m. James **HICKOX**, Sept. 30, 1815 419

Page

SMITH, (cont.)

James, s. Joseph & Rhoda, b. Apr. 17, 1769; bp. Apr. 23, [1769] 318,395

Jesse, s. Joseph, bp. Dec. 10, [1775] 325

John, s. Stephen, bp. Sept. 9, [1722] 258

John, s. Stephen, bp. Sept. [ ], 1728 263

John, s. John, bp. Aug. 29, 1736, at Haddam, Conn. 272

John, bp. Nov. 11, 1753 294

Jonathan, s. Stephen, Jr., bp. Dec. 13, 1741 280

Joseph, m. Rhoda **PICKET**, b. of Durham, Sept. 10, [1767], by Rev. Elizur Goodrich 330,395

Landon, s. Daniel, bp. Mar. 10, 1744/5 284

Lewis, s. John, bp. Nov. 11, 1753 294

Lucena, twin with Lucretia, d. John, bp. July 3, 1740 278

Lucretia, twin with Lucena, d. John, bp. July 3, 1740 278

Lucy, d. Stephen, bp. Sept. 23, 1739 276

Mary, d. John, bp. Sept. 16, 1733 268

Mercy, m. Hezekiah **PARMALEE**, June 10, 1756 382

Nathan, s. Stephen, bp. July 26, 1730 264

Phebe, m. Clement **PARSONS**, Apr. 30, 1828 434

Polycarp, s. Daniel & Lydia, bp. May 6, [1759] 309

Sam[ue]l, s. Stephen, bp. Oct. 23, 1726 261

Sarah, d. Stephen, bp. Oct. 11, 1724 260

Sarah, w. of John, bp. Aug. 8, 1731 266

Sarah, d. Stephen, bp. July 9, 1732 267

Sarah, d. Daniel, bp. Oct. 5, 1740 278

Seth, s. Daniel & Lydia, bp. Apr. 24, [1757] 306

Simeon Parsons, s. Rev. David & Catharine, b. July 31, 1809 417

Timothy, m. Harriet **RANSOM**, b. of Durham, Aug. 17, 1846 442

William, s. Dan[ie]l, bp. Sept. 24, 1738 275

----, w. of John, bp. Nov. 11, 1753 294

SMITHSON, Ann, d. Lieut. William & Ann, bp. Aug. 3, 1746 286

Ann, m. Moses **GRISWOLD**, b. of Durham, Feb. 3, 1768, by Rev. Elizur Goodrich 330,392

Anne, d. Lieut. William & Anne, b. July 19, 1746 364

Anne, d. Robert & Phebe, bp. Oct. 20, 1771 321

Anne, m. Daniel **BATES**, Oct. 24, 1790 404

John, s. Lieut. William & Anne, b. Feb. 19, 1742/3; bp. Feb. 20, 1742/3 281,364

Phebe, d. Robert, bp. Apr. 30, [1775] 325

Phebe, d. Robert, bp. Mar. 28, [1779] 326

Rhoda, d. Robert & Phebe, bp. Oct. 30, [1768] 318

Rhoda, m. Israel **CAMP**, May 3, 1789 407

Robert, s. Lieut. William & Anne, b. June 25, 1744; bp. July 1, 1744 283,364

Robert, m. Mehetabel **HULL**, Mar. 25, 1778, by Rev. Elizur Goodrich 333

Sally, m. George **LYMAN**, Mar. 7, 1801 426

SNOW, Hannah, d. Abner, bp. Jan. 6, 1754 294

	Page
SNOW, (cont.)	
Joseph, s. Abner, bp. June [ ], 1751	292
SOTHERN, Joseph, bp. Oct. 27, 1751	293
Joseph, s. Joseph & Mary, bp. Apr. 14, 1754	295
Ruth, d. Joseph & Mary, bp. Dec. 1, 1751	293
----, w. of Joseph, bp. Oct. 27, 1751	293
SOUTHMAYD, Abiah, m. -----**RUTTY**, Nov. 12, 1826	433
Daniel, m. Tamson **HICKOX**, Dec. 25, 1838	438
Eunice B., m. Lyman **BUTLER**, May 23, 1823	431
Freeman Bailey, s. Joseph & Cynthia, b. May 26, 1801	410
Hannah, m. Samuel **BATES**, Jr., Nov. 13, 1786	404
Huntington, m. Mary **BRAINARD**, Apr. 24, 1834	436
John [B.], s. Joseph & Cynthia, b. June 11, 1794	410,413
Jonathan, s. Joseph & Cynthia, b. Mar. 2, 1797	410
Phebe A., m. Henry **ROBINSON**, Sept. 2, 1835	436
William, m. Mary **TUCKER**, May 23, 1833	436
SOUTHWARD, John, s. Joseph, bp. Mar. 26, [1769]	318
SOUTHWICK, Nathan G. R., m. Sarah Ann **NETTLETON**, Sept. 28, 1845	441
SOUTHWORTH, Concurrence, d. Joseph, bp. May 16, 1756	298
Joseph, s. Joseph & Mary, b. Apr. 7, 1754	372
Mary, d. Joseph & Mary, b. June 19, [1763]	313
Persis, m. Henry **CROWELL**, July 30, 1821	430
Rosanna, d. Joseph & Mary, bp. Dec. 10, [1758]	308
Ruth, d. Joseph & Mary, b. Nov. 27, 1751	372
Ruth, m. Abraham **HAND**, [1772], by Rev. Elizur Goodrich	332
SPELMAN, Aaron, [s. Thomas & Sarah], b. Jan. 22, 1733/4	365
Aaron, s. Thomas & Sarah, b. Jan. 22, 1735	357
Aaron, s. Thomas & Sarah, bp. Jan. 26, 1734/5	270
Amy, d. Richard & Margery, bp. Dec. 14, 1729	264
Amy, d. Richard & Margery, bp. July 7, 1734	269
Ann, [d. Phinehas & Elisabeth], b. Jan. 27, 1757	400
Anne, d. Richard & Margery, b. July 3, 1734	357
Anne, d. Phinehas & Eliz[abeth], bp. Jan. 30, [1757]	306
Annie, d. Richard & Margerie, b. Dec. 7, 1729	349
Ashael, s. John, bp. July 4, 1736	272
Charles, [s. Thomas & Sarah], b. Dec. 24, 1743; bp. Dec. 25, 1743	282,366
Daniel, [s. Thomas & Sarah], b. July 12, 1738; bp. July 15, 1738	275,365
David, s. John, of Bedford, bp. Nov. 3, 1754	296
Elizabeth, [d. Thomas & Sarah], b. July 14, 1740; bp. Aug. 10, [1740]	278,365
Elisabeth, [d. Phinehas & Elisabeth], b. May 13, 1774; bp. [1774]	324,400
Elizur, [s. Phinehas & Elisabeth], b. Aug. 7, 1780	400
Hannah, [d. Phinehas & Elisabeth], b. Mar. 26, 1755; bp. Mar. 30, 1755	297,400
Huldah, d. Richard & Margery, b. July 9, 1732; bp. July 16, 1732	267.354
John, s. John, bp. Mar. 8, 1740	279

Page

SPELMAN, (cont.)

Martha, [d. Thomas & Sarah], b. Mar. 21, 1742/3; bp. Mar. 28, 1742 280,366
Mary, d. Thomas & Sarah, b. Aug. 18, 1736 357,365
Mary, d. Thomas & Sarah, bp. Aug. 22, 1736 272
Nathan, s. John, bp. June 8, 1746 286
Nathan, [s. Phinehas & Elisabeth], b. Sept. 23, 1777; bp. Oct. 26, 1777 326,400
Oliver, s. John, bp. Feb. 25, 1738/9 276
Phinehas, s. Richard & Margery, b. Feb. 9, 1736; bp. Feb. 13, 1736/7 273,357
Phinehas, s. John, bp. Mar. 4, 1743/4 283
Phinehas, d. Dec. 31, 1783 400
Richard, [s. Phinehas & Elisabeth], b. Dec. 3, 1758; bp. Dec. 3, [1758] 308,400
Robert, [s. Phinehas & Elisabeth], b. Feb. 7, 1767; bp. Feb. 8, 1767 316,400
Sarah, d. Tho[mas] & Sarah, bp. Jan. 29, 1747/8 288
Sarah, [d. Thomas & Sarah], b. Jan. 30, 1747/8 366
Sarah, m. Samuel **BATES**, b. of Haddam, May 17, [1764], by Rev. Elizur Goodrich 329
Stephen, [s. Thomas & Sarah], b. Dec. 5, 1745; bp. Dec. 8, 1745 285,366

SPENCER, Augustus, s. Stephen & Rhoda, bp. June 28, 1772 322
Elizabeth, d. Stephen & Rhoda, bp. Sept. 18, [1768] 317
Elizabeth, m. Elias **CAMP**, Jr., Oct. 17, 1788 405
Hannah, wid., of Durham, m. Capt. William **WARD**, of Middletown, July 4, 1771, by Rev. Elizur Goodrich 331
Martha, m. James **TIBBALS**, Apr. 4, 1744 370
Phebe, m. Nathan O. **CAMP**, May 16, 1787 403
Rachel, d. Stephen & Rhoda, bp. May 27, [1770] 319
Roger, s. Stephen & Rhoda, bp. June 28, 1767 316
Samuel S., of Middletown, m. Mary A. **JACKSON**, of Durham, Oct. 1, 1848 442
Stephen, of Killingworth, m. Rhoda **SQUIRE**, of Durham, Dec. 5, 1766, by Rev. Elizur Goodrich 330
Stephen, s. Stephen & Rhoda, bp. Dec. 12, [1773] 323

SPINER, Eunice, m. John W. **HOUSEMAN**, [ ], 1837 438

SQUIRE, SQUIER, SQUIRES, Abiathar, s. Samuel & Abigail, bp. Aug. 14, 1734 269
Abiathar, s. Samuel & Abigail, b. Nov. 15, 1740; bp. Nov. 16, [1740] 278,396
Abiathar, m. Mary **DUDLEY**, Mar. 9, 1763 396
Abiathar, [s. Abiathar & Mary], b. May 19, 1768; bp. May 29, [1768] 317,396
Abigail, d. George & Jane, bp. Apr. [ ], [1713/14] 253
Abigail, d. Samuel & Abigail, b. Mar. 19, 1750 368
Abigail, d. Samuel & Sarah, bp. Mar. 25, 1750 291
Abigail, of Durham, m. Joel **PALMER**, of Greenwich, Mar. 1, 1779, by Rev. Elizur Goodrich 333

Page

SQUIRE, SQUIER, SQUIRES, (cont.)

Ambrose, [s. Abiathar & Mary], b. Aug. 2, 1766; bp. Aug. 10, 1766 316,396
Anne, d. Sam[ue]l & Anne, bp. Feb. 20, [1757] 306
Anne, d. Samuel & Anne, b. Feb. 20, 1759 376
Anne, d. Samuel & Anne, b. Apr. 30, 1760; bp. May 4, [1760] 310,376
Anne, m. Phinehas **PICKET**, Oct. 4, 1778, by Rev. Elizur Goodrich 333
Anne, d. Ebenezer & Lucy, b. Aug. 26, 1791 406
Asher, [s. Abiathar & Mary], b. Nov. 16, 1763; bp. Nov. 27, [1763] 313,396
Bishop, s. David & Huldah, bp. May 26, [1771] 320
Catharine, d. Samuel & Ann, b. July 21, 1765 385
Charles, s. Samuel & Abigail, b. Aug. 28, 1732; bp. Sept. 3, 1732 267,369
Charles, s. Charles & Mary, bp. Nov. 6, [1763] 313
Clary, d. Samuel & Anne, bp. Mar. 15, [1772] 321
Clement, s. [Josiah & Sarah], b. Nov. 22, 1750; bp. Nov. 25, 1750 292,368
Dan, s. Dan & Patience, bp. Jan. [ ], 1730 265
Daniel, s. Sam[ue]l & Sarah, bp. Oct. 12, 1716 286
Daniel, m. Patience **BARNES**, Sept. 1, 1730, by John Russell, J. P. 356
Daniel, s. Samuel & Abigail, b. Oct. 11, 1746 368
Daniel, s. Ebenezer & Lucy, b. Sept. 12, 1780 406
David, s. Samuel & Abigail, bp. Feb. 18, 1738/9 276
David, m. Huldah **BISHOP**, Feb. 9, 1761 381
David, s. David & Huldah, b. Oct. 8, 1762; bp. Nov. 28, 1762 312,386
Desire, d. Daniel & Patience, bp. Oct. 24, 1736 272
Dudley, [s. Abiathar & Mary], b. Mar. 31, 1765; bp. Apr. 28, [1766] 315,396
Ebenezer, s. Samuel & Abigail, b. Apr. 7, 1745 368
Ebenezer, m. Lucy **WILCOX**, Nov. 26, 1778 406
Ebenezer, s. Ebenezer & Lucy, b. Dec. 14, 1782 406
Edmund Adams, s. Charles & Mary, bp. Jan. 16, [1757] 306
Edward Adams, s. Charles & Mary, b. Jan. 15, 1757 373
Eleazar, s. Daniel & Patience, bp. Aug. 14, 1734 269
Esther, d. George & Jane, bp. Jan. 17, 1719/20 256
George, s. Josiah & Betty, bp. Nov. 15, [1772] 322
Israel, s. Daniel & Patience, b. June 27, 1732; bp. July 2, 1732 267,355
Jane, m. Job **WHEELER**, Apr. 29, 1731 355
Jerusha, d. Abiathar, bp. Mar. 5, [1775] 325
John,, s. George, bp. Apr. 12, 1724 259
John, s. [Josiah & Sarah], b. July 19, 1747; bp. July 26, 1747 287,368
Jonathan, s. Samuel & Abigail, b. July 21, 1748 368
Jonathan, m. Sarah **INGRAHAM**, May 9, 1774, by Rev. Elizur Goodrich 332
Josiah, s. George & Jane, bp. Jan. 15, [1715/16] 254
Josiah, bp. Feb. 5, 1737/8 274
Josiah, s. Josiah & Sarah, bp. Feb. 22, 1740 278
Josiah, s. [Josiah & Sarah], b. Sept. 15, 1742; bp. Sept. 17, 1742 281,368
Josiah, of Durham, m. Betty **DUDLEY**, of Guilford, Dec. 5,

Page

SQUIRE, SQUIER, SQUIRES, (cont.)

1766. by Rev. Elizur Goodrich | 330
Josiah, s. Josiah, bp. May 1, [1774] | 324
Justice (Justus), s. Charles & Mary, b. Nov. 20, 1758; bp. Nov. 26, [1758] | 308,374
Katharine, d. Samuel & Ann, b. Apr. 5, 1762; bp. Apr. 11, [1762]; d. June 8, 1762 | 312,383
Katharine, d. Samuel & Anne, bp. July 21, [1765] | 315
Katharine, d. Ebenezer & Lucy, b. Dec. 6, 1787 | 406
Lydia, d. Charles & Mary, bp. Jan. 31, 1762 | 311
Martha, d. Josiah & Sarah, bp. Feb. 12, 1748/9 | 289
Martha, d. [Josiah & Sarah], b. Feb. 7, 1749/50 | 368
Mary, d. Charles & Mary, b. Sept. 4, 1754; bp. Sept. 8, 1754 | 296,373
Mary, d. Abiathar, bp. Sept. 7, [1777] | 326
Medad, s. David & Huldah, bp. Oct. 23, 1774 | 324
Millesant, d. David & Huldah, bp. Mar. 12, [1769] | 318
Nathan, s. Josiah & Betty, bp. Nov. 15, [1772] | 322
Noah, [s. Abiathar & Mary], b. May 25, 1772 | 396
Olive, d. Samuel & Anne, bp. Oct. 22, [1769] | 319
Orpha M., m. Nathaniel P. **MASON**, July 1, 1839 | 438
Phebe, d. Samuel, bp. Sept. 27, [1767] | 317
Phinehas, s. David & Huldah, b. Apr. 13, 1761; bp. Sept. 20, [1761] | 311,381
Rebecca, d. Josiah & Betty, bp. Nov. 15, [1772] | 322
Rhoda, d. [Josiah & Sarah], b. Nov. 25, 1745; bp. Dec. 1, 1745 | 285,368
Rhoda, of Durham, m. Stephen **SPENCER**, of Killingworth, Dec. 5, 1766, by Rev. Elizur Goodrich | 330
Ruth, d. George & Jane, bp. Feb. 9, 1717/18 | 255
Ruth, d. Josiah & Sarah, bp. Dec. 24, [1739] | 277
Ruth, d. [Josiah & Sarah], b. May 25, 1744; bp. May 27, 1744 | 283,368
Samuel, s. Samuel & Abigail, bp. Mar. 21, 1735 | 272
Samuel, s. Samuel & Abigail, bp. May 29, 1737 | 273
Samuel, d. Mar. 13, 1751 | 351
Samuel d. Mar. 13, 1752 | 351
Samuel, m. Anne **BISHOP**, Sept. 30, 1756 | 377
Samuel, s. Samuel & Ann, b. May 16, 1763; bp. May 22, 1763 | 313,383
Samuel Stent, s. Ephraim & Mehetabel, b. June 15, 1733; bp. June 17, 1733 | 268,357
Santon, s. Samuel & Anne, bp. June 4, [1758] | 307
Sarah, d. [Josiah & Sarah], b. Nov. 22, 1737; bp. Feb. 5, 1737/8 | 274,368
Sarah, m. John **SUTLIF**, Jan. 19, 1754 | 371
Sarah, d. Jonathan & Sarah, bp. Dec. 25, 1774 | 325
Sarah, m. Charles P. **CHEDSY**, June 2, 1840 | 439
Saxton, s. Samuel & Anne, b. June 4, 1758 | 376
Saxton, m. Dorcas **BULKLEY**, Feb. 8, 1779, by Rev. Elizur Goodrich | 333
Statira, [d. Abiathar & Mary], b. Mar. 6, 1769; bp. Mar. 11, 1770 | 319,396
Thaddeus, s. David & Hulda[h], bo. Aug. 19, 1764; bp. Aug. 19, [1764] | 314,386
Tryphene, d. David & Huldah, b. Nov. 9, 1766; bp. Nov. 16, 1766 | 316,389

	Page
STONE, (cont.)	
Timothy Sherman, s. Timothy & Eunice, b. Oct. 21, 1820	417
Urania E., of Durham, m. Rev. Rollin S. **STONE**, of Brooklyn, N. Y., Nov. 27, 1835	437
STOWE, STOW, Abijah, s. Sumner & Sarah, b. May 14, 1746; bp. May 18, 1746 (Incorrectly written "**HOWE**" in the birth)	286,371
Abraham, s. Sumner & Sarah, b. Mar. 5, 1740; bp. Mar. 9, 1739/40	277,359
Abraham, m. Rachel **SEWARD**, Feb. 25, 1779, by Rev. Elizur Goodrich	333
Daniel, s. Sumner & Sarah, b. Oct. 9, 1751 (Incorrectly written "**HOWE**")	371
Daniel Sumner, s. Sumner & Sarah, bp. Oct. 13, 1751	293
Prudence, d. Sumner, bp. May 2, [1756]	298
Rachel, d. Timothy, bp. July 6, [1777]	326
Rachel, w. of Abraham, d. Sept. 20, 1800	409
Rebeckah, d. Timothy & Rebeckah, b. Dec. 4, 1774; bp. Dec. 18, 1774	325,397
Rebecca, see Schuyler & Nathan **MEEKER**	320
Robert, s. Sumner & Sarah, bp. Nov. 6, 1747	288
Robert, s. Sumner & Sarah, b. Nov. 2, 1748 (Incorrectly written "**HOWE**")	371
Sarah, d. Sumner & Sarah, b. Feb. 10, 1737	359
Sarah, w. of Sumner, bp. Aug. 6, 1749	289
Sumner, m. Sarah **SEWARD**, Dec. 1, 1736	359
Timothy, s. Sumner & Sarah, bp. Apr. 24, 1742	280
Timothy, s. Sumner & Sarah, b. Apr. 27, 1742	360
Timothy, m. Rebeckah **MEEKER**, June 13, 1769	392
Timothy, s. Timothy & Rebecca, bp. May 26, [1771]	320
Timothy, d. Mar. 16, 1808	411
STRONG, Asahel, s. Eliakim & Remembrance, b. July 27, 1781	425
Asahel, m. Sally **MUNSON**, May 12, 1803	425
Asahel, s. Asahel & Sally, b. Aug. 6, 1812; d. Sept. 6, 1812	425
Bela, s. Huit, bp. Aug. 6, 1732	267
Beulah (Balah), d. Eliakim & Hannah, b. Mar. 13, 1757; bp. Mar. 13, [1757]	306,373
Beulah, m. Ashur **WRIGHT**, May 22, [1775], by Rev. Elizur Goodrich	333
Catharine, m. Bryan **ROSSETER**, Sept. 2, 1736	367
Damaris, m. John **CAMP**, Jr., [ ], 1730	379
Eliakim, d. Jan. 24, 1745	350
Eliakim, m. Hannah **SEWARD**, June 4, 1751	371
Eliakim, s. Eliakim & Hannah, b. Oct. 6, 1751; bp. Oct. 13, 1751	293,371
Eliakim, Jr., m. Remembrance **WRIGHT**, Mar. 16, 1775, by Rev. Elizur Goodrich	333
Eliza A., m. George **CRUTTENDEN**, May 19, 1824	431
Eliza F., d. Russel H. & Sarah, b. Aug. 24, 1802	411
Elizabeth, m. Seth B. **COOPER**, Aug. 6, 1837	438

Page

STRONG, (cont.)

Eunice, d. Thomas & Phebe, b. Aug. 16, 1752 — 376
Experience, d. Eliakim, bp. Jan. 3, 1730/1 — 265
Experience, m. Noah **NORTON**, Dec. 29, [1757], by Rev. Elizur Goodrich — 327
Guernsey, m. Amanda **PARSONS**, Sept. 7, 1823 — 431
Hannah, d. Lieut. Eliakim & Hannah, bp. Sept. 9, [1770] — 320
Hannah, d. Lieut. Eliakim & Hannah, b. July 4, 1773; bp. Sept. 19, [1773] — 323,397
John, s. Eliakim & Hannah, b. May 7, 1755; bp. May 11, 1755 — 297,371
Katharine, d. Thomas & Phebe, b. Apr. 14, 1759; bp. Apr. 15, [1759] — 308,377
Lois, d. Huit & Dinah, bp. Nov. 2, 1735 — 271
Lois, d. Thomas & Phebe, b. July 1, 1750; bp. July 8, 1750 — 291,367
Lois, d. Eliakin & Hannah, b. May 29, 1764; bp. June 3, 1764 — 314,384
Lorain (Lorraine), d. Thomas & Phebe, b. Mar. 18, 1757; bp. Mar. 20, 1757 — 306,376
Lucy, d. Huit & Dinah, bp. Apr. 6, 1729 — 263
Lucy, d. Thomas & Phebe, bp. Feb. 19, 1764 — 313
Lucy, d. Thomas & Phebe, b. Mar. 4, 1764 — 388
Lucy, d. Asahel & Sally, b. Feb. 6, 1807 — 425
Lucy, m. Edwin **HUBBARD**, Sept. 17, 1825 — 432
Mary, d. Eliakim & Mehetabel, bp. Sept. 8, 1734 — 270
Mary, m. Rowland **ROSSETTER**, Apr. 11, 1753 — 371
Mary, d. Ashael & Sally, b. May 8, 1817 — 425
Mary A., m. Benj[amin] H. **CARRIER**, May 2, 1842 — 440
Medad, s. Eliakim & Hannah, b. July 4, 1753 — 371
Medad, m. Hannah **KELSEY**, b. of Durham, Feb. 9, 1775, by Rev. Elizur Goodrich — 333
Mehetabel, m. Aaron **ALVORD**, Nov. 6, 1739 — 362
Munson, s. Asahel & Sally, b. Feb. 26, 1804 — 425
Nancy, d. Asahel & Sally, b. Apr. 16, 1815 — 425
Nancy E., m. David P. **CAMP**, Aug. 11, 1833 — 436
Nathan, s. Thomas & Phebe, b. Jan. 3, 1762; bp. Jan. 3, 1762; d. Apr. 28, 1763 — 311,388
Nathan, s. Thomas & Phebe, b. Oct. 13, 1766; bp. Oct. 26, 1766; d. Nov. 23, 1767 — 316,388
Nathan, s. Thomas & Phebe, b. June 29, 1769; bp. July 2, [1769] — 318,392
Phebe, d. Thomas & Phebe, b. Nov. 1, 1754; bp. Nov. 3, 1754 — 296,376
Phebe, w. of Thomas, d. Feb. 3, 1787 — 402
Rachel, d. Huit & Dinah, bp. Aug. 20, 1727 — 262
Sarah, d. Thomas & Phebe, b. Feb. 20, 1747; bp. Feb. 22, 1746/7 — 287,367
Sarah, d. Asahel & Sally, b. Apr. 19, 1823 — 425
Sarah, of Durham, m. Elijah **LOVELAND**, of Middletown, June 19, 1843 — 440
Selah, s. Eliakim & Hannah, b. Jan. 6, 1759; bp. Jan. 7, 1759 — 308,376
Seth, s. Eliakim & Hannah, b. May 8, 1761; bp. May 10, [1761] — 310,380

	Page
STRONG, (cont.)	
Stephen, s. Eliakim & Hannah, b. May 8, 1763; bp. May 8, [1763]; d. June 4, 1763	313,382
Stephen, s. Eliakim* & Hannah, b. May 12, 1766; bp. May [ ], [1766]; d. Sept. 26, 1767 *(Ens. Eliakim)	315,388
Stephen, s. Lieut. Eliakim & Hannah, b. July 31, 1768; bp. Aug. 7, [1768]	317,397
Tabatha, m. Joseph **COLLINS**, Oct. 19, 1824	432
Thomas, m. Phebe **SEWARD**, Jan. 16, 1746	361
Thomas, s. Thomas & Phebe, b. July 23, 1748	367
----, w. of Asahel, d. Oct. 27, [ ]62	336
STURTEVANT, Maria W., m. Nathan H. **PARSONS**, b. of Durham, May 14, 1846	442
Peris, m. Caroline D. **CAMP**, Apr. 28, 1824	431
SUL[L]IVAN, Hannah, m. Henry E. **BEMUS**, Sept. 28, 1860	443
SUTLIEF, SUTLEIF, STULIF, SUTLIFF, Anna, d. Nath[anie]ll & Sarah b. May 30, 1715; bp. June 5, [1715]	254,344
Benjamin, s. Sergt. John & Sarah, b. Aug. 23, 1755; bp. Aug. 24, 1755	297,371
David, s. Samuel & Eunice, bp. July 20, [1760]	310
Deborah, d. John & Hannah, b. Apr. 10, 1710	340
Dinah, d. John & Hannah, bp. Sept. 2, [1716]	254
Dinah, d. John & Hannah, b. Sept. 7, 1716	345
Elizabeth, of Durham, m. William **PARK**, of Haddam, May 29, 1755	351
Eunice, d. Nathaniel, b. Aug. 7, 1706	339
Eunice, had, d. Sybilla, bp. May 10, 1724	259
Eunice, d. Samuel & Eunice, bp. Mar. 22, [1767]	316
Gad, s. John, Jr. & Lucy, b. Jan. 2, 1756	373
Hannah, d. Samuel & Eunice, bp. Dec. 19, 1762	312
Jehiel, s. Judith, b. Mar. [ ], [1723]	259
John, s. John & Hannah, b. Mar. 9, 1713/14; bp. Mar. 20, [1713/14]	253,341
John, s. John & Mehetabel, bp. July 23, 1726	261
John, s. John & Mahethabel, b. Jan. 28, 1727/8; bp. Jan. 28, 1727/8	262,348
John, m. Sarah **SQUIRE**, Jan. 19, 1754	371
John, m. Lucy **STOCKING**, Apr. 23, 1754	350
John had grandson, bp. Feb. 8, 1756	298
John, d. May 18, 1757	351
Joseph, s. Nathaniel & Sarah, b. June 29, 1710; d. June 22, 1711	340,341
Joseph, s. Nath[aniel] & Sarah, bp. July 27, [1712]	252
Joseph, s. Joseph & Sarah, b. Jan. 1, 1733; bp. Dec. 7, 1740	278,360
Levi, s. Samuel & Eunice, bp. May 28, [1769]	318
Martha, d. John & Hannah, b. Apr. 19, 1712; bp. May 24, [1712]	252,342
Mary, d. Nathaniel & Sarah, b. July 16, 1708	339
N----, Capt., had negro Dan, s. Cambridge, bp. July 3, [1757]	306

Page

SUTLIEF, SUTLEIF, SUTLIF, SUTLIFF, (cont.)
Nathan, s. Samuel & Eunice, bp. June 18, 1758, by Mr. Seaward 307
Nathaniel, Capt., had negro Peter, bp. Sept. 10, 1732 267
Nathaniel, s. Joseph & Sarah, bp. Dec. 7, 1740 278
Rhoda, d. Samuel & Eunice, bp. Feb. 16, 1772 321
Samuel, of Haddam, m. Eunice **CURTISS**, of Durham, Mar. 21, [1735], by Rev. Elizur Goodrich 327
Samuel, s. Samuel & Eunice, bp. Apr. 14, 1765 315
Sarah, d. Joseph & Sarah, bp. Dec. 7, 1740 278
Sarah, d. John, Jr., bp. June* 7, 1754 (*July) 296
Sybilla, d. Eunice, bp. May 10, 1724 259
----, Capt., had negro Deborah, d. Cambridge, bp. Dec. [ ], 1749 290
----, Capt., had negro Thankful, d. Cambridge, bp. Oct. 27, [1754] 296
----, Capt., had negro Phebe, d. Cambridge & C[h]loe, bp. Aug. 5, [1759] 309

SWADDLE, [see also **SWATHEL**], Esther, m. Samuel **TIBBALS**, Apr. 27, 1794 408
Susannah, m. John **COE**, Dec. 10, 1797 408

SWATHEL, [see also **SWADDLE**], Eliza, m. Jehiel U. **HAND**, May 12, 1829 434
Elizabeth, d. John & Phebe, b. Mar. 24, 1809 422
Hannah, m. Lewis **NORTON**, Dec. 16, 1805 414
Jane Maria, d. John, Jr. & Sophronia, b. May 2, 1821 416
John, s. John & Phebe, b. Sept. 8, 1799 422
John, Jr., m. Sophronia **ROBINSON**, Nov. 3, 1820 416
John William, s. John, Jr. & Sophronia, b. Jan. 25, 1822 416
Lydia, m. Oliver **COE**, Jan. 1, 1794 410
Margaret, d. John & Phebe, b. June 30, 1811 422
Margaret, of Durham, m. Wedworth **WADSWORTH**, of Monroe, Mich., Dec. 25, 1833 436
Mary Ann, d. John & Phebe, b. Oct. 1, 1806 422
Mary Ann, m. Ebenezer G. **BATES**, Mar. 26, 1823 431
Phebe, d. John & Phebe, b. Nov. 6, 1815 423
Phinehas, s. John & Phebe, b. Aug. 17, 1814 422
Sally, m. Allen **CLARKE**, Sept. 22, 1803 411

TAINTOR, TAINTER, Benjamin, m. Hannah **NORTON**, Jan. 17, 1779, by Rev. Elizur Goodrich 333
Sarah, m. John **NORTON**, Mar. 24, 1774 397

TALCOTT, TALCOT, Ann, d. Hezekiah & Jemima, b. Sept. 6, 1725 346
Ann, m. Israel **CAMP**, Dec. 24, 1747 352
Anne, d. David & Anne, bp. Aug. 5, [1770] 320
Annes, d. Hezekiah & Jemima, bp. Sept. [ ], 1725 260
David, s. John & Sarah, bp. Oct. 21, 1744 284
David, m. Anne **LYMAN**, b. of Durham, Sept. 16 (17), [1767], by Rev. Elizur Goodrich 330.389

Page

TALCOTT, TALCOT, (cont.)
Eunice, d. Hezekiah & Jemimah, b. Feb. 1, 1735; bp. Feb. 8, 1735 272,356,357
Eunice, m. Elnathan **CAMP**, May 23, [1759], by Rev. Elizur Goodrich 327,379
Hezekiah, s. John & Sarah, b. June 19, 1739; bp. June 24, 1739 276,358
Hezekiah, d. Feb. 13, 1764 383
Hezekiah, of Durham, m. Sarah **JOHNSON**, of Middletown, Mar. 28, 1765, by Rev. Elizur Goodrich 329,387
Jemimah, d. Hezekiah & Jemimah, b. Nov. 20, 1719; bp. Nov. 22, [1719] 256,345
Jemimah, w. of Hezekiah, d. Feb. 2, 1757 350
John, s. Hez[ekiah] & Jemima, b. Nov. last, 1712 252
John, s. Hezekiah & Jemima, b. Nov. 26, 1712 341
Mary, d. Hezekiah & Jemima, b. Feb. 16, 1722/3; bp. Feb. 17, 1722/3 258,236
Noah, s. David & Anne, b. Aug. 7, 1768; bp. Dec. 4, [1768] 318,390
Phebe, d. Hezkeiah & Sarah, b. May 29, 1766; bp. July 13, [1766] 316,387
Rachel, d. Hez[ekiah] & Jemima, b. Sept. 30, 1728; bp. Oct. 6, 1728 263,346
Rachel, m. Job **CAMP**, Dec. 28, 1752 353
Rachel, d. David, bp. [ ], [1774] 324
Rhoda, d. Hezekiah & Jemima, bp. Feb. 6, 1731/2 266
Rhoda, m. Jesse **COOK**, Oct. 27, 1766, by Rev. Elizur Goodrich 329,387
Rhoda, d. David & Anne, bp. Aug. 23, [1772] 322
Sally, d. Hezekiah, b. July 30, 1768 408
Sally, m. Joel **COE**, Jan. 31, 1791 408
Sarah, d. John & Sarah, b. Sept. 1, 1741; bp. Sept. 6, 1741 279,360
----, had negro Peter, bp. Oct. 20, 1751 293

TERRY, John, s. Richard, bp. Oct. 19, 1777 326

THAYER, Lucius Fowler, s. Nathaniel & Anne, b. June 21, 1797 407
Lydia Maria, m. Leveret Marsden **LEACH**, b. of Durham, Feb. 7, 1844 440
Nathaniel, m. Anne **FOWLER**, Nov. 6, 1791 407
William Austin, s. Nathaniel & Anne, b. Aug. 5, 1792 407

THOMAS, Abraham, s. Abraham & Hannah, b. Jan. 9, 1732; bp. Jan. 9, 1731/2 266,354
Ann, d. Abraham & Hannah, bp. Feb. 22, 1740 279
Benjamin, m. Eliza **CROWELL**, June 2, 1830 434
Betsey Ann, m. Jerome **SHELLEY**, b. of Durham, Jan. 9, 1848 442
Hannah, d. Abraham & Hannah, b. Apr. 23, 1728; bp. July 14, 1728 263,346
Jerusha, d. Abraham & Hannah, b. Mar. 10, 1730; bp. May 3, 1730 264,353
Jerusha, m. David **JOHNSON**, Jr., Mar. 14, 1751 377
Mary, d. Abr[aham] & Hannah, bp. June 26, 1737 274
Mary, m. Abraham **BISHOP**, b. of Durham, Oct. 7, 1773.

	Page
THOMAS, (cont.)	
by Rev. Elizur Goodrich	332
Phebe, d. Abraham & Hannah, bp. Apr. 17, [1743]	282
Phebe, m. Timothy **COE**, b. of Durham, July 29, 1766, by Rev. Elizur Goodrich	329
Sarah, d. Abrham & Hannah, bp. Aug. 10, 1733	268
Sarah, m. Moses **SEAWARD**, b. of Durham, Apr. 9, 1761, by Rev. Elizur Goodrich	328,380
William, m. Clarissa Ann **CHAMBERLAIN**, Aug. 26, 1829	434
THOMPSON, Andrew Jackson, s. Charles & Lydia, b. Feb. 17, 1821, in Killingworth	422
Arelno, m. Betsey **LYNN**, Sept. 11, 1842	440
Charles, of Guilford, m. Lydia **NETTLETON**, of Killingworth, Apr. 5, 1810	422
Charles Benjamin, s. Andrew J. & Betsey Ann, b. Oct. 28, 1843	429
Daniel, s. Charles & Lydia, b. Jan. 24, 1811, in Killingworth	422
David, d. July 24, 1828	427
Edward, s. Charles & Lydia, b. Mar. 24, 1817; d. Nov. 6, 1825	422,427
Lucy A., of Durham, m. Franklin S. **SMITH**, of Middletown, Sept. 27, 1846	442
Lucy Ann, d. Charles & Lydia, b. July 23, 1826	427
Lydia D., m. Thomas **FRANCIS**, Nov. 15, 1836	437
Lydia Diana, d. Charles, b. Dec. 13, 1814, at Guilford	422
Prudence, Melora, d. Charles & Lydia, b. Jan. 1, 1824	426
Thankful, m. David **CURTISS**, Jan. 22, 1747	352
William, s. Charles & Lydia, b. Oct. 14, 1812, in Killingworth	422
TIBBALS, THEOBALD, THEOBALDS, TIBBALDS, TYBBALS, Abel, s. Abner & Sarah, b. Mar. 4, 1750; bp. Mar. 18, 1749/50	291,369
Abel, m. Jane **KELSEY**, Oct. 7, 1776	399
Abigail, d. Joseph & Abigail, b. July 1, 1725; bp. July 4, 1725	260,367
Abigail, d. James & Martha, b. Nov. 27, 1752	370
Abigail, [d. Ebenezer & Submit], b. Mar. 22, 1761; bp. Mar. 22, [1761]	310,391
Abner, m. Sarah **CRITTENDEN**, Aug. 26, 1747	368
Abner, bp. Jan. 24, 1747/8	287
Abner, s. Abner, bp. May 16, [1756]	298
Abner, s. Abner & Sarah, b. May 29, 1756	373
Alpheus, s. Seth & Diana, b. Apr. 14, 1812	424
Alpheus Chalker, s. Seth & Diana, b. Feb. 15, 1809; d. Apr. 19, 1809	424
Amelia, d. Seth & Diana, b. June 3, 1810	424
Angus, s. John & Eunice, b. Nov. 19, 1805	421
Anna, d. Abel & Jane, b. May 7, 1778	399
Anna, d. James & Hannah, b. May 2, 1806	415
Asher, s. James & Martha, b. Apr. 4, 1748	370
Asher, s. James & Hannah, b. Nov. 14, 1802	415

Page

TIBBALS, THEOBALD, THEOBALDS, TIBBALDS, TYBBALS,(cont.)

Concurrence, d. John & Eunice, b. Aug. 15, 1798 421
Concurrence, d. Mar. 22, 1822 421
David, s. Joseph & Esther, bp. Sept. 25, 1743 282
David, s. James & Hannah, b. Mar. 5, 1801 415
Diana, w. of Seth, d. Sept. 5, 1813 425
Diana, d. Seth & Sally, b. Dec. 12, 1814 425
Ebenezer, s. Joseph & Abigail, b. Jan. 19, 1730; bp. Jan. 25, 1729/30 264,367
Ebenezer, m. Submit **SEAWARD**, May 23, 1754 391
Ebenezer, [s. Ebenezer & Submit], b. Oct. 16, 1755; bp. Oct. 19, 1755 298,391
Ebenezer, d. May 25, 1819 422
Eber, s. Abner & Sarah, b. Dec. 27, 1751; bp. Dec. 29, 1751 293,369
Elizabeth, d. Joseph & Esther, bp. Sept. 29, 1745 285
Elizabeth, of Middlefield, m. Amos **MILLER**, Jr., Apr. 7, 1766, by Rev. Elizur Goodrich 329
Elnathan, s. Joseph & Esther, bp. Dec. 3, 1749 290
Esther, d. Ebenezer & Submit, bp. Dec. 1, 1771 321
Esther, m. Ebenezer **GOOLTHRAIGHT**, Sept. 8, 1828 434
Eunice, d. James, bp. Jan. 11, 1746/7 287
Eunice, d. John & Eunice, b. Jan. 22, 1808 421
Hannah, [d. Ebenezer & Submit], b. July 22, 1765 391
Hannah, d. Abel & Jane, b. Oct. 7, 1779 399
Henry, s. Seth & Sally, b. Dec. 29, 1822 425
James, s. Joseph & Abigail, b. July 21, 1720 367
James, m. Martha **SPENCER**, Apr. 4, 1744 370
James, bp. Aug. 26, 1744 283
James, s. James & Martha, b. May 7, 1754 415
James, s. James & Martha, b. May 23, 1754 397
James, s. James, bp. May 26, 1754 295
James, m. Hannah **RICHMOND**, Apr. 21, 1799 415
James, s. James & Hannah, b. June 6, 1808 415
John, s. Joseph & Abigail, b. Oct. 29, 1727; bp. Oct. 29, 1727 262,367
John, s. John & Eunice, b. Jan. 4, 1812 421
Joseph, s. Joseph & Abigail, b. May 27, 1718 367
Joseph, s. James & Martha, b. Nov. 10, 1750; bp. Nov. 11, 1750 292,370
Joseph, m. Mrs. Elizabeth **LANE**, Oct. [ ], 1752 391
Loise, d. John & Eunice, b. July 26, 1816 421
Martha, bp. Aug. 26, 1744 283
Mary, d. Joseph & Abigail, bp. Dec. 3, 1732 267
Mary, d. Joseph & Abigail, b. Nov. 20, 1733 367
Mary, d. Abner & Sarah, b. Oct. 2, 1747; bp. Jan. 24, 1747/8 287,369
Mary, [d. Ebenezer & Submit], b. Apr. 30, 1763; bp. May 8, 1763 313,391
Mary, m. Heth **CAMP**, Nov. 20, 1766, by Rev. Elizur Goodrich 329
Mary, d. Seth & Sally, b. Feb. 21, 1817 425
Nathan, s. Abner & Elisabeth, b. May 16, 1786 410
Noah, s. Thomas & Rachel, bp. Aug. 17, [1760] 310

	Page
TIBBALS, THEOBALD, THEOBALDS, TIBBALDS, TYBBALS, (cont.)	
Olive, d. James & Hannah, b. Nov. 30, 1804	415
Ozias, s. Abel & Jane, b. Aug. 20, 1783	400
Phebe, [d. Ebenezer & Submit], b. May 7, 1757; bp. May 8, [1757]	306,391
Rachel, d. Joseph & Esther, bp. Nov. 22, 1747	288
Ruth, d. Abner & Sarah, b. May 3, 1761; bp. May 3, [1761]	310,379
Samuel, s. Joseph & Abigail, b. May 29, 1735; bp. June 1, 1735	271,367
Samuel, s. Thomas & Rachel, b. Nov. 2, 1751; bp. Nov. 3, 1751	293,370
Samuel, s. Abner & Sarah, b. Mar. 9, 1765; bp. Mar. 10, 1765	314,384
Samuel, [s. Ebenezer & Submit], b. June 18, 1769; bp. June 18, [1769]	318,392
Samuel, m. Esther **SWADDLE**, Apr. 27, 1794	408
Samuel G., m. Harriet **HALL**, Sept. 8, 1828	434
Samuel Hall, s. Seth & Sally, b. May 11, 1821	425
Sarah, d. James & Martha, bp. Sept. 1, 1745	285
Sarah,, d. James & Martha, b. Sept. 5, 1745	370
Sarah, bp. Jan. 24, 1747/8	287
Sarah, d. Abner & Sarah, bp. June 16, [1754]	295
Sarah, of Durham, m. Reuben **HOPSON**, of Wallingford, Nov. 7, [1771], by Rev. Elizur Goodrich	331
Sarah, d. Seth & Sally, b. Mar. 19, 1819	425
Seth, s. Eber, b. May 28, 1782, at Haddam	424
Seth, s. John & Eunice, b. May 21, 1801	421
Seth, m. Diana **HULL**, June 11, 1807	424
Seth, m. Sally **GILLUM**, Mar. 6, 1814	425
Stephen, s. Thomas & Rachel, b. Feb. 8, 1749/50; bp. Feb. 11, 1749/50; d. Mar. 28, 1751	290,369
Stephen, s. Abner & Sarah, b. Aug. 2, 1758; bp. Aug. 20, [1758], by Mr. Ely	307,375
Stephen, [s. Ebenezer & Submit], b. June 23, 1767; bp. June 28, 1767	316,391
Stephen, m. Adah **CAMP**, Dec. 8, 1822	430
Submit, [d. Ebenezer & Submit], b. May 8, 1759; bp. May 13, [1759]	309,391
Thomas, s. Joseph & Abigail, b. Sept. 25, 1722; bp. Sept. [ ], [1722]	258,367
Thomas, m. Rachel **DOUD**, Dec. 22, 1748	369
Thomas, bp. Jan. 7, 1749/50	290
Thomas, s. Thomas & Rachel, b. Jan. 10, 1754; bp. Jan. 13, 1754	294,370
-----, w. of Thomas, bp. Jan. 7, 1749/50	290
TORREY, TORRY, Ann, m. Hazael **HINMAN**, May 11, 1756	373
Sarah had d. Nabby **HENMAN**, bp. Oct. 29, [1758]	308
Sarah had s. Torry, b. Oct. 6, 1761; bp. Feb. 28, 1762	311,384
Sarah had s. Aaron **HENMAN**, bp. Aug. 31, 1767; m. Samuel **WILKINSON**, [ ]	317
Torry, s. Sarah, b. Oct. 6, 1761; bp. Feb. 28, 1762	311,384

	Page
TRENCH, James, s. W[illia]m & Rhoda, bp. Sept. 17, 1775	325
Rhoda, wid., of Durham, m. Judah **BENJAMIN**, of Milford, June 2, 1779, by Rev. Elizur Goodrich	334
William, m. Rhoda **HICKOX**, Nov. 10, 1773, by Rev. Elizur Goodrich	332
TUCKER, Henry, m. Rosella **RIDEL**, [ ]	438
Mary, m. William **SOUTHMAYD**, May 23, 1833	436
TURNER, Abigail, m. Jeremiah **LEMING**, July 4, 1716, by Thomas Ward, J. P.	343
Danforth, d. John & Elisabeth, b. Jan. 3, 1795	408
Elisabeth, w. of John, d. Dec. 13, 1798	408
Hannah Eli, d. John & Elisabeth, b. Aug. 26, 1793	408
John, m. Elizabeth **CHATFIELD**, Oct. 18, 1792	408
Oreb, s. John & Elisabeth, b. Dec. 21, 1796	408
TUTTLE, Elijah Coe, s. Joseph & Margaret, b. Dec. 22, 1821	417
Eliza Merrel, d. Joseph & Margaret, b. Mar. 3, 1824	426
Joseph, m. Margaret **COE**, Dec. 25, 1820	429
Stephen, of New Haven, m. Rhoda **COE**, of Durham, Nov. 19, [1772], by Rev. Elizur Goodrich	332
VINTON, Asher, s. Samuel, bp. Aug. 15, [1756]	298
WACKLEY, [see under **WALKLEY**]	
WADSWORTH, Abigail, w. of James, Jr., d. Feb. 14, 1748	351
Abigail, d. Capt. James & Catharine, b. Dec. 8, 1757; bp. Dec. 25, 1757; d. Feb. 2, 1759	307,351
Catharine, d. Capt. James & Katharine, b. Jan. 19, 1760; d. May 28, 1763	352
Catharine, w. of Gen. James, d. Dec. 13, 1813	352
Esther, wid., had negro Nilit, d. Jin, b. May 7, 1784; Mille, b. May 5, 1787	402
James, s. James & Abigail, bp. July 12, 1730	264
James, Capt., m. Katharine **GURNSEY**, Jan. 13, [1735], by Rev. Elizur Goodrich (1757?)	327
James, Capt., d. Jan. 10, 1756	351
James, Capt., m. Katharine **GUERNSEY**, Jan. 13, 1757, by Rev. Elizur Goodrich	351
James, s. Capt. John Noyes & Esther, bp. Apr. 28, 1768	317
James, Capt., had negro Jenny, bp. Mar. 17, 1771	320
James, d. July 21, 1777	352
James, Gen., d. Sept. 22, 1817	3562
James, m. Rosetta E. **ROBINSON**, Sept. 8, 1845	441
John, of New York City, m. Maria **CHEDSEY**, of Durham, Aug. 21, 1834	436
John Noyes, s. James & Abigail, bp. July 26, 1732	267
John Noyes, m. Esther **PARSONS**, Oct. 27, [1757], by Rev. Elizur Goodrich	327
John Noyes, s. John Noyes & Esther, bp. Oct. 1, [1758]	308
Katharine, d. Capt. James & Ruth, bp. Jan. 20, 1760	309
Ruth, d. James & Abigail, bp. May 22, 1743	282

Page

WADSWORTH, (cont.)
Ruth, wid. of Col. James, d. June 5, 1774 352
Wedworth, of Monroe, Mich., m. Margaret **SWATHEL**, of Durham, Dec. 25, 1833 436
William, s. John Noyes & Esther, bp. July 12, [1761] 311
WALKLEY, WACKLEY, WACKLY, WALKLY, Abigail, d. Simeon & Sarah, bp. Dec. 19, 1762 312
Anne, d. Jonathan, bp. Aug. 13, [1775] 325
Hannah, d. Jonathan & Anne, b. Jan. 18, 1769; bp. Jan. 29, 1769 318,392
Jonathan, m. Anne **BATES**, Sept. 17, 1767 (See also Timothy) 392
Sarah, wid., of Haddam, m. Reuben **BISHOP**, of Durham, Dec. 12, [1768], by Rev. Elizur Goodrich 331
Sarah, d. Jonathan & Ann, bp. Jan. 19, 1772 321
Timothy*, of Durham, m. Anne **BATES**, of Haddam, Sept. 17, [1767], by Rev. Elizur Goodrich (*Note gives "Jonathan") 330
Zebulon, s. Simeon & Sarah, bp. June 3, 1764 314
WAMSLEY, Harriet M., m. Henry W. **SMITH**, Apr. 25, 1842 440
WARD, Albert, of Durham, m. Harriet **BEARDSLEY**, of Meriden, Oct. 7, 1831 435
Elizabeth, m. Jess **AUSTIN**, Jan. 26, 1758 379
Henry, of Middletown, m. Maria A. **NEWTON**, of Durham, May 13, 1852 443
Jennette S., m. Jerome **SHELLEY**, Aug. 22, 1844 441
Joseph, m. Charlotte M. **HYDE**, Sept. 24, 1821 430
William, Capt., of Middletown, m. wid. Hannah **SPENCER**, of Durham, July 4, 1771, by Rev. Elizur Goodrich 331
WARNER, Gideon, s. Gideon & Mary, bp. Dec. 1, 1754 296
Olive, d. Gideon & Freelove, bp. June 12, [1763], by Mr. Huntington 313
WATROUS, Jacob, bp. Nov. 30, 1735 271
WAY, Allen, m. Sally **SIMONS**, Oct. 7, 1831 435
WEBB, Rachel, m. Samuel **ROBERTS**, Mar. 22, 1716/17, by James Wadsworth, J. P. 345,358
WEEKS, Samuel, of Woodbury, m. Abigail **HULL**, of Durham, Feb. 14, 1775, by Rev. Elizur Goodrich 333
WELD, Anne, d. Daniel & Elizabeth, b. Feb. 21, 1758; bp. Mar. 27, [1759] 308,396
Anne, d. Daniel & Elizabeth, bp. Apr. 3, 1768 317
Elizabeth, d. Daniel & Elizabeth, b. May 26, 1754; bp. June 2, 1754 295,374
Hannah, d. Daniel & Elizabeth, bp. Jan. 21, 1749/50 290
Hannah, d. Daniel & Elizabeth, b. Jan. 27, 1750/51 369
Mary, d. Daniel & Elizabeth, bp. July 5, 1747 287
Mary, d. Daniel & Elizabeth, b. July 9, 1747 369
Olive, d. Daniel & Elizabeth, b. May 2, 1770; bp. May 6, [1770] 319,396
Olive, m. Dr. Lyman **NORTON**, June 18, 1795 410
Phinehas, s. Daniel & Elizabeth, b. Nov. 25, 1748; bp. Dec. 4, 1748; d. Jan. 1, 1749 288,369
Samuel, s. Daniel & Elizabeth, b. Mar. 10, 1757; bp. Mar. 13,

Page

WELD, (cont.)
[1757] 306,374
Sarah, d. Daniel & Elizabeth, b. Mar. 20, 1752 374
Sarah, d. Samuel & Eliz[abeth], bp. Mar. 22, 1751/2 294
Sarah, d. Daniel & Elizabeth, b. Mar. 20, 1752/3 369
----, d. Daniel, bp. Mar. 24, [1756] 298
WELLS, WELLES, Abigail, d. Jonathan & Mehethabel, b. June 21, 1715; bp. June 25, [1715] 254,344
Elizabeth, of Haddam, m. Daniel **MERWIN**, Jr., of Durham, Dec. 20, 1738, by Henry Brainard, J. P. 358
Elizabeth, d. Jonathan & Mary, b. June 25, 1744; bp. June 25, 1744 283,377
Elizabeth, m. Aaron **HINMAN**, b. of Durham, Oct. 21, 1765, by Rev. Elizur Goodrich 329
Israel, s. Rhoda, b. Apr. 29, 1766; bp. Jan. 25, 1767 316,390
John, s. Jonathan & Mehetabel, bp. Aug. 4, [1718] 255
Jonathan, s. John & Sarah, b. Dec. 14, 1682 344
Jonathan, s. Jonathan & Mehethabel, b. Nov. 16, 1712; bp. Dec. 14, 1712 252,253,344
Jonathan, s. Jonathan, Jr. & Mary, b. July 28, 1736 356
Jonathan, s. Jonathan, Jr. & Mary, b. Apr. 1, 1742; bp. Apr. 4, 1742; d. Sept. 9, 1746 280,360
Jonathan, s. Jonathan & Mary, b. Jan. 24, 1754; bp. Jan. 27, 1754 295,377
Jonathan, d. May 12, 1755 350
Jonathan, d. Nov. 7, 1760 350
Mary, d. Jonathan & Mehetabel, bp. Feb. 17, 1711/12 252
Mary, d. Jonathan & Mary, b. Mar. 17, 1739; bp. Mar. 23, 1739/40 277,360
Mehithabel, d. Jonathan & Mary, b. Sept. 9, 1751; bp. Sept. 29, 1751 293,377
Mehethabel, s. [Jonathan], d. Apr. 16, 1759 350
Rachel, d. Sergt. Jonathan & Mary, bp. Sept. 10, 1749 290
Rachel, d. Jonathan & Mary, b. Sept. 24, 1749 377
Rachel, [b. Sept. 20, 1750]; m. Eliakim **HULL**, Mar. 14, 1787 404
Rhoda, d. Jonathan & Mary, b. July 15, 1746; bp. July 20, 1746 286,377
Rhoda, had s. Israel, bp. Jan. 25, 1767 316
Sarah, d. Jonathan & Mahetabel, b. Feb. 26, 1709/10; bp. Feb. 17, 1711/12 252,340
Sarah, d. Jonathan, Jr. & Mary, b. Feb. 2, 1737; bp. Feb. 5, 1737/8 274,357
Statira, d. Benjamin & Sarah, bp. Mar. 11, 1749/50 291
WELTON, Eunice, bp. Nov. 25, 1722 258
George H., m. Mary **NICHOLS**, b. of Waterbury, Jan. 28, 1844 440
WETMORE, WHETMORE, [see also **WHITMORE**], Abigail, m. Ephriam **SEWARD**, Oct. 19, 1743 363
Amy, d. Jabez & Abigail, bp. Sept. 21, 1734 270
Anne, d. Jabez & Abigail, b. Sept. 29, 1734 356
Asher, s. Samuel B. & Anne, bp. Feb. 20, 1774 323
Catharine, d. Jabez & Abigail, b. July 20, 1736 356

Page

WETMORE, WHETMORE, (cont.)
Elihu, s. David, bp. Aug. 15, 1762, at Middlefield 312
Ira, s. Jabez & Abigail, b. Apr. 3, 1740; bp. Apr. 6, 1740 277,358
Katharine, d. Jabez & Abig[ai]l, bp. July 25, 1736 272
Lois, of Middletown, m. Ebenezer **BALDWIN**, of Granville, Mar. 5, 1759, by Rev. Elizur Goodrich 327
Nathan, s. Samuel Bowman & Anne, bp. July 22, [1770] 320
Polly, d. Daniel, bp. Feb. 17, 1771 320
Samuel Bowman, m. Anna **CANFIELD**, Nov. 7, 1768, by Rev. Elizur Goodrich 331
WHEDON, WHEADON, Chipman, s. Jared & Sarah, b. Feb. 9, 1771; bp. Mar. 17, 1771 320,393
Concurrence, d. Jared & Sarah, b. Apr. 19, 1769; bp. Apr. 23, [1769] 318,391
Elizabeth, d. Jared & Sarah, b. Apr. 28, 1765; bp. May 12, [1765] 315,384
Jared, m. Sarah **CHIPMAN**, b. of Durham, May 24, [1764], by Rev. Elizur Goodrich 329,384
Jared, s. Jared & Sarah, b. Oct. 24, 1773 396
John, s. Jared & Sarah, b. Apr. 26, 1777 398
Samuel, s. Jared & Sarah, b. Dec. 27, 1766; bp. Dec. 27, 1766 316,387
WHEELER, Ann, d. Joseph & Ann, bp. May 18, 1735 271
Elenour, m. Joseph **SEWARD**, Jan. 14, 1713/14, by Rev. Nath[anie]l Chauncey 343
Emily, m. Giles H. **ROBINSON**, Oct. 13, 1825 432
Jane, d. Job & Jane, b. Feb. 15, 1732; bp. Feb. 20, 1731/2 266,355
Job., m. Jane **SQUIRE**, Apr. 29, 1731 355
John, s. Joseph & Prudence, bp. Aug. 23, 1747 288
Joseph, m. Prudence, **GRAVES**, Apr. 13, 1732 355
Joseph, s. Joseph & Prudence, bp. July 8, 1744 283
Mary, of Durham, m. Samuel **PARSONS**, uncle of Moses **PARSONS**, of Northampton, Mass., [Dec. 15], 1711, by Rev. Nath[anie]ll Chauncey 342,352
Mary, d. Job & Jane, bp. Sept. 30, [1733] 268
Mary, d. Joseph & Prudence, bp. Aug. 6, 1738 275
Phebe, d. Thomas & Mary, b. [ ] 1, 1711; bp. June 1, [1712] 252,341
Prudence, d. Joseph & Prudence, bp. June 20, 1740 278
Sarah, d. Joseph & Prudence, b. Feb. 18, 1732/3; bp. Apr. 28 or 29, [1733] 268,355
Thomas, s. Joseph & Prudence, bp. Sept. 22, 1751 292
WHITE, Alice, d. Dan[iel] & Alice, of Middletown, bp. Aug. 14, [1714] 253
Elizabeth, m. Isaac W. **HICKOX**, June 6, 1843 440
Jane, m. Henry **PARSONS**, Sept. 7, 1834 436
Jennett, of Durham, m. Lucius P. **BRYAN**, of Waterbury, Aug. 25, 1836 437
Seymour, m. Phebe C. **MERWIN**, Oct. 5, 1836 437
WHITMORE, [see also **WETMORE**], Daniel, s. Daniel & Sarah, b. Sept. 4, 1772; bp. Sept. 6, [1772] 322,395

Page

WHITMORE, (cont.)
Hope had s. James **GURDON**, b. Oct. 30, 1779 402
Polly, d. Daniel & Sarah, b. Nov. 7, 1770 395
WILCOX, WILCOCKS, WILLCOKS, Hannah, m. Joel **ROBINSON**, Apr. 3, 1774, by Rev. Elizur Goodrich 332
Lucy, m. Ebenezer **SQUIRE**, Nov. 26, 1778 406
Martha, m. Joseph **HICKOX**, Dec. 8, 1748 376
Samuel, m. Eliza A. **PARSONS**, July 20, 1836 437
WILKINSON, John Edwards, s. Samuel & Sarah, b. Apr. 2, 1766; bp. Aug. 31, 1767 317,391
Samuel, m. Sarah **TORRY**, [ ] 317
Sarah, d. Sarah, bp. July 31, [1775] 325
Sarah had d. Sarah, bp. July 31, [1775] 325
WILLIAMS, Silas, m. Elizabeth **BATES**, of Durham, May 1, 1834 436
WINSHIP, Joseph, of Hartford, m. Mary **IVES**, of Durham, Feb. 10, 1833 435
WOOD, David, of Greenwich, m. Mary **BROWN**, of Haddam, Nov. 1, [1759], by Rev. Elizur Goodrich 327
Eunice, d. David & Mary, bp. Oct. 29, [1760] 310
WOODING, Horace, of Hamden, Conn., m. Catharine **BAILEY**, of Durham, Oct. 1, 1848 443
WORTHINGTON, Rhoda Ann, m. Abraham W. **RICE**, July 30, 1828 434
WRIGHT, RIGHT, Aaron, s. John & Lucy, bp. Feb. 4, 1738/9 276
Aaron, s. John & Lucy, bp. Feb. 28, 1747/8 288
Abigail, d. James & Bathiah, bp. Dec. 26, 1720 257
Abigail, d. Daniel & Lucy, bp. Apr. 22, [1759] 309
Ann, d. John & Lucy, bp. Apr. 17, 1737 273
Anne, m. Reuben **BISHOP**, Mar. 9, 1758 384
Asher, s. Daniel & Lucy, b. May 9, 1755; bp. May 11, 1755 297,370
Ashur, m. Beulah **STRONG**, May 22, [1775], by Rev. Elizur Goodrich 333
Caroline E., m. Henry C. **CAMP**, Sept. 6, 1829 434
Catharine, d. Jonathan & Phebe, bp. Dec. 28, 1729 264
Daniel, s. James, bp. June 23, [1723] 259
Daniel, m. Lucy **STEVENS**, Nov. 9, 1752 369
David, s. Joseph & Hellena, bp. Mar. 29, 1747 287
Ebenezer, s. James & Hannah, b. Feb. 26, 1715/16; bp. Mar. 18, 1715/16 254,344
Ele[a]nor, d. Joseph & Ele[a]nor, b. May 2, 1740 362
Eleanor, of Durham, m. Nathaniel **PAGE**, of Goshen, Nov. 5, 1760, by Rev. Elizur Goodrich 328
Hannah, twin with Sarah, d. James, bp. Dec. 10, 1727 262
Hannah, d. Jonathan & Phebe, bp. Mar. 12, 1731/2 266
Helena, d. Joseph & Helena, bp. May 4, 1740 277
Huldah, d. Joseph & Helen, bp. Nov. 24, 1754 296
Ichabod, s. Joseph, Jr. & Sarah, bp. Apr. 11, [1773] 322
Isabel, d. Jonathan & Phebe, bp. Dec. 7, 1734 270
James, bp. Apr. 28 or 29, [1733] 268
Joel, s. John & Lucy, bp. Apr. 6, 1735 271

Page

WRIGHT, RIGHT, (cont.)

Joel, s. John, bp. Dec. 27, 1741 280
John, s. John & Lucy, bp. Apr. 6, 1755 297
Jonathan, s. Jonathan & Phebe, bp. May 1, 1737 273
Joseph, s. James & Hannah, b. Nov. 1, 1713; bp. Nov. 1, 1713 253,344
Joseph, s. Joseph & Helen, bp. May 6, 1744 283
Joseph, Jr., of Durham, m. Sarah **BISHOP**, of Guilford, Dec. 17, [1767], by Rev. Elizur Goodrich 330,389
Lucy, d. John & Lucy, bp. Nov, 2, 1735 271
Lucy, w. of Daniel, d. Nov. 8, 1760 351
Margery, d. Joseph & Ele[a]nor, b. Jan. 5, 1741/2 362
Margery, d. Joseph & Helen, bp. Jan. 24, 1741/2 280
Rachel, d. John & Lucy, bp. June 3, 1744 283
Remembrance, d. Daniel & Lucie, b. Aug. 22, 1753 350
Remembrance, m. Eliakim **STRONG**, Jr., Mar. 16, 1775, by Rev. Elizur Goodrich 333
Ruth, d. Sam[ue]l, bp. Aug. 9, 1747 287
Sally, d. Joseph, Jr. & Sarah, b. Dec. 3, 1769; bp. Dec. 10, [1769] 319,391
Samuel, s. James & Bethiah, bp. July 13, [1718] 255
Samuel, s. James & Bethiah, bp. July 4, 1725 260
Samuel, s. Daniel & Lucy, b. June 22, 1757; bp. July 3, [1757] 306,374
Sarah, twin with Hannah, d. James, bp. Dec. 10, 1727 262
Sarah, d. John, bp. Aug. 3, 1746 286
------, w. of James, d. Mar. 11, 1715/16 343

NO SURNAME

Abigail, d. John, bp. Mar. 17, 1754 295
Bertha, d. Jeremy, negro, bp. Jan. 24, 1747/8 287
Clarissa, m. Curtiss **BATES**, Dec. 14, 1776 404
Dolphin, negro, bp. June 2, [1771] 320
Elah had negro Chloe, d. Sharp & Phyllis, bp. Aug. 29, 1773 323
Lucy, m. Aaron **PARSONS**, Oct. 3, 1782 401
Mary, m. Jesse **ATWELL**, June 16, 1767 401
Shem, bp. Mar. 29, 1747 287
Thankful, d. Cuff & Kate, negroes, bp. Dec. 24, 1749 290
Zillah, w. of Dolphin, negro, bp. June 2, [1771] 320

EASTFORD VITAL RECORDS
1847 - 1851

	Vol.	Page
ADAMS, Addina, b. Ashford, res. Eastford, d. Apr. 16, [1850], ae 44	2	23-4
Dwight R., of Conestia, N. Y., m. Sarah J. **HOUGH**, of Eastford, Oct. 7, 1849, by Charles Peabody. Intention published.	1	19
ALLEN, Eliza, farmer's wife, b. Hampton, res. Eastford, d. Mar. 5, [1848], ae 39	2	11-12
Fielder, medical student, b. Eastford, res. Boston, d. Jan. 12, 1848, ae 21	2	11-12
Harriet C., m. Moses G. **LEONARD**, June 6, 1852, by Rev. Tubal Wakefield. Intention published.	1	37
Woodard B., merchant, d. June 19, [1848], ae 34	2	11-12
AMES, Beriah, b. Ashford, res. Eastford, d. Aug. 9, 1847, ae 7 m.	2	11-12
AMIDON, John, of New York, m. Nancy H. **SOUTHWORTH**, of Eastford, Dec. 7, 1849, by Rev. Lyman Leffingwell	1	19
John, merchant, ae 32, b. Ashford, res. New York, m. Nancy H. **SOUTHWORTH**, ae 26, b. Ashford, res. New York, Dec. 7, [1849], by Lyman Leffingwell	2	25-6
ANGELL, Oliver M., of Eastford, m. Cemantha **HOUGHTON**, of Union, Nov. 21, 1852, by Rev. Tubal Wakefield	1	37
ARNOLD, George, m. Lydia Ann **PLACE**, b. of Eastford, Feb. 14, 1854, by John B. Adams, J. P.	1	41
Harriet, ae 23, b. Eastford, m. Alfred **BURR**, shoemaker, ae 21, b. Mass., res. Eastford, May 12, [1850], by Lyman Leffingwell	2	25-6
Harriet L., m. Alfred P. **BOSS**, b. of Eastford, May 12, 1850, by Rev. Lyman Leffingwell	1	20
James L., s. Ezra, boot manufacturer, ae 23, & Esther, ae 24, b. Aug. 7, 1847	2	7-8
Robert, s. Ezra P., bootmaker, ae 25, & Esther, ae 26, b. Sept. 29, [1849]	2	21-2
BACKUS, Jerah, shoemaker, ae 23, b. Chaplin, res. Eastford, m. Susan **DODGE**, ae 17, of Eastford, May 25, [1850], by Rev. Henry Forbush	2	33-4
Jirah L., m. Susan M. **DODGE**, b. of Eastford, May 25, 1851, by Rev. Henry Forbush	1	36
Zilpha W., m. Henry **WHITAKER**, b. of Eastford, June 22, 1861, in Palmer, Mass., by Rev. Joseph Hall, of the Cong. Church, at Palmer Depot, Mass.	1	43
BAKER, Arthur A., s. Benjamin L., farmer, ae 35, & Susan M., ae 29, b. Sept. 22, [1848]	2	13-4
Emma, d. Jerome W., shoemaker, ae 28, & Emily E., ae 19, b. Feb. [ ], [1850]	2	31-2

	Vol.	Page
BAKER, (cont.)		
Ethan, s. Solomon, farmer, ae 25, & Zuriah, ae 25, b. Apr. 3, [1850]	2	23-4
George H., s. Benj[ami]n, shoemaker, ae 37, & Susan, ae 31, b. Oct. 2, [1850]	2	31-2
N., s. Solomon H., shoemaker, ae 26, & Zeruah R., ae 25, b. June 23, [1850]	2	31-2
Oscar R., s. Solomon, shoemaker, ae 23, & Zeraih, ae 22, b. July 15, [1848]	2	9-10
Sarah, m. George **WHITMAN**, Jan. [ ], 1849, by Francis Williams	1	5
Sophia, d. W[illia]m, laborer, ae 33, & Sarah A., ae 30, b. Apr. 13, 1848	2	9-10
BALLARD, H. S., d. Lorenzo, merchant, & Harriet, b. Oct. 25, [1850]	2	29-30
BARROWS, Cha[rle]s, s. Charles, shoemaker, ae 35, & Susan, ae 34, b. Mar. 4, 1848	2	7-8
Clark Edwin, s. Joseph D., b. Sept.7, 1843, at Ashford, New Eastford	1	5
George M., s. Joseph D., farmer, ae 31, & Mary, ae 33, b. May 4, [1849]	2	13-14
George W., d. Sept. 22, [1850], ae 1	2	33-4
Is[a]bel, d. Sept. 11, [1847], ae 5 1/2	2	11-2
-----, s. Joseph D., farmer, ae 33, & Mary K., ae 35, b. May 18, [1850]	2	29-30
BARTLETT, Arthur N., s. Ephraim, ae 25, of Brimfield, Mass., & Pamia, ae 20, b. Oct. 25, [1850]	2	31-2
Betsey, d. Apr. 12, [1848], ae 66	2	11-2
BASS, [see also **BOSS**], Cyrus M., m. Caroline **THOMAS**, b. of Ashford, May 8, 1853, by Rev. Daniel Dorchester, Jr.	1	39
Loiza M., m. Albert M. **MUMFORD**, b. of Eastford, June 23, 1851, by Rev. H. Forbush	1	36
Louisa, ae 24, b. Middlebury, Mass., res. Eastford, m. Albert **MANFORD**, manufacturer, ae 21, of Eastford, June 23, [1850], by Rev. Henry Forbush	2	33-4
Medora, b. Rutland, Mass., d. Dec. 4, [1850], ae 16	2	33-4
BATES, Adeline A., colored, d. Mar. 28, [1848], ae 1	2	11-2
Joseph, s. W[illia]m, farmer, black, ae 36, & Maria F., ae 33, b. May 30, [1849]	2	15-6
Robert S., s. William, farmer, colored, ae 35, & Maria, ae 37, b. June 27, [1850]	2	29-30
BAXTER, Augustus, m. Susan **LYON**, Dec. 26, 1847, by Isaac Sherman	1	1
Calvin A., laborer, ae 22, b. Coventry, res. Eastford, m. Susan E. **LYON**, ae 16, of Eastford, Dec. 26, 1847, by Rev. Isaac Sherman	2	9-10
Everett R., s. Samuel R., merchant, ae 33, & Sarah, ae 25, b. Jan. 7, 1849	2	13-14

	Vol.	Page
BAXTER, (cont.)		
Henry A., d. Oct. 18, [1850], ae 2	2	33-4
-----, d. Calvin, laborer, & Susan, b. May [ ], [1850]	2	23-4
BENNETT, Betsey, m. Newton A. **LEWIS**, b. of Eastford, Dec. 29, 1850, by Rev. Lyman Leffingwell	1	20
Betsey, ae 23, b. England, res. Eastford, m. Newton **LEWIS**, tanner, ae 21, of Eastford, Dec. 30, [1850], by Rev. Lyman Leffingwell	2	33-4
BIGGS, Edwin A., m. Mirrinda **MILLER**, Feb. 29, 1852, by Isaac Sherman	1	35
BLISS, Eunice, m. Samuel **FRANCES**, b. of Eastford, Nov. 24, 1853, by Rev. Daniel Dorchester, Jr.	1	40
BOLLES, Jane, d. Sept. 5, [1850], ae 1 m.	2	33-4
BOSS, [see also **BASS**], Alfred P., m. Harriet L. **ARNOLD**, b. of Eastford, May 12, 1850, by Rev. Lyman Leffingwell	1	20
BOSWORTH, Benjamin, d. July 2, [1850], ae 88	2	25-6
Eben[eze]r, farmer, b. Ashford, res. Eastford, d. Sept. 20, [1848], ae 78	2	17-8
Hiram, farmer, d. Nov. 3, [1847], ae 42	2	11-2
Hiram E., s. Ezra H., farmer, ae 46, & Lucretia, ae 44, b. Mar. 11, 1850	2	23-4
Samuel D., m. Elizabeth L. **BURT**, b. of Eastford, Jan. 11, 1852, by Francis Williams	1	35
BOTHAM, Lewis, s. Lyman, shoemaker, & Maria, b. Mar. 14, [1850]	2	31-2
BOUTELLE, BOUTELL, Emily, ae 21, b. Ashford, res. Eastford, m. Henry **WHITAKER**, farmer, ae 28, b. Ashford, res. Eastford, Mar. 6, [1849], by Rev. Cha[rle]s Peabody	2	15-6
Emily E., m. Henry **WHITAKER**, b. of Eastford, Mar. 6, 1849, by Charles Peabody	1	5
BOWEN, A. M., s. Oliver, farmer, ae 42, & Betsey B., ae 36, b. Feb. 7, [1850]	2	31-2
Francis D., s. Jabez, farmer, ae 47, b. Feb. 24, 1850	2	21-2
Mary E., d. May 10, [1850], ae 10	2	25-6
Nancy Ann, d. Oliver, farmer, ae 39, & Betsey, ae 34, b. Sept. 13, 1847	2	7-8
Richard H., s. Jabez, farmer, ae 45, & Mary Ann, ae 36, b. Oct. 5, 1847	2	7-8
William J., m. Harriet R. **BROWN**, Apr. 6, 1851, by Isaac Sherman	1	27
Wyman, fisher, d. Aug. 28, [1847], ae 41	2	11-2
BOWERS, Uriel M., m. Jane **DAY**, b. of Eastford, Jan. 1, 1854, by Rev. Tubal Wakefield. Intention published in the Cong. Church by Rev. H. Honmer	1	41
BRADWAY, Martha, d. William, farmer, ae 27, & Sarah, ae 22, b. Nov. 18, [1849]	2	21-2
Martha A., d. Aug. 8, [1850], ae 9 m.	2	33-4
BRAYMAN, Frances, d. Daniel, shoemaker, ae 46, & Lucinda, ae		

	Vol.	Page
BRAYMAN, (cont.)		
45, b. Aug. 4, 1849	2	21-2
----, d. Dan[ie]l, shoemaker, ae 44, & Lorinda, ae 42, b. Aug. 9, 1848	2	13-4
BROWN, Harriet R., m. William J. **BOWEN**, Apr. 6, 1851, by Isaac Sherman	1	27
Mary, housework, of Ashford, d. [1848], ae 64	2	17-8
BUCK, Franklyn, basketmaker, colored, b. Columbia, res. Eastford, d. Sept. 20, [1847], ae 47	2	11-2
BUCKING, BUCKIN, William P., s. Charles & Mary, b. Feb. 23, [1850]	2	21-2
-----, s. Charles, farmer, ae 27, of Ashford, & Mary, ae 26, of Eastford, Apr. [ ], [1850]	2	29-30
BUGBEE, Alvin, of Eastford, m. Mary E. **LUMMIS**, of Worcester, Mass., June 11, 1849, by Francis Williams	1	6
Alvin, farmer, ae 31, of Eastford, m. 2d w., Mary E. **LUMMIS**, ae 25, b. Hampton, res. Eastford, June 11, [1849], by Rev. F. Williams	2	17-8
Maria, b. Ashford, res. Eastford, d. June 19, [1848], ae 39	2	11-2
Maria Lucinda, d. Alvan, farmer, b. Nov. 4, [1850]	2	29-30
Nancy, m. Harvey **DEAN**, June 27, 1847, by Francis Williams	1	1
Susan, b. Woodstock, res. Eastford, d. June 13, [1848], ae 26	2	11-2
W[illia]m H., s. Alvin, farmer, & Sarah, ae 26, b. Mar. [ ], 1848	2	7-8
W[illia]m W., d. Feb. 10, [1848 or 9], ae 11 m.	2	17-8
-----, child of E. G., d. Aug. 29, [1847], ae 3 m.	2	11-2
BULLARD, Sarah K., d. Lorenzo, merchant, ae 43, & Harriet, ae 34, b. Apr. 3, [1849]	2	13-4
BURNHAM, Chester, of Willington, m. Mrs. Prudy **SNOW**, of Eastford, Oct. 24, 1854, by Rev. Charles Chamberlain	1	42
Danforth E., s. Hiram B., merchant, ae 38, & Harriet H., ae 29, b. Dec. 10, [1849]	2	21-2
Joseph B., s. Joseph, trader, ae 26, & Sarah Ann, ae 22, b. Mar. 5, 1848	2	7-8
BURR, Alfred, shoemaker, ae 21, b. Mass., res. Eastford, m. Harriet **ARNOLD**, ae 23, b. Eastford, May 12, [1850], by Lyman Leffingwell	2	25-6
Polly, b. Mass., res. Eastford, d. May 6, [1850], ae 55	2	25-9
BURRBY (?), Francis, of Belchertown, Mass., m. Sarah **SNOW**, of Eastford, Sept. 14, 1851, by Francis Williams	1	35
BURT, Elizabeth L., m. Samuel D. **BOSWORTH**, b. of Eastford, Jan. 11, 1852, by Francis Williams	1	35
BUTTON, Hiram A., s. Hiram, farmer, ae 46, & Catharine, ae 34, b. May 30, [1849]	2	15-6
Hiram W., d. Sept. 20, [1850]	2	33-4
John, d. Dec. 17, [1850], ae 88	2	35-6
CADY, Horace, b. Wrentham, res. Hampton, d. June 21, [1850], ae		

	Vol.	Page
CADY, (cont.)		
20	2	33-4
CARPENTER, Ellen B., d. Uriah L., shoemaker, ae 30, & Emily A., ae 24, b. May 17, [1849]	2	15-6
Fancelia A., ae 18, m. William P. **SPAULDING**, house carpenter, ae 24, b. Southbridge, Mass., res. Killingly, Jan. 19, [1850], by Rev. Rennsalear O. Putney	2	33-4
Fanelia A., of Eastford, m. W[illia]m P. **SPAULDING**, of Killingly, Jan. 18, 1851, by Rev. Rennsalear C. Putney	1	27
Judson, of Eastford, m. Clarissa **PERRIN**, of Woodstock, Apr. 10, 1853, by Rev. B. M. Walker	1	39
Martha, d. Aug. 29, [1847], ae 1 1/2 y.	2	11-2
Mary C., m. Samuel A. **JOHNSON**, b. of Eastford, Sept. 1, 1851, by Rev. Shubael Wakefield. Intention published	1	28
-----, child of Lucius, shoemaker, ae 34, & Cornelia, ae 22, b. Dec. 17, 1847	2	7-8
CHAFFEE, CHAFFE, Adaline, b. Ashford, res. Eastford, d. Sept. 20, [1848], ae 1 1/2 y.	2	17-8
Amos, farmer, b. Ashford, res. Eastford, d. Feb. 20, [1848], ae 79	2	17-8
George M., s. Amos, ae 45, & Mary, ae 34, b. Mar. 13, [1850]	2	31-2
CHAMBERLAIN, Chester E., s. Whitman, innkeeper, ae 51, & Maria, ae 43, b. Apr. 25, [1849]	2	13-4
M. J., of Eastford, m. Albert **UNDERWOOD**, of Pomfret, Nov. 30, 1848, by Francis Williams	1	5
Marion J., ae 21, b. Woodstock, res. Pomfret, m. Albert **UNDERWOOD**, carpenter, ae 24, of Pomfret, Nov. 30, [1849], by Rev. F. Williams	2	15-6
CHAPIN, Mary L., m. Asaph **WEEKS**, b. of Eastford, Nov. 16, 1852, by Rev. H. Forbush	1	36
CHAPMAN, Amelia, ae 38, b. Fisher's Island, m. Moses M. **KENSTER**, shoemaker, ae 34, b. New Bedford, res. Eastford, Apr. 8, [1850], by Rev. F. Williams	2	33-4
Amelia A., of Eastford, m. Moses W. **McKINSTOEY**, of Southbridge, Mass., Apr. 6, 1851, by Francis Williams	1	27
Elvira E., m. Dr. Newton W. **PRESTON**, b. of Eastford, Mar. 7, 1848, by Rev. Rennsalear O. Putney	1	4
Elvira E., ae 19, b. Ashford, res. Stafford, m. Newton W. **PRESTON**, physician, ae 23, b. Ashford, res. Stafford, Mar. 7, 1848, by Rev. R. O. Putney	2	9-10
Harriet C., ae 18, of Ashford, m. Royal **CHAPMAN**, shoemaker, ae 25, of Ashford, Nov. 5, [1849], by Rev. Cha[rle]s Peabody	2	15-6
Lois, m. Jesse T. **HALL**, farmer, b. Ashford, res. Windsor, Ct., Apr. 4, [1850], by Ezekiel Skinner	2	25-6
Royal, shoemaker, ae 25, of Ashford, m. Harriet C. **CHAPMAN**, ae 18, of Ashford, Nov. 5, [1849], by Rev. Cha[rles] Peabody	2	15-6

	Vol.	Page
CHAPMAN, (cont.)		
Susan A., ae 17, b. Eastford, res. Ashford, m. Edwin P. **LEWIS**, farmer, ae 30, b. Eastford, res. Ashford, Nov. 5, [1849], by Rev. Cha[rle]s Peabody	2	15-6
W[illia]m, of Ashford, m. Roxy **DEAN**, of Eastford, Feb. 25, 1849, by W[illia]m S. Simmons	1	5
CHENEY, Mary, b. Mansfield, res. Eastford, d. July 17, [1850], ae 17	2	33-4
Mary B., d. Apr. 5, [1848]	2	17-8
----, child of W[illia]m E., carriage maker, ae 43, & Clarissa, ae 40, b. May 5, 1848	2	9-10
CHILDS, Isaac M., m. Sarah K. **JOHNSON**, b. of Eastford, Dec. 26, 1847, by Francis Williams	1	2
Mary A., d. Isaac M., shoemaker, ae 30, & Mary, ae 27, b. Oct. 20, [1850]	2	29-30
Thomas Snow, of Ashford, d. Apr. 1, [1848]	2	17-8
CLARK, Mary, b. Canterbury, res. Eastford, d. Feb. 7, [1850], ae 66	2	23-4
Nelson P., m. Emily E. **HOLMAN**, b. of Eastford, Mar. 10, 1850, by Francis Williams	1	19
COLE, Sarah E., m. Patrick G. **WEEKS**, b. of Eastford, Dec. 13, 1851, by Rev. H. Forbush	1	36
CONANT, -----, s. H., d. Sept. 14, [1847], ae 1 1/2 m.	2	11-2
CONVERSE, Betsey, of Stafford, m. Wilson **WEEKS**, of Eastford, Aug. 25, 1851, by Francis Williams	1	28
Laranie, of Ashford, m. L. Bruce **WATKINS**, of Eastford, Mar. 27, 1853, by Rev. Tubal Wakefield. Intention published.	1	38
COOLEY, Mira, b. Ashford, res. Eastford, d. Mar. [ ], [1850], ae 59	2	23-4
Rouse, farmer, of Eastford, ae 60, m. 2d w. Chloe **LYON**, ae 57, of Eastford, Mar. 24, [1850], by Isaac Sherman	2	25-6
Rowe, m. Chloe B. **LYON**, b. of Eastford, Mar. 24, 1850, by Rev. Lyman Leffingwell	1	20
COPELAND, Harvey, farmer, ae 21, b. Hampton, res. Hampton, m. Clara **LYON**, ae 17, b. Ashford, res. Hampton, Apr. 29, [1849], by Rev. F. Williams	2	17-8
Harvey, of Hampton, m. Clara (?) S. **LYON**, of Eastford, May 20, 1849, by Francis Williams	1	6
CORBIN, Maria, d. Apr. 29, [1850], ae 36	2	23-4
COREY, Emmy Ann, d. Mason, farmer, ae 35, & Chloe, ae 39, b. Mar. 10, [1850]	2	29-30
W[illia]m Mason, s. W[illia]m Mason, laborer, ae 32, & Clarissa, ae 35, b. Feb. 24, 1848	2	7-8
CURTIS, Harriet, ae 24, b. Ashford, res. Union, m. Ira **MORSE**, farmer, & shoemaker, ae 24, of Union, Jan. 12, 1850, by Asa Willey, Esq.	2	25-6
Henry, farmer, of Ashford, d. June 21, [1848], ae 57* (*Perhaps 77?)	2	17-8
Ruth, b. Scituate, res. Ashford, d. May 19, [1848], ae 88	2	11-2

	Vol.	Page
DAVIS, Almira C., d. Henry, laborer, colored, ae 30, & Melissaa A., ae 24, b. May 9, [1850]	2	23-4
Francis, m. Mary **MALBONE**, Feb. 11, 1849, by Isaac Sherman	1	5
Francis, farmer, colored, ae 34, b. Boston, Mass., res. Eastford, m. 2d w. Mary **MALBONE**, ae 33, Feb. 11, 1849, by Rev. Isaac Sherman	2	15-6
DAY, Albert S., s. George A., carpenter, ae 29, & Sarah J., ae 24, b. Dec. 14, [1849]	2	21-2
Elbridge G., of Thompson, m. Fidelia D. **LEWIS**, of Eastford, Mar. 17, 1850, by Francis Williams	1	19
Jane, m. Uriel M. **BOWERS**, b. of Eastford, Jan. 1, 1854, by Rev. Tubal Wakefield. Intention published in the Cong. Church by Rev. H. Honmer.	1	41
Julia, of Eastford, m. Milton D. **HOWARD**, of Union, Sept. 25, 1853, by Rev. Tubal Wakefield. Intention published Sept. 25, 1853, by Rev. Samuel J. Curtis.	1	39
DEAN, Charles R., of Woodstock, m. Olive S. **LEONARD**, of Union, Nov. 15, 1847, by Rev. Rennsalear O. Putney	1	3
Harvey, m. Nancy **BUGBEE**, June 27, 1847, by Francis Williams	1	1
Irene, housework, b. Ashford, res. Eastford, d. Feb. 15, [1848], ae 78	2	17-8
Roxy, of Eastford, m. W[illia]m **CHAPMAN**, of Ashford, Feb. 25, 1849, by W[illia]m S. Simmons	1	5
----, s. Harvey, sailor, ae 38, & Nancy, ae 38, b. July 24, 1848	2	9-10
DILLABAR, DILLABEE, DILLEBAR, Laura, b. Willington, res. Ashford, d. Mar. [ ], [1850], ae 45	2	33-4
Mary, b. Woodstock, res. Ashford, d. Oct. [ ], 1850, ae 70	2	33-4
-----, d. Thomas C., shoemaker, ae 45, of Ashford, m. Loisa, ae 45, b. Mar. [ ], [1850]	2	29-30
DODGE, Nancy, of Eastford, m. Luke **HISCOX**, of West Woodstock, Aug. 13, 1854, by Rev. Rubal Wakefield. Intention published Aug. [ ], 1854.	1	42
Nathan, d. Sept. 27, [1850], ae 1	2	33-4
Nathan B., s. Augustus, farmer, ae 44, & Mary, ae 35, b. May 4, [1849]	2	13-4
Susan, ae 17, of Eastford, m. Jerah **BACKUS**, shoemaker, ae 23, b. Chaplin, res. Eastford, May 25, [1850], by Rev. Henry Forbush	2	33-4
Susan M., m. Jirah L. **BACKUS**, b. of Eastford, May 25, 1851, by Rev. Henry Forbush	1	36
----, st. b. d. Augustus, farmer, ae 46, & Mary, ae 35, b. June [ ], [1850]	2	29-30
DONAGHUE, Patrick, m. Martha K. **LAMB**, b. of Eastford, Mar. 27, 1853, by Rev. W[illia]m M. Birchard	1	38
DOWLEY, Levi, farmer, ae 16, b. Watertown, N. Y., res. unknown,		

	Vol.	Page
DOWLEY, (cont.)		
m. Jane **WEEKS**, ae 22, res. unknown, Sept. 24, [1849], by Isaac Sherman	2	15-6
Levi S., m. Betsey Jane **WEEKS**, Sept. 24, 1848, by Isaac Sherman	1	4
EDGARTON, Mindwell, b. N. Brookfield, Mass., res. Eastford, d. Feb. 12, [1848], ae 68	2	17-8
ELDREDGE, John, b. Eastford, res. Ashford, d. Sept. 8, [1848], ae 4 1/2 m.	2	17-8
FARNHAM, Patience, of Eastford, m. John S. **MURREY**, of Woodstock, Feb. 27, 1848, by Rennsalear O. Putney, at his residence	1	3
FITCH, Ruby, b. Canterbury, res. Eastford, d. Feb. 5, [1850], ae 63	2	23-4
FITTS, Duty, of Eastford, m. Betsey **HUNTINGTON**, of Ashford, Jan. 7, 1849, by Francis Williams	1	5
Edward B., s. Benj[ami]n S., shoemaker, ae 34, & Elizabeth, ae 31, b. July 21, [1849]	2	15-6
Henrietta, d. Benj[ami]n T., boot & shoemaker, ae 32, & Elizabeth, ae 30, b. Jan. 4, 1848	2	7-8
Henrietta, d. Mar. 13, [1848], ae 10 w.	2	11-2
John A., shoemaker, ae 27, of Eastford, m. Caroline A. **SKINNER**, ae 17, of Eastford, Aug. 29, 1847, by Rev. Henry Menn, N. Y. City	2	9-10
Olive, farmer's wife, d. Apr. 9, [1848], ae 59	2	11-12
----, s. John A., shoemaker, ae 30, & Caroline N., ae 20, b. July 31, [1850]	1	23-4
FRANCES, Samuel, m. Eunice **BLISS**, b. of Eastford, Nov. 24, 1853, by Rev. Daniel Dorchester, Jr.	1	40
FULLER, Harriet, m. Daniel R. **SHIRTLEFF**, Apr. 29, 1849, by Isaac Sherman	1	6
Harriet, m. Daniel R. **SHIRTLEFF**, farmer, ae 36, of Ashford, Apr. 29, [1849], by Rev. Isaac Sherman	2	15-6
GIFFORD, Mary A., of Ashford, m. James R. **SLY**, of Eastford, Dec. 25, 1853, by Rev. Daniel Dorchester, Jr.	1	41
GOODALE, [see also **GOODELL**], Ludiocea, d. Sept. 13, [1850], infant	2	33-4
Virgil, farmer, d. Mar. 7, [1850], ae 44	2	33-4
GOODELL, [see also **GOODALE**], Ludentia, d. Virgil M., shoemaker, ae 45, & Marcia, ae 35, b. Mar. 3, [1850]	2	23-4
Maranda, d. Virgil M., shoemaker, ae 37, & Maria, ae 30, b. Aug. 30, 1847	2	7-8
GORTON, GORTEN, Thomas, of Eastford, m. Nancy **LEWIS**, of Frances Town, N. H., Jan. 5, 1852, by Rev. H. Forbush	1	36
Thomas L., s. Nathan S., shoemaker, ae 23, & Emma L., ae 20, b. Nov. 19, [1848]	2	13-4
GRIGGS, John Phillips, Jr., b. Nov. 4, 1845, in Eastford	1	19
HALL, Emerson, s. Jesse, farmer, ae 26, of Ashford, & Lois, ae 25, b. Mar. 10, [1850]	2	31-2

	Vol.	Page
HALL, (cont.)		
George B., of Chaplin, m. Esther E. **LYON**, of Eastford, Nov. 28, 1850, by Rev. Lyman Leffingwell	1	20
George B., farmer, ae 20, b. Hampton, res. Chaplin, m. Esther E. **LYON**, ae 20, b. Eastford, res. Eastford, Nov. 28, 1850, by Rev. Lyman Leffingwell	2	33-4
James W., m. Laruna **LAMB**, b. of Eastford, Mar. 14, 1852, by Rev. H. Forbush	1	37
Jesse T., farmer, b. Ashford, res. Windsor, Ct., m. Lois **CHAPMAN**, Apr. 4, [1850], by Ezekiel Skinner	2	25-6
------, d. Joseph, farmer, ae 50, & Mary, ae 44, b. Mar. 8, [1849]	2	13-4
HARWOOD, C[h]loe, b. Sutton, Mass., res. Eastford, d. Aug. 11, 1849, ae 78	2	23-4
HAVENS, Harty, tailoress, ae 36, b. Eastford, res. Eastford, m. Samuel E. **SKINNER**, farmer, ae 32, b. Stafford, res. Eastford, Dec. 25, 1847, by Rev. Edward A. Lyon	2	9-10
Harty E., m. Samuel **SKINNER**, Dec. 26, 1847, by Rev. Edward A. Lyon	1	3
Zilpha E., of Eastford, m. John R. **MILLER**, of Plainfield, Nov. 12, 1854, by Rev. D. Dorchester	1	42
HENRY, ------, s. George, manufacturer, ae 27, & Mary A., ae 23, b. July 26, [1849]	2	15-6
HISCOX, Luke, of West Woodstock, m. Nancy **DODGE**, of Eastford, Aug. 13, 1854, by Rev. Tubal Wakefield. Intention published Aug. [ ], 1854	1	42
HODGKIN, Nathan D., shoemaker, ae 20, b. Eastford, res. Willimantic, m. Alice **ROBBINS**, ae 21, b. Ashford, res. Willimantic, Feb. [ ], [1850], by Rev. Dr. Ezekiel Skinner	2	25-6
HOLLINGWORTH, Benj[amin], manufacturer, b. England, res. Eastford, d. Aug. 20, [1847], ae 24	2	11-2
HOLMAN, Emily E., m. Nelson P. **CLARK**, b. of Eastford, Mar. 10, 1850, by Francis Williams	1	19
HORTON, Alvira, ae 23, b. Union, res. Eastford, m. Thomas P. **LEONARD**, shoemaker, ae 23, b. Union, res. Eastford, June 29, [1850], by Rev. Shubael Wakefield	2	33-4
Elvira, of Union, m. Thomas P. **LEONARD**, of Eastford, June 29, 1851, by Rev. Shuael Wakefield	1	27
HOUGH, Sarah J., of Eastford, m. Dwight R. **ADAMS**, of Conestia, N. Y., Oct. 7, 1849, by Charles Peabody. Intention published.	1	19
HOUGHTON, Cemantha, of Union, m. Oliver M. **ANGELL**, of Eastford, Nov. 21, 1852, by Rev. Tubal Wakefield	1	37
HOWARD, Abby M., d. Ezra, farmer, ae 45, & Betsey, ae 35, b. Dec. 19, [1848]	2	13-4
Abigail, b. Ashford, res. Eastford, d. Aug. 5, [1847], ae 84	2	11-2
Betsey, housework, b. Ashford, res. Eastford, d. Feb. 22,		

	Vol.	Page
HOWARD, (cont.)		
[1848], ae 96	2	17-8
Milton D., of Union, m. Julia **DAY**, of Eastford, Sept. 25, 1853, by Rev. Tubal Wakefield. Intention published Sept. 25, 1853, by Rev. Samuel J. Curtis.	1	39
Reuben, b. Ashford, now Eastford, res. Eastford, d. Apr. 23, [1850], ae 23	2	25-6
HOWLETT, Mary M., m. Marcus J. **WEEKS**, Dec. 27, 1852, by Rev. W[illia]m M. Birchard	1	38
HUNTINGTON, Betsey, of Ashford, m. Duty **FITTS**, of Eastford, Jan. 7, 1849, by Francis Williams	1	5
Lucia, d. Elisha, house carpenter, ae 27, & Lucia, ae 25, b. Nov. 12, 1847	2	7-8
Lucy Ann, m. Andrew **WEEKS**, Jan. 23, 1848, by Isaac Sherman	1	1
Lucy Ann, ae 15, b. Eastford, res. Pomfret, m. Andrew **WEEKS**, laborer, ae 20, b. Eastford, res. Pomfret, Jan. 23, 1848, by Rev. Isaac Sherman	2	9-10
JANES, Lucius R., farmer, d. Mar. 17, [1848], ae 39	2	17-8
JOHNSON, Mary E., d. Aug. 28, [1848], ae 16 m.	2	17-8
Samuel A., m. Mary C. **CARPENTER**, b. of Eastford, Sept. 1, 1851, by Rev. Shubael Wakefield. Intention published	1	28
Sarah K., m. Isaac M. **CHILDS**, b. of Eastford, Dec. 26, 1847, by Francis Williams	1	2
JUSTIN, Julia A., of Eastford, m. Jared **WHITFORD**, of Waterford, Apr. 23, 1849, by Francis Williams	1	6
Julia Ann, ae 36, b. Ashford, res. Thompson, m. Jared **WHITFORD**, mason, ae 44, res. Thompson, Apr. 23, [1849], by Rev. F. Williams	2	15-6
KEITH, Edward W., s. Merit A., manufacturer, ae 40, & Mary W., ae 37, b. Nov. 8, [1849]	2	21-2
KENSTER, Moses M., shoemaker, ae 34, b. New Bedford, res. Eastford, m. Amelia **CHAPMAN**, ae 38, b. Fisher's Island, Apr. 8, [1850], by Rev. F. Williams	2	33-4
KEYES, Danforth, farmer, b. Union, res. Eastford, d. Nov. 6, [1849], ae 62	2	23-4
Frank E., s. Edward, farmer, & Mary, b. Sept. 16, [1850]	2	29-30
Joseph F., farmer, b. Ashford, res. Eastford, d. Nov. 20, [1848], ae 45	2	17-8
Sarah Ann, of Eastford, m. Lyman **MORSE**, Jr., of Sturbridge, Mass., Nov. 7, 1849, by Rev. Rennsalear O. Putney	1	19
Sarah Ann, ae 33, b. Eastford, Mass., m. Lyman **MORSE**, Jr., farmer, ae 35, b. Sturbridge, Mass., res. Sturbridge, Mass., Nov. 7, 1849, by Rennsalear C. Putney	2	25-6
KNIGHT, Darius, of Chaplin, m. Abigail A. **PAYNE**, of Eastford, Nov. 25. 1852, by Rev. W[illia]m M. Birchard	1	37
LAMB. Laruna, m. James W. **HALL**, b. of Eastford, Mar. 14, 1852, by Rev. H. Forbush	1	37

	Vol.	Page
LAMB, (cont.)		
Martha K., m. Patrick **DONAGHUE**, b. of Eastford, Mar. 27, 1853, by Rev. W[illia]m M. Birchard	1	38
LAMPHEAR, Andrew, of Ashford, m. Eliza A. **WHITE**, of Eastford, Oct. 23, 1853, by Rev. Daniel Dorchester, Jr.	1	40
LEONARD, Moses G., m. Harriet C. **ALLEN**, June 6, 1852, by Rev. Tubal Wakefield. Intention published	1	37
Olive S., of Union, m. Charles R. **DEAN**, of Woodstock, Nov. 15, 1847, by Rev. Rennsalear O. Putney	1	3
Thomas P., of Eastford, m. Elvira **HORTON**, of Union, June 29, 1851, by Rev. Shubael Wakefield	1	27
Thomas P., shoemaker, ae 23, b. Union, res. Eastford, m. Alvira **HORTON**, ae 23, b. Union, res. Eastford, June 29, [1850], by Rev. Shubael Wakefield	2	33-4
W[illia]m H., Dr., b. in Mansfield, ae 27, now of Orangeville, N. Y., m. Jane A. **PRESTON**, b. in Glastenbury, ae 25, now of Eastford, Oct. 11, 1853, by Rev. Alvan Underwood, of Woodstock. Residence after marriage Orangeville, N. Y.	1	40
LEWIS, Edwin P., farmer, ae 30, b. Eastford, res. Ashford, m. Susan A. **CHAPMAN**, ae 17, b. Eastford, res. Ashford, Nov. 5, [1849], by Rev. Cha[rle]s Peabody	2	15-6
Fidelia D., of Eastford, m. Elbridge G. **DAY**, of Thompson, Mar. 17, 1850, by Francis Williams	1	19
Israel, farmer, b. Richmond, R. I., res. Ashford, d. June 7, [1850], ae 100	2	25-6
Nancy, of Frances Town, N. H., m. Thomas **GORTEN**, of Eastford, Jan. 5, 1852, by Rev. H. Forbush	1	36
Newton, tanner, ae 21, of Eastford, m. Betsey **BENNETT**, ae 23, b. England, res. Eastford, Dec. 30, [1850], by Rev. Lyman Leffingwell	2	33-4
Newton A., m. Betsey **BENNETT**, b. of Eastford, Dec. 29, 1850, by Rev. Lyman Leffingwell	1	20
[LOOMIS], LUMMIS, Mary E., of Worcester, Mass., m. Alvin **BUGBEE**, of Eastford, June 11, 1849, by Francis Williams	1	6
Mary E., ae 25, b. Hampton, res. Eastford, m. Alvin **BUGBEE**, farmer, ae 31, of Eastford, June 11, [1849], by Rev. F. Williams	2	17-8
LYON, Ann, d. Nathan, farmer, ae 60, & Sophia, ae 38, b. June 3, [1850]	2	29-30
Chloe, ae 57, of Eastford, m. 2d h. Rouse **COOLEY**, farmer, ae 60, of Eastford, Mar. 24, [1850], by Isaac Sherman	2	25-6
Chloe B., m. Rowe **COOLEY**, b. of Eastford, Mar. 24, 1850, by Rev. Lyman Leffingwell	1	20
Clara, ae 17, b. Ashford, res. Hampton, m. Harvey **COPELAND**, ae 21, farmer, b. Hampton, res. Hampton, Apr. 29, [1849], by Rev. F. Williams	2	17-8

	Vol.	Page
LYON, (cont.)		
Clara(?), S., of Eastford, m. Harvey **COPELAND**, of Hampton, May 20, 1849, by Francis Williams	1	6
Daniel, d. Sept. 25, [1850], ae 4	2	33-4
Ebenezer, farmer, d. Sept. [ ], 1850, ae 37	2	33-4
Elvin, b. Brookfield, Mass., res. Eastford, d. Apr. 27, [1850], ae 48	2	23-4
Esther E., of Eastford, m. George B. **HALL**, of Chaplin, Nov. 28, 1850, by Rev. Lyman Leffingwell	1	20
Esther E., ae 20, b. Eastford, res. Eastford, m. George B. **HALL**, farmer, ae 20, b. Hampton, res. Chaplin, Nov. 28, 1850, by Rev. Lyman Leffingwell	2	33-4
Henry, s. W[illia]m, farmer, ae 47, & Minerva, ae 35, b. Jan. 29, [1849]	2	13-4
James, 2d, s. Willard, boot manufacturer, ae 36, & Harriet P., ae 37, b. Jan. 18, [1850]	2	21-2
Mary, d. Willard, boot & shoemaker, ae 34, & Harriet, ae 36, b. June 15, 1848	2	9-10
Mary E., d. Jan. 17, 1850, ae 1 1/2	2	23-4
Paulena, d. Nov. 9, [1850], ae 28	2	35-6
Susan, m. Augustus **BAXTER**, Dec. 26, 1847, by Isaac Sherman	1	1
Susan B., ae 16, of Eastford, m. Calvin A. **BAXTER**, laborer, ae 22, b. Coventry, res. Eastford, Dec. 26, 1847, by Rev. Isaac Sherman	2	9-10
Susan M., of Eastford, m. Erastus M. **TUCKER**, of Pomfret, Jan. 9, 1853, by Rev. B. M. Walker	1	38
MALBONE, Mary, m. Francis **DAVIS**, Feb. 11, 1849, by Isaac Sherman	1	5
Mary, ae 33, m. Francis **DAVIS**, farmer, colored, ae 34, b. Boston, Mass., res. Eastford, Feb. 11, 1849, by Rev. Isaac Sherman	2	15-6
MANFORD, Albert, manufacturer, ae 21, of Eastford, m. Louisa **BASS**, ae 24, b. Middlebury, Mass., res. Eastford, June 23, [1850], by Rev. Henry Forbush	2	33-4
MASON, Hepsy, of Killingly, d. Jan. 6, [1848], ae 88	2	17-8
McKINSTOEY, Moses W., of Southbridge, Mass., m. Amelia A. **CHAPMAN**, of Eastford, Apr. 6, 1851, by Francis Williams	1	27
MILLER, Esther, factory hand, b. New York, res. Eastford, d. Sept. 4, [1847], ae 18	2	11-2
George D., s. William D., mechanic, ae 27, & T[ ], ae 20, b. Mar. [ ], [1850]	2	31-2
John R., of Plainfield, m. Zilpha E. **HAVENS**, of Eastford, Nov. 12, 1854, by Rev. D. Dorchester	1	42
Mirrinda, m. Edwin A. **BIGGS**, Feb. 29, 1852, by Isaac Sherman	1	35
MOORE, Esther M., m. Lorenz M. **WHITNEY**, b. of Ashford,		

	Vol.	Page
MOORE, (cont.)		
Sept. 11, 1853, by Rev. D. Dorchester, Jr.	1	39
MORSE, Albert H., farmer, ae 21, of Union, m. Laura **ROBBINS**, ae 24, b. Ashford, res. Union, Sept. 26, 1847, by Dr. Ezekiel Skinner	2	9-10
Ira, farmer, & shoemaker, ae 24, of Union, m. Harriet **CURTIS**, ae 24, b. Ashford, res. Union, Jan. 12, 1850, by Asa Willey, Esq.	2	25-6
Lyman, Jr., of Sturbridge, Mass., m. Sarah Ann **KEYES**, of Eastford, Nov. 7, 1849, by Rev. Rennsalear O. Putney	1	19
Lyman, Jr., farmer, ae 35, b. Sturbridge, Mass., res. Sturbridge, Mass., m. Sarah Ann **KEYES**, ae 33, b. Eastford, Mass., Nov. 7, 1849, by Rennsalear C. Putney	2	25-6
MUMFORD, Albert M., m. Loiza M. **BASS**, b. of Eastford, June 23, 1851, by Rev. H. Forbush	1	36
Nancy M., of Eastford, m. Charles H. **SMITH**, of Derry, N. H., Nov. 24, 1853, by Rev. D. Dorchester, Jr.	1	40
MURREY, John S., of Woodstock, m. Patience, **FARNHAM**, of Eastford, Feb. 27, 1848, by Rennsalear O. Putney, at his residence	1	3
ORMSBEE, John B., m. Mary E. **WARREN**, Aug. 25, 1847, by Francis Williams	1	2
John B., manufacturer, ae 21, of Eastford, m. Mary E. **WARREN**, ae 18, b. Pomfret, res. Eastford, Aug. 25, 1847, by Rev. Francis Williams	2	9-10
OWEN, Mary A., d. Elijah F., farmer & shoemaker, of Ashford, & Lucinda, b. Nov. [ ], [1849]	2	21-2
PAINE, PAYNE, Abigail A., of Eastford, m. Darius **KNIGHT**, of Chaplin, Nov. 25, 1852, by Rev. W[illia]m M. Birchard	1	37
Anna, [w. Noah], b. Ashford, res. Eastford, d. Dec. 29, [1847], ae 75	2	11-2
Noah, farmer, b. Ashford, res. Eastford, d. Dec. 25, [1847], ae 69	2	11-2
PALMER, Hannah S., of Ashford, m. Thompson **RICHMOND**, of Merton, Wis., Apr. 28, 1850, by Rev. Lyman Leffingwell	1	20
PAYNE, [see under **PAINE**]		
PERRIN, Clarissa, of Woodstock, m. Judson **CARPENTER**, of Eastford, Apr. 10, 1853, by Rev. B. M. Walker	1	39
PHELPS, Charles D., s. John D., shoemaker, ae 25, & Abigail D., ae 21, b. Apr. 9, 1848	2	7-8
----, s. John D., d. Aug. 30, [1847], ae 4 m.	2	11-2
----, s. John, shoemaker, ae 27, & Abigail, ae 24, b. Mar. 29, [1850]	2	29-30
PIERCE, Emmy Ann, d. Jeremiah, colored, ae 37, & Mary, ae 19, b. Oct. 8, [1850]	2	29-30
PIKE, Sarah M., d. Calvin, shoemaker, b. [Oct.] 14, [1849]	2	21-22
----, d. Calvin, shoemaker, ae 39, & Amey, ae 30, b. June 25, [1850]	2	31-2

	Vol.	Page
PLACE, Lydia Ann, m. George **ARNOLD**, b. of Eastford, Feb. 14, 1854, by John B. Adams, J. P.	1	41
PRESTON, Charles C., s. W[illia]m E., shoemaker, ae 26, & Lovina, ae 24, b. Nov. 5, 1847	2	7-8
Charles C., d. Oct. 8, [1850 or 51], ae 3	2	33-4
Jane A., b. in Glastenbury, ae 25, now of Eastford, m. Dr. W[illia]m H. **LEONARD**, b. in Mansfield, ae 27, now of Orangeville, N. Y., Oct. 11, 1853, by Rev. Alvan Underwood, of Woodstock. Residence after marriage Orangeville, N. Y.	1	40
Mary L., d. William E., shoemaker, ae 28, & Lovina, ae 26, b. June 21, [1850]	2	23-4
Newton W., Dr., m. Elvira E. **CHAPMAN**, b. of Eastford, Mar. 7, 1848, by Rev. Rennsalear O. Putney	1	4
Newton W., physician, ae 23, b. Ashford, res. Stafford, m. Elvira E. **CHAPMAN**, ae 19, b. Ashford, res. Stafford, Mar. 7, 1848, by Rev. R. O. Putney	2	9-10
Zephaniah, farmer, b. Ashford, res. Eastford, d. Mar. 16, [1848], ae 84	2	17-8
RANDALL, Lucy, of Eastford, m. Joseph J. **WAITE**, of Norwich, Conn., Dec. 31, 1854, by Rev. D. Dorchester	1	43
RICHARDS, James Albert, s. William, of Ashford, & Mary, b. Nov. 16, [1849]	2	21-2
RICHMOND, Thompson, of Merton, Wis., m. Hannah S. **PALMER**, of Ashford, Apr. 28, 1850, by Rev. Lyman Leffingwell	1	20
ROBBINS, Alice, ae 21, b. Ashford, res. Willimantic, m. Nathan D. **HODGKIN**, shoemaker, ae 20, b. Eastford, res. Williamantic, Feb. [ ], [1850], by Rev. Dr. Ezekiel Skinner	2	25-6
Fanny E., ae 18, b. Ashford, res. Eastford, m. William **ROWAND**, shoemaker, ae 23, b. Pomfret, res. Eastford, Dec. 27, 1847, by Dr. Ezekiel Skinner	2	9-10
Laura, ae 24, b. Ashford, res. Union, m. Albert H. **MORSE**, farmer, ae 21, of Union, Sept. 26, 1847, by Dr. Ezekiel Skinner	2	9-10
ROWAND, William, shoemaker, ae 23, b. Pomfret, res. Eastford, m. Fanny E. **ROBBINS**, ae 18, b. Ashford, res. Eastford, Dec. 27, 1847, by Dr. Ezekiel Skinner	2	9-10
SHERMAN, Laton, of Chicopee, Mass., m. Arsina **TROWBRIDGE**, of Eastford, Aug. 28, 1849, by Rev. Augustus Bolles	1	6
SHIPPEE, SHIPPEY, Emeline M., d. Horace, farmer, ae 45, & Loiza, ae 29, b. Jan. [ ], [1850]	2	31-2
William H., s. Horace, farmer, ae 38, & Louisa, ae 26, b. June 17, 1847	2	9-10
SHIRTLEFF, Daniel R., m. Harriet **FULLER**, Apr. 29, 1849, by Isaac Sherman	1	6
Daniel R., farmer, ae 36, of Ashford, m. Harriet **FULLER**, Apr. 29, [1849], by Rev. Isaac Sherman	2	15-6

	Vol.	Page
SIMMONS, William, farmer, d. Oct. 22, [1847], ae 70	2	11-2
SKINNER, Caroline A., ae 17, of Eastford, m. John A. **FITTS**, shoemaker, ae 27, of Eastford, Aug. 29, 1847, by Rev. Henry Menn, N. Y. City	2	9-10
Samuel, m. Harty E. **HAVENS**, Dec. 26, 1847, by Rev. Edward A. Lyon	1	3
Samuel E., farmer, ae 32, b. Stafford, res. Eastford, m. Harty **HAVENS**, ae 36, tailoress, b. Eastford, res. Eastford, Dec. 25, 1847, by Rev. Edward A. Lyon	2	9-10
Susan, d. Samuel E., ae 35, & Katy, ae 39, b. May 2, [1850]	2	31-32
-----, d. Jonathan, manufacturer, ae 53, & Mary, ae 37, b. June 8, [1850]	2	29-30
SLY, James R., of Eastford, m. Mary A. **GIFFORD**, of Ashford, Dec. 25, 1853, by Rev. Daniel Dorchester, Jr.	1	41
SMITH, Charles H., of Derry, N. H., m. Nancy M. **MUMFORD**, of Eastford, Nov. 24, 1853, by Rev. D. Dorchester, Jr.	1	40
SNOW, Almeda S., d. Apr. 8, [1848], ae 2 1/2	2	11-2
Christiana L., d. Hezekiah, shoemaker, ae 26, b. May 1, [1850]	2	23-4
John, of Ashford, d. Sept. 28, [1847], ae 97	2	11-2
Minerva, m. Sylvanus **WEEKS**, b. of Eastford, Nov. 13, 1848, by Francis Williams	1	4
Molly, b. Ashford, res. Eastford, d. Feb. [ ], [1850], ae 90	2	23-4
Prudy, Mrs., of Eastford, m. Chester **BURNHAM**, of Willington, Oct. 24, 1854, by Rev. Charles Chamberlain	1	42
Sarah, of Eastford, m. Francis **BURRBY**(?), of Belchertown, Mass., Sept. 14, 1851, by Francis Williams	1	35
----, s. Thomas, blacksmith, ae 35, & Caroline, ae 24, b. Oct. 24, [1848]	2	13-4
SOUTHWORTH, Ezra, s. Mason S., farmer, & Sophia, b. Mar. 4, [1850]	2	23-4
Herbert, d. Dec. 15, [1850], ae 7	2	33-4
Martha, d. Marvin S., farmer, ae 33, & Sophia L., ae 26, b. Feb. 6, 1848	2	7-8
Nancy H., of Eastford, m. John **AMIDON**, of New York, Dec. 7, 1849, by Rev. Lyman Leffingwell	1	19
Nancy H., ae 26, b. Ashford, res. New York, m. John **AMIDON**, merchant, ae 32, b. Ashford, res. New York, Dec. 7, [1849], by Lyman Leffingwell	2	25-6
SPAULDING, Albert J., s. Harvey G., carriage maker, ae 25, & Dianna, ae 25, b. July 16, [1849]	2	15-6
W[illia]m P., of Killingly, m. Fanelia A. **CARPENTER**, of Eastford, Jan. 18, 1851, by Rev. Rennsalear C. Putney	1	27
William P., house carpenter, ae 24, b. Southbridge, Mass., res. Killingly, m. Fancelia A. **CARPENTER**, ae 18, Jan. 19, [1850], by Rev. Rennsalear O. Putney	2	33-4
SPRAGUE, George, s. George, bootmaker, & Mary, b. Dec. [ ], [1850]	2	31-2

	Vol.	Page
SPRAGUE, (cont.)		
Mary A., b. Northampton, res. Eastford, d. July 29, [1850]	2	25-6
SQUIER, SQUER, Francis, b. Mansfield, res. Woodstock, d. May 26, [1848], ae 21	2	11-2
Philip, of Ashford, d. Nov. 14, [1847], ae 94	2	11-2
STEAD, Amey, housework, b. Pomfret, res. Ashford, d. May 14, [1848], ae 70	2	17-8
STEBBINS, Fanny, d. Aug. 11, 1848, ae 18 m.	2	17-8
STEPHENS, Chloe Elisabeth, d. Moses, farmer, b. Nov. 7, [1850]	2	29-30
STEVENSON, Emma, d. Henry, manufacturer, ae 33, & Emeline, ae 30, b. Aug. 17, [1849]	2	21-2
STORRS, Henry C., m. Jane M. **UTLEY**, b. of Chaplin, May 2, 1849, by Francis Williams	1	6
Henry C., of Chaplin, m. Jane M. **UTLEY**, of Chaplin, May 2, [1849], by Rev. F. Williams	2	17-8
TAFT, Charles P., s. Thomas J., of Ashford, & Anna E., b. Sept. 22, [1849]	2	21-2
Martha J., d. Thomas J., miller, ae 44, & Anna E., ae 39, b. Oct. 24, [1848]	2	13-4
Martha Jane, of Ashford, d. Nov. 20, [1848], ae 1 m.	2	17-8
Rosina C., b. Ashford, res. Eastford, d. Dec. 11, [1849], ae 21	2	23-4
----, child of Thomas J., miller, ae 44, of Ashford, & Loisa, ae 29, of Ashford, Apr. [ ], [1850]	2	29-30
TANNER, -----, s. Stephen, farmer, colored, ae 41, & Mary A., ae 37, b. May 18, [1849]	2	15-6
TAYLOR, Deborah, housework, b. Canterbury, res. Eastford, d. June 13, [1848], ae 73	2	17-8
THOMAS, Caroline, m. Cyrus M. **BASS**, b. of Ashford, May 8, 1853, by Rev. Daniel Dorchester, Jr.	1	39
Clifford W., s. Henry, manufacturer, ae 29, & Almira, ae 31, b. Feb. 9, [1849]	2	13-4
Mary Jane, m. Ira B. **WILSON**, b. of Eastford, Nov. 28, 1853, by Rev. Daniel Dorchester, Jr.	1	41
William C., s. Clifford, merchant, & Laura, b. Jan. 29, 1850	2	21-2
----, Mrs., b. R. I., res. Eastford, d. Jan. 17, [1850], ae 93	2	35-6
THOMPSON, Brainard, machinist, b. Killingly, res. Eastford, d. June 13, [1848], ae 26	2	11-2
David B., d. [1848], ae 7 m.	2	17-8
David Brainard, s. Brainard, merchant, ae 26, & Sarah, ae 22, b. Feb. 11, 1848	2	7-8
Prescott, m. Althea **TROWBRIDGE**, b. of Eastford, Nov. 5, 1848, by Francis Williams	1	4
Sarah, d. Nov. 11, [1849], ae 25	2	23-4
TROWBRIDGE, Althea, m. Prescott **THOMPSON**, b. of Eastford, Nov. 5, 1848, by Francis Williams	1	4
Arsina, of Eastford, m. Laton **SHERMAN**, of Chicopee, Mass., Aug. 28, 1849, by Rev. Augustus Bolles	1	6

	Vol.	Page
TROWBRIDGE, (cont.)		
Diantha A., m. Amos **WHITAKER**, b. of Eastford, Dec. 7, 1847, by Charles Peabody	1	3
Diantha A., ae 21, b. Ashford, res. Eastford, m. Amos **WHITAKER**, farmer, ae 26, of Eastford, Dec. 7, 1847, by Rev. Cha[rle]s Peabody	2	9-10
John P., s. Philander, farmer, ae 42, & Harriet, ae 39, b. Dec. 10, [1849]	2	21-2
Sarah, d. July 12, [1848], ae 8	2	11-2
Willard, s. Joseph, farmer, ae 37, & Delia A., ae 23, b. June 6, [1850]	2	31-2
TUCKER, Erastus M., of Pomfret, m. Susan M. **LYON**, of Eastford, Jan. 9, 1853, by Rev. B. M. Walker	1	38
TUFTS, Mariette, of Eastford, m. Joseph L. **WATSON**, of Mansfield, Apr. 2, 1849, by Francis Williams	1	6
Mariaetta, ae 29, b. Ashford, res. Eastford, m. Lyman **WATSON**, farmer, ae 39, b. R. I., res. Mansfield, Apr. 2, [1849], by Rev. F. Williams	2	15-6
UNDERWOOD, Albert, of Pomfret, m. M. J. **CHAMBERLAIN**, of Eastford, Nov. 30, 1848, by Francis Williams	1	5
Albert, carpenter, of Pomfret, ae 24, m. Marian J. **CHAMBERLAIN**, ae 21, b. Woodstock, res. Pomfret, Nov. 30, [1849], by Rev. F. Williams	2	15-6
UTLEY, Jane M., m. Henry C. **STORRS**, b. of Chaplin, May 2, 1849, by Francis Williams	1	6
Jane M., of Chaplin, m. Henry C. **STORRS**, of Chaplin, May 2, [1849], by Rev. F. Williams	2	17-8
WAITE, Joseph J., of Norwich, Conn., m. Lucy **RANDALL**, of Eastford, Dec. 31, 1854, by Rev. D. Dorchester	1	43
WALKER, Ellen P., d. Palmer, farmer, ae 49, & Mary, ae 39, b. Sept. 19, [1848]	2	13-4
Mary, b. Ashford, now Eastford, res. Eastford, d. May 23, [1850], ae 40	2	25-6
WARREN, Mary E., m. John B. **ORMSBEE**, Aug. 25, 1847, by Francis Williams	1	2
Mary E., ae 18, b. Pomfret, res. Eastford, m. John B. **ORMSBEE**, manufacturer, ae 21, of Eastford, Aug. 25, 1847, by Rev. Francis Williams	2	9-10
Samuel F., of Conway, Mass., m. Lucinda S. **WILLIAMS**, of Greenfield, Mass., May 21, 1848, by Francis Williams	1	4
Samuel F., ae 32, res. Conway, Mass., m. 2d w. Lucinda S. **WILLIAMS**, ae 31, res. Greenfield, Mass., May 13, 1848, by Rev. Francis Williams	2	9-10
----, d. Wid. Serapta, tailoress, ae 32, of Thompson, b. Nov. 23, [1849]	2	21-2
WATKINS, L. Bruce, of Eastford, m. Laramie **CONVERSE**, of Ashford, Mar. 27, 1853, by Rev. Tubal Wakefield. Intention published.	1	38

	Vol.	Page
WATSON, Joseph L., of Mansfield, m. Mariette **TUFTS**, of Eastford,Apr. 2, 1849, by Francis Williams	1	6
Lyman, farmer, ae 39, b. R. I., res. Mansfield, m. 2d w. Mariaetta **TUFTS**, ae 29, b. Ashford, res. Eastford, Apr. 2, [1849], by Rev. F. Williams	2	15-6
WEBSTER, Chester, Jr., s. Chester, farmer, black, ae 30, & Hannah A., ae 27, b. June 8, [1849]	2	15-6
Emma A., black, d. Aug. 19, [1848], ae 16 m.	2	17-8
Luther, of Charlotte, N. Y., m. Martha **WHITNEY**, of Eastford, Oct. 1, 1848, by Francis Williams	1	4
Luther, farmer, b. Woodstock, res. Charlotte, N. Y., ae 24, m. Maria **WHITNEY**, school teacher, ae 25, b. Eastford, res. Charlotte, N. Y., Oct. 1, [1849], by Rev. F. Williams	2	15-6
Mary L., b. Burlington, N. J., res. Eastford, d. May 21, [1850], ae 17	2	33-4
WEEKS, WEEKES, Abzina Bosworth, d. Percy, ae 17, b. Sept. 21, [1850]	2	29-30
Andrew, m. Lucy Ann **HUNTINGTON**, Jan. 23, 1848, by Isaac Sherman	1	1
Andrew, laborer, ae 20, b. Eastford, res. Pomfret, m. Lucy Ann **HUNTINGTON**, ae 15, b. Eastford, res. Pomfret, Jan. 23, 1848, by Rev. Isaac Sherman	2	9-10
Asaph, m. Mary L. **CHAPIN**, b. of Eastford, Nov. 16, 1852, by Rev. H. Forbush	1	36
Betsey Jane, m. Levi S. **DOWLEY**, Sept. 24, 1848, by Isaac Sherman	1	4
Burton S., s. Rufus W., laborer, & Mehetable B., b. Feb. 12, [1850]	2	21-2
Charlotte, m. Ashley **YOUNG**, b. of Eastford, Oct. 12, 1854, by Rev. D. Dorchester	1	42
Clarissa, m. Josiah W. **WHITNEY**, July 11, 1847, by Isaac Sherman	1	1
Eli E., s. Amos, farmer, ae 36, & Lucretia, ae 30, b. Aug. 20, 1847	2	7-8
Elijah R., s. Frances, farmer, ae 30, & Lucretia, ae 25, b. June 3, [1850]	2	23-4
Frances E., child of David D. N., house carpenter, ae 44, & Almira, ae 40, b. Oct. 21, 1847	2	7-8
Jane, ae 22, res. unknown, m. Levi **DOWLEY**, farmer, ae 16, b. Watertown, N. Y., res. unknown, Sept. 24, [1849], by Isaac Sherman	2	15-6
Jane M., m. Jonathan O. **WEEKS**, b. of Eastford, Aug. 12, 1851, by Francis Williams	1	28
Jonathan O., m. Jane M. **WEEKS**, b. of Eastford, Aug. 12, 1851, by Francis Williams	1	28
Marcus J., m. Mary M. **HOWLETT**, Dec. 27, 1852, by Rev. W[illia]m M. Birchard	1	38

	Vol.	Page
WEEKS, WEEKES, (cont.)		
Martha A., d. Rufus, laborer, ae 29, & Mehetable, ae 25, b. Feb. 11, 1848	2	7-8
Mary, b. R. I., res. Eastford, d. July 17, [1850]], ae 49	2	25-6
Minerva M., ae 22, m. Sylvanus L. **WEEKS**, farmer, ae 28, of Eastford, Nov. 13, [1849], by Rev. F. Williams	2	15-6
Patrick G., m. Sarah E. **COLE**, b. of Eastford, Dec. 13, 1851, by Rev. H. Forbush	1	36
Sophronia, of Eastford, m. Alfred **WITHEY**, of Pomfret, Aug. 15, 1852, by Rev. W[illia]m M. Birchard	1	37
Sylvanus, m. Minerva **SNOW**, b. of Eastford, Nov. 13, 1848, by Francis Williams	1	4
Sylvanus L., farmer, ae 28, of Eastford, m. 2d w. Minerva M. **WEEKS**, ae 22, Nov. 13, [1849], by Rev. F. Williams	2	15-6
Wilson, of Eastford, m. Betsey **CONVERSE**, of Stafford, Aug. 25, 1851, by Francis Williams	1	28
-----, d. Jon[atha]n, farmer, ae 41, & Philanda, ae 39, b. Feb. 25, [1849]	2	13-4
WHITAKER, Amos, m. Diantha A. **TROWBRIDGE**, b. of Eastford, Dec. 7, 1847, by Charles Peabody	1	3
Amos, farmer, ae 26, of Eastford, m. Diantha A. **TROWBRIDGE**, ae 21, b. Ashford, res. Eastford, Dec. 7, 1847, by Rev. Cha[rle]s Peabody	2	9-10
Diantha, d. Amos, farmer, & Diantha, b. Oct. [ ], 1849	2	21-2
Diantha, d. July [ ], [1850], ae 24	2	33-4
Dianthia A., b. Ashford, res. Eastford, d. July 25, [1850], ae 23	2	25-6
Henry, m. Emily E. **BOUTELLE**, b. of Eastford, Mar. 6, 1849, by Charles Peabody	1	5
Henry, farmer, ae 28, b. Ashford, res. Eastford, m. Emily **BOUTELL**, ae 21, b. Ashford, res. Eastford, Mar. 6, [1849], by Rev. Cha[rle]s Peabody	2	15-6
Henry, m. Zilpha W. **BACKUS**, b. of Eastford, June 22, 1861, in Palmer, Mass., by Rev. Joseph Hall, of the Cong. Church at Palmer Depot, Mass.	1	43
WHITE, Eliza A., of Eastford, m. Andrew **LAMPHEAR**, of Ashford, Oct. 23, 1853, by Rev. Daniel Dorchester, Jr.	1	40
WHITFORD, Jared, of Waterford, m. Julia A. **JUSTIN**, of Eastford, Apr. 23, 1849, by Francis Williams	1	6
Jared, mason, ae 44, res. Thompson, m. 2d w. Julia Ann **JUSTIN**, ae 36, b. Ashford, res. Thompson, Apr. 23, [1849], by Rev. F. Williams	2	15-6
WHITMAN, George, m. Sarah **BAKER**, Jan. [ ], 1849, by Francis Williams	1	5
Roxana L., d. W[illia]m, farmer, ae 25, & Jane M., ae 20, b. Sept. 13, [1848]	2	13-4
WHITNEY, Calvin, surveyor, b. Killingly, res. Eastford, d. Apr. 10, [1850], ae 62	2	23-4

	Vol.	Page
WHITNEY, (cont.)		
Horace S., s. Josiah W., mule spinner, ae 22, & Clarissa, ae 17, b. June 20, 1848	2	9-10
Josiah W., m. Clarissa **WEEKES**, July 11, 1847, by Isaac Sherman	1	1
Lorenz M., m. Esther M. **MOORE**, b. of Ashford, Sept. 11, 1853, by Rev. D. Dorchester, Jr.	1	39
Maria, school teacher, ae 25, b. Eastford, res. Charlotte, N. Y., m. Luther **WEBSTER**, farmer, ae 24, b. Woodstock, res. Charlotte, N. Y., Oct. 1, [1849], by Rev. F. Williams	2	15-6
Martha, of Eastford, m. Luther **WEBESTER**, of Charlotte, N. Y., Oct. 1, 1848, by Francis Williams	1	4
William S., s. William, laborer, b. Apr. [ ], [1850]	2	23-4
WILBUR, Mary, b. Pomfret, res. Eastford, d. Sept. 8, [1849], ae 67	2	23-4
Orrin E., s. Dan[ie]l, shoemaker, ae 42, & Roxana, ae 32, b. Aug. 25, [1848]	2	13-4
WILLETT, Fanny, b. Warwick, R. I., res. Oxford, Mass., d. May 20, [1848], ae 52	2	11-2
WILLIAMS, Charles H., s. Francis, Congregational minister, ae 34, & Mahala, ae 27, b. May 7, 1848	2	9-10
Lucinda S., of Greenfield, Mass., m. Samuel F. **WARREN**, of Conway, Mass., May 21, 1848, by Francis Williams	1	4
Lucinda S., ae 31, res. Greenfield, Mass., m. 2d h. Samuel F. **WARREN**, ae 32, res. Conway, Mass., May 13, 1848, by Rev. Francis Williams	2	9-10
----, d. Frances, clergyman, ae 37, & Mahala, ae 29, b. May 18, [1850]* (*1849?)	2	29-30
----, s. Francis, clergyman, ae 36, & Mahala, ae 28, b. June 7, [1850]	2	23-4
----, s. Francis, d. June 8, [1850, ae 1 d.	2	25-6
WILSON, Aaron, b. Killingly, res. Eastford, d. Oct. 4, [1847], ae 2 y.	2	11-2
Ira B., m. Mary Jane **THOMAS**, b. of Eastford, Nov. 28, 1853, by Rev. Daniel Dorchester, Jr.	1	41
Seaman C., s. Orrin, laborer, & Amanda, b. Sept. 28, [1849]	2	21-2
WITHEY, Alfred, of Pomfret, m. Sophronia **WEEKS**, of Eastford, Aug. 15, 1852, by Rev. W[illia]m M. Birchard	1	37
Edmund, s. Jeremiah, shoemaker, ae 28, & Amanda, b. Apr. 28, [1850]	2	31-2
-----, s. Samuel, shoemaker, ae 28, & Amanda, ae 19, b. June [ ], [1849]	2	15-6
YOUNG, Amey Elizabeth, d. Thomas S., farmer, ae 27, & Esther R., ae 28, b. Aug. 13, 1847	2	7-8
Ashley, m. Charlotte **WEEKS**, b. of Eastford, Oct. 12, 1854, by Rev. D. Dorchester	1	42
Cha[u]nc[e]y G., s. William, farmer, ae 31, & Sarah, ae 22, b. Dec. [ ], [1850]	2	31-2

	Vol.	Page
YOUNG, (cont.)		
Edward M., s. Ashby, shoemaker, ae 39, & Tryphena, ae 35, b. Aug. 10, 1847	2	7-8

EAST HADDAM VITAL RECORDS
1743 - 1857

	Vol.	Page
ABBEY, Julius, of Saybrook, m. Lucy Ann **LORD**, of East Haddam, May 14, 1834, by R. S. Crampton, V. D. M.	3	134
ABELL, Lucy A., ae 18, b. at East Hampton, res. East Haddam, m. Frederick W. **LEE**, ae 22, of Guilford, Oct. 19, 1856, by Rev. Nelson Goodrich. Int. pub.	4	104
ACKLEY, ACKLE, ACKLEE, ACKLY, ACLY, Abigail, d. Gideon & Hannah, b. Nov. 29, 1738	LR2	1115
Abigail, m. Robertson **WILLIAMS**, May 7, 1741	LR3	7
Abigail, d. Elijah & Abigail, b. Jan. 28, 1749/50	LR3	1
Abigail, m. Thomas **KNOWLTON**, b. of East Haddam, Aug. 25, 1754	LR6	506
Abigail had s. Thomas **ACKLEY**, b. Mar. 30, 1776; father Thomas **ACKLEY**	2	28
Abigail, m. Cyrus **WILLEY**, b. of East Haddam, Apr. 6, 1788	2	190
Abigail Fuller, d. Amasa & Sarah, b. June 5, 1769	LR7	413
Ahira, s. Nathaniel, 3rd, & Lucretia, b. Apr. 22, 1761	LR6	503
Alathea Ann, d. [Ansel & Lydia], b. Sept. 9, 1821	3	126
Albin, s. Amasa & Sarah, b. June 27, 1778	LR7	413
Alfrad, s. Simeon, Jr. & Sarah, b. June 23, 1770	2	88
Ales, d. Simeon & Ales, d. Aug. 6, 1746	LR3	2
Alice, d. Stephen & Alice, b. Feb. 20, 1775	2	32
Alvin, m. Eunice **WATSON**, b. of East Haddam, Apr. 1, 1821, by Rev. Simeon Dickinson, at the house of Asa Watson	3	4
Amasa, s. Elijah & Abigail, b. Feb. 17, 1747/8	LR3	1
Amasa, m. Sarah **FULLER**, Nov. 11, 1766	LR7	413
Amasa, s. Amasa & Sarah, b. Apr. 12, 1772	LR7	413
Andrew J., mechanic, b. in Haddam, res. East Haddam, d. Mar. 17, 1848, ae 19	4	7-8
Ann, d. Job & Elizabeth, b. May 20, 1737	LR3	510
Anna, d. W[illia]m & Hannah, b. Mar. 9, 1776	2	251
Anna, d. Elijah, Jr. & Anna, b. Feb. 12, 1781	2	24
Anna, d. Elijah, Jr. & Anna, d. May 13, 1781	2	25
Anna, d. Elijah, Jr. & Anna, b. Mar. 30, 1782	2	24
Anna Maria, d. Isaac & Rebeckah, b. Dec. 21, 1836	3	161
Anne, d. Thomas & Han[n]ah, b. Sept. 17, 1698	LR1	3
Ansel, m. Lydia **ROWLEY**, Aug. 3, 1818, by Rev. Solomon Blakesley	3	126
Anson, m. Azubah **BURNHAM**, b. of East Haddam, Mar. 17, 1822, by Rev. W[illia]m Lyman	3	23
Asenath, d. Thomas, 2d & Huldah, b. Jan. 25, 1799	2	255
Bazaleel, s. Samuell & Bethiah, b. Feb. 14, 1723/4	LR2	1096

	Vol.	Page
ACKLEY, ACKLE, ACKLEE, ACKLY, ACLY, (cont.)		
Benajah, s. James & Elizabeth, b. July 10, 1729	LR1	582
Benjamin, Jr., m. Hannah **HIGGINS**, b. of East Haddam, Jan. 15, 1756	LR5	562
Bethiah, d. Elijah & Abigail, b. May 31, 1754	LR3	1
Bethiah, wid. of Samuel, d. Mar. 12, 1764	LR3	19
Bithiah, of East Haddam, m. Israel **DEWEY**, of Colchester, Dec. 14, 1775	2	32
Bethier, m. Ephraim **WILLEY**, Jr., Aug. 14, 1781	2	166
Betsey, d. Isaac C. & Ruth, b. Feb. 20, 1794	2	134
Bezaleel, see under Bazeleel		
Candis, d. Nathaniel & Mary, b. July 20, 1756	LR5	560
Caroline, d. [Ansel & Lydia], b. Feb. 24, 1831	3	126
Caroline, school-teacher, d. Feb. 19, 1850, ae 19	4	29-30
Chaunc[e]y, s. Isaac C. & Ruth, b. Apr. 10, 1792	2	134
C[h]loe, d. Benjamin, Jr. & Hannah, b. Feb. 2, 1763	LR5	562
C[h]loe, d. Benjamin, Jr. & Hannah, d. Dec. 9, 1764	LR5	562
C[h]loe, d. Benjamin, Jr. & Hannah, b. July 28, 1765	LR5	562
Claressa, d. Elijah & Anna, b. Sept. 19, 1775	2	24
Clarissa, see also Larissa		
Daniel, s. Amasa & Sarah, b. Apr. 12, 1776	LR7	413
David, s. Lemuel & Hannah, b. Apr. 23, 1730	LR2	1111
Deborah, d. Samuell & Bethiah, b. July 11, 1709	LR1	7
Deborah, d. Gideon & Deborah, b. June 13, 1766	LR2	1115
Deborah, d. Nathaniel, 3rd, & Lucosey, b. Feb. 19, 1771	2	34
Deborah, of East Haddam, m. Simeon **DICKINSON**, of Richmond, Mass., Nov. 6, 1783	2	148
Demmis, d. Isaac & Ruth, b. Feb. 16, 1745/6	LR3	19
Dimmes, m. David **WICKHAM**, b. of East Haddam, Aug. 23, 1764	LR7	4
Electa, m. Joseph **WHITMORE**, June 17, 1804	3	60-61
Elijah, s. Samuell & Bethyah, b. Mar. 28, 1719	LR1	572
Elijah, m. Abigail **BLACKLEY**, Oct. 12, 1741	LR3	1
Elijah, s. Elijah & Abigail, b. June 23, 1745	LR3	1
Elijah, Jr., m. Ann **OSBORN**, Jan. 31, 1765	LR7	5
Elijah, s. Capt. Elijah & Anna, b. Dec. 3, 1783	2	24
Elizabeth, d. James & Elizabeth, b. Jan. 16, 1721/22	LR1	579
Elizabeth, d. Samuell & Hannah, b. Apr. 15, 1731	LR2	1131
Elizabeth, m. Richard **ANDREWS**, July 10, 1740	LR2	1106
Elizabeth, d. Nathaniel & Mary, b. Mar. 16, 1745	LR5	560
Elizabeth, d. Simeon & Ales, b. Dec. 25, 1747	LR3	2
Elizabeth, d. Elijah & Abigail, b. Feb. 12, 1756	LR3	1
Elizabeth, d. Elijah & Abigail, d. Mar. 20, 1764	LR3	1
Elizabeth, d. Elijah, Jr. & Ann, b. Mar. 15, 1766	LR7	5
Elizabeth, d. Elijah, Jr. & Ann, d. Apr. 25, 1766	LR7	5
Elizabeth, d. Amasa & Sarah, b. May 6, 1767	LR7	413
Elizabeth F., of East Haddam, m. Lorenzo **BAILEY**, of Middletown, Feb. 4, 1825, by Rev. Isaac Parsons	3	70-1

	Vol.	Page
ACKLEY, ACKLE, ACKLEE, ACKLY, ACLY, (cont.)		
Ellen Eliza, d. [Ansel & Lydia], b. Aug. 7, 1836	3	126
Ephraim, s. Nathaniel & Mary, b. Feb. 25, 1751/2	LR5	560
Ephraim, s. Capt. Ephraim & Hannah, b. Feb. 26, 1781	2	227
Eveline Addie, of East Haddam, m. William **WATROUS**, of Mereden, Sept. 4, 1842, by Rev. Isaac Parsons	3	191
Eveline Cornelia, d. Joseph O. & Temperance, b. Aug. 3, 1808	2	219
Eveline Cornelia, m. William B. **BOYD**, Apr. 17, 1827, by Rev. Isaac Parsons	3	95
Ezra, s. Job & Elizabeth, b. Mar. 31, 1744	LR3	510
Fluvia, d. Isaac C. & Ruth, b. July 6, 1787	2	134
Fluvia, m. Matthew **SMITH**, Jan. 1, 1805	3	112-3
Gibbons Jewett, s. Capt. Ephraim & Hannah, b. Oct. 2, 1789	2	227
Giddian, s. James, b. Apr. 14, 1716	LR1	582
Gideon, m. Hannah **ANDREWES**, Mar. 24, 1737	LR2	1115
Gideon, of East Haddam, m. Deborah **ROWLE**, of Colchester, Oct. 27, 1763	LR2	1115
Hannah, d. Thomas & Han[n]ah, b. Oct. 24, 1696	LR1	3
Han[n]ah, m. Benjamin **STRAWBRIDGE**, July 9, 1705	LR1	3
Hannah, alias Hannah **HUNGERFORD**, m. David **GATES**, Sept. 17, 1731	LR2	1111
Hannah, d. Gideon & Hannah, b. Mar. 18, 1742	LR2	1115
Hannah, d. Simeon & Ales, b. July 27, 1744	LR3	2
Hannah, d. Job & Elizabeth, b. Apr. 17, 1746	LR3	510
Hannah, d. Simeon & Ales, d. Nov. 17, 1749	LR3	2
Hannah, m. Silvanus **CONE**, Nov. 13, 1755	LR5	267
Hannah, d. Benjamin, Jr. & Hannah, b. Nov. 21, 1756	LR5	562
Hannah, d. Simeon & Elizabeth, b. Apr. 13, 1760	LR3	2
Hannah, w. of Gideon, d. July 5, 1763	LR2	1115
Hannah, d. William & Hannah, b. July 13, 1767	2	251
Hannah, d. W[illia]m & Hannah, d. Dec. 11(?), 1769	2	252
Hannah, d. W[illia]m & Hannah, b. July 15, 1773	2	251
Hannah, 2d, d. W[illia]m & Hannah, d. June 24, 1792. "Was drowned in Salmon River"	2	252
Hannah, d. Thomas, 2d, & Elizabeth, b. Nov. 5, 1805	2	255
Hannah, of East Haddam, m. David **WRIGHT**, of Saybrook, June 16, 1825, by Rev. Isaac Parsons	3	76-7
Harriet, d. [Ansel & Lydia], b. Feb. 15, 1828	3	126
Harriet, tailorest, ae 22, m. Lewellyn **GLADWIN**, ship joiner, ae 21, b. of E. Haddam, Oct. 31, 1849, by Alpheas Geer	4	19-20
Harriet, m. Lewellyn **GLADWIN**, Dec. 31, 1849, by Rev. Alpheas Geer	3	222
Henry, s. Nathaniel & Mary, b. Sept. 1, 1747	LR5	560
Henry, s. Capt. Ephraim & Hannah, b. Sept. 28, 1785	2	227
Henry Cyrenius, s. [Ansel & Lydia], b. Aug. 8, 1819	3	126
Huldah, d. Nathaniel, 3rd, & Lucretia, b. Apr. 6, 1768	LR6	503
Huldah, d. Thomas, 2d, & Huldah, b. Sept. 30, 1800	2	255
Huldah, w. of Thomas, 2d, d. Nov. 9, 1800	3	256

	Vol.	Page
ACKLEY, ACKLE, ACKLEE, ACKLY, ACLY, (cont.)		
Ichabod, s. Benjamin, Jr. & Hannah, b. Feb. 7, 1761	LR5	562
Ichabod, s. Benjamin, Jr. & Hannah, d. Aug. 23, 1764	LR5	562
Irenie, d. Nathaniel, 3rd, & Lucretia, b. Feb. 24, 1778	LR6	503
Isaac, s. Samuell & Bethyah, b. Oct. 6, 1721	LR1	572
Isaac, m. Ruth **GATES**, Apr. 25, 1745	LR3	19
Isaac, s. Isaac C. & Ruth, b. Feb. 26, 1789	2	134
Isaac, m. Rebeckah **CONE**, Oct. 23, 1833, at Shawcatetes, N.Y.	3	161
Isaac, Jr., adopted s. Isaac & Rebeckah, b. July 17, 1834	3	161
Isaac C., m. Ruth **BURR**, b. of East Haddam, Apr. 27, 1785	2	134
Isaac C., farmer, d. Nov. 3, 1848, ae 88	4	17-18
Isaac Chalker, s. Isaac & Ruth, b. Mar. 16, 1760	LR3	19
Israel Dutton, s. Isaac & Ruth, b. June 1, 1762; d. Oct. 13, 1764	LR3	19
James, s. James & Elizabeth, b. July 17, 1707	LR1	7
Jedidah, d. Capt. Elijah & Anna, b. Dec. 29, 1787	2	24
Jedidah, d. Capt. Elijah & Anna, d. Aug. 21, 1788	2	25
Jeremiah, m. Caroline E. **PURPLE**, Feb. 16, 1851, by Rev. Jacob Gardner	3	230
Jeremiah, ae 31, b. at Chatham, Ct., res. East Haddam, m. Sarah **LORD**, ae 26, of East Haddam, Nov. 20, 1856, by Rev. S. W. Robbins. Int. pub. Nov. 17, 1856	4	113-4
Jerusha, d. James* & Bethiah, b. Mar. 29, 1707 (*Samuel?)	LR1	7
Jerusha, m. Jedediah **GRAVES**, Mar. [ ], 1728	LR3	14
Job. s. Thomas & Han[n]ah, b. Mar. 14, 1702	LR1	3
Job. m. Elizabeth **FULLER**, Dec. 3, 1735	LR3	510
John C., d. Nov. 5, 1849, ae 15 m.	4	29-30
John Crowell, s. Henry C., carpenter, ae 29, & Lucia C., ae 26, b. Aug. 14, 1848	4	13-14
Joseph O., of East Haddam, m. Mrs. Sally **BRAINARD**, of Haddam, Sept. 24, 1812	2	219
Joseph Osborn, m. Temperance **SMITH**, b. of East Haddam, Oct. 31, 1805	2	219
Julia Ann F., of East Haddam, m. Stephen **RUSSELL**, of Haddam, Aug. 30, 1840, by Isaac Parson, V. D. M.	3	182-3
Julius, s. Capt. Ephraim & Hannah, b. Aug. 17, 1787	2	227
Larissa, d. Isaac D. & Ruth, b. Sept. 22, 1802	2	134
Larissa, m. Charles C. **OLMSTED**, b. of East Haddam, May 27, 1832, by Rev. Peter G. Clarke	3	124
Larissa, see also Clarissa		
Lucinda, d. Amasa & Sarah, b. Sept. 18, 1784	LR7	413
Lucretia, d. Nathaniel, 3rd, & Lucretia, b. July 1, 1759	LR6	503
Lucy, d. Isaac & Ruth, b. Oct. 9, 1757	LR3	19
Lucy, m. Israel **CONE**, b. of East Haddam, Apr. 13, 1784	2	154
Lydeah, d. Samuell & Bethyah, b. Aug. 14, 1712	LR1	572
Lydiah, alias Lydiah **ROBINSON**, m. Jonathan **HINKLEY**, Sept. 6, 1733	LR2	1129
Lydia, d. Simeon & Ales, b. Dec. 18, 1742	LR3	2
Lidia, d. Nathaniel & Mary, b. Aug. 28, 1749	LR5	560

	Vol.	Page
ACKLEY, ACKLE, ACKLEE, ACKLY, ACLY, (cont.)		
Lydia, d. Simeon & Ales, d. Nov. 10, 1749	LR5	560
Lydia, d. Simeon & Elizabeth, b. Nov. 13, 1757 (Arnold Copy has "son")	LR3	2
Maria L., m. Edwin B. **GRIFFIN**, b. of East Haddam, Dec. 2, [1840] by Nathaniel Miner. Int. pub.	3	185
Mary, d. Nathaniel & Mary, b. May 27, 1735	LR5	560
Mary, m. David **BELDEN**, b. of East Haddam, Apr. 17, 1760	LR6	504
Mary, d. Gideon & Deborah, b. Sept. 14, 1767	LR2	1115
Mary, d. Nathaniel, 3rd, & Lucretia, b. Feb. 24, 1775	LR6	503
Mary C., of Haddam Neck, m. Daniel W. **MITCHELL**, of East Haddam, Sept. 8, 1850,by Rev. Jacob Gardner, in Moodus	3	227
Molly, d. Elijah, Jr. & Ann, b. Mar. 9, 1768	LR7	5
Nathan, s. Amasa & Sarah, b. Apr. 16, 1781	LR7	413
Nathaniel, d. Feb. 27, 1709/10	LR1	8
Nathaniel, s. James, b. Sept. 7, 1712	LR1	8
Nathaniell, s. Samuell & Bethiah, b. June 14, 1726	LR2	1096
Nathaniel, m. Mary **WILLIAMS**, b. of East Haddam, Apr. 16, 1734	LR5	560
Nathaniel, s. Nathaniel & Mary, b. Apr. 19, 1740	LR5	560
Nathaniel, 3rd, m. Lucretia **WILLEY**, Feb. 16, 1756	LR6	503
Nathaniel, s. Nathaniel & Mary, d. Dec. 2, 1759	LR5	560
Nathaniel, s. Nathaniel, 3rd, & Lucretia, b. Aug. 8, 1765	LR6	503
Nicholas, s. James & Elizabeth, b. Dec. 16, 1708	LR1	7
Olive, d. Isaac & Ruth, b. Aug. 26, 1767	LR3	19
Olive, m. Daniel **CONE**, 3rd, b. of East Haddam, Apr. 28, 1785	2	134
Othamer, s. Nathaniel, 3rd, & Lucretia, b. July 13, 1763	LR6	503
Phebe, d. Job & Elizabeth, b. July 17, 1742	LR3	510
Prudence, d. Isaac & Ruth, b. Aug. 5, 1754	LR3	19
Rachel, d. Benjamin, Jr. & Hannah, b. Dec. 5, 1758	LR5	562
Rachel Crosby, d. [Ansel & Lydia], b. Sept. 20, 1825	3	126
Rebeckah, m. Thomas **MARSHAL**, b. of East Haddam, Feb. 6, 1770	2	198
Rhoda, d. Isaac & Ruth, b. Nov. 10, 1747	LR3	19
Rhoda, m. Jehiel **SAXTON**, b. of East Haddam, Jan. 15, 1765	LR7	417
Rhoda, d. W[illia]m & Hannah, b. Oct. 8, 1785	2	251
Rhoda, d. W[illia]m & Hannah, d. May 8, 1788	2	252
Ruth, d. Nathaniel & Mary, b. Dec. 3, 1737/8	LR5	560
Ruth, d. Isaac & Ruth, b. Mar. 23, 1752	LR3	19
Ruth, d. W[illia]m & Hannah, b. June 7, 1779	2	251
Ruthy, d. Isaac C. & Ruth, b. Jan. 25, 1791	2	134
Ruth, w. Isaac, d. Dec. 25, 1789, in the 69th y. of her age	2	9
Ruth, m. Simon **ELY**, Dec. 8, 1805	2	241
Samuell, s. Samuell & Bethiah, b. Dec. 8, 1703	LR1	5
Samuell, Jr., m. Hannah **HUNGERFORD**, Nov. 22, 1727	LR2	1131
Samuell, s. Samuell & Hannah, b. Nov. 30, 1728	LR2	1131
Samuel, s. Simeon & Ales, b. Oct. 3, 1740	LR3	2
Samuel, d. Apr. 27, 1745	LR3	19

	Vol.	Page
ACKLEY, ACKLE, ACKLEE, ACKLY, ACLY, (cont.)		
Samuel, s. Elijah, Jr. & Anna, b. Apr. 1, 1769	LR7	5
Samuel, s. Elijah, Jr. & Anna, d. Dec. 7, 1770	2	25
Samuel, s. Elijah, Jr. & Anna, b. Sept. 20, 1771	2	24
Samuel O., of East Haddam, m. Cynthia N. **SAWYER**, of Lyme, Oct. 13, 1833, by Rev. Joseph Vaill, of Hadlyme	3	47
Sarah, m. Selvanus **CONE**, 2d, b. of East Haddam,June 26,1760	LR6	507
Sarah, d. Simeon & Sarah, b. Feb. 17, 1772	2	88
Sarah, d. W[illia]m & Hannah, b. Dec. 25, 1781	2	251
Sarah, m. Judah **GATES**, b. of East Haddam, Feb. 3, 1813	2	281
Sarah A., ae 20, b. in Haddam, res. East Haddam, m. Samuel S. **HASTINGS**, ae 22, b. in Suffield, Ct., res. Hartford, Jan. 2, 1857, by Rev. Nelson Goodrich, of Moodus. Int. pub. Jan. 2, 1857	4	115-6
Sarah Brainerd, d. Isaac & Rebeckah, b. Apr. 14, 1840	3	161
Sarah Fuller, d. Stephen & Alice, b. Mar. 20, 1778	2	32
Sarah Jane, of East Haddam, m. Washington A. **BAILEY**, of Chatham, Aug. 30, 1840, by Isaac Parson, V. D. M.	3	182-3
Simeon, m. Ales **FULLER**, Nov. 8, 1739	LR3	2
Simeon, of East Haddam, m. Elizabeth **CROCKER**, of Colchester, May 25, 1747	LR3	2
Simeon, s. Simeon & Ales, b. Apr. 15, 1749	LR3	2
Simeon, Jr., m. Sarah **BEEBE**, Mar. 1, 1770	2	88
Simson*, s. Samuell & Bethuah, b. Jan. 10, 1714 (*Simeon?)	LR1	572
Sophia, d. Thomas, 2d, & Huldah, b. Oct. 14, 1797	2	255
Sophia, d. Thomas & Huldah, d. June 25, 1800	2	256
Sophia Smith, d. Joseph O. & Temperance, b. May 27, 1810	2	219
Stephen, s. Samuell & Bethyah, b. July 25, 1717	LR1	572
Stephen, s. Job & Elizabeth, b. Sept. 9, 1739	LR3	510
Stephen, s. Elijah & Abigail, b. Aug. 19, 1742	LR3	1
Stephen, s. Elijah & Abigail, d. Dec. 5, 1749	LR3	1
Stephen, s. Elijah & Abigail, b. Sept. 6, 1750	LR3	1
Stephen, s. Simeon & Elizabeth, b. July 6, 1753	LR3	2
Stephen, of East Haddam, m. Alice **FULLER**, of Colchester, Nov. 6, 1770	2	32
Stephen, s. Stephen & Alice, b. Aug. 17, 1771	2	32
Stephen, s. Simeon, d. Oct. 1, [1775], at Roxbury, in the 23rd y. of his age. Enlisted in Gen. Spencer's Co., 1775, in the 15th reign of George 3rd.	2	99
Stephen, Jr., m. Deborah **BECKWITH**, b. of East Haddam, Feb. 12, 1794	2	249
Temperance, d. Isaac & Ruth, b. Sept. 27, 1749	LR3	19
Thankfull, d. Gideon & Hannah, b. June 1, 1737	LR2	1115
Thankfull, m. Thomas **SPENCER**, b. of East Haddam, Aug. 27, 1760	LR6	508
Thankfull, m. Matthew **SMITH**, Jr., b. of East Haddam, May 13, 1761	LR6	505
Thomas, s. Thomas & Han[n]ah, b. Jan. 28, 1700	LR1	3

	Vol.	Page
ACKLEY, ACKLE, ACKLEE, ACKLY, ACLY, (cont.)		
Thomas, d. Jan. 16, 1703/4	LR1	3
Thomas, s. Job & Elizabeth, b. June 6, 1740	LR3	510
Thomas, s. Simeon & Elizabeth, b. May 25, 1755	LR3	2
Thomas, s. W[illia]m & Hannah, b. Jan. 5, 1771	2	251
Thomas, s. Thomas & Abigail, b. Mar. 30, 1776	2	28
Thomas, the elder, d. Nov. 30, 1789	2	252
Thomas, 2d, m. Huldah **HURD**, b. of East Haddam, Dec. 14, 1796	2	255
Thomas 2d, m. Elizabeth **SPENCER**, b. of East Haddam, Nov. 2, 1802	2	255
Thomas, s. Thomas, 2d, & Elizabeth, b. Aug. 22, 1807	2	255
Thomas, 3rd, m. Mary **WILLIAMS**, Feb. 11, 1830, by Rev. Isaac Parsons	3	104
Vincey Louisa, [d. Ansel & Lydia], b. Nov. 24, 1823	3	126
Walter, s. Simeon, Jr. & Sarah, b. Mar. 25, 1774	2	88
Warren, s. Nathaniel & Mary, b. Oct. 26, 1756	LR5	560
Warrin, s. Capt. Ephraim & Hannah, b. Aug. 18, 1783	2	227
William, m. Hannah **LORD**, Nov. 13, 1766	2	251
William, s. W[illia]m & Hannah, b. Jan. 30, 1769	2	251
William Nichols, s. [Ansel & Lydia], b. Oct. 31, 1840	3	126
-----y, d. James & Elizabeth, b. Feb. 24, 1718/19	LR1	579
-----, Mrs., d. Mar. 11, 1853, ae 18	LR3	49-50
ADAMS, Samuell, s. Thomas & Sarah, b. Feb. 19, 1745/6	LR5	3
Sarah, w. Tho[ma]s, d. Sept. 30, 1751	LR3	560
Thomas, m. Mrs. Sarah **HOSMOER**, May 10, 1744		3
William, ae 23, b. at Montevella, Ireland, res. East Haddam, m. Alice **WHITE**, ae 21, b. at Castle Conner, Ireland, res. East Haddam, Oct. 26, 1856, by John Lynch, at Moodus. Int. pub. Oct. 11, 1856, at East Haddam	4	105
ALBEE, William, of Lyme, m. Mary A. **BANNING**, of East Haddam, Mar. 29, 1835, by Rev. Hiram Walden	3 4	137
ALBISTON, Lavinia, d. Roger, clergyman, b. July 29, 1851	4	33-4
ALDEN, -----, child of [ ], joiner, b. Aug. 28, 1853		47-8
ALEXANDER, Livingston, m. Jerusha R. B. **BURNHAM**, Apr. 1, 1832, by Rev. Isaac Parsons	3 2	122
ALLEN, ALLYN, Ann, m. Erastus **SMITH**, June 4, 1818		317
Ann G., Mrs., m. Jonathan B. **PARSONS**, b. of East Haddam, Jan. 9, 1833, by Rev. Peter G. Clarke	3	128
Azubah, of Win[d]sor, m. Eli **WARNER**, of East Haddam, Dec. 18, 1754	LR5 LR3	560
Elizabeth, m. Jedediah **GRAVES**, June [ ], 1737		14
Frederick, of Windham, m. Ann G. **PALMER**, of East Haddam, Mar. 18, 1828, by Rev. Isaac Parsons	3	99
Oliver, of Norwich, m. Jerusha C. **GOODSPEED**, of East Haddam, Mar. 18, 1828, by Rev. Isaac Parsons	3	99
Thomas H., of Willimantic, m. Clarissa E. **PEMBERTON**, of Bradford, Mass., June 2, 1850, by Rev. Isaac Parsons	3	225

	Vol.	Page
ALLEN, ALLYN, (cont.)		
Thomas H., shoemaker, ae 21, b. Windham, res. E. Haddam, m. Clara C. **PEMBERTON**, ae 21, b. in Bradford, Mass., res. E. Haddam, June 2, 1850, by Isaac Parsons	4	19-20
ALLYN, [see under **ALLEN**]		
ALMANG, Phebe, alias **SMITH**, m. Bazaliel **BRAINARD**, May 19, 1749	LR2	1092
ANDERSON, Anna, d. Robert & Anna, b. Feb. 24, 1780	2	204
Polly, d. Robert & Anna, b. Feb. 4, 1785	2	204
Polly, m. Israel **CONE**, Jr., Nov. 10, 1807	2	66
Reed, m. Sophia **FOX**, b. of East Haddam, Oct. 14, 18[ ]	2	315
Robert, m. Anna **HUNGERFORD**, b. of East Haddam, May 7, 1776	2	204
Robert, s. Robert & Anna, b. July 17, 1778	2	204
Robert, Capt., d. Feb. 4, 1833, ae 78	3	123
Wel[l]s, s. Robert & Anna, b. Jan. 23, 1788	2	204
ANDRESSE, [see also **ANDREWS**], Eleanor, m. Robert **HURD**, Jr., b. of East Haddam, Apr. 23, 1761	LR6	506
ANDREWS, ANDREW, ANDREWES, ANDREWSS, ANDRUS, [see also **ANDRESSE**], Abiga[i]ll, d. Samuell & Ele[a]ner, b. Aug. 5, 1723	LR2	1127
Abigail, d. Richard & Elizabeth, b. Apr. 27, 1755	LR2	1106
Abijah, s. Joseph & Mable, b. May 1, 1785	2	78
Almira, m. Austin **BURNHAM**, b. of East Haddam, Nov. 26, 1850, by Rev. Geo[rge] W. Brewster, Moodus	3	229
Almyra E., apprentice in cotton mill, m. David A. **BURNHAM**, shoemaker, Nov. 26, 1851, by George W. Brewster	4	37-8
Ann, m. Daniel **SMITH**, Dec. 15, 1767	LR7	412
Asa, s. Zepheniah & Mercy, b. Feb. 11, 1767	2	28
Asahel, s. Richard & Elizabeth, b. Feb. 20, 1742/3	LR2	1106
Asahel, m. Sarah **ROWLEE**, b. of East Haddam, Oct. 8, 1764	LR7	415
Asael, s. Asael & Sarah, b. Feb. 15, 1776	2	88
Benjamin, s. Zepheniah & Mercy, b. Apr. 29, 1775	2	28
Calvin, s. John & Lucy, b. June 27, 1784	2	128
Calvin, 1st, s. John & Lucy, d. Mar. 15, 1787	2	129
Calvin, 2d, s. John & Lucy, b. Jan. 16, 1791	2	128
Charlotte A., of East Haddam, m. Halsey B. **LUCAS**, of Manchester, June 16, 1852, by Rev. Warren Emmerson	3	236
Ebenezer, s. Samuell & Eleanor, b. May 3, 1730; d. May 3, 1730	LR2	1127
Ebenezer, d. Richard & Elizabeth, b. May 10, 1741	LR2	1106
Ebenezer, s. Thomas & Anne, b. June 8, 1743	LR2	1094
Eli, s. Nehemiah & Hannah, b. Feb. 21, 1753	LR3	13
Elizabeth, d. Samuell & Lydia(?), b. Apr. 15, 1709(?)	LR1	583
Elizabeth, d. Richard & Elizabeth, b. June 24, 1750	LR2	1105
Elizabeth, d. Richard & Elizabeth, b. June 24, 1750	LR2	1106
Elizabeth, d. Samuell & Elizabeth, d. Dec. 24, 1751	LR1	583
Elizabeth, d. Asahel & Sarah, b. Mar. 29, 1769	LR7	415

	Vol.	Page
ANDREWS, ANDREW, ANDREWES, ANDREWSS, ANDRUS, (cont.)		
Elizabeth, m. Noah **WILLEY**, Jr., b. of East Haddam, Oct. 25, 1770	2	180
Elizabeth C., ae 18, b. in East Haddam, m. Albert J. **THOMAS**, joiner, ae 23, b. in East Haddam, res. Chatham, Oct. 17, 1848, by Henry Forbush	4	9-10
Ellenah, d. Samuell & Ellenah, b. Mar. 12, 1713	LR1	9
Ephraim H., s. Ephraim R., ae 35, & Rhoda, ae 36, b. Jan. 15, 1849	4	11-12
Ephraim R., m. Rhoda A. **SCOVILL**, b. of East Haddam, Jan. 2, 1837, by Rev. Stephen Beach	3	151
Ephraim R., ship carpenter, d. Nov. 9, 1848, ae 35	4	17-18
Ephraim Robbins, s. [Gideon Spencer & Jemima Hill], b. Feb. 1, 1813	3	171
Esther, d. Richard & Esther, b. June 15, 1738	LR2	1118
Esther, w. of Richard, d. June 25, 1738	LR2	1118
Esther, d. Joseph & Mable, b. Jan. 10, 1779	2	78
Esther, m. Jonathan **MARTIN**, b. of East Haddam, Apr. 29, 1802	2	273
Eunice, d. Samuel & Jemima, b. July 9, 1742	LR2	1107
Ezra, s. Samuel & Mary Lee, b. Mar. 3, 1787	2	162
Finette, m. Albert C. **COFFIN**, Apr. 20, 1834, by Rev. Stephen Beach	3	133
Fuller, m. Harriet **BOOGE**, Oct. 17, 1826, by Rev. Simeon Dickinson, at the house of John Booge	3	88-9
Gideon S., s. [Gideon Spencer & Jemima Hill], b. Feb. 8, 1817	3	171
Gideon Spencer, s. John & Mable, b. Jan. 17, 1792	2	78
Gideon Spencer, m. Jemima Hill **SAWYER**, May 7, 1812	3	171
Hannah, d. Samuell & Ellener, b. July 18, 1714	LR3	9
Hannah, m. Gideon **ACKLY**, Mar. 24, 1737	LR2	1115
Hannah, d. Nehemiah & Hannah, b. May 23, 1748	LR3	13
Harriet L., ae 22, b. in Glastonbury, res. East Haddam, m. Alden **BEEBE**, joiner, ae 24, of East Haddam, Nov. 18, 1848, by Henry Forbush	4	9-10
James, s. Zepheniah & Mercy, b. Jan. 22, 1769	2	28
Jedidah, m. Nehemiah **CONE**, b. of East Haddam,Jan. 17, 1765	LR7	417
John, s. Richard & Elizabeth, b. July 17, 1746	LR2	1106
John, s. Asael & Sarah, b. Oct. 20, 1780	2	88
John, m. Lucy **CONE**, b. of East Haddam, Sept. 26, 1781	2	128
John, s. John & Lucy, b. July 9, 1782	2	128
Joseph, s. Richard & Elizabeth, b. Nov. 3, 1752	LR2	1106
Joseph, of East Haddam, m. Mable **ROBERTS**, of Middletown, May 17, 1774	2	78
Joseph, s. Joseph & Mable, b. Jan. 19, 1781	2	78
Joseph Richard, [s. Gideon Spencer & Jemima Hill], b. June 29, 1821	3	171

	Vol.	Page
ANDREWS, ANDREW, ANDREWES, ANDREWSS, ANDRUS, (cont.)		
Joseph Rowley, s. Asael & Sarah, b. July 25, 1778	2	88
Lebbeus, s. Zepheniah & Mercy, b. Dec. 31, 1770	2	28
Lois, d. Samuel & Jemima, b. Feb. 5, 1739/40	LR2	1107
Lois, d. Samuel & Jemima, d. June 27, 1743	LR2	1107
Lois, d. Samuel & Jemima, b. Aug. 31, 1744	LR2	1107
Lucy, d. John & Lucy, b. Sept. 14, 1788	2	128
Lucy, 1st, d. John & Lucy, d. Dec. 17, 1788	2	129
Lucy, 2d, d. John & Lucy, b. Feb. 1, 1793	2	128
Mable, d. Joseph & Mable, b. Dec. 2, 1787	2	78
Marcy, d. Zephaniah & Marcy, b. Aug. 13, 1761	LR6	510
Marcy, m. Josiah **LYON**, b. of East Haddam, Oct. 10, 1785	2	114
Marquis, s. John & Lucy, b. Sept. 21, 1786	2	128
Mary, d. Samuell & Ellener, b. Dec. 2, 1710	LR1	9
Mary, d. Richard & Elizabeth, b. Aug. 7, 1745	LR2	1106
Mary, d. Richard & Elizabeth, d. Sept. 5, 1745	LR2	1106
Mary, d. Zephaniah & Marcy, b. May 21, 1765	LR6	510
Mary, d. Ashael & Sarah, b. Apr. 14, 1767	LR7	415
Mary, m. Samuel **LORD**, b. of East Haddam, Apr. 27, 1785	2	142
Mary, d. Samuel & Mary Lee, b. Sept. 10, 1785	2	162
Mehittabell, d. Samuell & Eleanor, b. May 11, 1724	LR2	1127
Mehetabel, d. Nehemiah & Hannah, b. Sept. 4, 1746	LR3	13
Melissa Cone, d. [Gideon Spencer & Jemima Hill], b. Mar. 4, 1824	3	171
Nathaniel, s. Samuel, Jr. & Jemima, b. Apr. 30, 1749	LR4	475
Nathaniel, s. Samuel, Jr. & Jemima, d. Sept. 2, 1753	LR4	475
Nehemiah, s. Samuell & Ele[a]ner, b. May 18, 1722	LR2	1127
Nehemiah, m. Hannah **BORDEN**, Oct. 31, 1745	LR3	13
Nehemiah, s. Nehemiah & Hannah, b. June 29, 1750	LR3	13
Oliver, s. Thomas & Anne, b. July 29, 1741	LR2	1094
Oliver Robards, s. Joseph & Mable, b. Apr. 21, 1783	2	78
Phylamon, s. Zephaniah & Marcy, b. May 7, 1763	LR6	510
Rachel, d. Samuel & Elliner, b. Aug. 17, 1732	LR2	1119
Rachel, m. Jason **MILLARD**, b. of East Haddam, May 17, 1750	LR6	509
Richard, s. Samuell & Ellener, b. Jan. 17, 1711/12	LR1	9
Richard, m. Esther **CONE**, June 16, 1737	LR2	1118
Richard, m. Elizabeth **ACKLEY**, July 10, 1740	LR2	1106
Richard, d. Oct. 29, 1785, in the 74th y. of his age	2	101
Samuel, m. Eliner **LOE**, Nov. 18, 1708	LR1	6
Samuell, s. Samuell & Ellener, b. Sept. 20, 1709	LR1	9
Samuel, m. Mary **HOLMES**, June 1, 1736	LR2	1119
Samuel, Jr., m. Jemima **CONE**, Nov. 23, 1738	LR2	1107
Samuel, s. Samuel & Jemima, b. June 16, 1746	LR2	1107
Samuel, s. Samuel, Jr. & Jemima, d. Aug. 21, 1750	LR4	475
Samuel, s. Samuel, Jr. & Jemima, b. Apr. 12, 1751	LR4	475
Samuel, s. Samuel, Jr. & Jemima, d. Sept. 11, 1753	LR4	475

	Vol.	Page
ANDREWS, ANDREW, ANDREWES, ANDREWSS, ANDRUS, (cont.)		
Samuel, s. Nehemiah & Hannah, b. Jan. 18, 1755	LR3	13
Samuell, d. Dec. 14, 1758	LR2	1127
Samuel, s. Zephaniah & Marcy, b. Feb. 23, 1760	LR6	510
Samuel, m. Mary Lee **KNOWLTON**, b. of East Haddam, Apr. 10, 1783	2	162
Samuel, s. Samuel & Mary Lee, b. May 4, 1784	2	162
Sarah, d. Samuell & Ellener, b. Feb. 13, 1715/16	LR1	9
Sarah, m. Christopher **HOLMES**, Mar. 2, 1736	LR2	1103
Sarah, d. Asahel & Sarah, b. Aug. 3, 1765	LR7	415
Sarah A., m. Benjamin F. **AYRES**, Aug. 30, 1841, by Nathaniel Miner	3	186
Seymour L., merchant, d. Jan. 1, 1850, ae 25	4	29-30
Statira, d. Joseph & Mable, b. Mar. 30, 1776	2	78
Susannah, d. Samuell & Ele[a]nor, b. Oct. 11, 1726	LR2	1127
Susannah, d. Asael & Sarah, b. Apr. 7, 1771	2	88
Temperance P., m. Timothy Wheeler **PELLET**, Sept. 30, 1832, by Rev. Isaac Parsons	3	125
Temperance Pamelia, d. [Gideon Spencer & Jemima Hill], b. Jan. 30, 1815	3	171
Thomas, s. Samuell & Elizabeth, b. Mar. 3, 1720	LR1	583
Thomas, m. Anne **CONE**, May 29, 1740	LR2	1094
Thomas, s. Thomas & Anne, b. Aug. 15, 1746	LR2	1094
Timothy Fuller, s. Zepheniah & Mercy, b. July 20, 1778	2	28
Uriel, s. Zephaniah & Mercy, b. Feb. 3, 1773	2	28
Warren, s. Zepheniah & Mercy, b. July 20, 1781	2	28
Wells, s. John & Lucy, b. Jan. 6, 1796	2	128
Wells, s. John & Lucy, d. Dec. 7, 1801	2	129
Wells C., of Haddam, m. Delia C. **LAY**, of East Haddam, Mar. 29, 1848, by Rev. Levi H. Wakeman	3	212
William Wright, [s. Gideon Spencer & Jemima Hill], b. Jan. 17, 1819	3	171
Zefeniah, s. Samuell & Ele[a]nor, b. May 9, 1728	LR2	1127
Zephaniah, of East Haddam, m. Marcy **TUBBS**, of Lyme, Apr. 17, 1759	LR6	510
-----, s. Samuell & Elizabeth, b. Oct. 24, 1718	LR1	583
ANDRUS, [see under **ANDREWS**]		
ANNABLE, ANABLE, Abigail, d. David & Esther, b. Dec. 13, 1758	LR5	b
Abner, s. David & Esther, b. Nov. 26, 1752	LR5	b
Abraham, s. David & Esther, b. Aug. 17, 1760	LR5	b
Anna, m. Calvin **SMITH**, b. of East Haddam, Jan. 15, 1784	2	204
Anne, d. Cornielius & Experience, b. Feb. 23, 1728/9	LR3	507
Ansel, s. Cornielius & Experience, b. Jan. 29, 1736/7	LR3	507
Asenath, d. Joseph & Temperance, b. Feb. 4, 1756	LR4	471
Aseneth, d. John & Hannah, b. Apr. 6, 1783	2	200
Cornielius, s. Cornielius & Experience, b. Apr. 28, 1736	LR3	507
David, m. Esther **CHAPMAN**, Jan. 13, 1751	LR5	b

	Vol.	Page
ANNABLE, ANABLE, (cont.)		
Elijah, s. Cornielius & Experience, b. June 27, 1741	LR3	507
Esther, d. David & Esther, b. Nov. 3, 1756	LR5	b
Esther, see also Esther **ISHAM**	2	9
Hannah, d. John & Hannah, b. Nov. 16, 1775	2	200
Henry, s. John & Hannah, b. July 8, 1788	2	200
John, s. Cornielius & Experience, b. Apr. 18, 1744	LR3	507
John, s. John & Hannah, b. Mar. 16, 1780	2	200
Joseph, s. John & Hannah, b. July 18, 1773	2	200
Martha, d. Joseph & Temperance, b. Aug. 20, 1748	LR4	471
Mary, d. Joseph & Temperance, b. Feb. 25, 1752	LR4	471
Mary, m. Nathan **BURNHAM**, b. of East Haddam (or said to be) Feb. 7, 1771	LR8	4
Mehitable, d. Corneilius & Experience, b. Sept. 4, 1731	LR3	507
Mehitable, m. Jeremiah **BRAINERD**, Sept. 30, 1750	LR4	469
Reuben, s. John & Hannah, b. Mar. 7, 1771	2	200
Reuben, s. John & Hannah, d. Mar. 29, 1777	2	201
Rhoda Jewett, d. John & Hannah, b. Dec. 30, 1777	2	200
Samuel, s. John & Hannah, b. Mar. 30, 1786	2	200
Sarah, d. Joseph & Temperance, b. Apr. 25, 1754	LR4	471
Susannah, d. Cornielius & Experience, b. Apr. 23, 1733	LR3	507
Susannah had s. Gideon **BUCKINGHAM**, b. Sept. 22, 1786; reputed father Gideon **BUCKINGHAM**	2	4
Temperance, d. Cornielius & Experience, b. Apr. 15, 1747	LR3	507
Temparance, d. John & Hannah, b. Mar. 5, 1769	2	200
Temparance, d. John & Hannah, d. Feb. 9, 1785	2	201
ARCHER, ARCKER, Mary, m. Crippen **HURD**, Jan. 18, 1749/50	LR4	473
Sarah, m. Peter **FREEMAN**, Oct. 7, 1781	2	10
ARCKER, [see under **ARCHER**]		
ARNOLD, Aaron, s. Enoch & Abigail, b. Feb. 9, 1759	LR3	12
Almira P., of East Haddam, m. David S. **RANNY**, of Chatham, June 2, 1850, by Rev. Isaac Parsons	3	225
Almira P., ae 22, b. in Saybrook, res. E. Haddam, m. David S. **RAMSEY**, shoemaker, ae 22, b. in Middle Haddam, res. E. Haddam, June 2, 1850, by Isaac Parsons	4	19-20
Anna, d. Enoch & Dorothy, b. Jan. 1, 1750	LR3	12
Caroline E., of East Haddam, m. Seth **HIGGINS**, of Chatham, Mar. 3, 1833, by Nathaniel Miner	3	131
Charles, 2d, of Haddam, m. Eliza Ann **BINGHAM**, of East Haddam, May 19, 1839, by Charles William Bradley	3	172
Charlotte, d. Joseph, Jr. & Lucy, b. Sept. 13, 1763	LR7	7
Curtis S., of East Haddam, m. Phebe **TUCKER**, of Haddam, Sept. 13, 1840, by Rev. Moses Stoddard	3	182-3
Curtis S., of East Haddam, m. Irene H. **FLOOD**, of Middle Haddam, Nov. 26, 1848, by Rev. Levi H. Wakeman	3	215
Curtis S., shoemaker, ae 25, b. East Haddam, res. Haddam, m. Irena **FLOOD**, ae 24, b. in Haddam, res. Haddam, Nov. 20, 1848, by Levi H. Wakeman	4	9-10

	Vol.	Page
ARNOLD, (cont.)		
Curtis S., ae 63, b. in Haddam, res. East Haddam, m. Mrs. Eleanor P. **BULLONIA**, ae 50, b. in Willimantic, res. East Haddam, Aug. 31, 1856, by Jonathan O. Cone, J. P. Int. pub. Aug. 31, 1856	4	93-94
Cynthia M., of East Haddam, m. Benjamin F. **BREWSTER**, of Springfield, Mass.,May 8, 1842, by Augustus Olmsted,J. P.	3	190
Daniel, s. Enoch & Abigail, b. June 9, 1757	LR3	12
Dorothy, d. Enoch & Dorothy, b. June 2, 1746	LR3	12
Dorothy, w. of Enoch, d. June 24, 1754	LR3	12
Dorothy, m. Joseph **GILBERT**, b. of East Haddam, May 18, 1769	2	70
Eliphalet L., of Haddam, m. Clarissa H. **CONE**, of East Haddam, Nov. 12, 1826, by Rev. Simeon Shailer	3	90
Elizabeth, [twin with Lidiah], d. Josiah & Lydia, b. Nov. 15, 1743	LR2	1097
Elizabeth, m. Elijah **WHITE**, Jr., May 9, 1767	LR7	412
Elizabeth M., m. Lyman **BURKE**, b. of East Haddam, Dec. 12, 1853, by Rev. W. Emerson	3	238a
Emeline, m. William L. **FULLER**, Sept. 17, 1845, by Nathaniel Miner, Millington	3	203
Enoch, m. Dorothy **EM[M]ONS**, b. of East Haddam, June 16, 1743	LR3	12
Enoch, of East Haddam, m. Abigail **WILLIAMS**, of Colchester, Apr. 23, 1755	LR3	12
Flavia, see under Fluvia		
Fluvia A., m. Lord W. **CONE**, b. of East Haddam, Jan. 1, 1837, by Rev. Nathaniel Miner	3	146
Fluvia A., m. Lord W. **CONE**, Jan. 1, 1837	3	242
Horace, m. Polly Maria **STEPHENS**, b. of East Haddam, Oct. 30, 1836, by W[illia]m Marsh, J. P.	3	145
Isaiah, s. Joseph & Lucy, b. Dec. 29, 1772	LR7	7
Jira, s. Enoch & Abigail, b. Dec. 22, 1761	LR3	12
John, m. Mrs, Elisabeth **FULLER**, b. of East Haddam, Nov. 13, 1785	2	82
Jonathan, s. Enoch & Dorothy, b. May 21, 1754	LR3	12
Joseph, Jr., m. Lucy **BARN**, b. of East Haddam, May 13, 1761	LR7	7
Joseph, s. Joseph & Lucy, b. Oct. 16, 1766	LR7	7
Joseph, m. Mary F. **BLISH**, Feb. 11, 1824, by Russell Dutton, J. P.	3	54-5
Joseph H., m. Harriet M. **SWAN**, b. of East Haddam, Sept. 25, 1854, by Rev. Nathaniel Miner	3	240
Joseph H., cooper, ae 28, m. Harriet M. **SWAN**, ae 16, b. of E. Haddam, Sept. 25, 1854, by Rev. Nathaniel Miner	4	41-2
Joseph H., cooper, ae 28, m. Harriet M. **SWAN**, ae 16, Sept. 25, 1854, by Rev. Nathaniel Miner	4	51-2
Josiah, m. Lydia **SMITH**, Feb. 24, 1742/3	LR2	1097
Josiah, s. Josiah & Lydia, b. Aug. 29, 1745	LR2	1097

	Vol.	Page
ARNOLD, (cont.)		
Josiah, m. Hannah **CONTE**, May 29, 1755	LR5	562
Justin, m. Sarah **BLISH**, b. of East Haddam, Feb. 4, 1840, by Rev. Nathaniel Miner	3	174
Lucy, d. Joseph & Lucy, b. Feb. 24, 1769	LR7	7
Lidiah, [twin with Elizabeth], d. Josiah & Lydia, b. Nov. 15, 1743	LR2	1097
Lydia, w. Josiah, d. May 31, 1747	LR2	1097
Lydiah, m. Ezekiel **CROCKER**, b. of East Haddam, Feb. 28, 1765	LR7	7
Mary, d. Enoch & Dorothy, b. Feb. 1, 1748	LR3	12
Mary, d. Joseph & Lucy, b. July 21, 1774	LR7	7
Nancy, m. Cha[rle]s **MINER**, b. of East Haddam, June 13, [1841], by [Rev. Nathaniel Miner]	3	186
Olive, m. William **BURKE**, b. of East Haddam, [May] 27, [1821], by Rev. W[illia]m Lyman	3	5
Phebe, b. in Haddam, res. East Haddam, married, d. Oct. 8, 1855, ae 54 y.	4	73
Phebe A., m. David **POTTER**, b. of East Haddam, Sept. 19, 1847, by Rev. Levi H. Wakeman	3	210
Phebe A., of East Haddam, m. David **POTTER**, mechanic, ae 23, of East Haddam, Sept. [ ], 1848, by L. H. Wakeman	4	1-2
Ruth, d. Enoch & Dorothy, b. Apr. 26, 1744	LR3	12
Ruth, d. Enoch & Dorothy, d. Oct. 7, 1744	LR3	12
Ruth, m. Philip **WILLIAMS**, b. of East Haddam, Feb. 24, 1761	LR3	4
Samuel, d. Mar. 20, 1739	LR2	1116
Sarah, m. Richard **BOOGE**, Jan. 22, 1729/30	LR2	1128
Sarah, m. Isaiah **BARNES**, b. of East Haddam, Jan. 12, 1756	LR6	504
Sarah, of East Haddam, m. John **WATSON**, of Lebanon, Feb. 26, 1761	LR6	504
Sarah, d. Joseph, Jr. & Lucy, b. Mar. 22, 1762	LR7	7
Selden, of Haddam, m. Dorothy **OLMSTED**, of East Haddam, Nov. 12, 1839, by Rev. Isaac Parsons	3	173
Serena A., s. Horace E., shoemaker, b. Mar. 3, 1851	4	33-4
Serena A., d. Apr. 8, 1853, ae 2 y. 1 m.	4	49-50
Stella, Mrs., of East Haddam, m. Dr. David **JOHNSON**, of Colchester, Apr. 29, 1799, by Rev. W[illia]m Lyman	2	261
Theodosia, of East Haddam, m. Jonathan S. **GREEN**, Rev., of Andover, Mass., Sept. 20, 1827, by Rev. Isaac Parsons	3	95
-----, s. Edward, dentist, ae 30, & Francis M., ae 27, b. Aug. 18, 1856	4	100
ARTHUR, Alexander, of Chatham, m. Rebecca R. **WORTHINGTON**, of East Haddam, Jan. 18, 1832, by Rev. Isaac Parsons	3	121
ASHCRAFT, Abby J., m. Henry T. **HOLMES**, b. of East Haddam, Mar. 17, 1850, by Rev. Levi H. Wakeman	3	223
Abby T., ae 32, m. Henry J. **HOLMES**, farmer, ae 35, b. of E. Haddam, Mar. 25, 1850, by E. H. Wakeman	4	19-20

	Vol.	Page
ASHCRAFT, (cont.)		
Laura, m. Joshua Brainerd **ELY**, Nov. 29, 1837, by Rev.Isaac Parsons	3	159
Phebe H., of East Haddam, m. Ezra M. **LAY**, of Lyme, June 22, 1845, by Rev. W[illia]m S. Simmons, at the Methodist Chapel, Moodus	3	202
ATWELL, ATWEL, Anna, m. William **BEAN**, June 7, 1762	LR6	a
Betsey A., ae 16, of East Haddam, m. Ja[me]s **STEPHENS**, farmer, ae 24, b. in Colchester, res. East Haddam, Aug. 5, 1848, by David Chapman	4	9-10
Betsey Ann, m. Joseph S. **STEPHENS**, Aug. 5, 1849, by David A. Chapman	3	219
Sahpenus, d. Hezekiah & Anne, b. Dec. 30, 1757	LR5	a
----, s. Benjamin, factory operative, ae 28, & Clarissa, ae 28, b. June 18, 1850	4	23-4
ATWOOD, ATTWOOD, Alice, d. Elijah & Anna, b. Apr. 12, 1772	LR7	5
Alice, d. Elijah & Anna, b. Apr. 12, 1772	2	206
Almira, m. Epaphroditus **DICKINSON**, Dec. 21, 1825, by Rev. Simeon Dickinson, at the house of Capt. Oliver Attwood	3	83
Ann Eliza, d. Whiting & Deborah, b. Dec. 22, 1810	2	262
Anna, d. Elijah & Anna, b. Feb. 14, 1757	LR7	5
Anna, d. Elijah & Anna, b. Feb. 16, 1757	2	206
Anna, w. of Elijah, d. Apr. 12, 1774, ae 40 y.	2	207
Anna, d. Elijah & Anne, d. July 16, 1791, ae 34 y.	2	207
Anna, d. Oliver & Dorothy, b. Oct. 4, 1792	2	259
Anna, d. Oliver & Dorothy, m. Richard **LORD**, Sept. 29, 1811	2	260
Annette M., d. Whiting & Deborah, b. July 28, 1826	2	262
Annette M., d. Whiting & Deborah, d. July 27, 1844	2	262
Bertha Palmer, d. [Julius & Catharine], b. Aug. 21, 1864	2	262
Bertha Palmer, d. Julius & Catharine P., b. Aug. 21, 1864	3	245-6
Charles, s. Oliver & Dorothy, b. Mar. 19, 1795	2	259
Charles, m. Mary **HOLMES**, b. of East Haddam, Nov. 29, 1832, by R. S. Crampton, V. D. M.	3	128
Charles, of East Haddam, m. Julia A. **CHAPMAN**, of Whateley, Mass., Dec. 31, 1837, by John C. Palmer, J. P.	3	160
Daniel, of East Haddam, m. Meriam **WILLEY**, of Lyme, Dec. 4, 1764	LR8	5
Deborah, w. of Whiting, d. Mar. 21, 1860	2	262
Deborah Purple, w. of Whiting, b. Apr. 25, 1788	2	262
Deliverance, [twin with Meriam], d. Daniel & Meriam, b. Aug. 15, 1768	LR8	5
Edward P., s. Whiting & Deborah, b. Feb. 10, 1818	2	262
Elijah, m. Anna **GOODSPEED**, b. of East Haddam, Nov. 21, 1754	LR7	5
Elijah, m. Anna **GOODSPEED**, b. of East Haddam, Nov. 21, 1754	2	206
Elijah, s. Elijah & Anna, b. Nov. 5, 1760	LR7	5

	Vol.	Page
ATWOOD, ATTWOOD, (cont.)		
Elijah, s. Elijah & Anna, b. Nov. 5, 1760	2	206
Elijah, of East Haddam, m. Mrs. Mary **BAILEY**, of Haddam, Nov. 10, 1774	2	206
Elijah, Jr., Capt., d. June 9, 1806, ae 46	2	207
Elijah, Capt., d. Aug. 4, 1806, ae 82	2	207
Elijah Whiting, s. Whiting & Deborah, b. Nov. 26, 1815	2	262
Eliza Ann, m. Ahira D. **WHEELER**, Mar. 7, 1831, by Rev. Isaac Parsons	3	115
Elizabeth had d. Elizabeth **LYON**, b. Aug. 1, 1762; reputed father Humphrey **LYON**	LR8	5
Esther, d. Whiting & Deborah, b. Oct. 18, 1813	2	262
Esther, w. of Elijah, Jr., d. Dec. 23, 1813, ae 53	2	207
Esther, d. Whiting & Deborah, d. Sept. 24, 1817	2	262
Frederick J., [s. Julius & Sarah A.], b. Aug. 19, 1853, at Stony Brook	2	262
Frederick Julius, s. Julius & Sarah A., b. Aug. 18, 1853, at Stony Brook, L. I.	3	245-6
Harriet, d. Elijah, Jr., d. Jan. 24, 1810, ae 21	2	207
Harriet L., d. Whiting & Deborah, b. Jan. 29, 1809	2	262
Isaac, s. Elijah & Anna, b. Oct. 10, 1763	LR7	5
Isaac, s. Elijah & Anna, b. Oct. 10, 1763	2	206
John, s. Elijah & Anna, b. Apr. 8, 1755	LR7	5
John, s. Elijah & Anna, b. Apr. 8, 1755	2	206
Joseph, s. Elijah & Anna, b. Aug. 14, 1767	LR7	5
Joseph, s. Elijah & Anna, b. Aug. 14, 1767	2	206
Joseph, s. Elijah & Anna, d. July 7, 1773	2	207
Joseph, s. Elijah & Mary, b. Sept. 30, 1775	2	206
Julia, m. William Wyllys **PRATT**, June 12, 1825, by Rev. William Jarvis	3	76-7
Julius, s. Whiting & Deborah, b. Feb. 23, 1824	2	262
Julius, b. Feb. 23, 1824; m. Sarah A. **GOULD**, Oct. 3, 1852, at Stony Brook, L. I.	2	262
Julius, b. Feb. 23, 1824	3	245-6
Julius, m. Sarah Antoinette **GOULD**, Oct. 3, 1852, by Rev. Frederick M. Noll, at Stony Brook, L. I.	3	245-6
Julius, m. Catharine **PALMER**, d. of Brainard & Eunice, Oct. 22, 1862	2	262
Julius, m. Catharine **PALMER**, Oct. 22, 1862	3	245-6
Kelly, s. Elijah & Mary, b. Mar. 12, 1777	2	206
Lusenda, d. Elijah & Anna, b. June 19, 1769	LR7	5
Lucenda, d. Elijah & Anna, b. June 19, 1769	2	206
Lucinda, d. Elijah & Anna, d. July 15, 1773	2	207
Lucynda, d. Elijah & Anna, b. Mar. 4, 1774	2	206
Maria, d. Oliver & Dorothy, b. July 20, 1796	2	259
Meriam, [twin with Deliverance], d. Daniel & Meriam, b. Aug. 15, 1768	LR8	5
Oliver, s. Elijah & Anna, b. Oct. 12, 1765	LR7	5

	Vol.	Page
ATWOOD, ATTWOOD, (cont.)		
Oliver, s. Elijah & Anna, b. Oct. 12, 1765	2	206
Oliver, m. Dorothy **CHAPMAN**, b. of East Haddam, Jan. 23, 1792	2	259
Rachel, d. Elijah & Mary, b. Jan. [ ], 1779	2	206
Sally, d. Elijah & Mary, b. Mar. 30, 1783	2	206
Sarah, d. Daniel & Meriam, b. Mar. 29, 1766	LR8	5
Sarah A., w. of Julius, d. Apr. 5, 1860	2	262
Sarah Antoinette, d. Apr. 5, 1860	3	247
Sarah C., m. Amos S. **HARVEY**, Dec. 10, 1849, by Rev. Alpheas Geer	3	220
Sarah E., ae 23, of E. Haddam, m. Amos S. **HARVEY**, mechanic, ae 25, b. in Colchester, res. E. Haddam, Dec. 10, 1849, by Rev. Alpheas Geer	4	21-2
Temperance, d. Elijah & Mary, b. July 23, 1785	2	206
Whiting, s. Elijah, Jr. & Esther, b. May 17, 1787	2	262
Whiting, d. June 27, 1829	2	262
William H., s. Whiting & Deborah, b. Feb. 21, 1830	2	262
AUSTIN, Peter, m. Eliza Ann **RANSOM**, June 9, 1839, by David D. Field, in Millington. Int. pub. in Bozrahville, by H. Mowry	3	172
AVERY, Abby G., m. Joseph H. **CONKLING**, b. of Lyme, Nov. 20, 1836, by Rev. Nathaniel Miner	3	146
Darius, b. in Groton, res. East Haddam, d. Dec. 13, 1847, ae 58	4	7-8
David, of Chaplin, m. Rebecca B. **MORGAN**, of East Haddam, Apr. 11, 1830, by Isaac Parsons	3	107
Eunice, of Grotton, m. Caleb **BEEBE**, Jr., of East Haddam, Jan. 21, 1761	LR6	a
AYER, AYRES, AYERS, Aaron Lyon, s. [Hubart & Susannah], b. May 14, 1810	3	111
Amelia J., ae 21, b. at East Haddam, res. East Haddam, m. Edwin B. **CHIPMAN**, ae 28, b. at New London, res. New London, Apr. 1, 1856, by Rev. Nathaniel Miner. Int. pub. Mar. 31, 1856	4	85
Benjamin F., m. Sarah A. **ANDREWS**, Aug. 30, 1841, by Nathaniel Miner	3	186
Benjamin Franklin, s. [Hubart & Susannah], b. Jan. 10, 1816	3	111
Elizabeth E., ae 19, m. Harlow **MARTIN**, farmer, ae 28, of E. Haddam, Apr. 15, 1851, by Nathaniel Miner	4	37-8
George Levi, s. [Hubart & Susannah], b. Mar. 18, 1827	3	111
Hannah, of Saybrook, m. Gibbons **JEWETT**, of East Haddam, June 12, 1760; d. Dec. 25, 1760	LR6	510
Henry S., ae 24, b. in East Haddam, res. East Haddam, m. Eliza G. **BRAINERD**, ae 19, b. in East Haddam, res. East Haddam, Aug. 24, 1856, at the Parsonage, by Rev. Nelson Goodrich. Int. pub. Aug. 22, 1856	4	93
Herbert, m. Laura **MARTIN**, Jan. 19, 1840, by Rev. Charles William Bradley	3	174

	Vol.	Page
AYER, AYRES, AYERS, (cont.)		
Hubart, m. Susannah **LYON**, [1807?]	3	111
Huldah Abby, d. [Hubart & Susannah], b. May 3, 1818	3	111
Joshua Bulkley, s. [Hubart & Susannah], b. Mar. 10, 1820	3	111
Julia Louisa, m. Harlow **MARTIN**, b. of East Haddam, Apr. 13, 1851, by Nathaniel Miner	3	232
Lydia Alzina, d. [Hubart & Susannah], b. Nov. 10, 1813	3	111
Mariah M., m. Ozias H. **PARKER**, b. of East Haddam, Nov. 29, 1849, by Nathaniel Miner	3	221
Mary E., m. Casper S. **GLADWIN**, b. of East Haddam, Dec. 19, 1850, by Charles Attwood, J. P.	3	229
Mary Eliza, ae 14, m. Casper **GLADWIN**, joiner, ae 16, of E. Haddam, [ ], 1851, by Charles Atwood	4	37-8
Mary Louisa, d. [Hubart & Susannah], b. July 18, 1822	3	111
Mary M., ae 21, m. Ozias **PARKER**, tanner, ae 26, b. of East Haddam, Nov. 29, 1849, by Rev. Nathaniel Miner	4	19-20
Mercy Maria, d. [Hubart & Susannah], b. May 28, 1829	3	111
Ribinah, child of Urial A., farmer, ae 35, & Maria, ae 35, b. July 4, 1848	4	3-4
Thomas Andrews Lyon, s. [Hubart & Susannah],b. Oct. 16,1824	3	111
Uriel Andrews, s. [Hubart & Susannah], b. Feb. 27, 1812	3	111
William Hubart, s. [Hubart & Susannah], b. Aug. 25, 1808	3	111
William Hubart, m. Julia Ann **MARTIN**, Sept. 5, 1830, by Rev. Alvan Ackley	3	108
AYRAULT, Allen, of Moscow, N. Y., m. Bethia **LYMAN**, of East Haddam, Sept. 9, 1822, by Rev. W[illia]m Lyman	3	26-7
BABCOCK, Ellen S., m. Hobart C. **PALMER**, Jan. 8, 1850, by Rev. Alpheas Geer	3	222
Josephine A., of East Haddam, m. Samuel S. **GILLETT**, of Colchester, Aug. 29, 1838, by Rev. Isaac Parsons	3	166
Julia Ann, m. Waite **EASTON**, Sept. 1, 1836, by Jed[edia]h R. Gardiner, J. P.	3	145
Lucy A., dressmaker, ae 23, b. in Lebanon, res. Norwich, m. Joseph E. **HOWELL**, farmer, ae 22, of Hadlyme, Sept. 1, 1850, by Nathan Weldman	4	37-8
William, of Salem, m. Charlotte **THOMPSON**, of East Haddam, Nov. 21, 1837, by Nathan Jewett, Jr., J. P.	3	160
BACKEN, Elizabeth, m. James **PASAVELL**, July 9, 1730	LR2	1126
BAILEY, BAYLE, Charles D., of Hartford, m. Elizabeth S. **GATES**, of Hartford, Nov. 19, 1854, by Rev. Nathaniel Miner	3	241
Charles D., merchant, ae 35, b. in Middletown, res. Hartford, m. Elizabeth L. **GATES**, dressmaker, ae 31, b. in E. Haddam, res. Hartford, Nov. 19, 1854, by Rev. Nath[anie]l Miner	4	51-2
Elizabeth, m. John **BOOGE**, May 1, 1735	LR2	1120
Elizabeth. m. William **CONE**, Dec. 31, 1747	LR3	508
Elisabeth, of Killingsworth, m. Jonah **SPENCER**, of East Haddam, June 22, 1775	2	14

	Vol.	Page
BAILEY, BAYLE, (cont.)		
Jane E., ae 20, b. at Middle Haddam, res. East Haddam, m. J. Lewis **KING**, ae 23, b. at Athol, Mass., res. Brooklyn, N. Y., Oct. 1, 1855, at Moodus, by Rev. James M. Phillips. Int. Pub. Oct. 1, 1855	4	65
Josiah B., manufacturer, ae 21, of Glastonbury, m. Dinah B. **BAKER**, ae 21, of E. Hampton, Aug. 4, 1853, by Jacob Garner	4	45-6
Julia, m. Henry G. **SHAW**, b. of East Haddam, Nov. 26, 1843, by Rev. Samuel M. Emory, of Portland, in St. Stephen's Church, East Haddam	3	196
Lorenzo, of Middletown, m. Elizabeth F. **ACKLEY**, of East Haddam, Feb. 4, 1825, by Rev. Isaac Parsons	3	70-1
Mary, Mrs., of Haddam, m. Elijah **ATTWOOD**, of East Haddam, Nov. 10, 1774	2	206
Sarah Jane, Mrs., ae 35 y., b. at East Haddam, res. East Haddam, m. Elijah **WATROUS**, ae 38 y., b. at Colchester, res. Colchester, Dec. 6, 1855, at Leesville, by Rev. J. E. Heald. Int. Pub. Dec. 3, 1855	4	67-8
Washington A., of Chatham, m. Sarah Jane **ACKLEY**, of East Haddam, Aug. 30, 1840, by Isaac Parsons, V. D. M.	3	182-3
Washington A., stone cutter, b. in Chatham, res. E. Haddam, d. Jan. 14, 1850, ae 33	4	29-30
BAKER, Alice, d. Josiah J. & Alice, b. May 17, 1810	2	243
Alice, housekeeper, b. in Colchester, res. E. Haddam, d. Nov. 12, 1849, ae 69	4	29-30
Bayze, of East Haddam, m. Joanna **MINOR**, of Lyme, Oct. 22, 1791	2	243
Bets[e]y, w. of Josiah J., d. Apr. 24, 1804	2	244
Betsey, d. Josiah J. & Alice, b. Mar. 27, 1813	2	243
Constantine, s. Samuel & Mary, b. Nov. 4, 1749	LR3	12
Constantine, s. Samuel & Mary, b. Oct. 21, 1754	2	8
Dinah B., ae 21, of E. Hampton, m. Josiah B. **BAILEY**, manufacturer, ae 21, of Glastonbury, Aug. 4, 1853, by Jacob Gardner	4	45-6
Eliza, d. Josiah, J. & Bets[e]y, b. Dec. 20, 1803	2	243
Jacob, s. Samuel & Mary, b. Aug. 29, 1747	LR3	12
Jason H., ae 23, b. at Bloomfield, N. Y., res. East Haddam, m. Sarah E. **RANSOM**, ae 20, b. at East Haddam, res. East Haddam, Oct. 17, 1855, at Salem, by Rev. B. B. Hopkinson. Int. pub. Oct. 16, 1855, at East Haddam	4	64
Jeremiah, s. William & Marcy, b. Dec. 1, 1773	2	34
Jewett, s. Bayze & Joanna, b. Sept. 7, 1792	2	243
John, s. William & Marcy, b. Aug. 23, 1775	2	34
John, s. Josiah J. & Alice, b. Mar. 6, 1815	2	243
Josiah J., m. Bets[e]y **CHADWICK**, b. of East Haddam, Jan. 13, 1791	2	243
Josiah J., m. Alice **FOX**, Sept. 22, 1805	2	243

	Vol.	Page
BAKER, (cont.)		
Josiah Jewett, s. William & Marcy, b. Sept. 17, 1763	LR7	417
Marcy, d. William & Marcy, b. July 3, 1764	LR7	417
Nathaniel, s. Josiah J. & Alice, b. Dec. 1, 1807	2	243
Ruby, d. Josiah J. & Alice, b. June 26, 1806	2	243
Samuel, s. Joseph, of Tolland, m. Mary **SPENCER**, d. John, of East Haddam, Oct. 28, 1746	LR3	12
Samuel, s. Samuel & Mary, b. June 19, 1752	LR3	12
Samuel, s. Samuel & Mary, b. June 19, 1752	2	8
Sophia, d. Josiah J. & Bets[e]y, b. Jan. 26, 1792	2	243
William, m. Marcy **JEWETT**, June 12, 1760	LR7	417
William, d. Nov. 4, 1776	2	35
William, s. Josiah J. & Bets[e]y, b. Mar. 26, 1801	2	243
BALCOM, BALCAM, Helen, ae 21, b. in Mansfield, res. East Haddam, m. Nelson **BOWERS**, ae 21, b. in Norwich, res. East Haddam, May 22, 1856, by Rev. Isaac Parsons. Int. pub. May 7, 1856	4	87-8
Mary, of Winchester, m. Noadiah Brainard **GATES**, formerly of East Haddam, now of Barkhempstead, June 4, 1787	2	285
BALDWIN, Heman, of Chester, m. Julia E. **CHAPMAN**, of East Haddam, Aug. 5, 1838, by Rev. Isaac Parsons	3	164-5
BANNING, Abby M., of East Haddam, m. George W. **LAY**, of Lyme, Mar. 28, 1841, by Rev. Hiram Walden	3	185
Brainerd, s. Joseph & Susannah, b. May 6, 1785	2	184
David, s. Marvin & Allice, b. July 9, 1800	2	269
Elizabeth, of East Haddam, m. Amasa **JOHNSON**, of Manchester, May 19, 1839, by Rev. George Carrington, of Hadlyme	3	173
Irena, of Lyme, m. Joseph **WILLEY**, 2d, of East Haddam, Mar. 3, 1764	2	174
Joseph, of Lyme m. Susannah **WARNER**, of East Haddam, Dec. 2, 1773	2	184
Joseph, s. Joseph & Susannah, b. Mar. 2, 1780	2	184
Joseph, s. Marvin & Alice, b. Sept. 1, 1802	2	269
Marven, s. Joseph & Susannah, b. Nov. 1, 1774	2	184
Marvin, of East Haddam, m. Allice **PECK**, of Lyme, Oct. 2, 1799	2	269
Mary A., of East Haddam, m. William **ALBEE**, of Lyme, Mar. 29, 1835, by Rev. Hiram Walden	3	137
Mary E., m. William S. **BOGUE**, b. of Lyme, Oct. 18, 1843, by Rev. Stephen Alonzo Loper, of Hadlyme	3	195
Philemon Fuller, s. Joseph & Susannah, b. Apr. 10, 1787	2	184
Samuel, of East Haddam, m. Mrs. Catharine **BANTA**, of South Lyme, Apr. 23, 1857, at Hadlyme, by W[illia]m Harris	4	120
Sarah, m. Cha[rle]s **BROOKS**, [Mar.] 27, [1844], by Rev. Nathaniel Miner, Millington	3	200
Selden, s. Joseph & Susannah, b. Sept. 27, 1782	2	184
Susannah, d. Joseph & Susannah, b. Oct. 28, 1776	2	184

	Vol.	Page
BANTA, Catharine, Mrs., of South Lyme, m. Samuel **BANNING**, of East Haddam, Apr. 23, 1857, at Hadlyme, by W[illia]m Harris	4	120
BARBER, Epaphras Lord, s. Josiah & Sophia, b. Nov. 25, 1802	2	291
Harriet Eliza, d. Josiah & Sophia, b. Aug. 13, 1809	2	291
John G., ae 21, b. in Hebron, res. East Haddam, m. Leonora L. **FOWLER**, of East Haddam, Oct. 15, 1856, at Hartford, by Rev. W[illia]m Watton. Int. pub. Oct. 14, 1856, in East Haddam	4	103
Sophia Lord, d. Josiah & Sophia, b. Apr. 1, 1806	2	291
BARNARD, George, of Hartford, m. Mary B. **SMITH**, of East Haddam, May 25, 1831, by Rev. Isaac Parsons	3	116
BARNES, BARNS, Aaron, [twin with Ann], s. William & Mary, b. Sept. 20, 1740	LR2	1105
Aaron, s. Isaiah & Sarah, b. Dec. 1, 1766	LR6	504
Abigail, d. William & Mary, b. Jan. 2, 1704/5	LR1	5
Abigaill, m. Stephen **CONE**, June 6, 1724	LR2	e
Abigail, d. Isaiah & Sarah, b. Jan. 15, 1759	LR6	504
Ann, [twin with Aaron], d. William & Mary, b. Sept. 20, 1740	LR2	1105
Dan, s. Thomas & Rebeckah, b. Jan. 3, 1735/6	LR2	1115
Dorcas, d. Thomas & Rebeckah, b. Nov. 6, 1743	LR2	1115
Ellenner, d. Thomas & Rebeckah, b. Feb. 10, 1729/30	LR2	1115
Esther, d. Samuel & Lucy, b. June 3, 1738	LR3	13
Eunice, d. William & Mary, b. Nov. 11, 1736	LR2	1105
Eunice, d. Samuel & Lucy, b. May 20, 1746	LR3	13
Han[n]ah, d. William, b. Oct. (?) 15, 1709	LR1	8
Isaiah, s. Samuel & Lucy, b. Oct. [ ], 1734	LR3	13
Isaiah, m. Sarah **ARNOLD**, b. of East Haddam, Jan. 12, 1756	LR6	504
James, s. William & Mary, b. Mar. 28, 1738	LR2	1105
Jemima, d. Samuel & Lucy, b. Apr. 24, 1744	LR3	13
John, s. William & Mary, b. Apr. 12, 1725	LR2	e
Jonah, s. Thomas & Rebeckah, b. July 11, 1741	LR2	115
Lois, d. Isaiah & Sarah, b. May 15, 1761	LR6	504
Lucy, d. Samuel & Lucy, b. Apr. 14, 1740	LR3	13
Lucy, m. Joseph **ARNOLD**, Jr., b. of East Haddam, May 13, 1761	LR7	7
Lucy, w. Samuel, d. Jan. 20, 1766	LR3	13
Marcy, d. William & Mary, b. Mar. 9, 1733	LR2	1105
Mary, w. of William, d. Nov. 18, 1714	LR1	2
Mary, m. Daniell **CONE**, Dec. 25, 1718	LR2	1130
Mary, d. William & Mary, b. Jan. 11, 1726	LR2	e
Mary, d. Samuel & Lucy, b. Apr. 3, 1742	LR3	13
Mary, m. Matthew **CONE**, b. of East Haddam, June 24, 1760	LR6	505
Rebeckah, d. Thomas & Rebeckah, b. Dec. 16, 1737	LR2	1115
Samuel, m. Lucy **CONE**, b. of East Haddam, Nov. [ ], 1733	LR6	13
Samuel, s. Isaiah & Sarah, b. Jan. 12, 1757	LR6	504
Samuel, s. Isaiah & Sarah, d. Jan. 14, 1757	LR6	504

	Vol.	Page
BARNES, BARNS, (cont.)		
Samuel, s. Isaiah & Sarah, b. Sept. 18, 1763	LR6	504
Sarah, d. Samuel & Lucy, b. Mar. 20, 1736	LR3	13
Sarah, m. Simeon **CHAPMAN**, b. of East Haddam, May 21, 1760	LR6	504
Stephen, s. William & Mary, b. Nov. 5, 1730	LR2	e
Susan[n]ah, d. Thomas & Rebeckah, b. Aug. 14, 1739	LR2	1115
Thomas, s. William & Mary, b. Mar. 26, 1706	LR1	5
Thomas, m. Rebeckah **CONE**, Mar. 14, 1729	LR2	1115
Thomas, s. Thomas & Rebeckah, b. May 12, 1733	LR2	1115
William, m. Mary **CONE**, July 2, 1724	LR2	e
William, s. William & Mary, b. Jan. 16, 1728/9	LR2	e
BARRY, Carlos, s. [Samuel & Mary], b. June 28, 1830	3	117
Caroline Augusta, d. [Samuel & Mary], b. May 3, 1829	3	117
Francis, s. [Samuel & Mary], b. June 25, 1827	3	117
Samuel, m. Mary **WOODWORTH**, Nov. 3, 1823, by Rev. Daniel Austin, at Bozrah	3	117
Samuel Dewitt Clinton, s. [Samuel & Mary], b. Oct. 3, 1824	3	117
Wallace, s. [Samuel & Mary], b. Sept. 17, 1825	3	117
BARTHOLOMEY, Martha, of Wallingford, m. Timothy **DUTTON**, of East Haddam, Nov. 1, 1758	LR6	512
BARTLETT, Lucy, of Lebanon, m. Andrew **CHAMPION**, of East Haddam, Jan. 27, 1791	2	229
Smith, of Windham, m. Nancy Melinda **SNOW**, of East Haddam, Mar. 1, 1835, by Rev. Isaac Parsons	3	136
BARTMAN, Almira L., m. George **DANIELS**, Feb. 20, 1848, by Rev. Benjamin G. Goff	3	212
Ezra, farmer, ae 39, b. in Lyme, res. E. Haddam, d. Apr. 14, 1851, ae 39	4	39-0
Ezra W., m. Sarah **PAGEWOOD**, b. of East Haddam, May 3, 1846, by Rev. Alpheas Geer	3	205
John J., sailmaker, b. in London, res. E. Haddam, d. Apr. 1, 1850, ae 88	4	29-30
Sarah, housewife, ae 42, of E. Haddam, m. 2d h. Eleazer **SPENCER**, mechanic, ae 45, b. in Haddam, res. Chatham, Mar. 19, 1854	4	41-42
Sarah, house work, ae 42, of E. Haddam, m. 2d h. Eleazer **SPENCER**, mechanic, ae 45, b. in Haddam, res. Chatham, Mar. 19, 1854	4	51-52
------, s. William, ae 50, res. East Haddam, b. June 4, 1855	4	76
BASSETT, Clarissa A., of Guilford, m. George M. **STAPLES**, of Colchester, Jan. 1, 1839, by Rev. Isaac Parsons	3	167
BATELLE, Nathaniel, of Montgomery, Ala., m. Amanda G. **JOHNSON**, of East Haddam, Aug. 1, 1824, by Rev. Isaac Parsons	3	62-63
BATES, BATE, Abigail, d. James & Mary, b. Feb. 21, 1717/8	LR2	1119
Abigail, w. of Clement, d. July 4, 1734	LR2	1124
Abigail, d. Clement & Mary, b. Apr. 10, 1737	LR2	1124

	Vol.	Page
BATES, BATE, (cont.)		
Clement, m. Mary **STROBRIDGE**, Jan. 1, 1734/5	LR2	1124
Dorothy, d. Joseph & Elizabeth, b. Feb. 25, 1731/2	LR2	e
Dorothy, m. Ichabod **OLMSTEAD**, July 23, 1747	LR3	18
Elizabeth, d. Joseph & Elizabeth, b. Jan. 31, 1730/31	LR2	e
Ephraim, s. John & Marcy, b. Oct. 17, 1715	LR2	1129
Eunice, d. James & Mary, b. June 11, 1722	LR2	1119
Hannah, d. John & Marcy, b. Oct. 16, 1721	LR2	1129
Hannah, d. James & Dorothy, b. Sept. 13, 1737	LR2	1114
Hannah, d. John & Phebe, b. Oct. 11, 1757	LR5	270
James, s. John, Sr. & Han[n]ah, b. July 18, 1703	LR1	3
James, m. Dorothy **SPENCER**, Dec. 13, 1734	LR2	1114
James, s. James & Dorothy, b. Mar. 7, 1736	LR2	1114
John, s. John, Sr. & Han[n]ah, b. Dec. 8, 1694	LR1	3
John, 3rd, m. Mary **KNOWLTON**, Nov. 3, 1714	LR2	1129
John, s. Clement & Abigail, b. June 30, 1734	LR2	1124
John, 2d, d. Feb. 3, 1739/40	LR2	1109
John, Jr., m. Phebe **CLARK**, b. of East Haddam, July 8, 1756	LR5	270
John, of Haddam, m. Mary Ann **CLARK**, of East Haddam,		
Apr. 26, 1837, by Rev. Stephen Beach	3	151
Joseph, s. John, Sr. & Han[n]ah, b. May 24, 1698	LR1	3
Joseph, m. Elizabeth **SPENCER**, Oct. 12, 1727	LR2	e
Joseph, s. Joseph & Elizabeth, b. Sept. 13, 1728	LR2	e
Joseph, Jr., m. Mary **OLMSTED**, Aug. 29, 1746	LR3	18
Mary, d. Clement & Mary, b. Aug. 21, 1735	LR2	1124
Mary, d. Joseph, Jr. & Mary, b. Nov. 24, 1747	LR3	18
Mary, m. Jonathan **WILLEY**, b. of East Haddam, May 4, 1758	2	60
Mary, of Saybrook, m. Francis **CHAPMAN**, of East Haddam,		474
Sept. 16, 1761	LR4	
Mary, m. Humphr[e]y **LYON**, b. of East Haddam, Apr. 25,		6
1765	LR7	1129
Mehittabell, d. John & Marcy, b. June 9, 1727	LR2	
Orphila M., of East Haddam, m. S. J. **TILEY**, of Essex, Mar. 5,		239
1854, by Rev. Isaac Parsons	3	
Orphelia M., music teacher, ae 19, b. in E. Haddam, m. S. J.		
TILEY, merchant, ae 23, b. in Essex, res. E. Haddam,		41-2
Mar. 5, 1854	4	
Ophelia M., music teacher, ae 19, of E. Haddam, m. S. J.		51-2
TILEY, merchant, ae 23, of Essex, Mar. 5, 1854	4	
Polly, Mrs., m. Humphr[e]y **LYON**, b. of East Haddam,		146
Apr. 25, 1765	2	1129
Rebeckah, d. John & Marcy, b. Jan. 5, 1729	LR2	e
Ruth, m. Ebenezer **GIBES**, May 10, 1726	LR2	e
Samuel, s. Joseph & Elizabeth, b. May 3, 1735	LR2	1129
Sarah, d. John & Marcy, b. May 22, 1718	LR2	1124
Susannah, d. Clement & Mary, b. June 14, 1748	LR2	1
Sybel, m. Jared **BRAINERD**, Apr. 19, 1763	LR7	1124
Thomas, s. Clement & Mary, b. Apr. 23, 1739	LR2	

	Vol.	Page
BATES, BATE, (cont.)		
------, child of Anson, mechanic, b. Aug. 25, 1853	4	47-8
------, d. Anson, mechanic, res. East Haddam, b. Mar. 5, 1856	4	96
------, d. Anson, b. in East Haddam, res. East Haddam, d. Mar. 27, 1856, ae 16 d.	4	97
BAXTER, William, of Pittsfield, Mass., m. Abigail **DEWEY**, of Colchester, Mar. 7, 1784	2	130
BEAN, Sarah, d. William & Anna, b. Apr. 5, 1763	LR6	a
William, m. Anna **ATWEL[L]**, June 7, 1762	LR6	a
BECKWITH, Abigail, d. Nathaniell & Abigail, b. Nov. 12, 1730	LR2	1104
Abigail, wid., m. Joseph **SELDEN**, b. of East Haddam, Nov. 25, 1777	2	168
Abigail Olmsted, d. Elisha & Abigail, b. Aug. 6, 1766	LR7	5
Abigail Warner, d. Asa & Abigail, b. May 12, 1772	2	168
Alvin, of Lyme, m. Nancy A. **REDDING**, of Langdon, N. H., May 11, 1851, of Rev. W[illia]m Harris	3	233
Anna, d. Job & Mehitabel, b. Nov. 15, 1784	2	208
Anna, d. Job & Mehitabel, d. Mar. 26, 1785	2	209
Asa, s. Joseph & Mary, b. June 3, 1753	LR8	4
Asa, s. Joseph, 2d, & Rebekah, b. Aug. 18, 1765	2	118
Asa, s. Joseph, 2d, & Rebekah, d. Aug. 19, 1765	2	119
Asa, d. Oct. 9, 1776	2	169
Baruch, s. Barzillai & Mary, b. Sept. 6, 1779	2	196
Barack, s. Samuel & Anna, b. Aug. 24, 1781	2	188
Barzillai, s. Barzillai & Mary, b. Nov. 19, 1765	2	196
Bethael, s. Nathaniell & Abigail, b. Dec. 22, 1741	LR2	1104
Betsey, d. Ezekiel B[rockway] & Jane, b. Dec. 19, 1791	2	202
Butler, s. Barzillai & Mary, b. Feb. 14, 1772	2	196
Charles, s. Elisha & Abigail, b. Oct. 22, 1760	LR7	5
Chauncey, s. Joseph & Mary, b. Apr. 29, 1768	LR8	4
Cha[u]nc[e]y, of East Haddam, m. Silence **PHELPS**, of Lyme, Nov. 29, 1787	2	198
Deborah, m. Stephen **ACKLEY**, Jr., b. of East Haddam, Feb. 12, 1794	2	249
Dorkis, d. Joseph & Mary, b. Sept. 20, 1759	LR8	4
Dorcas, d. Cha[u]nc[e]y & Silence, b. May 30, 1789	2	198
Eliot, s. Joseph & Mary, b. July 6, 1762	LR8	4
Elisha, s. Nathaniell & Abigail, b. Jan. 26, 1735/6	LR2	1104
Elisha, m. Abigail **WILLEY**, b. of East Haddam, Aug. 16, 1759	LR7	5
Elisha, s. Elisha & Abigail, b. July 24, 1764	LR7	5
Eliza, m. Henry **CHESTER**, Mar. 14, 1828*, by Rev. Tubal Wakefield (*Probably Mar. 14 is an error as it was recorded Mar. 11, 1828	3	96
Elizabeth, [twin with Ezra], d. Job & Mary, b. May 10, 1738	LR2	1121
Elizabeth, d. Barzillai & Mary, b. Feb. 23, 1777	2	196
Elizabeth Conkling, d. Ephraim & Caralina, b. Sept. 12, 1787	2	170
Emily Cordelia, d. Jonathan & Nancy, b. Aug. 16, 1823	2	319
Ephraim, s. Joseph & Mary, b. Apr. 14, 1765	LR8	4

	Vol.	Page
BECKWITH, (cont.)		
Ephraim, of East Haddam, m. Carolina **WOOD**, of Lyme, Dec. 29, 1783	2	170
Esther, d. Asa & Abigail, b. Feb. 27, 1776	2	168
Esther, m. Dr. Christopher **HOLMES**, b. of East Haddam, Mar. 14, 1793	2	247
Eunice, d. Nathaniel & Abigail, b. Feb. 9, 1739/40	LR2	1104
Ezekiel Brockway, of East Haddam, m. Jane **BECKWITH**, of Lyme, Aug. 25, 1773	2	202
Ezra, [twin with Elizabeth], s. Job & Mary, b. May 10, 1738	LR2	1121
George, s. Barzillai & Mary, b. Feb. 6, 1764	2	196
George Augustus, s. Jonathan & Nancy, b. July 16, 1829	2	319
Henry Edwin, s. Jonathan & Nancy, b. July 1, 1831	2	319
Jane, of Lyme, m. Ezekiel Brockway **BECKWITH**, of East Haddam, Aug. 25, 1773	2	202
Jerus[h]a, d. Nathaniell & Sarah, b. June 10, 1709	LR1	7
Job, s. Nathaniell & Sarah, b. May 22, 1705	LR1	7
Job, m. Mary **BIGS**, Jan. 24, 1727	LR2	1121
Job, s. Job & Mary, b. Nov. 22, 1730	LR2	1121
Job, m. Mehitabel **CHAMPION**, b. of East Haddam, Mar. 23, 1780	2	208
Jonathan, s. Barzillai & Mary, b. Sept. 21, 1783	2	196
Jonathan, m. Nancy **LORD**, Feb. 18, 1813	2	319
Jonathan Butler, s. Jonathan & Nancy, b. Feb. 21, 1821	2	319
Joseph, s. Nathaniell & Sarah, b. Dec. 11, 1715	LR1	582
Joseph, m. Sarah **WILLEY**, b. of East Haddam, (or said to be), Oct. 9, 1737	LR8	4
Joseph, s. Joseph & Sarah, b. Feb. 17, 1739	LR8	4
Joseph, m. Mrs. Mary **SCOVEL**, b. of East Haddam, (or said to be), Mar. 3, 1751	LR8	4
Joseph, 2d, m. Rebeckah **CROSBY**, b. of East Haddam, Mar. 17, 1757	2	118
Joseph, s. Joseph & Rebekah, b. Sept. 19, 1767	2	118
Joseph, s. Joseph, 2d, & Rebekah, d. Aug. 16, 1774	2	119
Lucy, d. Nathaniell & Abigail, b. May 5, 1732	LR2	1104
Luck*, m. Daniel **SCOVEL**, b. of East Haddam, Sept. 24, 1758 (Lucy?)	LR6	507
Mailin, s. Nathaniell & Abigail, b. Feb. 10, 1737/8	LR2	1104
Mary, d. Job & Mary, b. Aug. 6, 1734	LR2	1121
Mary, m. Jacob **COWDREY**, b. of East Haddam, Dec. 18, 1755	LR5	267
Mary, d. Barzillai & Mary, b. Dec. 16, 1769	2	196
Mary, d. Asa & Abigail, b. Apr. 27, 1774	2	168
Mary Brainard, m. Asa **SMITH**, b. of East Haddam, Nov. 24, 1802	2	273
Mary H., ae 38, of East Haddam, m. Richard **PRATT**, ae 56, b. at Saybrook, Ct., res. Shelbourne Falls, Mass., Nov. 25, 1856, by Rev. Nath[anie]l Miner. Int. pub. Nov. 21, 1856	4	113

	Vol.	Page
BECKWITH, (cont.)		
Mary Hyde, d. Jonathan & Nawncy, b. Apr. 29, 1818	2	319
Melicient, d. Elisha & Abigail, b. Apr. 22, 1775	2	36
Moses D., m. Lydia **PILGRIM**, b. of East Haddam, Sept. 2, 1827, by Rev. Simon Shailer, of Haddam	3	94
Nancy Lord, d. Jonathan & Nancy, b. Aug. 24, 1814	2	319
Naomi, d. Samuel & Anna, b. Nov. 22, 1787	2	188
Nathan, s. Job & Mary, b. Dec. 7, 1728	LR2	1121
Nathan, s. Ezekiel B. & Jane, b. Apr. 20, 1775	2	202
Nathaniell, m. Sarah [ ], Jan. 20, 1703	LR1	6
Nathaniell, s. Nathaniell & Sarah, b. Jan. 6, 1707	LR1	7
Nathaniell, d. Mar. 17, 1717	LR2	1103
Nathaniell, m. Abigail **HUNTLEY**, Apr. 11, 1728	LR2	1104
Nathaniell, s. Nathaniell & Abigail, b. Dec. 11, 1728	LR2	1104
Nathaniel, s. Samuel & Anna, b. Oct. 13, 1785	2	188
Nathaniel Brown, s. Barzillai & Mary, b. Sept. 25, 1781	2	196
Patience, [twin with Prudence], d. Joseph & Sarah, b. Mar. 18, 1748	LR8	4
Polley, d. Elisha & Abigail, b. May 2, 1771	2	36
Prudence, [twin with Patience], d. Joseph & Sarah, b. Mar. 18, 1748	LR8	4
Prudence, d. Joseph, 2d, & Rebekah, b. Apr. 20, 1772	2	118
Prudence, d. Joseph, 2d, & Rebekah, d. Aug. 27, 1774	2	119
Prudence, d. Stephen & Elizabeth, b. Feb. 27, 1782	2	200
Rachel, d. Nathaniell & Abigail, b. May 24, 1734	LR2	1104
Rebekah, d. Barzillai & Mary, b. Dec. 22, 1767	2	196
Rebeckah, d. Stephen & Elizabeth, b. June 4, 1780	2	200
Rhoda, d. Barzilla & Mary, b. Feb. 4, 1786	2	196
Rhoda, m. William E. **CONE**, b. of East Haddam, Apr. 21, 1831, by Rev. Nathaniel Miner	3	127
Roger S., d. Jan. 21, 1850, ae 10 m.	4	29-30
Salle Anne, d. Ezekiel B[rockway] & Jane, b. Nov. 26, 1777	2	202
Samuel, of East Haddam, m. Anna **RANSOM**, of Lyme, June 14, 1774	2	188
Samuel, s. Samuel & Anna, b. July 31, 1783	2	188
Sarah, d. Nathaniell, b. Aug. 13, 1712	LR1	9
Sarah, d. Job & Mary, b. May 13, 1736	LR2	1121
Sarah, w. of Nathaniell, d. Jan. 9, 1739/40	LR2	1103
Sarah, d. Joseph & Sarah, b. May 26, 1745	LR8	4
Sarah, w. of Joseph, d. Aug. 3, 1750	LR8	4
Sarah, of East Haddam, m. John **BEEBE**, of Saybrook, July 12, 1764	2	178
Sarah, d. Barzillai & Mary, b. June 3, 1774	2	196
Sarah, d. Joseph, 2d, & Rebekah, b. June 26, 1775	2	118
Sarah Ann, m. Chauncey **FULLER**, b. of East Haddam, Mar. 21, 1826, by Rev. Joseph Vaill, of Hadlyme	3	84-5
Shobal, s. Samuel & Anna, b. Oct. 9, 1775	2	188
Simeon Wood, s. Ephraim & Carolina, b. Mar. 29, 1785	2	170

	Vol.	Page
BECKWITH, (cont.)		
Stephen, s. Joseph, 2d, & Rebekah, b. Jan. 3, 1759	2	118
Stephen, s. Samuel & Anna, b. Apr. 7, 1778	2	188
Stephen, s. Samuel & Anna, d. June 2, 1778	2	189
Stephen, s. Samuel & Anna, b. June 5, 1779	2	188
Stephen, of East Haddam, m. Elizabeth **DRAKE**, of Long Island, July 20, 1779	2	200
Susanna, m. Abraham **WILLEY**, b. of East Haddam, Jan. 12, 1773	2	64
William, s. Job & Mary, b. Oct. 14, 1732	LR2	1121
Wilson, of Palmyra, N. Y., m. Emeline L. **TIFFANY**, of Lyme, Mar. 17, 1841, by Rev. George Carrington, of Hadlyme	3	185
----, child of [Stephen] & Elizabeth, b. July 7, 1785	2	200
----, child of Stephen & Elizabeth, d. July 16, 1785	2	201
----, child of Denison P., mechanic, ae 26, & Sarah E., ae 27, b. Aug. 24, 1847	4	5-6
BEEBE, BEEBEE, Abigail, m. Abner **CHAPMAN**, b. paupers, of E. Haddam, with the consent of the Selectmen of said town, Dec. 2, 1827, by Herman L. Vaill	3	79
Alden, joiner, ae 24, of East Haddam, m. Harriet L. **ANDREWS**, ae 22, b. in Glastonbury, res. East Haddam, Nov. 18, 1848, by Henry Forbush	4	9-10
Allen Chester, s. Ezra & Lydia, b. Aug. 4, 1816	2	297
Almira J., m. Robert W. **CHAPMAN**, Mar. 29, 1835, by Isaac Parsons	3	137
Alvin, cooper, d. Jan. 18, 1850, ae 90	4	29-30
Anne, d. William & Phebe, b. Jan. 27, 1731	LR7	6
Anne, m. Jabez **CHAPMAN**, b. of East Haddam, Apr. 2, 1752	LR7	6
Annes, d. John & Sarah, b. Sept. 15, 1766	2	178
Annes, d. John & Sarah, d. [ ], 1776	2	179
Ancel, s. Silas & Elizabeth, b. Mar. 13, 1760	LR7	416
Ansel, Jr., m. Mary E. **STARR**, Oct. 31, 1821, by Rev. W[illia]m Lyman	3	36-37
Ansel, farmer, d. Apr. 19, 1849, ae 90	4	17-18
Austin, m. Lucy **HAYES**, b. of East Haddam, Mar. 25, 1832, by Rev. Alvan Ackley	3	122
Brockway, s. Joshua & Hannah, b. Sept. 12, 1735	LR4	467
Brockway, m. Pheebe **DUTTON**, b. of East Haddam, Feb. 10, 1757	LR5	267
Caleb, of East Haddam, m. Phebe **BUCKINGHAM**, of Saybrook, Mar. 6, 1737	LR5	559
Caleb, s. Caleb & Phebe, b. June 4, 1737	LR5	559
Caleb, Jr., of East Haddam, m. Eunice **AVERY**, of Grotton, Jan. 21, 1761	LR6	a
Caleb, d. Feb. 12, 1761	LR5	559
Caleb S., of East Haddam, m. M. J. **HURLBURT**, of East Haddam, Nov. 22, 1854, by Rev. Nathaniel Miner	3	242
Caleb S., ae 30, b. in E. Haddam, res. California, m.		

	Vol.	Page
BEEBE, BEEBEE, (cont.)		
M. J. **HURBURT**, ae 22, of E. Haddam, Nov. 22, 1854, by Rev. N. Miner	4	51-2
Clarissa, m. Benjamin B. **BURR**, Feb. 14, 1839, by Francis Griffin, J. P.	3	168
Clark, d. Dec. 10, 1810	2	298
Clark Beckwith, s. Ezra & Lydia, b. Apr. 27, 1803	2	297
Content, d. Caleb, Jr. & Eunice, b. Feb. 19, 1763	LR6	a
Demas, see under Dimmis		
Diadama, d. Silas & Elizabeth, b. July 19, 1764	LR7	416
Dimmis, d. Joshua & Hannah, b. July 31, 1740	LR4	467
Dimmis, m. Jeremiah **DUTTON**, b. of East Haddam, Jan. 21, 1758	2	18
Demas, m. Jeremiah **DUTTON**, b. of East Haddam, Jan. 24, 1753	LR6	513
Dorothy A., m. Jabez A. **PHELPS**, Aug. 4, 1833, by Rev. Benjamin G. Goff	3	132
Elizabeth, d. Silas & Elizabeth, b. Oct. 29, 1753	LR7	416
Elizabeth, m. Timothy **PATTERSON**, b. of East Haddam, Mar. 13, 1760	LR6	506
Elizabeth, w. Silas, d. Oct. 15, 1765	LR7	416
Elisabeth, d. John & Sarah, b. Feb. 7, 1770	2	178
Erastus, [see under Rastus]		
Esther, alias Esther **PAINE**, late of Southhold, L. I., m. Horace **HAYDEN**, of East Haddam, [Oct.] 13, [1824], by William Gelston, J. P.	3	66-67
Ezra, s. Clark & Patience, b. Mar. 12, 1780	2	297
Ezra, s. Ezra & Lydia, b. Apr. 6, 1801	2	297
Ezra, s. Ezra & Lydia, d. Jan. 31, 1812	2	298
Ezra, of East Haddam, m. Lydia **CHAPPELL**, of Waterford, [1798?]	2	297
Gideon, s. Joshua & Hannah, b. June 17, 1742	LR4	467
Harriet N., of East Haddam, m. Henry E. **BURR**, of Haddam, Nov. 4, 1838, by Rev. Erastus Denison	3	167
Henry Perkins, s. Ezra & Lydia, b. Sept. 11, 1812	2	297
Henry Perkins, s. Ezra & Lydia, b. Mar. 9, 1819	2	298
Huldah, of Lyme, m. Samuel **POST**, of East Haddam, Jan. 6, 1774	2	58
Isaac Bigelow, s. Reuben & Mary, b. Mar. 20, 1768	2	120
Jehiel, s. Silas & Elizabeth, b. Apr. 5, 1755	LR7	416
Jerusha, d. Joshua & Hannah, b. Aug. 11, 1746	LR4	467
John, of Saybrook, m. Sarah **BECKWITH**, of East Haddam. July 12, 1764	2	178
John W., of Lebanon, m. Dorothy S. **PHELPS**, of East Haddam. Oct. 22, 1840, by Rev. George Carrington, of Hadlyme	3	184
Joshua, m. Hannah **BROCKWAY**, Oct. 18, 1733	LR4	467
Joshua, s. Joshua & Hannah, b. Oct. 10. 1738	LR4	467

	Vol.	Page
BEEBE, BEEBEE, (cont.)		
Judah, s. Caleb & Phebe, b. Sept. 25, 1749	LR5	559
Leve, s. Caleb & Phebe, b. Apr. 25, 1743	LR5	559
Levi, m. Martha **CONE**, b. of East Haddam, Nov. 20, 1769	2	30
Lucy, d. Ezra & Lydia, b. Nov. 15, 1799	2	297
Lucy B., m. Rufus W. **SWAN**, Nov. 21, 1822, by Rev. W[illia]m Lyman, Millington	3	30-1
Lucy L., of Colchester, m. Andrew J. **TREADWAY**, of Salem, Nov. 30, 1854, by Rev. Nathaniel Miner	3	242
Lucy L., ae 20, b. in E. Haddam, res. Colchester, m. Andrew J. **TREADWAY**, merchant, ae 30, of Salem, Nov. 30, 1854, by Rev. N. Miner	4	51-2
Lidia, d. Reuben & Mary, b. Feb. 15, 1764	LR7	3
Lydia, d. Reuben & Lydia, b. Jan. 16, 1780	2	120
Manley, of East Haddam, m. Abby **HAYES**, Mar. 11, 1823, by Russell Dutton, J. P.	3	38-9
Mary, d. Reuben & Mary, b. Apr. 10, 1771	2	120
Mary, d. Reuben & Mary, d. Aug. 24, 1771	2	121
Mary, w. of Reubin, d. Oct. 25, 1773	2	121
Mercy C., of East Haddam, m. John **TEW**, of Salem, Jan. 1, 1830, by Russell Dutton, J. P.	3	104
Mercy Crocker, d. Ezra & Lydia, b. Feb. 15, 1805	2	297
Molley, d. Reuben & Lydia, b. Mar. 20, 1775	2	120
Nathan, s. Caleb & Phebe, b. Apr. 2, 1739	LR5	559
Nathan, m. Abigail **TRACY**, Oct. 25, 1825, by Russell Dutton, J. P.	3	79
Ollive, d. Silas & Elizabeth, b. Apr. 13, 1752	LR7	416
Patience, d. Ezra & Lydia, b. June 19, 1810	2	297
Patience, wid. d. Aug. 11, 1823	3	46
Patience, of East Haddam, m. Gurdon **THOMPSON**, of Saybrook, Oct. 1, 1830, by Russell Dutton, J. P.	3	108
Phebe, m. Ebenezer **DUTTON**, b. of East Haddam, Apr. 26, 1753	LR6	510
Phebe, d. Caleb & Phebe, b. Aug. 9, 1754	LR5	559
Prudence, d. Joshua & Hannah, b. Aug. 3, 1737	LR4	467
Rastus, [twin with Roderick], s. Reuben & Lydia, b. Oct. 20, 1777	2	120
Reuben, s. Caleb & Phebe, b. Feb. 14, 1741	LR5	559
R[e]uben, of East Haddam, m. Mary **BIGGSLOW**, of Colchester, Sept. 9, 1761	LR7	3
Reube[n], s. Reuben & Mary, b. Oct. 22, 1762	LR7	3
Reuben, s. Reuben & Mary, b. Apr. 11, 1766	LR7	3
Reuben, of East Haddam, m. Lydia **WATERS**, of Hebron, Apr. 21, 1774	2	120
Robert, s. Caleb & Phebe, b. Aug. 5, 1747	LR5	559
Rode. d. Silas & Elizabeth, b. Apr. 20, 1761	LR7	416
Rodrick, [twin with Rastus], s. Reuben & Lydia, b. Oct. 20. 1777	2	120

	Vol.	Page
BEEBE, BEEBEE, (cont.)		
Rube, d. Reuben & Mary, d. Sept. 30, 1775	2	121
Ruth, m. Gurdon **ROGERS**, b. of East Haddam, Sept. 11, 1782	LR8	1
Salley, d. John & Sarah, b. Jan. 28, 1768	2	178
Salley, d. John & Sarah, d. [ ], 1776	2	179
Salley Annes, d. John & Sarah, b. July 15, 1771	2	178
Sarah, d. Caleb & Phebe, b. Mar. 24, 1745	LR5	559
Sarah, d. Caleb & Phebe, d. Mar. 19, 1750	LR5	559
Sarah, d. Caleb & Phebe, b. Sept. 1, 1752	LR5	559
Sarah, m. Simeon **ACKLEY**, Jr., Mar. 1, 1770	2	88
Sarah M., m. Francis A. **CHAPMAN**, b. of East Haddam, Mar. 30, 1845, by Isaac Parsons, V. D. M.	3	201
Silas, m. Elizabeth **EM[M]ONS**, Jan. 5, 1752	LR7	416
Sophia Fox, d. Ezra & Lydia, b. Sept. 11, 1814	2	297
Starling Waters, s. Reuben & Lydia, b. Sept. 23, 1781	2	120
Susannah, m. Judah **SPENCER**, b. of East Haddam, Mar. 5, 1767	2	118
Thomas, s. Abner & Apphiah, b. Apr. 16, 1754	LR5	265
----, d. Joseph A., mechanic, ae 25, & Harriet L., ae 23, b. Apr. 1, 1850	4	27-8
----, s. Alden J., joiner & farmer, ae 30, & Harriet, ae 27, b. Oct.. 31, 1856	4	112
BEERS, Caroline, factory operative, b. in Marlborough, res. E. Haddam, d. Sept. 26, 1849, ae 21	4	29-30
Simon P., of Chatham, m. Elizabeth J. **TOMPKINS**, of Lyme, Sept. 20, 1840, by Isaac Parsons, V. D. M.	3	182-3
BELDEN, BELDING, David, m. Mary **ACKLEY**, b. of East Haddam, Apr. 17, 1760	LR6	504
David, of East Haddam, m. Marget **CLARK**, of Lyme, Jan. 10, 1776	2	136
David Ackley, s. David & Mary, b. July 14, 1764	LR6	504
Elisabeth, d. David & Marget, b. Mar. 1, 1777	2	136
Elizabeth, m. John Lathrop **PECK**, b. of East Haddam, Nov. 16 1800	2	267
Henry, s. David & Marget, b. Feb. 26, 1781	2	136
James, s. David & Marget, b. May 18, 1785	2	136
Mary, w. of David, d. July 14, 1764	LR6	504
Obedience, d. David & Marget, b. May 22, 1783	2	136
Sarah, m. Thomas **GRIFFIS**, Feb. 12, 1718/19	LR1	574
Stephen, s. David & Mary, b. Mar. 24, 1761	LR6	504
BENNETT, -----, s. John, stonemason, ae 41, & Harriet N., ae 34, b. Sept. 13, 1856	4	111
BERTLE, Hannah, d. William & Arving, b. Jan. 1, 1743/4	LR2	1095
BEVINS, Isaac A., m. Huldah Ann **SNOW**, b. of East Haddam, Nov. 7, 1830, by Rev. Isaac Parsons	3	115
BIDWELL, Eliza, b. in Shenang, N. Y., res. East Haddam, d. July 15, 1848, ae 34	4	17-18
Francis O., of Chatham, m. Elsey **WILLIAMS**, of East		

	Vol.	Page
BIDWELL, (cont.)		
Haddam, Oct. 27, 1834, by Rev. Isaac Parsons. Witness: N. L. Foster	3	135
Francis O., m. Olive M. **CRITTENDEN**, b. of East Haddam, Jan. 14, 1850, by Rev. Moses Chase	3	222
BIGELOW, BIGGSLOW, Aaron, s. Joel & Lucretia, b. May 19, 1796	2	221
Austin, s. Joel & Lucretia, b. Feb. 13, 1792	2	221
Ebenezer Lathrop, s. Joel & Lucretia, b. Dec. 6, 1806* (*Perhaps "1800")	2	221
Eli, m. Esther **GATES**, May 19, 1825, by Rev. William Jarvis	3	76-7
Eunice, of Colchester, m. William **LEFFINGWELL**, Mar. 25, [1830], by Rev. Alvan Ackley	3	104
Mary, of Colchester, m. R[e]uben **BEEBE**, of East Haddam, Sept. 9, 1761	LR7	3
Mary, of Colchester, m. Elijah **SPENCER**, of Lyme, Sept. 5, 1824, by Simeon Dickinson	3	87
Phebe, d. Joel & Lucretia, b. Sept. 16, 1789	2	221
Roxy, m. Joseph **GOODSPEED**, b. of East Haddam, Sept. 13, 1833, by Isaac Parsons	3	132
Virtue, d. Elisha & Thankful, b. Feb. 28, 1790	2	42
BIGS, Mary, m. Job **BECKWITH**, Jan. 24, 1727	LR2	1121
BILL, Joshua, s. Edward & Zurviah, b. Feb. 10, 1735	LR2	1120
BINGHAM, Abel, m. Jemima **ELY**, b. of East Haddam, Sept. 9, 1784	2	219
Anna, d. Abel & Jemima, b. May 26, 1788	2	219
Carile C., of East Haddam, m. Alline S. **NEWELL**, of Dummerstown, Vt., May 25, 1846, by Rev. Isaac Parsons	3	205
Elijah W., m. Rozilla **DANIELS**, Apr. 5, 1835, by Isaac Parsons	3	137
Elijah W., m. Rozilla **DANIELS**, Apr. 5, 1835	3	147
Elisha, s. Abel & Jemima, b. May 22, 1786	2	219
Elisha C., m. Julia E. **CONE**, b. of East Haddam, June 4, 1837, by Rev. Isaac Parsons	3	152
Elisha C., ae 41, b. in East Haddam, res. East Haddam, m. Martha M. **GATES**, ae 35, b. in Glastonbury, res. East Haddam, May 20, 1856, by Rev. Henry Forbush. Int. pub. May 14, 1856	4	88
Eliza Ann, of East Haddam, m. Charles **ARNOLD**, 2d, of Haddam, May 19, 1839, by Charles William Bradley	3	172
Ely, s. Abel & Jemima b. July 17, 1793	2	219
Fanny G., m. Jonah C. **CHAPMAN**, Dec. 6, 1843, by Rev. Isaac Parsons	3	196
Floretta, m. Gamaleel R. **TRACY**, Jr., b. of East Haddam, Mar. 20, 1842, by Thomas G. Salter	3	189
Jemima, d. Abel & Jemima, b. Nov. 12, 1791	2	219
Julia A., b. in East Haddam, res. East Haddam, married, d. Jan. 31, 1855, ae 39	4	71

	Vol.	Page
BINGHAM, (cont.)		
Lucy, b. Chester, res. East Haddam, d. Sept. 25, 1849, ae 36	4	17-8
Sarah, d. [William B. & Amelia], b. Nov. 15, 1846	3	117
Susannah Elizabeth, d. [Elijah W. & Rozilla], b. Aug. 21, 1836	3	147
Tracy, s. [William B. & Amelia], b. Oct. 24, 1852	3	117
William B., m. Amelia **SMITH**, Nov. [ ], 1837, at Portland, Conn.	3	117
-----, s. Elisha C., farmer, ae 34, & Julia, ae 34, b. May 22, 1850	4	27-8
BLACKLEY, [see also **BLAKSLEE**], Abigail, m. Elijah **ACKLY**, Oct. 12, 1741	LR3	1
BLAGUE, Joshua, m. Jemima **RAND**, July 26, 1826, by Ozias Holmes, J. P.	3	87
BLAKSLEE, BLAKESLEY, [see also **BLACKLEY**], Daniel Chapman, s. Rev. Solomon & Anna, b. Jan. 15, 1796	2	256
Daniel Chapman, m. Betsey **BURNHAM**, b. of East Haddam, Jan. 27, 1817, by Rev. Solomon Blakslee, of New London	2	305
Edward Solomon, s. Rev. Solomon & Ann, b. Dec. 10, 1798	2	256
Edward Solomon, of East Haddam, m. Lucy **WESTON**, Oct. 11, 1821, by Rev. Russell Wheeler, at Butternuts, N. Y.	3	53
Elizabeth Ann, d. Rev. Solo[mo]n & Ann, b. Aug. 18, 1801	2	256
Eveline, d. Rev. Solo[mo]n & Ann, b. Mar. 7, 1805	2	256
George N., of Plymouth, m. Harriet **GREEN**, of East Haddam, Dec. 22, 1823, by Rev. Isaac Parsons	3	49
Helen Louisa, d. Edward & Lucy, b. Sept. 23, 1822	3	53
Henrietta, d. Rev. Solo[mon] & Ann, b. Feb. 11, 1808	2	256
Solomon, Rev., m. Mrs. Anna **CHAPMAN**, b. of East Haddam, Apr. 8, 1795	2	256
BLISH, [see also **BLISS** and **BLUSH**], Mary F., m. Joseph **ARNOLD**, Feb. 11, 1824, by Russell Dutton, J. P.	3	54-5
Nancy, m. Calvin B. **WICKHAM**, Sept. 14, 1830, by Rev. Alvan Ackley	3	108
Sarah, m. Justin **ARNOLD**, b. of East Haddam, Feb. 4, 1840, by Rev. Nathaniel Miner	3	174
BLISS, [see also **BLISH** and **BLUSH**], Sylvester, of Long Meadow, Mass., m. Nancy C. **WARNER**, of East Haddam, Sept. 27, 1848, by Rev. Alpheas Geer	3	214
Sylvester, farmer, ae 29, b. in Longmeadow, Mass., res. Longmeadow, Mass., m. Nancy C. **WARNER**, ae 30, b. in East Haddam, res. Longmeadow, Mass., Sept. 27, 1848, by Rev. Alpheas Geer	4	9-10
William, m. Harriet **PALMER**, Oct. 13, 1831, by Rev. Isaac Parsons	3	120
BLUSH, [see also **BLISH** and **BLISS**], Rachel, Mrs., of Colchester, m. Philip **WILLIAMS**, of East Haddam, June 11, 1788	2	14
BLY, Paddis Pamelia, of Lebanon, m. David Leonard **ROGERS**, of Lyme, Feb. 14, 1836, by Rev. George Carrington, of Hadlyme	3	142

	Vol.	Page
BLYTHE, Mary E., ae 28, of Marlborough, m. Moses C. **HILLS**, ae 30, b. at Portland, Ct., res. East Haddam, Nov. 15, 1856, by Jonathan O. Cone, J. P. Int. pub. Nov. 8, 1856	4	106
BOAG, [see under **BOOGE]**		
BOARDMAN, BORDMAN, Ada, d. Frances, manufacturer, ae 22, & Mary, ae 19, b. Jan. 26, 1851	4	31-2
Ashbel, of Wethersfield, m. Eveline **PALMER**, of East Haddam, Feb. 11, 1823, by Rev. Isaac Parsons	3	38-9
Ashbel, s. Ashbel & Eveline, b. Nov. 19, 1823	3	38-9
Francis R., clerk, ae 22, of E. Haddam, m. Mary **DOUGLASS**, ae 18, of E. Haddam, May 28, 1850, at Greensport, L. I., by Rev. Woodbridge	4	21-2
John C. Palmer, s. Ashbel, laborer, ae 33, res. East Haddam, b. Jan. 25, 1856	4	82
Nathaniel C., of Plymouth, m. Emeline C. **BROWNELL**, of East Haddam, Aug. 9, 1852, by Rev. Isaac Parsons	3	237
Thomas C., m. Sophronia **PALMER**, b. of East Haddam, Jan. 6, 1822, by Rev. Isaac Parsons	3	21
BOLLES, Francis, of Waterford, m. Nancy C. **MORGAN**, of East Haddam, Nov. 9, 1831, by Rev. Isaac Parsons	3	120
Horatio N., of Marlborough, m. Phebe A. **MACK**, of East Haddam, Sept. 9, 1838, by Isaac Parsons, V. D. M.	3	166
BOND, Joseph W., of Lyme, m. Harriet W. **SANFORD**, of Wethersfield, Aug. 9, 1852, by James Noyes, Hadlyme	3	236
BONFOY, Esther, d. Pormoit & Esther, b. Oct. 18, 1784	2	6
Hannah, d. Pormoit & Esther, b. June 11, 1787	2	6
Penelope, d. Pormoit & Esther, b. Mar. 25, 1792	2	6
Phebe, d. Pormoit & Esther, b. Aug. 22, 1789	2	6
BOOGE, BOAG, BOOG, BOGE, [see also **BOGUE]**, Aaron, s. John & Anna, b. Apr. 16, 1803	2	305
Abiga[i]ll, d. John & Hannah, b. Jan. 13, 1717/18	LR1	570
Amos, s. John, b. Jan. 17, 1724/5	LR1	570
Amos, m. Eunice **MAYO**, Nov. 22, 1750	LR4	472
Amos, m. Mrs. Hannah **FULLER**, b. of East Haddam, Feb. 28, 1776	2	12
Amos, m. Mrs. Hannah **FULLER**, b. of East Haddam, Feb. 28, 1776	2	82
Amos, d. Apr. 18, 1777	2	83
Amos, s. Timothy & Rebekah, b. Mar. 23, 1778	2	44
Anna, d. John & Anna, b. Jan. 11, 1813	2	305
Caroline, d. John & Anna, b. June 11, 1811	2	305
Caroline, m. Luther **HUBBARD**, b. of East Haddam, Dec. 24, 1832, by Isaac Parsons, M. G.	3	128
Clark, s. James, b. Mar. 30, 1771	2	188
Daniell, m. Lidea **WILLE**, Nov. 29, 1722	LR1	571
Daniell, s. Daniell & Lidea, b. Feb. 27, 1727/8	LR1	571
Daniel, d. July 11, 1748	LR3	509
Dorothy, d. William & Dorothy, b. Mar. 31. 1727	LR2	1117

	Vol.	Page
BOOGE, BOAG, BOOG, BOGE, (cont.)		
Dorothy, m. William **SELBY**, Feb. 26, 1749/50	LR3	4
Dorothy, d. Jonathan & Lucretia, b. Apr. 10, 1753	LR4	468
Dorothy, d. Jonathan & Lucretia, d. Apr. 11, 1758	LR4	468
Dorothy, d. Jonathan & Lucretia, b. May 20, 1759	LR4	468
Dorothy, m. Abraham **OSBORN**, b. of East Haddam, Jan. 10, 1782	2	62
Ebenezer, s. John, b. May 9, 1716	LR1	10
Edwin, s. John & Anna, b. Mar. 19, 1806	2	305
Eleazer, s. Daniell & Lidea, b. Jan. 22, 1724/5	LR1	571
Eliazer, of East Haddam, m. Lidia **BURT**, of Lebanon, Mar. 19, 1728	LR5	266
Elijah, s. James, b. June 14, 1769	2	188
Eliphib, s. Daniel & Lidea, b. Aug. 23, 1726	LR1	571
Elizabeth, d. William & Dorothy, b. Nov. 17, 1723	LR2	1117
Ephraim, s. John & Hannah, b. Feb. 18, 1722/3; d. June 15, 1725	LR1	570
Ephraim, s. William & Dorothy, b. Jan. 26, 1735	LR2	1117
[E]unice, d. John & Hannah, b. Oct. 10, 1722; d. Nov. 26, same year	LR1	570
Eunice, w. of Amos, d. Dec. 20, 1774	2	83
George Washington, s. John & Anna, b. Feb. 4, 1815	2	305
Hannah, d. John & Rebeckah, b. Aug. 27, 1708	LR1	6
Hannah, d. John & Hannah, b. Oct. 31, 1719	LR1	570
Hannah, wid. of Amos, d. Apr. 27, 1777	2	83
Harriet, d. John & Anna, b. July 16, 1804	2	305
Harriet, m. Fuller **ANDREWS**, Oct. 17, 1826, by Rev. Simeon Dickinson, at the house of John Booge	3	88-9
Henry, s. John & Anna, b. Apr. 24, 1824	2	305
Ichabod, s. Daniel & Lydia, b. Sept. 23, 1745	LR1	571
James, s. John & Rebeckah, b. Oct. 26, 1710	LR1	8
James, m. Sarah **HODGE**, Dec. 29, 1737	LR2	1110
James, s. James & Sarah, b. Sept. 3, 1738	LR2	1110
James, m. Anna **TRO[W]BRIDGE**, Nov. 21, 1739	LR3	10
James, Jr., of East Haddam, m. Eunice **CLARK**, of Lyme, Feb. 6, 1759	LR7	2
James, s. James, b. May 23, 1767	2	188
James, m. Marietta L. **EDWARDS**, Feb. 3, 1839, by Rev. George Carrington, of Hadlyme	3	167
Jeremiah, s. Daniell & Lidea, b. Feb. 4, 1729/30	LR1	571
John, Jr., m. Hannah **LORD**, Apr. 11, 1717	LR1	570
John, s. Daniell & Lidea, b. Jan, 26, 1731/2	LR1	571
John, m. Elizabeth **BAYLE**, May 1, 1735	LR2	1120
John, d. Aug. 21, 1748	LR3	1
John, d. Mar. 4, 1763	LR1	570
John, s. James, b. July 6, 1765	2	188
John, s. Timothy & Rebeckah, b. June 22, 1772	2	44
John, of East Haddam, m. Anna **TAYLOR**, of Colchester,		

	Vol.	Page
BOOGE, BOAG, BOOG, BOGE, (cont.)		
Dec. 5, 1802, by John Isham	2	305
Jonathan, s. William & Dorothy, b. Sept. 11, 1729	LR2	1117
Jonathan, m. Lucretia **GILBERT**, Sept. 13, 1750	LR4	468
Joshua, s. Daniel & Lidea, b. Oct. 22, 1735	LR1	571
Louisanna, d. James, Jr. & Eunice, b. Apr. 10, 1760	LR7	2
Lydia, d. Daniel & Lidea, b. Oct. 26, 1738	LR1	571
Mary, d. Jonathan & Lucretia, b. Jan. 12, 1750/51	LR4	468
Rebeckah, d. John & Rebeckah, b. Mar. 17, 1712	LR1	10
Rebeckah, m. Thomas **DIBBLE**, Sept. 14, 1734	LR3	9
Rebeckah, d. Daniel & Lydea, b. Sept. 14, 1741	LR1	571
Rebeckah, d. James, Jr. & Eunice, b. May 16, 1762	LR7	2
Rebeckah, d. Timothy & Rebekah, b. Feb. 21, 1782	2	44
Richard, m. Sarah **ARNOLD**, Jan. 22, 1729/30	LR2	1128
Richard, m. Johanna **MACK**, Mar. 12, 1731	LR2	1119
Richard, s. Daniel & Lidea, b. Sept. 19, 1733	LR1	571
Richard, d. Feb. 25, 1733/4	LR2	1119
Sally, d. John & Anna, b. Dec. 28, 1807	2	305
Samuell, s. William & Dorothy, b. Sept. 27, 1721; d. Feb. 10, 1721/2	LR1	578
Samuell, s. John, Jr. & Hannah, b. Jan. 2, 1729/30	LR1	570
Sarah, d. John & Rebeckah, b. Aug. 3, 1704	LR1	3
Sarah, m. Micajah **SPENCER**, Dec. 27, 1722	LR1	584
Sarah, d. John, Jr. & Hannah, b. Apr. 26, 1726	LR1	570
Sarah, d. Richard & Johanna, b. Dec. 12, 1732	LR2	1119
Sarah, d. James & Anna, b. Nov. 17, 1744	LR3	10
Sophia, d. John & Anna, b. July 1, 1817	2	305
Thomas, m. Huldah **SPENCER**, b. of East Haddam, Apr. 10, 1831, by Rev. Nathaniel Miner	3	127
Thomas Murphy, s. Timothy & Rebeckahes, b. June 19, 1775	2	44
Timothy, s. William & Dorothy, b. Nov. 11, 1733	LR2	1117
Timothy, of East Haddam, m. Rebeckah **STANCLIFF***, of Middletown, May 7, 1766 (*corrected from **STANTELY**, in handwritting in original manuscript)	2	44
William, m. Dorothy **LORD**, Dec. 6, 1720	LR1	578
William, s. William & Dorothy, b. Jan. 8, 1722	LR2	1117
William, m. Eunice **WILLIAMS**, Oct. 17, 1745	LR3	3
William, s. Timothy & Rebeckah, b. Dec. 29, 1769	2	44
William, d. Oct. 7, 1771	2	45
BOGUE, [see also **BOOGE**], George Washington, of East Haddam, m. Mary **INGRAHAM**, of Chatham, Feb. 24, 1840, by Isaac Parsons, V. D. M.	3	176-7
Lucy, ae 19, m. John W. **BRADLEY**, shoemaker, ae 24, b. in Hamstead, Mass., res. E. Haddam, June 12, 1851, by Elder Gardner	4	37-8
Lucy A., of East Haddam, m. John W. **BRADLEY**, of Hamsted, N. H., June 12, 1851, by Rev. Jacob Gardner	3	232
Mariette, m. Thomas **RAND**, Nov. 23, 1836, by Rev. George		

	Vol.	Page
BOGUE, (cont.)		
Carrington, of Hadlyme	3	151
Sally, of Colchester, m. Eleazer **SCRANTON**, of East Haddam, June 18, 1838, by Rev. Isaac Parsons	3	162-3
William S., m. Mary E. **BANNING**, b. of Lyme, Oct. 18, 1843, by Rev. Stephen Alonzo Loper, of Hadlyme	3	195
-----, d. Henry, shoemaker, ae 27, & Martha R., ae 19, b. Apr. 16, 1851	4	33-4
BORDEN, Asahel, s. John & Mary, b. June 18, 175[ ]	LR5	561
Daniel, s. John & Mary, b. Apr. 9, 1763	LR5	561
Elisha, m. Susannah **SELBY**, Nov. 6, 1743	LR3	2
Ezekiel, s. Elisha & Susannah, b. Dec. 4, 1749	LR3	2
Hannah, m. Nehemiah **ANDREWS**, Oct. 31, 1745	LR3	13
John, m. Mary **CONE**, Apr. 30, [ ]	LR5	561
Lois, d. John & Mary, b. Nov. 30, 175[ ]	LR5	561
Louisa, d. Elisha & Susannah, b. May 1, 1745	LR3	2
Rachel, d. Elisha & Susannah, b. Nov. 26, 1751	LR3	2
Russell, s. John & Mary, b. Jan. 16, 1759	LR5	561
Russell, s. John & Mary, d. Aug. 3, 1760	LR5	561
Russel[l], s. John & Mary, b. May 10, 1761	LF5	561
BORDMAN, [see under **BOARDMAN**]		
BOWERS, Frances A., factory operative, ae 18, b. in Hartford, res. East Haddam, m. Joel **LEE**, shoemaker, ae 23, of East Haddam, Mar. 30, 1850, by Rev. Levi H. Wakeman	4	19-20
Frances A., m. Joel L. **LEE**, b. of East Haddam, Mar. 31, 1850, by Rev. Levi H. Wakeman	3	223
Mary M., ae 17, b. at E. Haddam, res. E. Haddam, m. Henry A. **BROOKS**, ae 21, b. at E. Haddam, res. E. Haddam, Dec. 30, 1855, by Rev. J. E. Heald. Int. pub. Dec. 24, 1855. Consent given Nov. 30, 1855, by Paris H. **BROOKS***, father of Mary M. **BOWERS**. (*Probably meant for "**BOWERS**")	4	70
Nelson, ae 21, b. in Norwich, res. East Haddam, m. Helen **BALCOM**, ae 21, b. in Mansfield, res. East Haddam, May 22, 1856, by Rev. Isaac Parsons. Int. pub. May 7, 1856	4	87-8
BOYD, William B., m. Eveline Cornelia **ACKLEY**, Apr. 17, 1827, by Rev. Isaac Parsons	3	95
BOYER, Margaret, d. of Owen, farmer, of E. Haddam, & Bridget, formerly of Ireland, b. June* 30, 1850 (*Perhaps Jan.)	4	27-8
BRADLEY, John W., of Hamsted, N. H., m. Lucy A. **BOGUE**, of East Haddam, June 12, 1851, by Rev. Jacob Gardner	3	232
John W., shoemaker, ae 24, b. in Hamstead, Mass., res. E. Haddam, m. 2d w. Jucy **BOGUE**, ae 19, June 12, 1851, by Elder Gardner	4	37-8
Sarah, of Hartford, m. Erastus W. **PRATT**, of Essex, Oct. 8, 1837, by Rev. Stephen Beach	3	159
BRAINARD, BRAINERD, Abba, of East Haddam, m. Enoch S. **BRAINERD**, of Lebanon, [Aug.] 17, [1820], by Rev.		

	Vol.	Page
BRAINARD, BRAINERD, (cont.)		
Isaac Parsons	2	319
Abigail Lucinda, d. [William & Lucy D.], b. Jan. 1, 1835	3	92
Alfred K., of East Haddam, m. Hannah M. **SMALL**, of Willimantic, Feb. 20, 1853, by Rev. Isaac Parsons	3	238
Alfred K., shoemaker, ae 24, of E. Haddam, m. Hannah M. **SMALL**, worker in cotton mill, ae 20, b. in Willimantic, res. E. Haddam, Feb. 20, 1853, by Rev. Isaac Parsons	4	43-4
Amasa, s. Joshua, Jr. & Mehitabell, b. Aug. 9, 1742	LR2	1111
Amasa, m. Jedidah **OSBORN**, b. of East Haddam, Dec. 22, 1763	LR7	1
Amasa, m. Jedidah **OSBORN**, b. of East Haddam, Dec. 22, 1763	2	24
Amasa, s. Amasa & Jedidah, b. Sept. 19, 1778	2	24
Amasa, Lieut., d. Nov. 26, 1815, ae 73	2	25
Amasa, s. Amasa & Jedidah, d. [ ]	2	25
Ammaziah, s. Bezaleel & Hannah, b. May 16, 1761	LR6	508
Anna, w. of Daniel, 2d, d. Jan. 31, 1772	2	43
Anna Marsh, d. Daniel, 2d, & Anna, b. Feb. 6, 1769	2	42
Anne, d. Amasa & Jedidah, b. June 29, 1772	2	24
Anne, m. Darius **GATES**, Oct. 7, 1799	2	210
Asa, s. Eleazer & Mary, b. Feb. 21, 1773	2	210
Asahel, s. Daniel & Esther, b. Mar. 20, 1737	LR2	1110
Asahel, s. Daniel & Esther, d. Dec. 31, 1739	LR2	1110
Asahel, s. Daniel & Esther, b. Nov. 1, 1755	LR4	475
Barzillai, s. Daniel & Esther, b. Aug. 8, 1757	LR4	475
Bazaleel, s. Daniell & Susan[n]a, b. Apr. 17, 1701	LR1	4
Bazaliell, m. Mary **GATES**, [ ], 1727	LR2	b
Bazaliel, s. Bazaliel & Mary, b. Apr. 15, 1737	LR2	b
Bazaliel, m. Elizabeth **WARNER**, June 17, 1744	LR2	1092
Bazaliel, m. Phebe **ALMANG**, alias **SMITH**, May 19, 1749	LR2	1092
Bazaliel, Capt., d. Oct. 9, 1749	LR2	1092
Bezaleel, of East Haddam, m. Hannah **BRAINERD**, of Colchester, June 22, 1758	LR6	508
Bezaleel, s. Bezaleel & Hannah, b. Jan. 24, 1759	LR6	508
Bezaleel, Jr., of East Haddam, m. Lydia **DEMING**, of Norwich, Oct. 21, 1787	2	166
Bezaleel, d. June 25, 1827, ae 68	2	167
Betsey, d. Amasa & Jedidah, b. Aug. 18, 1770	2	24
Bezaleel, see under Bazaleel		
Charity, d. Joshua, Jr. & Susannah, b. Aug. 4, 1767	2	26
Chauncey, s. Amasa & Jedidiah, b. Oct. 26, 1768	LR7	1
Chauncey, s. Silas & Lucinda, b. Oct. 5, 1795	2	279
Chevers, s. Amasa & Jedidah, b. Oct. 26, 1768	2	24
Cynthia L., m. Sylvester N. **WILLIAMS**, b. of East Haddam, Feb. 25, 1834, by Rev. Isaac Parsons	3	133
Daniell, s. Daniell & Susan[n]a, b. Sept. 28, 1690	LR1	4
Daniell, m. Hannah **SELDIN**, Feb. 2, 1715	LR1	581

	Vol.	Page
BRAINARD, BRAINERD, (cont.)		
Daniell, s. Joshua & Mehettabell, b. July 17, 1715	LR1	573
Daniell, s. Daniell & Hannah, b. Feb. 24, 1720/21	LR1	581
Daniell, Jr., d. Sept. 28, 1728	LR1	581
Daniel, m. Esther **SPENCER**, Jan. 6, 1736/7	LR2	1110
Daniel, s. Daniel & Esther, b. Sept. 17, 1739	LR2	1110
Daniel, s. Daniel & Esther, d. Jan. 12, 1740/41	LR2	1110
Daniell, Dea., d. [ ] 28, 1742/3	LR1	4
Daniel, Jr., m. Hannah **GATES**, July 7, 1743	LR2	1098
Daniel, s. Daniel & Hannah, b. Mar. 10, 1744	LR2	1098
Daniell, s. Bazaliel & Elizabeth, b. Mar. 17, 1746	LR2	1092
Daniel, s. Daniel & Esther, b. July 3, 1748	LR2	1110
Daniel, s. Daniel & Esther, d. Sept. 21, 1749	LR2	1110
Daniel, Jr., m. Esther **GATES**, Aug. 15, 1751	LR4	469
Daniel, s. Daniel & Esther, b. Mar. 14, 1752	LR4	475
Daniel, s. Daniel & Esther, b. June 13, 1755	LR4	469
Daniel, s. Daniel, Jr. & Hannah, d. Aug. 15, 1755	LR2	1098
Daniel, 2d, m. Anna **MARSH**, Apr. 16, 1768	2	42
Daniel, of East Haddam, m. Prudence **GRIDLEY**, of Farmington, June 6, 1771	2	36
Daniel, 2d, m. Darkis **GILBART**, b. of East Haddam, Dec. 31, 1773	2	42
Daniel, Judge of Probate, d. Jan. 10, 1777, in the 55th y. of his age	2	37
Daniel, s. David & Rachel, b. Mar. 13, 1784	2	164
Daniel Adams, s. Daniel, 2d, & Anna, b. Dec. 31, 1771	2	42
Darius, s. Bazaleel & Hannah, b. July 29, 1767	LR6	508
David, s. Joshua, Jr. & Mehitabell, b. Sept. 5, 1750	LR2	1111
David, m. Rachel **SMITH**, b. of East Haddam, June 5, 1783	2	164
David, s. David & Rachel, b. June 25, 1786	2	164
Deborah, d. Joshua & Mehettabell, b. Aug. 12, 1714; d. Sept. 2, 1714	LR1	573
Deborah, d. Joshua & Mahettabell, b. June 20, 1724	LR1	573
Deborah, m. Henry **CHAMPION**, Jr., b. of East Haddam, Dec. 25, 1746	LR6	509
Dolly, d. David & Rachel, b. Aug. 22, 1791	2	164
Dyer, s. Amasa & Jedidah, b. May 25, 1774	2	24
Ebenezer, s. Daniel & Esther, b. May 4, 1760	LR4	475
Edwin, m. Lucy Ann **WHITMORE**, b. of East Haddam, Nov. 24, 1831, by Rev. Isaac Parsons	3	121
Ealieazer, s. Joshua & Mehettabell, b. Nov. 10, 1719 (Eleazer)	LR1	573
Eliza G., ae 19, b. in East Haddam, res. East Haddam, m. Henry S. **AYRES**, ae 24, b. in East Haddam, res. East Haddam, Aug. 24, 1856, at the Parsonage, by Rev. Nelson Goodrich. Int. pub. Aug. 22, 1856	4	93
Elizabeth, 3rd, d. Noadiah & Hannah, b. Aug. 12, 1731	LR1	575
Elizabeth, 3rd, d. Noadiah & Hannah, d. June 15, 1731/2	LR1	575
Elizabeth, 4th, d. Noadiah & Hannah, b. Jan. 27, 1732/3	LR2	575

	Vol.	Page
BRAINARD, BRAINERD, (cont.)		
Elizabeth, d. Noadiah & Hannah, d. June 13, 1733	LR1	575
Elizabeth, w. of Bazaliel, d. Oct. 5, 1746	LR2	1092
Elizabeth, of Middletown, m. George **CONE**, Jr., of East Haddam, May 21, 1761	LR6	503
Elizabeth, m. Noadiah **EMMONS**, b. of East Haddam, May 1, 1777	2	176
Elizabeth, of East Haddam, m. Daniel **ROL[L]O**, of Burlington, N. Y., May 4, 1829, by Rev. Isaac Parsons	3	102
Ellen A., of East Haddam, m. William B. **YOUNG**, of Chatham, Sept. 5, 1852, by Rev. Isaac Parsons	3	237
Enoch, s. Bazaliel & Phebe, b. Sept. 9, 1749	LR2	1092
Enoch S., of Lebanon, m. Abba **BRAINERD**, of East Haddam, [Aug.] 17, 1820, by Rev. Isaac Parsons	2	319
Enos L., m. Emily **SCOVEL**, Dec. 27, 1829, by Isaac Parsons	3	104
Epaphroditis, s. Jared & Sybil, b. Mar. 4, 1777	LR7	1
Easter, d. Bazaliell & Mary, b. Oct. 21, 1729	LR2	b
Esther, d. Bazaliel & Mary, d. Dec. 19, 1737	LR2	b
Esther, d. Daniel & Esther, b. Oct. 14, 1741	LR2	1110
Esther, d. Daniel & Esther, d. Sept. 22, 1749	LR2	1110
Esther, d. Daniel & Esther, b. July 2, 1750	LR4	475
Esther, d. Daniel & Esther, b. Aug. 7, 1757	LR4	469
Esther, w. of Daniel, d. May 11, 1769	LR4	469
Fanna, d. Silas & Lusinda, b. Feb. 26, 1799	2	279
Fanny, of East Haddam, m. George **LEWIS**, 2d, of Chatham, Jan. 15, 1824, by Rev. Isaac Parsons	3	50-1
Frederick, butcher, ae 24, of E. Haddam, m. Elizabeth **CLARK**, ae 23, Jan. 23, 1851, by Mr. Geer	4	37-8
Frvin*, d. Bazaliell & Mary, b. Apr. 15, 1733 (*Fruin)	LR2	b
Gideon, s. Daniel & Esther, b. Dec. 2, 1752	LR4	469
Gideon, s. Daniel, d. Oct. 25, 1775, in the 23rd y. of his age at Roxbury, Mass.	2	37
Gideon, s. Daniel & Esther, d. Oct. 25, [1775], at Roxbury, in the 23rd y. of his age. Enlisted in Gen. Spencer's Co., 1775, in the 15th reign of George 3d	2	99
Han[n]ah, d. Daniell & Susan[n]a, b. June 12, 1694	LR1	4
Hannah, d. Daniell & Hannah, b. Nov. 28, 1718	LR1	581
Hannah, m. Joseph **GATES**, Jan. 8, 1718/19	LR1	573
Hannah, d. Noadiah & Hannah, b. Apr. 24, 1725	LR1	575
Hannah(?), [d. Daniel, Jr. & Hannah], d. [Jan. or Feb. 1726(?)]	LR1	581
Hannah, d. Daniell, Jr., b. Aug. 9, 1726	LR1	581
Hannah, d. Bazaliell & Mary, b. Aug. 26, 1728	LR2	b
Hannah, d. Daniell, Jr. & Hannah, b. Apr. 17, 1729	LR1	581
Hannah, alias **SELDIN**, m. Jonathan **CHAPMAN**, Dec. 3, 1730	LR2	1120
Hannah, d. Bazaliel & Mary, d. Sept. 29, 1736	LR2	b
Hannah, w. of Noadiah, d. May 14, 1744	LR2	1097
Hannah, m. William **SELBY**, Dec. 26, 1744	LR3	4
Hannah, w. of Daniel, Jr., d. May 5, 1746	LR2	1098

	Vol.	Page
BRAINARD, BRAINERD, (cont.)		
Hannah, m. Jabez **WARNER**, May 9, 1749	LR4	471
Hannah, of Middletown, m. Joel **CONE**, of East Haddam, June 9, 1757	LR5	267
Hannah, m. Joel **CONE**, June 9, 1757	LR7	411
Hannah, of Colchester, m. Bezaleel **BRAINERD**, of East Haddam, June 22, 1758	LR6	508
Hannah, d. Daniel & Esther, b. Aug. 25, 1761	LR4	469
Hannah, d. Jared & Sybel, b. Dec. 31, 1764	LR7	1
Hannah, d. Bezaleel & Hannah, b. Aug. 13, 1765	LR6	508
Hannah, d. Bezaleel & Hannah, d. Oct. 27, 1776	2	39
Hannah, m. Daniel Hurlbut **WHITE**, b. of East Haddam, Aug. 31, 1780	2	12
Hannah, d. Bezaleel, Jr. & Lydia, b. Dec. 4, 1790	2	166
Hannah, w. of Bezaleel, d. Aug. 26, 1819	2	39
Harriet, wid. of Darius, of East Haddam, m. Amasa **CARRIER**, of Marlborough, Feb. 18, 1852, by Rev. Isaac Parsons	3	235
Huldah, d. Joshua & Mehitabell, b. Feb. 14, 1744/5	LR2	1111
Huldah, m. David Brainerd **SPENCER**, Feb. 2, 1769	LR7	410
Huldah, m. David B. **SPENCER**, Feb. 2, 1769	2	38
James Frederick, m. Ann Elizabeth **CLARK**, b. of East Haddam, Jan. 27, 1851, by Rev. Alpheas Geer	3	229
Jared, s. Noadiah & Hannah, b. Sept. 17, 1730	LR1	575
Jared, m. Sybel **BATE**, Apr. 19, 1763	LR7	1
Jared S., m. Mrs. Mariah **CONE**, June 9, 1822, by Rev. Simeon Dickinson, at the house of Wid. Peggy Cone	3	25
Jedidah, d. Amasa & Jedidah, b. July 13, 1781	2	24
Jedidah, d. Amasa & Jedidah, d. Oct. 10, 1787	2	25
Jeremiah, m. Mehitable **ANNABLE**, Sept. 20, 1750	LR4	469
Jeremiah, s. Jeremiah & Mehitable, b. Dec. 25, 1751	LR4	469
Jeremiah Gates, s. Daniel & Esther, b. July 28, 1759	LR4	469
Jerusha, m. Samuell **SPENCER**, Dec. 19, 1732	LR2	1126
John, s. Joshua, Jr. & Mehitabell, b. Dec. 13, 1752	LR2	1111
John M., of Chatham, m. Olive **SILLIMAN**, of East Haddam, Jan. 1, 1829, by Rev. Isaac Parsons	3	101
John S., of East Haddam, m. Mary C. **CLARK**, of Haddam, Jan. 1, 1851, by Rev. Jacob Gardiner, Moodus	3	229
John S., housejoiner, ae 20, of E. Haddam, m. Mary C. **CLARK**, ae 20, b. in Haddam, Jan. 1, 1851, by Elder Gardner	4	37-8
Jonah, s. Joshua, Jr. & Mehitabell, b. Apr. 2, 1747	LR2	1111
Joseph, m. Sophia **SMITH**, b. of East Haddam, Feb. 13, 1812, by Rev. Elijah Parsons	2	303
Joseph Sluman, s. Amasa & Jedidah, b. Sept. 5, 1776	2	24
Joshua, m. Mahittabell **DUDLEY**, July 12, 1710	LR1	573
Joshua, Jr., m. Mehitabell **CHURCH**, Mar. 31, 1737	LR2	1111
Joshua, s. Joshua, Jr. & Mehitabell, b. May 31, 1738	LR2	1111
Joshua, Capt., d. May 13, 1755, in the 84th y. of his age	LR1	573

	Vol.	Page
BRAINARD, BRAINERD, (cont.)		
Joshua, Jr., m. Susannah **CHAPMAN**, b. of East Haddam, Aug. 26, 1762	LR6	503
Joshua, Jr., m. Susannah **CHAPMAN**, b. of East Haddam, Aug. 26, 1762	2	26
Joshua, s. Joshua, Jr. & Susannah, b. Apr. 30, 1763	LR6	503
Joshua, s. Joshua, Jr. & Susannah, b. Apr. 30, 1763	2	26
Julia A., of East Haddam, m. William E. **MERRICK**, of Hartford, Mar. 22, 1847, by Rev. Isaac Parsons	3	209
Julia E., m. Charles T. **HAMILTON**, b. of East Haddam, Apr. 24, 1856, by Rev. James M. Phillips	3	244
Julia E., ae 20, b. in East Haddam, res. East Haddam, m. Charles T. **HAMILTON**, ae 24, b. at Montville, res. East Haddam, Apr. 24, 1856, by Rev. James M. Phillips. Int. pub. Apr. 24, 1856	4	86
Laura, d. Bezaleel, Jr. & Lydia, b. July 19, 1788	2	166
Laura, m. Erastus **COMSTOCK**, Nov. 27, 1805	2	293
Lois, d. Silas & Lusinda, b. Nov. 18, 1802	2	279
Lusinda, d. Silas & Lusinda, b. Oct. 27, 1800	2	279
Lucy, d. Bezaleel & Hannah, b. May 26, 1769	LR6	508
Lucy, d. Bezaleel & Hannah, d. Oct. 1, 1776	2	39
Lucy, d. Bezaleel, Jr. & Lydia, b. July 17, 1793	2	166
Lucy D., m. William **BRAINERD**, Sept. 16, 1824, by Rev. Jacob Scales, at Colchester	3	92
Lidea, d. Joshua & Mehettabell, b. Sept. 1, 1717	LR1	573
Lydia, m. Joshua **GATES**, July 8, 1736	LR2	1110
Lydia, d. Daniel & Esther, b. Apr. 26, 1746	LR2	1110
Lydiah, d. Daniel & Esther, d. Sept. 18, 1749	LR2	1110
Lidiah, m. Samuel **MACK**, b. of East Haddam, Feb. 14, 1758	LR6	513
Martha, m. Joseph **SPENCER**, Jr., Aug. 2, 1738	LR2	1112
Mary, d. Daniell & Susan[n]a, b. Sept. 10, 1703	LR1	4
Mary, w. Joshua, d. Dec. 25, 1704	LR1	3
Mary, d. Joshua & Mahettabell, b. Oct. 6, 1721	LR1	573
Mary, d. Daniell & Hannah, b. Sept. 24, 1723	LR1	581
Mary, 2d, d. [Daniel, Jr. & Hannah], d. [Jan. or Feb. 1726?]	LR1	581
Mary(?), d. Daniell, Jr., d. Jan. or Feb. [ ], 1726	LR1	581
Mary, d. Noadiah & Hannah, b. Apr. 24, 1727	LR1	575
Mary, m. William **OLMSTEAD**, July [ ], 1728	LR3	6
Mary, d. Bazaliell & Mary, b. June 3, 1731	LR2	b
Mary, d. Bazaliel & Mary, d. Jan. 10, 1738/9	LR2	b
Mary, d. Bazaliel & Mary, b. July 7, 1740	LR2	b
Mary, w. of Bazaliel, d. Mar. 1, 1742	LR2	b
Mary, m. Ebenezer **CONE**, Jr., b. of East Haddam, Jan. 8, 1746	LR3	17
Mary, m. Bazaleel **GATES**, Feb. 26, 1749/50	LR4	475
Mary, of Middletown, m. John **PARSEVEL**, Jr., of East Haddam, Nov. 7, 1754	LR7	4
Mary, d. Bezaleel & Hannah, b. July 4, 1763	LR6	508
Mary, d. Daniel & Prudence, b. Sept. 1, 1776	2	36

	Vol.	Page
BRAINARD, BRAINERD, (cont.)		
Mary, d. Amasa & Jedidah, b. May 29, 1783	2	24
Mary, d. David & Rachel, b. Apr 29, 1788	2	164
Mary, m. Isaac **CHAPMAN**, Jr., b. of East Haddam, Sept. 27, 1801	2	267
Mary, [d. Jared & Sybel]	LR7	1
Mary, see also Mary **CHAPMAN**	2	268
Mary E., of East Haddam, m. Joseph **CLARKE**, of Haddam, July 1, 1852, by Rev. W. Emmerson	3	236
Mehittabell, d. Joshua & Mehittabell, b. Nov. 7, 1712	LR1	573
Mehitabell, d. Joshua, Jr. & Mehitabel, b. June 21, 1740	LR2	1111
Mehitabell, d. Joshua, Jr. & Mehitabell, d. May 13, 1758	LR2	1111
Mehetable, d. Amasa & Jedidah, b. Feb. 2, 1766	LR7	1
Mehitabel, d. Amasa & Jedidah, b. Feb. 2, 1766	2	24
Mehitable, w. of Joshua, d. July 23, 1771	2	27
Mehetabel, m. Calvin **SPENCER**, b. of East Haddam, Nov. 1, 1789	2	210
Morris M., m. Eliza D. **HARROW**, June 13, 1825, by Rev. Isaac Parsons	3	78
Nehemiah, s. Bezaleel & Hannah, b. Mar. 18, 1774	2	38
Nehemiah, s. Bezaleel & Hannah, d. Sept. 27, 1776	2	39
Noadiah, s. Daniell & Susan[n]a, b. Apr. 4, 1697	LR1	4
Noadiah, m. Hannah **CONE**, June 4, 1724	LR1	575
Noadiah, s. Noadiah & Hannah, b. Mar. 10, 1729	LR1	575
Noadiah, s. Dr. Noadiah & Hannah, d. Mar. 31, 1750	LR2	1097
Noadiah, [s. Jared & Sybel,]	LR7	1
Oliver, of Greenwich, m. Mary Snow, of East Haddam, May 7, 1838, by Rev. Isaac Parsons	3	164-5
Phebe had s. John **MARSH**, b. Jan. 31, 1756; father John **MARSH**	LR6	503
Phebe, m. John **MARSH**, b. of East Haddam, May 9, 1757	LR6	503
Phebe, d. Bezaleel & Lydia, b. Dec. 11, 1798	2	166
Phebe, of East Haddam, m. Silas A. **NICHOLS**, of Norwich, Nov. 11, 1822, by Rev. Isaac Parsons	3	28-9
Prudence, d. Daniel & Prudence, b. July 31, 1774	2	36
Raymond Hastings, s. Silas & Fanny, b. Dec. 25, 1821	2	279
R[e]uben, s. Joshua, Jr. & Susannah, b. Apr. 14, 1765	LR6	503
Reubin, s. Joshua, Jr. & Susannah, b. Apr. 14, 1765	2	26
Rhoda, d. Daniel & Esther, b. Mar. 18, 1763	LR4	475
Rhodiah, d. Daniel & Esther, b. Feb. 22, 1743/4	LR2	1110
Rhodiah, d. Daniel & Esther, d. Sept. 20, 1749	LR2	1110
Sally, Mrs., of Haddam, m. Joseph O. **ACKLEY**, of East Haddam, Sept. 24, 1812	2	219
Sarah, [d. Jared & Sybel,]	LR7	1
Silas, s. Silas & Lusinda, formerly of Middle Haddam, b. Dec. 31, 1793	2	279
Silas, m. Fanny **CHAPMAN**, b. of East Haddam, Nov. 27, 1820, by Rev. Isaac Parsons	2	279

	Vol.	Page
BRAINARD, BRAINERD, (cont.)		
Steven, s. Daniell & Susan[n]a, b. Feb. 27, 1699	LR1	4
Susanna, d. Daniell & Susan[n]a, b. Aug. 9, 1689	LR1	4
Susan[n]ah, d. Daniell & Hannah, b. Nov. 21, 1716	LR1	581
Susan[n]ah, [d. Daniel, Jr. & Hannah], d. [Jan. or Feb. 1726?]	LR1	581
Susannah, d. Bezaliel & Mary, b. Dec. 14, 1734	LR2	b
Susannah, d. Bazaliel & Mary, d. Dec. 22, 1737	LR2	b
Susannah, d. Daniell, Jr. & Hannah, d. Sept. 14, 1751	LR1	581
Susannah, w. of Dr. Daniel, d. Jan. 26, 1754	LR5	265
Susannah, d. Daniel & Esther, b. Feb. 1, 1766	LR4	469
Susannah, d. Daniel & Esther, d. May 9, 1769	LR4	469
Susannah, d. Joshua, Jr. & Susannah, b. Aug. 28, 1769	2	26
Susannah, d. Daniel & Prudence, b. June 21, 1772	2	36
Susannah, of Farmington, m. Timothy **GATES**, 3rd, of East Haddam, May 18, 1791	2	235
Sybil, d. Noadiah & Hannah, b. June 7, 1736	LR1	575
Sibbel, m. Aaron **CLEVELAND**, Oct. 24, 1751	LR4	470
Sibel, [d. Jared & Sybel]	LR7	1
Timothy, s. Joshua & Mahittabell, b. Mar. 18, 1729	LR1	573
Uri, s. Bezaleel & Hannah, b. Aug. 18, 1771	2	38
Uri, s. Bezaleel & Hannah, d. Oct. 4, 1776	2	39
Ursula, m. Russell E. **WILLIAMS**, b. of East Haddam, Apr. 26, 1835, by Nathaniel Miner	3	138
Washington, of Haddam Neck, m. Abigail M. **CLARK**, of Haddam Neck, July 12, 1845, by Rev. William S. Simmons, Leesville	3	202
William, s. Bezaleel, Jr. & Lydia, b. Oct. 29, 1795	2	166
William, m. Lucy D. **BRAINERD**, Sept. 16, 1824, by Rev. Jacob Scales, at Colchester	3	92
William Oren, s. [William & Lucy D.], b. Apr. 25, 1829	3	92
William S., m. Julia A. **CHAPMAN**, Nov. 15, 1836, by Rev. Isaac Parsons	3	146
Zeno, m. Mary **HILLIARD**, June 23, 1833, by Rev. N. E. Shailer	3	132
----iah, s. Joshua & Mahittabell, b. Mar. 14, 1727	LR1	573
------, d. W[illia]m H., painter, ae 47, of Haddam & Emily M. ae 40, b. July 2, 1850	4	25-6
-----, s. W. O., farmer, b. Jan. 17, 1853	4	47-8
-----, wid., d. [ ], 1853, ae 90	4	49-0
-----, s. Wilson, mechanic, ae 35, res. E. Haddam, & [ ], ae 35, b. Oct. 18, 1855	4	77
BRAMBLE, Joseph, m. Jane Ann **REYNOLDS**, b. of Lyme, July 13, 1841, by Ozias Holmes, J. P.	3	186
-----, d. Nelson, farmer, ae 27, & Laura, ae 21, b. Aug. 20, [1856]	4	110
BRAY, Han[n]ah, m. Abell **WILLEE**, July 17, 1703	LR1	4
BREWSTER, Benjamin F., of Springfield, Mass., m. Cynthia M. **ARNOLD**, of East Haddam, May 8, 1842, by Augustus		

	Vol.	Page
BREWSTER, (cont.)		
Olmsted, J. P.	3	190
BRIGHT, Juletee, d. John **BRIGHT** & Dorothy **CONE**, b. Jan. 31, 1787	2	14
BROCKWAY, BROCKWEY, Bette, of Lyme, m. Selden **WARNER**, of East Haddam, June 30, 1785	2	164
Carroline, d. Enoch & Mary, b. Oct. 3, 1783	2	206
Enoch, m. Mary **HUNGERFORD**, b. of East Haddam, May 1, 1781	2	206
Hannah, m. Joshua **BEEBE**, Oct. 18, 1733	LR4	467
Isaiah M., s. Charles E. L., farmer, ae 39, of Hadlyme, & Caroline M., ae 42, b. Aug. 13, 1850	4	35-6
Jane, of Lyme, m. Joseph **GATES**, 2d, of East Haddam, Aug. 13, 1772	2	108
Joseph B., m. Catharine J. **CLARK**, Jan. 16, 1825, by Rev. William Jarvis	3	69
Mary, of Lyme, m. Jeremiah **CONE**, of East Haddam, Aug. 10, 1773	2	106
Mary, d. Enoch & Mary, b. Jan. 15, 1782	2	206
Mary, d. Enoch & Mary, d. Dec. 9, 1784	2	207
Mary, d. Enoch & Mary, b. Nov. 23, 1788	2	206
Mary, [m.] Hezekiah **MACK**, Jr., b. of East Haddam, [ ]	2	46
Samuel M., m. Temperance C. **SPENCER**, b. of Lyme, Sept. 27, 1825, by Rev. Joseph Vaill, of Hadlyme	3	78
BROOKS, Abigail, wid., m. Isaac **CHAPMAN**, Dec. 24, 1786	2	34
Alvan, of Exeter, N. Y., m. Susannah **FULLER**, of East Haddam, Feb. 7, 1832, by Rev. Isaac Parsons	3	121
Aristarchos Smith, s. [Charles & Naomi], b. Oct. 3, 1810	3	111
Carlton, s. Revillo, polisher, ae 26, & Lucretia, ae 24, b. Nov. 30, 1849	4	11-2
Catharine H., of East Haddam, m. Nathaniel P. **CARD**, of Norwich, Oct. 21, 1832, by Rev. Isaac Parsons	3	125
Catharine Hope, d. [Charles & Naomi], b. Oct. 18, 1812	3	111
Charles, s. Elisabeth **SPENCER**, single woman, b. Apr. 18, 1779	2	8
Charles, m. Naomi **TROWBRIDGE**, Apr. 9, 1809, by Rev. Ezra Stiles Ely	3	111
Cha[rle]s, m. Sarah **BANNING**, [Mar.] 27, [1844], by Rev. Nathaniel Miner, Millington	3	200
Charles William, s. [Charles & Naomi], b. Jan. 12, 1826	3	111
Daniel, 2d, of East Haddam, m. Clarissa **SQUIRE**, of East Haddam, Mar. 31, 1839, by Rev. Isaac Parsons	3	168
Elizabeth, Mrs., m. Noadiah **EMMONS**, b. of East Haddam, Apr. 4, 1802	2	309
George Washington, s. [Charles & Naomi], b. Feb. 7, 1815	3	111
Henry A., ae 21, b. in East Haddam, res. East Haddam, m. Mary M. **BOWERS**, ae 17, b. at East Haddam, res. East Haddam, Dec. 30, 1855, by Rev. J. E. Heald. Int.		

	Vol.	Page
BROOKS, (cont.)		
pub. Dec. 24, 1855. Consent given Nov. 30, 1855, by Paris H. **BROOKS***, father of Mary M. **BOWERS**. (*Probably "**BOWERS**")	4	70
Huldah, ae 54, b. in Colchester, res. Hadlyme, m. 2d h. Samuel **BROOKS**, tanner, ae 76, b. in Lyme, res. Hadlyme, Mar. 19, 1850, by Rev. Stephen A. Loper	4	21-2
Jasper S., of Saybrook, m. Harriet **CHAPMAN**, of East Haddam, May 10, 1838, by Rev. Isaac Parsons	3	164-5
Leroy, mechanic, ae 21, of E. Haddam, m. Harriet **DIBBLE**, ae 20, b. in Saybrook, res. E. Haddam, Dec. 30, 1849, by Rev. Isaac Parsons	4	21-2
Leroy D., of East Haddam, m. Harriet A. **DIBBLE**, of Saybrook, Dec. 30, 1849, by Rev. Isaac Parsons	3	221
Louisa C., m. George **PALMER**, b. of East Haddam, Oct. 26, 1828, by Rev. Isaac Parsons	3	100
Ogden Moseley, s. [Charles & Naomi], b. Apr. 24, 1819	3	111
Palmer C., s. Ogden M., manufacturer, ae 30, & Henrietta, ae 26, b. May 10, 1849	4	11-2
Rachel, m. Joseph **CHURCH**, Sr., Sept. 5, 1841, by Charles William Bradley	3	188
Richard V., of Lyme, m. Harriet **DANIELS**, of East Haddam, Oct. 7, 1832, by Rev. Isaac Parsons	3	125
Rivillo, of Haddam, m. Lucretia G. **HUBBARD**, of East Haddam, July 16, 1846, by Rev. Isaac Parsons	3	206
Samuel, of Lyme, m. Huldah R. **HUNGERFORD**, of East Haddam, Mar. 19, 1850, by Rev. Stephen A. Loper, of Hadlyme	3	223
Samuel, tanner, ae 76, b. in Lyme, res. Hadlyme, m. 2d w. Huldah **BROOKS**, ae 54, b. in Colchester, res. Hadlyme, Mar. 19, 1850, by Rev. Stephen A. Loper	4	21-2
William D., s. Leroy **de DELOS**, manufacturer, ae 22, & Harriet A., ae 20, b. Nov. 11, 1850	4	31-2
William E., s. Charles W., house carpenter, ae 25, & Esther C., ae 22, b. Aug. 25, 1850	4	33-4
------, st. b. s. Jasper S., mason, ae 37, & Harriet, ae 37, b. Aug. 23, 1850	4	23-4
------, d. Ogden, mechanic, ae 37, & Henrietta, ae 32, b. Mar. [ ], 1855	4	80
-----, s. Charles W., joiner, ae 31, & Esther C., ae 28, b. Nov. 4, 1856	4	112
BROWN, Ann Elvira, d. [Halsey & Louisa], b. Oct. 16, 1838	3	179
Celia, of Chatham, m. Charles A. **CHESTER**, of East Haddam, [Oct.] 24, [1852], by A. E. Denison	3	238
Cephas C., of Colchester, m. Emeline F. **SELDEN**, Apr. 14, 1835, by Rev. Isaac Parsons	3	138
Elizabeth M., of Chatham, m. Oliver W. **MACK**, of Portland, Dec. 3, 1854, by Rev. John S. Sheffield	3	241

	Vol.	Page
BROWN, (cont.)		
Eunice, ae 19, b. in Colchester, res. Colchester, m. Arnold **WETMORE**, ae 23, b. in East Haddam, res. East Haddam, May 24, 1856, by Rev. Henry Torbush. Int. pub. May 20, 1856	4	89
Francis E., s. Cephas C., farmer, ae 40, & Emeline E., ae 37, b. Aug. 21, 1848	4	13-4
Halsey, of Chatham, m. Louisa **WHITMORE**, of East Haddam, Nov. 24, 1831, by Rev. Isaac Parsons	3	121
Halsey, m. Louisa **WHITMORE**, Nov. 24, 1831	3	179
Hannah, of Colchester, m. Peter **SPENCER**, of East Haddam, June 4, 1741	LR4	464
Harriet M., ae 21, b. at Haddam, res. E. Haddam, m. George L. **CHAPMAN**, ae 20, b. of Newfield, N. Y., res. E. Haddam, Aug. 5, 1855, by Rev. L. W. Blood. Int. pub. Aug. 1, 1855	4	60
Henry, m. Lavinia **DERBY**, b. of East Haddam, Oct. 9, 1842, by Stephen Alonzo Loper, in Hadlyme	3	192
Jeremiah V., of Haddam, m. Clarissa **MITCHELL**, of East Haddam, Nov. 18, 1827, by Rev. Isaac Parsons	3	96
Lucina P. M., d. Halsey, farmer, ae 44, & Lucena P., ae 42, b. Dec. 1, 1848	4	13-4
Malsey, m. Lucena P. **PECK**, Nov. 22, 1843, by Rev. Nathaniel Miner	3	196
Malsey, see also Halsey		
Mary S., m. William P. **MAYNARD**, b. of East Haddam, Mar. 24, 1850, by Rev. Stephen A. Loper, of Hadlyme	3	224
Mary S., ae 21, of Lyme, m. W[illia]m P. **MAYNARD**, farmer, ae 32, b. in E. Haddam, res. Lyme, Mar. 24, 1850, by Rev. Soper	4	19-20
Mehetibel, of Sandisfield, m. Gideon **GATES**, of East Haddam, Oct. 11, 1787	2	142
Parses, m. Rowland **CROCKER**, b. of East Haddam, May 24, 1763	LR7	1
Sarah, of Essex, m. Henry **FOX**, of Hartford, June 11, 1850, by Rev. W[illia]m Harris	3	226
-----, d. Cephas C., farmer, b. Nov. 5, 1851	4	33-4
BROWNELL, Charles Edward, s. Edward P. & Anst (?) C., b. Oct. 26, 1827	3	7
Emeline C., of East Haddam, m. Nathaniel C. **BOARDMAN**, of Plymouth, Aug. 9, 1852, by Rev. Isaac Parsons	3	237
Emeline Canfield, d. James H. & Louisa M., b. Oct. 16, 1831	3	48
Franklin Clinton, s. James H. & Louisa M., b. Feb. 11, 1830	3	48
Harriet Louisa, d. James H. & Louisa M., b. Aug. 17, 1834	3	48
Jane Maria, d. James H. & Louisa M., b. Mar. 11, 1833	3	48
Mary M., m. William C. **SPENCER**, b. of East Haddam, Sept. 27, 1854, by Rev. Isaac Parsons	3	240
Mary U., teacher, ae 23, of E. Haddam, m. William C.		

	Vol.	Page
BROWNELL, (cont.)		
SPENCER, merchant, ae 30, b. in Lyme, res. E. Haddam, Sept. 27, 1854	4	51-2
Mary Updike, d. E[dward] P. & A[nst] C., b. Mar. 28, 1831	3	7
Prudence Crary, d. E[dward] P. & A[nst] C., b. Nov. 26, 1833	3	7
Susan Ellen, d. James H. & Louisa M., b. July 16, 1836	3	48
BUCK, Sarah, m. William **STEWARD**, May 8, 1744	LR5	559
BUCKINGHAM, Gideon, reputed s. Gideon **BUCKINGHAM**, & Susannah **ANNABLE**, b. Sept. 22, 1786	2	4
Phebe, of Saybrook, m. Caleb **BEEBE**, of East Haddam, Mar. 6, 1737	LR5	559
BUELL, Emily F., of East Haddam, m. Julius A. **FULLER**, of Columbia, Conn., Sept. 26, 1852, by Rev. Warren Emmerson	3	237
Randalo, child of Joseph N., farmer, ae 37, of Colchester, & Susan A., ae 33, b. Feb. 10, 1847	4	3-4
BULKELEY, BULKLEY, Adelia, of Manchester, m. James **CONE**, of East Haddam, Sept. 4, 1842, by Rev. Simon Shaler, of Haddam	3	192
Ann A., of East Haddam, m. Geo[rge] R. **ROBERTS**, of Chicago, Ill., July 30, 1851, by Rev. Alpheas Geer	3	233
Ann A., ae 26, m. George R. **ROBERTS**, merchant. ae 32, b. Bridgewater, N. Y., res. Chicago, Ill., [ ], 1851, by Alpheas Geer	4	37-8
James, of Waterford, m. Adelia A. **WHITMORE**, of East Haddam, Jan. 1, 1824, by Rev. Isaac Parsons	3	50-1
Mary, m. Richard S. **PRATT**, Apr. 25, 1836	3	157
Mary, m. Richard S. **PRATT**, Apr. 25, 1836, by Rev. Isaac Parsons	3	142
Virginia, ae 25, b. in Colchester, res. East Haddam, m. George **WAKEMAN**, ae 29, b. in Wilton, Conn., res. East Haddam, June 12, 1856, by Levi H. Wakeman. Int. pub. June 10, 1856	4	89-90
BULL, William N., of Mereden, m. Myra M. **CHAPMAN**, of East Haddam, July 2, 1851, by Rev. Isaac Parsons	3	233
BULLONIA, Eleanor P., Mrs., ae 50, b. in Willimantic, res. East Haddam, m. Curtis S. **ARNOLD**, ae 63, b. in Haddam, res. East Haddam, Aug. 31, 1856, by Jonathan O. Cone, J. P. Int. pub. Aug. 31, 1856	4	93-94
BURDICK, Albert A., ae 21, of East Haddam, m. Mary E. **SPENCER**, ae 20, of East Haddam, Aug. 31, 1856, by Rev. Nelson Goodrich. Int. pub. Aug. 26, 1856	4	98
Denison P., of West Killingly, m. Sarah E. **CONE**, of East Haddam, Sept. 8, 1844, by Rev. W[illia]m S. Simmons	3	200
Mary Ann, Mrs., m. Elijah **HARVEY**, b. of East Haddam, June 27. 1849, by Rev. Moses Chace (Perhaps "**BURDICT**"]	3	218
BURKE, Edward G., m. Mary **FOWLER**, Mar. 29, 1835, by Isaac		

	Vol.	Page
BURKE, (cont.)		
Parsons	3	137
Frederick H., d. Mar. 18, 1850, ae 3	4	29-30
George A., s. Samuel, shoe manufacturer, & Sarah, d. Jan. 10, 1849, ae 8 m.	4	11-12
Lydia, of East Haddam, m. Hiram **WOODRUFF**, of Middletown, Oct. 31, 1821, by Rev. W[illia]m Lyman	3	17
Lyman, m. Elizabeth M. **ARNOLD**, b. of East Haddam, Dec. 12, 1853, by Rev. W. Emerson	3	238a
Martha M., of East Haddam, m. Erastus A. **MINER**, of Bozrah, July 4, 1847, by Rev. Isaac Parsons	3	210
Samuel, m. Sarah **LANNINGHAM**, Mar. 1, 1846, by Rev. Isaac Parsons	3	204
Samuel W., m. Lucy **SPENCER**, Jan. 8, 1843, by Nathaniel Miner	3	193
William, m. Olive **ARNOLD**, b. of East Haddam, [May] 27, [1821], by Rev. W[illia]m Lyman	3	5
-----, d. Sam[ue]l, mechanic, res. East Haddam, b. May 29, 1856	4	95
BURNHAM, Aaron H., of East Haddam, m. Eliza A. **DRASON**, of Vermont, Jan. 18, 1852, by Rev. Isaac Parsons	3	234
Abigail, d. Jacob & Mary, b. Aug. 12, 1734	LR4	456
Abigail, bd. Jan. 7, 1855, in Hadlyme	4	57
Anna, d. Joshua & Margret, b. Dec. 22, 1755	LR7	3
Anna, m. Calvin C. **MACK**, Jan. 7, 1812	3	129
Austin, m. Almira **ANDREWS**, b. of East Haddam, Nov. 26, 1850, by Rev. Geo[rge] W. Brewster, Moodus	3	229
Azubah, m. Anson **ACKLEY**, b. of East Haddam, Mar. 17, 1822, by Rev. W[illia]m Lyman	3	23
Betsey, d. Nathan & Mary, b. Nov. 21, 1784	LR8	4
Betsey, m. Daniel Chapman **BLAKSLEE**, b. of East Haddam, Jan. 27, 1817, by Rev. Solomon Blakslee, of New London	2	305
Catharine, ae 17, b. in Colchester, res. East Haddam, m. W[illia]m **LYMAN**, mechanic, ae 22, b. in Henderson, N. Y., res. East Haddam, May 3, 1848, by Isaac Parsons	4	1-2
Catharine M., m. William **LYMAN**, b. of East Haddam, Apr. 23, 1848, by Rev. Isaac Parsons	3	212
David A., shoemaker, m. Almyra E. **ANDREWS**, apprentice in cotton mill, Nov. 26, 1851, by George W. Brewster	4	37-8
Dyer, s. Nathan & Mary, b. July 23, 1771	LR8	4
Griswold, of Hebron, m. Eliza J. **SWAN**, of East Haddam, Mar. 26, 1838, by Rev. Isaac Parsons	3	160
Israel D., m. Mary Adeline **CHESTER**, b. of East Haddam, Mar. 19, 1840, by Rev. George Carrington, of Hadlyme	3	176-7
James A. m. Sabra A. **GATES**, b. of East Haddam, May 2, 1847, by Rev. Isaac Parsons	3	209
Jerusha R. B., m. Livingston **ALEXANDER**, Apr. 1, 1832, by Rev. Isaac Parsons	3	122

	Vol.	Page
BURNHAM, (cont.)		
John, m. Lucretia J. **MANTLE**, b. of East Haddam, Oct. 4, 1835, by Rev. Nathaniel Miner	3	140-1
Joshua, s. Jacob & Mary, b. May 20, 1732	LR4	465
Joshua, of East Haddam, m. Margret **PHELPS**, of Lyme, Jan. 9, 1755	LR7	3
Mary, d. Nathan & Mary, b. Jan. 26, 1776	LR8	4
Nathan, s. Jacob & Mary, b. Feb. 3, 1737	LR4	465
Nathan, s. Joshua & Margret, b. Oct. 11, 1758	LR7	3
Nathan, m. Mary **ANNABLE**, b. of East Haddam, (or said to be), Feb. 7, 1771	LR8	4
Nathan Crocker, s. Nathan & Mary, b. Dec. 28, 1788	LR8	4
Rebeckah, d. Joshua & Margret, b. Aug. 28, 1761	LR7	3
Ruth A., ae 18, b. in East Haddam, res. East Haddam, m. Warren **CULVER**, ae 21, b. in Marlborough, res. East Haddam, July 14, 1856, by Rev. Isaac Parsons. Int. pub. July 11, 1856	4	90
Sarah, d. Nathan & Mary, b. Nov. 27, 1782	LR8	4
-----, d. James A., shoemaker, ae 24, & Sabra, ae 20, b. Feb. 12, 1850	4	23-4
------, d. Aaron, shoemaker, & Eliza, b. Apr. 9, 1855	4	68
BURNS, Minnie, d. John & Ellen, b. May 24, 1856, as certified by Garrett Kieff, of Glastonbury, Ct., Jan. 29, 1868	4	117
BURR, Abigail, m. Jeremiah **SPENCER**, Jan. 7, 1747/8	LR3	508
Abigail, m. Jonathan **WILLIAMS**, b. of East Haddam, Mar. 29, 1764	LR7	4
Benjamin B., m. Clarissa **BEEBE**, Feb. 14, 1839, by Francis Griffin, J. P.	3	168
Hannah, m. Daniel **FOX**, Oct. 15, 1747	LR6	507
Henry E., of Haddam, m. Harriet N. **BEEBE**, of East Haddam, Nov. 4, 1838, by Rev. Erastus Denison	3	167
Horace, of Westbrook, m. Louisa N. **HUNGERFORD**, of East Haddam, Dec. 13, 1847, by Rev. Stephen Alonzo Loper, of Hadlyme	3	211
Ruth, m. Isaac D. **ACKLEY**, b. of East Haddam, Apr. 27, 1785	2	134
Thankfull, m. Jonathan **HINKLY**, Jr., Nov. 28, 1741	LR4	471
BURROWS, Urban, of Penn., m. Emeline Eliza **LORD**, of East Haddam, Sept. 23, 1824, by Rev. W[illia]m Jarvis	3	64-5
BURT, Dorothy, m. John **PERCIVAL**, 3rd, b. of East Haddam, May 24, 1781	2	138
Lidia, of Lebanon, m. Eliazer **BOOGE**, of East Haddam, Mar. 19, 1728	LR5	266
Zilpha, d. Richard, & Sarah, b. Sept. 18, 1748, in Barkley, R. I.	2	40
Zilpha, of Canterbury, m. Obadiah **GATES**, of East Haddam, Aug. 15, 1771	2	40
BUTLER, Mehetable D., domestic, b. in Haddam, res. East Haddam, married, d. Sept. 11, 1856, ae 38	4	94
BUTTON, [see also **BUTLER**], Mehetable, married, d. Sept. 11,		

	Vol.	Page
BUTTON, (cont.)		
1856, ae 38	4	99
-----, s. Nelson, spoon polisher, ae 27, & Maria, ae 24, b. June 19, 1856	4	109
-----, d. Benjamin, farmer, ae 48, & Mehitable, ae 38, b. Sept. 6, 1856	4	101
CADY, Zalmon, stone cutter, ae 41, of Chatham, m. 2d w. Sylvia Eliza **LEWIS**, ae 23, b. in Haddam, res. E. Haddam, Mar. 6, 1853, by Jacob Gardner	4	43-4
CALHOUN, Diodate G., alias **COON**, m. Mary O. **WILLARD**, b. of East Haddam, Apr. 23, 1843, by Rev. Charles William Bradley	3	194
Georgia, d. Diodate G., ae 36, & Mary, ae 26, b. Jan. 20, 1849	4	11-2
CALKINS, [see under **CAULKINS**]		
CAMBRIDGE, Fanny, colored, d. Jan. 18, 1835, ae about 50	3	46
CAMMEL, Amos, s. John & Axe, b. Oct. 13, 1811	2	289
Claris[s]a Maria, d. John & Axe, b. Dec. 18, 1809	2	289
John, alias Punch, m. Axe Mason (negro), b. of East Haddam, Oct. 16, 1803 (People of color but free)	2	289
John, s. John & Axe, b. June 20, 1805	2	289
Mary Ann, d. Punch alias John & Axe, b. Dec. 1, 1803	2	289
William Mason, s. John & Axe, b. Sept. 24, 1807	2	289
CAMPBELL, Hannah, m. William **STEWARD**, Feb. 2, 1732	LR5	559
CANFIELD, Harriet M., m. Humphrey **LYON**, b. of East Haddam, Jan. 8, 1821, by Rev. Solomon Blakesley	3	1
Marcy, of Saybrook, m. John **HOLMES**, of East Haddam, Apr. 22, 1762	LR7	417
CAPLES, George G., of East Haddam, m. Caroline C. **WILLIAMS**, of Lyme, Sept. 24, 1848, by Nathaniel Miner	3	216
Joseph W., s. George, farmer, colored, ae 28, & Caroline, ae 21, b. Dec. 31, 1849	4	25-6
Lucretia, of East Haddam, m. Luman T. **PELHAM**, of Hartford, Jan. 20, 1849, by Rev. Nathaniel Miner	3	174
Ray, of Saybrook, m. Mary R. **HUBBARD**, of East Haddam, Aug. 18, 1830, by Rev. Isaac Parsons	3	108
----, s. George G., farmer, colored, ae 25, & Caroline, ae 22, b. Mar. 9, 1851	4	33-4
CARD, Almira O., m. Jonathan O. **CONE**, Dec. 7, 1836, by Rev. Alfred Gates	3	151
Almira Olive, d. [Stanton S. & Olive], b. Jan. 4, 1817	3	109
Elijah Bradford, s. [Stanton S. & Olive], b. Aug. 25, 1815	3	109
Elijah Bradford, s. Stanton S. & Olive, d. Apr. 15, 1830	3	110
Eliza Ann, d. [Stanton S. & Olive], b. Oct. 1, 1820	3	109
Eliza Ann, of East Haddam, m. Emory **JOHNSON**, of Middle Haddam, Oct. 24, 1838, by Rev. Ebenezer Loomis	3	166
Gurdon, s. Stanton S. & Olive, d. Sept. 5, 1824	3	110
Gurdon S., s. [Stanton S. & Olive], b. Aug. 26, 1824	3	109
Nathaniel P., of Norwich, m. Catharine H. **BROOKS**, of East		

	Vol.	Page
CARD, (cont.)		
Haddam, Oct. 21, 1832, by Rev. Isaac Parsons	3	125
Stanton S., b. Dec. 26, 1790; m. Olive **PARKHURST**, Jan. 2, 1814, at Plainfield	3	109
CAREW, Simon S., of Stonington, m. Julia A. **EMMONS**, of East Haddam, Nov. 4, [1846], by Nathaniel Miner	3	208
CARRIER, CARIER, [see also **CARVER**], Amasa, of Marlborough, m. Mrs. Harriet **BRAINERD**, wid. of Darius, of East Haddam, Feb. 18, 1852, by Rev. Isaac Parsons	3	235
Ellen G., m. Jones P. **GATES**, June 6, 1847, by Rev. Isaac Parsons	3	210
Jerusha B., of Colchester, m. Richardson **FULLER**, of East Haddam, Sept. 14, 1835, by W[illia]m Marsh, J. P.	3	140-1
Mary, m. Samuel **LORD**, b. of Colchester, Jan. 3, 1750	LR3	3
Stephen A., of Chatham, m. Sarah **RANSOM**, of East Haddam, [June] 5, [1850], by Nathaniel Miner	3	225
Stephen A., tanner, ae 28, of Chatham, m. Sarah **RANSOM**, ae 24, b. in E. Haddam, res. Chatham, June 2, 1850, by Nathaniel Miner	4	19-20
CARTER, Charles Henry, [s. William & Ann], b. Dec. 2, 1824	3	56-57
Edward Oliver, [s. William & Ann], b. July 23, 1826	3	56-57
Orpha Ann, m. Nathan **PRATT**, Jr., Nov. [ ], 1827, by Rev. John Marsh, at Haddam	3	139
William, m. Ann **SOUTHWORTH**, Feb. 23, 1824, by Rev. Simeon Dickinson, at the house of John Southworth	3	56-57
CARVER, [see also **CARRIER**], Frances R., d. Lucian B., farmer, ae 36, of Hebron, & Hannah E., ae 28, b. Feb. 7, 1851	3	33-34
Lucien B., of Hebron, m. Hannah C. **OLMSTED**, of East Haddam, May 31, [1848], by Nath[anie]l Miner	3	213
Lucian B., farmer, ae 32, b. in Hebron, res. Hebron, m. Hannah E. **OLMSTED**, ae 25, b. in East Haddam, res. Hebron, May 31, 1848, by Nath[anie]l Miner	4	1-2
------, st. b. s. Lucien B., farmer, ae 35, & Hannah E., ae 26, b. July 28, 1849	4	15-16
CAULKINS, CALKINS, Abigail, m. Jonah **SPENCER**, Aug. 20, 1767	LR7	410
Isaac Newton, of New York State, m. Sophia Esther **CHADWICK**, of East Haddam, Apr. 28, 1825, by Josiah Griffin, J. P.	3	76-77
Lucy, d. Aquilla & Desire, b. May 1, 1762	LR6	511
Molly, d. Aquilia & Desire, b. June 19, 1759	LR6	511
CHADWICK, Anson Gillett, s. Silas, 2d, & Sophia, b. July 29, 1801	2	309
Bets[e]y, m. Josiah J. **BAKER**, b. of East Haddam, Jan. 13, 1791	2	243
Esther, w. of Silas, d. Mar. 3, 1819, ae 72	2	316
George H., of Lyme, m. Mehitable S. **CONE**, of East Haddam, Apr. 21, 1825, by Rev. Herman L. Vaill	3	74-75
George Latimer, s. James & Rachel, b. Mar 22, 1803	2	311

	Vol.	Page
CHADWICK, (cont.)		
Israel Coleman, s. Silas & Sophia, b. Mar. 8, 1806	2	309
James, of East Haddam, m. Rachel **LATIMER**, of Montville, May 1, 1800, by Andrew Griswold, J. P.	2	311
James, d. Mar. 26, 1839	2	312
James Madison, s. James & Rachel, b. Nov. 6, 1813	2	311
Lydia, m. Griswold C. **PHELPS**, b. of East Haddam, Jan. 16, 1825, by Rev. Simeon Shailer, of Haddam	3	70-71
Mary, of East Haddam, m. Henry R. **WATROUS**, of Lyme, Nov. 22, 1821, by Josiah Griffin, J. P.	3	19
Mary Hunt, d. James & Rachel, b. Feb. 18,. 1801	2	311
Orris Church, d. Silas & Sophia, b. July 20, 1810	2	309
Rachel S., m. Epaphroditus G. **GATES**, Mar. 25, 1838, by Rev. Nathaniel Miner, of Millington	3	164-5
Rachel S., m. Epaphroditus G. **GATES**, Mar. 25, 1838	3	180-1
Rachel Smith, d. James & Rachel, b. Feb. 14, 1808	2	311
Sophia Esther, d. Silas & Sophia, b. Apr. 24, 1803	2	309
Sophia Esther, of East Haddam, m. Isaac Newton **CAULKINS**, of New York State, Apr. 28, 1825, by Josiah Griffin, J. P.	3	76-77
CHALKER, Alice A., m. Elijah B. **PURPLE**, b. of East Haddam, Dec. 14, 1834, by Rev. Stephen Beach	3	136
Deborah, m. Thomas **HUNGERFORD**, Jan. 7, 1739	LR4	472
Harriet A., m. Joseph **CHURCH**, Jr., Sept. 18, 1848	3	158
Harriet A., m. Joseph **CHURCH**, Jr., b. of East Haddam, Sept. 18, 1848, by Rev. Alpheas Geer	3	214
John, shoemaker, b. in Durham, res. E. Haddam, married, d. Oct. 30, 1852, ae 67	4	49-50
Marilla, m. John **SQUIRES**, Dec. 13, 1840, by Isaac Parsons, V. D. M.	3	184
CHAMBERLAIN, Benjamin, m. Lydia **HUNGERFORD**, b. of East Haddam, Sept. 17, 1821, by Isaac Chester, J. P.	3	11
Meriam, of Colchester, m. Daniel **SCOVEL**, of East Haddam, July 1, 1756	LR6	507
CHAMPION, CHAMPEN, Andrew, s. Israel & Mehitable, b. Sept. 5, 1766	LR5	561
Andrew, of East Haddam, m. Lucy **BARTLETT**, of Lebanon, Jan. 27, 1791	2	229
Ann, d. Israel & Mehitable, b. Mar. 4, 1763	LR5	561
Clarissa, d. Epaphroditus & Lucretia, b. Feb. 24, 1785	2	144
Clarissa, d. Gen. Epa[phroditu]s & Lucretia, d. Oct. 22, 1801	2	145
Ebenezer, s. Henry & Mahittabell, b. Jan. 27, 1718	LR2	a
Ebenezer, s. Henry & Mehetable, d. Jan. 16, 1789	2	15
Elizabeth, d. Henry & Mahittabell, b. June 26, 1734	LR2	a
Epaphraditus, s. Henry, Jr. & Deborah, b. Apr. 16, 1749	LR6	509
Epaphroditus, of East Haddam, m. Lucretia **HUBBARD**, of Hatfield. Dec. 17, 1781	2	144
Epaphroditus, s. Epaphroditus & Lucretia, b. Oct. 21, 1786	2	144
Epaphroditus, Gen., d. Dec. 22, 1834, ae 79	2	145

	Vol.	Page
CHAMPION, CHAMPEN, (cont.)		
Hallet, s. Andrew & Lucy, b. Mar. 27, 1803	2	229
Henry, m. Mahittabell **ROWLE**, Jan. 16, 1717	LR2	a
Henry, s. Henry & Mahittabell, b. Jan. 19, 1723	LR2	a
Henry, Jr., m. Deborah **BRAINERD**, b. of East Haddam, Dec. 25, 1746	LR6	509
Henry, s. Henry, Jr. & Deborah, b. Oct. 23, 1747	LR6	509
Henry, s. Henry, Jr. & Deborah, d. Jan. 26, 1750	LR6	509
Henry, d. Nov. 26, 1779	2	15
Ichabod, s. Israel & Mehitable, b. Nov. 23, 1757	LR5	561
Ichabod, s. Israel & Mehitabel d. Sept. 9, 1775	2	17
Ichabod, s. Andrew & Lucy, b. Mar. 25, 1801	2	229
Ichabod, of Rome, O., m. Lucretia **COFFIN**, of East Haddam, Oct. 11, 1830, by Isaac Parsons	3	108
Israel, s. Henry & Mahittabell, b. Dec. 20, 1726	LR2	a
Israel, m. Mehitable **FULLER**, Apr. 29, 1756	LR5	561
Judah, s. Henry & Mahittabell, b. Aug. 20, 1729	LR2	a
Judah, s. Israel & Mehitabel, b. Nov. 29, 1770	2	16
Judah, s. Israel & Mehitable, d. Aug. 21, 1776	2	17
Lucretia, d. Epaphroditus & Lucretia, b. Feb. 17, 1783	2	144
Lucretia, wid. of Gen. Epaphroditus, d. June 20, 1836, ae 76	2	145
Lucy, d. Andrew & Lucy, b. Aug. 26, 1799	2	229
Lucy, of East Haddam, m. Jeremiah R. **STARK**, of Lebanon, Nov. 28, 1822, by Rev. W[illia]m Jarvis	3	34-5
Martha, d. Israel & Mehitable, b. May 19, 1768	LR5	551
Martha, d. Israel & Mehitabel, d. June 20, 1771	2	17
Martha, d. Israel & Mehitable, b. Apr. 17, 1773	2	16
Mary, d. Henry & Mahittabell, b. Nov. 28, 1731	LR2	a
Mary, d. Israel & Mehitable, b. Sept. 21, 1764 church records Sept. 25 (handwritten in margin in original manuscript	LR5	561
Mary, d. Andrew & Lucy, b. Jan. 26, 1806	2	229
Mahittabell, d. Henry & Mahittabell, b. Feb. 25, 1720	LR2	a
Mehitable, d. Israel & Mehitable, b. Dec. 24, 1760	LR5	561
Mehetable, w. of Henry, d. Oct. 5, 1775	2	15
Mehitabel, m. Job **BECKWITH**, b. of East Haddam, Mar. 23, 1780	2	208
Noadiah, s. Israel & Mehitable, b. Jan. 5, 1775	2	16
Noahiah, s. Israel & Mehitable, d. Oct. 16, 1775	2	17
R[e]uben, s. Israel & Mehitable, b. Mar. 31, 1759	LR5	561
Reuben, m. Rhoda **JEWETT**, b. of East Haddam, Nov. 12,1782	2	124
Reuben, s. Andrew & Lucy, b. Nov. 16, 1794	2	229
Rhoda, d. Andrew & Lucy, b. Apr. 17, 1793	2	229
CHAMPLAIN, CHAMPLIN, Abby E., of East Haddam, m. William C. **SERRALL**, of Guilford, May 2, 1850, by Rev. Isaac Parsons	3	224
Charles A., m. Sarah Ann **CLARK**, b. of East Haddam, Apr. 28, 1839, by Rev. Isaac Parsons	3	172
Esther, of East Haddam, m. Seth C. **WHEELER**, of Hebron,		

	Vol.	Page
CHAMPLAIN, CHAMPLIN, (cont.)		
Nov. 26, 1835, by Rev. Joseph Harvey, of Colchester	3	140-1
Huldah A., of East Haddam, m. Frederick **FITCH**, of Salem, N. Y., Apr. 16, 1837, by G. A. Calhoun	3	151
CHANDLER, Lucy, of Groton, m. John **SAWYER**, of East Haddam, Aug. 6, 1832, by Ralph S. Crampton, V. D. M.	3	125
CHAPMAN, Aaron, s. Robert & Mary, b. May 25, 1744	LR5	561
Aaron Cone, s. Isaac & Abigail, b. Sept. 25, 1789	2	34
Aaron Cone, s. Isaac & Abigail, d. Jan. 18, 1790	2	35
Abigail, d. David & Abigail, b. Aug. 26, 1731	LR2	1131
Abigail, w. of David, d. Jan. 27, 1767, in the 61st y. of her age	LR2	1131
Abigail, d. Isaac & Abigail, b. Nov. 23, 1794	2	34
Abigail, of East Haddam, m. Solomon **DOWD**, of Colchester, Jan. 25, 1835, by Rev. Nathaniel Miner	3	136
Abner, m. Abigail **BEEBE**, b. paupers of E. Haddam, with the consent of the Selectmen of said town, Dec. 2, 1827, by Herman L. Vaill	3	79
Adaline, d. Roderick U., manufacturer, ae 38, & Amelia D., ae 34, b. Aug. 13, 1847	4	5-6
Albert P., m. Caroline S. **CHAPMAN**, b. of East Haddam, Oct. 1, 1843, by Rev. Lyman Strong	3	195
Albert Robbins, s. Erastus & Prudence R., b. Aug. 7, 1815	2	301
Alfred, m. Mary **WILLEY**, b. of East Haddam, Nov. 14, 1820, by Rev. W[illia]m Lyman	2	327
Alfred Hamilton, s. Alfred & Mary, b. Aug. 2, 1821	2	327
Almira L., of East Haddam, m. Washington K. **SMITH**, of Haddam, Jan. 7, 1840, by Tho[mas] W. Gile	3	174
Amanda, d. Ozias & Abigail, b. Dec. 21, 1784	2	16
Ann, m. Joseph **SELDIN**, [ ] 19, 1706	LR1	582
Ann, of East Haddam, m. Charles W. **LEANTRY**, of Chatham, Sept. 16, 1832, by Rev. Peter G. Clarke	3	125
Ann E., m. Rob[er]t S. **CONE**, Nov. [1], 1849, by Rev. Isaac Parsons	3	220
Ann E., school teacher, ae 24, m. Rob[er]t S. **CONE**, turner, ae 29, b. of East Haddam, Nov. 4, 1849, by Rev. Isaac Parsons	4	19-0
Ann Elisa, m. Alphonso S. **HYDE**, b. of East Haddam, Sept. 14, 1842, by Isaac Parsons, V. D. M.	3	191
Annah, m. Jonathan **CONE**, Oct. 30, 1745	LR3	4
Anna, Mrs., m. Rev. Solomon **BLAKSLEE**, b. of East Haddam, Apr. 8, 1795	2	256
Anne, d. Jabez & Anne, b. Sept. 22, 1759	LR7	6
Ancel, s. Timothy & Sarah, b. Apr. 19, 1781	2	20
Ansel, farmer, b. in E. Haddam, res. Rochester, N. Y., d. Oct 4, 1849, ae 68	4	29-30
Asa, s. Caleb, Jr. & Elizabeth, b. Feb. 12, 1753	LR7	414
Asa, m. Mary **WILLIAMS**, b. of East Haddam, Nov. 26, 1778	2	122
Asa, s. Asa & Mary, b. Feb. 28, 1784	2	122

	Vol.	Page
CHAPMAN, (cont.)		
Asa, d. May 14, 1827, in the 44th y. of his age. "Killed instantly by the limb of a tree"	2	123
Azubah K., of East Haddam, m. Ackmon **POST**, of Saybrook, Oct. 20, 1830, by Rev. Isaac Parsons	3	108
Benjamin, s. Ozias & Abigail, b. May 24, 1789	2	18
Betsey, m. Alanson **GATES**, b. of East Haddam, Sept. 17, 1821, by Rev. Isaac Parsons	3	12
Calib, s. Robert & Mary, b. Aug. 21, 1704	LR1	9
Calib, m. Elizabeth **CHURCH**, Feb. 11, 1731	LR2	1125
Calib, s. Caleb & Elizabeth, b. Apr. 19, 1732	LR2	1125
Caleb, Jr., m. Elizabeth **CLARK**, b. of East Haddam, Oct. 4, 1751	LR7	414
Caleb, s. Caleb, Jr. & Elizabeth, b. Aug. 20, 1759	LR7	414
Caleb, see m. of Elisha **CLARK** to Mary **CLEVELAND**	LR2	1101
Calvin, s. Samuel & Zilpah, b. Apr. 19, 1787	2	223
Caroline S., m. Albert P. **CHAPMAN**, b. of East Haddam, Oct. 1, 1843, by Rev. Lyman Strong	3	195
Cassandra, d. Daniel & Esther, b. Nov. 11, 1796	2	112
Charles, s. Zachariah & Isabella, b. Aug. 28, 1776	2	68
Chloe, d. Francis & Mary, b. Mar. 25, 1768	LR4	474
Chloe, d. Isaac & Tabitha, b. Mar. 31, 1781	2	34
Chloe, m. Joshua **CONE**, b. of East Haddam Jan. 17, 1790	2	277
Claressa, d. Zechariah & Isaballa, b. Feb. 17, 1770	2	68
Claris[s]a Shailor, d. Daniel & Esther, b. Oct. 3, 1788	2	112
Claris[s]a Shailor, d. Daniel & Esther, d. Dec. 23, 1788	2	113
Cynthia E., m. Samuel **MITCHELL**, b. of East Haddam, Oct. 19, 1842, by Isaac Parsons, V. D. M.	3	192
Cyrus W., m. Jane C. **CONE**, b. of East Haddam, June 23, 1850, by Nathaniel Miner. Int. pub.	3	226
Cyrus W., farmer, ae 23, m. Jane **CONE**, ae 29, b. of E. Haddam, June [ ], 1850, by Rev. N. Miner	4	19-20
Cyrus W., m. Cornielia A. **HUNGERFORD**, b. of East Haddam, Sept. 5, 1853, by Rev. William Harris	3	238a
Cyrus Willey, s. Alfred & Mary, b. Oct. 26, 1826	2	327
Daniel, s. Francis & Temperance, b. Dec. 20, 1751	LR4	474
Daniel, s. Ozias & Abigail, b. Aug. 30, 1771	2	16
Daniel, s. Zachariah & Isabella, b. Apr. 19, 1775	2	68
Daniel, s. Zechariah & Isabella, d. Apr. 19, 1775	2	69
Daniel, of East Haddam, m. Esther **SHAILER**, of Haddam, Nov. 18, 1778	2	112
Daniel, d. June 10, 1799	2	113
Daniel, m. Orrice **CONE**, Apr. 25, 1824, by Elijah Parsons	3	60-1
Daniel Brainard, s. Isaac, Jr. & Mary, b. June 2, 1807	2	267
Daniel C., s. Robert C., farmer, ae 25, & Elizabeth, ae 23, b. June 22, 1849	4	11-2
Daniel Shailor, s. Daniel & Esther, b. July 18, 1794	2	112
David, s. Robert & Mary, b. Dec. 13, 1698	LR1	9

	Vol.	Page
CHAPMAN, (cont.)		
David, m. Abigail **LEE**, Feb. 5, 1723/4	LR2	1131
David, s. David & Abigail, b. Nov. 6, 1726	LR2	1131
David, Jr., d. Aug. 8, 1768, in the 42nd y. of his age	LR7	413
Deborah, d. Robert & Mary, b. Feb. 15, 1707	LR1	9
Deborah, d. Robert & Mary, b. Oct. 14, 1730	LR1	583
Dorothy, d. Ozias & Abigail, b. Feb. 29, 1775	2	16
Dorothy, m. Oliver **ATTWOOD**, b. of East Haddam, Jan. 23, 1792	2	259
Ebenezer, s. David & Abigail, b. Nov. 10, 1740	LR2	1111
Ebenezer, s. David & Abigail, d. Sept. 4, 1760, in the 70th y. of his age	LR6	507
Edward, s. David & Abigail, b. June 18, 1751	LR2	1131
Edward S., d. Apr. 28, 1848, ae 3	4	7-8
Eleazer, s. Robert & Mary, b. Mar. 20, 1746	LR5	561
Elexsira, d. Daniel & Esther, b. Sept. 11, 1784	2	112
Eliza, m. Hezekiah S. **COOK**, b. of Middle Haddam, Dec. 13, 1846, by Rev. Isaac Parsons	3	208
Elizabeth, s.[sic] Calib & Elizabeth, b. Sept. 22, 1738	LR2	1125
Elizabeth, d. Caleb & Elizabeth, d. June last day, 1740	LR2	1101
Elizabeth, d. Caleb & Elizabeth, b. Dec. 17, 1747	LR2	1114
Elizabeth, d. Zechariah & Isabella, b. Apr. 19, 1781	2	68
Elizabeth, d. Ozias & Abigail, b. June 14, 1792	2	18
Emeline L., m. Henry C. **RANSOM**, July 10, 1849, by Rev. Isaac Parsons	3	219
Emeline L., of East Haddam, m. Henry C. **RANSOM**, merchant, b. in Salem, Ct., res. East Haddam, July 10, 1849, by Isaac Parsons	4	9-10
Emma E., d. William W., mechanic, ae 23, & Harriet, ae 19, b. Dec. 15, 1848	4	5-6
Emma T., of East Haddam, m. Frederick W. **MORGAN**, of Clarksburg, Va., Oct. 20, 1842, by Isaac Parsons, V. D. M.	3	192
Eppaphras, s. Isaac & Abigail, b. Apr. 26, 1792	2	34
Erastus, s. Ozias & Abigail, b. Feb. 14, 1787	2	16
Erastus, of East Haddam, m. Prudence Robbins **LOOMIS**, of Colchester, June [ ], 1814	2	301
Easter, d. Jabez & Easter, b. Jan. 4, 1727/8	LR2	1131
Esther, m. David **ANNABLE**, Jan. 13, 1751	LR5	b
Esther, d. John & Mary, b. June 5, 1762	LR4	468
Esther, d. Daniel & Esther, b. Jan. 14, 1790	2	112
Esther, d. Daniel & Esther, d. Jan. 18, 1790	2	113
Esther W., of East Haddam, m. George **WAY**, of Colchester, [Aug.] 14, [1820], by Rev. Isaac Parsons	2	321
Esther Whittlesey, d. Daniel & Esther, b. June 28, 1792	2	112
Eunice, d. David & Abigail, b. Mar. 8, 1745	LR2	1131
[E]unice, d. Isaiah & Hezsidiah, b. Nov. 20, 1772	2	8
Eveline E., d. W[illia]m H., shoemaker, ae 25, & Jane, ae 26, b. Jan. 8, 1850	4	25-6

	Vol.	Page
CHAPMAN, (cont.)		
Ezekiel, s. David & Abigail, b. Feb. 21, 1733/4	LR2	1131
Fanny, d. Ozias & Abigail, b. Dec. 6, 1782	2	16
Fanny, m. Silas **BRAINARD**, b. of East Haddam, Nov. 27, 1820, by Rev. Isaac Parsons	2	279
Farozina, d. Isaac & Abigail, b. Sept. 30, 1787	2	34
Francis, s. Robert & Mary, b. Dec. 23, 1712	LR1	9
Francis, m. Susannah **ROWLEY**, Sept. 24, 1741	LR2	1102
Francis, m. Temperance **JONES**, Oct. 10, 1749	LR4	474
Francis, of East Haddam, m. Mary **BATES**, of Saybrook, Sept. 16, 1761	LR4	474
Francis, s. Daniel & Esther, b. Jan. 10, 1783	2	112
Francis, d. Dec. 9, 1794, in the 83rd y. of his age	LR4	474
Francis A., m. Sarah M. **BEEBE**, b. of East Haddam, Mar. 30, 1845, by Isaac Parsons, V. D. M.	3	201
George L., ae 20 y., b. at Newfield, N. Y., res. East Haddam, m. Harriet M. **BROWN**, ae 21 y., b. at Haddam, res. East Haddam, Aug. 5, 1855, by Rev. L. W. Blood. Int. pub. Aug. 1, 1855	4	60
Gideon, of Saybrook, m. Julia **COMSTOCK**, of East Haddam, May 19, 1824, by Rev. Isaac Parsons	3	58-9
Hannah, d. Robert & Mary, b. Mar. 26, 1733	LR1	583
Hannah, w. of Jonathan, d. Mar. 17, 1742	LR2	1120
Hannah, m. Fradrick **SPENCER**, b. of East Haddam, Apr. 1, 1762	LR7	2
Hannah, m. Jonathan **KILBORN**, Jr., b. of East Haddam, Oct. 2, 1766	LR7	414
Harriet, of East Haddam, m. Jasper S. **BROOKS**, of Saybrook, May 10, 1838, by Rev. Isaac Parsons	3	164-5
Henrietta M., m. Rufus W. **SWAN**, Mar. 26, 1828, by Rev. Isaac Parsons	3	99
Hester, of Saybrook, m. Robert **CHAPMAN**, of East Haddam, Apr. 22, 1766	LR5	561
Hester Kirtland, d. Isaac & Tabitha, b. June 17, 1773	2	34
Horatio Dana, s. [Robert W.], b. Aug. 7, 1826	3	153
Hosea, s. Jabez & Anne, b. Mar. 8, 1755	LR7	6
Huldah L., m. Oliver W. **MACK**, b. of East Haddam, Feb. 25, 1850, by Rev. Moses Chase	3	223
Ichabod, s. Isaac & Tabitha, b. Apr. 3, 1779	2	34
Isaac, s. Robert & Mary, b. Jan. 7, 1739	LR5	561
Isaac, s. Isaac & Tabathy, b. Apr. 12, 1771	2	34
Isaac, m. Wid. Abigail **BROOKS**, Dec. 24, 1786	2	34
Isaac, Jr., m. Mary **BRAINARD**, b. of East Haddam, Sept. 27, 1801	2	267
Isaac, s. Isaac, Jr. & Mary, b. Aug. 2, 1804	2	267
Isaac, s. Isaac, Jr. & Mary, b. Aug. 3, 1807	2	268
Isaac, d. Feb. 14, 1811, in the 73rd y. of his age	2	35
Isaac, of East Haddam, m. Mrs. Prudence **GLEASON**, of		

	Vol.	Page
CHAPMAN, (cont.)		
Farmington, Sept. 29, 1816, by Rev. Mrs. Porter, at Farmington	2	267
Isaiah, s. David & Abigail, b. July 17, 1743	LR2	1111
Isaiah, of East Haddam, m. Hezzediah **SOYER**, of Lyme, Oct. 29, 1764	LR7	4
Isaiah, s. Isaiah & Heszediah, b. Oct. 4, 1766	2	8
Jabez, s. Jonathan & Hannah, b. Aug. 24, 1731	LR2	1120
Jabez, m. Anne **BEEBE**, b. of East Haddam, Apr. 2, 1752	LR7	6
Jabez, s. Jabez & Anne, b. June 17, 1764	LR7	6
James, s. Jonathan & Mary, b. Aug. 11, 1766	2	28
James Dyer, s. Zechariah & Isaballa, b. Dec. 13, 1771	2	68
Jane, see Jane **CONE**	4	91-2
Jedediah, s. Robert & Mary, b. Sept. 28, 1736	LR5	561
Jedediah, s. Robert & Mary, b. Sept. 27, 1741	LR5	561
Jedediah, s. Robert & Mary, d. Nov. 7, 1745	LR5	561
Jedadiah, s. Isaac & Tabitha, b. Oct. 20, 1776	2	34
Jenette G., ae 17, b. in Glastonbury, res. East Haddam, m. William H. **STEVENS**, ae 24, b. in Hebron, res. East Haddam, Oct. 5, 1856, by Rev. N. Goodrich. Int. pub. Oct. 4, 1856	4	102
John, s. Jonathan & Hannah, b. Nov. 10, 1739	LR2	1120
John, b. Nov. 10, 1739; d. Dec. 10, 1833, ae probably upwards of 100 years. (Arnold Note: "By above however he was not quite 94 years")	3	46
John, m. Mary **HOWARD**, Feb. 25, 1752	LR4	468
Jonah C., m. Fanny G. **BINGHAM**, Dec. 6, 1843, by Rev. Isaac Parsons	3	196
Jonathan, s. David & Abigail, b. Sept. 27, 1729	LR2	1131
Jonathan, m. Hannah **BRAINERD**, alias **SELDEN**, Dec. 3, 1730	LR2	1120
Jonathan, s. Jonathan & Hannah, b. Jan. 21, 1733/4	LR2	1120
Jonathan, d. Aug. 23, 1742	LR2	1120
Jonathan, s. Jonathan & Mary, b. Apr. 24, 1768	2	28
Joseph, s. Jonathan & Hannah, b. Sept. 6, 1736	LR2	1120
Joseph, s. Ozias & Abigail, b. Mar. 15, 1791	2	18
Josiah, s. Francis & Mary, b. Apr. 30, 1763	LR4	474
Josiah A., m. Huldah O. **SWAN**, b. of East Haddam, May 5, 1825, by Rev. Herman L. Vaill	3	74-75
Julia A., m. William S. **BRAINERD**, Nov. 15, 1836, by Rev. Isaac Parsons	3	146
Julia A., of Whateley, Mass., m. Charles **ATTWOOD**, of East Haddam, Dec. 31, 1837, by John C. Palmer, J. P.	3	160
Julia Ann, d. Oren & Penelope, b. June 4, 1816	2	313
Julia E., of East Haddam, m. Heman **BALDWIN**, of Chester, Aug. 5, 1838, by Rev. Isaac Parsons	3	164-5
Julias, s. Ozias & Abigail, b. May 6, 1785	2	16
Keziah, of East Win[d]sor, m. Daniel **CONE**, 3rd, of East		

	Vol.	Page
CHAPMAN, (cont.)		
Haddam, Aug. 3, 1775	2	116
Laura A., m. Joseph B. **EMMOS**, b. of East Haddam, Dec. 5, 1847, by Rev. Isaac Parsons	3	211
Laura A., m. Joseph B. **EMMONS**, b. of East Haddam, Dec. 5, 1847, by Rev. Isaac Parsons	3	243
Laura Ann, m. Stephen **FULLER**, Feb. 8, 1843, by Isaac Parsons, V. D. M.	3	193
Laurene, d. Ozias & Abigail, b. July 15, 1794	2	18
Lavina A., ae 19, b. in Chatham, res. East Haddam, m. Joseph B. **EMMONS**, mechanic, ae 22, of East Haddam, Dec. 5, 1847, by Isaac Parsons	4	1-2
Lavinia R., m. Joseph **SILLIMAN**, Oct. 7, 1841, by Isaac Parsons, V. D. M.	3	187
Lois, d. David & Abigail, b. Sept. 13, 1747	LR2	1131
Lois M., m. Oliver C. **PALMER**, b. of East Haddam, Oct. 19, 1823, by Rev. Isaac Parsons	3	47
Louisa, d. Dec. 22, 1849, ae 20	4	29-30
Lovina, d. Ozias & Abigail, b. Apr. 23, 1779	2	16
Lucinda, d. Asa & Mary, b. Feb. 5, 1780	2	122
Lucretia, ae 22, m. Oliver W. **MACK**, stone business, ae 22, b. of East Haddam, Feb. 24, 1850, by Rev. Charles Chase	4	19-20
Lucy, m. Charles W. **LAY**, b. of East Haddam, Aug. 25, 1836, by Rev. George Carrington, of Hadlyme	3	145
Lurinda, d. Daniel & Esther, b. Aug. 2, 1779	2	112
Lurinda, d. Daniel & Est[h]er, d. June 23, 1794	2	113
Lydia, d. Jabez & Easter, b. Apr. 19, 1728	LR2	1131
Lydia, m. John **CHURCH**, Jr., Feb. 10, 1736/7	LR2	1103
Lidiah, m. Daniel **LORD**, Oct. 11, 1751	LR4	470
Lydia, d. Caleb, Jr. & Elizabeth, b. Jan. 11, 1763	LR7	414
Marcy, d. David & Abigail, b. May 18, 1738	LR2	1111
Margaret R., ae 27, b. in East Haddam, res. East Haddam, m. John L. **MERRILL**, ae 32, b. in Newbury, Mass., res. Brooklyn, N. Y., May 14, 1856, by Rev. Isaac Parson. Int. pub. May 13, 1856	4	87
Maria H., m. John S. **WELLES**, b. of East Haddam, Mar. 26, 1840, by Isaac Parsons, V. D. M.	3	176-7
Martin, of Haddam, m. Almina **WHITMORE**, of East Haddam, Nov. 24, 1835, by Stephen A. Loper	3	140-1
Mary, d. Robert & Mary, b. Jan. 9, 1726	LR1	583
Mary, d. Francis & Temperance, b. May 11, 1753	LR4	474
Mary, d. Francis & Temperance, d. June 10, 1753	LR4	474
Mary, d. Francis & Temperance, b. Apr. 11, 1755	LR4	474
Mary, d. Simeon & Sarah, b. Apr. 5, 1761	LR6	504
Mary, w. of Robert, d. June 5, 1764, in the 90th y. of her age	LR6	514
Mary, w. of Robert, d. Nov. 19, 1764	LR5	561
Mary, d. Timothy & Sarah, b. Oct. 5, 1773	2	20

	Vol.	Page
CHAPMAN, (cont.)		
Mary, m. Isaac **HUMPHR[E]Y**, b. of East Haddam, Oct. 5, 1775	2	104
Mary, w. of Francis, d. Jan. 10, 1791	LR4	474
Mary, w. of Isaac, and d. of Daniel **BRAINARD**, d. Aug. 25, 1815, in the 39th y. of her age	2	268
Mary Elizabeth, d. [Robert W.], b. Apr. 22, 1825	3	153
Mary Jane, d. Alfred & Mary, b. July 4, 1823	2	327
Mary Tabitha, d. Isaac, Jr. & Mary, b. Feb. 3, 1810	2	267
Miriam, d. Caleb & Elizabeth, b. Mar. 2, 1750	LR2	1114
Meriam, m. Dr. Francis **PERCIVAL**, b. of East Haddam, May 24, 1774	2	86
Minerva, ae 19, b. at Glastonbury, res. East Haddam, m. Warren B. **DROWN**, ae 26, b. at Lyndon, Vt., res. East Haddam, Nov. 18, 1856, by Rev. Nelson Goodrich. Int. pub. Nov. 17, 1856	4	107-8
Miriam, see under Meriam		
Myra M., of East Haddam, m. William N. **BULL**, of Mereden, July 2, 1851, by Rev. Isaac Parsons	3	233
Nancy, d. Francis & Mary, b. May 23, 1777	LR4	474
Nancy, of East Haddam, m. Hezekiah M. **SELDEN**, of Chatham, Feb. 22, 1826, by Isaac Parsons	3	84-85
Nancy, m. Alfred **DEAN**, b. of East Haddam, Mar. 1, 1832, by Rev. Alvan Ackley	3	121
Nathan, s. Robert & Mary, b. Aug. 18, 1702	LR1	9
Olive, d. Caleb, Jr. & Elizabeth, b. July 10, 1766	LR7	414
Oliver, s. Jabez & Anne, b. Feb. 20, 1753	LR7	6
Oliver, s. Jabez & Anne, d. Apr. 15, 1756	LR7	6
Oliver, s. Jabez & Anne, b. June 25, 1756	LR7	6
Oliver, s. Caleb, Jr. & Elizabeth, b. Feb. 15, 1765	LR7	414
Oren, of Haddam, m. Penelope **GATES**, of East Haddam, Nov. 12, 1812	2	313
Orian, s. Ozias & Abigail, b. Aug. 6, 1780	2	16
Ozias, s. Caleb & Elizabeth, b. Sept. [ ], 1742	LR2	1114
Ozias, s. Caleb & Elizabeth, b. Sept. 25, 1742	LR2	1101
Ozias, m. Abigail **FULLER**, b. of East Haddam, Aug. 10, 1769	2	16
Phebe, d. David & Abigail, b. Sept. 9, 1736	LR2	1131
Phebe Ann, d. Zachariah & Isabella, b. Nov. 19, 1778	2	68
Polly, d. Asa & Mary, b. Dec. 7, 1782	2	122
Prudence, d. Robert & Mary, b. Oct. 27, 1748	LR5	561
Rebeckah, d. Jabez & Easter, b. May 16, 1725	LR2	1131
Rebeckah, m. Job **SPENCER**, Nov. 13, 1746	LR4	466
Reuben, s. Caleb, Jr. & Elizabeth, b. Nov. 10, 1757	LR7	414
Reuben, s. Ozias & Abigail, b. Mar. 25, 1777	2	16
Reuben, of East Haddam, m. Jane Maria **ROWLEY**, of Chatham, Nov. 27, 1836, by Rev. Stephen Beach	3	146
Reuben Gates, s. Oren & Penelope, b. July 24, 1813	2	313
Rhodalthe*, d. David & Abigail, b. Feb. 27, 1735		

	Vol.	Page
CHAPMAN, (cont.)		
(*Probably "Rhoda the")	LR2	1131
Rhoda, d. David & Abigail, d. Feb. 9, 1760	LR6	510
Rhoda Maria, of Geneva, O., m. Caleb R. **CORSER**, of Gates, N. Y., Oct. 11, 1841, by Isaac Parsons, V. D. M.	3	187
Robert, s. Robert & Mary, b. Sept. 30, 1700	LR1	9
Robert, m. Mary **CHURCH**, Mar. 17, 1726	LR1	583
Robert, s. Robert & Mary, b. Oct. 27, 1734	LR5	561
Robert, d. Nov. 4, 1760, in the 86th y. of his age	LR6	514
Robert, d. Dec. 4, 1760, in the 86th y. of his age	LR6	507
Robert, of East Haddam, m. Hester **CHAPMAN**, of Saybrook, Apr. 22, 1766	LR5	561
Robert, s. Francis & Mary, b. Feb. 22, 1773	LR4	474
Robert C., m. Elizabeth S. **GATES**, Apr. 28, 1844, by Rev. Isaac Parsons	3	199
Robert W., m. Almira J. **BEEBE**, Mar. 29, 1835, by Isaac Parsons	3	137
Robert W., m. [ ]	3	153
Robert Wolcott, s. [Robert W.], b. Nov. 13, 1828	3	153
Robert Wolcott, s. Robert W., d. June 14, 1830, in his 2nd y.	3	154
Rosena, d. Jabez & Anne, b. Feb. 10, 1758	LR7	6
Russel[l], s. Timothy & Sarah, b. Oct. 9, 1769	2	20
Russel[l], s. Timothy & Sarah, d. Jan. 9, 1771	2	21
Russel[l], s. Timothy & Sarah, b. Apr. 16, 1778	2	20
Ruth, of Chatham, m. Horatio **EARL**, of East Greenwich, R. I., Dec. 7, 1828, by Rev. Isaac Parsons	3	101
Sally, m. Russel[l] **DUTTON**, b. of East Haddam, Oct. 14, 1788	2	180
Samuel, s. Caleb & Elizabeth, b. Sept. 21, 1745	LR2	1114
Samuel, s. Caleb & Elizabeth, d. Aug. 15, 1748	LR2	1114
Samuel, s. Francis & Temperance, b. Aug. 5, 1750	LR4	474
Samuel, s. Caleb, Jr. & Elizabeth, b. Jan. 12, 1755	LR7	414
Samuel, m. Zilpah **GATES**, b. of East Haddam, Mar. 4, 1783	2	223
Samuel, s. Daniel & Esther, b. Dec. 9, 1786	2	112
Samuel, s. Samuel & Zilpah, b. Apr. 21, 1789	2	223
Sarah, d. Jabez & Easter, b. Sept. 8, 1720	LR2	1131
Sarah, d. Robert & Mary, b. Dec. 3, 1728	LR1	583
Sarah, m. Moses **ROWLEE**, Jr., Sept. 25, 1729	LR3	16
Sarah, m. Shubael **FULLER**, June 12, 1755	LR5	562
Sarah, d. Simeon & Sarah, b. Sept. 17, 1762	LR6	504
Sarah, d. Timothy & Sarah, b. Oct. 19, 1771	2	20
Sarah, w. of Timothy, d. Sept. 18, 1787	2	21
Sarah, b. in E. Haddam, res. New London, d. June [ ], 1851	4	39-40
Sarah Stanton, d. Zechariah & Isaballa, b. Sept. 16, 1768	2	68
Selina, m. Rufus **WILLEY**, b. of East Haddam, Dec. 31, 1821, by Josiah Griffing, J. P.	3	19
Silvanus, s. Samuel & Zilpah, b. Oct. 14, 1783	2	223
Simeon, m. Sarah **BARNS**, b. of East Haddam, May 21, 1760	LR6	504

	Vol.	Page
CHAPMAN, (cont.)		
Sophia, d. Samuel & Zilpah, b. July 19, 1785	2	223
Statira, d. Timothy & Sarah, b. Feb. 2, 1776	2	20
Statira, m. Thomas **FULLER**, Aug. 26, 1793	2	303
Susannah, d. Francis & Susannah, b. Oct. 10, 1742	LR2	1102
Susannah, w. of Francis, d. Jan. 20, 1743/4	LR2	1102
Susannah, m. Joshua **BRAINERD**, Jr., b. of East Haddam, Aug. 26, 1762	LR6	503
Susannah, m. Joshua **BRAINERD**, Jr., b. of East Haddam, Aug. 26, 1762	2	26
Sylvester, s. Ozias & Abigail, b. May 22, 1770	2	16
Sylvester M., m. Elizabeth H. **SPENCER**, Feb. 18, 1838, by Rev. Isaac Parsons	3	160
Sylvina, of East Haddam, m. Samuel **NORTON**, of Hebron, Aug. 20, 1823, by Ebenezer Blake, Elder, of Hebron	3	44-45
Tabathy, d. Isaac & Tabathy, b. Aug. 6, 1769	2	34
Tabitha, w. of Isaac, d. Nov. 8, 1785	2	35
Temperance, w. of Francis, d. Mar. 8, 1758	LR4	474
Temperance, d. Francis & Mary, b. Dec. 5, 1765	LR4	474
Temperance Jones, d. Daniel & Esther, b. Mar. 4, 1781	2	112
Thankfull, d. Jabez & Easter, b. Aug. 2, 1715	LR1	582
Timothy, s. Calib & Elizabeth, b. Oct. 3, 1736	LR2	1125
Timothy, m. Sarah **FULLER**, b. of East Haddam, Jan. 26, 1764	LR7	414
Timothy, m. Sarah **FULLER**, b. of East Haddam, Jan. 26, 1764	2	20
Timothy, s. Timothy & Sarah, b. Nov. 13, 1765	LR7	414
Timothy, s. Timothy & Sarah, b. Nov. 13, 1765	2	20
Uitilla, d. Jabez & Anne, b. Aug. 4, 1761	LR7	6
Warren, s. Jabez & Anne, b. Oct. 1, 1765	LR7	6
Warren, s. Timothy & Sarah, b. July 7, 1767	2	20
Warren W., dentist, b. in Hanover, N. J., res. N. Y., d. May 10, 1848, ae 22	4	7-8
Wealthy, d. Isaac & Tabitha, b. Jan. 26, 1783	2	34
William, s. Ozias & Abigail, b. Aug. 5, 1773	2	16
William A., of Middle Haddam, m. Harriet A. **MARTIN**, of East Haddam, Dec. 13, 1846, by Rev. Isaac Parsons	3	208
William H., of New London, m. Sarah W. **HUTCHINS**, of East Haddam, Sept. 13, [1843], by Rev. Isaac Parsons	3	195
William H., m. Jane **NICHOLS**, Mar. 3, 1846, by Rev. Isaac Parsons	3	204
William H., ae 37, b. in East Haddam, res. New London, m. Ellen **TYLER**, ae 30, b. in Haddam, res. East Haddam, Sept. 24, 1856, by Cha[rle]s H. Bullard, of Rockville. Int. pub. Sept. 23, 1856	4	99
Worthy, s. Isaac & Tabith[a], b. Jan. 27, 1785	2	34
Zachariah, s. Calib & Elizabeth, b. Dec. 3, 1734	LR2	1125
Zachariah, s. Calib & Elizabeth, d. Feb. 22, 1736/7	LR2	1125
Zachariah, s. Calib & Elizabeth, b. Aug. 2, 1740	LR2	1125
Zachariah, s. Caleb, Jr. & Elizabeth, b. Feb. 29, 1761(sic)	LR7	414

	Vol.	Page
CHAPMAN, (cont.)		
Zachariah, of East Haddam, m. Isaballa **STANTON**, of the Island of Barbados, July 19, 1767	2	68
-----, child of Henry, mechanic, b. July 18, 1853	4	47-8
CHAPPELL, CHAPEL, Lydia, of Waterford, m. Ezra **BEEBE**, of East Haddam, [1798?]	2	297
Mary, m. Jeremiah **GATES**, b. of East Haddam, Nov. 24, 1785	2	154
CHAUNCEY, CHANCEY, Dorothy, m. Ira **CHURCH**, b. of East Haddam, Oct. 10, 1763	LR7	7
Jerusha, Mrs., m. Rev. Hobart **ESTABROOK**, Aug. 4, 1747	LR3	3
Michael, m. Dorothy **CONE**, b. of East Haddam, Dec. 22, 1813	2	301
CHESTER, CHETESTER, Catharine, d. Mar. 28, 1850, ae 5	4	29-30
Charles A., of East Haddam, m. Celia **BROWN**, of Chatham, [Oct.] 24, [1852], by A. E. Denison	3	238
Charles D., s. Charles A., mechanic, ae 23, of Hadlyme, & Martha E., ae 23, b. Nov. 12, 1849	4	27-28
Charlotte A., of Erie, Pa., m. George H. **LEE**, of East Haddam, Sept. 23, 1850, by Rev. Alpheas Geer	3	226
Henry, m. Eliza **BECKWITH**, Mar. 14, 1828*, by Rev. Tubal Wakefield (*Probably an error as it was recorded Mar. 11, 1828)	3	96
Laura, of East Haddam, m. Andrew **STARK**, of Lyme, Mar. 28, 1825, by Rev. Simeon Dickinson, at the house of Isaac Chester	3	72-73
Mary Adeline, m. Israel D. **BURNHAM**, b. of East Haddam, Mar. 19, 1840, by Rev. George Carrington, of Hadlyme	3	176-7
CHIPMAN, Edwin B., ae 28, b. at New London, res. New London, m. Amelia J. **AYRES**, ae 21, b. at East Haddam, res. East Haddam, Apr. 1, 1856, by Rev. Nathaniel Miner. Int. pub. Mar. 31, 1856	4	85
Perry Green, of East Haddam, m. Lucinda C. **ROWLEY**, of Chatham, Jan. 31, 1842, by Rev. Alonzo G. Shears	3	188
CHURCH, Ambrose, s. Capt. William & Hannah, d. Aug. 22, 1775, at Roxbury. Enlisted in Gen. Spencer's Co., 1775, in the 15th year of the reign of George, 3rd	2	99
Ann F., of Millington, m. Roswell **TUPPER**, of Campton, N. H., Mar. 25, 1838, by Rev. Nathaniel Miner, of Millington	3	164-5
Azel, s. Samuel & Elizabeth, b. July 12, 1765	LR4	474
Betsey, d. Capt. Jo[seph], of East Haddam, m. Silas H. **POST**, of Saybrook, Oct. 27, 1822, by Rev. Isaac Parsons	3	28-9
Calvin, s. Joseph & Phebe, b. Jan. 27, 1766	LR7	411
Charles, of Ogden, N. Y., m. Amanda **JEWETT**, of East Haddam, Oct. 4, 1826, by Rev. Herman L. Vaill	3	86
Diodate Ackley, m. Mary **PALMER**, b. of East Haddam, Apr. 17, 1823, by Rev. Isaac Parsons	3	38-9
Dorothy, d. Ira & Dorothy, b. Aug. 10, 1764	LR7	7
Ebenezer, s. Samuel & Elizabeth, b. Dec. 14, 1750	LR4	474

	Vol.	Page
CHURCH, (cont.)		
Elihu, s. John & Lydia, b. Feb. 11, 1756	LR2	1103
Elizabeth, d. John & Elizabeth, b. July 8, 1709	LR1	7
Elizabeth, d. John & Elizabeth, b. Aug. 8, 1709	LR1	583
Elizabeth, m. Calib **CHAPMAN**, Feb. 11, 1731	LR2	1125
Elizabeth, w. of John, d. Dec. 22, 1749	LR4	469
Elizabeth, d. Samuel & Elizabeth, b. Mar. 25, 1763	LR4	474
George, of Greenwich, N. Y., m. Margaret S. **HALL**, of East Haddam, Feb. 28, 1847, by Rev. Levi H. Wakeman	3	208
Harriet Holt, [d. Joseph, Jr. & Harriet], b. May 24, 1847	3	158
Ira, s. John, Jr. & Lydia, b. May 19, 1741	LR2	1103
Ira, s. Samuel & Elizabeth, b. Sept. 1, 1760	LR4	474
Ira, m. Dorothy **CHA[U]NC[E]Y**, b. of East Haddam, Oct. 10, 1763	LR7	7
Jabez, s. John, Jr. & Lydia, b. Aug. 23, 1747	LR2	1103
James, s. John, Jr. & Park*, b. Nov. 6, 1762 (*Probably "Jane **PARK**")	LR7	7
Jane, of Lyme, m. John **HUNTINGTON**, of East Haddam, Mar. 2, 1757	LR6	512
Jddo(?), s. Samuel & Elizabeth, b. Feb. 14, 1756	LR4	474
John, m. Elizabeth **OLMSTEAD**, Feb. 5, 1707	LR1	583
John, s. John & Elizabeth, b. July 29, 1711	LR1	583
John, Jr., m. Lydia **CHAPMAN**, Feb. 10, 1736/7	LR2	1103
John, s. John, Jr. & Lydia, b. Nov. 22, 1737	LR2	1103
John, d. Mar. 21, 1751	LR4	469
John, Jr., m. Jane **PARK**, b. of East Haddam, Jan. 21, 1762	LR7	7
John, s. John, Jr. & Park*, b. June 22, 1764 (*Probably "Jane **PARK**")	LR7	7
Jonathan, s. Samuel & Elizabeth, b. Apr. 12, 1758	LR4	474
Joseph, s. John & Elizabeth, b. Jan. 14, 1726	LR1	583
Joseph, of East Haddam, m. Phebe **STARLING**, of Lyme, Jan. 24, 1765	LR7	411
Joseph, s. Joseph & Phebe, b. Apr. 1, 1770	2	48
Joseph, s. Sarah **SELBY**, 2d, b. Aug. 2, 1793	2	14
Joseph, Sr., m. Rachel **BROOKS**, Sept. 5, 1841, by Charles William Bradley	3	188
Joseph, Jr., m. Harriet **HOLT**, Apr. 4, 1843	3	158
Joseph, Jr., m. Harriet **HOLT**, b. of East Haddam, Apr. 4, 1843, by Rev. Russell Jennings	3	194
Joseph, Jr., m. Harriet **HOLT**, Apr. 4, 1843	3	197
Joseph, Jr., m. Harriet A. **CHALKER**, Sept. 18, 1848	3	158
Joseph, Jr., m. Harriet A. **CHALKER**, b. of East Haddam, Sept. 18, 1848, by Rev. Alpheas Geer	3	214
Joseph, agriculturist, married, d. Nov. 6, 1853, ae 83	4	49-50
Lazarus, [twin with Lydia], s. John & Lydia, b. Nov. 21, 1753	LR2	1103
Lydia, [twin with Lazarus], d. John & Lydia, b. Nov. 21, 1753	LR2	1103
Manere, m. Hubbard **SWAN**, b. of East Haddam, May 23, 1833, by Nathaniel Miner	3	131

	Vol.	Page
CHURCH, (cont.)		
Maria Jenette, [d. Joseph, Jr. & Harriet A.], b. Oct. 22, 1853	3	158
Mary, d. John & Mary, b. Dec. 22, 1706	LR1	7
Mary, m. Ebenezer **ROWLE**, June 6, 1719	LR2	1121
Mary, m. Robert **CHAPMAN**, Mar. 17, 1726	LR1	583
Mary L., d. Joseph, farmer, ae 38, & Harriet, ae 26, b. Aug. 6, 1849	4	23-4
Mary Louisa, [d. Joseph, Jr. & Harriet A.], b. Aug. 6, 1849	3	158
Mehittabell, d. John & Elizabeth, b. Mar. 7, 1714	LR1	583
Mehitabell, m. Joshua **BRAINERD**, Jr., Mar. 31, 1737	LR2	1111
Phebe, d. Joseph & Phebe, b. Oct. 13, 1767	LR7	411
Phebe, w. of Joseph, d. Aug. 1, 1770	2	49
Phebe, m. Elijah **CROSBY**, b. of East Haddam, Nov. 13, 1787	2	194
Rachel, d. John & Elizabeth, b. Sept. 5, 1732	LR1	583
Rachel, m. Hezekiah **MACK**, Nov. 14, 1751	LR4	469
Samuell, s. John & Elizabeth, b. July 5, 1720	LR1	583
Samuel, m. Elizabeth **FULLER**, Nov. 12, 1747	LR4	474
Samuel, s. Samuel & Elizabeth, b. Jan. 28, 1748/9	LR4	474
Sarah, d. John & Elizabeth, b. July 4, 1724	LR1	583
Sarah, m. Matthew **SMITH**, Jr., Jan. 16, 1745/6	LR3	15
Selden, s. John, Jr. & Lydia, b. Sept. 2, 1744	LR2	1103
Sophronia, m. Jeremiah H. **DANIELS**, Mar. 3, 1839, by Rev. George Carrington, of Hadlyme	3	168
Stephen, of Groton, m. Eliza A. **EDWARDS**, of East Haddam, Sept. 10, 1837, by Ethan A. Willey, J. P.	3	152
Thomas, s. John, Jr. & Lydia, b. Aug. 14, 1750	LR2	1103
Thomas, s. Samuel & Elizabeth, b. Feb. 19, 1754	LR4	474
William, s. John & Elizabeth, b. Nov. 7, 1716	LR1	583
-----, s. Truman, mechanic, ae about 30 y., res. East Haddam & Emma, ae about 30 y., b. Jan. 1, 1855	4	74
CIDIS, Mary, of Hebron, m. Grisham **ROWLEE**, of East Haddam, Dec. 14, 1758	LR6	510
CLARK, CLARKE, Abigail, d. Samuel & Ruth, b. Dec. 6, 1786	2	182
Abigail M., m. Washington **BRAINERD**, b. of Haddam Neck, July 12, 1845, by Rev. William S. Simmons, Leesville	3	202
Amasa B., m. Julia S. **SPENCER**, b. of East Haddam, Nov. 25, 1840, by Rev. Moses Stoddard	3	184
Ann Elizabeth, m. James Frederick **BRAINERD**, b. of East Haddam, Jan. 27, 1851, by Rev. Alpheas Geer	3	229
Arnold, of Lyme, m. Mary S. **SMITH**, of East Haddam, Jan. 1, 1822, by Rev. Isaac Parsons	3	21
Asa, s. Silas & Ele[a]ner, b. Feb. 10, 1766	LR5	270
Asa, of Haddam, m. Mary **WATSON**, of East Haddam, Oct. 4, 1829, by Rev. Alvan Ackley	3	102
Catharine J., m. Joseph B. **BROCKWAY**, Jan. 16, 1825, by Rev. William Jarvis	3	69
Champion, s. Dan & Esther, b. Nov. 6, 1760	LR6	505

	Vol.	Page
CLARK, CLARKE, (cont.)		
Charles, s. Silas & Ele[a]ner, b. Jan. 13, 1751	LR5	270
Charles, of Northampton, m. Hannah **HEATH**, of East Haddam, Aug. 27, 1773	2	62
Charles M., d. Dec. 31, 1850, ae 11	4	39-4
Dan, of East Haddam, m. Esther **SWADDLE**, of Middletown, Jan. 3, 1760	LR6	505
David H., of Columbia, m. Samantha S. **WATROUS**, of Saybrook, Sept. 25, 1836, by Rev. Isaac Parsons	3	145
Delia, of East Haddam, m. Orren H. **MAYNARD**, of Waterford, Feb. 15, 1835, by Thomas C. Bordman, J. P.	3	136
Elisha, m. Mary **CLEVELAND**, Sept. 17, 1741 (Arnold Copy note: "Over this item is written 'Caleb **CHAPMAN**'")	LR2	1101
Elisha, s. Elisha & Mary, b. Apr. 23, 1744	LR2	1101
Elizabeth, ae 23, m. Frederick **BRAINERD**, butcher, ae 24, of E. Haddam, Jan. 23, 1851, by Mr. Geer	4	37-8
Elizabeth, m. Caleb **CHAPMAN**, Jr., b. of East Haddam, Oct. 4, 1751	LR7	414
Elisabeth, m. Daniel **WARNER**, b. of East Haddam, July 28 1774	2	62
Elizabeth A., m. Albert D. **WHITMAN**, May 21, 1844, by Rev. Isaac Parsons	3	199
Erastus S., m. Hannah M. **PURPLE**, b. of East Haddam, July 5, 1846, by Rev. Alpheas Geer	3	206
Eunice, of Lyme, m. James **BOOGE**, Jr., of East Haddam, Feb. 6, 1759	LR7	2
Eunice, d. Silas & Ele[a]ner, b. Aug. 28, 1764	LR5	270
Ezekiel S., of Haddam, m. Lucy W. **SWAN**, of East Haddam, Dec. 9, 1824, by Rev. Isaac Parsons	3	69
Ezra S., of Saybrook, m. Julia A. **HUBBARD**, of East Haddam, Nov. 21, 1833, by Rev. Isaac Parsons	3	133
Foster P. Church, s. Truman F., blacksmith, ae 27, & Emma A. ae 27, b. Feb. 5, 1850	4	25-6
Frederick W., s. Erastus S., pedlar, ae 26, & Matilda H., ae 19, b. Dec. 24, 1847	4	5-6
Hannah, d. Samuel & Ruth, b. Jan. 28, 1776	2	182
Jabez, s. Sterlin & Sarah, b. Apr. 27, 1792	2	239
Jonathan E., farmer, d. Dec. 30, 1850, ae 31	4	39-40
Jonathan E., s. Jonathan E., & Esther M., b. Jan. 1, 1851	4	33-34
Joseph, of Haddam, m. Mary E. **BRAINERD**, of East Haddam, July 1, 1852, by Rev. W. Emmerson	3	236
Juliette, of East Haddam, m. Gustavus **KELLOGG**, of Glastonbury, Dec. 2, 1845, by Rev. Alpheas Geer	3	203
Leonard S., m. Esther P. **MARTIN**, Feb. 26, 1843, by Rev. Stephen Alonzo Loper, of Hadlyme	3	194
Luceney, d. Samuel & Ruth, b. July 16, 1782	2	182
Lucena, of Lyme, m. Ezekiel Yarrington **PECK**, of East Haddam, Dec. 25, 1800	2	293

	Vol.	Page
CLARK, CLARKE, (cont.)		
Lydia, m. Gamaleel R. **TRACY**, May 17, 1821, by Rev. Solomon Blakesley	3	7
Lyne, d. Samuel & Ruth, b. June 20, 1780	2	182
Mable, m. Samuel **LORD**, b. of Colchester, Apr. 12, 1753	LR3	3
Marget, of Lyme, m. David **BELDING**, of East Haddam, Jan. 10, 1776	2	136
Mary, d. Elisha & Mary, b. Apr. 4, 1749	LR2	1101
Mary, d. Sterlin & Sarah, b. Apr. 19, 1789	2	239
Mary Ann, of East Haddam, m. John **BATES**, of Haddam, Apr. 26, 1837, by Rev. Stephen Beach	3	151
Mary C., of Haddam, m. John S. **BRAINERD**, of East Haddam, Jan. 1, 1851, by Rev. Jacob Gardiner, Moodus	3	229
Mary C., ae 20, b. in Haddam, m. John S. **BRAINERD**, house joiner,ae 20, of E. Haddam, Jan. 1, 1851, by Elder Gardner	4	37-8
Nathaniel, s. Silas & Ele[a]ner, b. Nov. 26, 1759	LR5	270
Olive, d. Silas & Ele[a]ner, b. Mar. 9, 1757	LR5	270
Oliver C., m. Cynthia M. **SWAN**, Oct. 11, 1831, by Rev. Isaac Parsons	3	120
Phebe, m. John **BATES**, Jr., b. of East Haddam, July 8, 1756	LR5	270
Phebe, m. Richard H. **GLADWIN**, b. of East Haddam, July 25, 1849, by Rev. Alpheas Geer	3	219
Reuben, s. Silas & Ele[a]ner, b. June 4, 1748	LR5	270
Reuben, s. Charles & Hannah, b. Jan. 29, 1775	2	62
Ruth, d. Samuel & Ruth, b. Aug. 19, 1772	2	182
Samuel, s. Samuel & Ruth, b. Dec. 31, 1788	2	182
Samuel, of New York, m. Nancy **PRATT**, of East Haddam, Sept. 16, 1827, by Rev. Isaac Parsons	3	95
Sarah, d. Samuel & Ruth, b. July 29, 1784	2	182
Sarah, ae 57, b. in Chatham, res. East Haddam, m. Ephraim **MEECH**, farmer, ae 59, b. in Stonington, res. East Haddam, Mar. 1, 1848, by William Russell	4	9-10
Sarah Ann, m. Charles A. **CHAMPLAIN**, b. of East Haddam, Apr. 28, 1839, by Rev. Isaac Parsons	3	172
Silas, m. Ele[a]ner **WILLIAMS**, Mar. 26, 1747	LR5	270
Silas, s. Silas & Ele[a]ner, b. Sept. 2, 1753	LR5	270
Silvester, s. Uzzel & Azubah, b. Aug. 21, 1778	2	108
Starling, s. Samuel & Ruth, b. Mar. 18, 1767	2	182
Sterlin, m. Sarah **WARNER**, b. of East Haddam, Oct. [1787?]	2	239
Sterlin, s. Sterlin & Sarah, b. July 17, 1790	2	239
Susan[n]ah, m. Stephen **CONE**, 3rd, Feb. 21, 1732/3	LR2	1123
Sylvester, see under Silvester		
Uzel, s. Silas & Ele[a]ner, b. Apr. 18, 1755	LR5	270
Uzzel, m. Azubah **KNOWLTON**, b. of East Haddam, Nov. 20, 1777	2	108
Watrous, s. Elisha & Mary, b. June 30, 1742	LR2	1101

	Vol.	Page
CLARK, CLARKE, (cont.)		
William, s. Elisha & Mary, b. Aug. 19, 1746	LR2	1101
William, of Madison, m. Almira **SMITH**, of Clinton, June 16, 1840, by John C. Palmer, J. P.	3	178
William B., of Norwich, m. Julia **SNOW**, of East Haddam, Nov. 29, 1832, by Isaac Parsons	3	127
Zera, of Saybrook, m. Maria **HORSON**, of East Haddam, Oct. 26, 1823, by Rev. Isaac Parsons	3	47
-----, s. James, farmer, ae 35 y., res. East Haddam, & [ ], ae 35, b. Apr. 5, 1855	4	75
CLEVELAND, Aaron, m. Sibbel **BRAINERD**, Oct. 24, 1751	LR4	470
Aaron, m. Eunice **SPENCER**, b. of East Haddam, Sept. 4, 1755	LR4	470
Dyer, s. Aaron & Eunice, b. June 6, 1756	LR4	470
Joanna, d. Josiah & Joanna, b. June 15, 1739	LR2	1109
John, s. Josiah & Joanna, b. Sept. 26, 1746	LR2	1109
Mary, m. Elisha **CLARK**, Sept. 17, 1741 (Arnold Copy note: "Over this item is written 'Caleb **CHAPMAN**'")	LR2	1101
Noadiah, s. Aaron & Sibble, b. Aug. 11, 1753	LR4	470
Ollive, d. Aaron & Eunice, b. June 1, 1758	LR4	470
Sybel, w. of Aaron, d. July 5, 1755	LR4	470
Sybel, d. Aaron & Eunice, b. July 19, 1760	LR4	470
COATES, Martin S., of New London, m. Lucy H. **CONE**, of East Haddam, Feb. 27, 1828, by Rev. Peter G. Clarke	3	100
COFFIN, Albert C., m. Finette **ANDREWS**, Apr. 20, 1834, by Rev. Stephen Beach	3	133
Frederick A., m. Caroline A. **MACK**, Apr. 20, 1834, by Rev. Stephen Beach	3	133
Lucretia, of East Haddam, m. Ichabod **CHAMPION**, of Rome, O., Oct. 11, 1830, by Isaac Parsons	3	108
COGGESHALL, William, of Brooklyn, m. Rebecca **DOANE**, of East Haddam, Feb. 18, 1840, by Rev. Tho[ma]s W. Gile	3	176-7
COLLINS, COLLINGS, Bennajah, of Liverpool, m. Susannah **TRACY**, of East Haddam, Mar. 29, 1770	2	26
George, s. Bennaiah & Susannah, b. Jan. 17, 1771	2	26
Julia, m. Enos B. **YOUNG**, b. of East Haddam, Dec. 7, 1845, by Rev. Stephen A. Loper, of Hadlyme	3	204
COLT, Lucretia, of Lyme, m. Isaac **SPENCER**, Jr., of East Haddam, Nov. 15, 1781	2	132
COMSTOCK, Almeda Elvira, d. Erastus & Laura, b. Nov. 2, 1811	2	293
Ann, of East Haddam, (Hadlyme Parish),m. Thomas P. **DIXON**, of Deep River, Conn., Nov. 30, 1852, by James Noyes	3	238
Balinda, d. Joseph & Dammaries, b. July 15, 1751	LR3	506
Chinathe, d. Joseph & Dammaries, b. May 17, 1757	LR3	506
Eliza, [twin with Erastus], d. Erastus & Laura, b. Sept. 10, 1808	2	293
Eliza, m. William **RAYNER**, Mar. 27, 1831, by Rev. Isaac Parsons	3	116
Erastus, m. Laura **BRAINARD**, Nov. 27, 1805	2	293

	Vol.	Page
COMSTOCK, (cont.)		
Erastus, [twin with Eliza], s. Erastus & Laura, b. Sept. 10, 1808	2	293
Erastus, d. July 14, 1812, ae 29	2	294
Ethan, s. Joseph & Dammaries, b. Dec. 16, 1748	LR3	506
Israel, m. Anna **SELDEN**, b. of East Haddam, Mar. 15, 1775	2	160
Israel Selden, s. Israel & Anna, b. July 10, 1785	2	160
Jonathan, s. Joseph & Dammaries, b. Apr. 2, 1747	LR3	506
Jude, d. Joseph & Dammaris, b. Dec. 29, 1745	LR3	506
Julia, of East Haddam, m. Gideon **CHAPMAN**, of Saybrook, May 19, 1824, by Rev. Isaac Parsons	3	58-59
Laura Brainard, d. Erastus & Laura, b. Nov. 7, 1806	2	293
Lucy, of East Haddam, m. John **WARNER**, of Saybrook, Sept. 25, 1827, by Rev. Simon Shailer, of Haddam	3	95
Mehitabel, d. Israel & Anna, b. Apr. 19, 1777	2	160
Ruth, of Lyme, m. Levi **CROSBY**, of East Haddam, Mar. 1, 1763	2	52
Samuel P., m. Almyra C. **THOMPSON**, Sept. 29, 1844, by Rev. Stephen Alonzo Loper, of Hadlyme	3	200
Samuel W., s. Samuel P., farmer, ae 28, of Hadlyme, & Almira C., ae 31, b. Aug. 16, 1849	4	27-8
Silence Sears, m. John **MAYNARD**, Sept. 21, 1802	2	281
Sophia, m. Samuel **FOX**, June 7, 1821, by Rev. J. Vaill, of Hadlyme	3	5
Temperance, of Lyme, m. Jeremiah **SMITH**, of East Haddam, June 17, 1784	2	136
Victory, s. Jabez, farmer, ae 58, & Margaret, ae 43, b. Jan. 19, 1850, of Hadlyme	4	27-8
CONDAL, Samuel, of Colchester, m. Elizabeth **JEFFERY**, of East Haddam, Nov. 28, last [1822], by Josiah Griffen, J. P.	3	33
CONE, Aaron, s. Jonah & Elizabeth, b. Dec. 30, 1747	LR3	5
Aaron, s. Jonah & Elizabeth, d. Aug. 18, 1749	LR3	5
Abigail, d. Daniell, b. June 27, 1706	LR1	574
Abiga[i]ll, d. Stephen & Abiga[i]ll, b. June 2, 1725	LR2	e
Abigail, d. Jared & Ruth, b. Aug. 18, 1753	LR5	563
Abigail, d. Timothy & Abigail, b. Mar. 9, 1768	2	217
Abigail, d. Elisha & Elizabeth, b. May 13, 1791	2	239
Abigail, of East Haddam, m. Franklin G. **CROCKER**, of New London, Nov. 3, 1839, by Rev. Charles William Bradley	3	173
Achsah, d. Daniel & Keziah, b. July 17, 1789	2	116
Allas, d. Joseph, Jr. & Martha, b. Feb. 8, 1762	LR6	507
Alice, d. James, 2d & Alice, b. May 10, 1783	2	138
Ambrose, s. James, Jr. & Alice, b. Apr. 6, 1781	2	138
Annah, d. Jonathan & Annah, b. Nov. 25, 1752	LR3	4
Anna, d. Jonah & Elizabeth, b. May 29, 1755	LR3	5
Anner, d. Timothy & Abigail, b. May 27, 1764	2	217
Anna, d. George, Jr. & Elizabeth, b. May 28, 1767	LR6	503
Anna, d. George, Jr. & Elizabeth, d. July 28, 1770	2	7

	Vol.	Page
CONE, (cont.)		
Anna, d. George, Jr. & Damaris, b. Oct. 1, 1778* *(Entry has been crossed out)	2	6
Anna, d. George, 2d, & Demeris, b. Oct. 1, 1778	2	110
Anne, m. Thomas **ANDREWS**, May 29, 1740	LR2	1094
Anne, m. James **OLMSTED**, b. of East Haddam, June 18, 1763	LR7	417
Anne, d. Roswel[l] & Sarah, b. June 1, 1780	2	66
Anne, d. Daniel, 4th & Marcy, b. June 21, 1785	2	215
Asa, s. Daniel, 3rd, & Keziah, b. Apr. 19, 1778	2	116
Aseni, d. Silvanus & Hannah, b. Nov. 23, 1757	LR5	267
Ashbel, s. Joseph & Mary, b. Aug. 2, 1747	LR3	508
Azel, s. Rufus & Esther, b. June 30, 1763	LR6	508
Azubah, wid. of William, d. Jan. 14, 1835, at Hartford, ae 76	2	159
Azubah Ann, m. Warren S. **SPENCER**, Aug. 4, 1833, by Rev. Stephen Beach	3	132
Azubah L., of East Haddam, m. Nathan L. **FOSTER**, of Mass., May 30, 1810, by Rev. William Lyman	2	299
Azubah Louisa, d. William, Jr. & Azubah, b. Jan. 14, 1788	2	158
Benjamin, s. Joseph & Mary, b. Sept. 20, 1739	LR2	1123
Benjamin, s. Joseph & Mary, d. Oct. 16, 1758	LR3	508
Benjamin, s. Nathaniel, Jr. & Mary, b. Mar. 26, 1766	LR3	5
Bethia, d. Thomas & Mehitable, b. Aug. 28, 1741	LR2	1112
Bets[e]y, d. Samuel, 2d, & Phebe, b. Oct. 11, 1784	2	172
Bettee, d. William & Elizabeth, b. Aug. 2, 1759	LR3	508
Bettee, d. William & Elizabeth, d. June 27, 1760	LR3	508
Carisle M., of East Haddam, m. Rev. Zolva **WHITMORE**, of North Guilford, Oct. 16, 1821, by Rev. Isaac Parsons (Carile?)	3	15
Carile Mary, d. Dr. Jonah, 3rd, & Mary, b. Nov. 26, 1797	2	279
Cephas, s. Jonathan & Annah, b. May 23, 1750	LR3	4
Cephas, s. Jonathan & Annah, d. June 2, 1753	LR3	4
Charity, of Haddam, m. Elijah **HURD**, of East Haddam, Mar. 13, 1794, by Nehemiah Brainerd, in Haddam	2	295
Charity, of East Haddam, m. Russell **UFFORD**, of Chatham, Sept. 12, 1824, by Rev. W[illia]m Jarvis	3	64-5
Charles, s. Robart & Margaret, b. Sept. 12, 1791	2	148
Charles C., m. Mrs. Mary **ROBERT**, b. of East Haddam, Feb. 12, 1829, by Alvan Ackley	3	101
Chloe, w. of Joshua, d. Aug. 9, 1800	2	278
Chloe Chapman, d. Joshua & Sally, b. Oct. 1, 1808	2	277
Clare, d. Judah & Lydia, b. Apr. 1, 1775	2	172
Claracy, d. Rufus & Esther, b. Dec. 9, 1767	LR6	508
Clarressee, d. Zechariah & Jemima, b. Aug. 14, 1783	2	70
Clarissa H., of East Haddam, m. Eliphalet L. **ARNOLD**, of Haddam, Nov. 12, 1826, by Rev. Simeon Shailer	3	90
Conant, s. Joseph, Jr. & Martha, b. July 6, 1760	LR6	507
Cyrus, s. Nathaniel, Jr. & Mary, b. July 28, 1761	LR3	5
Daniell, m. Mary **GATES**, Feb. 14, 1693	LR1	574

	Vol.	Page
CONE, (cont.)		
Daniell, s. Dea. Daniell, b. Dec. 26, 1693	LR1	574
Daniell, m. Mary **BARNS**, Dec. 25, 1718	LR2	1130
Daniell, Dea., d. June 15, 1725, in the 60th y. of his age	LR2	1096
Daniel, Jr., m. Mary **SPENCER**, Mar. 14, 1728	LR2	1119
Daniel, s. Daniel, Jr. & Mary, b. Nov. [ ], 1728	LR2	1119
Daniell, s. Daniell & Mary, b. June 21, 1733	LR2	1130
Daniel, s. Jared & Ruth, b. Feb. 2, 1755	LR5	563
Daniel, Jr., m. Dorothy **SPENCER**, May 15, 1755	LR5	561
Daniel, s. Nathaniel, Jr. & Mary, b. July 7, 1759	LR3	5
Daniel, of East Haddam, m. Abigail **GRISWOLD**, of Weathersfield, May 7, 1760	LR5	559
Daniel, [twin with Mary], s. Jonah & Elizabeth, b. Aug. 28, 1763	LR3	5
Daniel, 3rd, of East Haddam, m. Keziah **CHAPMAN**, of East Win[d]sor, Aug. 3, 1775	2	116
Daniel, 4th, of East Haddam, m. Marcy **OTIS**, of Colchester, Sept. 15, 1784	2	215
Daniel, 3rd, m. Olive **ACKLEY**, b. of East Haddam, Apr. 28, 1785	2	134
Daniel, 4th, d. Sept. 27, 1786, in the 24th y. of his age	2	216
Daniel, s. Stephen & Mary, b. Aug. 17, 1818	2	321
Daniel, m. Phebe **SISSON**, Aug. 22, 1841, by Charles William Bradley	3	187
Daniel Clark, s. Horatio & Polly, b. Sept. 9, 1821	2	285
Darius, s. Nathaniel, Jr. & Mary, b. Sept. 2, 1763	LR3	5
David, s. Daniell, b. Feb. 12, 1715	LR1	574
David S., m. Eliza E. **SPENCER**, b. of East Haddam, Dec. 27, 1835, by Rev. Isaac Parsons	3	140-1
Deborah, d. Stephen & Mary, b. Apr. 2, 1718	LR2	1116
Delight, d. Nathaniel, Jr. & Mary, b. Sept. 3, 1757	LR3	5
Delight had d. Martha, b. Mar. 21, 1783; reputed f. Nathan **STEWART**, Jr., of Litchfield	2	78
Delina, d. Daniel, 4th, & Marcy, b. Jan. 31, 1787	2	215
Demeris, d. George, 2d, & Demeris, b. July 11, 1781	2	110
Dorithy, d. Daniell, b. Apr. 29, 1704	LR1	574
Dorothy, m. Thomas **GATES**, Jr., Aug. 17, 1722	LR2	c
Dorothy, d. Stephen & Abigail, b. Sept. 16, 1732	LR2	1114
Dorothy, d. Silvanus, 2d, & Sarah, b. Jan. 11, 1763	LR6	507
Dorothy, had d. Juletee **BRIGHT**, b. Jan. 31, 1787; reputed father John **BRIGHT**	2	14
Dorothy, Mrs., of East Haddam, m. Elias **WORTHINGTON**, of Colchester, Jan. 10, 1790	2	265
Dorothy had s. Ithamer **HARVEY**, b. Jan. 12, 1790	2	14
Dorothy, d. William & Azubah, b. Oct. 15, 1792	2	158
Dorothy, m. Michael **CHAUNCEY**, b. of East Haddam, Dec. 22, 1813	2	301
Ebenezer, Jr., m. Mary **BRAINARD**, b. of East Haddam, Jan.		

	Vol.	Page
CONE, (cont.)		
8, 1746	LR3	17
Ebenezer, s. Ebenezer, Jr. & Mary, b. Jan. 30, 1748	LR3	17
Ebenezer, s. Timothy & Abigail, b. Oct. 8, 1776	2	217
Ebenezer, d. Feb. 1, 1788	2	218
Elle[a]ner, d. Stephen & Mary, b. Dec. 25, 1710	LR2	1116
Elle[a]ner, d. Stephen & Mary, d. Apr. 9, 1730	LR2	1116
Ele[a]ner, d. Stephen, 3rd, & Susan[n]ah, b. Feb. 5, 1740/41	LR2	1098
Eleazer, s. George & Mehettabell, b. July 2, 1740	LR2	1124
Elisha, s. Stephen & Abiga[i]ll, b. Dec. 1, 1726	LR2	e
Elisha, m. Elizabeth **TRACY**, b. of East Haddam, Sept. 28, 1786 (Entry crossed out)	2	157
Elisha, m. Elizabeth **TRACY**, b. of East Haddam, Sept. 28, 1786	2	239
Elizabeth, d. Jonah & Elizabeth, b. July 3, 1751	LR3	5
Elizabeth, d. Joseph & Mary, b.Aug. 22, 1751	LR3	508
Elizabeth, m. Joseph **WARNER**, b. of East Haddam, Jan. 24, 1760	LR6	505
Elizabeth, d. George, Jr. & Elizabeth, b. Jan. 20, 1763	LR6	503
Elisabeth, m. Levi **PALMER**, b. of East Haddam, July 21, 1768	2	128
Elizabeth, d. Timothy & Abigail, b. Mar. 24, 1770	2	217
Elisabeth, w. of George, Jr., d. Dec. 5, 1773	2	111
Elisabeth, m. Reubin **SPENCER**, b. of East Haddam, Mar. 17, 1774	2	80
Elisabeth, d. William, Jr. & Azubah, b. July 2, 1778	2	158
Elisabeth, d. William, Jr. & Azuba[h], d. Apr. 5, 1781	2	159
Elisabeth, 2d, d. William, Jr. & Azubah, b. Aug. 30, 1784	2	158
Elisabeth, w. of Capt. William, d. Feb. 26, 1786	2	159
Elisabeth, d. Robert & Margaret, b. Sept. 11, 1787	2	148
Elisabeth, d. William & Azubah, d. Apr. 28, 1850, at Hartford, ae 66	2	159
Elizabeth C., of East Haddam, m. David R. **MARVIN**, of Lyme, Jan. 27, 1853, by Rev. Nathaniel Miner, of Millington	3	238
Elizabeth C., ae 27, of Millington, m. David R. **MARVIN**, agriculturist, ae 30, of Lyme, Jan. 27, 1853, by Rev. Nathaniel Miner	4	43-4
Elizabeth J., of East Haddam, m. Daniel **TOMPKINS**, of Middletown, Sept. 3, 1837, by Roswell Davison, J. P.	3	152
Emeline E., d. [Lord W. & Fluvia A.], b. Jan. 6, 1840	3	242
Ephraim, s. Matthew & Lydia, b. Aug. 25, 1771	2	58
Erastus, s. Israel & Lucy, b. Sept. 29, 1788	2	154
Erastus, of East Haddam, m. Lucy S. **TINKER**, of Lyme, Mar. 18, 1833, by Nathaniel Miner	3	131
Esther, m. Richard **ANDREWES**, June 16, 1737	LR2	1118
Esther, d. James & Grace, b. Feb. 21, 1739/40	LR2	1122
Esther, d. Jonathan & Annah, b. Aug. 23, 1746	LR3	4
Esther, d. George, Jr. & Elizabeth, b. Nov. 28, 1768	LR6	503

	Vol.	Page
CONE, (cont.)		
Esther, d. Rufus & Esther, b. Sept. 10, 1770	2	14
Esther, d. George, Jr. & Elisabeth, d. Aug. 15, 1771	2	7
Esther, d. Daniel & Keziah, b. Oct. 15, 1786	2	116
Eunice, d. Daniell & Mary, b. May 24, 1727	LR2	1130
Eunice, d. Daniell & Mary, d. Nov. 21, 1741, in the 15th y. of her age	LR2	1130
Eunice, d. William & Elizabeth, b. Dec. 31, 1748	LR3	508
Eunice, d. William & Elizabeth, d. Mar. 19, 1761	LR3	508
Eunice, wid., d. Oct. 21, 1819	2	331
Fanny W., of East Haddam, m. Edwin B. **GRISWOLD**, of West Hartford, Mar. 31, 1847, by Nathaniel Miner	3	209
Festus, s. Nathaniel & Mary, b. July 24, 1772	2	78
Festus, s. Nathaniel & Mary, d. Sept. 6, 1778	2	79
Filenia, d. Rufus & Esther, b. Jan. 8, 1762	LR6	508
Fluvia A., m. Joseph **PADDOCK**, b. of East Haddam, Mar. 6, 1832, by Nathaniel Miner	3	124
Frederick Tylee, s. Joshua & Sally, b. Sept. 10, 1803	2	277
Garrard, s. Stephen & Mary, b. Mar. 10, 1713	LR2	1116
Garrard, s. Stephen & Mary, d. Sept. 27, 1714	LR2	1116
Garade, s. Stephen, 3rd, & Susannah, b. Dec. 21, 1733	LR2	1123
George, m. Mehittabell **EM[M]ONS**, Jan. 31, 1733/4	LR2	1124
George, s. George & Mehittabell, b. Jan. 3, 1738	LR2	1124
George, Jr., of East Haddam, m. Elizabeth **BRAINERD**, of Middletown, May 21, 1761	LR6	503
George, 2d, of East Haddam, m. Demeris **SAXTON**, of Colchester, Sept. 5, 1776	2	110
George, s. George, 2d, & Damaris, b. Oct. 23, 1784	2	110
George, d. Aug. 8, 1793, in the 86th y. of his age	2	71
George G., of East Haddam, m. Frances **WELLES**, of Lyme, Nov. 8, 1854, by Rev. S. A. Loper, of Higganum	3	241
George G., salesman, ae 26, b. in Euclid, Ohio, res. E. Haddam, m. Frances **WELLS**, ae 25, of Lyme, Nov. 8, 1854, by Rev. Stephen A. Loper	4	51-2
Gideon, m. Huldah **LISK**, b. of East Haddam, Mar. 20, 1776	2	116
Grace Spencer, d. Rufus & Esther, b. Apr. 14, 1765	LR6	508
Gurdon, s. James, 2d, & Alice, b. Oct. 19, 1769	2	138
Hannah, m. Noadiah **BRAINARD**, June 4, 1724	LR1	575
Hannah, m. Shubael **FULLER**, Jr., June 28, 1744	LR3	8
Hannah, d. Thomas & Mehitable, b. Aug. 12, 1744	LR2	1112
Hannah, m. Josiah **ARNOLD**, May 29, 1755	LR5	562
Hannah, d. Joel & Hannah, b. May 23, 1766	LR7	411
Hannah, d. George, Jr. & Elizabeth, b. Oct. 25, 1770	2	6
Hannah, m. Samuel **HALL**, Jr., July 9, 1789	2	307
Hannah, b. in E. Haddam, res. Millington, d. Jan. 18, 1851, ae 74	4	39-40
Hannah Andrewes, d. Silvanus & Hannah, b. Feb. 26, 1763	LR5	267
Harriet Elizabeth, d. Horatio & Polly, b. Nov. 6. 1812	2	285

	Vol.	Page
CONE, (cont.)		
Helon, s. George, 2d, & Demeris, b. Sept. 9, 1789	2	110
Henrietta, d. Joshua & Chloe, b. May 9, 1795	2	277
Henryetta, d. Horatio & Polly, b. May 31, 1807	2	285
Henrietta, m. Robert U. **WICKHAM**, b. of East Haddam, Sept. 4, 1831, by Rev. Isaac Parsons	3	120
Henry, s. Daniell, b. July 16, 1709	LR1	574
Hezekiah Selden, s. Horatio & Polly, b. Oct. 30, 1809	2	285
Hiram Francis, s. Joshua & Chloe, b. Sept. 5, 1797	2	277
Hopsy, d. James & Alice, b. Jan. 18, 1789	2	138
Horice, d. James, 2d, & Alice, b. Jan. 2, 1768	2	138
Horice, d. James, 2d, & Alice, d. Nov. 28, 1775	2	139
Horice, 2d, d. James, Jr. & Alice, b. Dec. 28, 1778	2	138
Horace, m. Sarah C. **SPENCER**, b. of Haddam, July 23, 1837, by Roswell Davison, J. P.	3	152
Horatio, s. Zechariah & Jemima, b. Sept. 22, 1777	2	70
Horatio, of East Haddam, m. Polly **SELDEN**, of Chatham, Sept. 25, 1803	2	285
Huldah, d. James & Grace, b. Mar. 9, 1732	LR2	1122
Huldah, m. Thomas **EM[M]ONS**, May 21, 1751	LR7	416
Huldah, m. Thomas **EM[M]ONS**, May 21, 1751	LR7	417
Huldah, d. George, Jr. & Elizabeth, b. Sept. 5, 1764	LR6	503
Isaac, s. Timothy & Abigail, b. July 28, 1772	2	217
Israel, s. Nathaniel, Jr. & Mary, b. Dec. 21, 1749	LR3	5
Israel, m. Lucy **ACKLEY**, b. of East Haddam, Apr. 13, 1784	2	154
Israel, s. Israel & Lucy, b. July 9, 1786	2	154
Israel, Jr., m. Polly **ANDERSON**, Nov. 10, 1807	2	66
Israel, Jr., Dea., d. Apr. 6, 1827, ae 41	2	67
Israel, Dea., d. Apr. 7, 1827, ae 41 y. Certified by J. Attwood, he having seen the records of the Cong. Church in Millington Soc. of East Haddam and the family Bible of the late Polly **CONE**	3	92
James, s. James & Grace, b. Sept. 4, 1742	LR2	1122
James, Jr., m. Alice **CROCKER**, b. of East Haddam, May 3, 1764	2	138
James, s. James, Jr. & Alice, b. Dec. 13, 1771	2	138
James, d. July 24, 1797	2	139
James, s. Stephen & Mary, b. July 27, 1816	2	321
James, of East Haddam, m. Adelia **BULKLEY**, of Manchester, Sept. 4, 1842, by Rev. Simon Shaler, of Haddam	3	192
Jane, ae 29, m. Cyrus W. **CHAPMAN**, farmer, ae 23, b. of E. Haddam, June [ ], 1850, by Rev. N. Miner	4	19-20
Jane, Mrs., divorced from Cyrus W. **CHAPMAN**, ae 32, b. in East Haddam, res. East Haddam, m. Jared A. **SPENCER**, ae 40, b. in Westbrook, res. Westbrook, June 30, 1856, by Rev. Nath[anie]l Miner. Int. pub. June 28, 1856	4	91-92
Jane C., m. Cyrus W. **CHAPMAN**, b. of East Haddam, June		

	Vol.	Page
CONE, (cont.)		
23, 1850, by Nathaniel Miner. Int. pub.	3	226
Jared, m. Ruth **SMITH**, Dec. [ ], 1738	LR3	11
Jared, m. Ruth **NEWELL**, June 7, 1752	LR5	563
Jared, d. Oct. 10, 1781	2	117
Jared, s. Nehemiah & Jedidah, b. Dec. 21, 1781	2	120
Jemima, m. Samuel **ANDREWS**, Jr., Nov. 23, 1738	LR2	107
Jemima, d. Jonathan & Annah, b. Sept. 16, 1754	LR3	4
Jennett, of East Haddam, m. Ebenezer H. **ROSE**, of Saybrook, Ct., Mar. 24, 1857, by Rev. S. W. Robbins	4	119
Jeremiah, s. Daniell & Mary, b. Jan. 15, 1720	LR2	1130
Jeremiah, s. Joseph & Mary, b. Feb. 17, 1750	LR3	508
Jeremiah, of East Haddam, m. Mary **BROCKWAY**, of Lyme, Aug. 10, 1773	2	106
Joel, s. Thomas & Mehitable, b. Feb. 26, 1735/6	LR2	1112
Joel, of East Haddam, m. Hannah **BRAINERD**, of Middletown, June 9, 1757	LR5	267
Joel, m. Hannah **BRAINERD**, June 9, 1757	LR7	411
Joel, d. Jan. 3, 1788	2	278
Joel, farmer, d. Nov. 14, 1847, ae 73	4	7-8
John, s. Stephen & Mary, b. Oct. 25, 1720	LR2	1116
John, s. Stephen, 3rd & Susannah, b. May 26, 1746	LR2	1098
Jonah, s. Daniell & Mary, b. Mar. 7, 1721	LR2	1130
Jonah, m. Elizabeth **GATES**, June 20, 1745	LR3	5
Jonah, s. Jonah & Elizabeth, b. Apr. 9, 1746	LR3	5
Jonah, s. Jonah & Elizabeth, d. Aug. 17, 1749	LR3	5
Jonah, s. Jonah & Elizabeth, b. Apr. 16, 1753	LR3	5
Jonah, s. Joel & Hannah, b. May 17, 1763	LR7	411
Jonah, 3rd, Dr., m. Mary **HALL**, b. of East Haddam, Jan. 11, 1797, by Rev. William Lyman	2	279
Jonah, Dr., d. Sept. 17, 1830, ae 67	2	280
Jonathan, m. Annah **CHAPMAN**, Oct. 30, 1745	LR3	4
Jonathan, s. Jonathan & Annah, b. July 9, 1748	LR3	4
Jonathan O., m. Almira O. **CARD**, Dec. 7, 1836, by Rev. Alfred Gates	3	151
Jonathan Olmsted, s. Stephen & Mary, b. Oct. 18, 1814	2	321
Joseph, s. Daniell, b. Mar. 20, 1711	LR1	574
Joseph, m. Mary **SMITH**, Nov. 28, 1734	LR2	1123
Joseph, s. Joseph & Mary, b. Nov. 2, 1735	LR2	1123
Joseph, Jr., m. Martha **SPENCER**, b. of East Haddam, June 14, 1759	LR6	507
Joseph A., of New London, m. Harriet E. **GOFF**, of East Haddam, Mar. 10, 1839, by Rev. Charles William Bradley	3	168
Joseph Henry, s. Stephen & Sarah, b. Nov. 8, 1834	2	321
Joseph Olmsted, s. Samuel & Elizabeth, b. Dec. 19, 1756	LR7	1
Joshua, s. Thomas & Mehitable, b. Feb. 10, 1738/9	LR2	1112
Joshua, s. Joel & Hannah, b. July 6, 1758	LR7	411
Joshua, m. Chloe **CHAPMAN**, b. of East Haddam, Jan. 17,		

	Vol.	Page
CONE, (cont.)		
1790	2	277
Joshua, of East Haddam, m. Sally **RANNEY**, of Middletown, Jan. 18, 1802	2	277
Judah, s. Samuel & Elizabeth, b. July 26, 1753	LR7	1
Judah, m. Lydia **CONE**, b. of East Haddam, Apr. 10, 1774	2	172
Julia, d. Joshua & Chloe, b. Feb. 5, 1791	2	277
Julia E., m. Elisha C. **BINGHAM**, b. of East Haddam, June 4, 1837, by Rev. Isaac Parsons	3	152
Juliett, d. Israel, Jr. & Polly, b. Jan. 4, 1814	2	66
Julius, s. James, Jr. & Alice, b. Sept. 3, 1785	2	138
Laura, m. David **MARTIN**, b. of East Haddam, Oct. 24, 1820, by Rev. Isaac Parsons	2	323
Laura S., d. [Lord W. & Fluvia A.], b. May 8, 1848	3	242
Laura S., d. Lord W., farmer, ae 33, & Fluvia, ae 28, b. Apr. 15, 1848	4	5-6
Lois, d. Daniell & Mary, b. Aug. 9, 1731	LR2	1130
Lord W., m. Fluvia A. **ARNOLD**, b. of East Haddam, Jan. 1, 1837, by Rev. Nathaniel Miner	3	146
Lord W., m. Fluvia A. **ARNOLD**, Jan. 1, 1837	3	242
Lord Wellington, s. Isra[e]l, Jr. & Polly, b. July 26, 1815	2	66
Lucy, m. Samuel **BARNS**, b. of East Haddam, Nov. [ ], 1733	LR3	13
Lucy, d. Stephen & Abigail, b. Mar. 9, 1737	LR2	1114
Lucy, d. Matthew & Mary, b. July 20, 1761	LR6	505
Lucy, d. Timothy & Abigail, b. Dec. 16, 1774	2	217
Lucy, d. Capt. Timothy & Abigail, d. Sept. 4, 1775	2	218
Lucy, d. Timothy & Abigail, b. Feb. 2, 1779	2	217
Lucy, m. John **ANDREWES**, b. of East Haddam, Sept. 26, 1781	2	128
Lucy, d. Israel & Lucy, b. May 27, 1785	2	154
Lucy Ann, d. Israe[l], Jr. & Polly, b. Feb. 21, 1809	2	66
Lucy Ann, of East Haddam, m. George **RANSOM**, of Lyme, Feb. 26, 1834, by Rev. Nathaniel Miner	3	133
Lucy H., of East Haddam, m. Martin S. **COATES**, of New London, Feb. 27, 1828, by Rev. Peter G. Clarke	3	100
Lydia, d. Daniel, Jr. & Mary, b. Feb. 5, 1732/3	LR2	1119
Lydia, d. Ebenezer, Jr. & Mary, b. Aug. 28, 1754	LR3	17
Lydia, m. Judah **CONE**, b. of East Haddam, Apr. 10, 1774	2	172
Lydia, d. Daniel & Keziah, b. Aug. 25, 1784	2	116
Lydia, of Hadlyme, d. Nov. 3, 1850, ae 85	4	39-40
Mariah, Mrs., m. Jared S. **BRAINERD**, June 9, 1822, by Rev. Simeon Dickinson, at the house of Wid. Peggy Cone	3	25
Martha, d. Joseph & Mary, b. Apr. 10, 1744	LR2	1123
Martha, m. Levi **BEEBE**, b. of East Haddam, Nov. 20, 1769	2	30
Martha, reputed d. of Nathan **STEWART**, Jr., of Litchfield, & Delight **CONE**, b. Mar. 21, 1783	2	78
Martin, s. Joseph & Mary, b. May 15, 1742	LR2	1123
Martin, m. Rebeckah **SPENCER**, b. of East Haddam, June 5,	LR7	7

	Vol.	Page
CONE, (cont.)		
1764	LR7	7
Mary, d. Daniell, b. Jan. 6, 1701	LR1	574
Mary, d. Stephen & Mary, b. Nov. 5, 1702	LR2	1116
Mary, m. Matthias **FULLER**, June 16, 1722	LR2	1099
Mary, m. William **BARNS**, July 2, 1724	LR2	e
Mary, d. Daniell & Mary, b. Oct. 12, 1729	LR2	1130
Mary, d. Joseph & Mary, b. Mar. 27, 1738	LR2	1123
Mary, d. Stephen, 3rd, & Susannah, b. Mar. 20, 1743	LR2	1098
Mary, w. of Dea. Daniell, d. May 12, 1743, in the 68th y. of her age	LR2	1096
Mary, d. Ebenezer, Jr. & Mary, b. Mar. 8, 1746	LR3	17
Mary, m. William **OLMSTEAD**, Jr., Mar. 20, 1746	LR3	10
Mary, d. Ebenezer, Jr. & Mary, d. June 6, 1747	LR3	17
Mary, d. Ebenezer, Jr. & Mary, b. Sept. 15, 1750	LR3	17
Mary, w. of Daniell, d. Sept. 2, 1753	LR2	1130
Mary, m. Daniel **EMMONS**, Apr. 2, 1762	LR7	416
Mary, [twin with Daniel], d. Jonah & Elizabeth, b. Aug. 28, 1763	LR3	5
Mary, w. of Matthew, d. Apr. 27, 1768	2	59
Mary, d. Nehemiah & Jedidah, b. July 10, 1774	2	120
Mary, w. of Jeremiah, d. Sept. 23, 1775	2	107
Mary, d. Daniel, 3rd, & Keziah, b. Jan. 17, 1780	2	116
Mary, d. Israel & Lucy, b. Apr. 25, 1799	2	154
Mary, d. Israel, Jr. & Polly, b. Sept. 14, 1817		66
Mary, w. of Stephen, d. Mar. 6, 1830, in the 37th y. of her	2	
age	2	322
Mary, wid. of Dr. Jonah, d. Aug. 13, 1836, ae 68	3	280
Mary, m. Rufus W. **SWAN**, Apr. 16, 1840, by Nathaniel Miner	LR5	178
Mary, m. John **BORDEN**, Apr. 30, [ ]		561
Mary Ann C., m. Nelson C. **RICHMOND**, Sept. 22, 1835, by	3	
Rev. Isaac Parsons	3	140-1
Mary E., d. [Lord W. & Fluvia A.], b. Jan. 7, 1851	4	242
Mary E., d. Lord W., farmer, & Flavia, b. Jan. 15, 1851		33-4
Mary E., ae 23, b. in East Haddam, res. East Haddam, m. Samuel H. **FULLER**, ae 25, b. in East Haddam, res. East Haddam, Aug. 14, 1856, at Hadlyme, b. Rev. E. B.	4	
Hillard. Int. pub. Aug. 13, 1856	2	92
Matilda, d. Israel & Lucy, b. Aug. 15, 1790		154
Matilda, of East Haddam, m. Ephraim **UFFORD**, of Chatham,	3	
Sept. 5, 1824, by David Selden	LR3	62-3
Matthew, s. Jared & Ruth, b. Oct. 15, 1739	LR3	11
Matthew, s. Jared & Ruth, d. Dec. 15, 1739(sic)	LR3	11
Matthew, s. Jared & Ruth, b. Oct. 14, 1740	LR6	11
Matthew, m. Mary **BARNS**, b. of East Haddam, June 24, 1760	2	505
Matthew, s. Matthew & Mary, b. Oct. 7, 1767	2	58
Matthew, m. Lydia **GATES**, b. of East Haddam, Sept. 13, 1770	LR1	58
Mehittabell, d. Daniell, b. June 27, 1699	LR2	574

	Vol.	Page
CONE, (cont.)		
Mehitable, d. Stephen & Mary, b. July 14, 1715	LR2	1116
Mehitable, m. Weeks **WILLIAMS**, Dec. 25, 1718	LR2	1094
Mehittable, d. James & Grace, b. Aug. 11, 1729	LR2	1122
Mehitable, m. Thomas **CONE**, Feb. 20, 1734/5	LR2	1112
Mehetable, d. Joel & Hannah, b. Apr. 17, 1760	LR7	411
Mehetable, d. Silvanus & Hannah, b. Sept. 13, 1760	LR5	267
Mehetable, w. of George, d. July 6, 1796, in the 87th y. of her age	2	71
Mehitable S., of East Haddam, m. George H. **CHADWICK**, of Lyme, Apr. 21, 1825, by Rev. Herman L. Vaill	3	74-5
Melissa, d. Israel & Lucy, b. Aug. 7, 1792	2	154
Nancy, d. Capt. Timothy & Abigail, b. June 15, 1781	2	217
Nancy, m. Gad **SMITH**, b. of East Haddam, [1838?], in New London	3	180-1
Nancy J., d. [Lord W. & Fluvia A.], b. May 26, 1842	3	242
Nathaniel, Jr., m. Mary **GRAVES**, Dec. 5, 1745	LR3	5
Nathaniel, s. Nathaniel, Jr. & Mary, b. June 22, 1748	LR3	5
Nehemiah, s. Jared & Ruth, b. Sept. 14, 1742	LR3	11
Nehemiah, m. Jedidah **ANDREWS**, b. of East Haddam, Jan. 17, 1765	LR7	417
Newel, s. Jared & Ruth, b. Aug. 3, 1762	LR5	563
Newel, s. Jared & Ruth, d. Mar. 13, 1764	LR5	563
Newel, s. Matthew & Mary, b. Aug. 28, 1765	LR6	505
Nuel, s. Nehemiah & Jedidah, b. Sept. 2, 1779	2	120
Noadiah, s. Thomas & Mehitable, b. Sept. 17, 1750	LR2	1112
Noadiah, d. Nov. 19, 1825, ae 75	2	278
Octavianus, s. James & Alice, b. June 22, 1792	2	138
Olive, d. William & Elizabeth, b. Sept. 19, 1755	LR3	508
Olive, d. Ebenezer, Jr. & Mary, b. Mar. 24, 1759	LR3	17
Olive, d. William & Elizabeth, d. June 4, 1760	LR3	508
Ollive, d. Jonah & Elizabeth, b. Nov. 27, 1760	LR3	5
Oliver, s. Daniell & Mary, b. May 28, 1736; d. Dec. 17, 1755, at Sharon	LR2	1130
Oliver, s. Nathaniel, Jr. & Mary, b. Dec. 2, 1755	LR3	5
Oliver, s. Jonah & Elizabeth, b. June 26, 1757	LR3	5
Oliver, s. Eliakim & Dorothy, b. May 24, 1772	2	32
Oliver, 2d, d. Sept. 26, 1782, in the 26th y. of his age	2	15
Oris, d. Judah & Lydia, b. July 27, 1777	2	172
Oris, m. Eliphalet **HOLMES**, Jr., b. of East Haddam, Mar. 14, 1798	2	259
Orrice, m. Daniel **CHAPMAN**, Apr. 25, 1824, by Elijah Parsons	3	60-1
Peleg, s. Zachariah & Jemima, b. Oct. 28, 1778	2	70
Peleg, s. Zachariah & Jemima, d. Mar. 14, 1797, in the 19th y. of his age	2	71
Peleg, s. Horatio & Polly, b. Feb. 22, 1805	2	285
Phebe, m. Matthew **MILLARD**, Mar. 31, 1735/6	LR2	1106

	Vol.	Page
CONE, (cont.)		
Phebe, d. Roswel & Sarah, b. Mar. 2, 1774	2	66
Phebe, d. Roswel & Sarah, d. June 17, 1776	2	67
Phebe, d. Roswel & Sarah, b. Aug. 30, 1778	2	66
Phebe, d. Israel & Lucy, b. Oct. 6, 1796	2	154
Phebe, of East Haddam, m. Orson **GOODRICH**, of Glastenbury, Nov. 30, 1832, by Rev. Peter Gilchrist Clarke	3	128
Phebe M., of East Haddam, m. William **PARMLEE**, of Chatham, Feb. 26, 1837, by Roswell Davison, J. P.	3	152
Philena, of East Haddam, m. Amos **GILLETT**, of Mt. Morris, N. Y., Nov. 9, 1834, by Rev. Nathaniel Miner	3	135
Phinehas, s. Ebenezer, Jr. & Mary, b. Sept. 27, 1752	LR3	17
Phyloxia, d. Joshua & Chloe, b. Jan. 16, 1793	2	277
Polley, d. Jeremiah & Mary, b. Oct. 13, 1774	2	106
Polley, d. Jeremiah & Mary, d. Sept. 21, 1775	2	107
Rachill, m. Samuell **DUTTON**, Nov. 17, 1725	LR1	584
Rachel, d. Daniel, Jr. & Mary, b. Oct. 9, 1736	LR2	1119
Rachel, m. Nathaniel **HUNGERFORD**, Dec. 8, 1756	LR5	269
Rachel Starlin, d. Benjamin & Rachel, b. July 16, 1786	2	176
Rebeckah, d. Stephen & Mary, b. Mar. 6, 1704	LR2	1116
Rebeckah, m. Thomas **BARNS**, Mar. 14, 1729	LR2	1115
Rebeckah, m. Isaac **ACKLEY**, Oct. 23, 1833, at Shawcatetes, N. Y.	3	161
Rueben, s. Stephen & Mary, b. May 30, 1723	LR2	1116
Rhoda, d. Daniel, 3rd, & Keziah, b. Aug. 4, 1776	2	116
Robert, b. Dec. 19, 1760, at Middletown, m. Margaret **PAGET**, of Middletown, July 29, 1783	2	148
Robert, s. Robert & Margaret, b. Aug. 13, 1785	2	148
Robert Dickson, s. Timothy & Abigail, b. Mar. 12, 1766	2	217
Robert Dickson, s. Capt. Timothy & Abigail, d. Aug. 11, 1781	2	218
Robert Dickson, s. Capt. Timothy & Abigail, b. Jan. 21, 1784	2	217
Robert Goodloe Harper, s. Israel, Jr. & Polly, b. Sept. 3, 1810	2	66
Rob[er]t S., m. Ann E. **CHAPMAN**, Nov. [1], 1849, by Rev. Isaac Parsons	3	220
Rob[er]t S., turner, ae 29, m. Ann E. **CHAPMAN**, school-teacher, ae 24, Nov. 4, 1849, by Rev. Isaac Parsons	4	19-20
Roswel[l], m. Sarah **SPENCER**, Nov. 22, 1773	2	66
Rufus, s. James & Grace, b. Oct. 10, 1737	LR2	1122
Rufus, m. Esther **STEWART**, b. of East Haddam, Dec. 18, 1761	LR6	508
Ruth, m. Samuell **EM[M]ONS**, Jr., Sept. 14, 1721	LR2	d
Ruth, d. Stephen & Abigail, b. Oct. 15, 1734	LR2	1114
Ruth, d. Jared & Ruth, b. July 28, 1745	LR3	11
Ruth, w. of Jared, d. Oct. 13, 1748	LR3	11
Ruth Newell, d. Daniel, 3rd, & Keziah, b. Apr. 26, 1782	2	116
Sally, m. Samuel **HARVEY**, b. of East Haddam, Apr. 10, 1802	2	275
Salmon, s. James, Jr. & Alice, b. Feb. 27, 1777	2	138
Samuel, m. Elizabeth **WILLEY**, b. of East Haddam, Sept. 23,		

	Vol.	Page
CONE, (cont.)		
1747	LR7	1
Sam[ue]l, s. Samuel & Elizabeth, b. Feb. 20, 1748	LR7	1
Samuel, s. Nathaniel, Jr. & Mary, b. Mar. 13, 1754	LR3	5
Samuel, s. Nathaniel, Jr. & Mary, d. Dec. 25, 1756	LR3	5
Samuel, s. Nathaniel & Mary, b. Oct. 9, 1769	2	78
Samuel, 2d, m. Phebe **MARSH**, b. of East Haddam, Dec. 2, 1783	2	172
Samuel Crocker, s. James, Jr. & Alice, b. Sept. 2, 1773	2	138
Samuel Crocker, s. James, Jr. & Alice, d. Sept. 19, 1773	2	139
Samuel Crocker, 2d, s. James, 2d, & Alice, b. June 2, 1775	2	138
Samuel W., ae 27 y., b. in East Haddam, res. East Haddam, m. Lucy L. **MACK**, ae 23, b. in East Haddam, res. East Haddam, June 27, 1855, at Moodus, by Rev. James M. Phillips. Int. pub. June 21, 1855	4	59
Sarah, d. Daniell, b. June 27, 1697	LR1	574
Sarah, m. Daniel **GATES**, June 13, 1723	LR2	1128
Sarah, d. Nathaniel, Jr. & Mary, b. Jan. 16, 1747	LR3	5
Sarah, d. Jared & Ruth, b. Mar. 19, 1748	LR3	11
Sarah, w. of Nathaniell, d. Sept. 25, 1753	LR3	4
Sarah, d. Silvanus, 2d, & Sarah, b. Oct. 7, 1761	LR6	507
Sarah, m. Jeremiah **SELBY**, b. of East Haddam, Mar. 29, 1769	2	12
Sarah, d. Nehemiah & Jedidah, b. Oct. 8, 1777	2	120
Sarah, m. William **GATES**, b. of East Haddam, June 2, 1852, by Rev. Isaac Parsons	3	235
Sarah E., of East Haddam, m. Denison P. **BURDICK**, of West Killingly, Sept. 8, 1844, by Rev. W[illia]m S. Simmons	3	200
Sherwood A., s. [Lord W. & Fluvia A.], b. Oct. 23, 1844	3	242
Silvanus, s. James & Grace, b. Jan. 21, 1734/5	LR2	1122
Silvanus, s. George & Mehittable, b. Aug. 16, 1735	LR2	1124
Silvanus, m. Hannah **ACKLEY**, Nov. 13, 1755	LR5	267
Selvanus, 2d, m. Sarah **ACKLEY**, b. of East Haddam, June 26, 1760	LR6	507
Solomon, s. Joseph & Mary, b. Sept. 2, 1745	LR2	1123
Spencer, s. Roswel[l] & Sarah, b. Apr. 16, 1788	2	66
Statira, d. Daniell & Mary, b. Jan. 13, 1740/41	LR2	1130
Statira, d. Daniell & Mary, d. Mar. 30, 1749, in the 9th y. of her age	LR2	1130
Statira, d. Jonah & Elizabeth, b. July 9, 1749	LR3	5
Statira, m. Uriel **HOLMES**, July 1, 1764	LR7	2
Statira, d. Nehemiah & Jedidah, b. May 1, 1772	2	120
Stephen, m. Mary **HUNGERFORD**, Feb. 5, 1702	LR2	1116
Stephen, s. Stephen & Mary, b. Mar. 11, 1706	LR2	1116
Stephen, m. Abigaill **BARNS**, June 6, 1724	LR2	e
Stephen, 3rd, m. Susan[n]ah **CLARK**, Feb. 21, 1732/3	LR2	1123
Stephen, s. Stephen, 3rd, & Susannah, b. Mar. 24, 1737	LR2	123
Stephen, s. Elisha & Elizabeth, b. Sept. 18, 1787* (*Entry crossed out)	2	157

	Vol.	Page
CONE, (cont.)		
Stephen, s. Elisha & Elizabeth, b. Sept. 18, 1787	2	239
Stephen, m. Mary **FULLER**, b. of East Haddam, Feb. 6, 1812	2	321
Stephen, m. Sarah **ISHAM**, Sept. 12, 1833, at Watertown, N. Y.	2	321
Stephen, d. Nov. 23, 1847, in the 60th y. of his age	2	322
Stephen Isham, s. Stephen & Sarah, b. Nov. 20, 1845	2	321
Susan[n]ah, d. Stephen & Mary, b. July 15, 1708	LR2	1116
Susannah, d. Stephen, 3rd, & Susannah, b. Apr. 1, 1735	LR2	1123
Susannah S., m. David B. **PIKE**, b. of East Haddam, Apr. 16, 1832, by Rev. Isaac Parsons	3	122
Sylvester, s. Zachariah & Jemima, b. Apr. 4, 1780	2	70
Temperance, d. Daniel, Jr. & Mary, b. Sept. 29, 1730	LR2	1119
Thankfull, d. Nathaniel, Jr. & Mary, b. May 7, 1752	LR3	5
Theodora, d. Joseph & Mary, b. Aug. 12, 1755	LR3	508
Theodore, s. Joshua & Chloe, b. Oct. 2, 1799	2	277
Thomas, s. Stephen & Abigail, b. Feb. 22, 1729/30	LR2	1114
Thomas, m. Mehitable **CONE**, Feb. 20, 1734/5	LR2	1112
Timothy, of East Haddam, m. Abigail **DIXON**, of Middletown, Sept. 9, 1761	LR6	503
Timothy, s. Timothy & Abigail, b. Dec. 10, 1762	2	217
Tryphena T., of East Haddam, m. John B. **HARVEY**, of Cooperstown, N. Y., Dec. 1, 1840, by Rev. Isaac Parsons	3	184
Uriel, s. Nathaniel & Mary, b. May 18, 1768	2	78
Uriel, s. Nathaniel & Mary, d. June 15, 1772	2	79
Walter Rutherford, s. Silvanus & Hannah, b. Nov. 26, 1764	LR5	267
William, s. Daniell & Mary, b. Mar. 14, 1723	LR2	1130
William, m. Elizabeth **BAILEY**, Dec. 31, 1747	LR3	508
William, s. William & Elizabeth, b. Mar. 14, 1753	LR3	508
William, Jr., m. Azubah **OLMSTED**, b. of East Haddam, Apr. 23, 1775	2	100
William, Jr., m. Azubah **OLMSTED**, b. of East Haddam, Apr. 23, 1775	2	158
William, Capt., d. Apr. 22, 1793, ae 71 y.	2	159
William, s. Robart & Margaret, b. May 16, 1794	2	148
William, s. Israel & Lucy, b. Sept. 24, 1794	2	154
William, d. Jan. 18, 1827, ae 74	2	159
W[illia]m A., m. Vincey B. **MACK**, b. of East Haddam, June 14, 1842, by Rev. Alonzo G. Shears, in Middletown	3	191
William Albert, s. William Edwin, manufacturer, ae 42, & Rhoda, ae 35, b. Sept. 24, 1847	4	5-6
William E., m. Rhoda **BECKWITH**, b. of East Haddam, Apr. 21, 1831, by Rev. Nathaniel Miner	3	127
William H., m. Silenda **FOX**, Jan. 18, 1824, by Russell Dutton, J. P.	3	54-5
William Hungerford, [s. Lord W. & Fluvia A.], b. Jan. 12, 1838	3	242
Zachariah, s. Stephen, 3rd, & Susannah, b. Feb. 23, 1738/9	LR2	1123
Zachariah, s. George & Mehettabell, b. Feb. 11, 1743	LR2	1124
Zachariah, m. Mrs. Jemima **HALL**, b. of East Haddam, Dec.		

	Vol.	Page
CONE, (cont.)		
5, 1776	2	70
Zecheriah, d. Mar. 19, 1814, ae 70	2	71
Zechariah, s. Horatio & Polly, b. Aug. 18, 1818	2	285
Zenus, s. Matthew & Mary, b. Nov. 18, 1763	LR6	505
CONKLING, Joseph H., m. Abby G. **AVERY**, b. of Lyme, Nov. 20, 1836, by Rev. Nathaniel Miner	3	146
CONVIS, Susannah, m. Thomas **KNOWLTON**, Jr., Dec. 24, 1724	LR1	584
COOK, Anne, d. Gideon & Huldah, b. Mar. 14, 1777	2	116
David Brainerd, s. William & Jerusha, b. July 23, 1808	2	303
Ebenezer, of Haddam, m. Louisa P. **EMMONS**, of East Haddam, Dec. 13, 1832, by Isaac Parsons	3	128
Gideon, s. Gideon & Huldah, b. Nov. 28, 1780	2	116
Hezekiah S., m. Eliza **CHAPMAN**, b. of Middle Haddam, Dec. 13, 1846, by Rev. Isaac Parsons	3	208
Jerusha Ann, d. William & Jerusha, b. June 23, 1811	2	303
John, s. Gideon & Huldah, b. Dec. 11, 1778	2	116
Mary, m. Thomas **ROGERS**, Feb. 19, 1756	LR7	4
Olive M., of East Haddam, m. Charles **CRUTTENDEN**, of Chatham, Apr. 8, 1840, by Isaac Parsons, V. D. M.	3	178
Ora Agnesia, d. William & Jerusha, b. Apr. 21, 1814	2	303
Rebeckah, m. Samuel **MITCHEL[L]**, b. of East Haddam, Nov. 10, 1762	2	30
Sarah E., d. of a physician, b. in Portland, res. East Haddam, d. Feb. 9, 1849, ae 16	4	17-18
Walter, s. Samuel, mechanic, ae 31, & Caroline, ae 28, b. Apr. 29, 1850	4	27-8
William, s. Gideon, b. Feb. 11, 1785; m. Jerusha **SPENCER**, Oct. 1, 1807	2	303
William Henry, s. William & Jerusha, b. Dec. 5, 1809	2	303
COON, Diodate G., alias **CALHOUN**, m. Mary C. **WILLARD**, b. of East Haddam, Apr. 23, 1843, by Rev. Charles William Bradley	3	194
Electa A., m. James W. **WRIGHT**, b. of East Haddam, Apr. 13, 1835, by Nathaniel Miner	3	137
CORBY, CORBE, CORBEE, Abigail, w. of Samuel, d. Nov. 29, 1764	LR7	1
Mary, d. Samuel & Mary, b. Nov. 13, 1691	LR1	3
Samuell, d. Apr. 10, 1692	LR1	3
Samuell, s. Sam[ue]ll & Mary, b. Dec. 10, 1692	LR1	3
Samuell, m. Abigail [ ], Jan. 21, 1724/5	LR1	571
Samuel, d. Sept. 15, 1757	LR7	1
COREY, CORY, William, of Colchester, m. Caroline E. **WARES**, of East Haddam, Nov. 24, 1844, by Rev. W[illia]m S. Simmons	3	201
William L., worker in cotton mill, ae 25, b. Valley Falls, R. I. res. Portland, m. Huldah A. **EVANS**, ae 20, b. Chatham, Ct., June 12, 1850, by Jacob Gardner	4	37-8

	Vol.	Page
COREY, CORY, (cont.)		
William L., of East Greenwich, R. I., m. Huldah A. **EVANS**, of East Haddam, June 12, 1851, by Rev. Jacob Gardner	3	232
CORNWELL, Jerusha, of Chatham, m. William **LORD**, 2d, of East Haddam, Apr. 20, 1802	2	283
Mary, alias Mary **ROWLE**, m. John **FULLER**, May 10, 1721	LR1	572
CORSER, Caleb R., of Gates, N. Y., m. Rhoda Maria **CHAPMAN**, of Geneva, O., Oct. 11, 1841, by Isaac Parsons, V. D. M.	3	187
COWDREY, COWDERY, COWDRY, Abby A., m. Ozias E. **PALMER**, b. of East Haddam, June 10, 1849, by Rev. Alpheas Geer, in St. Stephen's Church	3	217
Ann, d. Moses & Martha, b. Nov. 11, 1759	LR6	508
Asa, s. Moses & Martha, b. Feb. 19, 1758	LR6	508
Ezubah, d. Jacob & Mary, b. Aug. 1, 1756 (Azubah)	LR5	267
Diadama, d. William & Hannah, b. Dec. 29, 1768	2	10
Huldah, d. Nathaniell & Mehittabell, b. Dec. 14, 1733	LR2	1124
Huldah, m. Obadiah **GATES**, b. of East Haddam, Sept. 14, 1762	LR7	3
Jacob, m. Mary **BECKWITH**, b. of East Haddam, Dec. 18, 1755	LR5	267
Lorin, m. Catharine A., **GARDNER**, b. of East Haddam, Nov. 30, 1854, by Rev. Isaac Parsons	3	241
Loren, manufacturer, ae 25, b. in Plainfield, N. Y., res. E. Haddam, m. Catharine A. **GARDNER**, ae 19, of E. Haddam, Nov. 30, 1854, by Rev. Isaac Parsons	4	51-2
Lidia, d. Jacob & Mary, b. Oct. 24, 1757	LR5	267
Mehittabell, d. Nathaniell & Mehittabell, b. July 24, 1735	LR2	1124
Olive, d. William & Hannah, b. June 23, 1767	2	10
------, s. Loren, cotton manufacturer, ae 26, & Catharine, ae 21, b. Sept. 4, 1856	4	110
CRAMPTON, Alvaline Sarah, d. Rev. Ralph S. & Tirzah J., b. Apr. 24, 1832	3	126
John, s. John & Sarah, b. Apr. 25, 1731	LR2	1112
Sarah, d. John & Sarah, b. Mar. 16, 1738	LR2	1112
CRIPPEN, Elizabeth, d. Thomas, Jr. & Mary, b. June 14, 1699	LR1	4
Hannah, d. Thomas, Jr. & Mary, b. May 25, 1703	LR1	4
Hannah, m. James **SPENCER**, Jan. 14, 1720	LR1	584
Mary, w. of Thomas, d. Oct. 25, 1732	LR2	1109
Thomas, s. Thomas, Jr. & Mary, b. Dec. 3, 1696	LR1	4
CRITTENDEN, CRUTTENDEN, Charles, of Chatham, m. Olive M. **COOK**, of East Haddam, Apr. 8, 1840, by Isaac Parsons, V. D. M.	3	178
Olive M., m. Francis O. **BIDWELL**, b. of East Haddam, Jan. 14, 1850, by Rev. Moses Chase	3	222
CROCKER, CROCKAH, Alice, m. James **CONE**, Jr., b. of East Haddam, May 3, 1764	2	138
Ann, d. Isaac & Ann, b. June 29, 1722	LR1	575
Dorothy, d. Rowland & Parsis, b. Oct. 20, 1765	LR7	1

	Vol.	Page
CROCKER, CROCKAH, (cont.)		
Ebenezer, s. Ebenezer & Ann, b. June 25, 1751	LR4	471
Elizabeth, d. Isaac & Elizabeth, b. Aug. 26, 1727	LR2	1128
Elizabeth, of Colchester, m. Simeon **ACKLEY**, of East Haddam, May 25, 1747	LR3	2
Ezekiel, m. Lydiah **ARNOLD**, b. of East Haddam, Feb. 28, 1765	LR7	7
Franklin G., of New London, m. Abigail **CONE**, of East Haddam, Nov. 3, 1839, by Rev. Charles William Bradley	3	173
Hannah, m. Shuball **FFULLER**, Dec. 7, 1708	LR1	578
Hannah, d. Isaac & Ann, b. Sept. 22, 1719	LR1	575
Hannah, m. Philip **WILLIAMS**, Feb. 13, 1745/6	LR3	4
Isaac, m. Ann **SMITH**, Dec. 13, 1718	LR1	575
Isaac, m. Elizabeth **FULLER**, Oct. 31, 1726	LR2	1128
Joannah, m. Stephen **SPENCER**, b. of East Haddam, Mar. 8, 1759	LR6	511
Joseph, s. Isaac & Ann, b. Nov. or Dec. 20, 1724	LR1	575
Lydia, of Colchester, m. Levi **GATES**, of East Haddam, May 29, 1760	LR6	509
Mary, d. Isaac & Elizabeth, b. Apr. 30, 1729	LR2	1128
Oliver, s. Ezekiel & Lydiah, b. June 14, 1765	LR7	7
Ozias, s. Rowland & Parsis, b. Mar. 17, 1764	LR7	1
Ozias, s. Rowland & Parsis, d. Apr. 10, 1770	LR7	1
Rowland, m. Parses **BROWN**, b. of East Haddam, May 24, 1763	LR7	1
Rowland, s. Rowland & Parsis, b. Mar. 28, 1767; d. May 2, 1767	LR7	1
Rowland, s. Rowland & Parsis, b. June 10, 1768	LR7	1
Samuel, s. Ebenezer & Ann, b. June 2, 1753	LR4	471
Thankfull, of Colchester, m. Timothy **SCOVEL**, of East Haddam, Sept. 3, 1760	LR6	504
CROSBY, Anna, d. Levi & Ruth, b. June 29, 1770	2	52
Anna, d. Levi & Ruth, d. Jan. 30, 1774	2	53
Anna, d. Levi & Ruth, b. Aug. 6, 1777	2	52
Benjamin, s. Simeon & Lydia, b. Jan. 11, 1755	LR4	467
Benjamin, s. Increase & Rachel, b. June 24, 1767	2	66
Benjamin, of East Haddam, m. Jemima **PECK**, of Lyme, Nov. 25, 1788	2	186
Calvin, s. Elijah & Phebe, b. May 10, 1793	2	194
Cyrenius, [s.] Increase & Rachal, b. Apr. 18, 1760	2	66
Dorothy, d. Simeon & Lidia, b. Aug. 26, 1757	LR4	467
Ely, s. Increase & Rachal, b. Dec. 20, 1757	2	66
Eli, s. Levi, 2d, & Mary, b. Jan. 12, 1782	2	140
Eliab*, s. Levi & Ruth, b. May 20, 1766 (*Eliel?)	2	52
Eliel, s. Levi & Ruth, d. Jan. 30, 1774	2	53
Elial, s. Elijah & Phebe, b. Mar. 22, 1797	2	194
Elijah, s. Levi & Ruth, b. May 13, 1764	2	52
Elijah, m. Phebe **CHURCH**, b. of East Haddam, Nov. 13, 1787	2	194

	Vol.	Page
CROSBY, (cont.)		
Elijah, s. Elijah & Phebe, b. May 20, 1797* (*Overwritten 1799)	2	194
Elijah, s. Elijah & Phebe, d. Jan. 28, 1804	2	195
Elijah, s. Elijah & Phebe, b. Feb. 14, 1805	2	194
Ely, see under Eli		
Increase, m. Rachel **GRAVES**, b. of East Haddam, Feb. 13, 1755	LR5	563
Increase, s. Increase & Rachel, b. June 13, 1765	2	66
James, s. Simeon & Lidiah, b. Aug. 19, 1750	LR4	467
Jane S., of East Haddam, m. William M. **SMITH**, of Lyme, Apr. 19, 1825, by Rev. Isaac Parsons	3	76-77
Joseph, s. Elijah & Phebe, b. May 10, 1801	2	194
Levi, of East Haddam, m. Ruth **COMSTOCK**, of Lyme, Mar. 1, 1763	2	52
Levi, s. Elijah & Phebe, b. Apr. 2, 1803	2	194
Levi, d. Aug. 13, 1804	2	53
Lovina, d. Elijah & Phebe, b. May 4, 1795	2	194
Lucinde, d. Elijah & Phebe, b. Aug. 21, 1791	2	194
Mary, d. Simeon & Lidiah, b. Nov. 16, 1751	LR4	467
Mary, d. Levi, 2d, & Mary, b. Oct. 16, 1785	2	140
Obed, s. Simeon & Lydia, b. July 22, 1753	LR4	467
Phebe Sterlin, d. Elijah & Phebe, b. Oct. 12, 1789	2	194
Rachel, d. Increase & Rachel, b. Feb. 24, 1772	2	66
Rebeckah, m. Joseph **BECKWITH**, 2d, b. of East Haddam, Mar. 17, 1757	2	118
Ruth, d. Levi & Ruth, b. Jan. 21, 1775	2	52
Ruth, wid. of Dea. Samuel, d. Nov. 14, 1789	2	19
Ruth, w. of Levi, d. Apr. 18, 1804	2	53
Samuel, Dea., d. Jan, 12, 1756	LR5	265
Simeon, m. Lidiah **GRAVES**, Aug. 10, 1749	LR4	467
Susannah, d. Increase & Rachel, b. Mar. 22, 1763	2	66
CROUCH, Sarah, d. Joseph & Hannah, b. Sept. 4, 1741	LR2	1101
CROWELL, CROWEL, Anna C., m. Joshua B. **EMMONS**, s. of Daniel, b. of East Haddam, Oct. 12, 1820, by Rev. Solomon Blakesley	3	1
David, [twin with Samuel], s. W[illia]m & Ruth, b. Apr. 21, 1805	2	255
Ezekiel, s. W[illia]m & Ruth, b. Oct. 25, 1797	2	255
Jerusha, d. William & Ruth, b. June 3, 1793	2	255
John, s. W[illia]m & Ruth, b. Sept. 15, 1801	2	255
Ruth, d. W[illia]m & Ruth, b. Oct. 13, 1799	2	255
Samuel, [twin with David], s. W[illia]m & Ruth, b. Apr. 21, 1805	2	255
Samuel, s. William & Ruth, d. May 5, 1805	2	205
Sibbel, d. W[illia]m & Ruth, b. Jan. 25, 1795	2	255
Susan, d. W[illia]m & Ruth, b. Sept. 24, 1803	2	255
William, of East Haddam, m. Ruth **PECK**, of Lyme, Aug. 26,		

	Vol.	Page
CROWELL, CROWEL, (cont.)		
1792	2	255
William, s. William & Ruth, b. Aug. 7, 1796	2	255
CRUTTENDEN, [see under **CRITTENDEN**]		
CULVER, Warren, ae 21, b. in Marlborough, res. East Haddam, m. Ruth A. **BURNHAM**, ae 18, b. in East Haddam, res. East Haddam, July 14, 1856, by Rev. Isaac Parsons. Int. pub. July 11, 1856	4	90
CUNNINGHAM, Hannah, m. Elisha **LEWIS**, b. of Middletown, Sept. 25, 1823, by Rev. Simeon Dickinson, at the house of Richard Lord	3	44-45
CURTIS, Frederic, Jr., of Hampton, m. Ann O. **SPENCER**, of East Haddam, May 29, 1827, by Rev. Isaac Parsons	3	86
DALTON, Susannah, m. Jeremiah **SOLBY**, June 12, 1716	LR1	581
DAMMAN, [see under **DUMMAN**]		
DANIELS, Amasa, s. [Lemuel C. & Eunice], b. Nov. 15, 1822	3	97
Aristorchus, s. [Lemuel C. & Eunice], b. May 9, 1802, in Chatham	3	97
Bartlett, of East Hampton, m. Florella **FULLER**, of East Haddam, May 6, 1830, by Rev. Timothy Stone	3	107
David, s. [Lemuel C. & Eunice], b. Aug. 27, 1817	3	97
David, s. Lemuel C. & Eunice, d. Mar. 2, 1818	3	98
Edmund, s. [Lemuel C. & Eunice], b. Oct. 16, 1826	3	97
Erastus, s. [Lemuel C. & Eunice], b. Aug. 13, 1824	3	97
Esther Ann, [twin with Rozilla], d. [Lemuel C. & Eunice], b. Feb. 23, 1811	3	97
Eunice, d. [Lemuel C. & Eunice], b. Mar. 30, 1819	3	97
Eunice, of East Haddam, m. James M. **LETTS**, of DeRuyter, N. Y., May 15, 1841, by Isaac Parsons, M. V. D.	3	185
George, m. Almira L. **BARTMAN**, Feb. 20, 1848, by Rev. Benjamin G. Goff	3	212
Harriet, d. [Lemuel C. & Eunice], b. Mar. 17, 1805	3	97
Harriet, of East Haddam, m. Richard V. **BROOKS**, of Lyme, Oct. 7, 1832, by Rev. Isaac Parsons	3	125
Jeremiah H., m. Sophronia **CHURCH**, Mar. 3, 1839, by Rev. George Carrington, of Hadlyme	3	168
Jerusha, m. Oliver **OLCOTT**, Feb.* 23, 1800 (*Preceding this the words "Oct. 23" have been crossed out)	2	287
Lemuel, m. Hannah **FULLER**, Sept. 10, 1739	LR2	1106
Lemuel C., m. Eunice **YOUNG**, Dec. 13, 1801, by Rev. David Selden, in Chatham	3	97
Lemuel C., d. Feb. 10, 1830, ae 55 y.	3	98
Levi, s. [Lemuel C. & Eunice], b. Nov. 20, 1813	3	97
Oliver*, m. Abner **HURD**, Nov. 16, 1800 (*Perhaps Olive)	2	269
Rozilla, [twin with Esther Ann], d. [Lemuel C. & Eunice], b. Feb. 23, 1811	3	97
Rozilla, m. Elijah W. **BINGHAM**, Apr. 5, 1835, by Isaac Parsons	3	137

	Vol.	Page
DANIELS, (cont.)		
Rozilla, m. Elijah W. **BINGHAM**, Apr. 5, 1835	3	147
Sarah E., d. George, merchant, ae 25, & Lydia A., ae 20, b. Oct. 25, 1849	4	27-8
Seth, s. [Lemuel C. & Eunice], b. Nov. 29, 1806	3	97
DARLING, Lucy, m. Denison **HALL**, b. of East Haddam, Apr. 5, 1847, by Nathaniel A. Cowdrey, J. P.	3	215
DAVENPORT, Guy, of Canterbury, m. Betsey A. **WARNER**, of East Haddam, Apr. 8, 1827, by Rev. William Jarvis	3	95
DAVIS, Jesse S., m. Rhoda A. **SNOW**, b. of East Haddam, Sept. 7, 1834, by Rev. Stephen Beach	3	136
Roxa, m. Isaac **FOWLER**, Oct. 15, 1826, by Isaac Parsons	3	88-89
DAVISON, Huber Dixon, s. [Roswell & Prudence C.], b. Aug. 26,, 1836	3	157
John Weaver, s. [Roswell & Prudence C.], b. Feb. 11, 1834	3	157
Roswell, of Brooklyn, N. Y., m. Prudence C. **WRIGHT**, of East Haddam, May 26, 1831, by Rev. Peter G. Clarke	3	116
Roswell, m. Prudence C. **WRIGHT**, May 26, 1831	3	157
DAWES, Howland, of Windsor, Mass., m. Harriet **WILBUR**, of East Haddam, Apr. 30, 1837, by Nathaniel Miner	3	151
DAY, Elijah, of Colchester, m. Rebeckah E. **HUNGERFORD**, of East Haddam, Oct. 18, 1827, by Rev. Joseph Vaill, of Hadlyme	3	95
Sarah, of Colchester, m. Jehiel **FULLER**, of East Haddam, Jan. 11, 1759	LR6	506
Sarah Maria, of East Haddam, m. Francis Edwin **GATES**, of Lyme, Oct. 17, 1854, by Rev. Isaac Parsons	3	241
Sarah Maria, ae 22, of E. Haddam, m. Francis Edwin **GATES**, farmer, ae 27, of Lyme, Oct. 17, 1854, by Rev. Isaac Parsons	4	51-2
Stephen O., of Colchester, m. Mary P. **WILLEY**, of East Haddam, Oct. 6, 1834, by Joseph Vaill, of Hadlyme, Minister	3	135
DAYTON, Andrew J., of South Glastonbury, m. Henrietta, E. **HAYDEN**, of East Haddam, Mar. 3, 1852, by Rev. Alpheas Geer	3	234
DEAN, Alfred, m. Nancy **CHAPMAN**, b. of East Haddam, Mar. 1, 1832, by Rev. Alvan Ackley	3	121
DEMAY, Robert C., of Lyme, m. Mary Ann **SPENCER**, of East Haddam, Sept. 9, 1821, by Rev. Isaac Parsons	3	9
DEMING, Lydia, of Norwich, m. Bezaleel **BRAINERD**, Jr., of East Haddam, Oct. 21, 1787	2	166
DERBY, Lavinia, m. Henry **BROWN**, b. of East Haddam, Oct. 9, 1842, by Stephen Alonzo Loper, in Hadlyme	3	192
DEWEY, Abigail, of Colchester, m. William **BAXTER**, of Pittsfield, Mass., Mar. 7, 1784	2	130
Abigail Ackley, d. Israel & Bithiah, b. Sept. 21, 1791	2	32
Francis B., of West Springfield, Mass., m. Asa M. **HOLT**,		

	Vol.	Page
DEWEY, (cont.)		
M. D., of East Haddam, Mar. 29, 1846, by Rev. Levi H. Wakeman	3	204
Israel, of Colchester, m. Bithiah **ACKLEY**, of East Haddam, Dec. 14, 1775	2	32
Israel, s. Israel & Bithiah, b. May 19, 1784	2	32
Israel, s. Israel & Bithiah, d. July 13, 1791	2	33
Lucy, d. Israel & Bithiah, b. Oct. 24, 1781	2	32
DeWOLF, George, of Lyme, m. Lydia A. **FURGERSON**, of East Haddam, Aug. 21, 1842, by Rev. William A. Cone	3	191
DIBBLE, DIBBELL, Eunice, d. Thomas & Rebeckah, b. May 12, 1740	LR3	9
Eunice, d. Thomas & Rebeckah, b. May 13, 1740	LR5	560
Eunice, m. Zacheas **SPENCER**, b. of East Haddam, May 9, 1762	LR7	2
George, s. Thomas & Rebeckah, b. June 10, 1733 (sic)	LR3	9
George, s. Thomas & Rebeckah, b. June 10, 1735	LR5	560
Harriet, ae 20, b. in Saybrook, res. E. Haddam, m. Leroy **BROOKS**, mechanic, ae 21, of E. Haddam, Dec. 30, 1849, by Rev. Isaac Parsons	4	21-2
Harriet A., of Saybrook, m. Leroy D. **BROOKS**, of East Haddam, Dec. 30, 1849, by Rev. Isaac Parsons	3	221
Isaiah, s. Thomas & Rebeckah, b. July 16, 1737	LR3	9
Isaiah, s. Thomas & Rebeckah, b. July 18, 1737	LR5	560
Isajah, s. Thomas & Rebeckah, d. July some time, 1760	LR5	564
Martin, s. Thomas & Rebeckah, b. Feb. 25, 1741/2	LR3	9
Martin, s. Thomas & Rebeckah, b. Sept. 4, 1742	LR5	560
Martin, s. Thomas & Rebeckah, d. Nov. 3, 1760	LR5	564
Thomas, m. Rebeckah **BOOGE**, Sept. 14, 1734	LR3	9
Thomas, d. Oct. 16, 1755	LR5	564
DICKINSON, [see also **DIXON**], Abigail, d. William & Betsy, b. Oct. 18, 1796	2	142
Abigail, d. William & Betsy, d. Apr. 20, 1797	2	143
Abigail, d. William & Betsy, b. Mar. 30, 1798	2	142
Bets[e]y, d. William & Bets[e]y, b. Oct. 26, 1791	2	142
Clary, d. William & Bets[e]y, b. Mar. 24, 1800	2	142
Emma, d. William & Bets[e]y, b. July 29, 1805	2	142
Epaphroditus, m. Almira **ATTWOOD**, Dec. 21, 1825, by Rev. Simeon Dickinson, at the house of Capt. Oliver Attwood	3	83
Gideon Ackley, s. Simeon & Deborah, b. Jan. 25, 1788	2	148
Jonathan, s. Simeon & Deborah, b. Jan. 1, 1792	2	148
Josiah Simeon, s. [Lemuel & Mary], b. June 24, 1829	3	13
Lemuel, s. Simeon & Deborah, b. Mar. 6, 1794	2	148
Lemuel, m. Mary **LYON**, Mar. 9, 1819, by Rev. Simeon Dickinson, at the house of Josiah Lyon	3	13
Lemuel Lorenzo, s. Lemuel & Mary, b. Mar. 27, 1822	3	13
Levi, s. Simeon & Deborah, b. June 1, 1796	2	148
Martin L., ae 35, b. at Hadley, Mass., res. West Troy,		

	Vol.	Page
DICKINSON, (cont.)		
N. Y., m. Helen F. **SHALER**, ae 25, b. at East Haddam, res. East Haddam, Oct. 17, 1855, by Rev. James M. Phillips. Int. pub. Oct. 17, 1855	4	65-6
Mary, d. Simeon & Deborah, b. Dec. 19, 1785	2	148
Mary, of East Haddam, m. Justin **LUMMIS**, of Saybrook, July 29, 1820, by Rev. Simeon Dickinson, at the house of Mrs. Mary Lyon	2	321
Mary, d. May 6, 1851, ae 77	4	39-40
Mary, d. June 25, 1851, ae 55	4	39-40
Mary E., ae 22, b. at E. Haddam, res. E. Haddam, m. Lauiston M. **STARK**, ae 24, b. at E. Haddam, res. E. Haddam, Oct. 18, 1855, by Rev. James M. Phillips. Int. pub. Oct. 17, 1855	4	66
Mary Elizabeth, d. [Lemuel & Mary], b. Oct. 14, 1833	3	13
Oliver, s. Simeon & Deborah, b. Sept. 15, 1798	2	148
Oliver, m. Jerusha **FULLER**, June 22, 1823, by Rev. Simeon Dickinson, at the house of Stephen Fuller	3	40-41
Rebeckah, of Chatham, m. Samuel **WRIGHT**, of East Haddam, Dec. 22, 1773 (First written "**DIXON**")	2	86
Samuel, s. William & Bets[e]y, b. June 9, 1794	2	142
Simeon, of Richmond, Mass., m. Deborah **ACKLEY**, of East Haddam, Nov. 6, 1783	2	148
Simeon, s. Simeon & Deborah, b. Dec. 31, 1789	2	148
Thomas Newton, s. [Lemuel & Mary], b. June 19, 1825	3	13
Walter, s. William & Betsey, b. Jan. 21, 1789	2	142
DIMOCK, Hannah, m. Thomas **FULLER**, 4th, Nov. 15, 1748	LR4	472
DINGWELL, Henry, m. Tryphenia **SPENCER**, Oct. 3, 1822, by Rev. Elijah Parsons	3	33
DINSMORE, John B., of Ripley, N. Y., m. Elizabeth **GRIFFIN**, of East Haddam, June 14, 1832, by Nathaniel Miner	3	124
DIXON, DICKSON, [see also **DICKINSON**], Abigail, of Middletown, m. Timothy **CONE**, of East Haddam, Sept. 9, 1761	LR6	503
Alexander, s. James & Margaret, b. Oct. 21, 1770	2	8
Elisabeth, d. James & Margaret, b. June 4, 1773	2	8
James, s. James & Marg[a]ret, b. Apr. 7, 1768	LR6	504
Marg[a]ret, d. James & Marg[a]ret, b. June 21, 1761	LR6	504
Mary, d. James & Marg[a]ret, b. Oct. 30, 1765	LR6	504
Nancy, d. James & Margaret, b. Nov. 24, 1777	2	8
Phebe, d. James & Marg[a]ret, b. Nov. 23, 1763	LR6	504
Rebeckah, of Chatham, m. Samuel **WRIGHT**, of East Haddam, Dec. 22, 1773 (Overwritten "**DICKINSON**")	2	86
Thomas P., of Deep River, Conn., m. Ann **COMSTOCK**, of East Haddam (Hadlyme Parish), Nov. 30, 1852, by James Noyes	3	238
DOANE, DOAN, Mary E., of Essex, m. Zelotes **YOUNG**, of Killingly, Nov. 30, 1837, by Rev. David Todd	3	160

	Vol.	Page
DOANE, DOAN, (cont.)		
Rebecca, of East Haddam, m. William **COGGESHALL**, of		176-7
Brooklyn, Feb. 18, 1840, by Rev. Tho[ma]s W. Gile	3	
DONAHUE, Ann, ae 22, b. at County Tyrone, Ireland, res. East		
Haddam, m. Stephen **KEENAN**, ae 24, b. at Alvally,		
Ireland, res. E. Haddam, Sept. 2, 185[5], at Moodus, by		62
Rev. John Lynch, of Chester. Int. pub. Aug. 27, 1855	4	
DORR, Sarah, Mrs., of Lyme, m. Elkanah **HIGGINS**, of East		82
Haddam, Aug. 4, 1785	2	1104
DOUGLASS, John, s. John & Elizabeth, b. Mar. 1, 1739/40	LR2	
Mary, ae 18, of E. Hddam, m. Frances R. **BORDMAN**, clerk,		
ae 22, of E. Haddam, May 28, 1850, at Greensport, L. I.,		21-2
by Rev. Woodbridge	4	
DOWD, Solomon, of Colchester, m. Abigail **CHAPMAN**, of East		136
Haddam, Jan. 25, 1835, by Rev. Nathaniel Miner	3	
DRAKE, Elizabeth, of Long Island, m. Stephen **BECKWITH**, of		200
East Haddam, July 20, 1779	2	
DRASON, Eliza A., of Vermont, m. Aaron H. **BURNHAM**, of East		234
Haddam, Jan. 18, 1852, by Rev. Isaac Parsons	3	268
DRIGGS, David, s. Daniel & Elizabeth, b. Feb. 15, 1754	LR5	
Elisabeth, m. Roswell **GRAVES**, b. of East Haddam, Nov.		96
15, 1763	2	268
Esther, d. Daniel & Elizabeth, b. Apr. 11, 1756	LR5	268
Mary, d. Daniel & Elizabeth, b. Mar. 14, 1749	LR5	268
Sarah, d. Daniel & Elizabeth, b. Feb. 1, 1751	LR5	
DROWN, Warren B., ae 26, b. at Lydon, Vt., res. E. Haddam, m.		
Minerva **CHAPMAN**, ae 19, b. at Glastonbury, Ct., res.		
E. Haddam, Nov. 18, 1856, by Rev. Nelson Goodrich.		107-8
Int. pub. Nov. 17, 1856	4	573
DUDLEY, Mahittabell, m. Joshua **BRAINARD**, July 12, 1710	LR1	a
DUMMAN, Daniell, s. Benjamin & Marcy, b. Feb. 12, 1728	LR2	510
DUTTON, Ambrose, s. Ebenezer & Phebe, b. July 18, 1760	LR6	510
Ammasa, s. Ebenezer & Phebe, b. Jan. 28, 1754	LR6	
Anna, m. Rosel **KNOWLTON**, b. of East Haddam, Apr. 15,		5
1760	LR7	510
Asa, s. Ebenezer & Phebe, b. Oct. 30, 1755	LR6	18
Bettee, d. Jeremiah & Dimmis, b. Mar. 29, 1770	2	18
Calvin, s. Jeremiah & Dimmis, b. Oct. 20, 1767	2	18
Cone, s. Jeremiah & Dimmis, b. Nov. 22, 1764	2	513
Cone, s. Jeremiah & Demas, b. Nov. 27, 1764; d. Dec. 16, 1768	LR6	19
Cone, s. Jeremiah & Dimmis, d. Dec. 16, 1768	2	584
Ebenezer, s. Samuell & Rachill, b. Jan. 23, 1732/3	LR1	510
Ebenezer, m. Phebe **BEEBE**, b. of East Haddam, Apr. 26, 1753	LR6	513
Jeremiah, m. Demas **BEEBE**, b. of East Haddam, Jan. 24, 1753	LR6	
Jeremiah, m. Dimmis **BEEBEE**, b. of East Haddam, Jan. 21,		18
1758	2	584
Joseph, s. Samuell & Rachill, b. June 27, 1731	LR1	1128
Mary, w. of Joseph, d. Mar. 26, 1744	LR2	

	Vol.	Page
DUTTON, (cont.)		
Mary, m. William **MARTIN**, Aug. 18, 1812, by Rev. William Lyman	2	311
Oliver, s. Jeremiah & Dimmis, b. Mar. 11, 1760	2	18
Phebe, d. Samuel & Rachel, b. Dec. 28, 1734	LR2	1113
Pheebe, m. Brockway **BEEBE**, b. of East Haddam, Feb. 10, 1757	LR5	267
Rachill, d. Samuell & Rachill, b. Nov. 6, 1727	LR1	584
Russel[l], s. Ebenezer & Phebe, b. Feb. 18, 1763	LR6	510
Russel[l], m. Sally **CHAPMAN**, b. of East Haddam, Oct. 14, 1788	2	180
Ruth, d. Joseph & Mary, b. Aug. 14, 1704	LR1	5
Ruth, m. Thomas **MILLERD**, Jr., July 16, 1724	LR2	1130
Salley, d. Jeremiah & Demas, b. Feb. 12, 1763	LR6	513
Salley, d. Jeremiah & Dimmis, b. Feb. 12, 1763	2	18
Sally, d. Jan. 14, 1833, ae 55	3	46
Samuell, s. Joseph & Mary, b. Feb. 13, 1705	LR1	5
Samuell, m. Rachill **CONE**, Nov. 17, 1726	LR1	584
Samuell, s. Samuell & Rachill, b. July 27, 1729	LR1	584
Thomas, s. Joseph, b. Mar. 1, 1707	LR1	6
Timothy, s. Samuel & Rachel, b. Jan. 7, 1736/7	LR2	1113
Timothy, of East Haddam, m. Martha **BARTHOLOMEY**, of Wallingford, Nov. 1, 1758	LR6	512
EARL, Horatio, of East Greenwich, R. I., m. Ruth **CHAPMAN**, of Chatham, Dec. 7, 1828, by Rev. Isaac Parsons	3	101
EASTON, Waite, m. Julia Ann **BABCOCK**, Sept. 1, 1836, by Jed[edia]h R. Gardiner, J. P.	3	145
EC[C]ELSTON, Ira, m. Matilda R. **HURLBURT**, Oct. 8, 1840, by Francis Griffin, J. P.	3	184
EDWARDS, Eliza A., of East Haddam, m. Stephen **CHURCH**, of Groton, Sept. 10, 1837, by Ethan A. Willey, J. P.	3	152
Marietta L., m. James **BOOGE**, Feb. 3, 1839, by Rev. George Carrington, of Hadlyme	3	167
Richard, of Portland, m. Mary J. **JONES**, of East Haddam, May 7, 1851, by Rev. Alpheas Geer, in St. Stephen's Church	3	231
Timothy, s. Samuel H., cabinet maker, ae 24, & Harriet, ae 22, b. Mar. 28, 1851	4	31-2
Timothy, d. Apr. 8, 1851	4	39-40
------, d. Henry, laborer, ae 37, res. E. Haddam, b. Jan. 26, 1856	4	83
EGAN, Thomas, b. in Ireland, res. E. Haddam, m. Rose **WATSON**, b. in Ireland, res. East Haddam, Apr. 8, 1855, in Chester, by Rev. John Lynch, of Chester. Int. pub. Apr. 3, 1855, in East Haddam	4	55
ELLIOTT, Emma, of East Haddam, m. John **MAY**, of Haddam, Apr. 14, 1835, by Nathaniel Miner	3	138
ELY, Abner S., m. Fanny **GRIFFIN**, June 24, 1824, by Josiah Hawes, J. P.	3	131

	Vol.	Page
ELY, (cont.)		
Adelaide A., m. Edward A. **LEE**, b. of East Haddam, July 31, 1853, by Rev. Isaac Parsons	3	238a
Adalaide C., shoe binder, ae 18, m. Edward N. **LEE**, mechanic, ae 21, b. of E. Haddam, July 31, 1853, by Rev. Isaac Parsons	4	45-6
Alonzo B., ae 21, b. in E. Haddam res. E. Haddam, m. Mary E. **SNOW**, ae 19, b. in E. Haddam, res. E. Haddam, Jan. 21, 1856, by Rev. James M. Phillips. Int. pub. Jan. 19, 1856	4	80-1
Ella N., d. Sylvester N., mechanic, ae 36, & Mary E., ae 37, b. Aug. 15, 1847	4	3-4
Gurdon, of Lyme, m. Mrs. Sarah **RUSSELL**, of Essex, May 7, 1826, by Rev. Joseph Vaill, of Hadlyme	3	86
Jemima, m. Abel **BINGHAM**, b. of East Haddam, Sept. 9, 1784	2	219
Joshua Brainerd, m. Laura **ASHCRAFT**, Nov. 29, 1837, by Rev. Isaac Parsons	3	159
Margaret B., m. Henry C. **SPENCER**, b. of East Haddam, July 9, 1854, by Rev. Isaac Parsons	3	240
Margaret B., ae 17, m. Henry C. **SPENCER**, ae 18, b. of E. Haddam, July 9, 1854, by Rev. Isaac Parsons	4	51-2
Nelson S., shoemaker, d. Apr. 3, 1848, ae 37	4	17-18
Roxana E., m. Alfred G. **SILLIMAN**, b. of East Haddam, Dec. 21, 1842, by Isaac Parsons, V. D. M.	3	148
Selden M., of Ripley, N. Y., m. Statira E. **GRIFFIN**, of East Haddam, May 10, 1825, by Rev. Herman L. Vaill	3	74-5
Simon, m. Ruth **ACKLEY**, Dec. 8, 1805	2	241
Sylvester A., d. Apr. 16, 1850, ae 6	4	29-30
Sylvester N., m. Orinda H. **RUSSELL**, b. of East Haddam, Aug. 27, 1833, by Rev. Isaac Parsons	3	132
EMMONS, EMONS, Abigail, d. Jonathan & Rachell, b. July 28, 1726	LR2	d
Abigail, of East Haddam, m. Hiram **YOUNG**, of Chatham, Apr. 12, 1825, by Rev. Isaac Parsons	3	72-73
Alexander Hamilton, s. Noadiah & Elizabeth, b. Dec. 12, 1816	2	309
Anna, d. Thomas & Huldah, b. Mar. 6, 1757	LR7	416
Anna, d. Nath[anie]l & Huldah, b. Mar. 6, 1757	LR7	417
Anne, d. Joseph & Lois, b. June 20, 1773	2	30
Anne, m. Noadiah **GATES**, 2d, b. of East Haddam, Apr. 14,	2	249
1793	3	2
Anne C., w. Joshua B., d. Jan. 7, 1835, ae 37	2	265
Asa. m. Orpasia **OLMSTED**, b. of East Haddam, Aug. 7, 1806	2	176
Augustin, s. Noadiah & Elizabeth, b. Dec. 26, 1791		
Augustine, d. Feb. 19, 1844. Information given from Family	3	244
Record and oath of Lavina **EMMONS**	LR2	1106
Benjamin, s. Jonathan & Rachel, b. Feb. 4, 1744/5	2	176
Brainerd, s. Noadiah & Elizabeth, b. Sept. 20, 1782	3	2
Charles Henry, s. Joshua B. & Anne C., b. Dec. 1, 1833	3	1

	Vol.	Page
EMMONS, EMONS, (cont.)		
Clarissa Crowell, d. Joshua B. & Anne C., b. Dec. 10, 1823	3	1
Clarissa Crowell, d. Joshua B. & Anne C., d. Dec. 18, 1823	3	2
Daniel, m. Mary **CONE**, Apr. 2, 1762	LR7	416
Daniel, s. Daniel & Mary, b. June 21, 1765	LR7	416
Daniel Spencer, s. Ebenezer & Susannah, b. Oct. 9, 1757	LR5	562
David, s. Capt. Noadiah & Elizabeth, b. Jan. 9, 1797	2	176
David B., ae 23, of East Haddam, m. Lucena P. **SWAN**, ae 20, of East Haddam, Mar. 25, 1857, by Rev. Nathaniel Miner. Int. pub. Mar. 21, 1857	4	118
Dorothy, d. Samuell & Ruth, b. Sept. 18, 1722	LR2	d
Dorothy, m. Enoch **ARNOLD**, b. of East Haddam, June 16, 1743	LR3	12
Dorothy, d. Thomas & Huldah, b. Apr., 4, 1753	LR7	416
Dorothy, d. Nath[anie]l & Huldah, b. Apr. 4, 1753	LR7	417
Dyar, s. Joseph & Loes, b. Aug. 8, 1769	2	30
Ebenezer, s. Samuell & Ruth, b. Sept. 18, 1725	LR2	d
Ebenezer, m. Susannah **SPENCER**, Apr. 4, 1754	LR5	562
Edwin A., ae 28 y., b. in E. Haddam, res. E. Haddam, m. Clarissa M. **PECK**, ae 21, b. in East Haddam, res. E. Haddam, Dec. 25, 1855, at Millington, by Rev. Nathaniel Miner. Int. pub. Dec. 20, 1855	4	79
Edwin Norton, s. [Joseph B. & Laura A.], b. Jan. 24, 1851	3	243
Eliphalet, s. Thomas & Huldah, b. Feb. 25, 1752	LR7	416
Eliphalet, s. Nathaniel & Huldah, b. Feb. 25, 1752	LR7	417
Eliphalet, m. Mary M. **SWAN**, Mar. 26, 1838, by Rev. Nathaniel Miner, of Millington	3	164-5
Elizabeth, d. Samuell & Ruth, b. Mar. 6, 1724	LR2	d
Elizabeth, d. Nathaniel & Elizabeth, b. Jan. 9, 1732/3	LR2	1113
Elizabeth, m. Peter **SPENCER**, b. of East Haddam, Feb. 1, 1749/50	LR4	464
Elizabeth, m. Silas **BEEBE**, Jan. 5, 1752	LR7	416
Elizabeth, w. of Nathaniel, d. Sept. 27, 1768	LR2	1113
Elizabeth B., m. William M. **WILLEY**, b. of East Haddam, Oct. 10, 1832, by Nathaniel Miner	3	127
Elizabeth Brainerd, d. Noadiah & Elizabeth, b. Apr. 26, 1809	2	309
Emeline E., of East Haddam, m. Augustus P. **JONES**, of Hebron, Feb. 21, 1827, by Rev. Herman L. Vaill	3	93
Florella, m. William **PALMER**, Jr., b. of East Haddam, Feb. 18, 1818, by Rev. Isaac Parsons	3	87
Frederic Augustus, s. Noadiah & Elizabeth, b. Apr. 20, 1805	2	309
Hannah, m. Nathaniell **LORD**, June 12, 1712	LR2	d
Hannah, d. Jonathan & Rachel, b. Oct. 18, 1734	LR2	1106
Hannah, d. Jonathan & Rachel, b. Oct. 18, 1734	LR2	1122
Harriet N., of East Haddam, m. Theodore B. **SHELTON**, of New Haven, June 9, 1834, by Rev. Nathaniel Miner	3	134
Henry, s. Noadiah & Elizabeth, b. May 7, 1785	2	176
Huldah, d. Thomas & Huldah, b. Nov. 6, 1763	LR7	416

	Vol.	Page
EMMONS, EMONS, (cont.)		
Huldah, d. Nath[anie]l & Huldah, b. Nov. 6, 1763	LR7	417
Ichabod, s. Noadiah & Elizabeth, b. Mar. 18, 1778	2	176
Jeremiah, s. Jonathan & Rachel, b. July 30, 1748	LR2	1106
John, d. Dec. 1, 1841, ae 60	3	195
Jonathan, m. Rachell **GRISWOULD**, Jan. 2, 1723	LR2	d
Jonathan, s. Jonathan & Rachel, b. Apr. 5, 1737	LR2	1106
Jonathan, Jr., m. Desire **HARRIS**, b. of East Haddam, Jan. 11, 1759	LR6	511
Jonathan, s. Jonathan, Jr. & Desire, b. Dec. 30, 1761	LR6	511
Jonathan Lyman, s. Capt. Noadiah & Elizabeth, b. Mar. 11, 1794	2	176
Joseph, s. Jonathan & Rachel, b. Sept. 9, 1739	LR2	1106
Joseph, of East Haddam, m. Lois **GILBART**, of Middletown, Jan. 6, 1763	LR7	410
Joseph B., m. Laura A. **CHAPMAN**, b. of East Haddam, Dec. 5, 1847, by Rev. Isaac Parsons	3	211
Joseph B., m. Laura A. **CHAPMAN**, b. of East Haddam, Dec. 5, 1847, by Rev. Isaac Parsons	3	243
Joseph B., mechanic, ae 22, of East Haddam, m. Lavina A. **CHAPMAN**, ae 19, b. in Chatham, res. East Haddam, Dec. 5, 1847, by Isaac Parsons	4	1-2
Joseph Brainerd, s. Joshua B. & Anne C., b. Nov. 24, 1825	3	1
Joseph Gilbart, s. Joseph & Lois, b. Oct. 5, 1767	LR7	410
Joshua B., s. Daniel, m. Anna C. **CROWELL**, b. of East Haddam, Oct. 12, 1820, by Rev. Solomon Blakesley	3	1
Joshua B., m. Olive **HARDING**, b. of East Haddam, Feb. 21, 1836, by Rev. Stephen Beach	3	142
Julia A., of East Haddam, m. Simon S. **CAREW**, of Stonington, Nov. 4, [1846], by Nathaniel Miner	3	208
Louisa P., of East Haddam, m. Ebenezer **COOK**, of Haddam, Dec. 13, 1832, by Isaac Parsons	3	128
Lydia, d. Jonathan & Rachel, b. July 9, 1742	LR2	1106
Mary, m. Jeremiah **GATES**, Dec. 7, 1721	LR2	c
Mary, d. Samuell & Ruth, b. Feb. 6, 1729/30	LR2	d
Mary, d. Ebenezer & Susannah, b. Apr. 1, 1764	LR5	562
Mary, d. Jonathan, Jr. & Desire, b. Apr. 27, 1766	LR6	511
Mary, d. Franklin, mechanic, ae 33, & Mary, ae 25, b. Feb. 19, 1847	4	3-4
Mary E., ae 21, b. in East Haddam, res. East Haddam, m. Henry T. **FULLER**, July 10, 1855, by Rev. Isaac Parsons. Int. pub. July 7, 1853	4	59-60
Mary M., d. Oct. 2, 1848, ae 27	4	17-18
Mary Russell, d. Joshua B. & Anne C., b. Jan. 22, 1832	3	2
Mary S., m. Frederick A. **ROBERTS**, b. of East Haddam, May 6, 1834, by Rev. Nathaniel Miner	3	134
Mary Stirling, d. Noadiah & Elizabeth, b. Sept. 8, 1813	2	309
Mehittabell, m. George **CONE**, Jan. 31, 1733/4	LR2	1124

	Vol.	Page
EMMONS, EMONS, (cont.)		
Mehetable, d. Thomas & Huldah, b. Apr. 10, 1755	LR7	416
Mehetable, d. Nath[anie]l & Huldah, b. Apr. 10, 1755	LR7	147
Nathan, of East Haddam, m. Abigail **FULLER**, of Colchester, June 14, 1769	LR8	5
Nathaniel, m. Elizabeth **WELLS**, Sept. 21, 1727	LR2	1113
Nathaniel, Capt., d. Apr. 17, 1825	3	46
Noadiah, s. Ebenezer & Susannah, b. Feb. 23, 1755	LR5	562
Noadiah, m. Elizabeth **BRAINERD**, b. of East Haddam, May 1, 1777	2	176
Noadiah, s. Noadiah & Elizabeth, b. May 28, 1780	2	176
Noadiah, m. Mrs. Elizabeth **BROOKS**, b. of East Haddam, Apr. 4, 1802	2	309
Noadiah Franklin, s. Noadiah & Elizabeth, b. Feb. 23, 1807	2	309
Octavius, of Colchester, m. Wid. Elizabeth Ann **SMITH**, of East Haddam, Feb. 5, 1854, by Rev. Isaac Parsons	3	239
Octavius, farmer, ae 48, of Colchester, m. 2d w. Elizabeth Ann **SMITH**, tailoress, ae 34, of E. Haddam, Feb. 5, 1854, by [ ]	4	41-2
Octavius, farmer, ae 48, of Colchester, m. 2d w. Elizabeth Ann **SMITH**, tailoress, ae 34, of E. Haddam, Feb. 5, 1854, by [ ]	4	51-2
Olive, d. Joseph & Lois, b. Nov. 16, 1764	LR7	410
Olive, of East Haddam, m. Elisha **PECK**, of Lyme, Nov. 27, 1785	2	196
Olive, d. Oct. 5, 1849, ae 75	4	29-30
Oliver, s. Jonathan, Jr. & Desire, b. Dec. 15, 1759	LR6	511
Rachel, d. Jonathan & Rachel, b. Sept. 13, 1729	LR2	d
Samuell, Jr., m. Ruth **CONE**, Sept. 14, 1721	LR2	d
Samuell, s. Samuell, Jr. & Ruth, b. Nov. 20, 1725	LR2	d
Samuel, s. Jonathan, Jr. & Desire, b. Sept. 23, 1768	LR6	511
Samuel, farmer, d. July 2, 1850, ae 89	4	29-30
Samuel Crowell, s. Joshua B. & Anne C., b. Sept. 24, 1828	3	1
Sarah, d. Jonathan & Rachel, b. July 5, 1732	LR2	d
Sarah, m. John **HARVEY**, 2d, Dec. 27, 1753	LR5	564
Sarah, d. Jonathan, Jr. & Desire, b. Apr. 4, 1764	LR6	511
Sarah, of East Haddam, m. Henry A. **PERKINS**, of Hartford, May 24, 1831, by Rev. Nathaniel Miner	3	124
Silvester, s. Ebenezer & Susannah, b. Feb. 3, 1771	2	46
Sophia C., of East Haddam, m. Egbert **NEWBERRY**, of Brooklyn, June 3, 1824, by Rev. Isaac Parsons	3	62-3
Sophia Champion, d. Noadiah & Elizabeth, b. Dec. 5, 1802	2	309
Susannah, d. Ebenezer & Susannah, b. May 2, 1761	LR5	562
Susanna, d. Noadiah & Elizabeth, b. Feb. 24, 1788	2	176
Thomas, s. Nathaniel & Elizabeth, b. June 11, 1728	LR2	1113
Thomas, m. Huldah **CONE**, May 21, 1751	LR7	416
Thomas, m. Huldah **CONE**, May 21, 1751	LR7	417
Thomas, s. Thomas & Huldah, b. July 12, 1760	LR7	416

	Vol.	Vol.
EMMONS, EMONS, (cont.)		
Thomas, s. Nath[anie]l & Huldah, b. July 12, 1760	LR7	417
Wilbur Fiske, s. Joseph B. & Laura A., b. Oct. 4, 1848	3	243
Wilbur Fiske, s. Joseph B., shoemaker, ae 23, & Laura A., ae 20, b. Oct. 4, 1848	4	13-14
William O., m. Adelia A. **HILL**, b. of East Haddam, Dec. 6, 1847, by Rev. Abraham Holway	3	211
-----, child of Dyer, mechanic, ae 33, & Laura M., ae 27, b. Aug. 3, 1847	4	3-4
-----, s. Joseph G., farmer, ae 56, & Sarah, ae 38, b. Mar. 22, 1849	4	13-14
-----, d. James E., mechanic, ae 32, res. Moodus, & Caroline E., ae 26, b. Apr. 29, [1856]	4	86
ESTABROOK, Anna, d. Hobart & Hannah, b. Aug. 18, 1777	2	112
Anna, of East Haddam, m. Ambrose **NILES**, Jr., of Colchester, May 11, 1797	2	231
Anna, of East Haddam, m. Ambrose **NILES**, Jr., of Colchester, May 11, 1797* *(Entry crossed out)	2	265
Anne, d. Rev. Hobart & Sarah, b. May 1, 1746	LR3	3
Anne, d. Rev. Hobart & Sarah, d. Mar. 26, 1750	LR3	3
Chauncey, s. Rev. Hobart & Jerusha, b. July 20, 1758	LR3	3
Hannah, d. Hobart & Hannah, b. Feb. 15, 1774	2	112
Hobart, Rev. m. Mrs. Jerusha **CHA[U]NCEY**, Aug. 4, 1747	LR3	3
Hobart, s. Rev. Hobart & Jerusha, b. Jan. 13, 1748/9	LR3	3
Hobart, s. Hobart & Hannah, b. May 9, 1787	2	112
Jerusha, d. Rev. Hobart & Jerusha, b. July 23, 1755	LR3	3
Jerusha, d. Hobart & Hannah, b. Sept. 17, 1775	2	112
Mary, d. Hobart & Hannah, b. Dec. 9, 1785	2	112
Olive, d. Hobert & Hannah, b. June 23, 1782	2	112
Rhoda, d. Hobart & Hannah, b. May 10, 1790	2	112
Samuel, s. Rev. Hobart & Jerusha, b. Mar. 28, 1751	LR3	3
Sarah, w. of Rev. Hobart, d. June 25, 1746	LR3	3
Sarah, d. Hobert & Hannah, b. July 25, 1779	2	112
EVANS, Caroline C., d. Buel, mechanic, ae 42, & Mary, ae 40, b. Oct. 19, 1847	4	3-4
Huldah A., ae 20, b. in Chatham, Ct., m. William L. **COREY**, worker in cotton mill, ae 25, b. in Valley Falls, R. I., res. Portland, June 12, 1850, by Jacob Gardner	4	37-8
Huldah A., of East Haddam, m. William L. **COREY**, of East Greenwich, R. I., June 12, 1851, by Rev. Jacob Gardner	3	232
Mary H., of East Haddam, m. Aaron B. **HENRY**, of Holden, Mass., July 5, 1846, by Rev. Levi H. Wakeman	3	206
EVARTS, David, of Killingworth, m. Amanda **VAILL**, of East Haddam, Mar. 2, 1836, by Rev. George Carrington, of Hadlyme	3	142
FAIRCLOTH, James H., s. Peter, shoemaker, ae 36, b. Oct. 8, 1849	4	25-6
-----, d. John P., shoemaker, ae 41, & Olive S., ae 37, b. Nov. 28, 1856	4	115

	Vol.	Page
FARGO, Mary L., ae 23, of Montville, m. Orlando N. **RAYMOND**, ae 26, of Salem, Mar. 22, 1857, by Rev. Nathaniel Miner. Int. pub. Mar. 22, 1857	4	119
FINAGAN, Patrick, m. Mary **PATTERSON**, Oct. 10, 1841, by Rev. George Carrington, of Hadlyme	3	187
FISHER, Ann, d. Nathan & Hannah, b. Aug. 14, 1743	LR3	16
Eliazer, [twin with Hannah], s. Nathan & Hannah, b. Dec. 24, 1750	LR3	11
Elizabeth, d. Nathan & Hannah, b. Jan. 4, 1754	LR3	11
Hannah, d. Nathan & Hannah, b. Nov. 6, 1747	LR3	11
Hannah, d. Nathan & Hannah, d. Jan. 16, 1747/8	LR3	11
Hannah, [twin with Eliazer], d. Nathan & Hannah, b. Dec. 24, 1750	LR3	11
Nathan, m. Hannah **OLCUTT**, Sept. 28, 1741	LR3	11
Nathan, s. Nathan & Hannah, b. June 6, 1749	LR3	11
Olcutt, s. Nathan & Hannah, b. Apr. 8, 1745	LR3	16
FISKE, Warren C., Rev., m. Harriet M. **PARSONS**, May 19, 1847, by Rev. Isaac Parsons	3	209
FITCH, Frederick, of Salem, N. Y., m. Huldah A. **CHAMPLAIN**, of East Haddam, Apr. 16, 1837, by G. A. Calhoun	3	151
FLOOD, Eliza Ann, of Colchester, m. Levi **PALMER**, of East Haddam, Aug. 8, 1838, by Rev. George Carrington, of Hadlyme	3	166
Eliza Ann, m. Levi **PALMER**, Aug. 8, 1838	3	175
Irena, ae 24, b. in Haddam, res. Haddam, m. Curtis S. **ARNOLD**, shoemaker, ae 25, b. in East Haddam, res. Haddam, Nov. 20, 1848, by Levi H. Wakeman	4	9-10
Irene H., of Middle Haddam, m. Curtis S. **ARNOLD**, of East Haddam, Nov. 26, 1848, by Rev. Levi H. Wakeman	3	215
FOOT, Edwin, m. Abby Ann **LINDSLEY**, May 20, 1821, by Rev. Solomon Blakesley	3	7
Esther, of Colechester, m. Caleb **GATES**, of East Haddam, Oct. 17, 1775	2	92
Lucy, of Colchester, m. Joseph **GATES**, 3rd, of East Haddam, Nov. 3, 1774	2	92
FOSTER, Catharine Lunan Tonnele, d. Nathan L. & Azubah L., b. Feb. 8, 1828	2	299
Edgar Theodore, s. N[athan L.] & A[zubah] L., b. Apr. 7, 1823, in Hartford	2	299
Elisabeth Louisa, d. Nathan L. & Azubah Louisa, b. Jan. 7, 1815	2	299
Elizabeth Louisa, m. Eleazer Watrous **MATHER**, b. of East Haddam, June 18, 1837, by Rev. Stephen Beach	3	152
Elizabeth Louisa, m. Eleazer Watrous **MATHER**,June 18, 1837	3	175
Henry Lysander, s. N[athan] L. & A[zubah] L., b. Sept. 17, 1833	2	299
Joel William Lanesford, s. Nathan L. & Azubah Louisa, b. May 28, 1813	2	299

	Vol.	Page
FOSTER, (cont.)		
John Webster, s. Nathan L. & Azubah L., b. Feb. 19, 1821, in Hartford	2	299
Marie Antionette, d. Nathan L. & Azubah L., b. Nov. 29, 1818	2	299
Marie Antionette, m. John **HOLMES**, b. of East Haddam, Apr. 26, 1840, by Rev. Charles William Bradley	3	178
Mary Sophia, d. N[athan] L. & A[zubah] L., b. July 27, 1825	2	299
Nathan L., of Mass., m. Azubah L. **CONE**, of East Haddam, May 30, 1810, by Rev. William Lyman	2	299
Phebe, b. in Middletown, res. E. Haddam, d. Oct. 25, 1849, aged 96	4	29-30
Reginald Heber, s. Nathan L. & Azubah L., b. Sept. 10, 1831	2	299
William Cone, s. Nathan L. & Azubah L., b. May 8, 1817	2	299
William Cone, s. Nathan L. & Azubah L., d. Oct. 14, 1817, ae 5 m. 6 d.	2	300
FOWLER, Asa A., of East Haddam, m. Lucinda M. **TILLOTSON**, of Lyme, July 7, 1836, by Rev. Isaac Parsons	3	145
Asenath M., m. Zachariah L. **HUNGERFORD**, b. of East Haddam, Feb. 27, 1840, by Isaac Parsons, V. D. M.	3	176-7
David, s. Joseph & Margaret, b. May 4, 1777	2	42
Electa, d. Joseph & Sarah, b. July 7, 1767	LR8	3
Elisha Adams, s. Joseph & Sarah, b. Sept. 29, 1755	LR8	3
Elizabeth, d. Joseph & Sarah, b. Jan. 19, 1750; d. Feb. 13, 1750	LR8	3
Elizabeth, d. Joseph & Sarah , b. Oct. 17, 1751	LR8	3
Elizabeth, d. Joseph & Sarah, d. Sept. 19, 1762	LR8	3
Elizabeth, w. [Col.(?) Joseph], d. Nov. 21, 1768	LR8	3
Elizabeth, d. Joseph & Margaret, b. June 30, 1779	2	42
Ezra, s. Joseph & Margaret, b. May 20, 1774	2	42
George R., m. Esther **GATES**, Nov. 2, 1828, by Rev. Isaac Parsons	3	100
Gordon A., m. Mary **SMITH**, b. of East Haddam, Mar. 14, 1821, by Rev. Isaac Parsons	3	3
Isaac, m. Roxa **DAVIS**, Oct. 15, 1826, by Isaac Parsons	3	88-89
Isaac, of Vermillion, O., m. Prudence R. **SNOW**, of East Haddam, Sept. 6, 1852, by Rev. Warren Emmerson	3	237
Joseph, Jr., Rev., m. Sarah **MEDCALF**, Feb. 13, 1747	LR8	3
Joseph, s. Joseph & Sarah, b. Dec. 3, 1747	LR8	3
Joseph, Col.(?), d. June 23, 1768	LR8	3
Joseph, Rev., d. June 10, 1771	2	37
Joseph, m. Margaret **HALL**, b. of East Haddam, Oct. 21, 1771	2	42
Leonora L., of East Haddam, m. John G. **BARBER**, ae 21, b. in Hebron, res. E. Haddam, Oct. 15, 1856, at Hartford, by Rev. W[illia]m Watton. Int. pub. Oct. 14, 1856, in East Haddam	4	103
Mary, m. Edward G. **BURKE**, Mar. 29, 1835, by Isaac Parsons	3	137
Samuel K., m. Adelia H. **TRYON**, Oct. 14, 1829, by Isaac Parsons	3	103

	Vol.	Page
FOWLER, (cont.)		
Samuel W., of East Haddam, m. Abigail B. **MARKHAM**, of Chatham, June 18, 1848, by Rev. Isaac Parsons	3	213
Samuel W., mechanic, ae 21, b. East Haddam, res. East Haddam, m. Abby B. **MARKHAM**, ae 21, b. in Chatham, res. East Haddam, June 18, 1848, by Isaac Parsons	4	1-2
Sarah, d. Joseph & Sarah, b. Nov. 11, 1753	LR8	3
Sarah, m. Rev. Joseph **VAILL**, b. of East Haddam, Oct. 12, 1780	2	150
William, s. Joseph & Sarah, b. Dec. 27, 1757; d. July 16, 1759	LR8	3
William, s. Joseph & Sarah, b. Sept. 27, 1761	LR8	3
William, m. Caroline L. **GREEN**, Sept. 26, 1830, by Rev. Alvan Ackley	3	108
William L., Jr., m. Mary B. **PERCIVAL**, b. of East Haddam, Apr. 20, 1853, by Rev. Isaac Parsons	3	238a
William L., shoemaker, ae 22, m. Mary B. **PERCIVAL**, ae 22, b. of E. Haddam, Apr. 20, 1853, by Rev. Isaac Parsons	4	43-4
-----, d. Samuel W., b. Apr. 20, 1855	4	53-4
FOX, Aaron, Capt., d. July 10, 1831, ae 68	3	123
Alice, m. Josiah J. **BAKER**, Sept. 22, 1805	2	243
Allen, s. Daniel & Hannah, b. July 1, 1755	LR6	507
Amasa, s. Daniel & Elisabeth, b. Feb. 14, 1767	2	72
Ann, d. Thomas & Margeret, b. Apr. 15, 1737	LR5	265
Ansel, s. Daniel & Hannah, b. Feb. 16, 1759	LR6	507
Asa, s. Asa & Sarah, b. Oct. 29, 1787	LR8	2
Azubah, d. Nathan & Sarah, b. July 4, 1768	2	50
Candis, d. Daniel & Elisabeth, b. June 16, 1774	2	72
Charles, s. Warren & Charity, b. Jan. [ ], 1794	2	245
Daniel, m. Hannah **BURR**, Oct. 15, 1747	LR6	507
Daniel, m. Elisabeth **GATES**, Nov. 12, 1761	2	72
Daniel, s. Daniel & Elisabeth, b. July 27, 1770	2	72
Deborah, d. Nathan & Sarah, b. Jan. 21, 1759	2	50
Dimmis, d. Daniel & Hannah, b. May 13, 1757	LR6	507
Diodate, m. Clarissa **SPENCER**, b. of East Haddam, Aug. 2, 1832, by Oliver Green, J. P.	3	124
Dorcas, d. Nathan & Sarah, b. Apr. 19, 1764	2	50
Ebener, s. Nathan & Sarah, b. Apr. 27, 1770	2	50
Ebenezer, m. Anna **GRIFFIN**, b. of East Haddam, May 13, 1823, by Josiah Griffin, J. P.	3	40-1
Eliza, d. [Moses & Lucy], b. Apr. 15, 1838	3	157
Ellen C., m. John C. **SMITH**, b. of East Haddam, Nov. 11, 1832, by Nathaniel Miner	3	127
Ezekiel, s. Ezekiel & Sarah, b. Nov. 28, 1774	2	263
Ezra, s. Ezekiel & Sarah, b. May 3, 1779	2	263
Hannah, w. of Daniel, d. Aug. 17, 1761	2	73
Henry, of Hartford, m. Sarah **BROWN**, of Essex, June 11, 1850, by Rev. W[illia]m Harris	3	226
Hiel, s. Daniel & Elisabeth, b. Aug. 22, 1762	2	72

	Vol.	Page
FOX, (cont.)		
Hubbard, s. Daniel & Hannah, b. May 22, 1753	LR6	507
Leavitt, [twin with Leena], s. Daniel & Elisabeth, b. Sept. 10, 1764	2	72
Leena, [twin with Leavitt], d. Daniel & Elisabeth, b. Sept. 10, 1764	2	72
Lyna, d. Nathan & Sarah, b. Mar. 11, 1772	2	50
Mary Allice, d. [Moses & Lucy], b. Nov. 21, 1834	3	157
Mary E., ae 15, m. Henry **PURPLE**, ae 20, b. of E. Haddam, Oct. 12, 1851, by W. Alburtson	4	37-8
Matilda, d. [Moses & Lucy], b. Aug. 31, 1841	3	157
Mercy*, d. Nathan & Sarah, b. June 20, 1762 (*First written "Marcy")	2	50
Moses, of East Haddam, m. Lucy **MILLER**, of Lyme, Jan. 1, 1834, by Josiah Griffin, J. P.	3	133
Moses, m. Lucy **MILLER**, Jan. 1, 1834	3	157
Nathan, of East Haddam, m. Sarah **SANDERS**, of Lyme, Jan. 11, 1758	2	50
Nathan, s. Nathan & Sarah, b. June 6, 1766	2	50
Nathan, d. Jan. 16, 1773	2	51
Orange, d. Daniel & Elisabeth, b. Sept. 8, 1772	2	72
Reuben, s. Daniel & Hannah, b. July 8, 1751	LR6	507
Roxana, d. [Moses & Lucy], b. Apr. 16, 1836	3	157
Samuel, m. Sophia **COMSTOCK**, June 7, 1821, by Rev. J. Vaill, of Hadlyme	3	5
Sibble, d. Daniel & Hannah, b. July 3, 1749	LR6	507
Silenda, m. William H. **CONE**(?), Jan. 18, 1824, by Russell Dutton, J. P.	3	54-5
Simion, s. Nathan & Sarah, b. Nov. 16, 1760	2	50
Simeon, s. Nathan & Sarah, d. Sept. 14, 1761	2	51
Sophia, m. Reed **ANDERSON**, b. of East Haddam, Oct. 14, 18[ ]	2	315
T[h]eresa, m. Horace **PALMER**, b. of East Haddam, Oct. 19, 1820, by Rev. W[illia]m Lyman	2	325
Warren, m. Charity **SPENCER**, b. of East Haddam, Sept. 15, 1793	3	245
William Henry, of East Haddam, m. Nancy **REYNOLDS**, of New Haven, Feb. 1, 1835, by Rev. Nathaniel Miner		136
FRANKLIN, Almira, of Killingworth, m. Edward R. **WHITE**, of East Haddam, May 6, 1857, at Killingworth, by Rev. Hiram Bell. License issued May 1, 1857	4 2 2	121
FREEMAN, Alcey, d. Peter & Sarah, b. July 15, 1791	2	10
Amos, s. Peter & Sarah, b. Nov. 14, 1781	2	10
Amos, s. Peter & Sarah, d. Sept. 15, 1785	2	11
Deborah, d. Peter & Sarah, b. Feb. 23, 1797	2	10
Jerusha, d. Peter & Sarah, b. Aug. 16, 1794	2	10
Lois, d. Peter & Sarah, b. May 15, 1784	2	10
Peter, m. Sarah **ARCKER**, Oct. 7, 1781	2	10

	Vol.	Page
FREEMAN, (cont.)		
Peter, s. Peter & Sarah, b. Mar. 23, 1805	2	10
Peter, d. Apr. 3, 1805	2	11
Polle, d. Saun* & Clarressa, b. Sept. 17, 1794 (*Sam?)	2	96
Salle, d. Peter & Sarah, b. May 13, 1787	2	10
FRINK, Mary, of Stonington, m. John **MARSH**, of East Haddam, Sept. 27, 1788	2	241
Mary, of Stonington, m. John **MARSH**, of East Haddam, Nov. 27, 1788* (*Entry crossed out)	2	157
FULLER, FFULLER, Abby, m. Jehiel **INGRAHAM**, b. of East Haddam, Jan. 2, 1831, by Rev. Nathaniel Miner	3	127
Abby, of Colchester, m. Nathan **SCOVEL**, of East Haddam, Mar. 4, 1832, by Russell Dutton, J. P.	3	122
Abigail, d. Timothy & Sarah, b. July 5, 1704	LR1	4
Abiga[i]ll, d. Timothy & Mary, b. Oct. 19, 1718	LR2	a
Abigail, m. Joseph **GATES**, Jr., Dec. 4, 1746	LR3	14
Abigail, d. Thomas, Jr. & Martha, b. July 3, 1753	LR2	1113
Abigail, of Colchester, m. Nathan **EMMONS**, of East Haddam, June 14, 1769	LR8	5
Abigail, m. Ozias **CHAPMAN**, b. of East Haddam, Aug. 10, 1769	2	16
Alfred, s. Samuell & Marcy, b. Jan. 2, 1739/40	LR2	1125
Alfred, s. Jehiel & Sarah, b. Sept. 4, 1766	LR6	506
Alfred, s. [Gurdon & Harriet], b. Oct. 1, 1836	3	139
Ales, m. Simeon **ACKLEE**, Nov. 8, 1739	LR3	2
Alice, of Colechester, m. Stephen **ACKLEY**, of East Haddam, Nov. 6, 1770	2	32
Almira, d. [Gurdon & Harriet], b. Sept. 8, 1833	3	139
Andrew, s. John & Mary, b. Aug. 11, 1734	LR1	572
And[r]ew Cornwel, s. William & Rebeckah, b. Nov. 15, 1757	LR6	506
Anise, d. Jehiel & Sarah, b. Oct. 4, 1768	LR6	506
Ann, d. Ephraim & Sarah, b. July 23, 1745	LR4	471
Anna, d. Thomas & Martha, b. Feb. 8, 1748/9	LR2	1113
Anna, m. Abihu **MACK**, b. of East Haddam, July 4, 1768	LR8	5
Anne, d. Timothy, b. Aug. 29, 1707	LR1	6
Anne, d. Matthias & Mary, b. Feb. 17, 1736/7	LR2	1099
Anne, m. Samuel **GATES**, 2d, b. of East Haddam, Mar. 16, 1743	LR6	507
Anne, d. Matthias, Jr. & Mary, b. Sept. 1, 1757	LR7	417
Anne, d. Tho[ma]s, 4th, & Hannah, b. Feb. 11, 1763	LR4	472
Asenah, d. Jehiel & Sarah, b. Nov. 2, 1778	2	74
Austin, of Monson, Mass., m. Harriet **TAYLOR**, of East Haddam, Sept. 9, 1822, by Rev. Isaac Parsons	3	26-27
Benjamin, s. John & Mahittabell, b. Oct. 20, 1701	LR1	5
Benjamin, s. Thomas & Elizabeth, b. June 15, 1754	LR4	472
Bethuel, s. Thomas, 4th, & Hannah, b. Jan. 9, 1754	LR4	472
Bethuel, s. Thomas, 4th, & Hannah, d. July 14, 1755	LR4	472
Bethuel, s. Thomas, 4th, & Hannah, b. Mar. 10, 1756	LR4	472

	Vol.	Page
FULLER, FFULLER, (cont.)		
Bethuel, s. Dea. Thomas & Hannah, d. Sept. 19, [1775], in the 20th y. of his age.. Enlisted in Gen. Spencer's Co., 1775, in the 15th reign of George 3rd	2	99
Chaddeus, s. Samuell & Mercy, b. Nov. 8, 1743	LR2	1097
Chauncey, m. Sarah Ann **BECKWITH**, b. of East Haddam, Mar. 21, 1826, by Rev. Joseph Vaill, of Hadlyme	3	84-5
Daniel, s. Matthias & Mary, b. Feb. 5, 1731/2	LR2	1099
Daniel, s. Thomas, Jr. & Martha, b. Apr. 22, 1739	LR2	1113
Daniel, s. Jehiel & Sarah, b. July 16, 1764	LR6	506
Deborah, m. John **ROWLE**, Sept. 11, 1716	LR1	571
Deborah, d. Jehiel & Sarah, b. Mar. 1, 1774	2	74
Demis, d. Shubael, Jr. & Hannah, b. Dec. 20, 1746	LR3	8
Dorothy, d. Thomas, Jr. & Mary, b. Feb. 1, 1768	LR6	508
Ebenezer, s. Thomas & Elizabeth, b. Oct. 27, 1715	LR1	2
Edgar Willson, s. Stephen, mechanic, ae 26, & Laura A., ae 24, b. Mar. 14, 1847	4	3-4
Electa, d. Jehiel & Sarah, b. Jan. 30, 1781	2	74
Eliphalet, s. Thomas, 4th, & Hannah, b. Sept. 22, 1749	LR4	472
Elisha, s. Matthias & Mary, b. Mar. 4, 1727	LR2	1099
Eliza H., d. [Truman & Matilda], b. Feb. 13, 1826	3	112-3
Eliza H., m. David S. **PURPLE**, Sept. 11, 1844, by Rev. Isaac Parsons	3	200
Elizabeth, m. Isaac **CROCKER**, Oct. 31, 1726	LR2	1128
Elizabeth, m. Job **ACKLY**, Dec. 3, 1735	LR3	510
Elizabeth, d. Samuell & Mercy, b. Nov. 13, 1745	LR2	1097
Elizabeth, m. Samuel **CHURCH**, Nov. 12, 1747	LR4	474
Elisabeth, Mrs., m. John **ARNOLD**, b. of East Haddam, Nov. 13, 1785	2	82
Ephraim, s. Shuball & Hannah, b. Sept. 8, 1711	LR1	578
Ephraim, s. Ephraim & Sarah, b. Dec. 27, 1753	LR4	471
Erastus, s. Capt. Jehiel & Sarah, b. June 18, 1787	2	74
Erastus, s. Capt. Jehiel & Sarah, d. June 23, 1787	2	75
Esther, d. John & Mary, b. July 6, 1724	LR1	572
Ezra, s. Matthias & Mary, b. Aug. 24, 1734	LR2	1099
Ezra, s. Matthias & Mary, d. July [ ], 1736	LR2	1099
File, d. Capt. Jehiel & Sarah, b. Oct. 15, 1784	2	74
Flavia, see under Fluvia		
Flora, m. Chauncey B. **PHELPS**, b. of E. Haddam, Jan. 22, 1828, by Rev. Isaac Parsons	3	96
Flora L., d. [Truman & Matilda], b. June 21, 1829	3	112-3
Flora L., of East Haddam, m. Eber R. **RAY**, of Haddam, Nov. 25, 1847, by Rev. Isaac Parsons	3	211
Flora Lucinda, b. in East Haddam, res. Haddam, m. Eber **RAY**, mechanic, of Haddam, [ ], 1848, by Isaac Parsons	4	1-2
Florella, of East Hddam, m. Bartlett **DANIELS**, of East Hampton, May 6, 1830, by Rev. Timothy Stone	3	107

	Vol.	Page
FULLER, FFULLER, (cont.)		
Fluvia, d. Jabez & Lydia, b. Sept. 20, 1792 (Flavia?)	2	247
Gurdon, s. Jehiel & Sarah, b. June 13, 1776	2	74
Gurdon, m. Harriet **WILLEY**, June 7, 1832, by Nathaniel Miner	3	124
Gurdon, m. Harriet **WILLEY**, June 7, 1832	3	139
Hannah, d. Shuball & Hannah, b. Apr. 29, 1718	LR1	578
Hannah, d. Thomas & Elizabeth, b. Mar. 21, 1720	LR1	575
Hannah, d. Timothy & Mary, b. July 3, 1720	LR2	a
Hannah, m. Lemuel **DANIELS**, Sept. 10, 1739	LR2	1106
Hannah, d. Shubael, Jr. & Hannah, b. May 27, 1745	LR3	8
Hannah, w. of Shubael, d. Mar. 31, 1751	LR3	8
Hannah, d. Tho[ma]s, 4th, & Hannah, b. Aug. 15, 1760	LR4	472
Hannah, Mrs., m. Amos **BOOGE**, b. of East Haddam, Feb. 28, 1776	2	12
Hannah, Mrs., m. Amos **BOOGE**, b. of East Haddam, Feb. 28, 1776	2	82
Hannah, m. Philo **FULLER**, b. of East Haddam, Nov. 9, 1829, by Rev. Isaac Parsons	3	103
Hannah, of East Haddam, m. Eleazer **LEWIS**, of Haddam, June 30, 1831, by Rev. Isaac Parsons	3	119
Henry T., s. [Truman & Matilda], b. Aug. 4, 1831	3	112-3
Henry T., ae 24, b. in East Haddam, res. East Haddam, m. Mary E. **EMMONS**, ae 21, b. in East Haddam, res. East Haddam, July 10, 1855, by Rev. Isaac Parsons. Int. pub. July 7, 1853	4	59-60
Huldah, d. William & Rebeckah, b. Jan. 26, 1762	LR6	506
Huldah, of East Haddam, m. Rufus **GLASS**, of Canterbury, Nov. 16, 1779	2	88
Ichabod, s. Tho[ma]s, 4th, & Hannah, b. Mar. 23, 1758	LR4	472
Ithamer, s. Matthias, Jr. & Mary, b. Dec. 25, 1754	LR7	417
Jabez, s. Thomas & Elizabeth, b. Feb. 19, 1722	LR1	575
Jabez, m. Lydia **SMITH**, b. of East Haddam, Apr. 3, 1791	2	247
Jabez H., m. Lucy Ann **NORTHAM**, June 28, 1841, by Isaac Parsons, M. V. D.	3	186
Jedediah, s. Shubael & Sarah, b. Mar. 20, 1764	LR5	562
Jehiel, s. Thomas, Jr. & Martha, b. Mar. 25, 1735	LR2	1113
Jehiel, of East Haddam, m. Sarah **DAY**, of Colchester, Jan. 11, 1759	LR6	506
Jehiel, s. Jehiel & Sarah, b. Apr. 13, 1760	LR6	506
Jerusha, m. Oliver **DICKINSON**, June 22, 1823, by Rev. Simeon Dickinson, at the house of Stephen Fuller	3	40-41
Jethrow, s. Shubael & Sarah, b. Dec. 2, 1760	LR5	562
John, s. John & Mahittabell, b. Nov. 10, 1697	LR1	5
John, m. Mary **ROWLE**, alias Mary **CORNWELL**, May 10, 1721	LR1	572
John, s. John & Mary, b. Jan. 29, 1729	LR1	572
John, s. Shubael & Sarah, b. Sept. 23, 1762	LR5	562

	Vol.	Page
FULLER, FFULLER, (cont.)		
Jonathan, s. Shuball & Hannah, b. Sept. 10, 1724; d. Jan. 19, 1726	LR1	577
Jonathan, s. Thomas & Elizabeth, b. Jan. 12, 1725	LR2	575
Jonathan, s. Shubael & Sarah, b. Aug. 20, 1757	LR5	562
Joseph, s. John & Mahittabell, b. Mar. 1, 1699	LR1	5
Julius A., of Columbia, Conn., m. Emily F. **BUELL**, of East Haddam, Sept. 26, 1852, by Rev. Warren Emmerson	3	237
Lydia, d. Shuball & Hannah, b. Sept. 1, 1709	LR1	578
Lydia, m. Orrellana **MACK**, b. of East Haddam, Mar. 11, 1821, by Rev. Isaac Parsons	3	3
Marcy, d. Samuell & Marcy, b. Mar. 9, 1734/5	LR2	1125
Martha, d. Thomas, Jr. & Martha, b. July 27, 1746	LR2	1113
Martha, w. of Thomas, Jr., d. Mar. 13, 1760	LR2	1113
Martha, m. Noadiah **GATES**, Feb. 23, 1764	LR7	415
Mary, d. Timothy & Sarah, b. Dec. 19, 1697	LR1	4
Mary, d. John & Mary, b. Feb. 19, 1721/2	LR1	572
Mary, d. Timothy & Mary, b. Mar. 18, 1731	LR2	a
Mary, d. Matthias & Mary, b. Oct. 29, 1739	LR2	1099
Mary, w. of Matthias, d. Nov. 15, 1739	LR2	1099
Mary, d. Matthias & Mary, d. Feb. 2, 1739/40	LR2	1099
Mary, d. Shubael, Jr. & Hannah, b. Oct. 24, 1748	LR3	8
Mary, d. Timothy & Thankfull, b. Sept. 12, 1750	LR4	465
Mary, m. Jedediah **SPENCER**, Jan. 25, 1753	LR4	465
Mary, d. Thomas, Jr. & Mary, b. Sept. 27, 1761	LR6	508
Mary, d. Dea. Thomas & Hannah, b. Nov. 6, 1770	2	20
Mary, m. John **HOWARD**, b. of East Haddam, Oct. 26, 1772	2	60
Mary, m. David B. **SPENCER**, June 24, 1783	2	38
Mary, m. Stephen **CONE**, b. of East Haddam, Feb. 6, 1812	2	321
Matilda, b. Colchester, res. East Haddam, d. Jan. 13, 1848, ae 51	4	7-8
Matthew, s. Benjamin & Content, b. Mar. 6, 1723	LR2	1122
Matthias, s. Timothy & Sarah, b. Mar. 24, 1700	LR1	4
Matthias, m. Mary **CONE**, June 16, 1722	LR2	1099
Matthias, s. Matthias & Mary, b. Jan. 15, 1724/5	LR2	1099
Matthias, m. Jemima **HUNGERFORD**, alias **RICHARDSON**, Apr. 16, 1741	LR2	1099
Matthias, Jr., m. Mary **GRISWOLD**, June 27, 1764	LR7	417
Matthias, s. Matthias & Mary, b. Sept. 29, 1773	LR7	417
Mahittabell, d. John & Mahittabell, b. Apr. 16, 1706	LR1	5
Mehetable, d. John & Mary, b. Jan. 3, 1731/2	LR1	572
Mehitable, m. Israel **CHAMPION**, Apr. 29, 1756	LR5	561
Nathan, s. Thomas & Elizabeth, b. Apr. 20, 1719	LR1	575
Noadiah, s. Matthias & Mary, b. Sept. 3, 1729	LR2	1099
Ollive Green, d. Thomas, Jr. & Mary, b. Apr. 13, 1763	LR6	508
Ollive Green, d. Thomas, Jr. & Mary, d. Feb. 7, 1764	LR6	508
Ollive Green, d. Thomas, Jr. & Mary, b. Dec. 17, 1764	LR6	508
Oliver, s. Thomas, Jr. & Martha, b. Sept. 30, 1742	LR2	1113

	Vol.	Page
FULLER, FFULLER, (cont.)		
Patience, d. Benjamin & Content. b. Jan. 15, 1722/3	LR2	1122
Philemon, s. Timothy & Thankfull, b. Apr. 22, 1755	LR4	465
Philemon, s. Timothy & Thankfull, d. Nov. 21, [1775], at Roxbury, in the 21st y. of his age. Enlisted in Gen. Spencer's Co., 1775, in the reign of George 3rd	2	99
Philo, m. Hannah **FULLER**, b. of East Haddam, Nov. 9, 1829, by Rev. Isaac Parsons	3	103
Prudence, d. Shubael & Sarah, b. Mar. 13, 1759	LR5	562
Rachel, d. Shuball & Hannah, b. Feb. 24, 1727	LR1	577
Rebeckah, d. Thomas & Elizabeth, b. Sept. 2, 1752	LR4	472
Rebeckah, d. Thomas & Elizabeth, d. Oct. 15, 1752	LR4	472
Rebeckah, d. William & Rebeckah, b. Jan. 2, 1768	LR6	506
Richardson, of East Haddam, m. Jerusha B. **CARRIER**, of Colchester, Sept. 14, 1835, by W[illia]m Marsh, J. P.	3	140-1
Ruth, d. Thomas & Elizabeth, b. Nov. 21, 1750	LR4	472
Samuell, s. Timothy & Sarah, b. Sept. 1, 1711	LR2	a
Samuel, m. Marcy **PRICE**, Apr. 19, 1733/4	LR2	1125
Samuel, s. Samuell & Marcy, b. Oct. 16, 1733/4	LR2	1125
Samuel, s. Thomas, 4th, & Hannah, b. Oct. 10, 1751	LR4	472
Samuel H., ae 25, b. in East Haddam, res. East Haddam, m. Mary E. **CONE**, ae 23, b. in East Haddam, res. East Haddam, Aug. 14, 1856, at Hadlyme, by Rev. E. B. Hillard. Int. pub. Aug. 13, 1856	4	92
Sarah, d. Timothy & Sarah, b. Aug. 7, 1702	LR1	4
Sarah, d. Samuell & Marcy, b. Sept. 28, 1736	LR2	1125
Sarah, d. John & Mary, b. June 14, 1737	LR1	572
Sarah, m. John **PARKER**, b. of East Haddam, Nov. 21, 1760	2	237
Sarah, d. Jehiel & Sarah, b. Mar. 9, 1762	LR6	506
Sarah, m. Timothy **CHAPMAN**, b. of East Haddam, Jan. 26, 1764	LR7	414
Sarah, m. Timothy **CHAPMAN**, b. of East Haddam, Jan. 26, 1764	2	20
Sarah, m. Amasa **ACKLEY**, Nov. 11, 1766	LR7	413
Sarah, m. Isaac **TAYLOR**, b. of East Haddam, Nov. 8, 1781	2	202
Sarah D., of East Haddam, m. Loren **GATES**, of Unadilla, N. Y., Jan. 30, 1821, by Rev. Isaac Parsons	2	329
Sarah Whitmore, d. [Gurdon & Harriet], b. Sept. 16, 1834	3	139
Shuball, m. Hannah **CROCKER**, Dec. 7, 1708	LR1	578
Shubale, s. Shuball & Hannah, b. Jan. 6, 1720/21	LR1	578
Shubael, Jr., m. Hannah **CONE**, June 28, 1744	LR3	8
Shubael, d. May 29, 1748	LR3	509
Shubael, m. Sarah **CHAPMAN**, June 12, 1755	LR5	562
Shubael, s. Shubael & Sarah, b. Feb. 14, 1766	LR5	562
Statira, d. Oct. 5, 1848, ae 72	4	17-18
Stephen, s. William & Rebeckah, b. Mar. 29, 1764	LR6	506
Stephen, s. Truman & Matilda, b. Oct. 7, 1821	3	112-3
Stephen, m. Laura Ann **CHAPMAN**, Feb. 8, 1843, by Isaac		

	Vol.	Page
FULLER, FFULLER, (cont.)		
Parsons, V. D. M.	3	193
Susannah, m. Lemuel **WILLEY**, b. of East Haddam, Jan. 3, 1764	LR7	7
Susannah, of East Haddam, m. Alvan **BROOKS**, of Exeter, N. Y., Feb. 7, 1832, by Rev. Isaac Parsons	3	121
Sybel, d. Thomas, Jr. & Martha, b. July 3, 1737	LR2	1113
Sibble, d. Thomas, Jr. & Martha, d. Aug. 30, 1742	LR2	1113
Sibble, d. Thomas, Jr. & Martha, b. Jan. 29, 1743/4	LR2	1113
Sibble, d. Ephraim & Sarah, b. June 17, 1748	LR4	471
Sible, m. Rowland **PARSEVEL**, b. of East Haddam, June 30, 1763	LR7	4
Tamer, d. Shubael & Sarah, b. June 18, 1756	LR5	562
Thaddeus, see under Chaddeus		
Thankfull, d. Shuball & Hannah, b. July 10, 1713	LR1	578
Thankful, wid. of Timothy, d. Aug. 8, 1794	2	61
Theodore, ae 34, of East Haddam, m. Sarah W. **ROGERS**, ae 26, of East Haddam, Oct. 12, 1856, by Rev. Nelson Goodrich. Int. pub. Oct. 11, 1856	4	103-4
Thomas, s. Thomas & Elizabeth, b. Apr. 5, 1717	LR1	575
Thomas, s. Timothy & Mary, b. June 24, 1726	LR2	a
Thomas, Jr., m. Martha **ROWLEY**, Sept. 10, 1734	LR2	1113
Thomas, 4th, m. Hannah **DIMOCK**, Nov. 15, 1748	LR4	472
Thomas, Jr., m. Mary **HOSMER**, b. of East Haddam, Nov. 6, 1760	LR6	508
Thomas, s. Jehiel & Sarah, b. Nov. 14, 1771	2	74
Thomas, m. Statira **CHAPMAN**, Aug. 26, 1793	2	303
Thomas, Capt., d. Apr. 30, 1836	3	46
Timothy, s. Timothy & Sarah, b. Aug. 29, 1695	LR1	4
Timothy, s. Timothy & Mary, b. May 30, 1722	LR2	a
Timothy, s. Samuell & Marcy, b. Feb. 10, 1737/8	LR2	1125
Timothy, m. Thankfull **GRAY**, Nov. 29, 1749	LR4	465
Timothy, s. Timothy & Thankfull, b. July 25, 1752	LR4	465
Timothy, s. Timothy & Thankfull, d. Oct. 18, [1775], at Roxbury, in the 24th y. of his age. Enlisted in Gen. Spencer's Co. 1775, in the 15th reign of George 3rd	2	99
Truman, Jr., m. Lucy **HARDING**, b. of East Haddam, June 20, 1830, by Isaac Chester, J. P.	3	107
Warren, of Salem, m. Electa **WILLIAMS**, of East Haddam, Feb. 26, 1832, by Rev. Alven Ackley	3	121
William, s. John & Mary, b. June 16, 1729 (sic)	LR1	572
William, m. Rebeckah **SPENCER**, b. of East Haddam, Mar. 8, 1757	LR6	506
William, d. Dec. 25, 1768	LR6	506
William L., s. [Truman & Matilda], b. June 5, 1823	3	112-3
William L., m. Emeline **ARNOLD**, Sept. 17, 1845, by Nathaniel Miner, Millington	3	203
William Ward, s. William & Rebeckah, b. Feb. 23, 1760	LR6	506

	Vol.	Page
FULLER, FFULLER, (cont.)		
Zipporah, d. Samuel & Mercy, b. Dec. 2, 1741	LR2	1097
Zipporah, m. Daniel **GATES**, b. of East Haddam, Aug. 12, 1762	LR6	503
Zip[p]orah, m. Daniel **GATES**, 3rd, b. of East Haddam, Aug. 12, 1762	2	168
Zurbiah, d. Shuball & Hannah, b. Mar. 29, 1716	LR1	578
-----, d. Jabez H., farmer, ae 55, & Lucy A., ae 29, b. Nov. 28, 1849	4	23-4
------, d. Stephen, shoemaker, b. Feb. 28, 1851	4	33-4
FURGERSON, Lydia A., of East Haddam, m. George **DeWOLF**, of Lyme, Aug. 21, 1842, by Rev. William A. Cone	3	191
GALLUP, Lucy, m. Nathaniel **GATES**, b. of East Haddam, Feb. 3, 1788	2	152
Sarah Barber, m. Nathan **GRIFFIN**, Nov. 17, 1813	3	155
GARDNER, A. T., m. Henry F. **GARDNER**, farmer, of East Haddam, Mar. [ ], 1851, by Rev. Alpheas Geer	4	37-8
Angeline A., ae 18, of East Haddam, m. Lauriston D. **MACK**, ae 22, of East Haddam, Oct. 3, 1856, at Hadlyme, by Rev. E. B. Hillard. Int. pub. Oct. 2, 1856, in East Haddam	4	102-3
Catharine A., m. Lorin **COWDREY**, b. of East Haddam, Nov. 30, 1854, by Rev. Isaac Parsons	3	241
Catharine A., ae 19, of E. Haddam, m. Loren **COWDREY**, manufacturer, ae 25, b. in Plainfield, N. Y., res. E. Haddam, Nov. 30, 1854, by Rev. Isaac Parsons	4	51-2
Elizabeth C., of East Haddam, m. Jonathan **OLMSTED**, of Colchester, Apr. 10, 1838, by Rev. Isaac Parsons	3	164-5
Emeline M., m. Henry A. **PALMER**, Dec. 15, 1841, by Charles William Bradley	3	188
Emeline M., m. Henry A. **PALMER**, Dec. 15, 1841	3	213
Henry F., m. Ann T. **WRIGHT**, b. of East Haddam, Mar. 11, 1851, by Rev. Alpheas Geer	3	231
Henry F., farmer, m. A. T. **GARDNER***, Mar. [ ], 1851, by Rev. Alpheas Geer (***WRIGHT?**)	4	37-8
Polly, m. Elijah **HUNGERFORD**, Jr., b. of East Haddam, Oct. 30, 1798	2	261
GATES, Aaron, s. Joseph & Hannah, b. Oct. 20, 1733	LR1	573
Aaron, s. Joseph & Hannah, d. Aug. 14, 1740	LR2	1095
Aaron, s. Bezaleel & Mary, b. Aug. 31, 1753	LR4	475
Abiga[i]ll, d. Daniell, b. Mar. 18, 1714	LR1	10
Abigail, d. Joseph, Jr. & Abigail, b. Apr. 22, 1749	LR3	14
Abigail, d. Joseph, Jr. & Abigail, d. Oct. 9, 1758	LR3	14
Abigail, d. Joseph, Jr. & Abigail, b. Sept. 9, 1760	LR3	14
Abigail, Mrs., m. Capt. Ebenezer **HOLMES**, b. of East Haddam, Sept. 4, 1789	2	235
Abigail, d. Eph[rai]m & Susannah, b. Feb. 7, 1791	2	100
Achsah, d. Ep[hrai]]m & Susannah, b. June 5, 1784	2	100

	Vol.	Page
GATES, (cont.)		
Alenson, s. Phinehas & Anne, b. Oct. 25, 1788	2	94
Alanson, m. Betsey **CHAPMAN**, b. of East Haddam, Sept. 17, 1821, by Rev. Isaac Parsons	3	12
Alanson, d. Sept. 7, 1831, ae 43	3	12
Alfred, s. Noadiah, 2d, & Anne, b. Apr. 24, 1796	2	249
Alfred, s. Timothy, 3rd, & Susannah, b. Feb. 7, 1802	2	235
Alfred, m. Mary M. **SWAN**, Mar. 29, 1832, by Rev. Isaac Parsons	3	122
Alvah, s. Ep[hrai]m & Susannah, b. Nov. 21, 1795	2	100
Ann, d. Joseph & Hannah, b. Oct. 20, 1733	LR1	573
Ann, d. Joseph & Hannah, d. Aug. 18, 1740	LR2	1095
Anna, d. Daniel, Jr. & Anna, b. May 9, 1775	2	10
Anna, d. Daniel, Jr. & Anna, d. Feb. 2, 1778	2	11
Anna, d. Oliver & Mary, b. July 19, 1791	2	156
Anne, d. Joseph, Jr. & Abigail, b. Mar. 21, 1751	LR3	14
Anne, m. Eliphalet **HOLMES**, b. of East Haddam, Jan. 8, 1772	2	76
Anne, d. Phineas & Anne, b. May 13, 1786	2	94
Anne, d. Noadiah, 2d, & Anne, b. Dec. 20, 1793	2	249
Augustus E., ae 19, of East Haddam, m. Jacob R. **GREENFIELD**, painter, ae 25, b. in Middletown, res. East Haddam, July 2, 1849, by Iaac Parsons	4	9-10
Azel, s. Judah & Abigail, b. Nov. 17, 1765	LR3	506
Bazaliell, s. Joseph & Hannah, b. Oct. 14, 1726	LR1	573
Bazaleel, m. Mary **BRAINERD**, Feb. 26, 1749/50	LR4	475
Bezeleel, s. Bezaleel & Mary, b. Oct. 2, 1751	LR4	475
Bezaleel, Jr., d. Jan. 24, 1789	2	211
Benjamin Lewis, s. Samuel & Mary, b. Nov. 28, 1824	3	9
Beri, s. Noadiah B. & Mary, b. Nov. 23, 1793	2	285
Betsey, d. Eph[rai]m & Susannah, b. Aug. 15, 1793	2	100
Betsey, m. Uri **GATES**, b. of East Haddam, Apr. 19, 1813, by Rev. Elijah Parsons	3	94
Bezaleel, see under Bazaleel		
Brainard, s. Noadiah B. & Mary, b. Jan. 24, 1796	2	285
C. F., of Middletown, m. Mary E. **HUTCHINS**, of East Haddam, May 7, 1851, by Rev. Isaac Parsons	3	231
Caleb, s. Thomas & Dorothy, b. Mar. 22, 1738	LR2	c
Caleb, s. Joshua & Lydia, b. Apr. 1, 1746	LR2	1110
Caleb, s. Joshua & Lydia, d. Feb. 23, 1748/9	LR2	1110
Caleb, s. Joshua & Lidia, b. Jan. 29, 1749/50	LR4	474
Caleb, s. Thomas, Jr. & Sarah, b. June 1, 1765	LR7	3
Celeb, s. Thomas & Sarah, d. Dec. 19, 1765	2	13
Caleb, of East Haddam, m. Esther **FOOT**, of Colchester, Oct. 17, 1775	2	92
Caleb, s. Caleb & Esther, b. July 16, 1776	2	92
Caleb F., of Middletown, m. Mary E. **GATES**, May [ ], 1851, by Rev. Isaac Parsons	4	37-8
Calvin, s. Phineas & Anne, b. Jan. 22, 1784	2	94

	Vol.	Page
GATES, (cont.)		
Caroline A., m. Edward H. **PURPLE**, b. of East Haddam, Sept. 26, 1832, by Nathaniel Miner	3	127
Charles William Bradley, s. Alfred & Mary M., b. Sept. 9, 1840	3	68
Charles William Bradley, s. Alfred & Mary M., d. July 3, 1855, ae 14 y. 9 m. 24 d.	3	68
Charles Williams Bradly, b. in East Haddam, res. East Haddam, single, d. July 3, 1855, ae 14 y. 9 m. 21 d.	4	58
Charlotte Gleason, d. Alfred & Mary M., b. May 11, 1846	3	68
Chaunc[e]y, s. Noadiah & Martha, b. Jan. 18, 1786	2	80
Christopher C., m. Julia Jennings **SMITH**, b. of East Haddam, Oct. 15, 1818	2	313
Christopher Columbus, s. Timothy, 3rd, & Susannah, b. July 29, 1793	2	235
Claracia, d. Noadiah & Martha, b. Sept. 9, 1783	2	80
Daniell, s. Thomas, b. May 26, 1695	LR1	5
Daniel, s. Daniel, b. Feb. 5, 1706/7	LR1	6
Daniel, m. Sarah **CONE**, June 13, 1723	LR2	1128
Daniell, s. Daniell & Sarah, b. Mar. 9, 1727	LR2	1128
Daniel, s. Daniel & Lydia, b. Sept. 24, 1738	LR2	1125
Daniel, s. Joshua & Lydia, b. Nov. 3, 1739	LR2	1110
Daniell, s. Daniell & Sarah, d. Aug. 28, 1740	LR2	1128
Daniell, Capt., d. June 24, 1752	LR2	1128
Daniel, s. Paul & Mehetable, b. May 1, 1761	LR6	505
Daniel, d. Nov. 24, 1761	LR1	582
Daniel, m. Zipporah **FULLER**, b. of East Haddam, Aug. 12, 1762	LR6	503
Daniel, 3rd, m. Zip[p]orah **FULLER**, b. of East Haddam, Aug. 12, 1762	2	168
Daniel, s. Daniel, 3rd, & Zip[p]orah, b. Sept. 4, 1768	2	168
Daniel, Jr., of East Haddam, m. Anna **WHITE**, of Colchester, Aug. 27, 1770	2	10
Daniel, s. Daniel, 3rd, & Zip[p]orah, d. Oct. 28, 1774	2	169
Daniel, Dea., of Millington Soc., d. Oct. 5, 1775	2	109
Daniel, Jr., d. Jan. 7, 1777	2	11
Daniel, s. Daniel, Jr. & Anna, b. Mar. 13, 1777	2	10
Daniel, d. July 13, 1788	2	169
Daniel, s. Jeremiah & Mary, b. Dec. 7, 1789	2	154
Darius, m. Anne **BRAINARD**, Oct. 7, 1799	2	210
Darius, s. Jonah & Esther, b. Mar. 16, 1804	2	223
David, s. Daniell & Rebeckah, b. June 29, 1709	LR1	8
David, m. Hannah **ACKL[E]Y**, alias Hannah **HUNGERFORD**, Sept. 17, 1731	LR2	1111
David, s. Joseph & Hannah, b. Apr. 18, 1738	LR1	573
David, s. Joseph & Hannah, d. Aug. 12, 1740	LR2	1095
David, s. Levi & Lydiah, b. Apr. 6, 1761	LR6	509
Dorothy, d. Jeremiah & Mary, b. May 5, 1729	LR2	c
Dorothy, d. Thomas & Dorothy, b. Jan. 17, 1733	LR2	c

	Vol.	Page
GATES, (cont.)		
Dorothy, d. Thomas & Dorothy, b. Sept. 3, 1744	LR2	c
Dorothy, d. James & Deborah, b. Mar. 18, 1745	LR3	7
Dorothy, m. Eliakim **SPENCER**, b. of East Haddam, Apr. 16, 1761	LR6	503
Dorothy, m. James **PARSEVEL**, June 19, 1766	LR7	413
Dorothy, d. Timothy & Hannah, b. Jan. 9, 1767	LR6	504
Dorothy, wid., of Capt. Thomas, d. June 27, 1774, in the 71st y. of her age	2	13
Dorothy, m. Josiah **GRIFFIN**, b. of East Haddam,Feb. 22, 1791	2	227
Dorothy, d. Thomas, Jr. & Rachel, b. Mar. 3, 1791	2	152
Dorothy Anna, d. Jonah & Esther, b. Nov. 14, 1812	2	223
Dudley, s. Joseph, b. July 10, 1708	LR1	8
Edward Langdon, s. Alfred & Mary M., b. July 11, 1836	3	68
Edward* Timothy, s. Chris[tophe]r C. & Julia Jennings, b. Oct. 8, 1819 (*First written "George")	2	313
Eli, s. Joseph, 3rd, & Lucy, b. Dec. 2, 1788	2	92
Eliphaz, s. Joseph, 2d, & Jane, b. Oct. 9, 1775	2	108
Elephaz, s. Joseph, 2d, & Jane, d. Apr. 10, 1776	2	109
Eliphas, s. Joseph, 2d, & Jane, b. Apr. 18, 1788	2	108
Eliza A., of East Haddam, m. Jacob R. **GREENFIELD**, of Middletown, July 1, 1849, by Rev. Isaac Parsons	3	218
Eliza A., b. in East Haddam, m. Jacob R. **GREENFIELD**, painter, b. in Middletown, res. East Haddam, July 1, 1849, by Isaac Parsons	4	9-10
Elizabeth, d. Joseph, b. May 25, 1694	LR1	5
Elizabeth, d. Joseph & Hannah, b. Aug. 12, 1724	LR1	573
Elizabeth, d. David & Hannah, b. Jan. 15, 1733/4	LR2	1111
Elizabeth, m. Jonah **CONE**, June 20, 1745	LR3	5
Elizabeth, w. of Joseph, d. Nov. 17, 1759, in the 89th y. of her age	LR6	510
Elisabeth, m. Daniel **FOX**, Nov. 12, 1761	2	72
Elizabeth, Mrs., of East Haddam, m. Matthew **SMITH**, of Middlefield, Mass., July 30, 1826, by Rev. Isaac Parsons	3	86
Elizabeth L., dressmaker, ae 31, b. in East Haddam, res. Hartford, m. Charles D. **BAILEY**, merchant, ae 35, b. in Middletown, res. Hartford, Nov. 19, 1854, by Rev. Nath[anie]l Miner	4	51-2
Elizabeth L., ae 29, of East Haddam, m. Daniel C. **LORD**, ae 40, b. at Colchester, res. East Haddam, Dec. 2, 1856, at Hartford, by Rev. J. Hawes, of Hartford. Int. pub. Dec. 1, 1856	4	114
Elizabeth Lucy, d. Oren & Elizabeth, b. Dec. 26, 1822	2	283
Elizabeth S., m. Robert C. **CHAPMAN**, Apr. 28, 1844, by Rev. Isaac Parsons	3	199
Elizabeth S., m. Charles D. **BAILEY**, b. of Hartford, Nov. 19, 1854, by Rev. Nathaniel Miner	3	241

	Vol.	Page
GATES, (cont.)		
Ellen G., m. Asa M. **HARRIS**, b. of East Haddam, Mar. 31, 1857, at Moodus, by Rev. Amos D. Watrous	4	120
Ellen L., of East Haddam, m. George **LEE**, of Manchester, June 18, 1849, by Rev. Stephen A. Loper, of Hadlyme	3	218
Ellen L., ae 30, b. in East Haddam, Res. East Hartford, m. George **LEE**, merchant, ae 31, b. in Rome, Ohio, res. East Hartford, June 18, 1849, by Stephen A. Loper	4	9-10
Emma Maria, d. Christo[phe]r C. & Julia Jennings, b. July 4, 1836	2	313
Epaphroditus, s. Joseph, 3rd, & Lucy, b. Aug. 7, 1775	2	92
Epaphroditus, s. Joseph, 3rd, & Lucy, d. July 5, 1796	2	93
Epaphroditus G., m. Rachel S. **CHADWICK**, Mar. 25, 1838, by Rev. Nathaniel Miner, of Millington	3	164-5
Epaphroditus G., m. Rachel S. **CHADWICK**, Mar. 25, 1838	3	180-1
Epaphroditus Goold, s. Oren & Elizabeth, b. June 13, 1806	2	283
Ephraim, s. Daniell & Rebecka, b. Aug. 18, 1724	LR1	582
Ephraim, s. Judah & Lydiah, b. Dec. 13, 1749	LR3	506
Ephraim, m. Susannah **SPENCER**, b. of East Haddam, Feb. 19, 1775	2	100
Ephraim, s. Ephraim & Susannah, b. Apr. 17, 1780	2	100
Esther, d. Thomas, b. Feb. 24, 1701	LR1	5
Easter, d. Samuell, b. Feb. 26, 1718/19	LR1	10
Easter, d. Thomas, d. Dec. 1, 1720	LR1	10
Esther, m. Eli **BIGELOW**, May 19, 1825, by Rev. William Jarvis	3	76-7
Easter, d. Thomas & Dorothy, b. July 27, 1727	LR2	c
Esther, m. Samuel **GATES**, Apr. 19, 1739	LR2	1108
Esther, d. Samuel & Esther, b. Jan. 19, 1739/40	LR2	1108
Esther, d. Samuel & Esther, d. Apr. 23, 1739/40 (sic)	LR2	1108
Esther, s. Daniel **BRAINERD**, Jr., Aug. 15, 1751	LR4	469
Esther, w. Samuel, d. Aug. 26, 1757	LR2	1108
Esther, d. Bezaleel & Mary, b. Mar. 17, 1764	LR4	475
Esther, d. Timothy & Hannah, b. Sept. 25, 1770	LR6	504
Esther, d. Caleb & Esther, b. Mar. 1, 1791	2	92
Esther, d. Jonah & Esther, b. Sept. 22, 1809	2	223
Esther, d. Timothy, the elder, d. Mar. 8, 1826, in the 56th y. of her age	2	236
Esther, m. George R. **FOWLER**, Nov. 2, 1828, by Rev. Isaac Parsons	3	100
Eunice, d. Joshua & Lidia, b. Aug. 9, 1757	LR4	474
Fidelia, d. Gideon & Mehetable, b. July 25, 1789	2	142
Francis Edwin, of Lyme, m. Sarah Maria **DAY**, of East Haddam, Oct. 17, 1854, by Rev. Isaac Parsons	3	241
Francis Edwin, farmer, ae 27, of Lyme, m. Sarah Maria **DAY**, ae 22, of E. Haddam, Oct. 17, 1854, by Rev. Isaac Parsons	4	51-2
Frederick W., s. Alfred & Mary M., d. Apr. 7, 1860, ae 25 y.		

	Vol.	Page
GATES, (cont.)		
7 m. 2 d.	3	68
Frederick William, s. Alfred & Mary M., b. Sept. 3, 1834	3	68
George, m. Sarah **OMSTED**, Dec. 3, 1730	LR2	1126
George, s. George & Sarah, b. Oct. 18, 1737	LR2	1126
George, d. Dec. 29, 1756	LR2	1126
George, m. Sarah Ann **SWAN**, b. of East Haddam, Dec. 7, 1825, by Rev. Herman L. Vaill	3	80-1
George Dudley, s. Daniel, 3rd, & Zip[p]orah, b. Mar. 25, 1773	2	168
George Gleason, s. Christ[ophe]r C. & Julia Jennings, b. Dec. 25, 1825	2	313
Georgianna, d. George C., shoe manufacturer, ae 24, & Charlotte R., ae 19, b. Apr. 29, 1849	4	13-14
Gideon, s. Thomas & Dorothy, b. Sept. 13, 1747	LR3	508
Gideon, s. Thomas, Jr. & Sarah, b. Feb. 12, 1763	LR7	3
Gideon, s. Paul & Mehetabel, b. Sept. 17, 1778	2	8
Gideon, of East Haddam, m. Mehetibel **BROWN**, of Sandisfield, Oct. 11, 1787	2	142
Gideon, d. Sept. 12, 1791, in the 29th y. of his age	2	143
Girch, s. Levi & Lydiah, b. Oct. 10, 1763	LR6	509
Hannah, d. Thomas, b. Jan. 1, 1699	LR1	5
Hannah, d. Samuell & Easter, b. Feb. 4, 1713	LR1	10
Han[n]ah, d. Thomas, d. Oct. [ ], 1713	LR1	10
Hannah, d. Joseph & Hannah, b. Nov. 16, 1719	LR1	573
Hannah, d. Jeremiah & Mary, b. Oct. 23, 1723	LR2	c
Hannah, m. Thomas **SMITH**, Feb. 9, 1737/8	LR2	1107
Hannah, m. Daniel **BRAINERD**, Jr., July 7, 1743	LR2	1098
Hannah, w. of Joseph, d. Mar. 20, 1744	LR2	1095
Hannah, d. Daniel & Lydia, b. Sept. 9, 1744	LR2	1125
Hannah, m. Ebenezer **SPENCER**, Mar. 6, 1745/6	LR3	8
Hannah, d. Bazaleel & Mary, b. May 24, 1750	LR4	475
Hannah, d. Timothy & Hannah, b. Mar. 29, 1762	LR6	504
Hannah, d. Joseph, 2d, & Jane, b. Mar. 6, 1786	LR2	108
Hannah, d. Noadiah B. & Mary, b. Jan. 20, 1788	LR2	285
Hannah, d. Ep[hrai]m & Susannah, b. Oct. 11, 1788	2	100
Hannah, of East Haddam, m. Joseph **WHITE**, of Chatham, Mar. 29, 1791	2	84
Hannah, w. of Timothy, d. Aug. 13, 1810, in the 72nd y. of her age	2	236
Harriet, d. Jonah & Esther, b. Jan. 31, 1800	2	223
Henry, s. Bezaleel & Mary, b. Sept. 30, 1757	LR4	475
Henry Alfred, s. Alfred & Mary M., b. May 1, 1833	3	68
Henry Alfred, s. Alfred & Mary M., d. July 17, 1858, at the Retreat for the Insane, at Hartford, ae 25 y. 2 m. 16 d.	3	68
Hiram, s. Noadiah, 2d, & Anne, b. Feb. 14, 1798	2	249
Hiram, s. Noadiah, Jr. & Anna, d. Oct. 14, 1798	2	250
Hiram Stepney, s. Noadiah, 2d, & Anne, b. Oct. 4, 1799	2	249

	Vol.	Page
GATES, (cont.)		
Horace Spencer, s. Oren & Elizabeth, b. Nov. 16, 1814	2	283
Hubert Burnham, s. Alfred & Mary M., b. Apr. 7, 1838	3	68
Huldah, w. of Obadiah, d. Mar. 4, 1770	LR7	3
Ira, s. Noadiah & Martha, b. Oct. 15, 1776	2	80
James, s. Samuell & Easter, b. Aug. 29, 1721	LR1	572
James, m. Deborah **OLMSTEAD**, Nov. 6, 1743	LR3	7
James, s. James & Deborah, b. July 9, 1760	LR3	7
James, s. Noadiah & Martha, b. Aug. 3, 1781	2	80
James Perceval, s. Christ[ophe]r C. & Julia Jennings, b. Dec. 8, 1827	2	313
James S., s. James S. & Adaline, b. May 11, 1851	4	31-2
James Stranahan, s. Samuel & Mary, b. Mar. 9, 1822	3	9
Jedidah, d. Daniel & Zipporah, b. July 27, 1763	LR6	503
Jedidah, d. Daniel & Zip[p]orah, b. July 27, 1763	2	168
Jehiel, s. Judah & Abigail, b. Aug. 25, 1758	LR3	506
Jennet, d. Jonah & Esther, b. Oct. 3, 1794	2	223
Jeremiah, s. Thomas, b. Mar. 17, 1697	LR1	c
Jeremiah, m. Mary **EM[M]ONS**, Dec. 7, 1721	LR2	c
Jeremiah, s. Jeremiah & Mary, b. Mar. 17, 1732	LR2	c
Jeremiah, s. Jeremiah & Mary, d. Sept. 11, 1754, in the 23rd y. of his age	LR2	c
Jeremiah, s. Joshua & Lidia, b. Oct. 24, 1754	LR4	474
Jeremiah, s. Joshua & Lidia, b. Nov. 28, 1759	LR4	474
Jeremiah, Dea., d. Nov. 1, 1761	2	13
Jeremiah, s. Daniel, Jr. & Anna, b. Jan. 21, 1774	2	10
Jeremiah, m. Mary **CHAPEL**, b. of East Haddam,Nov. 24, 1785	2	154
Jeremiah, s. Jeremiah & Mary, b. July 18, 1791	2	154
Jerusha Jane, m. Ebenezer **SNOW**, 2d, Mar. 2, 1842, by Isaac Parsons, D. V. M.	3	189
Jesse, s. Daniel & Lydia, b. Apr. 5, 1734	LR2	1125
Jesse, of East Haddam, m. Elizabeth **LORD**, of Lyme, Mar. 2, 1758	LR5	266
John, s. Joseph, b. Sept. 20, 1698	LR1	5
Jonah, s. Thomas, Jr. & Sarah, b. Mar. 24, 1758	LR7	3
Jonah, s. James & Deborah, b. Sept. 20, 1762	LR3	7
Jonah, s. Thomas & Sarah, d. Feb. 9, 1777, in the 21st y. of his age. A soldier in the Continental Army	2	13
Jonah, m. Esther **SMITH**, b. of East Haddam, Feb. 25, 1790	2	223
Jonah, s. Jonah & Esther, b. May 17, 1806	2	223
Jonathan, s. Joseph, b. Dec. 17, 1703	LR1	5
Jones P., m. Ellen G. **CARRIER**, June 6, 1847, by Rev. Isaac Parsons	3	210
Joseph, s. Joseph , b. Dec. 28, 1696	LR1	5
Jos[eph], s. Thomas, b. Nov. 17, 1705	LR1	6
Jos[eph], s. Daniell, b. Sept. 7, 1716	LR1	582
Joseph, m. Hannah **BRAINARD**, Jan, 8, 1718/19	LR1	573
Joseph, s. Joseph & Hannah, b. Mar. 28, 1722	LR1	573

	Vol.	Page
GATES, (cont.)		
Joseph, Jr., m. Abigail **FULLER**, Dec. 4, 1746	LR3	14
Joseph, s. Joseph, Jr. & Abigail, b. May 9, 1754	LR3	14
Joseph, 2d, of East Haddam, m. Jane **BROCKWAY**, of Lyme, Aug. 13, 1772	2	108
Joseph, 3rd, of East Haddam, m. Lucy **FOOT**, of Colchester, Nov. 3, 1774	2	92
Joseph, s. Joseph, 2d, & Jane, b. Nov. 9, 1778	2	108
Joseph, s. Judah & Olive, b. Sept. 1, 1806	2	281
Joseph, d. Sept. 3, 1832, ae [ ]	3	123
Joseph Brainerd, s. Christ[ophe]r C. & Julia Jennings, b. Oct. 16, 1823	2	313
Joshua, s. Thomas, b. Apr. 26, 1708	LR1	6
Joshua, m. Lydia **BRAINERD**, July 8, 1736	LR2	1110
Joshua, s. Joshua & Lydia, b. Oct. 19, 1737	LR2	1110
Joshua, d. Dec. 22, 1791, in the 84th y. of his age	2	93
Judah, m. Lydia **HURD**, Jan. 19, 1748/9	LR3	506
Judah, m. Abigail **HURD**, Dec. 12, 1753	LR3	506
Judah, s. Judah & Abigail, b. May 8, 1761	LR3	506
Judah, d. June 25, 1767	LR3	506
Judah, s. Ephraim & Susannah, b. Apr. 22, 1776	2	100
Judah, m. Olive **GATES**, b. of East Haddam, Oct. 10, 1803	2	281
Judah, m. Sarah **ACKLEY**, b. of East Haddam, Feb. 3, 1813	2	281
Julia, d. Gideon & Mehetable, b. June 8, 1791	2	142
Julia Ann, d. Judah & Olive, b. Apr. 27, 1809	2	281
Julia S., of East Haddam, m. Strong A. **KELSEY**, of Plymouth, Aug. 27, 1850, by Rev. Warren C. Fiske	3	226
Julia Sophia, d. Christo[phe]r C. & Julia Jennings, b. Aug. 28, 1821	2	313
Laura C., d. Jan. 23, 1849, ae 26	4	17-18
Levi, s. David & Hannah, b. Feb. 23, 1735/6	LR2	1111
Levi, of East Haddam, m. Lydia **CROCKER**, of Colchester, May 29, 1760	LR6	509
Levi Crosby, s. Oren & Elizabeth, b. Nov. 8, 1817	2	283
Lois, d. Daniell & Sarah, b. May 24, 1731	LR2	1128
Lois, d. Daniell & Sarah, d. July 30, 1740	LR2	1128
Lois, d. Paul & Mehitable, b. Mar. 1, 1759	LR6	505
Loren, of Unadilla, N. Y., m. Sarah D. **FULLER**, of East Haddam, Jan. 30, 1821, by Rev. Isaac Parsons	2	329
Loring, s. Phineas & Anne, b. Mar. 1, 1782	2	94
Lucanda, d. Joseph, 2d, & Jane, b. Dec. 22, 1773	2	108
Lucanda, d. Joseph, 2d, & Jane, d. Oct. 11, 1775	2	109
Lucanda, d. Joseph, 2d, & Jane, b. Feb. 9, 1777	2	108
Lucretia Hanford, d. N. Ben, fisherman, ae 29, & Julia M., ae 22, b. Dec. 31, 1848	4	13-14
Lucy, d. Joseph, 3rd, & Lucy, b. Nov. 23, 1777	2	92
Lucy, d. Nathaniel & Lucy, b. July 2, 1789	2	152
Lucy Foot, d. Judah & Olive, b. Oct. 30, 1804	2	281

	Vol.	Page
GATES, (cont.)		
Lydia, d. Joshua & Lydia, b. Sept. 8, 1743	LR2	1110
Lidia, d. Judah & Lydiah, b. Nov. 19, 1751	LR3	506
Lydia, w. of Judah, d. Mar. 12, 1752	LR3	506
Lydia, m. Matthew **CONE**, b. of East Haddam, Sept. 13, 1770	2	58
Lydia, d. Noadiah & Martha, b. July 28, 1774	2	80
Lydia, wid. of Dea. Daniel, d. Aug. 14, 1778	2	109
Lydia, d. Joseph, 2d, & Jane, b. Sept. 1, 1780	2	108
Lydia, d. Eph[rai]m & Susannah, b. Apr. 24, 1782	2	100
Lydia, d. Jeremiah & Mary, b. Apr. 25, 1788	2	154
Lydia, of East Haddam, m. Hazard **GOTT**, of Hebron, Feb. 7, 1826, by Isaac Parsons	3	84-85
Maria, d. Capt. Timothy & Susannah, b. Feb. 15, 1796	2	235
Martha, d. Noadiah & Martha, b. Nov. 4, 1765	LR7	415
Martha M., ae 35, b. in Glastonbury, res. East Haddam, m. Elisha C. **BINGHAM**, ae 41, b. in East Haddam, res. East Haddam, May 20, 1856, by Rev. Henry Forbush. Int. pub. May 14, 1856	4	88
Mary, m. Daniell **CONE**, Feb. 14, 1693	LR1	574
Mary, d. Thomas, b. Aug. 20, 1703	LR1	6
Mary, d. Daniell, b. Mar. 29, 1719	LR1	582
Mary, d. Samuell, b. July 29, 1719	LR1	10
Mary, d. Jeremiah & Mary, b. Apr. 23, 1725	LR2	c
Mary, m. Bazaliell **BRAINARD**, [ ], 1727	LR2	b
Mary, d. David & Hannah, b. Oct. 22, 1738	LR2	1111
Mary, m. Hezekiah **SCOVEL**, Dec. 24, 1740	LR5	564
Mary, d. George & Sarah, b. Oct. 1, 1744	LR2	1126
Mary, d. James & Deborah, b. Mar. 23, 1749	LR3	7
Mary, d. Bezaleel & Mary, b. Nov. 9, 1755	LR4	475
Mary, m. Elkanah **HIGGINS**, b. of East Haddam, May 12, 1765	LR8	2
Mary had s. Amos **WHITE**, b. Feb. 9, 1767; reputed father Amos **WHITE**	LR7	412
Mary, wid. of Dea. Jeremiah, d. Feb. 26, 1773	2	13
Mary, d. Phineas & Anne, b. Nov. 5, 1777	2	94
Mary, m. Oliver **GATES**, b. of East Haddam, May 4, 1786	2	156
Mary, d. Jeremiah & Mary, b. Apr. 3, 1795	2	154
Mary, d. Oliver & Mary, b. Apr. 23, 1797	2	156
Mary, d. Oliver & Mary, d. Apr. 25, 1797	2	157
Mary B., of East Haddam, m. James **RAY**, of Haddam, May 10, 1846, by Rev. Isaac Parsons	3	205
Mary E., of East Haddam, m. Griswold E. **TOOKER**, of Saybrook, Nov. 17, 1845, by Rev. Isaac Parsons	3	203
Mary E., m. Caleb F. **GATES**, of Middletown, May [ ], 1851, by Rev. Isaac Parsons	4	37-8
Nathan, of East Haddam, m. Abigail **SEXTON**, of Colchester, Oct. 11, 1764	LR7	6
Nathan Sexton, s. Joseph, 2d, & Jane, b. July 23, 1784	2	108

	Vol.	Page
GATES, (cont.)		
Nathaniel, s. Thomas, Jr. & Sarah, b. Apr. 1, 1755	LR7	3
Nathaniel, s. Paul & Mehitable, b. Sept. 22, 1763	LR6	505
Nathaniel, m. Lucy **GALLUP**, b. of East Haddam, Feb. 3, 1788	2	152
Nathaniel, s. Nathaniel & Lucy, b. Feb. 12, 1791	2	152
Nathaniel, d. Nov. 7, 1793, at Kingstown, at the Susquahannah	2	153
Nehemiah, s. George & Sarah, b. July 6, 1732	LR2	1126
Nehemiah, of East Haddam, m. Ann **HART**, of Farmingtown, May 11, 1756	LR5	559
Noadiah, s. George & Sarah, b. July 10, 1742	LR2	1126
Noadiah, s. Bezaleel & Mary, b. Dec. 18, 1761	LR4	475
Noadiah, m. Martha **FULLER**, Feb. 23, 1764	LR7	415
Noadiah, s. Noadiah & Martha, b. Aug. 20, 1768	LR7	415
Noadiah, s. Noadiah B. & Mary, b. July 3, 1791	2	285
Noadiah, 2d, m. Anne **EMMONS**, b. of East Haddam, Apr. 14, 1793	2	249
Noadiah B., ae 28, of East Haddam, m. Julia M. **WRIGHT**, ae 21, b. in Winsted, Ms., Aug. 13, 1848, by H. Forbush	4	1-2
Noadiah Brainard, formerly of East Haddam, now of Barkhempstead, m. Mary **BALCAM**, of Winchester, June 4, 1787	2	285
Obadiah, s. Thomas & Dorothy, b. Dec. 18, 1740	LR2	c
Obadiah, m. Huldah **COWDREY**, b. of East Haddam, Sept. 14, 1762	LR7	3
Obadiah, of East Haddam, m. Zilpha **BURT**, of Canterbury, Aug. 15, 1771	2	40
Obadiah, d. Aug. 22, 1781, in the 41st y. of his age	2	41
Olive, d. Joseph, 3rd, & Lucy, b. Sept. 21, 1779	2	92
Olive, m. Judah **GATES**, b. of East Haddam, Oct. 10, 1803	2	281
Olive, w. of Judah, d. May 22, 1811	2	282
Olive, d. Judah & Sarah, b. Dec. 8, 1813	2	281
Olliver, s. Paul & Mehitable, b. July 27, 1770	LR6	505
Oliver, m. Mary **GATES**, b. of East Haddam, May 4, 1786	2	156
Oliver, s. Noadiah B. & Mary, b. July 3, 1798	2	285
Oliver, s. Oliver & Mary, b. Oct. 23, 1802	2	156
Oliver, m. Content **SQUIRES**, b. of East Haddam, Jan. 1, 1823, by Rev. Isaac Parsons	3	34-35
Olmsted, s. Noadiah & Martha, b. May 30, 1779	2	80
Oren, s. Joseph, 3rd, & Lucy, b. Mar. 11, 1781	2	92
Oren, m. Elizabeth **SPENCER**, b. of East Haddam, May 2, 1804	2	283
Oren Spencer, s. [Epaphroditus G. & Rachel S.], b. Jan. 17, 1839	3	180-1
Paul, s. Daniel & Sarah, b. July 8, 1729	LR2	1128
Paul, of East Haddam, m. Mehitable **ROGERS**, of Colchester, Jan. 11, 1759	LR6	505
Penelope, d. Jonah & Esther, b. Aug. 8, 1792	2	223
Penelope, of East Haddam, m. Oren **CHAPMAN**, of Haddam,		

	Vol.	Page
GATES, (cont.)		
Nov. 12, 1812	2	313
Phinehas, s. George & Sarah, b. Mar. 31, 1747	LR2	1126
Phineas, m. Anne **TAYLER**, b. of East Haddam, Dec. 14, 1773	2	94
Phineas, s. Phineas & Anne, b. Aug. 22, 1775	2	94
Prudence Emeline, d. Timothy, 2d, & Susannah, b. Mar. 3, 1805	2	235
Prudence Emeline, of East Haddam, m. Edward **LANGDON**, of Plymouth, Sept. 20, 1825, by Rev. Isaac Parsons	3	79
Rebeckah, d. Daniell & Rebeckah, b. June 27, 1711	LR1	8
Rebeckah, d. Judah & Abigail, b. May 11, 1756	LR3	506
Reuben, s. Jeremiah & Mary, b. Dec. 11, 1786	2	154
Robert William, s. Oren & Elizabeth, b. Sept. 1, 1820	2	283
Russel[l], s. Caleb & Esther, b. Jan. 27, 1786	2	92
Ruth, d. Daniell & Rebecka, b. Aug. 10, 1721	LR1	582
Ruth, m. Isaac **ACKLY**, Apr. 25, 1745	LR3	19
Sabra A., m. James A. **BURNHAM**, b. of East Haddam, May 2, 1847, by Rev. Isaac Parsons	3	209
Samuell, s. Joseph, b. Mar. 21, 1712	LR1	8
Samuell, s. Samuell, b. Aug. 14, 1715	LR1	10
Samuel, m. Esther **GATES**, Apr. 19, 1739	LR2	1108
Samuel, 2d, m. Anne **FULLER**, b. of East Haddam, Mar. 16, 1743	LR6	507
Samuel, s. James & Deborah, b. July 18, 1754	LR3	7
Samuel, m. Wid. Rachel **WILLEY**, b. of East Haddam (or said to be), Apr. 5, 1765	LR8	5
Samuel, s. Jonah & Esther, b. Aug. 14, 1797	2	223
Samuel, m. Mary **STRANAHAN**, Apr. 12, 1821, by Rev. Isaac Parsons	3	9
Samuel W., ae 23 y., b. in East Haddam, res. East Haddam, m. Martha A. **PHELPS**, ae 20, res. East Haddam, Aug. 12, 1855, by Rev. Moses Chace. Int. pub. July 9, 1855	4	61
Sarah, d. Joseph, b. Aug. 20, 1700	LR1	5
Sarah, w. of Capt. George, d. Nov. 7, 1709	LR1	7
Sarah, d. Samuell & Easter, b. July 15, 1712	LR1	10
Sarah, d. Daniel & Sarah, b. Apr. 11, 1725	LR2	1128
Sarah, d. George & Sarah, b. Aug. 6, 1739	LR2	1126
Sarah, d. Thomas, Jr. & Sarah, b. Nov. 3, 1760	LR7	3
Sarah, wid. of Capt. Daniel, d. Dec. 5, 1770	2	3
Sarah, only d. of Thomas & Sarah, d. Dec. 4, 1776, in the 17th y. of her age	2	13
Sarah, d. Phineas & Anne, b. Feb. 3, 1780	2	94
Selden, s. Caleb & Esther, b. Sept. 13, 1778	2	92
Sibble, d. Jeremiah & Mary, b. Sept. 22, 1748	LR2	c
Sibble, d. Jeremiah & Mary, d. Oct. 12, 1750, in the 3rd y. of her age	LR2	c
Sibbel, d. Bezeleel & Mary, b. Mar. 3, 1760	LR4	475
Silence, d. Paul & Mehitable, b. Mar. 31, 1766	LR6	505
Silvester, s. Timothy, 3rd, & Susannah, b. July 7, 1798	2	235

	Vol.	Page
GATES, (cont.)		
Sophia, of East Haddam, m. Daniel **HALL**, of Rome, O., May 26, 1831, by Rev. Peter G. Clarke	3	116
Statira, d. Timothy & Hannah, b. Dec. 28, 1764	LR6	504
Stephen, s. Samuell, b. June 30, 1723	LR1	572
Stephen, s. Oliver & Mary, b. Dec. 11, 1786	2	156
Susan, m. James **McARTHUR**, June 8, 1852, by Rev. Isaac Parsons	3	235
Susan[n]ah, d. Joseph, b. Sept. 21, 1705	LR1	5
Susannah, d. Joseph & Hannah, b. Nov. 24, 1730	LR1	573
Susannah, d. Joseph & Hannah, d. May 25, 1742	LR2	1095
Susannah, d. Joseph, Jr. & Abigail, b. Mar. 14, 1756	LR3	14
Susannah, d. Ephraim & Susannah, b. Apr. 29, 1778	2	100
Susannah, sister of Joseph, 3d, & d. of Joseph, d. Dec. 4, 1810	2	93
Susannah, wid. of Timothy, Jr., (called 3rd), d. Dec. 14, 1846, in the 75th y. of her age (*Perhaps 76th")	2	236
Sybil, see under Sibble		
Theopholus Lord, s. Jesse & Elizabeth, b. Apr. 13, 1759	LR5	266
Thomas, s. Thomas, b. Oct. 3, 1693	LR1	5
Thomas, Jr., m. Dorothy **CONE**, Aug. 17, 1722	LR2	c
Thomas, s. Thomas & Dorothy, b. Dec. 17, 1724	LR2	c
Thomas, Jr., m. Sarah **ROWLE**, b. of East Haddam, May 30, 1751	LR7	3
Thomas, s. Thomas, Jr. & Sarah, b. Jan. 3, 1752	LR7	3
Thomas, Capt., d. June 3, 1771, in the 78th y. of his age	2	13
Thomas, 2d, m. Rachel **SMITH**, b. of East Haddam, June 22, 1788	2	152
Thomas, Jr., d. Apr. 4, 1814, in the 51st y. of his age	2	236
Thomas, d. July 20, 1826	2	153
Tho[ma]s H., farmer, b. in East Haddam, res. East Haddam, single, d. June 8, 1855, ae 55	4	72
Timothy, s. Thomas & Dorothy, b. Apr. 29, 1730	LR2	c
Timothy, m. Hannah **PARSEVAL**, b. of East Haddam, June 18, 1761	LR6	504
Timothy, s. Timothy & Hannah, b. Sept. 20, 1763	LR6	504
Timothy, 3rd, of East Haddam, m. Susannah **BRAINERD**, of Farmington, May 18, 1791	2	235
Timothy, d. Oct. 9, 1819, in the 90th y. of his age	2	236
Trumendy, d. Nathaniel & Lucy, b. Nov. 30, 1793, at Kingstown, at the Susquahannah	2	152
Uri, s. Joseph, 3rd, & Lucy, b. Jan. 30, 1785	2	92
Uri, m. Betsey **GATES**, b. of East Haddam, Apr. 19, 1813, by Rev. Elijah Parsons	3	94
Uriah, s. Jesse & Elizabeth, b. Apr. 26, 1761	LR5	266
Vilecte, d. Daniel, Jr. & Anna, b. Feb. 23, 1771	2	10
Warren, s. Ep[hrai]m & Susannah, b. Oct. 8, 1786	2	100
William, s. Joseph, 2d, & Jane, b. Aug. 5, 1782	2	108
William, m. Sarah **CONE**, b. of East Haddam, June 2, 1852,		

	Vol.	Page
GATES, (cont.)		
by Rev. Isaac Parsons	3	235
William Richard, s. Christ[ophe]r C. & Julia Jennings, b. July 1, 1831	2	313
Zachariah, s. Thomas & Dorothy, b. June 3, 1735	LR2	c
Zachariah, s. Thomas, Jr. & Sarah, b. Dec. 29, 1753	LR7	3
Zechariah, s. Thomas, Jr. & Rachel, b. Oct. 8, 1789	2	152
Zilpah, m. Samuel **CHAPMAN**, b. of East Haddam, Mar. 4, 1783	2	223
----, s. Daniell & Rebecka, b. Aug. 2, 1727	LR1	582
GEERING, GEARING, George, of N. Y. m. Cynthia C. **HUBBARD**, of East Haddam, Dec. 27, 1848, by Rev. Alpheas Geer	3	216
George, machinist, ae 25, b. in New York, res. Meriden, m. Cynthia C. **HUBBARD**, ae 24, b. in Haddam, res. Meriden, Dec. 27, 1848, by Alpheas Geer	4	9-10
GELSTON, Abby Ann, of East Haddam, m. Henry E. **WEST**, of New London, June 9, 1846, by Rev. Alpheas Geer	3	205
Matilda, m. Timothy **WRIGHT**, Jan. 10, 1821, by Rev. Solomon Blakesley	3	1
Richard D., m. Cariste D. **PALMER**, Sept. 16, 1821, by Rev. Isaac Parsons	3	11
William, d. June 24, 1840	3	6
GEORGE(?), Eunice, d. William & Mary, b. July 21, 1707	LR1	7
GIBBERTS, [see also **GILBERT**], John, s. John & Mary, b. Mar. 20, 1736	LR5	a
Thomas, s. John & Mary, b. Sept. 20, 1737	LR5	a
GIBBS, GIBES, Deborah, of Lyme, m. Ebenezer **HINKLEY**, of East Haddam, July 6, 1785	2	2
Ebenezer, m. Ruth **BATE**, May 10, 1726	LR2	e
James, s. Ebenezer & Ruth, b. Mar. 5, 1727	LR2	e
GILBERT, GILBART, [see also **GIBBERTS**], Anna, d. John & Mehetabel, b. Aug. 12, 1769	2	6
Darkis, m. Daniel **BRAINERD**, 2d, b. of East Haddam, Dec. 31, 1773	2	42
Dorothy, d. Joseph & Dorothy, b. Apr. 7, 1772	2	70
Giles, s. William & Patience, d. Sept. 22, [1775], at Roxbury, in the 31st y. of his age. Enlisted in Gen. Spencer's Co., 1775, in the 15th reign of George 3rd	2	99
Joseph, m. Dorothy **ARNOLD**, b. of East Haddam, May 18, 1769	2	70
Joseph, s. Joseph & Dorothy, b. Jan. 2, 1774	2	70
Lois, of Middletown, m. Joseph **EMMONS**, of East Haddam, Jan. 6, 1763	LR7	410
Lucretia, m. Jonathan **BOOGE**, Sept. 13, 1750	LR4	468
Mary, d. Joseph & Dorothy, b. June 17, 1770	2	70
Mary M., m. Dr. Richard **WARNER**, [ ], at Mansfield (The words "brother of Selden" follow this entry.)	3	10

	Vol.	Page
GILBERT, GILBART, (cont.)		
Oliver, s. Samuel & Mary, b. Nov. 19, 1788	2	94
Russel[l], s. John & Mehetabel, b. Feb. 6, 1772	2	6
Samuel, s. Samuel & Mary, b. Jan. 17, 1787	2	94
Wealthy, Mrs., of Lebanon, m. Silvanus **TINKER**, of East Haddam, May 23, 1781	2	4
GILLETT, GILLET, Amos, of Mt. Morris, N. Y., m. Philena **CONE**, of East Haddam, Nov. 9, 1834, by Rev. Nathaniel Miner	3	135
Huntington, of Colchester, m. Tamzin **WILLARD**, of Saybrook, Dec. 8, 1824, by Rev. Isaac Parsons	3	66-7
Samuel S., of Colchester, m. Josephine A. **BABCOCK**, of East Haddam, Aug. 29, 1838, by Rev. Isaac Parsons	3	166
GLADWIN, Caroline Louisa Gardiner, d. James R., mechanic, ae 26, b. Feb. 27, 1850	4	27-8
Carroll C., s. Lewellyn, ship joiner, ae 21, & Harriet, ae 22, b. Dec. 30, 1849	4	23-4
Carrol Lewellin, d. Jan. 13, 1850, ae 5 m.	4	29-30
Casper, joiner, ae 16, of E. Haddam, m. Mary Eliza **AYRES**, ae 14, [ ], 1851, by Charles Atwood	4	37-8
Casper, s. Cooper*, joiner, ae 17, & Mary E., ae 14, b. May 3, 1851 (*Casper?)	4	31-2
Casper S., m. Mary E. **AYERS**, b. of East Haddam, Dec. 19, 1850, by Charles Attwood, J. P.	3	229
Lewellyn, ship joiner, ae 21, m. Harriet **ACKLEY**, tailorest, ae 22, b. of E. Haddam, Oct. 31, 1849, by Alpheas Geer	4	19-20
Lewellyn, m. Harriet **ACKLEY**, Dec. 31, 1849, by Rev. Alpheas Geer	3	222
Louis Bradford, s. James R., mechanic, ae 25, & Phebe Ann, ae 23, b. Aug. 27, 1847	4	3-4
Rebecca Stiles, d. Frederic, joiner, ae 25, & [ ], ae 25, b. Dec. 14, 1850	4	31-2
Richard H., m. Phebe **CLARK**, b. of East Haddam, July 25, 1849, by Rev. Alpheas Geer	3	219
-----, s. Rich[ar]d, joiner, b. Dec. 10, 1852	4	47-8
-----, child of James R., joiner, b. June 6, 1853	4	47-8
-----, child of Casper, joiner, b. Nov. 28, 1853	4	47-8
-----, child of Lewellyn, mechanic, ae about 24 y., res. East Haddam, & [ ], ae about 24 y., b. Jan. 25, 1855	4	75
-----, d. Frederic E., mechanic, ae 33, res. East Haddam, & Torzah, ae 33, b. Feb. 18, 1856	4	84
GLASS, Rufus, of Canterbury, m. Huldah **FULLER**, of East Haddam, Nov. 16, 1779	2	88
GLEASON, Prudence, Mrs., of Farmington, m. Isaac **CHAPMAN**, of East Haddam, Sept. 29, 1816, by Rev. Mr. Porter, at Farmington	2	267
GOBERT, Mrs., of New York, d. Apr. 13, 1787	2	232
GODDARD, Ira, of Hillsborough, Ga., m. Maria **SPENCER**, of		

	Vol.	Page
GODDARD, (cont.)		
Lyme, Sept. 23, 1824, by Rev. Joseph Vaill, of Hadlyme	3	66-7
GOFF, Asa, Jr., of Haddam, m. Harriet B. **MINER**, of East Haddam, Mar. 27, 1827, by Rev. Herman L. Vaill	3	93
Harriet E., of East Haddam, m. Joseph A. **CONE**, of New London, Mar. 10, 1839, by Rev. Charles William Bradley	3	168
Rachel, Mrs., of East Haddam, m. Timothy **TYLER**, of Haddam, Dec. 1, 1849, by Rev. Levi H. Wakeman	3	220
Sarah T., b. in Marlborough, res. E. Haddam, d. May 20, 1851, ae 42	4	39-40
Sylvester, m. Sarah J. **WORTHINGTON**, July 11, 1830, by Isaac Parsons	3	107
GOODRICH, GOODRIDGE, Elizabeth, ae 19, b. in Chatham, res. E. Haddam, m. Oliver **MEECH**, farmer, ae 22, of E. Haddam, June [ ], 1850	4	19-20
Orson, of Glastenbury, m. Phebe **CONE**, of East Haddam, Nov. 30, 1832, by Rev. Peter Gilchrist Clarke	3	128
-----, d. Nelson, clergyman, ae 40, & Sarah A., ae 39, b. Nov. 20, 1856	4	112
GOODSPEED, Anna, m. Elijah **ATWOOD**, b. of East Haddam, Nov. 21, 1754	LR7	5
Anna, m. Elijah **ATTWOOD**, b. of East Haddam, Nov. 21, 1754	2	206
Anna, d. Nathan & Mary, b. Feb. 8, 1779	2	56
George Edward, s. Joseph & Laura, b. Feb. 2, 1813	3	53
George Edward, m. Nancy Green **HAYDEN**, b. of East Haddam, Mar. 25, 1844, by Henry de Koven	3	199
Georgianna, d. George E., merchant, ae 35, & Nancy, ae 27, b. July 21, 1848	4	3-4
Jerusha C., of East Haddam, m. Oliver **ALLEN**, of Norwich, Mar. 18, 1828, by Rev. Isaac Parsons	3	99
Joseph, s. Nathan & Mary, b. Apr. 23, 1787	2	56
Joseph, of East Haddam, m. Laura **TYLER**, of Haddam, Sept. 26, 1811, by Rev. Solomon Blakesley	3	53
Joseph, m. Roxy **BIGELOW**, b. of East Haddam, Sept. 13, 1833, by Isaac Parsons	3	132
Joseph, merchant, d. Jan. 23, 1848, ae 61	4	7-8
Joseph Frederick, s. Joseph & Laura, b. Nov. 26, 1816	3	53
Laura Sophia, d. Joseph & Laura, b. Feb. 2, 1822	3	53
Louisa M., b. in Rocky Hill, res. E. Haddam, d. July 4, 1850, ae 26	4	29-30
Louisa Robbins, d. William H., merchant, ae 33, & Louisa M., ae 24, b. July 18, 1848	4	3-4
Mary, m. Elijah **METCALF**, b. of East Haddam, Sept. 13, 1773	2	36
Mary, d. Nathan & Mary, b. Nov. 27, 1776	2	56
Mary Ann, of East Haddam, m. Roland A. **ROBBINS**, of Hartford, Oct. 13, 1836, by Rev. Stephen Beach	3	146
Mary Anne, d. Joseph & Laura, b. June 12, 1818	3	53

	Vol.	Page
GOODSPEED, (cont.)		
Moses, s. Nathan & Mary, b. Apr. 11, 1786	2	56
Moses, s. Nathan & Mary, d. Aug. 18, 1786	2	57
Nathan, of East Haddam, m. Mary **KELLOGG**, of Colchester, Jan. 2, 1772	2	56
Nathan, s. Nathan & Mary, b. Oct. 15, 1774	2	56
Nathan, s. Nathan & Mary, d. Sept. 4, 1776	2	57
Nathan, s. Nathan & Mary, b. June 18, 1781	2	56
Nathan, Jr., m. Judith **HIGGINS**, b. of East Haddam, Oct. 31, 1802	2	271
Nathan Tyler, s. Joseph & Laura, b. Apr. 10, 1820	3	53
Samuel, s. Nathan & Mary, b. Apr. 4, 1773	2	56
Samuel, s. Nathan & Mary, d. Feb. 13, 1774	2	57
Sarah, d. Nathan & Mary, b. July 18, 1783	2	56
William Henry, s. Joseph & Laura, b. Dec. 29, 1814	3	53
William Robbins, s. W[illia]m H., merchant, ae 35, & Louisa M., ae 26, b. June 8, 1850	4	27-8
-------, d. Geo[rge] E., merchant, ae 41 y., res. East Haddam, & [ ], ae 41y., b. Nov. 9, 1855	4	78
GOTT, Hazard, of Hebron, m. Lydia **GATES**, of East Haddam, Feb. 7, 1826, by Isaac Parsons	3	84-5
GOULD, Anna, d. John & Mary, b. Mar. 4, 1780	2	106
Elizabeth, Mrs., of Lyme, m. Rev. Eleazer **SWEETLAND**, of East Haddam, Dec. 26, 1781	2	126
John, of Lyme, m. Mrs. Mary **SEARS**, of East Haddam, June 15, 1775	2	106
John, s. Jno. & Mary, b. July 20, 1790	2	106
Mary, d. John & Mary, b. Apr. 3, 1776, at Lyme	2	106
Matthew Sears, s. John & Mary, b. Apr. 13, 1778	2	106
Patty, d. John & Mary, b. Jan. 6, 1788	2	106
Sarah A., m. Julius **ATTWOOD**, Oct. 3, 1852, at Stony Brook, L. I.	2	262
Sarah Antoinette, m. Julius **ATTWOOD**, Oct. 3, 1852, by Rev. Frederick M. Noll, at Stony Brook, L. I.	3	245-6
GRAHAM, Emma, d. Oct. 18, 1848, ae 2	4	17-18
Emma, d. George W., tailor, ae 39, & Mary E., ae 33, b. May 1, 1849	4	11-12
Susan, of Lyme, m. William **LOVIY**, of Haddam, June 26, 1827, by Rev. Joseph Vaill, of Hadlyme	3	90
GRAVES, Allen, s. Jedediah & Elizabeth, b. May 1, 1738	LR3	14
Amos, s. Jedediah & Elizabeth, b. Dec. 10, 1753	LR3	14
Benjamin, s. Roswell & Elisabeth, b. July 25, 1769	2	96
Daniel, s. Roswell & Elisabeth, b. Nov. 4, 1773	2	96
Elizabeth, d. Jeremiah & Elizabeth, b. Feb. 21, 1740	LR3	14
Elisabeth, d. Roswell & Elisabeth, b. July 16, 1771	2	96
Esther. d. Jedediah & Jerusha, b. Jan. 9, 1731	LR3	14
Hulburt. s. Roswell & Elisabeth, b. July 4, 1765	2	96
Jedediah. m. Jerusha **ACKLY**, Mar. [ ], 1728	LR3	14

	Vol.	Page
GRAVES, (cont.)		
Jedediah, m. Elizabeth **ALLEN**, June [ ], 1737	LR3	14
Jerusha, w. of Jedediah, d. Aug. [ ], 1736	LR3	14
Jonah, s. Jedediah & Jerusha, b. June 20, 1728	LR3	14
Lucy, d. Jedediah & Elizabeth, b. Apr. 26, 1746	LR3	14
Lidiah, m. Simeon **CROSBY**, Aug. 10, 1749	LR4	467
Mary, m. Nathaniel **CONE**, Jr., Dec. 5, 1745	LR3	5
Mary, d. Jedediah & Elizabeth, b. May 28, 1748	LR3	14
Mary, wid. of Benjamin, d. Nov. 24, 1780	2	97
Rachel, d. Jedediah & Jerusha, b. Jan. 2, 1734	LR3	14
Rachel, m. Increase **CROSBY**, b. of East Haddam, Feb. 13, 1755	LR5	563
Rhoda, d. Jedediah & Elizabeth, b. Feb. 16, 1744	LR3	14
Roswell, m. Elisabeth **DRIGGS**, b. of East Haddam, Nov. 15, 1763	2	96
Roswell, s. Roswell & Elisabeth, b. Sept. 26, 1767	2	96
Russell, s. Jedediah & Elizabeth, b. Apr. 17, 1751	LR3	14
Stephen, s. Jedediah & Elizabeth, b. Feb. 7, 1742	LR3	14
Thankfull, m. William **STEWARD**, Apr. 7, 1746; d. Sept. [ ], 1746	LR5	559
GRAY, Jonathan, of New York, m. Mary Ann **HARRIS**, of East Haddam, Sept. 16, 1834, by Rev. Nathaniel Miner	3	134
Thankfull, m. Timothy **FULLER**, Nov. 29, 1749	LR4	465
GREEN, Benjamin, s. Capt. James & Ruth, b. Aug. 31, 1762	2	26
Caroline L., m. William **FOWLER**, Sept. 26, 1830, by Rev. Alvan Ackley	3	108
Catharine L., of East Haddam, m. Henry S. **TYLER**, of Haddam, June 11, 1845, by Rev. Isaac Parsons	3	202
Elizabeth, d. Richard & Sally, b. Aug. 28, 1816	3	80-1
Elizabeth, d. Richard & Sally, d. Feb. 1, 1818, in the 2nd y.	3	82
Frederick Warren, s. Richard & Sally, b. Aug. 16, 1813	3	80-1
Hannah, d. James & Ruth, b. Mar. 14, 1755	LR5	268
Hannah, m. Joseph **HUNGERFORD**, b. of East Haddam, Nov. 20, 1777	2	219
Hannah, of East Haddam, m. Daniel **TUTTLE**, of New York, Aug. 28, 1825, by Rev. Isaac Parsons	3	78
Harriet, of East Haddam, m. George N. **BLAKESLEY**, of Plymouth, Dec. 22, 1823, by Rev. Isaac Parsons	3	49
Henry, s. Richard & Sally, b. Sept. 5, 1805	3	80-1
James, m. Ruth **MARSHALL**, b. of East Haddam, Feb. 14, 1755	LR5	268
James Wilson, s. Richard & Sally, b. Mar. 20, 1809	3	80-1
Jonathan S., Rev., of Andover, Mass., m. Theodosia **ARNOLD**, of East Haddam, Sept. 20, 1827, by Rev. Isaac Parsons	3	95
Lucretia B., m. Sidney B. **WILLEY**, June 19, 1831, by Rev. Peter G. Clarke	3	119
Maria T., of East Haddam, m. Frederic W. **SHEPARD**, of Essex, Oct. 14, 1840, by Isaac Parsons, M. G.	3	182-3

	Vol.	Page
GREEN, (cont.)		
Mary, m. John **SPENCER**, Jr., Dec. 27, 1739	LR3	12
Mary, m. Robert **HOSMER**, Oct. 31, 1745	LR3	12
Mary, of Middletown, m. Thomas **SMITH**, Jr., of East Haddam, Dec. 11, 1760	LR6	503
Mary Ann, m. Daniel B. **WARNER**, Apr. 27, 1835, by Rev. Stephen Beach	3	137
Nancy, d. Capt. James & Ruth, b. Feb. 13, 1768	2	26
Nancy, m. Jared **SPENCER**, b. of East Haddam, Nov. 29, 1789	2	251
Nancy, m. Horace **HAYDEN**, Dec. 11, 1816, by Rev. Isaac Parsons	3	149
Oliver, s. Capt. James & Ruth, b. Aug. 16, 1773	2	26
Oliver, mechanic, d. Feb. 2, 1848, ae 74	4	7-8
Richard, s. Capt. James & Ruth, b. Mar. 10, 1765	2	26
Richard, of East Haddam, m. Sally **WEBB**, of Saybrook, May 1, 1803	3	80-1
Richard, farmer, d. Feb. 8, 1848, ae 83	4	7-8
Richard Gleason, s. Richard W. & Charlotte, b. June 29, 1829	3	106
Richard William, s. Richard & Sally, b. Mar. 28, 1804	3	80-1
Ruth, d. James & Ruth, b. May 12, 1756	LR5	268
Sarah Ann, d. Richard & Sally, b. Apr. 16, 1819	3	80-1
Sidney, s. Richard & Sally, b. Jan. 2, 1811	3	80-1
Timothy, s. Capt. James & Ruth, b. Aug. 31, 1771	2	26
Timothy, s. Capt. James & Ruth, d. Mar. 19, 1775	2	27
Timothy, s. Capt. James & Ruth, b. July 3, 1776	2	26
Timothy, farmer & merchant, d. June 15, 1853, ae 77	4	49-50
Timothy Franklin, Jr., s. Timothy F., manufacturer, ae 28, & Sarah M., ae 25, b. Oct. 14, 1849	4	27-8
William, s. Capt. James & Ruth, b. Aug. 26, 1760	2	26
William, m. Indiana **TINKER**, b. of East Haddam, Oct. 26, 1791	2	233
William Webb, s. Richard & Sally, b. Mar. 29, 1807	3	80-1
Wilson, s. Capt. James & Ruth, b. July 10, 1780	2	26
GREENFIELD, GRENFIELD, Jacob R., of Middletown, m. Eliza A. **GATES**, of East Haddam, July 1, 1849, by Rev. Isaac Parsons	3	218
Jacob R., painter, b. in Middletown, res. East Haddam, m. Eliza A. **GATES**, b. in East Haddam, July 1, 1849, by Isaac Parsons	4	9-10
Jacob R., painter, ae 25, b. in Middletown, res. East Haddam, m. Augustus* E. **GATES**, ae 19, of East Haddam, July 2, 1849, by Isaac Parsons (*Probably "Eliza")	4	9-10
Thomas W., d. Sept. 10, 1856, ae 3 y. 4 m. 9 d.	4	111
GRIDLEY, Keziah, of Farmington, m. Samuel **JONES**, of East Haddam, Nov. 30, 1762	2	74
Prudence, of Farmington, m. Daniel **BRAINERD**, of East Haddam, June 6, 1771	2	36
GRIFFIN, GRIFFING, GRIFFEN, [see also **GRIFFIS**], Albert		

	Vol.	Page
GRIFFIN, GRIFFING, GRIFFEN, (cont.)		
Morgan, s. [Nathan & Sarah Barber], b. June 3, 1826	3	155
Allen Willey, s. Lemuel, 2d, & Lydia, b. Aug. 20, 1769	2	160
Anna, m. John Maynard, [ ], 1779	2	281
Anna, m. Ebenezer **FOX**, b. of East Haddam, May 13, 1823, by Josiah Griffin, J. P.	3	40-1
Asahel, s. Lemuel, 2d, & Lydia, b. Aug. 7, 1767	2	160
Betsey Ann, d. [Nathan & Sarah Barber], b. Oct. 15, 1814	3	155
Betsey Ann, d. Maj. Nathan, d. Oct. 26, 1814	3	156
Betsey Beckwith, d. [Nathan & Sarah Barber], b. Feb. 26, 1822	3	155
Carlos, s. [Nathan & Sarah Barber], b. June 13, 1827	3	155
D----, s. Thomas & Sarah, b. Aug. 9, 1731	LR1	572
David, s. Lemuel, 2d, & Lydia, b. Sept. 7, 1785	2	160
Dorothea, of East Haddam, m. Dr. Richard **NOYES**, of Lyme, Mar. 25, 1830, by Rev. Chester Colton, of Lyme	3	107
Edwin B., m. Maria L. **ACKLEY**, b. of East Haddam, Dec. 2, [1840], by Nath[anie]l Miner. Int. pub.	3	185
Edwin Barber, s. [Nathan & Sarah Barber], b. Nov. 19, 1819	3	155
Elizabeth, of East Haddam, m. John B. **DINSMORE**, of Ripley, N. Y., June 14, 1832, by Nathaniel Miner	3	124
Fanny, m. Abner S. **ELY**, June 24, 1824, by Josiah Hawes, J. P.	3	131
Francis, of East Haddam, m. Mary M. **LORD**, of Lyme, Apr. 24, 1833, by Nathaniel Miner	3	131
Frances E., of East Haddam, m. Thomas **STRICKLAND**, of Montville, Feb. 21, 1842, by Rev. James Hepburn, of Montville	3	189
Frederick Wallace, s. [Nathan & Sarah Barber], b. Jan. 2, 1832	3	155
George Cone, s. [Nathan & Sarah Barber], b. Oct. 18, 1833	3	155
Henry, m. Jane **HARRISON**, b. of Lyme, June 15, 1840, by Rev. George Carrington, of Hadlyme	3	178
Henry Clinton, s. [Nathan & Sarah Barber], b. Feb. 8, 1824	3	155
Ichabod Comstock, s. Lemuel, 2d, & Lydia, b. Dec. 19, 1773	2	160
John G., m. Ursula **MACK**, Mar. 29, 1842, by Rev. Abraham Holway	3	190
John Gardner, s. [Nathan & Sarah Barber], b. Oct. 30, 1815	3	155
Josiah, s. Lemuel & Phebe, b. July 21, 1743	LR6	513
Josiah, m. Dorothy **GATES**, b. of East Haddam, Feb. 22, 1791	2	227
Lemuel, s. Lemuel, 2d, & Lydia, b. Sept. 11, 1771	2	160
Linus E., of East Haddam, m. Abigail S. **SMITH**, of Chatham, June 23, 1850, by Rev. Jacob Gardiner	3	227
Linus E., factory spinner, ae 22, b. in Wallingford, res. East Haddam, m. Abigail T. **SMITH**, factory operative, ae 21, b. in Chatham, res. East Haddam, June 23, 1850, by Rev. Jacob Gardner	4	19-20
Lydia, d. Lemuel, 2d, & Lydia, b. Aug. 15, 1782	2	160
Nathan. m. Sarah Barber **GALLUP**, Nov. 17, 1813	3	155
Phebe. d. Lemuel & Phebe, b. Jan. 26, 1741	LR6	513
Phebe, of East Haddam, m. Augustus **OLMSTED**, of West		

	Vol.	Page
GRIFFIN, GRIFFING, GRIFFEN, (cont.)		
Chester (Colchester), Sept. 25, 1834, by Nathaniel Miner	3	135
Phebe Sill, d. [Nathan & Sarah Barber], b. Nov. 8, 1829	3	155
Sarah Ann, d. [Nathan & Sarah Barber], b. Oct. 17, 1817	3	165
Sarah Ann, m. Julius C. **WILLIAMS**, Feb. 6, 1839, by Rev. Nathaniel Miner	3	168
Statira E., of East Haddam, m. Selden M. **ELY**, of Ripley, N. Y., May 10, 1825, by Rev. Herman L. Vaill	3	74-75
Walter, s. Lemuel, 2d, & Lydia, b. May 2, 1776	2	160
Zebulon, s. Lemuel, 2d, & Lydia, b. May 14, 1778	2	160
-----, d. Francis, farmer, ae 47, & Mary L., ae 34, b. Jan. 7, 1850	4	25-6
-----, d. John G., farmer, & Ursula M., b. Apr. 16, 1850	4	25-6
GRIFFIS, [see also **GRIFFIN**], Isbell, d. Thomas & Sarah, b. Feb. 19, 1726/7	LR1	574
John, s. Thomas & Sarah, b. June 12, 1724	LR1	574
Mary, d. Thomas, b. May 23, 1729	LR1	574
Sarah, d. Thomas & Sarah, b. Nov. 14, 1719	LR1	574
Thomas, m. Sarah **BELDEN**, Feb. 12, 1718/19	LR1	574
Thomas, s. Thomas & Sarah, b. Mar. 12, 1722	LR1	574
Thomas, s. Thomas, d. Mar. 20, 1728	LR1	574
GRIMSBURY, Frederick, s. Henry, machinist, ae 36, & Julia E., ae 34, b. Mar. 22, 1850	4	25-6
GRIMSHAW, Frederic, d. Nov. 20, 1852, ae 2 y. 8 m. 26 d.	4	49-50
GRISWOLD, Aaron, s. Aaron & Hannah, b. Apr. 10, 1754	LR6	508
Abigail, of Weathersfield, m. Daniel **CONE**, of East Haddam, May 7, 1760	LR5	559
Azariah, s. Ephraim & Mehitable, b. Sept. 10, 1727	LR2	1120
Deborah, m. Nathan **JEWETT**, b. of Lyme, Dec. 9, 1756	LR6	507
Edwin B., of West Hartford, m. Fanny W. **CONE**, of East Haddam, Mar. 31, 1847, by Nathaniel Miner	3	209
Elijah, s. Aaron & Hannah, b. Aug. 10, 1762	LR6	508
Ephraim, m. Mehitable **RYLE**, Dec. 19, 1726	LR2	1120
Ephraim, s. Ephraim & Mehitable, b. July 3, 1729	LR2	1120
Jabez, s. Ephraim & Mehitable, b. June 24, 1731	LR2	1120
Josiah, s. Aaron & Hannah, b. June 8, 1758	LR6	508
Mary, d. Aaron & Hannah, b. Sept. 22, 1760	LR6	508
Mary, m. Matthias **FULLER**, Jr., June 27, 1764	LR7	417
Moses, s. Aaron & Hannah, b. Sept. 14, 1755	LR6	508
Olive, d. Aaron & Hannah, b. Jan. 31, 1767	LR6	508
Rachell, m. Jonathan **EM[M]ONS**, Jan. 2, 1723	LR2	d
Rebeckah, d. Aaron & Hannah, b. Aug. 11, 1764	LR6	508
Sarah, d. Ephraim & Mehitable, b. Oct. 9, 1733	LR2	1120
Sarah, m. Amos **WHITE**, Apr. 8, 1767	LR7	412
Sarah, m. Amos **WHITE**, b. of East Haddam, Apr. 8, 1767	2	225
GROSS, Christian, m. Catharine S. **SWARTZ**, Sept. 12, 1836, by Rev. Isaac Parsons	3	145
GROVER, Aner, of Tolland, m. Mercy Ann **HUNGERFORD**, of Ea		

	Vol.	Page
GROVER, (cont.)		
East Haddam, Jan. 27, 1842, by Isaac Parsons, M. V. D.	3	188
Asa M., of East Hampton, m. Mary Ann **KIDDER**, of Moodus, Oct. 24, 1847, by Rev. Isaac Parsons	3	211
GUILD, Sarah A., b. [ ], at Stony Brook, [L. I.]	3	245-6
HADDAM*, Joseph, d. Mar. 31, 1747 (*Probably "Joseph **SPENCER**")	LR2	1108
HALL, Abner, m. Phebe **PERCIVEL**, b. of East Haddam, Nov. 29, 1772	2	54
Abner, s. Abner & Phebe, b. July 10, 1776	2	54
Abner, Jr., m. Elizabeth **OLMSTED**, b. of East Haddam, Nov. 22, 1801	2	271
Benjamin, s. Samuel & Sarah, b. May 4, 1745	LR3	17
Betsa, d. Samuel & Mary, b. Feb. 22, 1775	2	221
Chauncey, s. Sylvester & Elizabeth, b. Apr. 16, 1805	3	105
Daniel, of Rome, O., m. Sophia **GATES**, of East Haddam, May 26, 1831, by Rev. Peter G. Clarke	3	116
Dean, s. Daniel & Hannah, b. Apr. 5, 1784	2	100
Denison, m. Lucy **DARLING**, b. of East Haddam, Apr. 5, 1847, by Nathaniel A. Cowdrey, J. P.	3	215
Ebenezer, s. Thomas & Margaret, b. Sept. 2, 1739	LR2	1105
Ebenezer, s. Thomas & Margaret, b. Feb. 26, 1744	LR2	1105
Ebenezer, s. Abner & Phebe, b. May 20, 1778	2	54
Eliza, d. [Sylvester & Elizabeth], b. Dec. 30, 1807	3	105
Eliza B., of East Haddam, m. Ebenezer **MERRIMAN**, of Southington, Apr. 12, 1835, by Rev. Isaac Parsons	3	138
Elizabeth, w. of Sylvester, d. Jan. 16, 1819	3	105
Emmeline Spencer, d. Jedediah & Hannah, b. May 21, 1810	2	307
Esther, d. Tho]ma]s & Mary, b. June 7, 1791	2	30
Ezra Fowler, s. Capt. Abner & Phebe, b. July 2, 1793	2	54
George, s. Capt. Abner & Phebe, b. July 29, 1782	2	54
George, s. Abner, Jr. & Elizabeth, b. Dec. 1, 1803	2	271
Hannah, d. Tho[ma]s & Mary, b. Mar. 13, 1788	2	30
Herman, s. Samuel, Jr. & Hannah, b. May 6, 1790	2	307
Hope, d. Tho[ma]s & Mary, b. Nov. 16, 1793	2	30
Jedidiah, s. Samuel & Mary, b. Apr. 9, 1780	2	221
Jedediah, m. Hannah **SPENCER**, b. of East Haddam, Dec. 29, 1808	2	307
Jemima, d. Thomas & Mary, b. May 31, 1748	LR3	509
Jemima, Mrs., m. Zachariah **CONE**, b. of East Haddam, Dec. 5, 1776	2	70
Lovina, d. Tho[ma]s & Mary, b. Aug. 15, 1796	2	30
Lucia, d. Samuel & Mary, b. Apr. 19, 1773	2	221
Marg[a]ret, d. Thomas & Mary, b. June 13, 1746	LR3	509
Margaret, m. Joseph **FOWLER**, b. of East Haddam, Oct. 21, 1771	2	42
Margaret, d. Tho[ma]s & Mary, b. Aug. 7, 1785	2	30
Margaret, d. [Sylvester & Margaret], b. Dec. 27, 1802	3	105

	Vol.	Page
HALL, (cont.)		
Margaret, w. of Sylvester, d. Jan. 1, 1803	3	105
Margaret S., of East Haddam, m. George **CHURCH**, of Greenwich, N. Y., Feb. 28, 1847, by Rev. Levi H. Wakeman	3	208
Marvin, s. [Sylvester & Elizabeth], b. May 14, 1812	3	105
Mary, d. Samuel & Mary, b. Jan. 11, 1768	2	221
Mary, m. Dr. Jonah **CONE**, 3rd, b. of East Haddam, Jan. 11, 1797, by Rev. William Lyman	2	279
Mary, d. [Sylvester & Elizabeth], b. Mar. 12, 1815	3	105
Mary P., m. Joseph W. **HAYES**, b. of East Haddam, Sept. 6, 1835, by Rev. Joseph Hough	3	138
Ogden, twin with Ozborn, s. Sylvester & Margaret, b. Sept. 17, 1801	3	105
Orren, s. [Sylvester & Elizabeth], b. Sept. 17, 1806	3	105
Ozborn, twin with Ogden, s. Sylvester & Margaret, b. Sept. 17, 1801	3	105
Phebe, d. Abner & Phebe, b. May 24, 1780	2	54
Phebe, m. Benjamin **ISHAM**, b. of East Haddam, Nov. 15, 1801	2	170
Polly, d. Thomas & Mary, b. Aug. 19, 1783	2	30
Polly, of East Haddam, m. Benjamin **LEWIS**, of Colchester, Jan. 1, 1824, by Rev. Isaac Parsons	3	50-51
Rachel, d. Thomas & Margret, b. Feb. 9, 1758	LR3	509
Reuben, [s. Sylvester & Elizabeth], b. Oct. 22, 1816	3	105
Salla, d. Abner & Phebe, b. July 18, 1774	2	54
Samuel, s. Thomas & Margaret, b. Sept. 25, 1742	LR2	1105
Samuel, of East Haddam, m. Mary **PRAT[T]**, of Lebanon, Nov. 15, 1764	LR7	416
Samuel, s. Samuel & Mary, b. June 30, 1766	2	221
Samuel, Jr., m. Hannah **CONE**, July 9, 1789	2	307
Samuel, s. [Sylvester & Elizabeth], b. Oct. 5, 1813	3	105
Samuel, d. Mar. 10, 1828, ae 84	2	222
Sarah, d. Thomas & Margaret, b. Feb. 18, 1741	LR2	1105
Sarah, d. Samuel & Sarah, b. Dec. 5, 1747	LR3	17
Sarah, d. [Sylvester & Elizabeth], b. Jan. 2, 1811	3	105
Seth, s. Abner, Jr. & Elizabeth, b. Aug. 7, 1802	2	271
Simeon, s. [Sylvester & Elizabeth], b. Jan. 16, 1809	3	105
Statira, d. Thomas & Marg[a]ret, b. June 19, 1755	LR3	509
Statira, d. Samuel & Mary, b. Apr. 21, 1777	2	221
Statira, m. Capt. Samuel **SPENCER**, b. of East Haddam, Nov. 15, 1801	2	287
Selvester, s. Samuel & Mary, b. Jan. 10, 1770	2	221
Sylvester, m. Margaret **PLUMB**, Jan. 10, 1798	3	105
Sylvester, m. Elizabeth **WALKLEY**, July 5, 1804	3	105
Thomas, s. Thomas & Margaret, b. May 13, 1738	LR2	1105
Thomas, Jr., m. Polly **SMITH**, b. of East Haddam, Jan. 20, 1782	2	30

	Vol.	Page
HALL, (cont.)		
Thomas, [ ]	LR3	509
We[a]lthy, d. Samuel & Mary, b. Sept. 30, 1771	2	221
William, s. Samuel & Mary, b. June 2, 1782	2	221
------, widow, d. [ ], 1853, ae 95	4	49-50
HALLAM, Amos, of New London, m. Carisle **SCOVILLE**, of East Haddam, Mar. 14, 1852, by Rev. Isaac Parsons	3	235
HAMILTON, Charles T., m. Julia E. **BRAINERD**, b. of East Haddam, Apr. 24, 1856, by Rev. James M. Phillips	3	244
Charles T., ae 24, b. at Montville, res. East Haddam, m. Julia E. **BRAINERD**, ae 20, b. at East Haddam, res. East Haddam, Apr. 24, 1856, by Rev. James M. Phillips. Int. pub. Apr. 24, 1856	4	86
HARDING, Ethelinda, b. in New London, res. E. Haddam, d. Feb. 6, 1850, ae 84	4	29-30
Lucy, m. Truman **FULLER**, Jr., b. of East Haddam, June 20, 1830, by Isaac Chester, J. P.	3	107
Olive , m. Joshua B. **EMMONS**, b. of East Haddam, Feb. 21, 1836, by Rev. Stephen Beach	3	142
HARRIS, Albert, m. Eliza C. **WILLIAMS**, b. of East Haddam, [Feb.] 15, [1842], by Nathaniel Miner. Int. pub.	3	189
Ann S., ae 21, of East Haddam, m. James B. **MERRIMAN**, ae 25, of Wallingford, Ct., Dec. 25, 1856, by Rev. Isaac Parsons. Int. pub. Dec. 25, 1856	4	114a-5
Asa M., m. Ellen G. **GATES**, b. of East Haddam, Mar. 31, 1857, at Moodus, by Rev. Amos D. Watrous	4	120
Desire, m. Jonathan **EM[M]ONS**, Jr., b. of East Haddam, Jan. 11, 1759	LR6	511
Elizabeth C., m. Ephraim **MARTIN**, b. of Millington, May 28, 1848	3	213
Eunice T., m. Ephraim **MEECH**, Jan. 6, 1822, by Rev. John Hyde, at Preston	3	155
Henry C., of Middletown, m. Phebe **SMITH**, of East Haddam, May 26, 1842, by Isaac Parsons, V. D. M.	3	191
Hubbard, of Salem, m. Orpha **WATSON**, of East Haddam, Feb. 9, 1830, by Rev. Alvan Ackley	3	104
Lydia M., m. James E. **SWAN**, b. of East Haddam, Apr. 26, 1836, by Rev. Nathaniel Miner	3	142
Mary Ann, of East Haddam, m. Jonathan **GRAY**, of New York, Sept. 16, 1834, by Rev. Nathaniel Miner	3	134
Rachel Ann, m. Aaron T. **NILES**, July [ ], 1827, by Rev. Joseph Harvey	3	147
Viola, d. Henry C., joiner, ae 32, & Phebe, ae 32, b. May 12, 1850	4	23-4
-----, s. Willey O., farmer, b. Jan. 13, 1853	4	47-8
HARRISON, Jane, m. Henry **GRIFFIN**, b. of Lyme, June 15, 1840, by Rev. George Carrington, of Hadlyme	3	178
HARROW, Eliza D., m. Morris M. **BRAINERD**, June 13, 1825, by		

	Vol.	Page
HARROW, (cont.)		
Rev. Isaac Parsons	3	78
HART, Ann, of Farmingtown, m. Nehemiah **GATES**, of East Haddam, May 11, 1756	LR5	559
HARTSHORN, Henry, of Franklin, m. Dorothy **SMITH**, of East Haddam, June 1, 1843, by Rev. Alex[ander] Burguess	3	194
HARVEY, HARVY, Abigail, d. Robert & Rachel, b. May 14, 1766	2	192
Amasa, s. Robert & Rachel, b. Jan. 30, 1756	2	192
Amasa, s. Amasa & Eunice, b. Oct. 2, 1780	2	192
Amos S., m. Sarah C. **ATWOOD**, Dec. 10, 1849, by Rev. Alpheas Geer	3	220
Amos S., mechanic, ae 25, b. in Colchester, res. E. Haddam, m. Sarah E. **ATWOOD**, ae 23, of E. Haddam, Dec. 10, 1849, by Rev. Alpheas Geer	4	21-2
Ann, [twin with John], d. John & Elizabeth, b. Aug. 28, 1743	LR6	509
Asa, s. Thomas & Jane, b. Jan. 11, 1749	LR5	267
Asahel, s. Elisha & Zurviah, b. Jan. 6, 1760	LR5	b
Azuba, d. Robert & Rachel, b. June 15, 1776	2	192
Barthana, d. John & Elizabeth, b. June 6, 1745	LR6	509
Bethul, s. Amasa & Eunice, b. Sept. [ ], 1775	2	192
Brainerd, s. Amasa & Eunice, b. Apr. 18, 1774	2	192
Byron C., s. Daniel B., ae 29, & Attarista, ae 29, b. Oct. 11, 1847	4	3-4
Daniel, s. John, 2d, & Sarah, b. Jan. 27, 1759	LR5	564
Deborah, [twin with Josiah], d. Tho[ma]s & Jane, b. Oct. 19, 1745	LR5	267
Elaner, d. John & Elizabeth, b. May 8, 1758	LR6	509
Elanor, m. Amaziah **SPENCER**, b. of East Haddam, July 13, 1780	2	237
Elijah, m. Mrs. Mary Ann **BURDICK**, b. of East Haddam, June 27, 1849, by Rev. Moses Chace	3	218
Elisha, s. John & Elizabeth, b. Feb. 11, 1747	LR6	509
Elisha, m. Zurviah **HUNTINGTON**, Dec. 26, 1753	LR5	b
Elisha, s. Elisha & Zurviah, b. Jan. 8, 1755	LR5	b
Elizabeth, m. John **WILLE**, Oct. [ ], 1698	LR1	576
Elizabeth, d. John & Elizabeth, d. Oct. 14, 1765	LR6	509
Ezra, s. Thomas & Jane, b. Apr. 9, 1739	LR5	267
Ezra, s. Ezra (?) & Phebe, b. Jan. 28, 1761	LR6	509
Franklin, ae 28, of East Haddam, m. Delia **TOOKER**, ae 27, of Lyme, Jan. 11, 1857, by Isreal D. Burnham, J. P. Int. pub. Jan. 7, 1857	4	118
Huntington, s. Elisha & Zurviah, b. Oct. 15, 1756	LR5	b
Ichamer, s. Tho[ma]s & Jane, b. Feb. 11, 1743	LR5	267
Ithamer, s. Dorothy **CONE**, b. Jan. 12, 1790	2	14
James, s. Samuel & Sally, b. Sept. 5, 1805	2	275
John, [twin with Ann], s. John & Elizabeth, b. Aug. 28, 1743	LR6	509
John, 2d, m. Sarah **EM[M]ONS**, Dec. 27, 1753	LR5	564
John, s. John, 2d, & Sarah, b. Feb. 13, 1757	LR5	564

	Vol.	Page
HARVEY, HARVY, (cont.)		
John, s. John & Elizabeth, d. Dec. 3, 1760	LR6	509
John, m. Sarah **PHELPS**, b. of East Haddam, Mar. 26, 1767	LR7	413
John B., of Cooperstown, N. Y., m. Tryphena T. **CONE**, of East Haddam, Dec. 1, 1840, by Rev. Isaac Parsons	3	184
Jonathan, s. Thomas & Jane, b. Sept. 5, 1740	LR5	267
Jonathan, s. Robert & Rachel, b. Jan. 28, 1761	2	192
Jonathan, s. Thomas & Jane, d. Feb. 13, 1761	LR5	267
Josiah, [twin with Deborah], s. Tho[ma]s & Jane, b. Oct. 19, 1745	LR5	267
Levina, d. Elisha & Zurviah, b. Feb. 19, 1771	LR5	b
Lois, d. John & Elizabeth, b. Aug. 24, 1750	LR6	509
Losentha, d. Robert & Rachel, b. Oct. 10, 1781	2	192
Marcy, d. John & Elizabeth, b. Dec. 24, 1748	LR6	509
Mary, of Colchester, m. Eli **LORD**, of East Haddam, Sept. 8, 1822, by Isaac Chester, J. P.	3	26-27
Nathan, s. John & Elizabeth, b. Oct. 24, 1752	LR6	509
Olive, d. Elisha & Zurviah, b. July 19, 1762	LR5	b
Penelephe, d. John & Elizabeth, b. July 31, 1760	LR6	509
Prudence, d. Robert & Rachel, b. Nov. 22, 1770	2	192
Rachel, d. Thomas Harvey & Jemima Willey, 2d, b. June 24, 1786	LR8	6
Rhoda, d. Robert & Rachel, b. Dec. 4, 1758	2	192
Robert, s. Thomas & Jane, b. Dec. 26, 1731	LR5	267
Robert, s. Robert & Rachel, b. Apr. 25, 1760	2	192
Russel[l], s. Robert & Rachel, b. Mar. 9, 1767	2	192
Russell, Jr., m. Oris **HUNGERFORD**, b. of East Haddam, Dec. 28, 1820, by Rev. Joseph Vaill, of Hadlyme	2	327
Russell, d. Apr. 12, 1824, ae 56	3	46
Samuel, s. Elisha & Zurviah, b. Jan. 22, 1769	LR5	b
Samuel, m. Sally **CONE**, b. of East Haddam, Apr. 10, 1802	2	275
Samuel Cone, s. Samuel & Sally, b. May 31, 1803	2	275
Sarah, d. John & Elizabeth, b. Aug. 24, 1756	LR6	509
Sarah, w. of John, 2d, d. Jan. 21, 1762	LR5	564
Sarah, m. Jabez **WARNER**, 2d, b. of East Haddam, Dec. 25, 1786	2	162
Sarah, d. Amasa & Eunice, b. Aug. 24, 1787	2	192
Sibble, d. Elisha & Zurviah, b. Apr. 7, 1758	LR5	b
Sibble, d. Elisha & Zurviah, d. Nov. 21, 1759	LR5	b
Sibble, d. Elisha & Zurviah, b. Aug. 7, 1764	LR5	b
Thomas, m. Jane **HUNGERFORD**, Dec. 24, 1730	LR5	267
Walter, s. Amasa & Eunice, b. Dec. 26, 1778	2	192
William, s. John, 2d, & Sarah, b. Oct. 26, 1754	LR5	564
William, s. Amasa & Eunice, b. Feb. 13, 1783	2	192
Zachew, s. John & Elizabeth, b. Nov. 1, 1754	LR6	509
-----, s. Elijah, b. Oct. [ ], 1849	4	25-6
HASKELL, Edward, s. Silas, carpenter, ae 35, & Maria E., ae 32, b. Oct. 31, 1850	4	31-2

	Vol.	Page
HASKELL, (cont.)		
Ellen, d. Sept. 21, 1851, ae 4	4	39-40
Giles M., of East Haddam, m. Maria E. **NEWBERRY**, Mar. 20, 1842, by John C. Palmer, J. P.	3	184
Phebe, b. in East Haddam, res. East Haddam, wid., d. Mar. 26, 1855, ae 75	4	71
HASTINGS, Samuel S., ae 22, b. in Suffield, Ct., res. Hartford, m. Sarah A. **ACKLEY**, ae 20, b. in Haddam, res. East Haddam, Jan. 2, 1857, by Rev. Nelson Goodrich, of Moodus. Int. pub. Jan. 2, 1857	4	115-6
HATCH, Anna, d. Elnathan & Silance, b. June 19, 1780	2	186
Benjamin, s. Elnathan & Silance, b. Feb. 24, 1785	2	186
Elnathan, s. Elnathan & Silance. b. May 15, 1778	2	186
Grace, d. Elnathan & Silance, b. Aug. 26, 1773	2	186
Jemima, d. Elnathan & Silance, b. Jan. 25, 1776	2	186
Lovicy, d. Elnathan & Silance, b. Apr. 7, 1783	2	186
Silance, d. Elnathan & Silance, b. Feb. 3, 1772	2	186
Walter, s. Elnathan & Silance, b. Jan. 7, 1788	2	186
HAVENS, Clarissa, m. Alfred **WILLEY**, [Oct.] 11, [1829], by Josiah Griffin, J. P.	3	103
HAWLEY, Hannah, m. Samuel **SPENCER**, Apr. 9, 1751	LR4	468
HAYDEN, George Washington, s. Horace & Esther, b. Nov. 22, 1824	3	149
Henrietta E., of East Haddam, m. Andrew J. **DAYTON**, of South Glastonbury, Mar. 3, 1852, by Rev. Alpheas Geer	3	234
Henrietta Esther, d. Horace & Esther, b. Mar. 3, 1830	3	149
Horace, m. Nancy **GREEN**, Dec. 11, 1816, by Rev. Isaac Parsons	3	149
Horace, s. Horace & Nancy, b. May 28, 1822	3	149
Horace, of East Haddam, m. Esther **BEEBE**, alias Esther **PAINE**, late of Southhold, L. I., [Oct.] 13, [1824], by William Gelston, J. P.	3	66-7
Jane Maria, d. Horace & Esther, b. Apr. 27, 1828	3	149
Luther Paine, s. Horace & Esther, b. Jan. 18, 1833	3	149
Nancy, w. of Horace, d. July 3, 1822, ae 24	3	150
Nancy Green, d. Horace & Nancy, b. Oct. 29, 1820	3	149
Nancy Green, m. George Edward **GOODSPEED**, b. of East Haddam, Mar. 25, 1844, by Henry de Koven	3	199
Nehemiah, s. Horace & Nancy, b. Mar. 29, 1819	3	149
Nehemiah, Capt., of Mobile, Ala., m. Merebeth **POWERS**, of Saybrook, Conn., Sept. 17, 1829, by Rev. Peter G. Clarke	3	102
Richard W., m. Sarah W. **PRATT**, b. of Saybrook, Oct. 4, 1830, by Rev. Peter G. Clarke	3	115
Sarah Sill, d. Horace & Esther, b. Dec. 16, 1834	3	149
William Henry, s. Horace & Esther, b. June 15, 1826	3	149
William Henry, s. Horace, d. Oct. 17, 1828	3	150
HAYES, Abby, m. Manley **BEEBE**, Mar. 11, 1823, by Russell		

	Vol.	Page
HAYES, (cont.)		
Dutton, J. P.	3	38-39
Betsey, housekeeper, d. Aug. 29, 1849, ae 70	4	29-30
Joseph W., m. Mary P. **HALL**, b. of East Haddam, Sept. 6, 1835, by Rev. Joseph Hough	3	138
Lucy, m. Austin **BEEBE**, b. of East Haddam, Mar. 25, 1832, by Rev. Alvan Ackley	3	122
Mary F., m. Elijah E. **LOOMIS**, of Salem, Apr. 12, 1842, by Nathaniel Miner, Millington	3	190
HEATH, HETH, Abigail, d. Ezariah & Hannah, b. Nov. 23, 1763	LR5	560
Azariah, see under Ezariah		
Dyer, s. Azariah & Hannah, b. Sept. 8, 1772	2	4
Dyer, s. Azariah & Hannah, d. Nov. 20, 1773	2	5
Dyer, 2d, s. Azariah & Hannah, b. Feb. 9, 1775	2	4
Dyar, 2d, s. Azariah & Hannah, d. Feb. 26, 1778	2	5
Ezariah, m. Hannah **LAMB**, b. of East Haddam, Oct. 16, 1754	LR5	560
Ezariah, s. Ezariah & Hannah, b. Sept. 22, 1765	LR5	560
Hannah, d. Ezariah & Hannah, b. Oct. 22, 1756	LR5	560
Hannah, of East Haddam, m. Charles **CLARK**, of Northampton, Aug. 27, 1773	2	62
Josiah, s. Azariah & Hannah, b. Aug. 28, 1770	2	4
Lydia, d. Ezariah & Hannah, b. Mar. 26, 1761	LR5	560
Peleg, s. Thomas & Waight Still, b. Oct. 22, 1736	LR2	1118
Samuel Corbey, s. Ezariah & Hannah, b. Mar. 18, 1759	LR5	560
Sarah, d. Ezariah & Hannah, b. May 18, 1768	LR5	560
Thomas, s. Thomas & Waitstill, b. May 25, 1738	LR2	1118
HEFFLON, Susan A., ae 21, b. at Saybrook, res. East Haddam, m. Thomas G. **SWAN**, ae 23, of East Haddam, Oct. 23, 1856, by Rev. N. Goodrich. Int. pub. Oct. 22, 1856	4	105-6
HENRY, Aaron B., of Holden, Mass., m. Mary H. **EVANS**, of East Haddam, July 5, 1846, by Rev. Levi H. Wakeman	3	206
Elizabeth S., d. Mar. 2, 1850, ae 28	4	29-30
HETH, [see under **HEATH**]		
HEWIT[T], Hiram H. W., of Salem, m. Elizabeth **TOOKER**, of East Haddam, Apr. 30, 1849, by Rev. Simon Shailer	3	217
HICKOK, Eliphalet Holmes, s. Benjamin & Huldah, b. Mar. 13, 1768	LR7	411
HIDE, [see under **HYDE**]		
HIGGINS, Elisa, of East Haddam, m. James M. **WELSH**, of Chatham, Dec. 20, 1843, by Rev. Stephen Alonzo Loper, of Hadlyme	3	196
Elkanah, m. Mary **GATES**, b. of East Haddam, May 12, 1765	LR8	2
Elkanah, of East Haddam, m. Mrs. Sarah **DORR**, of Lyme, Aug. 4, 1785	2	82
George, s. Elkanah & Sarah, b. Sept. 4, 1785	2	82
Hannah, m. Benjamin **ACKLEY**, Jr., b. of East Haddam, Jan. 15, 1756	LR5	562
Judith, m. Nathan **GOODSPEED**, Jr., b. of East Haddam,		

	Vol.	Page
HIGGINS. (cont.)		
Oct. 31. 1802	2	271
Mary, w. of Elkanah , d. July 4, 1782, in the 38th y. of her age	LR8	2
Sarah D., m. Jared B. **SILLIMAN**, Dec. 10, 1848, by Rev. Isaac Parsons	3	216
Sarah D., m. Jared B. **SILLIMAN**, shoemaker, b. of East Haddam, Dec. 10, 1848, by Isaac Parsons	4	9-10
Seth, of Chatham, m. Caroline E. **ARNOLD**, of East Haddam, Mar. 3, 1833, by Nathaniel Miner	3	131
HILL, [see under **HILLS**]		
HILLIARD, Eliphalet, Dea., d. July 4, 1835, in his 64th y.	3	154
Lewis Griswold, s. [Lewis M. & Mary G.], b. Sept. 24, 1829	3	153
Lewis M., m. Mary G. **JONES**, Dec. 14, 1828	3	153
Margery, w. of Eliphalet, d. July 2, 1827, ae 53 y.	3	154
Marvin Lewis, m. Mary G. **JONES**, b. of East Haddam, Dec. 14, 1828, by Russell Dutton, J. P.	3	101
Mary, m. Zeno **BRAINERD**, June 23, 1833, by Rev. N. E. Shailer	3	132
Mary Chapman, d. [Lewis M. & Mary G.], b. May 27, 1834	3	153
Sophia, m. Ephraim **MEECH**, Oct. 14, 1813, at Preston, by Rev. John Hyde	3	.155
HILLS, HILL, Adelia A., m. William O. **EMMONS**. b. of East Haddam, Dec. 6, 1847, by Rev. Abraham Holway	3	211
Moses C., ae 30, b. at Portland, Ct., res. East Haddam, m. Mary E. **BLYTHE**, ae 28, of Marlborough, Nov. 15, 1856, by Jonathan O. Cone, J. P. Int. pub. Nov. 8, 1856	4	106
HINCKLEY, HINKLEY, Ebenezer, s. Jonathan, Jr. & Thankfull, b. June 11, 1750	LR4	471
Ebenezer, of East Haddam, m. Deborah **GIBBS**, of Lyme, July 6, 1785	2	2
Jonathan, m. Lydiah **ROBINSON**, alias Lydia **ACKLY**, Sept. 6, 1733	LR2	1129
Jonathan, Jr., m. Thankfull **BURR**, Nov. 28, 1741	LR4	471
Lydia, w. of Jonathan, d. Apr. 17, 1755	LR5	265
HOADLEY, Mary Ann, of New Haven, m. John C. **PALMER**, of East Haddam, May 1, 1831, by Rev. Mr. Merwin, in New Haven	3	139
Rebecca, of East Haddam, m. William **TAYLOR**, of Lee, Mass., May 6, 1846, by Rev. Stephen Geer	3	205
HODGE, Sarah, m. James **BOOG**, Dec. 29, 1737	LR2	1110
HOLCOMB, -----, s. George, b. Mar. 17, 1854	4	53-4
HOLDRIDGE, Watsell* Strong, of Colchester, m. Julia Ann **WATSON**, of East Haddam, Feb. 20, 1839, by Rev. Charles William Bradley. (* Watsell was crossed out in original manuscript)	3	167
HOLLISTER, HOLLESTER, David Belding, s. Elizur & Sarah, b. Apr. 25, 1764	LR6	507
Sarah. w. of Elizer, d. Nov. 21, 1776	2	3

	Vol.	Page
HOLMES, HOLMS, Abiga[i]ll, d. John & Mary, b. Aug. 1, 1729	LR2	1127
Abigail, d. Capt. Ebenezer & Abigail, b. July 31, 1792	2	235
Anne, d. Capt. Eliphalet & Anne, b. Jan. 30, 1781	2	76
Anne, d. Eliphalet & Anne, d. Aug. 31, 1795	2	77
Anne, d. Eliphalet, Jr. & Oris, b. Aug. 11, 1799	2	259
Charles H., d. Jan. 21, 1848, ae 5	4	7-8
Chauncey, s. John & Marcy, b. Nov. 15, 1766	LR7	417
Christopher, s. John, b. June 4, 1715 (Written "**HOLNIS**")	LR1	2
Christopher, m. Sarah **ANDREWSS**, Mar. 2, 1736	LR2	1103
Christopher, s. Christopher & Sarah, b. Sept. 17, 1739	LR2	1103
Christopher, s. Christopher & Sarah, d. Nov. 11, 1760	LR6	511
Christopher, s. Christopher & Sarah, b. July 5, 1762	LR6	511
Christopher, s. John & Marcy, b. Mar. 30, 1774	LR7	417
Christopher, Dea., d. Apr. 12, 1792, in the 77th y. of his age	2	77
Christopher, Dr., m. Esther **BECKWITH**, b. of East Haddam, Mar. 14, 1793	2	247
Christopher, s. Dr. Chris[tophe]r & Esther, b. Aug. 8, 1805	2	247
Christopher, see sixth book	LR2	1103
Cornelia H., of East Haddam, m. Henry R. **SMITH**, of Portland, Oct. 22, 1854, by Rev. James M. Phillips	3	240
Cornelia H., ae 38, b. in Lyme, res. E. Haddam, m. 3rd h. Henry R. **SMITH**, butcher, ae 36, b. in E. Hartford, res. Portland, Oct. 22, 1854, by Rev. James M. Phillips	4	51-2
Ebenezer, s. Christopher & Sarah, b. Sept. 24, 1755	LR6	511
Ebenezer, Capt., m. Mrs. Abigail **GATES**, b. of East Haddam, Sept. 4, 1789	2	235
Ebenezer, s. Capt. Ebenezer & Abigail, b. Aug. 1, 1797	2	235
Eleazer, d. Christopher & Sarah, b. Aug. 3, 1738	LR2	1103
Elifelet, s. John & Mary, b. July 12, 1722	LR2	1127
Eliphalet, m. Damaries **WATERHOUSE**, Jan. 25, 1742	LR3	1
Eliphalet, d. Nov. 30, 1743	LR3	1
Eliphalet, s. Thomas & Luca, b. July 17, 1744	LR2	1117
Eliphalet, s. Christopher & Sarah, b. Feb. 3, 1746/7	LR2	1103
Eliphalet, m. Anne **GATES**, b. of East Haddam, Jan. 8, 1772	2	76
Eliphalet, s. Capt. Eliphalet & Anne, b. Apr. 25, 1776	2	76
Eliphalet, Jr., m. Oris **CONE**, b. of East Haddam, Mar. 14, 1798	2	259
Eliza, d. Dr. Chris[tophe]r & Esther, b. July 14, 1803	2	247
Esther, d. Dr. Christopher & Esther, b. Sept. 24, 1797	2	247
Gilbert, s. Gilbert & Sarah, b. Dec. 19, 1791	2	264
Grace, d. John & Mary, b. Aug. 4, 1717	LR1	577
Grace, d. John & Mary, b. Aug. 4, 1717	LR2	1127
Grace, m. Robert **HUNGERFORD**, Mar. 2, 1736	LR3	509
Grace, d. Thomas & Luca, b. Sept. 26, 1736	LR2	1117
Harriet M., b. in Preston, res. East Haddam, d. Mar. 16, 1848, ae 33	4	17-18
Henry J., farmer, ae 35, m. 2d w. Abby T. **ASHCRAFT**, ae 32, b. of East Haddam, Mar. 25, 1850, by E. H.		

	Vol.	Page
HOLMES, HOLMS, (cont.)		
Wakeman	4	19-20
Henry T., of Griswold, m. Harriet N. **MEECH**, of East Haddam, Mar. 16, 1842, by Rev. Isaac Parsons	3	190
Henry T., m. Abby J. **ASHCRAFT**, b. of East Haddam, Mar. 17, 1850, by Rev. Levi H. Wakeman	3	223
Huldah, d. Eliphalet & Damaries, b. Aug. 19, 1743	LR3	1
Joel, s. John & Marcy, b. Feb. 5, 1765	LR7	417
John, Capt., s. of Thomas, d. May 29, 1734, in the 49th y. of his age	LR2	1117
John, s. Christopher & Sarah, b. Nov. 18, 1736	LR2	1103
John, of East Haddam, m. Marcy **CANFIELD**, of Saybrook, Apr. 22, 1762	LR7	417
John, s. John & Marcy, b. Feb. 22, 1763	LR7	417
John, s. Dr. Christopher & Esther, b. Jan. 30, 1808	2	247
John, m. Marie Antoinette **FOSTER**, b. of East Haddam, Apr. 26, 1840, by Rev. Charles William Bradley	3	178
Joseph, s. Eliphalet & Anne, b. May 13, 1791	2	76
Joseph, s. Eliphalet & Anna, d. Oct. 13, 1810	2	77
Joseph, s. Capt. Ozias & Betsey, b. Dec. 17, 1817	2	295
Joseph F., s. Henry J., farmer, ae 33, & Harriet N., ae 32, b. Dec. 3, 1847	4	3-4
Joseph T., d. Mar. 23, 1851, ae 3 1/2	4	39-40
Joseph Uriel, s. Dr. Christopher & Esther, b. July 6, 1812	2	247
Luca, d. Thomas & Luca, b. Sept. 26, 1733	LR2	1117
Lucreshe, d. Christopher & Sarah, b. Mar. 20, 1745	LR2	1103
Lucretia, d. Christopher & Sarah, d. Feb. 11, 1760	LR6	511
Lucretia, d. Capt. Eliphalet & Anne, b. Sept. 18, 1785	2	76
Lucretia, d. Eliphalet & Anne, d. Oct. 11, 1791	2	77
Lucretia, d. Capt. Ebenezer & Abigail, b. Mar. 2, 1794	2	235
Lucretia, m. Daniel **WOODWORTH**, Aug. 14, 1831, by Rev. Joseph Vaill	3	119
Marcy, d. Christopher & Sarah, d. June 25, 1753	LR6	511
Marcy, d. Christopher & Sarah, b. Feb. 8, 1754	LR6	511
Marcy, d. Christopher & Sarah, d. Oct. 3, 1754	LR6	511
Mary, [twin with Susannah], d. Thomas & Luca, b. May 26, 1735	LR2	1117
Mary, m. Samuel **ANDREWES**, June 1, 1736	LR2	1119
Mary, d. Christopher & Sarah, b. Jan. 9, 1751/2	LR2	1103
Mary, d. John & Marcy, b. Apr. 11, 1768	LR7	417
Mary, d. Dr. Chris[tophe]r & Esther, b. May 4, 1800	2	247
Mary, m. Charles **ATTWOOD**, b. of East Haddam, Nov. 29, 1832, by R. S. Crampton, V. D. M.	3	128
Mary Ann, d. Ozias & Betsey, b. Feb. 4, 1809	2	295
Mary Ann, of East Haddam, m. Joseph **WARNER**, of Lyme, Nov. 8, 1829, by Rev. Joseph Vaill	3	103
Mary E., d. Samuel, farmer, ae 56, & Cornelia, ae 37, b. Aug. 27, 1850	4	35-6

	Vol.	Page
HOLMES, HOLMS, (cont.)		
Mason, s. Gilbert & Sarah, b. Jan. 21, 1800	2	264
Mehetable, d. Christopher & Sarah, b. Oct. 3, 1748	LR2	1103
Mehitabel*, m. James **SPARROW**, b. of East Haddam, Dec. 12, 1770 *(First Written "Sarah")	2	90
Mehetable, d. Dr. Christopher & Esther, b. Apr. 20, 1810	2	247
Nancy, d. Capt. Eb[eneze]r & Abigail, b. Mar. 11, 1799	2	235
Nathaniel F., m. Sarah **STRANAHAN**, Nov. 25, 1830, by Rev. Isaac Parsons	3	115
Noadiah, s. Gilbert & Sarah, b. Dec. 14, 1793	2	264
Noah, s. Capt. Eb[eneze]r & Abigail, b. May 6, 1803	2	235
Ozias, s. Christopher & Sarah, b. July 24, 1757	LR6	511
Ozias, s. Dea. Christopher & Sarah, d. Dec. 24, 1776	2	77
Ozias, s. Capt. Eliphalet & Anne, b. Apr. 2, 1789	2	76
Ozias, of East Haddam, m. Betsey **TULLEY**, of Saybrook, Jan. 19, 1808, by Rev. Joseph Vail	2	295
Samuel, s. Christopher & Sarah, b. Apr. 11, 1750	LR2	1103
Samuel, s. Dr. Christopher & Esther, b. July 10, 1795	2	247
Sarah, d. John & Mary, b. May 14, 1726	LR2	1127
Sarah, d. Christopher & Sarah, b. Dec. 5, 1742	LR2	1103
Sarah, m. Edmond Grindall **RAWSON**, b. of East Haddam, Nov. 17, 1768	LR8	6
Sarah, w. of Dea. Christopher, d. Aug. 12, 1782	2	77
Sarah, d. Dr. Christopher & Esther, b. July 15, 1793	2	247
Sarah, d. Gilbert & Sarah, b. Aug. 8, 1796	2	264
Silas R., s. Timothy & Phebe R., b. Aug. 9, 1827	3	106
Silas R., teacher, ae 23, of Hadlyme, m. E. A. **ROSE**, ae 18, b. in N. Y., res. Williamsburgh, N. Y., June 9, 1851, by Thomas K. Beecher	4	37-8
Susannah, [twin with Mary], d. Thomas & Luca, b. May 26, 1735	LR2	1117
Thetford, s. Thomas & Luca, b. May 17, 1742	LR2	1117
Thirza, of Campton, N. H., m. Chauncey B. **PHELPS**, of East Haddam, Apr. 4, 1830, by Samuel Griswold	3	105
Thomas, Sr., d. Dec. 12, 1723, in the 98th y. of his age. "Was the first person in the burying place where he was laid"	LR2	1117
Thomas, m. Luca **KNOWLTON**, Jan. 9, 1732	LR2	1117
Thomas, s. Thomas & Luca, b. June 25, 1740	LR2	1117
Timothy, s. Eliphalet, Jr. & Oris, b. Feb. 24, 1802	2	259
Tryon A., of Norwalk, m. Carile **WHITMORE**, of East Haddam, May 12, 1839, by Rev. George Carrington, of Hadlyme	3	173
Uriel, s. Christopher & Sarah, b. June 11, 1741	LR2	1103
Uriel, m. Statira **CONE**, July 1, 1764	LR7	2
Uriel, s. Uriel & Statira, b. Aug. 26, 1764	LR7	2
Uriel, s. John & Marcy, b. Jan. 8, 1772	LR7	417
-----, d. Capt. Eb[eneze]r & Abagail, b. Sept. 30, 1801	2	235

	Vol.	Page
HOLMES, HOLMS,(cont.)		
-----, infant d. of Capt. Ebenezer & Abigail, d. Dec. 31, 1801	2	236
-----, s. John, farmer, ae about 47 y. res. East Haddam, & Antoinette, ae 43 y. b. Apr. 7, 1835* (*1855?)	4	75
-----, st. b. child of Christopher, farmer, ae 45, of Hadlyme, & Ellen E., ae 36, b. May 8, 1850	4	27-8
-----, s. Silas, farmer, b. Dec. 19, 1852	4	47-8
-----, d. Silas, farmer, ae 30, res. East Haddam, b. July 5, 1855	4	77
-----, d. John, mechanic, ae 34, res. East Haddam, b. Feb. 17, 1856	4	84
HOLNIS, [see under **HOLMES**]		
HOLT, Asa, s. Asa M. & Mercy, b. Nov. 24, 1819	3	197
Asa, of East Haddam, m. Hannah Choate **TUPPER**, of Campton, N. H., Oct. 17, 1841, by Rev. George Carrington, of Hadlyme	3	187
Asa M., Dr., of East Haddam, m. Mercy **TULLY**, of Saybrook, Sept. 18, 1816, by Rev. Fred W[illia]m Hotchkiss, of Saybrook	3	197
Asa M., M. D., of East Haddam, m. Francis B. **DEWEY**, of West Springfield, Mass., Mar. 29, 1846, by Rev. Levi H. Wakeman	3	204
Harriet, d. Asa M. & Mercy, b. Mar. 29, 1824; m. Joseph **CHURCH**, Jr., Apr. 4, 1843	3	197
Harriet, m. Joseph **CHURCH**, Jr., Apr. 4, 1843	3	158
Harriet, m. Joseph **CHURCH**, Jr., b. of East Haddam, Apr. 4, 1843, by Rev. Russell Jennings	3	194
John, s. Asa M. & Mercy, b. July 31, 1826	3	197
John, s. Asa M. & Mercy, d. Dec. 14, 1826	3	198
Mercy, w. of Asa M., d. Apr. 11, 1842	3	198
Theodore, s. Asa M. & Mercy, b. May 13, 1818	3	197
Theodore, of East Haddam, m. Maria Gustafson **LIND**, of New York City, Oct. 20, 1859, by Rev. Ira R. Steward, of New York City. Witnesses: Ira W. Steward, Emma J. Steward	3	243
William Tully, s. Asa M. & Mercy, b. May 17, 1822	3	197
HOOKER, Abigail, wid., and mother of John Harvey, Sr., d. July 2, 1762	LR6	509
HORSON, Maria, of East Haddam, m. Zera **CLARK**, of Saybrook, Oct. 26, 1823, by Rev. Isaac Parsons	3	47
HOSMER, HOSMORE, Dorothy, d. Steeven & Sarah, b. Dec. 6, 1703	LR1	4
Dorothy, d. Stephen & Sarah, b. Dec. 6, 1703	LR1	577
Mary, m. Thomas **FULLER**, Jr., b. of East Haddam, Nov. 6, 1760	LR6	508
Robert, s. Stephen & Sarah, b. Mar. 22, 1719/20	LR1	577
Robert, m. Mary **GREEN**, Oct. 31, 1745	LR3	12
Robert, d. Nov. 27, 1749	LR5	560
Sarah, d. Stephen & Sarah, b. Sept. 8, 1713	LR1	577
Sarah, Mrs., m. Thomas **ADAMS**, May 10, 1744	LR3	3

	Vol.	Page
HOSMER, HOSMORE, (cont.)		
Sarah, w. of Rev. Stephen, d. Sept. 30, 1749	LR5	560
Stephen, m. Mrs. Sarah **LONG**, Sept. 29, 1702	LR1	577
Stephen, s. Stephen & Sarah, b. Apr. 24, 1711	LR1	577
Stephen, Rev., d. June 16, 1749	LR5	560
Stephen, d. Dec. 20, 1751	LR5	560
Susannah, d. Rev. Stephen & Susannah, d. Aug. 16, 1748	LR5	560
Susannah, d. Robert & Mary, b. Nov. 9, 1748	LR3	12
Timothy, s. Robert & Mary, b. Oct. 30, 1746	LR3	12
Zachariah, s. Stephen & Sarah, b. Jan. 25, 1715/16	LR1	577
Zachariah, s. Rev. Stephen & Sarah, d. Feb. 13, 1737/8	LR5	560
HOUSE, ------, s. Chauncey, manufacturer, ae 31, & Jane, ae 31, b. Jan. 20, 1856	4	80
HOWARD, John, m. Mary **FULLER**, b. of East Haddam, Oct. 26, 1772	2	60
Mary, m. John **CHAPMAN**, Feb. 25, 1752	LR4	468
Mary, w. of John, d. Apr. 22, 1785	2	61
Philemon Fuller, s. John & Mary, b. Oct. 18, 1773	2	60
Philemon Fuller, s. John & Mary, d. Dec. 25, 1785	2	61
HOWELL, Charles, s. Edward & Abigail, b. Aug. 28, 1787	2	194
Daniel Kirtland, s. Edward & Abigail, b. May 12, 1780	2	194
Daniel Kirtland, m. Hannah **NORTH**, Feb. 12, 1816, at Berlin	3	117
Daniel Lyman, s. [Daniel Kirtland & Hannah], b. Aug. 28, 1824	3	117
Edward, of Long Island, m. Abigail **KIRTLAND**, of East Haddam, Apr. 15, 1778	2	194
George, s. [Daniel Kirtland & Hannah], b. Apr. 29, 1817	3	117
Joseph E., farmer, ae 22, of Hadlyme, m. Lucy A. **BABCOCK**, dressmaker, ae 23, b. in Lebanon, res. Norwich, Sept. 1, 1850, by Nathan Weldman	4	37-8
Joseph Edward, s. [Daniel Kirtland & Hannah], b. May 23, 1828	3	117
Joseph Vaill, s. [Daniel Kirtland & Hannah], b. Jan. 18, 1821	3	117
Joseph Vaill, s. Daniel K. & Hannah, d. Oct. 2, 1825	3	118
Phebe, d. Edward & Abigail, b. Mar. 27, 1785	2	194
Reynold, s. Edward & Abigail, b. Nov. 10, 1782	2	194
Sarah Abigail, d. [Daniel Kirtland & Hannah], b. Oct. 4, 1833	3	117
Sarah Abigail, d. Daniel K. & Hannah, d. Oct. 7, 1833	3	118
-----, d. Daniel K. & Hannah, b. Feb. 7, 1820	3	117
-----, d. Daniel K. & Hannah, d. Feb. 8, 1820	3	118
-----, s. Joseph E., farmer, ae 23, & Lucy A., ae 24, b. July 7, 1851	4	35-6
-----, child of Edward, farmer, b. June 28, 1853	4	47-8
HUBBARD, Catharine M., of East Haddam, m. Milton L. **VINING**, of Hartford, July 13, 1843, by Rev. Isaac Parsons	3	194
Cynthia C., of East Haddam, m. George **GEERING**, of N. Y., Dec. 27, 1848, by Rev. Alpheas Geer	3	216
Cynthia C., ae 24, b. in Haddam, res. Meriden, m. George **GEARING**, machinist, ae 25, b. in New York, res.		

	Vol.	Page
HUBBARD. (cont.)		
Meriden. Dec. 27, 1848, by Alpheas Geer	4	9-10
Elizabeth, of Middletown, m. Charles **WILLIAMS**, Jr., of East Haddam, Mar. 11, 1756	LR6	506
Julia A., of East Haddam, m. Ezra S. **CLARK**, of Saybrook, Nov. 21, 1833, by Rev. Isaac Parsons	3	133
Lucretia, of Hatfield, m. Epaphroditus **CHAMPION**, of East Haddam, Dec. 17, 1781	2	144
Lucretia G., of East Haddam, m. Rivillo **BROOKS**, of Haddam, July 16, 1846, by Rev. Isaac Parsons	3	206
Luther, m. Caroline **BOOGE**, b. of East Haddam, Dec. 24, 1832, by Isaac Parsons, M. G.	3	128
Mary R., of East Haddam, m. Ray **CAPLES**, of Saybrook, Aug. 18, 1830, by Rev. Isaac Parsons	3	108
HULBERT, [see under **HURLBURT**]		
[HUMPHREY], HUMPHRY, Isaac, m. Mary **CHAPMAN**, b. of East Haddam, Oct. 5, 1775	2	104
Isaac, s. Isaac & Mary, b. July 13, 1778	2	104
Mary, d. Isaac & Mary, b. Apr. 1, 1776	2	104
HUNGERFORD, HUNGARFORD, Anna, d. Robert & Grace, b. Mar. 13, 1739	LR3	509
Anna, d. Robert & Grace, d. Jan. 14, 1743/4	LR3	509
Anna, m. Robert **ANDERSON**, b. of East Haddam, May 7, 1776	2	204
Anne, d. Robert & Grace, b. Aug. 20, 1749	LR3	509
Ansel, s. Robert & Olive, b. Mar. 3, 1792	2	104
Ansel, s. Robert & Olive, d. May 24, 1800	2	105
Asa, s. Robert & Olive, b. Feb. 16, 1795	2	104
Asa, m. Eliza **PALMER**, Oct. 18, 1826, by Isaac Parsons	3	88-9
Benjamin, s. Thomas & Elizabeth, b. Dec. 15, 1705	LR1	7
Bettey, d. Tho[ma]s & Deborah, b. June 26, 1745	LR4	472
Calista, d. Robert, Jr. & Huldah, b. Nov. 27, 1825	3	6
Calista, d. Rob[er]t, Jr. & Huldah, d. Sept. 4, 1826	3	6
Charlotte, m. Ogden N. **PHELPS**, b. of East Haddam, Sept. 28, 1823, by Rev. Joseph Viall, of Hadlyme	3	44-5
Cornielia A., m. Cyrus W. **CHAPMAN**, b. of East Haddam, Sept. 5, 1853, by Rev. William Harris	3	238a
Daniel, s. Jonathan & Martha, b. Sept. 9, 1738	LR3	17
Deborah, m. John **HUNGERFORD**, Jr., Dec. 27, 1739	LR2	1105
Deborah, d. Robert & Grace, b. Oct. 14, 1743	LR3	509
Deborah, w. of Capt. John, d. Oct. 14, 1750	LR3	509
Edward Codrington, s. Robert, Jr. & Huldah, b. Nov. 19, 1827	3	6
Elijah, [twin with Elisha], s. Jonathan & Martha, b. July 5, 1743	LR3	17
Elijah, s. Robert & Grace, b. Nov. 10, 1756	LR3	509
Elijah, Jr., m. Polly **GARDNER**, b. of East Haddam, Oct. 30. 1798	2	261
Elisha, [twin with Elijah], s. Jonathan & Martha, b. July		

	Vol.	Page
HUNGERFORD, HUNGARFORD, (cont.)		
5, 1743	LR3	17
Elizabeth, d. Thomas & Elizabeth, b. Dec. 4, 1707	LR1	7
Elizabeth, d. Green & Jemima, b. July 25, 1730	LR2	1093
Elizabeth, d. Green & Elizabeth, b. Aug. 27, 1754	LR5	269
Elizabeth Selden, d. Robert, Jr. & Huldah, b. Nov. 12, 1821	3	6
Est[h]er, d. John & Dorcas, b. Oct. 14, 1709	LR1	7
Hester, d. Green & Jemima, b. May 22, 1728 (Esther)	LR2	1093
Grace, d. Robert & Grace, b. Jan. 5, 1755	LR3	509
Grace, d. Robert & Grace, d. Jan. 15, 1755	LR3	509
Grace, d. Robert & Grace, b. Aug. 16, 1759	LR3	509
Grace, d. Robert & Grace, d. Nov. 5, 1759	LR3	509
Green, m. Jemimah **RICHARDSON**, Mar. 3, 1709	LR1	7
Green, s. Green & Jemima, b. Jan. 4, 1718	LR2	1093
Green, m. Elizabeth **STEWARD**, Feb. 20, 1746	LR5	269
Han[n]ah, d. Thomas & Elizabeth, b. Aug. 16, 1700	LR1	7
Hannah, m. Samuell **ACKLEY**, Jr., Nov. 22, 1727	LR2	1131
Hannah, alias Hannah **ACKLY**, m. David **GATES**, Sept. 17, 1731	LR2	1111
Hannah, d. Joseph & Hannah, b. July 13, 1778	2	219
Hesther, see under Esther		
Huldah, d. Green & Elizabeth, b. Sept. 26, 1756	LR5	269
Huldah R., of East Haddam, m. Samuel **BROOKS**, of Lyme, Mar. 19, 1850, by Rev. Stephen A. Loper, of Hadlyme	3	223
James, s. Tho[ma]s & Deborah, b. Sept. 7, 1747	LR4	472
Jane, d. John & Dorcas, b. Jan. 27, 1708	LR1	6
Jane, m. Thomas **HARVEY**, Dec. 24, 1730	LR5	267
Jemimah, d. Green & Jemimah, b. Jan. 9, 1709/10	LR1	8
Jemima, alias **RICHARDSON**, m. Matthias **FULLER**, Apr. 16, 1741	LR2	1099
John, m. Deborah **SPENCER**, Dec. 3, 1702	LR1	4
John, s. John & Deborah, b. Aug. last day, 1712	LR1	10
John, s. John, d. July 30, 1714	LR1	10
John, s. Thomas & Elizabeth, b. Mar. 4, 1718	LR1	579
John, s. Robert & Grace, b. Feb. 21, 1736/7	LR3	509
John, Jr., m. Deborah **HUNGERFORD**, Dec. 27, 1739	LR2	1105
John, Capt., d. July 9, 1748	LR3	509
John, s. Lemuel R. & Abigail, b. Dec. 31, 1787	2	182
John Bigelow, s. [Zachariah & Anna], b. Oct. 26, 1819	3	143
Jonathan, m. Martha **WELLS**, Jan. 13, 1736/7	LR3	17
Joseph, s. Tho[ma]s & Deborah, b. Feb. 3, 1749	LR4	472
Joseph, m. Hannah **GREEN**, b. of East Haddam, Nov. 20, 1777	2	219
Joseph, s. Joseph & Hannah, b. Mar. 27, 1781	2	219
Joseph Ely, s. Robert, Jr. & Olive, b. July 28, 1784	2	104
Lemuel, [twin with Nathaniell], s. Green & Jemima, b. May 23, 1733	LR2	1093
Lemuel, m. Sarah **STEWARD**, b. of East Haddam, July 27, 1755	LR5	270

	Vol.	Page
HUNGERFORD, HUNGARFORD, (cont.)		
Levi, s. John, Jr. & Deborah, b. Dec. 28, 1740	LR2	1105
Louisa N., of East Haddam, m. Horace **BURR**, of Westbrook, Dec. 13, 1847, by Rev. Stephen Alonzo Loper, of Hadlyme	3	211
Lovice, w. of Robert, Jr., d. May 22, 1777	2	105
Lovice, d. Robert & Olive, b. Oct. 18, 1789	2	104
Lydia, d. Green & Jemima, b. Dec. [ ], 1712	LR2	1093
Lydia, d. Green & Jemima, b. Dec. 30, 1724	LR2	1093
Lydia, m. Benjamin **CHAMBERLAIN**, b. of East Haddam, Sept. 17, 1821, by Isaac Chester, J. P.	3	11
Marie Antoinette, d. Robert, Jr. & Huldah, b. Aug. 4, 1823	3	6
Marie Antoinette, of East Haddam, m. Hiram **HURLBURT**, of Utica, N. Y., Jan. 17, 1843, by Rev. George Carrington	3	172
Mary, m. Stephen **CONE**, Feb. 5, 1702	LR2	1116
Mary, d. John & Deborah, b. Nov. 3, 1703	LR1	4
Mary, d. Green & Jemima, b. Dec. 26, 1720	LR2	1093
Mary, d. Thomas & Deborah, b. Nov. 20, 1740	LR4	472
Mary, m. Enoch **BROCKWAY**, b. of East Haddam, May 1, 1781	2	206
Mercy Ann, d. [Zachariah & Anna], b. Jan. 28, 1822	3	143
Mercy Ann, of East Haddam, m. Aner **GROVER**, of Tolland, Jan. 27, 1842, by Isaac Parsons, M. V. D.	3	188
Miranda, of East Haddam, m. John K. **TIFFANY**, of Lyme, Aug. 18, 1825, by Rev. Joseph Vaill, of Hadlyme	3	78
Nathaniell, [twin with Lemuel], s. Green & Jemima, b. May 23, 1733	LR2	1093
Nathaniel, m. Rachel **CONE**, Dec. 8, 1756	LR5	269
Oris, m. Russell **HARVEY**, Jr., b. of East Haddam, Dec. 28, 1820, by Rev. Joseph Vaill, of Hadlyme	2	327
Prudence, d. Green & Jemima, b. Jan. 18, 1716	LR2	1093
Prudence, d. Green & Elizabeth, b. Feb. 10, 1751	LR5	269
Rachel, d. Green & Jemima, b. Oct. 12, 1722	LR2	1093
Rachel, m. Joseph **SPENCER**, June 24, 1736	LR2	1108
Rebeckah E., of East Haddam, m. Elijah **DAY**, of Colchester, Oct. 18, 1827, by Rev. Joseph Vaill, of Hadlyme	3	95
Rebeckah Ely, d. Robert & Olive, b. Apr. 20, 1804	2	104
Richard, s. Lemuel R. & Abigail, b. Dec. 8, 1788	2	182
Richard, s. Robert & Olive, b. Nov. 28, 1798	2	104
Richard, s. Lieut. Robert & Olive, d. Nov. 10, 1815, ae 17 y. Was killed when cutting a tree	2	105
Robert, s. John, b. Jan. 3, 1715/16	LR1	10
Robert, m. Grace **HOLMES**, Mar. 2, 1736	LR3	509
Robert, s. Robert & Grace, b. Jan. 23, 1751/2	LR3	509
Robart, Jr., of East Haddam, m. Lovice **WARNER**, of Lyme, Feb. 14. 1776	2	104
Robert. s. Robert, Jr. & Lovice, b. Jan. 17, 1777	2	104
Robert. Jr., Capt., of East Haddam, m. Huldah R. **SKINNER**,		

	Vol.	Page
HUNGERFORD,HUNGARFORD, (cont.)		
of Colchester, Dec. 28, 1820, by Rev. Jacob Scales, of Colchester	3	6
Robert Lawrence, s. Robert & Huldah, b. Apr. 4, 1837	3	6
Ruth, d. John & Deborah, b. Aug. 6, 1705	LR1	4
Sarah, d. Green & Jemima, b. Dec. 29, 1714	LR2	1093
Sarah, d. Green & Elizabeth, b. Jan. 16, 1747	LR5	269
Silence, d. Robert & Grace, b. May 6, 1747	LR3	509
Stephen, s. Green & Jemima, b. May 1, 1726	LR2	1093
Susannah, d. Green & Elizabeth, b. Jan. 10, 1749	LR5	269
Thankful, d. John & Deborah, b. Oct. 22, 1713	LR1	10
Thomas, s. Thomas & Elizabeth, b. July 11, 1702	LR1	7
Thomas, m. Deborah **CHALKER**, Jan. 7, 1739	LR4	472
Thomas, s. Tho[ma]s & Deborah, b. Feb. 12, 1742	LR4	472
Thomas, s. John, Jr. & Deborah, b. July 19, 1742	LR2	1105
Thomas, s. Jonathan & Martha, b. Aug. 8, 1747	LR3	17
Thomas, d. Sept. 29, 1750, ae 32 y. 8 m.	LR4	472
William, s. Robert, Jr. & Olive, b. Nov. 22, 1786	2	104
William Ezekiel, s. [Zachariah & Anna], b. Dec. 3, 1826	3	143
Zachariah, m. Anna **LORD**, May 21, 1815, by Rev. Nathaniel Dwight	3	143
Zachariah L., m. Asenath M. **FOWLER**, b. of East Haddam, Feb. 27, 1840, by Isaac Parsons, V. D. M.	3	176-7
Zachariah Lord, s. [Zachariah & Anna], b. June 28, 1817	3	143
Zaera, s. Robert & Grace, b. Mar. 20, 1741	LR3	509
-----, st. b. d. Zachariah C., farmer, & Asenath, b. June 20, 1849	4	11-12
-----, s. William E., farmer, ae 27, & Ellen F., ae 22, b. Aug. 3, 1854	4	53-4
HUNTINGTON, Abigail, d. John & Lucy, b. Nov. 21, 1776	2	40
Dorothy, m. William **SILLIMAN**, b. of East Haddam, Mar. 28, 1782	2	208
Eunice, d. John & Lucy, b. Oct. 31, 1784	2	40
Frances, s. John & Lucy, b. Jan. 21, 1770	2	40
Israel, s. John & Lucy, b. June 2, 1780	2	40
Jared Bliss, s. Jared & Elvira, b. May 2, 1809	2	8
John, of East Haddam, m. Jane **CHURCH**, of Lyme, Mar. 2, 1757	LR6	512
John, s. John & Jane, b. Feb. 25, 1759	LR6	512
John, s. John & Jane, d. Dec. 11, 1760	LR6	512
John, s. John & Lucy, b. Mar. 25, 1773	2	40
Jonathan, of East Haddam, m. Sarah **HUNTINGTON**, of Lebanon, Oct. 27, 1757	LR6	512
Jonathan, of East Haddam, m. Silence **TILDEN**, of Haddam, Sept. 17, 1767	2	6
Jonathan, s. Jonathan & Silence, b. July 2, 1770	2	6
Lucy, d. John & Lucy, b. Jan. 25, 1772	2	40
Mary, d. Sam[ue]ll & Dorothy, b. June 18, 1770	LR8	6

	Vol.	Page
HUNTINGTON, (cont.)		
Mason, s. Samuel, Jr. & Martha, b. Oct. 19, 1790	2	229
Rhoda, Mrs., of Lebanon, m. Rev. William **LYMAN**, of East Haddam, Dec. 24, 1789	2	233
Samuel, Jr., m. Martha **SEARS**, b. of East Haddam, Jan. 24, 1788	2	229
Samuel, s. Samuel, Jr. & Martha, b. Jan. 26, 1789	2	229
Samuel, of Middlefield, N. Y., m. Eliza G. **SILLIMAN**, of East Haddam, Mar. 31, 1852, by Rev. Isaac Parsons	3	235
Sarah, of Lebanon, m. Jonathan **HUNTINGTON**, of East Haddam, Oct. 27, 1757	LR6	512
Sarah, d. Jonathan & Sarah, b. Oct. 22, 1758	LR6	512
Sarah, d. Jonathan & Sarah, d. Oct. 24, 1758	LR6	512
Sarah, d. Jonathan & Sarah, b. Nov. 16, 1759	LR6	512
Silence, d. Jonathan & Silence, b. July 1, 1768	2	6
Zurviah, m. Elisha **HARVEY**, Dec. 26, 1753	LR5	b
HUNTLEY, Abigail, m. Nathaniell **BECKWITH**, Apr. 11, 1728	LR2	1104
Clarissa, m. Calvin F. **MINER**, b. of Lyme, June 22, 1823, by Rev. Joseph Vaill, of Hadlyme	3	42-43
George, m. Eunice Elizabeth **TAYLOR**, Apr. 30, 1855, by Rev. Isaac Parsons	4	55
George, ae 24, b. at Colchester, res. East Haddam, & Eunice Elizabeth **TAYLOR**, ae 22, b. at Bozrah, res. Colchester, had int. pub. Apr. 30, 1855	4	56
HURD, Abigail, m. Judah **GATES**, Dec. 12, 1753	LR3	506
Abner, s. Thomas & Mary, b. Aug. 16, 1779	2	122
Abner, m. Oliver* **DANIELS**, Nov. 16, 1800 (*Perhaps Olive)	2	269
Abner, of East Haddam, m. Nancy J. **WATROUS**, of Colchester, Nov. 12, 1848, by Rev. Isaac Parsons	3	214
Abner, shoemaker, of East Haddam, m. Nancy S. **WATROUS**, b. in Colchester, res. East Haddam, Nov. 12, 1848, by Isaac Parsons	4	9-10
Anna, [twin with Fanny], d. Thomas & Mary, b. June 15, 1794	2	122
Asenath, s. Justus & Rachel, b. Oct. 15, 1766	LR4	464
Crippen, s. Robert & Elizabeth, b. Oct. 28, 1727	LR2	1109
Crippen, m. Mary **ARCHER**, Jan. 18, 1749/50	LR4	473
Crippen, s. Crippen & Mary, b. Dec. 18, 1763	LR4	473
Crippen, 2d, m. Elisabeth **HURD**, b. of East Haddam, July 6, 1784	2	140
Crippen, of East Haddam, m. Thankful **WILCOX**, of Killingworth, June 5, 1798, by Rev. Henry Ely	2	22
Crippen, d. Dec. 14, 1845, ae 82	2	141
Dolly, d. Elijah & Charity, b. Dec. 31, 1795	2	295
Dolly, m. Gurdon **SPENCER**, b. of East Haddam, May 13, 1832, by Rev. Isaac Parsons	3	122
Dyar, s. Thomas & Mary, b. Aug. 18. 1790	2	122
Ebenezer, s. Justus & Rachel, b. Apr. 11, 1756	LR4	464
Eli, s. Elijah & Charity, b. May 23, 1801	2	295

	Vol.	Page
HURD, (cont.)		
Elijah, s. Crippen & Mary, b. Nov. 18, 1770	2	22
Elijah, of East Haddam, m. Charity **CONE**, of Haddam, Mar. 13, 1794, by Nehemiah Brainerd, in Haddam	2	295
Elijah, d. Feb. 19, 1816, ae 45 y. 3 m.	2	296
Elizabeth, d. Robert & Elizabeth, b. Sept. 15, 1730	LR2	1109
Elizabeth, m. Robertson **WILLIAMS**, Apr. 21, 1743	LR3	7
Elizabeth, m. Gideon **SPENCER**, Nov. 7, 1751	LR4	470
Elisabeth, m. Crippen **HURD**, 2d, b. of East Haddam, July 6, 1784	2	140
Elisabeth, d. Crippen, 2d, & Elisabeth, b. Dec. 9, 1786	2	140
Elizabeth, m. Abel **INGRAHAM**, Apr. 28, 1808	2	297
Erastus, s. Crippen, 2d, & Elisabeth, b. Feb. 22, 1792	2	140
Erastus, m. Eliza **PURPLE**, b. of East Haddam, June 23, 1850, by Nathaniel Miner. Int. pub.	3	226
Erastus L., farmer, ae 20, m. Elvira **PURPLE**, ae 21, b. of E. Haddam, June 25, 1850, by Nathaniel Miner	4	19-20
Esther, d. Crippen & Mary, b. Apr. 9, 1756	LR4	473
Fanny, [twin with Anna], d. Thomas & Mary, b. June 15, 1794	2	122
George Daniels, s. Abner & Olive, b. July 7, 1802	2	269
Hannah, d. Crippen & Mary, b. Nov. 12, 1750	LR4	473
Hannah E., m. Edmund C. **PURPLE**, b. of East Haddam, Nov. 22, 1846, by Rev. Levi H. Wakeman	3	207
Huldah, d. Justus & Rachel, b. Oct. 10, 1753	LR4	464
Huldah, d. Crippen & Mary, b. Oct. 29, 1774	2	22
Huldah, m. Thomas **ACKLEY**, 2d, b. of East Haddam, Dec. 14, 1796	2	255
Jabez, s. Crippen & Mary, b. Feb. 10, 1758	LR4	473
Joseph A., shoemaker, ae 31, m. Martha **WILLIAMS**, ae 16, b. of East Haddam, Mar. 25, 1850, by S. D. Jewett	4	19-20
Lucy, d. Crippen & Mary, b. Nov. 16, 1765	LR4	473
Lydia, d. Robert & Elizabeth, b. Dec. 20, 1725	LR2	1109
Lydia, m. Judah **GATES**, Jan. 19, 1748/9	LR3	506
Lidiah, d. Crippen & Mary, b. Mar. 18, 1752	LR4	473
Lydia, of East Haddam, m. John **WALES**, of Hopkenton, Mass., Oct. 17, 1775, by Rev. Mr. Parsons	2	88
Lydia, d. Crippen, b. Dec. 6, 181[ ]	2	315
Lyman, s. Elijah & Charity, b. June 28, 1798	2	295
Mary, d. Robert & Elizabeth, b. Aug. 29, 1733	LR2	1109
Mary, d. Crippen & Mary, b. Dec. 30, 1760	LR4	473
Mary, w. of Crippen, d. June 20, 1780	2	23
Mary, d. Thomas & Mary, b. Apr. 7, 1785	2	122
Noah Cone, s. Elijah & Charity, b. Mar. 13, 1804	2	295
Olive, m. Starling **ROOD**, Oct. 30, 1831, by Thomas C. Bordman, J. P.	3	121
Rachel, d. Justus & Rachel, b. Oct. 27, 1758	LR4	464
Robert, s. Robert & Elizabeth, b. Feb. 16, 1738	LR2	1109
Robert, Jr., m. Eleanor **ANDRESSE**, b. of East Haddam,		

	Vol.	Page
HURD, (cont.)		
Apr. 23, 1761	LR6	506
Robert, s. Crippen, 2d, & Elisabeth, b. Mar. 6, 1785	2	140
Robert Lane, s. Justus & Rachel, b. Feb. 29, 1764	LR4	.464
Sabra, d. Crippen & Mary, b. Dec. 11, 1767	LR4	473
Sarah, d. Robert & Elizabeth, b. Sept. 18, 1735	LR2	1109
Thankfull, w. of Crippen, d. Jan. 12, 1818, in the 79th y. of her age	2	23
Thomas, s. Crippen & Mary, b. Mar. 12, 1754	LR4	473
Thomas, of East Haddam, m. Mary **RAY**, of Haddam, Feb. 25, 1779	2	122
Thomas, s. Thomas & Mary, b. Dec. 7, 1782	2	122
Thomas, s. Thomas & Mary, d. Oct. 22, 1785	2	123
Thomas, s. Thomas & Mary, b. Mar. 16, 1787	2	122
Warren, s. Thomas & Mary, b. Feb. 4, 1781	2	122
Zadock, s. Justus & Rachel, b. Mar. 18, 1761	LR4	464
------, d. Robert, [ ], May 3, 1742	LR3	18
------, s. W[illia]m D., shoe manufacturer, ae 31, & Phebe E. ae 29, b. July 17, 1848	4	13-14
-----, st. b. s. Abner, shoe manufacturer, & Nancy, b. [1848?]	4	13-14
HURLBURT, HURBURT, HULBERT, Hiram, of Utica, N. Y., m. Marie Antoinette **HUNGERFORD**, of East Haddam, Jan. 17, 1843, by Rev. George Carrington	3	172
M. J., of East Haddam, m. Caleb S. **BEEBE**, of East Haddam, Nov. 22, 1854, by Rev. Nathaniel Miner	3	242
M. J., ae 22, of E. Haddam, m. Caleb S. **BEEBE**, ae 30, b. in E. Haddam, res. California, Nov. 22, 1854, by Rev. N. Miner	4	51-2
Matilda R., m. Ira **EC[C]ELSTON**, Oct. 8, 1840, by Francis Griffin	3	184
Sarah, m. Edward **JOHNSON**, b. of East Haddam, July 15, 1781	2	84
HUTCHINS, Charles Dresser, s. Jeremiah & Lucretia, b. Oct. 28, 1828	2	329
Jeremiah, m. Lucretia **SPALDING**, [ ]	2	329
Mary E., of East Haddam, m. C. F. **GATES**, of Middletown, May 7, 1851, by Rev. Isaac Parsons	3	231
Mary Eliza, d. Jeremiah & Lucretia, b. Oct. 5, 1825	2	329
Sarah, b. in Brooklyn, Conn., res. East Haddam, married, d. Apr. 1, 1855, ae 60	4	72
Sarah W., of East Haddam, m. William H. **CHAPMAN**, of New London, Sept. 13, [1843], by Rev. Isaac Parsons	3	195
Sarah Wright, d. Jeremiah & Lucretia, b. Mar. 9, 1822	2	329
William Spalding, s. Jeremiah & Lucretia, b. Feb. 22, 1818	2	329
HYDE, HIDE, Adaline S., of East Haddam, m. Charles **TAYLOR**, of Great Barrington, Mass., Jan. 2, 1842, by Thomas G. Salter	3	188
Alphonso M., m. Mary S. **WRIGHT**, b. of East Haddam, Mar.		

	Vol.	Page
HYDE, HIDE, (cont.)		
12, 1829, by Rev. Peter G. Clark	3	101
Alphonso S., m. Ann Elisa **CHAPMAN**, b. of East Haddam, Sept. 14, 1842, by Isaac Parson, V. D. M.	3	191
Avis, Mrs., of Lebanon, m. Col. David B. **SPENCER**, of East Haddam, Mar. 3, 1792	2	38
Rhoda, of Norwich, m. Gibbons **JEWETT**, of East Haddam, Oct. 6, 1761	LR6	510
------. d. Alphonso, mechanic, ae 38 y., res. East Haddam, & [ ], ae 38, b. Jan. 21, 1855	4	74
INGRAHAM, Abel, m. Elizabeth **HURD**, Apr. 28, 1808	2	297
Chauncey Edward, s. Abel & Elizabeth, b. Apr. 13, 1821	2	297
Eleanor Andrews, d. Abel & Elizabeth, b. Jan. 22, 1816	2	297
Eliza, m. Eleazer **SCRANTON**, b. of East Haddam, Apr. 5, 1835, by Josiah Griffin, J. P.	3	136
Eliza, m. Eleazer **SCRANTON**, Apr. 5, 1835	3	162-3
Elizabeth Mary, d. Abel & Elizabeth, b. Aug. 2, 1818	2	297
Hannah, m. Samuel **SPENCER**, Jan. 9, 1827, by Isaac Parsons	3	91
Huldah, d. Elkanah & Mary, b. May 6, 1785	2	50
Jehiel, m. Abby **FULLER**, b. of East Haddam, Jan. 2, 1831, by Rev. Nathaniel Miner	3	127
Leander H., m. Amanda **LORD**, Apr. 24, 1831, by Rev. Isaac Parsons	3	116
Leander Hurd, s. Abel & Elizabeth, b. Sept. 23, 1810	2	297
Mary, of Chatham, m. George Washington **BOGUE**, of East Haddam, Feb. 24, 1840, by Isaac Parsons, V. D. M.	3	176-7
Mary Ann, d. Nov. 22, 1863* (*1853?)	4	49-50
Selinda, of East Haddam, m. Frederick **TAYLOR**, of Salem, Aug. 3, 1834, by Russell Dutton, J. P.	3	134
Warren W., s. William & Mary Ann, b. Jan. 6, 1851	4	35-6
Wealthy A., d. William & Mary Ann, b. Dec. 22, 1845	4	35-6
Wells F., s. William & Mary Ann, b. Oct. 16, 1849	4	35-6
Wilbur, s. William & Mary Ann, b. Dec. 3, 1858	4	35-6
Wilhelmina, d. William & Mary Ann, b. June 19, 1853	4	35-6
Willianna, d. William & Mary Ann, b. May 3, 1860	4	35-6
ISHAM, Benjamin, m. Phebe **HALL**, b. of East Haddam, Nov. 15, 1801	2	170
Chauncey Foote, s. Benjamin & Phebe, b. June 19, 1805	2	170
Esther, w. of John, of Colchester, formerly w. of David **ANNABLE**, of East Haddam, d. Aug. 6, 1806	2	9
Lois Adam, d. Benj[ami]n & Phebe, b. June 30, 1803, in Colchester	2	170
Sarah, m. Stephen **CONE**, Sept. 12, 1833, at Watertown, N. Y.	2	321
JAMES, Caroline Sophia, of Chatham, m. Emory **LEWIS**, of East Haddam, Nov. 3, 1850, by Rev. Jacob Gardner	3	228
JEFFREY, Elizabeth, of East Haddam, m. Samuel **CONDAL**, of Colchester, Nov. 28, last [1822], by Josiah Griffen, J. P.	3	33
JEWETT, Albert, of New Hartford, m. Ann Maria **PALMER**, of		

	Vol.	Page
JEWETT, (cont.)		
East Haddam, Nov. 28, 1848, by Rev. Isaac Parsons	3	215
Amanda, of East Haddam, m. Charles **CHURCH**, of Ogden, N. Y., Oct. 4. 1826, by Rev. Herman L. Vaill	3	86
Anna, d. Nathan & Deborah, b. Feb. 21, 1764	LR6	507
Betty, d. Nathan & Deborah, b. June 4, 1759	LR6	507
Deby, d. Capt. Nathan & Deborah, b. Jan. 12, 1777	LR6	507
Dyar, s. Capt. Nathan & Deborah, b. Jan. 23, 1780	LR6	507
Emily, of East Haddam, m. Nathan **STARK**, 2d, of Lyme, Dec. 20, 1831, by Rev. Alvan Ackley	3	121
George, s. Gib[bon]s & Rhoda, b. Feb. 18, 1768	LR6	510
Gibbons, of East Haddam, m. Hannah **AYER**, of Saybrook, June 12, 1760	LR6	510
Gibbons, of East Haddam, m. Rhoda **HIDE**, of Norwich, Oct. 6, 1761	LR6	510
Gibbons, s. Gibbons & Rhoda, b. Apr. 16, 1766	LR6	510
Gibbons, Dr., d. Aug. 10, 1789	LR6	510
Hannah, d. Nathan & Deborah, b. Oct. 3, 1757	LR6	507
Hannah, w. of Gibbons, d. Dec. 25, 1760	LR6	510
Hannah, d. Gibbons & Rhoda, b. Oct. 11, 1762	LR6	510
John Griswold, s. Nathan & Deborah, b. Sept. 17, 1771	LR6	507
Laura M., m. Victor M. **JOHNSON**, Dec. 5, 1825, by Josiah Hawes, J. P.	3	131
Lurintha, d. Nathan & Deborah, b. Nov. 12, 1761	LR6	507
Marcy, m. William **BAKER**, June 12, 1760	LR7	417
Nathan, m. Deborah **GRISWOLD**, b. of Lyme, Dec. 9, 1756	LR6	507
Nathan, s. Nathan & Deborah, b. July 20, 1767	LR6	507
Rhoda, d. Gib[bo]n[s] & Rhoda, b. Apr. 12, 1764	LR6	510
Rhoda, m. Reuben **CHAMPION**, b. of East Haddam, Nov. 12, 1782	2	124
Samuel, s. Nathan & Deborah, b. July 21, 1769	LR6	507
JOELS, William H., m. Mary **THOMAS**, Oct. 26, 1831, by Rev. Benjamin G. Goff	3	120
JOHNSON, Almira, Mrs., ae 18, of East Haddam & Daniel **PURPLE**, ae 35, of East Haddam, had int. pub. Sept. 12, 1856	4	97
Almira, [of East Haddam], m. Daniel **PURPLE**, of East Haddam, Sept. 12, 1856, at Colchester, by Octavius Emmons, J. P.	4	98
Amanda G., of East Haddam, m. Nathaniel **BATELLE**, of Montgomery, Ala., Aug. 1, 1824, by Rev. Isaac Parsons	3	62-63
Amasa, of Manchester, m. Elizabeth **BANNING**, of East Haddam, May 19, 1839, by Rev. George Carrington, of Hadlyme	3	173
Benjamin L., of East Haddam, m. Nancy **MACK**, of Essex, Oct. 2. 1842, by Rev. Benjamin G. Goff	3	192
Caroline, d. Dr. David & Stella, b. Mar. 18, 1802	2	261
Catherine, d. David & Stella, b. July 5, 1807	2	261

	Vol.	Page
JOHNSON, (cont.)		
Daniel, of Chatham, m. Hannah **SPENCER**, of East Haddam, Dec. 14, 1834, by Rev. Isaac Parsons	3	135
David, Dr., of Colchester, m. Mrs. Stella **ARNOLD**, of East Haddam, Apr. 29, 1799, by Rev. W[illia]m Lyman	2	261
David, s. David & Stella, b. Mar. 23, 1804	2	261
Diodate, Rev., d. Jan. 15, 1773	2	37
Edward, m. Sarah **HULBERT**, b. of East Haddam, July 15, 1781	2	84
Edward, s. Edward & Sarah, b. Sept. 2, 1783	2	84
Emory, of Middle Haddam, m. Eliza Ann **CARD**, of East Haddam, Oct. 24, 1838, by Rev. Ebenezer Loomis	3	166
Jenet Louisa, d. David & Stella, b. Sept. 29, 1811	2	261
Joseph Arnold, s. David & Stella, b. Aug. 17, 1809	2	261
Mary, Mrs., of Middletown, m. Rev. Elijah **PARSONS**, of East Haddam, Nov. 5, 1792	2	150
Nelson L., m. Ann **YOUNG**, Nov. 28, 1839, by Edward P. Brownell, J. P.	3	174
Stella, d. David & Stella, b. Feb. 6, 1800	2	261
Victor M., m. Laura M. **JEWETT**, Dec. 5, 1825, by Josiah Hawes, J. P.	3	131
------, s. Joseph, mechanic, ae 34, res. East Haddam, b. May 1, 1856	4	95
JONES, Adosha, of East Haddam, m. Joshua Taylor, of Middle Haddam, Sept. 24, 1837, by Nathaniel Miner	3	159
Agnes, d. George W., merchant, ae 34, & Clarinda L., ae 33, b. Oct. 3, 1850	4	31-2
Asa, s. Diodate & Mary, b. Mar. 28, 1796	2	245
Augustus P., of Hebron, m. Emeline E. **EMMONS**, of East Haddam, Feb. 21, 1827, by Rev. Herman L. Vaill	3	93
Daniel, s. Samuel & Keziah, b. Dec. 28, 1770	2	74
Daniel, s. Samuel & Keziah, b. May 25, 1773	2	74
Daniel, s. Samuel & Keziah, d. Oct. 28, 1773	2	75
David, d. May 10, 1850, ae 9 m.	4	29-30
Diodate, m. Mary **SMITH**, b. of East Haddam, July 1, 1789	2	245
Diodate, s. Diodate & Mary, b. Nov. 12, 1791	2	245
Eliphalet Smith, s. Diodate & Mary, b. June 30, 1798	2	245
Emeline Emmons, d. [Augustus P. & Emeline E.], b. Nov. 2, 1839	3	93
Erastus, s. Diodate & Mary, b. Apr. 19, 1790	2	245
Frederic Cornelius, [s. Augustus P. & Emeline E.], b. Apr. 17, 1834	2	93
Frederick Cornelius, of New York City, m. Josephine Graham **YOUNG**, of New York City, June 15, 1859, at New York	3	94
Hannah S., m. John **STARK**, Jr., Dec. 25, 1826, by Russell Dutton	3	91
Hannah Smith, d. Diodate & Mary, b. Feb. 24, 1807	2	245
Henry, s. Diodate & Mary, b. Oct. 2, 1800	2	245

	Vol.	Page
JONES, (cont.)		
Maria B., m. Henry **PALMER**, b. of East Haddam, Apr. 23, 1843, by Rev. Cha[rle]s Thompson, of Salem	3	194
Mary, d. Samuel & Keziah, b. Nov. 24, 1767	2	74
Mary, w. of Capt. Diodate, d. Mar. 4, 1813, ae 46	2	246
Mary G., m. Marvin Lewis **HILLIARD**, b. of East Haddam, Dec. 14, 1828, by Russell Dutton, J. P.	3	101
Mary G., m. Lewis M. **HILLIARD**, Dec. 14, 1828	3	153
Mary J., of East Haddam, m. Richard **EDWARDS**, of Portland, May 7, 1851, by Rev. Alpheas Geer, in St. Stephen's Church	3	231
Samuel, of East Haddam, m. Keziah **GRIDLEY**, of Farmington, Nov. 30, 1762	2	74
Samuel, s. Samuel & Keziah, b. Nov. 19, 1763	2	74
Sarah Ann, b. in Glastenbury, resident of East Haddam, m. William P. **PETERS**, of Sheffield, Mass., Nov. 7, 1830, by Rev. Isaac Parsons	3	115
Temperance, m. Francis **CHAPMAN**, Oct. 10, 1749	LR4	474
Warren G., m. Clarine **OLMSTED**, b. of East Haddam, June 10, 1833, by Nathaniel Miner	3	131
Warren Green, s. Diodate & Mary, b. Nov. 2, 1802	2	245
William Albert, s. [William B. & Caroline], b. June 17, 1830	3	91
William B., m. Caroline **STARK**, Dec. 24, 1826, by Russell Dutton, J. P.	3	91
William Bradley, s. Diodate & Mary, b. Nov. 23, 1804	2	245
William Wallace, s. [Augustus P. & Emeline E.], b. May 13, 1831, at Marlborough	3	93
William Wallace, of La Cross, Wis., m. Mary Augustus **STROUT**, of Auburn, Me., Feb. 16, 1859, at Auburn, Me.	3	94
Wilson, s. Diodate & Mary, b. Sept. 20, 1793	2	245
JOSLING, Samuel, s. Samuel & Annis, b. Nov. 22, 1770	2	28
KEATING, James, farmer, b. in Tipperara, Ireland, res. E. Haddam, d. July 6, 1851, ae 21	4	39-40
KEECH, J. Waterman, of Pennington, N. J., m. Elizabeth A. **MARTIN**, of East Haddam, Dec. 31, 1848, by Rev. Alpheas Geer	3	217
KEENAN, Stephen, ae 24, b. at Alvally, Ireland, res. East Haddam, m. Ann **DONAHUE**, ae 22, b. at County Tyrone, Ireland, res. East Haddam, Sept. 2, 1855, by Rev. John Lynch, of Chester, at Moodus. Int. pub. Aug. 27, 1855	4	62
KEENEY, Abby J., ae 18, b. in Manchester, res. East Haddam, m. Jacob R. **MAYER**, ae 30, b. at Alabama, res. Barnwell District. S. C., Sept. 26, 1855, by Rev. Isaac Parsons. Int. pub. Sept. 26, 1855	4	61-62
Sarah A., b. in Manchester, res. East Haddam, single, d. Nov. 19, 1852, ae 19 y. 6 m. 14 d.	4	49-50
-----, child of Arnold, tavern keeper, ae [ ], res.		

	Vol.	Page
KEENEY, (cont.)		
East Haddam, b. May 4, 1855	4	76
-----, s. Bromley, tavern keeper, res. East Haddam, b. Mar. 26, 1856	4	94
-----, d. Steven, laborer, res. East Haddam, b. June 11, 1865	4	96
KELLOGG, Gustavus, of Glastonbury, b. Juliette **CLARK**, of East Haddam, Dec. 2, 1845, by Rev. Alpheas Geer	3	203
Mary, of Colchester, m. Nathan **GOODSPEED**, of East Haddam, Jan. 2, 1772	2	56
Seymour, of Colchester, m. Jane E. **WHITMORE**, of East Haddam, Feb. 9, 1840, by Isaac Parsons, V. D. M.	3	176-7
KELSEY, Strong A., of Plymouth, m. Julia S. **GATES**, of East Haddam, Aug. 27, 1850, by Rev. Warren C. Fiske	3	226
Susan, ae 30, b. at Haddam, res. Haddam, m. Richard **LORD**, ae 29, b. at East Haddam, res. East Haddam, Jan. 27, 1856, at Haddam, by Rev. Justus O. Worth. Int. Pub. Jan. 26, 1856	4	81
KIDDER, Ellen L., ae 26, b. Mass., res. East Haddam, m. William M. **WILLEY**, ae 51, b. at East Haddam, Nov. 28, 1855, at Hadlyme, by Rev. E. B. Hillard. Int. pub. Nov. 21, 1855	4	67
Mary Ann, of Moodus, m. Asa M. **GROVER**, of East Hampton, Oct. 24, 1847, by Rev. Isaac Parsons	3	211
KIEFF, Garrett, of Glastonbury, Ct., certified Jan. 29, 1868, that he was present at the birth of Minnie **BURNS**, d. of John & Ellen **BURNS**, and that it occurred May 24, 1856	4	117
KILBORN, KILBAM, KILBUM, Aaron, s. Jonathan, Jr. & Hannah, b. Feb. 14, 1772	2	44
Hannah, d. Jonathan, Jr. & Hannah, b. June 7, 1770	2	44
Jonathan, Jr., m. Hannah **CHAPMAN**, b. of East Haddam, Oct. 2, 1766	LR7	414
Jonathan, s. Jonathan & Hannah, b. Jan. 28, 1769	LR7	414
Mary, d. Jonathan & Mary, b. Sept. 10, 1767	LR7	414
KINERD, Elizabeth, m. John **SMITH**, Aug. 28, 1707	LR2	1129
KING, J. Lewis, ae 23, b. at Athol, Mass., res. Brooklyn, N. Y., m. Jane E. **BAILEY**, ae 20, b. at Middle Haddam, res. East Haddam Oct. 1, 1855, at Moodus, by Rev. James M. Phillips. Int pub. Oct. 1, 1855	4	65
Luther M., of Mass., m. Mariah E. **PHELPS**, of East Haddam, Dec. 16, 1849, by Rev. Alpheas Geer	3	221
Luther M., joiner, ae 35, b. W. Longmeadow, Mass., res. S. Wilbraham, Mass., m. 3rd w. Maria E. **PHELPS**, factory operative, ae 33, b. in E. Haddam, Oct. 18, 1849, by Alpheas Geer	4	19-20
KIRTLAND, Abigail, of East Haddam, m. Edward **HOWELL**, of Long Island, Apr. 15, 1778	2	194
KNIGHT, Dolly, d. Isaac & Eunice, b. Feb. 11, 1778	2	12
Phebe, of Waterford, m. Elisha **REYNOLDS**, of Martha's Vineyard, Oct. 11, 1829, by Rev. Isaac Parsons	3	102

	Vol.	Page
KNOWLES, Hezekiah, of Westbrook, m. Sophia H. **WHEELER**, of East Haddam, Oct. 20, 1844, by Rev. W[illia]m S. Simmons	3	201
KNOWLTON, Abigail, d. Thomas & Abigail, b. July 29, 1761	LR6	506
Azubah, m. Uzzel **CLARK**, b. of East Haddam, Nov. 20, 1777	2	108
Dorothy, d. Rosel & Anna, b. Mar. 18, 1765	LR7	5
Else, d. Rosel & Anna, b. Apr. 23, 1762	LR7	5
Elsene, d. Rosel & Anna, b. Apr. 15, 1761	LR7	5
Garrard, s. Thomas & Susannah, b. Feb. 8, 1726	LR2	1118
Gideon Ackley, s. Thomas & Abigail, b. Apr. 12, 1758	LR6	506
Hannah, d. Thomas & Susannah, b. Nov. 19, 1737	LR2	1118
Junia, d. Lieut. Thomas & Susan[n]a, b. Mar. 14, 1698	LR1	6
Luca, m. Thomas **HOLMES**, Jan. 9, 1732	LR2	1117
Lucy, d. Lieut. Thomas & Susan[n]a, b. Dec. 11, 1705	LR1	6
Lucy, d. Thomas & Susannah, b. Mar. 6, 1733	LR2	1118
Lucy, m. Ebenezer **PASEVEL**, Dec. 13, 1749	LR5	265
Mary, m. John **BATE**, 3rd, Nov. 3, 1714	LR2	1129
Mary Lee, m. Samuel **ANDREWES**, b. of East Haddam, Apr. 10, 1783	2	162
Patience, m. William **ROLLO**, Mar. 13, 1706	LR1	8
Robert, s. Thomas & Susannah, b. July 15, 1735	LR2	1118
Rosel, m. Anna **DUTTON**, b. of East Haddam, Apr. 15, 1760	LR7	5
Stephen, s. Thomas & Susannah, b. Aug. 26, 1730	LR2	1118
Thomas, s. Lieut. Thomas & Susan[n]a, b. Mar. 31, 1699	LR1	6
Thomas, Jr., m Susannah **CONVIS**, Dec. 24, 1724	LR1	584
Thomas, s. Thomas & Susannah, b. Sept. 30, 1728	LR2	1118
Thomas, m. Abigail **ACKLEY**, b. of East Haddam, Aug. 25, 1754	LR6	506
LAMB, Hannah, m. Ezariah **HETH**, b. of East Haddam, Oct. 16, 1754	LR5	560
Sibel, m. Zachariah **WILLIAMS**, b. of East Haddam, Nov. 21, 1769	LR8	4
LAMPHERE, Charles B., s. Charles B., mechanic, ae 27, & Fidelia, ae 34, b. Sept. 19, 1847	4	3-4
LANGDON, Edward, of Plymouth, m. Prudence Emeline **GATES**, of East Haddam, Sept. 20, 1825, by Rev. Isaac Parsons	3	79
LANGRELL, Bethiah, m. Daniel **ROWLEY**, Jan. 24, 1744/5	LR3	11
LANNINGHAN, Sarah, m. Samuel **BURKE**, Mar. 1, 1846, by Rev. Isaac Parsons	3	204
LATIMER, Rachel, of Montville, m. James **CHADWICK**, of East Haddam, May 1, 1800, by Andrew Griswold, J. P.	2	311
LAY, Charles W., m. Lucy **CHAPMAN**, b. of East Haddam, Aug. 25, 1836, by Rev. George Carrington, of Hadlyme	3	145
Delia C., of East Haddam, m. Wells C. **ANDREWS**, of Haddam, Mar. 29, 1848, by Rev. Levi H. Wakeman	3	212
Eliner, m. Samuel **ANDRUS**, Nov. 18, 1708 (Perhaps Eliner **LEE** or **LOE**)	LR1	6
Ezra M., of Lyme, m. Phebe H. **ACHCRAFT**, of East		

	Vol.	Page
LAY, (cont.)		
Haddam, June 22, 1845, by Rev. W[illia]m S. Simmons, at the Methodist Chapel Moodus	3	202
George W., of Lyme, m. Abby M. **BANNING**, of East Haddam, Mar. 28, 1841, by Rev. Hiram Walden	3	185
Pleiades B., m. William H. **WILLIAMS**, b. of Saybrook, Aug. 8, 1831, by Rev. Isaac Parsons	3	119
LEANTRY, Charles W., of Chatham, m. Ann **CHAPMAN**, of East Haddam, Sept. 16, 1832, by Rev. Peter G. Clarke	3	125
LEE, Abigail, m. David **CHAPMAN**, Feb. 5, 1723/4	LR2	1131
Diodate, of Lebanon, m. Harriet **SPENCER**, of East Haddam, Nov. 26, 1823, by Rev. Isaac Parsons	3	49
Edward A., m. Adelaide A. **ELY**, b. of East Haddam, July 31, 1853, by Rev. Isaac Parsons	3	238a
Edward N., mechanic, ae 21, m. Adalaide C. **ELY**, shoe binder, ae 18, b. of East Haddam, July 31, 1853, by Rev. Isaac Parsons	4	45-6
Eliner, m. Samuel **ANDRUS**, Nov. 18, 1708 (Perhaps Eliner **LAY** or **LOE**)	LR1	6
Frederick W., ae 22, of Guilford, m. Lucy A. **ABELL**, ae 18, b. at East Hampton, res. East Haddam, Oct. 19, 1856, by Rev. Nelson Goodrich. Int. pub.	4	104
George, of Manchester, m. Ellen L. **GATES**, of East Haddam, June 18, 1849, by Rev. Stephen A. Loper, of Hadlyme	3	218
George, merchant, ae 31, b. in Rome, Ohio, res. East Hartford, m. Ellen L. **GATES**, ae 30, b. in East Haddam, res. East Hartford, June 18, 1849, by Stephen A. Loper	4	9-10
George H., of East Haddam, m. Charlotte A. **CHETESTER**, of Erie, Pa., Sept. 23, 1850, by Rev. Alpheas Geer	3	226
Harriet E., m. Ralph **TRACY**, b. of East Haddam, Aug. 23, 1846, by Rev. Levi H. Wakeman	3	207
Joel, shoemaker, ae 23, of East Haddam, m. Frances A. **BOWERS**, factory operative, ae 18, b. in Hartford, res. East Haddam, Mar. 30, 1850, by Rev. Levi H. Wakeman	4	19-20
Joel L., m. Frances A. **BOWERS**, b. of East Haddam, Mar. 31, 1850, by Rev. Levi H. Wakeman	3	223
Nancy N., of East Haddam, m. Zalmond S. **MARKHAM**, of Chatham, Nov. 8, 1846, by Rev. Levi H. Wakeman	3	207
Susannah, b. in Chatham, res. East Haddam, d. [Jan.] [ ], 1848, ae 61	4	7-8
-----, d. Edmund, mechanic, ae 25, res. East Haddam, & [ ], ae about 25 y., b. Feb. 17, 1855	4	75
-----, d. Edwin, laborer, & Adalaide O., b. Feb. 17, 1856	4	84
LEFFINGWELL, William, m. Eunice **BIGELOW**, of Colchester, Mar. 25, [1830], by Rev. Alvan Ackley	3	104
LEONARD, Alvah, m. Phebe **PERCIVAL**, b. of East Haddam, June 23, 1823, by Rev. Isaac Parsons	3	42-43
Phebe A., of East Haddam, m. Robert W. **LOOMIS**, of		

	Vol.	Page
LEONARD, (cont.)		
Colchester, Nov. 28, 1850, by Rev. Isaac Parsons	3	228
LESTER, Clara Louisa, d. [George W. & Clarissa M.], b. Mar. 8, 1851	3	161
George S., s. George W., merchant, ae 30, & Clarissa M., ae 26, b. Aug. 25, 1849	4	27-8
George Seymour, s. [George W. & Clarissa M.], b. Aug. 25, 1849	3	161
George W., m. Clarissa M. **WHITMAN**, b. of East Haddam, Aug. 17, 1842	3	161
George W., m. Clarissa M. **WHITMORE**, b. of East Haddam, Aug. 17, 1842, by Isaac Parsons, M. G.	3	191
Mary, m. Oliver S. **SILLIMAN**, Nov. 26, 1829, by Isaac Parsons	3	104
Richard Whitman, s. [George W. & Clarissa M.], b. Jan. 16, 1844	3	161
------, d. George W., merchant, ae 31, & Clarissa M., b. Mar. 25, 1851	4	31-2
LETTS, James M., of DeRuyter, N. Y., m. Eunice **DANIELS**, of East Haddam, May 15, 1841, by Isaac Parsons, M. V. D.	3	185
LEWIS, Benjamin, of Colchester, m. Polly **HALL**, of East Haddam, Jan. 1, 1824, by Rev. Isaac Parsons	3	50-51
Benjamin, d. Mar. 10, 1840	3	52
Eleazer, of Haddam, m. Hannah **FULLER**, of East Haddam, June 30, 1831, by Rev. Isaac Parsons	3	119
Elisha, m. Hannah **CUNNINGHAM**, b. of Middletown, Sept. 25, 1823, by Rev. Simeon Dickinson, at the house of Richard Lord	3	44-45
Emory, of East Haddam, m. Caroline Sophia **JAMES**, of Chatham, Nov. 3, 1850, by Rev. Jacob Gardner	3	228
George, 2d, of Chatham, m. Fanny **BRAINERD**, of East Haddam, Jan. 15, 1824, by Rev. Isaac Parsons	3	50-51
Judah, d. Apr. 18, 1847	3	123
Sally, of Colchester, m. Gamaliel Ripley **TRACY**, of East Haddam, Oct. 15, 1789	2	215
Sylvia Eliza, ae 23, b. in Haddam, res. E. Haddam, m. Zalmon **CADY**, stone cutter, ae 41, of Chatham, Mar. 6, 1853, by Jacob Gardner	4	43-4
LIND, Maria Gustafson, of New York City, m. Theodore **HOLT**, of East Haddam, Oct. 20, 1859, by Rev. Ira R. Steward, of New York City. Witnesses: Ira W. Steward, Emma J. Steward	3	243
LINDSLEY, Abba Ann, d. Silvanus & Abigail, b. Aug. 2, 1802	2	257
Abby Ann, m. Edwin **FOOT**, May 20, 1821, by Rev. Solomon Blakesley	3	7
Abigail, of East Haddam, m. Samuel **TIBBALS**, of Meriden, May 20, 1822, by Reuben Ives. Int. pub. in Meriden	3	25
Edward Johnson, s. Silvanus & Abigail, b. Dec. 4, 1796	2	257

	Vol.	Page
LINDSLEY, (cont.)		
George White, s. Dr. Silvanus & Abigail, b. Mar. 5, 1794	2	257
Sally White, d. Silva[nu]s & Abigail, b. Dec. 15, 1803	2	257
Sylvanus, Dr., m. Mrs. Abigail **WHITE**, b. of East Haddam, Apr. 28, 1793	2	257
Sylvester Brainard, s. Dr. Sylvanus & Abigail, b. Dec. 17, 1798	2	257
LISK, Huldah, m. Gideon **COOK**, b. of East Haddam, Mar. 20, 1776	2	116
LITTLE, Anna, d. Dr. John & Anna, b. May 29, 1770	2	70
Betsey, d. John, b. Apr. 21, 1785	2	70
George, s. John & Anna, b. Jan. 19, 1782	2	70
John, s. John & Anna, b. June 16, 1776	2	70
Polly, d. John & Anna, b. Jan. 23, 1773	2	70
LOE*, Eliner, m. Samuel **ANDRUS**, Nov. 18, 1708 (*Perhaps "**LEE**" or "**LAY**")	LR1	6
LONG, Sarah, Mrs., m. Stephen **HOSMER**, Sept. 29, 1702	LR1	577
LOOKER, (?)*, Julia Amelia, of Lyme, m. Ralph H. **STODDARD**, of East Haddam, Mar. 29, 1847, by Rev. Alpheas Geer (***TOOKER**?)	3	209
LOOMIS, LUMMIS, Elias, of Salem, m. Sarah **MORGAN**, of East Haddam, Jan. 13, 1830, by Rev. Tubal Wakefield	3	104
Elijah E., of Salem, m. Mary F. **HAYES**, Apr. 12, 1842, by Nathaniel Miner. Millington	3	190
Justin, of Saybrook, m. Mary **DICKINSON**, of East Haddam, July 29, 1820, by Rev. Simeon Dickinson, at the house of Mrs. Mary Lyon	2	321
Lucretia Hubbard, m. Matthew Griswold **WARNER**, Nov. 30, 1825, by Rev. Jacob Scales, at Colchester	3	94
Maria, m. John **WILLIAMS**, b. colored, May 7, 1835, by Thomas C. Bordman, J. P.	3	137
Prudence Robbins, of Colchester, m. Erastus **CHAPMAN**, of East Haddam, June [ ], 1814	2	301
Robert W., of Colchester, m. Phebe A. **LEONARD**, of East Haddam, Nov. 28, 1850, by Rev. Isaac Parsons	3	228
LORD, Abby Ann, d. George & Ann, b. Feb. 1, 1803	2	275
Abial, s. Samuel & Mary, b. Oct. 16, 1799	2	142
Abiga[i]ll, d. Nathaniell & Hannah, b. July 14, 1720	LR2	d
Abigail, d. Samuel P. & Rachel, b. Feb. 25, 1764	LR6	503
Abigail, d. Samuel P. & Rachel, d. July 11, 1775, in the 12th y. of her age	2	23
Abigail, d. Samuel P. & Rachel, b. Aug. 13, 1775	2	22
Amanda, m. Leander H. **INGRAHAM**, Apr. 24, 1831, by Rev. Isaac Parsons	3	116
Anna, m. Zachariah **HUNGERFORD**, May 21, 1815, by Rev. Nathaniel Dwight	3	143
Benjamin, s. Daniel & Lydiah, b. Sept. 9, 1763	LR4	470
Charles W., ae 29, b. at Newburyport, Mass., res. Baltimore, Md., & Laura G. **ROBBINS**, ae 19, b. at Hartford, res. East Haddam, had int. pub. Nov. 18, 1856: license issued		

	Vol.	Page
LORD, (cont.)		
Nov. 18, 1856	4	117
Christopher, m. Patience **STRONG**, Apr. 15, 1747	LR3	506
Daniell, s. Nathaniell & Hannah, b. Apr. 14, 1726	LR2	d
Daniel, m. Lidiah **CHAPMAN**, Oct. 11, 1751	LR4	470
Daniel, s. Daniel & Lydiah, b. Mar. 4, 1754	LR4	470
Daniel C., ae 40, b. at Colchester, res. East Haddam, m. Elizabeth L. **GATES**, ae 29, of East Haddam, Dec. 2, 1856, at Hartford, by Rev. J. Hawes, of Hartford. Int. pub. Dec. 1, 1856	4	114
Dorothy, d. Nathaniell & Hannah, b. July 29, 1717	LR2	d
Dorothy, m. William **BOOGE**, Dec. 6, 1720	LR1	578
Eli, s. Samuel & Mary, b. July 2, 1790	2	142
Eli, of East Haddam, m. Mary **HARVEY**, of Colchester, Sept. 8, 1822, by Isaac Chester, J. P.	3	26-27
Eliza Ann, of East Haddam, m. Philetus Francis **MITCHELL**, of Middletown, Aug. 11, 1845, by Isaac Parsons, V. D. M.	3	202
Elizabeth, of Lyme, m. Jesse **GATES**, of East Haddam, Mar. 2, 1758	LR5	266
Emeline Eliza, d. George & Ann, b. June 20, 1804	2	275
Emeline Eliza, of East Haddam, m. Urban **BURROWS**, of Penn., Sept. 23, 1824, by Rev. W[illia]m Jarvis	3	64-65
Eppaphras, s. Samuel P. & Rachel, b. May 15, 1784	2	22
Epaphras, s. Sam[ue]ll P. & Rachel, d. Dec. 18, 1801	2	23
George, s. Samuel P. & Rachel, b. May 3, 1768	LR6	503
George, of East Haddam, m. Ann **RANDAL**, of West Chester, N. Y., May 9, 1802	2	275
Hannah, m. John **BOOGE**, Jr., Apr. 11, 1717	LR1	570
Hannah, m. William **ACKLEY**, Nov. 13, 1766	2	251
Hope, d. Samuel P. & Rac[h]el, b. Apr. 30, 1762	LR6	503
Jonah, s. Samuel & Mable, b. May 9, 1758	LR3	3
Jonah, s. Samuel & Mary, b. Mar. 24, 1786	2	142
Joseph Andrewes, s. Samuel & Mary, b. Aug. 31, 1797	2	142
Louice, d. Christopher & Patience, b. Feb. 11, 1748/9	LR3	506
Louise, d. Daniel & Lydiah, b. Oct. 8, 1760	LR4	470
Lucy Ann, of East Haddam, m. Julius **ABBEY**, of Saybrook, May 14, 1834, by R. S. Crampton, V. D. M.	3	134
Lydiah, d. Daniel & Lydiah, b. July 22, 1752	LR4	470
Lydia, d. Daniel & Lydiah, d. Nov. 3, 1754	LR4	470
Lydia, d. Daniel & Lydiah, b. Mar. 17, 1757	LR4	470
Lynde, of East Haddam, m. Phebe **SAWYER**, of Lyme, Mar. 27, 1821, by Rev. Joseph Vaill, of Hadlyme	3	4
Mable, d. Samuel & Mable, b. Oct. 4, 1759	LR3	3
Mary, d. Samuel & Mary, b. July 22, 1752	LR3	3
Mary, w. of Samuel, d. July 27, 1752	LR3	3
Mary, d. Samuel & Mary, b. May 4, 1795	2	142
Mary M., of Lyme, m. Francis **GRIFFIN**, of East Haddam, Apr. 24, 1833, by Nathaniel Miner	3	131

	Vol.	Page
LORD, (cont.)		
Nancy, m. Jonathan **BECKWITH**, Feb. 18, 1813	2	319
Nathaniell, m. Hannah **EM[M]ONS**, June 12, 1712	LR2	d
Nathaniel, s. Daniel & Lydiah, b. Nov. 10, 1755	LR4	470
Rachel, d. Samuel P. & Rachel, b. Oct. 6, 1770	2	22
Richard, s. Samuel & Mary, b. Sept. 20, 1801	2	142
Richard, s. Samuel P. & Rachel, b. Aug. 13, 1780	2	22
Richard, m. Anna **ATTWOOD**, d. Oliver & Dorothy, Sept. 29, 1811	2	260
Richard, ae 29, b. at East Haddam, res. East Haddam, m. Susan **KELSEY**, ae 30, b. at Haddam, res. Haddam, Jan. 27, 1856, by Rev. Justus O. Worth, in Haddam. Int. pub. Jan. 26, 1856	4	81
Samuell, s. Nathaniell & Hannah, b. Mar. 29, 1723	LR2	d
Samuel, m. Mary **CAR[R]IER**, b. of Colchester, Jan. 3, 1750	LR3	3
Samuel, m. Mable **CLERK**, b. of Colchester, Apr. 12, 1753	LR3	3
Samuel, s. Samuel & Mable, b. Sept. 23, 1755	LR3	3
Samuel, m. Mary **ANDREWES**, b. of East Haddam, Apr. 27, 1785	2	142
Samuel, d. Aug. 2, 1844, in the 89th y. of his age	2	143
Samuel Clark, s. Samuel & Mary, b. July 29, 1788	2	142
Samuel P., m. Rachel **WHITE**, b. of East Haddam, Aug. 30, 1761	LR6	503
Samuel P., had negro Cato, s. of Chance, b. June 19, 1786	2	28
Samuel Phillips, s. Samuel P. & Rachel, b. Feb. 9, 1766	LR6	503
Sarah, d. Samuel & Mary, b. Jan. 7, 1804	2	142
Sarah, ae 26, of East Haddam, m. Jeremiah **ACKLEY**, ae 31, b. at Chatham, Ct., res. East Haddam, Nov. 20, 1856, by Rev. S. W. Robbins. Int. pub. Nov. 17, 1856	4	113-4
Seymour, s. Samuel & Mary, b. Dec. 21, 1792	2	142
Sophia, d. Samuel P. & Rachel, b. June 28, 1773	2	22
William, s. Samuel P. & Rachel, b. May 4, 1778	2	22
William, 2d, of East Haddam, m. Jerusha **CORNWELL**, of Chatham, Apr. 20, 1802	2	283
William, s. William, 2d, & Jerusha, b. Apr. 22, 1803	2	283
William, s. William, 2d, & Jerusha, d. Dec. 8, 1803	2	284
William, s. Sam[ue]l P. & Rachel, d. July 4, 1804	2	23
William, 2d, d. July 4, 1804	2	284
William, s. William, 2d, & Jerusha, b. Oct. 4, 1804	2	283
LOTHROP, Bethiah, m. Samuel **PEEK**, Feb. 7, 1750/51	LR4	468
LOVELY, John, s. John Lovely & Eunice **SPENCER**, b. Sept. 17, 1769	LR8	1
LOVIT, William, of Haddam, m. Susan **GRAHAM**, of Lyme, June 26, 1827, by Rev. Joseph Vaill, of Hadlyme	3	90
LOWRY, Hugh, of Ashtabula, O., m. Mary **PADDOCK**, of East Haddam, Nov. 16, 1829, by Rev. John A. Hempsted, of Millington	3	103
LUCAS, Halsey B., of Manchester, m. Charlotte A. **ANDREWS**, of		

	Vol.	Page
LUCAS, (cont.)		
East Haddam, June 16, 1852, by Rev. Warren Emmerson	3	236
LUTHER, Mary S., m. Joseph P. **MACK**, b. of East Haddam, Mar. 29, 1829, by Rev. Benjamin G. Goff	3	101
Permelia, of East Haddam, m. Ely P. **WELLS**, of Lyme, Oct. 16, 1831, by Rev. Benjamin G. Goff	3	120
Sarah M., of Lyme, m. Samuel **SQUIRE**, of East Haddam, Feb. 25, 1828, by Rev. Peter G. Clarke	3	96
LYMAN, Bethiah, d. Rev. William & Rhoda, b. July 12, 1792	2	233
Bethia, of East Haddam, m. Allen **AYRAULT**, of Moscow, N. Y., Sept. 9, 1822, by Rev. W[illia]m Lyman	3	26-27
D. A., made affidavit to Alvin T. **DAVIS**, J. P., at Norwich, Ct., July 14, 1871, at Henry A. **LYMAN**, s. of Dwight A. & Alvira, was, b. Nov. 5, 1834	3	244
Dwight A., m. Alvira **WHITMORE**, b. of Leesville, Sept. 4, 1831, by Rev. Isaac Parsons	3	119
Henry A., s. Dwight A. & Alvira, b. Nov. 5, 1834. Affidavit made July 14, 1871, at Norwich, Conn., before Alvin T. Davis, J. P. by D. A. Lyman	3	244
Huntington, s. Rev. William & Rhoda, b. Apr. 25, 1803	2	233
Lucretia Caroline, d. Rev. William & Rhoda, b. July 1, 1806	2	233
Mary Barker, d. Rev. W[illia]m & Rhoda, b. Oct. 4, 1812	2	233
Ralston Walley, s. Rev. William & Rhoda, b. Oct. 4, 1809	2	233
Rhoda, d. Rev. William & Rhoda, b. Mar. 10, 1796	2	233
Rhoda, d. Rev. William & Rhoda, d. Mar. 15, 1798	2	234
Rhoda, d. Rev. William & Rhoda, b. July 5, 1801	2	233
Sarah, d. Rev. William & Rhoda, b. Jan. 26, 1791	2	233
William, Rev., of East Haddam, m. Mrs. Rhoda **HUNTINGTON**, of Lebanon, Dec. 24, 1789	2	233
William, s. Rev. William & Rhoda, b. Nov. 6, 1793	2	233
William, m. Catharine M. **BURNHAM**, b. of East Haddam, Apr. 23, 1848, by Rev. Isaac Parsons	3	212
W[illia]m, mechanic, ae 22, b. in Henderson, N. Y., res. East Haddam, m. Catharine **BURNHAM**, ae 17, b. in Colchester, res. East Haddam, May 3, 1848, by Isaac Parsons	4	1-2
------, child, of Howard, mechanic, ae 28, & Emeline, ae 24, b. July [ ], 1848	4	5-6
------, s. William, shoemaker, ae 24, & Catharine M., ae 19, b. Apr. 18, 1849	4	23-4
------, d. Sylvester H., carpenter, ae 26, of Lebanon, & Emeline ae 24, b. May 8, 1850	4	25-6
LYON, Aaron, s. Josiah & Susannah, b. Sept. 24, 1781	2	114
Abigail, m. Edward Granger **MACK**, b. of East Haddam, Apr. 5, 1825, by Rev. Simeon Dickinson, at his house	3	72-3
Almira, d. Humphry & Polly, b. Oct. 27, 1771	2	146
Almira, d. Humphry & Polly, d. July 20, 1773	2	147
Charles, s. Humphry & Polly, b. Jan. 30, 1776	2	146

	Vol.	Page
LYON, (cont.)		
Clara, d. Humphry & Mary, b. Sept. 23, 1767	LR7	6
Clara, d. Humphry & Polly, b. Sept. 23, 1767	2	146
Daniel, s. Humphry & Mary, b. Mar. 4, 1766	LR7	6
Daniel, s. Humphry & Polly, b. Mar. 4, 1766	2	146
Daniel, s. Capt. Humphry & Mary, d. Mar. 5, 1814, ae 48	2	147
Elizabeth, reputed d. Humphry **LYON**, & Elizabeth **ATWOOD**, b. Aug. 1, 1762	LR8	5
Humphry, m. Mary **BATE**, b. of East Haddam, Apr. 25, 1765	LR7	6
Humphry, m. Mrs. Polly **BATES**, b. of East Haddam, Apr. 25, 1765	2	146
Humphry, Capt., d. Dec. 13, 1794, ae 76	2	147
Humphrey, m. Harriet M. **CANFIELD**, b. of East Haddam, Jan. 8, 1821, by Rev. Solomon Blakesley	3	1
Josiah, m. Susannah **SELBY**, b. of East Haddam, Nov. 18, 1779	2	114
Josiah, m. Marcy **ANDREWES**, b. of East Haddam, Oct. 10, 1785	2	114
Josiah, d. Jan. 21, 1829	2	115
Julia, d. Capt. Hump[h]ry & Polly, b. May 4, 1780	2	146
Lucy, m. Lauriston B. **MACK**, b. of East Haddam, Dec. 30, 1828, by Alvan Ackley	3	101
Mary, d. Humphry & Polly, b. Jan. 27, 1774	2	146
Mary, wid. of Capt. Humphry, d. Mar. 7, 1814, in the 67th y. of her age	2	147
Mary, m. Lemuel **DICKINSON**, Mar. 9, 1819, by Rev. Simeon Dickinson, at the house of Josiah Lyon	3	13
Mercy, w. [Josiah], d. Feb. 13, 1829	2	115
Nancy, d. Capt. Humphry & Polly, b. Apr. 29, 1787	2	146
Robert, s. Humphrey & Mary, b. Dec. 29, 1769	LR7	6
Robert, s. Humphry & Polly, b. Dec. 29, 1769	2	146
Robert, s. Capt. Humphry & Mary, d. Jan. 4, 1799, ae 26	2	147
Sarah B., of New Haven, m. Rev. Isaac **PARSONS**, of East Haddam, Jan, 21, 1819	3	30-31
Sophia, d. Humphry & Polly, b. Feb. 8, 1778	2	146
Sophia, d. Capt. Humphry & Mary, d. Mar. 14, 1814, ae 36	2	147
Statira, m. Denison **STARK**, Oct. 11, 1821, by Rev. Simeon Dickinson	3	13
Susannah, w. of Josiah, d. Sept. 17, 1784	2	115
Susannah, d. Josiah & Marcy, b. Dec. 29, 1787	2	114
Susannah, m. Hubart **AYER**, [ ]	3	111
Thomas, s. Josiah & Susannah, b. Feb. 22, 1780	2	114
------, s. Humphry & Polly, b. Feb. 2, 1769	2	146
------, s. Humphry & Polly, d. Feb. 2, 1769	2	147
------, d. Josiah & Susannah, b. [ ]	2	114
------, d. Josiah & Susannah, d. [ ]	2	115
MACK, Abby Jane, d. [Edward Granger & Abigail], b. Sept. 25, 1834	3	72-73
Abigail, d. Samuel & Lidiah, b. Apr. 10, 1760	LR6	513

	Vol.	Page
MACK, (cont.)		
Abihu, m. Anna **FULLER**, b. of East Haddam, July 4, 1768	LR8	5
Abihu, d. Dec. 5, 1769	LR8	5
Amelia M., of East Haddam, m. Alfred **WATROUS**, of Mereden, Apr. 30, 1848, by Rev. Alpheas Geer	3	212
Ann, w. of Hezekiah, d. Oct. 2, 1824, ae 65	2	171
Ann E., single, d. Dec. 4, 1852, ae 20 y. 3 m. 26 d.	4	49-50
Ann Eliza, d. [Calvin C. & Anna], b. Aug. 8, 1832	3	129
Anna, w. of Calvin C., d. Aug. 23, 1832, ae 39	3	130
Anne, d. Hezekiah & Anne, b. May 27, 1778	2	170
Anne, d. Hezekiah & Anne, d. Nov. 7, 1779	2	171
Anne, d. Hezekiah & Anne, b. Sept. 26, 1787	2	170
Aurelia, ae 22, b. in East Haddam, res. Meriden, m. Alfred **WATROUS**, mechanic, ae 31, b. in Chester, res. Meriden, Apr. 13, 1848, by A. Geer	4	1-2
Aurelia Melinda, d. [Calvin C. & Anna], b. July 28, 1826	3	129
Calvin C., m. Anna **BURNHAM**, Jan. 7, 1812	3	129
Calvin Church, s. Hezekiah & Anna, b. Dec. 12, 1789	2	170
Caroline A., m. Frederick A. **COFFIN**, Apr. 20, 1834, by Rev. Stephen Beach	3	133
Caroline Almeda, d. [Calvin C. & Anna], b. Dec. 6, 1812	3	129
Edwards Granger, s. Hezek[ia]h & Anna, b. Oct. 23, 1801	2	170
Edward Granger, m. Abigail **LYON**, b. of East Haddam, Apr. 5, 1825, by Rev. Simeon Dickinson, at his house	3	72-73
Edward Granger, s. [Edward Granger & Abigail], b. June 19, 1826	3	72-3
Elijah S., m. Dorothy **SMITH**, Aug. 23, 1831, by Rev. Benjamin G. Goff	3	119
Eveline Elvira, d. [Calvin C. & Anna], b. May 15, 1818	3	129
Eveline Elvira, of East Haddam, m. Alfred **WATROUS**, of Chester, Feb. 8, 1843, by Rev. Alexander Burgess	3	193
Harriet Burnham, d. [Calvin C. & Anna], b. Nov. 18, 1822	3	129
Harriet Louisa, d. [Edward Granger & Abigail], b. Sept. 9, 1839	3	72-3
Henry, s. Hezekiah, Jr. & Mary, b. Nov. 20, 1808	2	46
Hezekiah, m. Rachel **CHURCH**, Nov. 14, 1751	LR4	469
Hezekiah , s. Hezekiah & Rachel, b. July 14, 1754	LR4	469
Hezekiah, m. Anna **SPENCER**, b. of East Haddam, Mar. 20, 1777	2	170
Hezekiah, s. Hezekiah & Anne, b. Jan. 14, 1785	2	170
Hezekiah, s. Hezekiah, Jr. & Mary, b. Aug. 17, 1810	2	46
Hezekiah, s. [Calvin C. & Anna], b. Jan. 5, 1815	3	129
Hezekiah, s. Calvin C. & Anna, d. Oct. 14, 1818	3	130
Hezekiah, Jr., m. Mary **BROCKWAY**, b. of East Haddam, [ ]	2	46
Hope, d. Hez[ekia]h & Anna, b. Feb. 5, 1792	2	170
Johanna, m. Richard **BOOGE**, Mar. 12, 1731	LR2	1119
John. s. Hezekiah & Rachel, b. Aug. 18, 1752	LR4	469
John, s. Hezekiah & Anne, b. Sept. 8, 1780	2	170
Joseph P., m. Mary S. **LUTHER**, b. of East Haddam, Mar.		

	Vol.	Page
MACK, (cont.)		
29, 1829, by Rev. Benjamin G. Goff	3	101
Lauriston B., m. Lucy **LYON**, b. of East Haddam, Dec. 30, 1828, by Alvan Ackley	3	101
Lauriston B., d. Aug. 1, 1832	3	130
Lauriston D., ae 22, of East Haddam, m. Angeline A. **GARDNER**, ae 18, of East Haddam, Oct. 3, 1856, at Hadlyme, by Rev. E. B. Hillard. Int. pub. Oct. 2, 1856, in East Haddam	4	102-3
Lauriston Lyon, s. Lauriston B. & Lucy, b. Sept. 27, 1829	3	129
Lauriston Lyon, s. Lauriston B. & Lucy, d. Jan. 24, 1831	3	130
Louisa M., m. Geo[rge] F. **SWAN**, Jan. 31, 1841, by Rev. Nathaniel Miner	3	186
Lucinda, m. Jesse **SQUIRE**, b. of East Haddam, July 3, 1823, by Rev. Isaac Parsons	3	42-43
Lucy L., ae 23, b. in East Haddam, res. East Haddam, m. Samuel W. **CONE**, ae 27, b. in East Haddam, res. East Haddam, June 27, 1855, at Moodus, by Rev. James, M. Phillips. Int. pub. June 21, 1855	4	59
Lucy Lyon, d. Lauriston B. & Lucy, b. Jan. 6, 1832	3	129
Lidiah, d. Samuel & Lidiah, b. Nov. 10, 1758	LR6	513
Maria Louisa, d. [Calvin C. & Anna], b. Dec. 24, 1820	3	129
Mary S., of East Haddam, m. Jonathan W. **MORGAN**, of Lyme, Jan. 6, 1839, by Rev. Benjamin G. Goff	3	167
Nancy, of Essex., m. Benjamin L. **JOHNSON**, of East Haddam, Oct. 2, 1842, by Rev. Benjamin G. Goff	3	192
Oliver W., stone business, ae 22, m. Lucretia **CHAPMAN**, ae 22, b. of East Haddam, Feb. 24, 1850, by Rev. Charles Chase	4	19-20
Oliver W., m. Huldah L. **CHAPMAN**, b. of East Haddam, Feb. 25, 1850, by Rev. Moses Chase	3	223
Oliver W., of Portland, m. Elizabeth M. **BROWN**, of Chatham, Dec. 3, 1854, by Rev. John S. Sheffield	3	241
Orellana, s. Hez[ekia]h & Anna, b. Sept. 5, 1794	2	170
Orrellana, m. Lydia **FULLER**, b. of East Haddam, Mar. 11, 1821, by Rev. Isaac Parsons	3	3
Permelia R., ae 20, b. in East Haddam, res. East Haddam, m. Charles A. **WARNER**, ae 23, b. in East Haddam, res. East Haddam, July 20, 1856, at Hadlyme Parish, by Rev. E. B. Hillard, Int. pub. July 17, 1856	4	91
Phebe, d. Abihu & Anne, b. Feb. 19, 1769	LR8	5
Phebe A., of East Haddam, m. Horatio N. **BOLLES**, of Marlborough, Sept. 9, 1838, by Isaac Parsons, V. D. M.	3	166
Rachel, d. Hez[ekia]h & Anna, b. Mar. 1, 1799	2	170
Rachel C., m. Samuel **MARTIN**, Mar. 25, 1818	3	97
Romantha, s. Hez[ekia]h & Anna, b. Nov. 21, 1796	2	170
Samuel, m. Lidiah **BRAINERD**, b. of East Haddam, Feb. 14, 1758	LR6	513

	Vol.	Page
MACK, (cont.)		
Sarah, m. Matthew **SMITH**, Nov. 28, 1706	LR1	9
Stephen, s. Hezekiah & Anne, b. Sept. 5, 1782	2	170
Ursula, m. John G. **GRIFFEN**, Mar. 29, 1842, by Rev. Abraham Holway	3	190
Vincey B., m. W[illia]m A. **CONE**, b. of East Haddam, June 14, 1842, by Rev. Alonzo G. Shears, in Middletown	3	191
-----, s. Edward, farmer, ae about 30, res. East Haddam, & Elizabeth, ae about 30, b. Jan. 20, 1855	4	74
MACKALL, [see also **MACKET**], Betty, d. John & Elizabeth, b. Aug. 16, 175[ ]	LR6	505
John, s. John & Elizabeth, b. May 21, 1756	LR6	505
Lydia, d. John & Elizabeth, b. Feb. 4, 175[ ]	LR6	505
Rozel, s. John & Elizabeth, b. July 12, 1751	LR6	505
Rozel, s. John & Elizabeth, d. Sept. 7, 175[ ]	LR6	505
MACKET, [see also **MACKALL** and **MUCKET**], Mary T., of East Haddam, m. Elliott J. **ROGERS**, of Lyme, Feb. 9, 1851, by Rev. Jacob Gardner	3	230
MANTLE, Lucretia J., m. John **BURNHAM**, b. of East Haddam, Oct. 4, 1835, by Rev. Nathaniel Miner	3	140-1
MARKHAM, Abby B., ae 21, b. in Chatham, res. East Haddam, m. Samuel W. **FOWLER**, mechanic, ae 21, b. in East Haddam, res. East Haddam, June 18, 1848, by Isaac Parsons	4	1-2
Abigail B., of Chatham, m. Samuel W. **FOWLER**, of East Haddam, June 18, 1848, by Rev. Isaac Parsons	3	213
Anne, d. James & Jane, b. Jan. 19, 1776	2	2
Betsey A., ae 18, b. in Chatham, res. East Haddam, m. Horace B. **SILLIMAN**, shoemaker, ae 20, of East Haddam, June 2, 1850, by Isaac Parsons	4	19-20
Betsey A. W., of Chatham, m. Horace B. **SILLIMAN**, of East Haddam, June 2, 1850, by Rev. Isaac Parsons	3	224
David, s. James & Jane, b. Apr. 1, 1771	2	2
David, s. James & Jane, d. June 26, 1771	2	3
David, s. James & Jane, b. June 5, 1772	2	2
Esther, d. James & Jane, b. Apr. 10, 1774	2	2
Huldah, d. William & Abigail, b. Nov. 23, 1763	LR6	503
James, of East Haddam, m. Jane **STARLING**, of Lyme, Nov. 17, 1763	2	2
James, s. James & Jane, b. Mar. 11, 1766	2	2
Jane, d. James & Jane, b. Nov. 3, 1767	2	2
John, s. James & Jane, b. July 24, 1769	2	2
Louis W., s. Zalmon S., manufacturer, ae 30, & Nancy S., ae 26, b. Apr. 23, 1850	4	23-4
Stephen, s. James & Jane, b. Sept. 20, 1764	2	2
William, m. Abigail Cone **WILLEY**, b. of East Haddam, June 4, 1761	LR6	503
William, s. William & Abigail, b. Aug. 19. 1762	LR6	503

	Vol.	Page
MARKHAM, (cont.)		
Zalmond S., of Chatham, m. Nancy N. **LEE**, of East Haddam, Nov. 8, 1846, by Rev. Levi H. Wakeman	3	207
MARSH, Anna, m. Daniel **BRAINERD**, 2d, Apr. 16, 1768	2	42
Elizabeth, m. Israel **SPENCER**, Oct. 18, 1753	LR5	b
John, s. John Marsh & Phebe Brainerd, b. Jan. 31, 1756	LR6	503
John, m. Phebe **BRAINERD**, b. of East Haddam, May 9, 1757	LR6	503
John, of East Haddam, m. Mary **FRINK**, of Stonington, Sept 27, 1788	2	241
John, of East Haddam, m. Mary **FRINK**, of Stonington, Nov. 27, 1788* (*Entry crossed out)	2	157
Lemuel, m. Hannah **SPENCER**, Nov. 17, 1763	LR7	416
Matilda A., of East Haddam, m. Walter **MERRYFIELD**, of New York, Nov. 20, 1839, by Luther Paine	3	174
Phebe, d. John & Phebe, b. Mar. 15, 1758	LR6	503
Phebe, d. John & Phebe, b. Mar. 16, 1758	2	100
Phebe, d. John & Phebe, d. Jan. 23, 1760	LR6	503
Phebe, m. Samuel **CONE**, 2d, b. of East Haddam, Dec. 2, 1783	2	172
Samuel, s. Lemuel & Hannah, b. Nov. 26, 1764	LR7	416
William, d. July 27, 1851, ae 58	4	39-40
MARSHALL, MARSHAL, Benjamin, s. Thomas & Rebeckah, b. Oct. 18, 1779	2	198
Betsey, d. Thomas & Rebec[c]ah, b. Jan. 13, 1772	2	198
Hope, d. Thomas & Rebeckah, b. Sept. 18, 1781	2	198
John, s. Thomas & Rebeckah, b. May 22, 1774	2	198
Lidda, d. Thomas & Rebec[c]ah, b. July 27, 1776	2	198
Rebeckah, d. Tho[ma]s & Rebeckah, b. Jan. 20, 1787	2	198
Ruth, m. James **GREEN**, b. of East Haddam, Feb. 14, 1755	LR5	268
Ruth, d. Thomas & Rebeckah, b. Mar. 14, 1789	2	198
Thomas, m. Rebeckah **ACKLEY**, b. of East Haddam, Feb. 6, 1770	2	198
William, s. Thomas & Rebeckah, b. Mar. 9, 1784	2	198
MARTIN, Abby, ae 25, b. at East Haddam, res. East Haddam, m. Silas A. **POST**, ae 27, b. at Westbrook, res. Westbrook, June 12, 1855, at Gelston Hotel, by Rev. George W. Nichols. Int. pub. June 11, 1855	4	57
Adaline, d. [Samuel & Rachel], b. June 7, 1830	3	97
Catharine Isabel, d. [Joseph & Livia], b. Dec. 26, 1834	3	161
Catharine S., d. Sept. 9, 1849, ae 8	4	29-30
Charles Huxford, s. William & Mary, b. May 6, 1824	2	311
Datus, s. [Joseph & Livia], b. Dec. 26, 1836	3	161
David, s. Jonathan & Hannah, b. Sept. 13, 1780	2	156
David, m. Laura **CONE**, b. of East Haddam, Oct. 24, 1820, by Rev. Isaac Parsons	2	323
David Austin, s. William & Mary, b. July 8, 1819	2	311
David C., pedlar, single, d. Jan. 13, 1856, ae 32	4	108
David Cone, s. David & Laura, b. Apr. 4, 1824	2	323
Edgar M., ae 25, of East Haddam, m. Azubah M. **WRIGHT**,		

	Vol.	Page
MARTIN, (cont.)		
ae 20, b. in Lyme, res. East Haddam, Oct. 1, 1856, by Rev. W[illia]m Harris. Int. pub. Sept. 26, 1856	4	101
Edgar Mandlebert, s. [Joseph & Livia], b. Sept. 10, 1830	3	161
Elihu, s. Jonathan & Hannah, b. May 31, 1774	2	156
Elihu, d. July 11, 1802, at Genesco, N. Y.	2	157
Elihu, s. Jonathan & Esther, b. June 29, 1803	2	273
Elizabeth A., of East Haddam, m. J. Waterman **KEECH**, of Pennington, N. J., Dec. 31, 1848, by Rev. Alpheas Geer	3	217
Ellen Maria, d. [Samuel & Rachel], b. Oct. 22, 1838	3	97
Emma, d. David & Laura, b. Aug. 18, 1821	2	323
Ephraim, s. Jonathan & Hannah, b. Jan. 31, 1788	2	156
Ephraim, s. [Joseph & Livia], b. Aug. 24, 1823	3	161
Ephraim, m. Elizabeth C. **HARRIS**, b. of Millington, May 28, 1848	3	213
Esther, d. Jonathan & Esther, b. Dec. 26, 1806	2	273
Esther, m. William **PADDOCK**, b. of East Haddam, Feb. 16, 1826, by Herman L. Vaill	3	84-85
Esther, s. [Joseph & Livia], b. July 4, 1826	3	161
Esther P., m. Leonard S. **CLARK**, Feb. 26, 1843, by Rev. Stephen Alonzo Loper, of Hadlyme	3	194
George Lemon, s. William & Mary, b. Oct. 1, 1817	2	311
George Lemon, s. William & Mary, d. July 22, 1822	2	312
George Lemon, s. David & Laura, b. May 29, 1826	2	323
Hannah, d. William & Lucy, b. Oct. 11, 1805, in Burlington, Conn.	2	311
Harlow, s. [Samuel & Rachel], b. Sept. 11, 1823	3	97
Harlow, m. Julia Louisa **AYERS**, b. of East Haddam, Apr. 13, 1851, by Nathaniel Miner	3	232
Harlow, farmer, ae 28, of E. Haddam, m. Elizabeth E. **AYRES**, ae 19, Apr. 15, 1851, by Nathaniel Miner	4	37-8
Harriet A., of East Haddam, m. William A. **CHAPMAN**, of Middle Haddam, Dec. 13, 1846, by Rev. Isaac Parsons	3	208
Harriet Augusta, d. David & Laura, b. Mar. 29, 1829	2	323
Henrietta, d. [Samuel & Rachel], b. Jan. 16, 1826	3	97
Henrietta, of East Haddam, m. Gamaleel R. **TRACY**, of New London, July 26, [1846?], by Nathaniel Miner, at Millington	3	206
Henry, b. in Millington, res. Millington, single, d. June 12, 1855, ae 38	4	58
Hezekiah, s. [Samuel & Rachel], b. Dec. 22, 1828	3	97
Hezekiah, s. Samuel & Rachel C., d. May 16, 1830	3	98
Hezekiah Mack, s. [Samuel & Rachel], b. Jan. 20, 1834	3	97
Isaac Austin, s. David & Laura, b. July 8, 1834	2	323
Jonathan, s. Jonathan & Hannah, b. Aug. 10, 1777	2	156
Jonathan, d. Nov. 7, 1795	2	157
Jonathan, m. Esther **ANDREWS**, b. of East Haddam, Apr. 29, 1802	2	273

	Vol.	Page
MARTIN, (cont.)		
Jonathan, s. Jonathan & Esther, b. Nov. 12, 1808	2	273
Jonathan Roberts, s. William & Lucy, b. Nov. 8, 1806, in Burlington, Conn.	2	311
Joseph, s. Jonathan & Hannah, b. Feb. 26, 1791	2	156
Joseph, s. Jonathan & Esther, b. Dec. 24, 1810	2	273
Joseph, m. Livia **PHELPS**, Oct. 1, 1817	3	161
Julia Ann, m. William Hubart **AYERS**, Sept. 5, 1830, by Rev. Alvan Ackley	3	108
Justin, s. William & Mary, b. July 8, 1815	2	311
Laura, m. Herbert **AYRES**, Jan. 19, 1840, by Rev. Charles William Bradley	3	174
Lucy, w. of William, d. Sept. 18, 1808, at Burlington, Conn., in the 27th y. of her age	2	312
Lucy Ann, d. Samuel, Jr., mechanic, b. Dec. 28, 1852	4	47-8
Lucy Maria, d. William & Mary, b. Dec. 28, 1821	2	311
Mabel, d. Jonathan & Esther, b. Dec. 23, 1804	2	273
Mariette, d. [Joseph & Livia], b. Jan. 13, 1819	3	161
Mary, d. [Samuel & Rachel C.], b. Sept. 13, 1819	3	97
Mary M., of East Haddam, m. Cephas B. **RUSS**, of Mansfield, [Oct.] 17, [1839], by Rev. Nathaniel Miner	3	173
Niles, s. [Joseph & Livia], b. Oct. 17, 1820	3	161
Oliver, s. Jonathan & Esther, b. Dec. 16, 1813	2	273
Oliver, m. Julia **SMITH**, b. of East Haddam, Apr. 1, 1850, by Nathaniel Miner	3	224
Peter, s. Jonathan & Hannah, b. Apr. 15, 1785	2	156
Samuel, s. Jonathan & Hannah, b. Aug. 13, 1794	2	156
Samuel, m. Rachel C. **MACK**, Mar. 25, 1818	3	97
Samuel, s. [Samuel & Rachel], b. Aug. 25, 1821	3	97
Samuel, m. Abby **TRACY**, b. of East Haddam, Jan. 1, 1852, by Rev. Nathaniel Miner	3	234
Warren Day, s. William & Mary, b. May 14, 1826	2	311
Wells, m. Julia A. **STOCKING**, of New York, Dec. 26, 1852, by Rev. Nathaniel Miner, of Millington	3	238
Wells, farmer, ae 30, of East Haddam, m. Julia A. **STOCKING**, ae 24, b. in Catskill, N. Y., res. N. Y., Dec. 26, 1852, by Rev. Nathaniel Miner	4	43-4
William, s. Jonathan & Hannah, b. Feb. 25, 1782	2	156
William, m. Lucy **ROBERTS**, July 4, 1804, by Rev. W[illia]m Lyman	2	311
William, m. Mary **DUTTON**, Aug. 18, 1812, by Rev. William Lyman	2	311
William Dutton, s. William & Mary, b. Aug. 11, 1813	2	311
-----, st. b. s. George, farmer, & Martha, b. Apr. 2, 1851	4	33-4
MARVIN, David R., of Lyme, m. Elizabeth C. **CONE**, of East Haddam, Jan. 27, 1853, by Rev. Nathaniel Miner, of Millington	3	238
David R., ae 30, b. in Lyme, m. [ ], Jan. 27, 1853	4	41-2

	Vol.	Page
MARVIN, (cont.)		
David R., agriculturist, ae 30, of Lyme, m. Elizabeth C. **CONE**, ae 27, of Millington, Jan. 27, 1853, by Rev. Nathaniel Miner	4	43-4
MASON, Abba, m. Abraham **PLATO**, Apr. 1, 1821, by Josiah Griffin, J. P.	3	6
Achsah, d. Cooley & [Clarenda], b. Feb. 22, 1784	2	34
Amos, s. Cooley & Clarenda, b. Oct. 6, 1789	2	96
Axe, m. Punch, alias John **CAMMEL**, (negro), b. of East Haddam, Oct. 16, 1803 (People of color but free)	2	289
Catherine, of New York, m. Noah **TUCKER**, Jr., of Haddam, Oct. 7, 1849, by Rev. Simon Shailor, of Haddam	3	220
Clarinda, d. Cooley & Clorenda, b. Sept. 13, 1779	2	96
Clarinda, m. John C. **MASON**, b. of East Haddam, [Jan.] 17, [1844] by Nathaniel Miner	3	196
Claressa, d. Cooley & Clorenda, b. Aug. 5, 1775	2	96
Cooley, m. Clarenda **ROBINS**, Oct. 7, 1781	2	34
Cooley, d. Jan. 29, 1795	2	97
George, of Lyme, m. Orris **STRONG**, of East Haddam, Nov. 28, 1822, by Rev. Isaac Parsons	3	33
Grace, [triplet with Olive & Oliver], d. Cooley & Clarenda, b. June 22, 1792	2	96
John C., m. Clarinda **MASON**, b. of East Haddam, [Jan.] 17, [1844], by Nathaniel Miner	3	196
John Robin, s. Cooley & [Clarenda], b. Feb. 5, 1787	2	34
Judith, d. Cooley & Clorenda, b. Aug. 22, 1782	2	96
Olive, [triplet with Oliver & Grace], d. Cooley & Clarenda, b. June 22, 1792	2	96
Oliver, [triplet with Oliver & Grace], s. Cooley & Clarenda, b. June 22, 1792	2	96
William, s. Cooley & Clorenda, b. Feb. 24, 1777	2	96
MATHER, A[u]gustus, Dr., of Lyme, m. Wid. Mehitabel **SPARROW**, Feb. 28, 1775	2	90
Augustus, s. Dr. Augustus & Mehetabel, b. Apr. 6, 1778	2	90
Augustus, Dr., m. Hannah **RANSOM**, May 8, 1811	2	90
Augustus, Dr., d. July 5, 1832, ae 84	3	46
Eleazer Watrous, s. Dr. Augustus & Hannah, b. Mar. 28, 1812	2	90
Eleazer Watrous, m. Elizabeth Louisa **FOSTER**, b. of East Haddam, June 18, 1837, by Rev. Stephen Beach	3	152
Eleazer Watrous, m. Elizabeth Louisa **FOSTER**, June 18, 1837	3	175
Elias, s. Richard & Deborah, b. Feb. 10, 1750	LR4	475
James, s. Dr. Augustus & Mehetabel, b. Dec. 30, 1783	2	90
Mary, d. Dr. Augustus & Mehetabel, b. Dec. 21, 1780	2	90
Mary Helen, d. [Eleazer Watrous & Elizabeth Watrous], b. Nov. 18, 1838	3	175
Mehitabel, d. Dr. A[u]gustus & Mehitabel, b. Nov. 21, 1775	2	90
Ozias, s. Dr. Augustus & Mehetabel, b. Jan. 22, 1787	2	90
------, child of E. W., butcher, b. Nov. 20, 1852	4	47-8

	Vol.	Page
MATSON, Lewis, m. Cynthia **SMITH**, Apr. 4, 1824, by Rev. Elijah Parsons	3	58-59
Lewis, m. Cynthia **SMITH**, b. of East Haddam, Nov. 12, 1837, by Roswell Davison, J. P.	3	159
MAY, John, of Haddam, m. Emma **ELLIOTT**, of East Haddam, Apr. 14, 1835, by Nathaniel Miner	3	138
MAYER, Jacob R., ae 30, b. at Alabama, res. Barnwell District, S. C., m. Abby J. **KEENEY**, ae 18, b. in Manchester, res. East Haddam, Sept. 26, 1855, by Rev. Isaac Parsons. Int. pub. Sept. 26, 1855	4	61-62
MAYNARD, Anna, [twin with David], d. Jno & Anna, b. Aug. 17, 1783	2	281
Anna, w. of John, d. Jan. 13, 1802	2	282
David, [twin with Anna], s. Jno & Anna, b. Aug. 17, 1783	2	281
James, s. John & Anna, b. May 24, 1789	2	281
John, m. Anna **GRIFFIN**, [ ], 1779	2	281
John, m. Silence Sears **COMSTOCK**, Sept. 21, 1802	2	281
Lois, d. John & Anna, b. Oct. 17, 1780	2	281
Lucy, d. John & Anna, b. Dec. 15, 1791	2	281
Nathan, s. Jno & Anna, b. Dec. 2, 1785	2	281
Orren H., of Waterford, m. Delia **CLARK**, of East Haddam, Feb. 15, 1835, by Thomas C. Bordman, J. P.	3	136
Sidney, m. Hannah **RANDALL**, Jan. 29, 1823, by Russell Dutton, J. P.	3	36-37
William P., m. Mary S. **BROWN**, b. of East Haddam, Mar. 24, 1850, by Rev. Stephen A. Loper, of Hadlyme	3	224
W[illia]m P., farmer, ae 32, b. in E. Haddam, res. Lyme, m. Mary S. **BROWN**, ae 21, of Lyme, Mar. 24, 1850, by Rev. Soper	4	19-20
MAYO, Eunice, m. Amos **BOOGE**, Nov. 22, 1750	LR4	472
McARTHUR, James, m. Susan **GATES**, June 8, 1852, by Rev. Isaac Parsons	3	235
McCANN, McCAN, Albert H., s. Willis, town laborer, ae 30, & Emily, b. Jan. 26, 1851	4	33-4
Ellen M., d. Willis A., farmer, ae 28, & Emily, ae 25, b. Mar. 2, 1848	4	5-6
George E., m. Abby **PURPLE**, b. of East Haddam, June 16, 1844, by W[illia]m March, J. P.	3	199
Willis, m. Emily M. **STODDARD**, Feb. 28, 1847, by W[illia]m Marsh, J. P.	3	208
McCARTHY, Mary, ae 19, b. in Lismore, Ireland, res. East Haddam. m. Frederick **SCHUB**, ae 24, b. in Prussia, res. East Haddam, April 8, 1855, by Rev. Isaac Parsons, Int. pub. Apr. 4, 1855	4	56
McCORMICK, -----, s. Patrick, laborer, ae 35, res. East Haddam, & [ ], ae 35, b. July 9, 1855	4	77
McINTOSH, Cynthia, m. Thomas **SILLIMAN**, Nov. 30, 1837, by Rev. Stephen Beach	3	159

	Vol.	Page
McINTOSH, (cont.)		
Ella, d. Ja[me]s, polisher, ae 25, & Jane A., ae 20, b. Apr. 25, 1849	4	11-12
Lester, d. Joseph, mechanic, ae 24, & Jane A., ae 19, b. Sept. 3, 1847	4	3-4
Sophronia, m. Oliver C. **TRACY**, b. of East Haddam, Dec. 27, 1832, by Rev. Isaac Parsons	3	128
------, d. Ansel, polisher, ae 31, & Lucy G., ae 18, b. June 10, 1849	4	11-12
------, s. Ansel, manufacturer, ae 34, & Lucy G., ae 20, b. Mar. 29, 1851	4	31-2
McLEAN, Alexander, ae 33, b. at Manchester, Ct., res. East Haddam, & Harriet G **ROGERS**, of East Haddam, had int. pub. Oct. 15, 1856* License dated Oct. 15, 1856 (*Written 1857)	4	116
McWILLIAMS, Mary, m. William **STEWARD**, Apr. 8, 1756	LR5	559
MEECH, Clarissa, d. Ephraim & Eunice T., b. Nov. 26, 1825	3	155
Clarissa, of East Haddam, m. Ralph T. **WETHERELL**, of Middletown, Oct. 7, 1846, by Rev. S. D. Jewett	3	207
Ephraim, m. Sophia **HILLIARD**, Oct. 14, 1813, at Preston, by Rev. John Hyde	3	155
Ephraim, m. Eunice T. **HARRIS**, June 6, 1822, by Rev. John Hyde, at Preston	3	155
Ephraim, farmer, ae 59, b. in Stonington, res. East Haddam, m. 3rd w. Sarah **CLARKE**, ae 57, b. in Chatham, res. East Haddam, Mar. 1, 1848, by William Russell	4	9-10
Eunice Eliza, d. Ephraim & Eunice T., b. Aug. 5, 1824	3	155
Eunice T., w. Ephraim, d. July 23, 1847	3	156
Harriet N., of East Haddam, m. Henry T. **HOLMES**, of Griswold, Mar. 16, 1842, by Rev. Isaac Parsons	3	190
Hesekiah, s. Ephraim & Sophia, d. Mar. 28, 1840, in Hudson. O.	3	156
Joseph Utley, s. Ephraim & Eunice T., b. Dec. 21, 1822	3	155
Lucy Ann, d. Ephraim & Sophia, b. Nov. 22, 1818	3	155
Lucy Ann, d. Ephraim & Sophia, d. Mar. [ ], 1841	3	156
Oliver, farmer, ae 22, of E. Haddam, m. Elizabeth **GOODRIDGE**, ae 19, b. in Chatham, res. E. Haddam, June [ ], 1850	4	19-20
Oliver Spicer, s. Ephraim & Eunice T., b. Jan. 29, 1828	3	155
Sophia, w. of Ephraim, d. Jan. 5, 1821	3	156
Sophia Hilliard, d. Ephraim & Sophia, b. Dec. 1, 1820	3	155
Sophia Hilliard, d. Ephraim & Sophia, d. July 13, 1840	3	156
MEIGS, Joseph F., of Madison, m. Elizabeth Ann **PILGRIM**, of East Haddam, Mar. 24, 1831, by Rev. Simon Shailer, of Haddam	3	116
MENTOR, MENTER, Linda, d. Christian, (mulatto), b. June 4, 1778	2	60
Lucynda had s. Ansel **SEARS**, b. Apr. 29, 1799, in Lyme	2	48

	Vol.	Page
MENTOR, MENTER (cont.)		
Lucynda had s. Benjamin **NEWBERRY**, b. Oct. 6, 1802	2	48
MERCHANT, Abraham, m. Mary Ann **ROBBINS**, Feb. 27, 1833, by Benjamin G. Goff	3	131
MERRIAM, [see also **MERRIMAN**], Josephus R., of Wallingford, m. Sarah A. **RATHBON**, of [Millington], June 6, [1847], by Rev. Nathaniel Miner, of Millington	3	210
MERRICK, William E., of Hartford, m. Julia A. **BRAINARD**, of East Haddam, Mar. 22, 1847, by Rev. Isaac Parsons	3	209
MERRILL, John L., ae 32, b. in Newbury, Mass., res. Brooklyn, N. Y., m. Margaret R. **CHAPMAN**, ae 27, b. in East Haddam, res. East Haddam, May 14, 1856, by Rev. Isaac Parsons. Int. pub. May 13, 1856	4	87
MERRIMAN, [see also **MERRIAM**], Ebenezer, of Southington, m. Eliza B. **HALL**, of East Haddam, Apr. 12, 1835, by Rev. Isaac Parsons	3	138
James B., ae 25, of Wallingford, Ct., m. Ann S. **HARRIS**, ae 21, of East Haddam, Dec. 25, 1856, by Rev. Isaac Parsons. Int. pub. Dec. 25, 1856	4	114a-5
MERRYFIELD, Walter, of New York, m. Matilda A. **MARSH**, of East Haddam, Nov. 20, 1839, by Luther Paine	3	174
METCALF, MEDCALF, Calvin, s. Elijah & Mary, b. July 4, 1779	2	36
Elijah, m. Mary **GOODSPEED**, b. of East Haddam, Sept. 13, 1773	2	36
Elijah H., s. Elijah & Mary, b. Sept. 8, 1778	2	36
Polley, d. Elijah & Mary, b. Oct. 17, 1783	2	36
Sarah, m. Rev. Joseph **FOWLER**, Jr., Feb. 13, 1747	LR8	3
Simeon, s. Elijah & Mary, b. Dec. 21, 1774	2	36
MILDRUM, -------, s. William H., ae 23, & Lydia M., ae 22, b. May 30, 1849	4	11-12
MILLARD, MILLERD, Andrews, s. Jason & Rachel , b. Jan. 21, 1751	LR6	509
Ann, d. Thomas & Ruth, b. May 25, 1742	LR2	1130
Huldah, d. Jason & Rachel, b. Dec. 2, 1758	LR6	509
Jason, s. Thomas & Ruth, b. May 21, 1727	LR2	1130
Jason, m. Rachel **ANDREWS**, b. of East Haddam, May 17, 1750	LR6	509
John, m. Mehitable **WILLEY**, Mar. 18, 1736	LR2	1115
John, s. John & Mehitable, b. Dec. 21, 1736	LR2	1115
Landon, s. Jason & Rachel, b. Oct. 22, 1762	LR6	509
Leavbitt, s. Jason & Rachel, b. May 8, 1760	LR6	509
Matthew, m. Phebe **CONE**, Mar. 31, 1735/6	LR2	1106
Matthew, s. Matthew & Phebe, b. Oct. 27, 1737	LR2	1106
Mehitable, d. John & Mehitable, b. Aug. 29, 1738	LR2	1115
Nathan, s. Thomas & Ruth, b. Dec. 5, 1737	LR2	1130
Oliver, s. Thomas & Ruth, b. May 22, 1744	LR2	1130
Phebe, w. of Matthew, d. Nov. 5, 1737	LR2	1106
Rebeckah, m. Stephen **SCOVEL**, b. of East Haddam, Jan. 16,		

	Vol.	Page
MILLARD, MILLERD, (cont.)		
1729	LR3	506
Robert, s. Thomas & Ruth, b. Nov. 5, 1739	LR2	1130
Samuel, s. Jason & Rachel, b. Apr. 10, 1755	LR6	509
Susannah, d. Jason & Rachel, b. May 5, 1753	LR6	509
Thomas, Jr., m. Ruth **DUTTON**, July 16, 1724	LR2	1130
Thomas, s. Thomas & Ruth, b. Nov. 14, 1728	LR2	1130
Thomas, d. Apr. 23, 1752	LR6	509
MILLER, Hazard H., farmer, b. in Lyme, res. East Haddam, d. May 28, 1850, ae 22	4	29-30
Laura J., m. Albert **SMITH**, b. of East Haddam, Nov. 24, 1845, by Rev. Philo Judson	3	203
Lucy, of Lyme, m. Moses **FOX**, of East Haddam, Jan. 1, 1834, by Josiah Griffin, J. P.	3	133
Lucy, m. Moses **FOX**, Jan. 1, 1834	3	157
Mary, m. George **REYNOLDS**, b. of Lyme, June 8, 1834, by R. S. Crampton, V. D. M.	3	134
Mary Ann, d. Nov. 7, 1849, ae 2	4	29-30
MILLERD, [see under **MILLARD**]		
MINOR, MINER, Abigail, d. Elihu & Keziah, b. Apr. 4, 1766	LR3	10
Amelia E., m. William E. **NEWBURY**, farmer, b. in E. Haddam, res. Millington, May 18, 1851, by Nathaniel Miner	4	37-8
Amelia Emeline, m. William E. **NEWBURY**, b. of East Haddam, May 18, [1851], by Nathaniel Miner	3	232
Asa, s. Elihu & Keziah, b. Feb. 20, 1747	LR3	10
Betsey, w. of a mechanic, b. in Lyme, res. East Haddam, d. Mar. 14, 1849, ae 46	4	17-18
Calvin F., m. Clarissa **HUNTLEY**, b. of Lyme, June 22, 1823, by Rev. Joseph Vaill, of Hadlyme	3	42-43
Cha[rle]s, m. Nancy **ARNOLD**, b. of East Haddam, June 13, [1841], by [Rev. Nathaniel Miner]	3	186
David, s. Elihu & Keziah, b. Aug. 22, 1752	LR3	10
Deliverance, d. Elihu & Keziah, b. Feb. 18, 1756	LR3	10
Elihu, m. Keziah **WILLEY**, Mar. 21, 1745	LR3	10
Elihu, s. Elihu & Keziah, b. Sept. 2, 1745	LR3	10
Eliza S., m. Cyrus W. **SWAN**, b. of East Haddam, Feb. 11, 1827, by Rev. Isaac Parsons	3	93
Erastus A., of Bozrah, m. Martha M. **BURKE**, of East Haddam, July 4, 1847, by Rev. Isaac Parsons	3	210
Griswold, of Lyme, m. Betsey **SPENCER**, of East Haddam, Sept. 5, 1831, by Rev. Isaac Parsons	3	120
Griswold, carpenter, ae 50, b. in Lyme, res. East Haddam, m. 2d w. Bets[e]y L. **WHITE**, ae 37, b, in Chatham, Mass., res. E. Haddam, June 5, 1853, by Jacob Gardner	4	43-4
Hannah B., m. James **STRANAHAN**, Jr., b. of East Haddam, Jan. 18, 1826, by Rev. Isaac Parsons	3	83
Harriet B., of East Haddam, m. Asa **GOFF**, Jr., of Haddam,		

	Vol.	Page
MINOR, MINER, (cont.)		
Mar. 27, 1827, by Rev. Herman L. Vaill	3	93
Harriet E., d. Charles, farmer, ae 31, & Nancy, ae 30, b. Oct. 3, 1849	4	25-6
Henry, m. Martha **STRANAHAN**, Jan. 17, 1827, by Isaac Parsons	3	93
Jabez, s. Elihu & Keziah, b. Oct. 10, 1748	LR3	10
Jared Spencer, s. Turner & Mary, b. July 8, 1789	2	178
Joanna, of Lyme, m. Bayze **BAKER**, of East Haddam, Oct. 22, 1791	2	243
Jonathan, s. Elihu & Keziah, b. Aug. 7, 1754	LR3	10
Joseph, s. Turner & Mary, b. May 19, 1791	2	178
Linus A., d. May 7, 1848, ae 3 m.	4	17-18
Linus A., s. William H., mechanic, ae 34, b. Feb. 7, 1849	4	11-12
Lovisa, of Lyme, m. Osmer **SAUNDERS**, of Saybrook, Jan. 15, 1844, by Rev. Stephen Alonzo Loper, of Hadlyme	3	196
Mehetable, d. Elihu & Keziah, b. June 28, 1759	LR3	10
Nathan Willey, s. Elihu & Keziah, b. Oct. 29, 1757	LR3	10
Sarah, d. Elihu & Keziah, b. May 3, 1750	LR3	10
Timothy, s. Elihu & Keziah, b. Apr. 20, 1762	LR3	10
Turner, m. Mary **SPENCER**, b. of East Haddam, Sept. 18, 1788	2	178
MITCHELL, MITCHEL, Abigail, d. Sam[ue]l & Rebeckah, b. Dec. 20, 1784	2	30
Angeline, Mrs., of East Haddam, m. Loren L. **ROBERTS**, of Torrington, Aug. 9, 1835, by Rev. Alfred Gates	3	138
Anna, d. Samuel & Rebeckah, b. Apr. 17, 1766	2	30
Clarissa, of East Haddam, m. Jeremiah V. **BROWN**, of Haddam, Nov. 18, 1827, by Rev. Isaac Parsons	3	96
Daniel W., of East Haddam, m. Mary C. **ACKLEY**, of Haddam Neck, Sept. 8, 1850, by Rev. Jacob Gardner, in Moodus	3	227
Diodate J., of Chatham, m. Eliza Ann **SKINNER**, of East Haddam, July 14, 1828, by Isaac Parsons	3	99
Emily Sophia, d. James S., laborer, ae 36, & Louisa, ae 27, b. Oct. 14, 1848	4	13-14
Eunice A., d. Sept. 25, 1847, ae 5 m.	4	7-8
Francis, s. Philetus, mariner, ae 36, & Eliza Ann, ae 23, b. Mar. 23, 1851	4	31-2
Gelston, s. Sam[ue]l & Rebeckah, b. Apr. 7, 1788	2	30
James, s. Samuel & Rebeckah, b. Mar. 15, 1764	2	30
James S., m. Sorepta A. **WATERS**, May 29, 1836, by Rev. Isaac Parsons	3	145
James S., of East Haddam, m. Louisa **WELLS**, of Marlborough, Mar. 15, 1846, by Rev. Isaac Parsons	3	204
Joseph, s. Samuel & Rebeckah, b. Mar. 8, 1782	2	30
Lydia, d. Samuel & Rebeckah, b. Mar. 11, 1770	2	30
Mary, d. Sam[ue]l & Rebeckah, b. Mar. 3, 1786	2	30
Phebe, d. Sam[ue]l & Rebeckah, b. Nov. 20, 1785	2	30
Philetus Francis, of Middletown, m. Eliza Ann **LORD**, of		

	Vol.	Page
MITCHELL, MITCHEL, (cont.)		
East Haddam, Aug. 11, 1845, by Isaac Parsons, V. D. M.	3	202
Rebeckah, d. Samuel & Rebeckah, b. Jan. 26, 1772	2	30
Ruth, d. Samuel & Rebeckah, b. Mar. 4, 1768	2	30
Samuel, m. Rebeckah **COOK**, b. of East Haddam, Nov. 10, 1762	2	30
Samuel, s. Samuel & Rebeckah, b. Jan. 24, 1774	2	30
Samuel, m. Cynthia E. **CHAPMAN**, b. of East Haddam, Oct. 19, 1842, by Isaac Parsons, V. D. M.	3	192
Selden, s. Samuel & Rebeckah, b. Nov. 3, 1776	2	30
Stephen Mix, of East Haddam, m. Sophia **WEIRE**, of Glastenbury, Nov. 4, 1832, by Hemon Perry	3	127
Warren, m. Amanda **PURPLE**, b. of East Haddam, Nov. 9, 1820, by Rev. Isaac Parsons	2	323
MOBBS, MOBS, Bathsheba, d. Peirce & Eunice, b. Feb. 18, 1772	2	102
Bathsheba, d. Peirce & Eunice, d. Sept. 8, 1776	2	103
John, s. Price & Eunice, b. June 10, 1767	LR7	2
Price, m. Eunice **SAWER**, Jan. 27, 1762	LR7	2
Samuel, s. Price & Eunice, b. June 10, 1765	LR7	2
Sarah, d. Price & Eunice, b. [ ] 9, 1763	LR7	2
MONSELL, [see under **MUNSELL**]		
MORGAN, Abby Jane, d. William J., farmer, b. Nov. 18, 1847	4	5-6
Emeline H., East Haddam, m. Avery **SMITH**, of Waterford, Oct. 27, 1824, by Rev. Isaac Parsons	3	66-67
Frederick W., of Clarksburg, Va., m. Emma T. **CHAPMAN**, of East Haddam, Oct. 20, 1842, by Isaac Parsons, V. D. M.	3	192
George, farmer, b. in Scotland, res. E. Haddam, d. Nov. 15, 1853, ae 83	4	49-50
George W[illia]m, s. William J., farmer, ae 32, res. East Haddam, b. Jan. 2, 1856	4	82
Jonthan W., of Lyme, m. Mary S. **MACK**, of East Haddam, Jan, 6, 1839, by Rev. Benjamin G. Goff	3	167
Mary Ann, of East Haddam, m. Simon **SMITH**, Jr., of Waterford, Mar. 26, 1828, by Rev. Isaac Parsons	3	99
Mary Ann, m. Nathan H. **SISSON**, b. of East Haddam, Oct. 30, 1838, by Rev. Erastus Denison	3	166
Mary Ann, d. William J., farmer, & L. G., b. Apr. 3, 1851	4	31-2
Nancy C., of East Haddam, m. Francis **BOLLES**, of Waterford, Nov. 9, 1831, by Rev. Isaac Parsons	3	120
Rebecca B., of East Haddam, m. David **AVERY**, of Chaplin, Apr. 11, 1830, by Isaac Parsons	3	107
Sarah, of East Haddam, m. Elias **LOOMIS**, of Salem, Jan. 13, 1830, by Rev. Tubal Wakefield	3	104
Sarah L., d. Willaim, farmer, & J., d. Feb. 9, 1849, ae 6 m.	4	11-12
Susan A., of East Haddam, m. Jehiel **RICHARDS**, of Waterford. Feb. 20, 1831, by Rev. Isaac Parsons	3	115
------, child of David, b. Mar. 23, 1853	4	47-48
------, W[illia]m J., farmer, b. Apr. 1, 1853	4	47-48

	Vol.	Page
MOSELEY, Alfred L., s. David, mechanic, black, ae 37, & Louisa, ae 21, b. Apr. 10, 1847	4	3-4
Charity W., of East Haddam, m. Hiram **WILLEY**, of New London, Sept. 6, 1843, by Rev. Stephen Alonzo Loper, of Hadlyme, in Hadlyme	3	195
Jennet, d. Maj. Jonathan O[gden] & Gitty, b. May 11, 1787	2	231
Jennet, d. Maj. Jonathan O. & Ditty, d. Oct. 26, 1789	2	232
John F., s. David, farmer, mulatto, b. Mar. 2, 1851	4	33-4
Jonathan O., Maj., had negro boy Charls Freeman, b. Mar. 11, 1789	2	231
Jonathan Ogden, s. Tho[ma]s & Phebe, b. Apr. 9, 1762	LR7	414
Jonathan Ogden, s. Maj. Jonathan O[gden] & Gitty, b. Mar. 27, 1791	2	231
Phebe, d. Jonathan O[gden] & Gitty, b. June 27, 1785	2	231
Phebe, w. of Dr. Thomas, d. Apr. 27, 1790	2	232
Phebe E., ae 23, of East Haddam, m. Frederick W. **WARNER**, ae 33, of East Haddam, Nov. 12, 1856, at Hadlyme, by Rev. E. B. Hillard. Int. pub. Nov. 11, 1856	4	107
Thomas, of East Haddam, m. Phebe **OGDEN**, of Elizabethtown, Sept. 27, 1759	LR7	414
Thomas, s. Jonathan Ogden & Gitty, b. Apr. 10, 1784	2	231
Thomas, s. Jonathan Ogden & Gitty, d. May 25, 1784	2	232
Thomas, s. Maj. Jonathan O[gden] & Gitty, b. Apr. 26, 1789	2	231
MOULTON, Ellen E., ae 18, m. William **SILLIMAN**, shoemaker, ae 20, b. of East Haddam, Jan. 23, 1851, by George W. Brewster	4	37-8
Henry K., m. Abigail **SNOW**, b. of East Haddam, Aug. 22, 1831, by Rev. Isaac Parsons	3	119
MUCKET, [see also **MACKET**], Martha, ae 20, b. in Durham, res. East Haddam, m. Morrison **ROBBINS**, blacksmith, ae 22, b. in Lyme, res. East Haddam, July 16, 1848. by Rev. Levi H. Wakeman	4	1-2
Martha A., of Chatham, m. Morrison **ROBBINS**, of East Haddam, July 15, 1848, by Rev. Levi H. Wakeman	3	213
Mary T., ae 19, b. in Durham, m. Elliott J. **ROGERS**, shoemaker, ae 23, of Lyme, Feb. [ ], 1850, by Jacob Gardner	4	37-8
MUNSELL, MONSELL, O. J., tanner, ae 25, of Riverheard, N. Y., m. J. L. **PALMER**, ae 18, b. in E. Haddam, Nov. 25, 1850, by Rev. Isaac Parsons	4	37-8
Oliver J., of Riverhead, N. Y., m. Jane L. **PALMER**, of East Haddam, Nov. 23, 1850, by Rev. Isaac Parsons	3	228
NEEDHAM, John, m. Hester **WILLEY**, b. of East Haddam, Aug. 11, 1763	LR7	6
John, s. John & Hester, b. Nov. 11, 1764	LR7	6
NEWBURY, NEWBERRY, Benjamin, s. Lucynda **MENTER**, b. Oct. 6. 1802	2	48
Charles C., ae 21 y., b. in East Haddam, res. East Haddam,		

	Vol.	Page
NEWBURY, NEWBERRY, (cont.)		
m. Emily A. **STARK**, ae 18, b. in East Haddam, res. East Haddam, Oct. 14, 1855, by Rev. Thomas Barbee. Int. pub. Oct. 13, 1855	4	63-64
Egbert, of Brooklyn, m. Sophia C. **EMMONS**, of East Haddam, June 3, 1824, by Rev. Isaac Parsons	3	62-63
Maria E., m. Giles M. **HASKELL**, Mar. 20, 1842, by John C. Palmer, J. P.	3	184
William E., m. Amelia Emeline **MINER**, b. of East Haddam, May 18, [1851], by Nathaniel Miner	3	232
William E., farmer, b. in East Haddam, res. Millington, m. Amelia E. **MINER**, May 18, 1851, by Nathaniel Miner	4	37-38
NEWCOMB, Electa, d. Israel Newcomb & Anna Taylor, b. Jan. 30, 1800	2	305
NEWELL, Alline S.,of Dummerstown, Vt.,m. Carile C. **BINGHAM**, of East Haddam, May 25, 1846, by Rev. Isaac Parsons	3	205
Ruth, m. Jared **CONE**, June 7, 1752	LR5	563
NICHOLS, Ellen, m. Watrous B. **SMITH**, Jr., b. of East Haddam, Mar. 16, 1851, by Rev. Isaac Parsons	3	230
Jane, m. William H. **CHAPMAN**, Mar. 3, 1846, by Rev. Isaac Parsons	3	204
Silas A., of Norwich, m. Phebe **BRAINERD**, of East Haddam, Nov. 11, 1822, by Rev. Isaac Parsons	3	28-29
NILES, Aaron Henry, s. [Aaron T. & Rachel Ann], b. Nov. 23, 1827	3	147
Aaron J., m. Asenath M. **PARKER**, b. of East Haddam, May 21, 1844, by Rev. Nathaniel Miner	3	199
Aaron T., m. Rachel Ann **HARRIS**, July [ ], 1827, by Rev. Joseph Harvey	3	147
Aaron Teabox, s. Ambrose & Anna, b. July 3, 1804	2	231
Ambrose, Jr., of Colchester, m. Anna **ESTABROOK**, of East Haddam, May 11, 1797	2	231
Ambrose, Jr., of Colchester, m. Anna **ESTABROOK**, of East Haddam, May 11, 1797* (*Crossed out)	2	265
Ambrose, Jr., d. [ ], 1804. "Tis said died on a voyage at sea"	2	232
Ambrose, Jr., d. [ ], 1804. It is said on a voyage at sea" (Entry crossed out)	2	266
Clark, m. Eunice **RICHARDS**, b. of East Haddam, Jan. 25, 1852, by Rev. Nathaniel Miner	3	234
Harriet Ann, [d. Aaron T. & Rachel Ann], b. Mar. 25, 1838	3	147
Henry A., m. Jane **ROGERS**, b. of Mon[t]ville, Conn., Jan. 8, 1852, by Rev. Nathaniel Miner	3	234
Hosford, Buell, s. [Aaron T. & Rachel Ann], b. Oct. 21, 1834	3	147
John M., s. [Aaron T. & Rachel Ann], b. May 15, 1843	3	147
Rachel Ann, w., of Aaron J., d. May 21, 1843, ae 37	3	148
William A., d. Jan. 10, 1850, ae 10 m.	4	29-30
William Henry, s. Ambrose, Jr. & Anna, b. Feb. 7, 1801	2	231

	Vol.	Page
NILES, (cont.)		
William Henry, s. Ambrose, Jr. & Anna, b Feb. 7, 1801 (Entry crossed out)	2	265
------, s. Aaron T., farmer, of Millington, & Maria, b. Feb. [ ], 1851	4	33-4
NOLAND, Benjamin, s. John & Mehettable, b. Nov. 12, 1746	LR3	1
NORTH, Hannah, m. Daniel Kirtland **HOWELL**, Feb. 12, 1816, at Berlin	3	117
NORTHAM, Lucy Ann, m. Jabez H. **FULLER**, June 28, 1841, by Isaac Parsons, M. V. D.	3	186
NORTON, Samuel, of Hebron, m. Sylvina **CHAPMAN**, of East Haddam, Aug. 20, 1823, by Ebenezer Blake, Elder, of Hebron	3	44-45
NOYES, Jos[eph], Capt., had negro Jim, s. Sylve, b. Apr. 25, 1806, formerly slave in the **DURFY** family	2	96
Richard, Dr., of Lyme, m. Dorothea **GRIFFIN**,of East Haddam, Mar. 25, 1830, by Rev. Chester Colton, of Lyme	3	107
NYE, Catharine A., d. Elisha B., physician, ae 36, & Caroline, ae 35, b. Mar. 10, 1848	4	5-6
O'BRIEN, Rhoda Ann, m. Joseph **PADDOCK**, b. of East Haddam, Dec. 11, 1836, by Rev. George Carrington, of Hadlyme	3	146
OGDEN, Anne, of Elizabethtown, N. J., m. Oliver **SPENCER**, of East Haddam, Jan. 22, 1758	LR6	505
Phebe, of Elizabethtown, m. Thomas **MOSELEY**, of East Haddam, Sept. 27, 1759	LR7	414
OLCOTT, OLCUTT, Eliza, d. Oliver & Jerusha, b. Jan. 27, 1803	2	287
Hannah, m. Nathan **FISHER**, Sept. 28, 1741	LR3	11
Har[r]iot, d. Oliver & Jerusha, b. Apr. 10, 1805	2	287
James Bacon, s. Thomas & Mary, b. Nov. 27, 1758	LR5	268
James Bacon, s. Thomas & Mary, d. Feb. 28, 1778, "at Prince Town, in the Jersier", in the 20th y. of his age. A Continental Soldier	2	7
Josiah, s. Thomas & Mary, b. June 23, 1772	2	6
Mary, d. Oliver & Jerusha, b. Jan. 4, 1801	2	287
Oliver, s. Thomas & Mary, b. May 30, 1769	2	6
Oliver, of East Haddam, m. Jerusha **DANIELS**, Feb. 23*, 1800 *(Preceding this the words "Oct. 23" have been crossed out)	2	287
Susannah, d. Thomas & Mary, b. Dec. 18, 1756	LR5	268
Thomas, m. Mary **PARSIVAL**, b. of East Haddam, Apr. 7, 1756	LR5	268
Thomas, d. Sept. 9, 1807, in the 83rd y. of his age	2	7
OLMSTED, OLMSTEAD, Aaron, s. William, Jr. & Mary, b. Jan. 26, 1756	LR3	10
Abigail (?), d. Samuell & Mary, b. June 10, 1716	LR1	579
Abigail, d. William & Mary, b. Sept. 10, 1735	LR3	6
Abigail, m. Silvanus **TINKER**, Sept. 24, 1755	2	4

	Vol.	Page
OLMSTED, OLMSTEAD, (cont.)		
Adonijah, m. Hannah E. **OLMSTED**, b. of East Haddam, Apr. 29, 1838, by Rev. Nathaniel Miner	3	164-5
Anna, m. Samuel **SPENCER**, b. of East Haddam, Sept. 22, 1795	2	287
Asahel, s. Ichabod & Dorothy, b. Dec. 18, 1750	LR3	18
Augustus, of West Chester, [Colchester], m. Phebe **GRIFFIN**, of East Haddam, Sept. 25, 1834, by Nathaniel Miner	3	135
Azubah, m. William **CONE**, Jr., b. of East Haddam, Apr. 23, 1775	2	100
Azubah, m. William **CONE**, Jr., b. of East Haddam, Apr. 23, 1775	2	158
Charles C., m. Larissa **ACKLEY**, b. of East Haddam, May 27, 1832, by Rev. Peter G. Clarke	3	124
Clarine, m. Warren G. **JONES**, b. of East Haddam, June 10, 1833, by Nathaniel Miner	3	131
Daniel, m. Rebeckah **SPENCER**, Dec. 28, 1738	LR2	1107
Deborah, d. Samuel & Mary, b. July 24, 1721	LR3	9
Deborah, m. James **GATES**, Nov. 6, 1743	LR3	7
Dorothy, d. Samuel & Mary, d. May 14, 1741	LR3	9
Dorothy, d. William & Mary, b. Feb. 29, 1741/2	LR3	6
Dorothy, d. William & Mary, d. Apr. 14, 1743	LR3	6
Dorothy, d. Ichabod & Dorothy, b. Feb. 1, 1748	LR3	18
Dorothy, of East Haddam, m. Selden **ARNOLD**, of Haddam, Nov. 12, 1839, by Isaac Parsons	3	173
Ebenezer, s. Ichabod & Dorothy, b. Aug. 22, 1756	LR3	18
Elizabeth, m. John **CHURCH**, Feb. 5, 1707	LR1	583
Elizabeth, d. Ichabod & Dorothy, b. Nov. 9, 175[ ]	LR3	18
Elizabeth, m. Abner **HALL**, Jr., b. of East Haddam, Nov. 22, 1801	2	271
Hannah C., of East Haddam, m. Lucien B. **CARVER**, of Hebron, May 31, [1848], by Nath[anie]l Miner	3	213
Hannah E., m. Adonijah **OLMSTED**, b. of East Haddam, Apr. 29, 1838, by Rev. Nathaniel Miner	3	164-5
Hannah E., ae 25, b. in East Haddam, res. Hebron, m. Lucian B. **CARVER**, farmer, ae 32, b. in Hebron, res. Hebron, May 31, 1848, by Nath[anie]l Miner	4	1-2
Ichabod, s. Samuel & Mary, b. Sept. 12, 1725	LR3	9
Ichabod, m. Dorothy **BATES**, July 23, 1747	LR3	18
Ichabod, d. May 17, 1851, ae 83	4	39-40
James, m. Anne **CONE**, b. of East Haddam, June 18, 1763	LR7	417
Jonathan, s. Samuell & Mary, b. Nov. 9, 1707	LR1	579
Jonathan, s. William & Anna, b. July 20, 1744	LR3	6
Jonathan, of Colchester, m. Elizabeth C. **GARDNER**, of East Haddam, Apr. 10, 1833, by Rev. Isaac Parsons	3	164-5
Lewis B., m. Hannah E. **SWAN**, b. of East Haddam, Oct. 31, 1821, by Rev. W[illia]m Lyman	3	36-37
Lucy, of Colchester, m. Nehemiah **TRACY**, of East Haddam,		

	Vol.	Page
OLMSTED, OLMSTEAD, (cont.)		
Oct. 14, 1789	2	212
Maria, of Colchester, m. Daniel **PECK**, of East Haddam, Nov. 5, 1832, by Rev. Joseph Harvey	3	143
Mary (?), d. Samuell & Mary, b. Mar. 21, 1715	LR1	579
Mary, d. William & Mary, b. Oct. 1, 1729	LR3	6
Mary, w. of William, d. Apr. 16, 1742	LR3	6
Mary, m. Joseph **BATE**, Jr., Aug. 29, 1746	LR3	18
Mary, d. William, Jr. & Mary, b. Apr. 20, 1761	LR3	10
Moses, s. Capt. William & Anna, d. Sept. 26, [1775], at Roxbury. Enlisted in Gen. Spencer's Co., 1775, in the 15th reign of George 3rd.	2	99
Nehemiah, s. William, Jr. & Mary, b. June 1, 1746	LR3	10
Orpasia, m. Asa **EMMONS**, b. of East Haddam, Aug. 7, 1806	2	265
R[e]uben, s. William, Jr. & Mary, b. Apr. 18, 1753	LR3	10
Samuell, m. Mary **ROWLE**, [ ], 1697	LR1	579
Samuell, d. Samuell & Mary, b. Sept. 8, 1703	LR1	579
Samuel, s. William & Mary, b. Sept. 13, 1737	LR3	6
Samuel, s. Ichabod & Dorothy, b. Feb. 24, 1753	LR3	18
Samuel, s. Ichabod & Dorothy, d. Jan. 19, 1754	LR3	18
Samuel, s. Ichabod & Dorothy, b. Dec. 6, 1754	LR3	18
Sarah, d. Samuell & Mary, b. Dec. 29, 1699	LR1	579
Sarah, d. Samuell & Mary, d. May 10, 1704	LR1	579
Sarah, m. George **GATES**, Dec. 3, 1730	LR2	1126
Sarah, d. William & Mary, b. Mar. 21, 1732/3	LR3	6
William, s. Samuell & Mary, b. Nov. 21, 1705	LR1	279
William, m. Mary **BRAINERD**, July [ ], 1728	LR3	6
William, s. William & Mary, b. Sept. 4, 1728	LR3	6
William, m. Anna **ROWLEE**, Nov. 5, 1743	LR3	6
William, Jr., m. Mary **CONE**, Mar. 20, 1746	LR3	10
William, s. William, Jr. & Mary, b. June 18, 1748	LR3	10
William, s. William, Jr. & Mary, d. Apr. 10, 1749	LR3	10
William, s. William, Jr. & Mary, b. Apr. 5, 1750	LR3	10
------, d. Samuell & Mary, b. Sept. 18, 1701	LR1	579
ORCHARD, Joseph, negro, b. in East Haddam, res. East Haddam, single, d. June 28, 1855, ae 23	4	72
Warren, laborer, black, b. in Salem, res. E. Haddam, d. Feb. [ ], 1850	4	29-30
OSBORN, Abraham, m. Dorothy **BOOGE**, b. of East Haddam, Jan. 10, 1782	2	62
Ann, m. Elijah **ACKLEY**, Jr., Jan. 31, 1765	LR7	5
Anne, of Middletown, m. Thomas **SMITH**, of East Haddam, May 27, 1750	LR2	1107
David Skellinger, s. Abraham & Dorothy, b. May 5, 1783	2	62
Jedidah, m. Amasa **BRAINERD**, b. of East Haddam, Dec. 22, 1763	LR7	1
Jedidah, m. Amasa **BRAINERD**, b. of East Haddam, Dec. 22, 1763	2	24

	Vol.	Page
OSBORN, (cont.)		
Sarah, of Long Island, m. Joseph **WARNER**, Jr., of East Haddam, Apr. [ ], 1783	2	212
OTIS, Charles, m. Mrs. Elisabeth **SWEETLAND**, b. of East Haddam, Mar. 19, 1788	2	126
Charles, s. Charles & Elisabeth, b. Apr. 14, 1791	2	126
Hannah, d. Charles & Elisabeth, b. Dec. 26, 1788	2	126
Marcy, of Colchester, m. Daniel **CONE**, 4th, of East Haddam, Sept. 15, 1784	2	215
PADDOCK, Hannah, of East Haddam, m. Anson **PRESCOTT**, of Whites Town, N. Y., Oct. 22, 1820, by Rev. W[illia]m Lyman	2	325
Joseph, m. Fluvia A. **CONE**, b. of East Haddam, Mar. 6, 1832, by Nathaniel Miner	3	124
Joseph, m. Rhoda Ann **O'BRIEN**, b. of East Haddam, Dec. 11, 1836, by Rev. George Carrington, of Hadlyme	3	146
Mary, of East Haddam, m. Hugh **LOWRY**, of Ashtabula, O., Nov. 16, 1829, by Rev. John A. Hempstead, of Millington	3	103
William, m. Esther **MARTIN**, b. of East Haddam, Feb. 16, 1826, by Herman L. Vaill	3	84-85
PAGET, Margaret, of Middletown, b. Jan. 28, 1766; m. Robert **CONE**, b. of Middletown, July 29, 1783	2	148
PAGEWOOD, Sarah, m. Ezra W. **BARTMAN**, b. of East Haddam, May 3, 1746, by Rev. Alpheas Geer	3	205
PAINE, PAYNE, Edward Harry, s. Harry & Cynthia, b. Sept. 25, 1838	3	169
Esther, see Esther **BEEBE**	3	66-67
PALMER, Aaron C., farmer, b. in East Haddam, res. East Haddam, married, d. Jan. 5, 1855, ae 82	4	71
Aaron Cone, s. Levi & Elizabeth, b. Feb. 5, 1773	2	128
Adaline A., m. George W. **SMITH**, Nov. 26, 1835, by Rev. Isaac Parsons	3	140-1
Adelaide, d. [John C. & Mary Ann], b. Oct. 30, 1833	3	139
Agnes G., d. Oliver, farmer, ae 34, & Jane, b. Oct. 5, 1849	4	23-4
Albert Gallatin, s. William & Dorothy, b. Mar. 20, 1824	3	40-1
Ann G., of East Haddam, m. Frederick **ALLEN**, of Windham, Mar. 18, 1828, by Rev. Isaac Parsons	3	99
Ann M., ae 20, b. in East Haddam, res. New Hartford, m. Albert **SWEET**, merchant, ae 28, of New Hartford, Nov. 26, 1848, by Isaac Parsons	4	9-10
Ann Maria, of East Haddam, m. Albert **JEWETT**, of New Hartford, Nov. 28, 1848, by Rev. Isaac Parsons	3	215
Anna, d. Capt. Levi & Elizabeth, b. Mar. 22, 1793	2	129
Augustus Henry, s. Henry A. & Emeline M., b. May 25, 1843	3	213
Carile D., d. William & Dorothy, b. Dec. 17, 1802	3	40-1
Cariste* D., m. Richard D. **GELSTON**, Sept. 16, 1821, by Rev. Isaac Parsons (*Carile?)	3	11

	Vol.	Page
PALMER, (cont.)		
Caroline W., of East Haddam, m. John G. **WAY**, of Colchester, Sept. 3, 1834, by R. S. Crampton, V. D. M.	3	135
Catharine, d. of Brainard & Eunice, m. Julius **ATTWOOD**, Oct. 22, 1862	2	262
Catharine, m. Julius **ATTWOOD**, Oct. 22, 1862	3	245-6
Charles O., d. Apr. 14, 1853, ae 1 m. 4 d.	4	49-50
Dorothy, d. Levi & Elisabeth, b. Nov, 21. 1768	2	128
Eliza, m. Asa **HUNGERFORD**, Oct. 18, 1826, by Isaac Parsons	3	88-89
Elisabeth, d. Levi & Elisabeth, b. Apr. 8, 1779	2	128
Esther, d. Levi & Elisabeth, b. Oct. 26, 1783	2	128
Eveline, d. William & Dorothy, b. Dec. 27, 1804	3	40-41
Eveline, of East Haddam, m. Ashbel **BORDMAN**, of Wethersfield, Feb. 11, 1823, by Rev. Isaac Parsons	3	38-39
Francis Mason, [s. William, Jr. & Florella], b. Aug. 13, 1821	3	87
Frederick Augustus, s. Levi & Eliza A., b. June 13, 1839	3	175
George, s. Levi & Elisabeth, b. May 22, 1781	2	128
George, m. Louisa C. **BROOKS**, b. of East Haddam, Oct. 26, 1828, by Rev. Isaac Parsons	3	100
Gertrude M., of East Haddam, m. Eldad **TAYLOR**, of Suffield, Sept. 19, 1832, by Rev. Isaac Parsons	3	125
Gertrude Moseley, d. William & Dorothy, b. Nov. 2, 1808	3	40-41
Harriet, m. William **BLISS**, Oct. 13, 1831, by Rev. Isaac Parsons	3	120
Henry, m. Maria B. **JONES**, b. of East Haddam, Apr. 23, 1843, by Rev. Cha[rle]s Thompson, of Salem	3	194
Henry A., m. Emeline M. **GARDNER**, Dec. 15, 1841, by Charles William Bradley	3	188
Henry A., m. Emeline M. **GARDNER**, Dec. 15, 1841	3	213
Henry Augustus, [s. William, Jr. & Florella], b. Sept. 11, 1819	3	87
Hobart C., m. Ellen S. **BABCOCK**, Jan. 8, 1850, by Rev. Alpheas Geer	3	222
Horace, s. Capt. Levi & Elizabeth, b. Feb. 24, 1797	2	129
Horace, m. Teresa **FOX**, b. of East Haddam, Oct. 19, 1820, by Rev. W[illia]m Lyman	2	325
Isaac, s. Levi & Elisabeth, b. Sept. 17, 1777	2	128
Isaac, s. Levi & Elisabeth, d. Sept. 23, 1777	2	129
Isabella, d. [John C. & Mary Ann], b. Feb. 16, 1842	3	189
J. L., ae 18, b. in E. Haddam, m. O. J. **MONSELL**, tanner, ae 25, of Riverhead, N. Y., Nov. 25, 1850, by Rev. Isaac Parsons	4	37-8
Jane L., of East Haddam, m. Oliver J. **MUNSELL**, of Riverhead, N. Y., Nov. 23, 1850, by Rev. Isaac Parsons	3	228
John C., of East Haddam, m. Mary Ann **HOADLEY**, of New Haven, May 1, 1831, by Rev. Mr. Merwin, in New Haven	3	139
John Cleveland. s. William & Dorothy, b. Nov. 17, 1806	3	40-41
John Cleveland. s. [John C. & Mary Ann], b. Dec. 18, 1836	3	139

	Vol.	Page
PALMER, (cont.)		
Julia, d. Capt. Levi & Elizabeth, b. Feb. 5, 1788	2	129
Julia F., m. Ebenezer **SNOW**, b. of East Haddam, July 22, 1852, by Rev. W. Emmerson	3	236
Levi, m. Elizabeth **CONE**, b. of East Haddam, July 21, 1768	2	128
Levi, s. Levi & Elisabeth, b. Dec. 28, 1770	2	128
Levi, of East Haddam, m. Eliza Ann **FLOOD**, of Colchester, Aug. 8, 1838, by Rev. George Carrington, of Hadlyme	3	166
Levi, m. Eliza Ann **FLOOD**, Aug. 8, 1838	3	175
Loren C., s. Ozias E., farmer, ae 25, & Abby Ann, b. Mar. 22, 1850	4	23-4
Maria C., d. Henry A., & Caroline M., b. Feb. 22, 1850	4	25-4
Maria Cordelia, d. Henry A. & Emeline M., b. Feb. 22, 1850	3	213
Mary, m. Diodate Ackley **CHURCH**, b. of East Haddam, Apr. 17, 1823, by Rev. Isaac Parsons	3	38-9
Oliver C., m. Lois M. **CHAPMAN**, b. of East Haddam. Oct. 19, 1823, by Rev. Isaac Parsons	3	47
Oliver Cone, s. Capt. Levi & Elizabeth, b. Feb. 10, 1791	2	129
Ozias E., m. Abby A. **COWDREY**, b. of East Haddam, June 10, 1849, by Rev. Alpheas Geer, in St. Stephen's Church	3	217
Ozias Emmons, [s. William, Jr. & Florella], b. July 3, 1825	3	87
Polle, d. Capt. Levi & Elisabeth, b. Dec. 3, 1785	2	128
Prudence, illeg., b. May [ ], 1851	4	31-2
Richard Warner, [s. William, Jr. & Florella], b. Aug. 17, 1823	3	87
Robert C., merchant, ae 24, of E. Haddam, m. Ellen S. **BABCOCK**, ae 20, b. in Colchester, res. E. Haddam, Jan. 8, 1849, by Rev. Alpheas Geer	4	21-2
Samuel, m. Dorothy **PHELPS**, Nov. 27, 1825, by Ozias Holmes, J. P.	3	80-1
Samuel, saddle & Harness maker, Revolutionary Pensioner, b. in Lyme or New London, res. East Haddam, d. June 21, 1849, ae 94	4	17-8
Sarah, b. in East Haddam, res. East Haddam, single, d. Feb. 11, 1856, ae 1 y. 5 m. 15 d.	4	83
Sarah, b. in East Haddam, res. East Haddam, d. Feb. 11, 1856, ae 1 y. 5 m. 15 d.	4	97
Sophronia, d. William & Dorothy, b. Feb. 5, 1799	3	40-1
Sophronia, m. Thomas C. **BORDMAN**, b. of East Haddam, Jan. 6, 1822, by Rev. Isaac Parsons	3	21
William, s. Levi & Elisabeth, b. Aug. 12, 1775	2	128
William, s. William & Dorothy, b. Mar. 27, 1797	3	40-1
William, Jr., m. Florella **EMMONS**, b. of East Haddam, Feb. 18, 1818, by Rev. Isaac Parsons	3	87
W[illia]m, 3rd, s. Francis M., farmer, ae 29, & Margaret, ae 25, b. Sept. 20, 1849	4	23-4
------, child of Francis M., tanner, b. Oct. 27, 1847	4	5-6
------, child of Frances M., tanner, b. Mar. 13, 1853	4	47-8
------, d. Henry A., tanner, b. Mar. 27, 1853	4	47-8

	Vol.	Page
PARK, Jane, m. John **CHURCH**, Jr., b. of East Haddam, Jan. 21, 1762	LR7	7
PARKER, Asenath M., m. Aaron J. **NILES**, b. of East Haddam, May 21, 1844, by Rev. Nathan Miner	3	199
Eliel, s. John & Sarah, b. Sept. 16, 1776	2	237
Francis Hubert, s. O. H., farmer, & Maria M., b. Sept. 23, 1850	4	33-4
Jabez D., of Chester, m. Louisa M. **SWAN**, of East Haddam, Nov. 23, 1845, by Rev. Alpheas Gear	3	203
John, m. Sarah **FULLER**, b. of East Haddam, Nov. 21, 1760	2	237
John, s. John & Sarah, b. Oct. 12, 1765	2	237
Lemuel, s. John & Sarah, b. Mar. 24, 1782	2	237
Lillis, d. John & Sarah, b. Aug. 17, 1770	2	237
Lucy, d. John & Sarah, b. Sept. 21, 1763	2	237
Lydia, m. Hezekiah **USHER**, Nov. 3, 1757	LR6	512
Mary, d. Joseph & Mary, b. Oct. 18, 1742. "Taken care of by the Townsmen of East Haddam, and put out to Joshua **LUTHER**? of Middletown"	LR3	5
Ozias, tanner, ae 26, m. Mary M. **AYRES**, ae 21, b. of E. Haddam, Nov. 29, 1849, by Rev. Nathaniel Miner	4	19-20
Ozias H., m. Mariah M. **AYRES**, b. of East Haddam, Nov. 29,1849, by Nathaniel Miner	3	221
Polley, d. John & Sarah, b. July 25, 1779	2	237
Richard, s. John & Sarah, b. Nov. 10, 1773	2	237
Salley, d. John & Sarah, b. July 17, 1768	2	237
Salley, d. John & Sarah, d. Oct. 24, 1774	2	238
Sarah, d. John & Sarah, b. Aug, 20, 1761	2	237
Sarah, d. John & Sarah, d. Apr. [ ], 1767	2	238
-----, s. Ozias H., farmer, b. Sept. 26, 1853	4	47-8
-----, d. Ozias, farmer, ae from 35 to 40 y., res. East Haddam, & Maria, ae from 35 to 40 y., b. Apr. 19, 1855	4	76
-----, s. Ozias H., farmer, res. East Haddam, b. Apr. 16, 1856	4	96
PARKHURST, Olive, b. May 20, 1788; m. Stanton S. **CARD**, Jan. 2, 1814, at Plainfield	3	109
PARMELEE, PARMELE, PARMLEE, PARMERLEE, Amasa, s. Phinehas & Prude, b. Nov. 19, 1769	2	190
Amasa, s. Phinehas & Prude, d. Oct. 6, 1774	2	191
Charity, d. Phinehas & Prude, b. Feb. 8, 1783	2	190
Gideon, s. Phinehas & Prude, b. Mar. 13, 1772	2	190
Gideon, s. Phinehas & Prude, d. Feb. 25, 1773	2	191
Phinehas, s. Phinehas & Prude, b. Apr. 23, 1766	2	190
Phinehas, s. Phinehas & Prude, d. Oct. 11, 1774	2	191
Prude, d. Phinehas & Prude, b. May 13, 1775	2	190
Samuel, s. Phinehas & Prude, b. Dec. 29, 1763	3	190
William, of Chatham, m. Phebe M. **CONE**, of East Haddam, Feb. 26, 1837, by Roswell Davison, J. P.	3	152
PARSONS, Elariza Jane Lord, d. [Isaac & Sarah B.], b. June 15,1831	2	30-31
Elijah, Rev., of East Haddam, m. Mrs. Elisabeth **ROGERS**,		

	Vol.	Page
PARSONS, (cont.)		
of Boston, Sept. 16, 1773	2	150
Elijah, Rev., of East Haddam, m. Mrs. Mary **JOHNSON**, of Middletown, Nov. 5, 1792	2	150
Elijah, Rev., m. Meliscent **SPENCER**, b. of East Haddam, Jan. 18, 1813	2	150
Elisabeth, w. of Rev. Elijah, d. Sept. 9, 1790	2	151
Harriet M., m. Rev. Warren C. **FISKE**, May 19, 1847, by Rev. Isaac Parsons	3	209
Harriet Mindwell, [d. Isaac & Sarah B.], b. Apr. 12, 1823	3	30-31
Henry Martyn, s. Isaac & Sarah B., b. Nov. 13, 1828	3	30-31
Isaac, Rev., of East Haddam, m. Sarah B. **LYON**, of New Haven, Jan. 21, 1819	3	30-31
Jonathan B., m. Mrs. Ann G. **ALLEN**, b. of East Haddam, Jan. 9, 1833, by Rev. Peter G. Clarke	3	128
Mary, w. of Rev. Elijah, d. Sept. 30, 1812	2	151
Mary M., of East Haddam, m. S. Everest **SWIFT**, M. D., of Colchester, Mar. 31, 1845, by Isaac Parsons, V. D. M.	3	201
Mary Underhill, d. Isaac & Sarah B., b. Dec. 3, 1821	3	30-31
PASCO, Lester, m. Sarah W. **PRATT**, Aug. 4, 1833, by Rev. Isaac Parsons	3	132
PATTERSON, Amzi, s. Timothy & Elisabeth, b. June 13, 1775	2	72
Ariel, s. Timothy & Elizabeth, b. July 8, 1764	LR6	506
Daniel, s. Timothy & Elisabeth, b. Sept. 2, 1777	2	72
Deborah, d. Timothy & Elisabeth, b. Aug. 1, 1769	2	72
Deborah, d. Timothy & Elisabeth, d. [ ], 1776	2	73
Elisabeth, d. Timothy & Elisabeth, b. Mar. 8, 1766	2	72
Ephraim, s. Timothy & Elisabeth, b. Nov. 12, 1779	2	72
Levi, s. Timothy & Elisabeth, b. May 19, 1773	2	72
Mary, m. Patrick **FINAGAN**, Oct. 10, 1841, by Rev. George Carrington, of Hadlyme	3	187
Molley, d. Timothy & Elizabeth, b. Feb. 8, 1761	LR6	506
Parnel, d. Timothy & Elisabeth, b. Sept. 29, 1767	2	72
Timothy, m. Elizabeth **BEEBE**, b. of East Haddam, Mar. 13, 1760	LR6	506
Timothy, s. Timothy & Elizabeth, b. Aug. 16, 1762	LR6	506
Timothy, s. Timothy & Elizabeth, d. Mar. 16, 1765	LR6	506
Timothy, s. Timothy & Elisabeth, b. Aug. 3, 1771	2	72
PAYNE, [see under **PAINE**]		
PECK, PEEK, PICK, Allice, of Lyme, m. Marvin **BANNING**, of East Haddam, Oct. 2, 1799	2	269
Anna Maria, d. John L. & Elizabeth, b. June 14, 1805	2	267
Barnibus, s. Samuel & Bethiah, b. Feb. 26, 1756	LR4	468
Clarissa M., m. Datus **WILLIAMS**, Aug. 25, 1824, by Rev. Noah C. Saxton	3	64-65
Clarissa M., ae 21, b. in East Haddam, res. East Haddam, m. Edwin A. **EMMONS**, ae 28, b. in East Haddam, res. East Haddam, Dec. 25, 1855, at Millington, by Rev.		

	Vol.	Page
PECK, PEEK, PICK, (cont.)		
Nathaniel Miner. Int. pub. Dec. 20, 1855	4	79
Claris[s]a Maria, d. Ezekiel Y. & Lucena, b. Oct. 23, 1803	2	293
Daniel, s. Ezek[ie]l Y. & Lucena, b. Oct. 4, 1801	2	293
Daniel, father of Ezekiel Y., d. Apr. 25, 1802	2	294
Daniel, of East Haddam, m. Maria **OLMSTED**, of Colchester, Nov. 5, 1832, by Rev. Joseph Harvey	3	143
Daniel Augustus, s. [Daniel & Maria], b. Nov. 14, 1833	3	143
David Belding, s. John L. & Elizabeth, b. Oct. 8, 1807	2	267
Elisha, of Lyme, m. Olive **EMMONS**, of East Haddam, Nov. 27, 1785	2	196
Eliza, d. John L. & Elizabeth, b. July 15, 1801	2	267
Eliza Ann, d. Ezekiel Y. & Lucena, b. June 18, 1820	2	293
Erastus F., m. Sophia **SWAN**, Mar. 13, 1832, by Nathaniel Miner	3	124
Erastus Franklin, s. Ezekiel Y. & Lucena, b. Feb. 6, 1811	2	293
Ezekiel Y., d. Dec. 24, 1831, ae 58	3	144
Ezekiel Yarrington, of East Haddam, m. Lucena **CLARK**, of Lyme, Dec. 25, 1800	2	293
Ezekiel Yarrington, s. Ezekiel Y. & Lucena, b. Dec. 23, 1808	2	293
Ezekiel Yarrington, d. Dec. 24, 1831, ae 58	2	294
Hannah, d. John & Hannah, b. Apr. 13, 1717	LR1	580
Hannah, w. of John, d. Feb. 5, 1759	LR6	513
Hannah, d. John & Hannah, d. Apr. 24, 1769	LR8	5
Horatio Henry, s. Ezekiel Y. & Lucena, b. July 28, 1822	2	293
James, s. Samuel & Bethiah, b. Mar. 2, 1754	LR4	468
Jemima, of Lyme, m. Benjamin **CROSBY**, of East Haddam, Nov. 25, 1788	2	186
Jerusha, w. of Daniel, d. Oct. 29, 1818	2	294
Jerusha Ann, d. Ezekiel Y. & Lucena, b. May 23, 1813	2	293
Jerusha Ann, d. Ezekiel Y. & Lucena, d. Aug. 3, 1813, ae 10 wks. 3 d.	2	294
John, s. Samuel & Bethiah, b. Dec. 22, 1751	LR4	468
John Lathrop, m. Elizabeth **BELDING**, b. of East Haddam, Nov. 16, 1800	2	267
John Lord, s. John Lathrop & Elizabeth, b. Apr. 12, 1803	2	267
Lathrop, s. Samuel & Bethiah, b. Oct. 8, 1758	LR4	468
Lathrop, s. Samuel & Bethiah, d. Oct. 22, 1759	LR4	468
Lucena P., m. Malsey **BROWN**, Nov. 22, 1843, by Rev. Nathaniel Miner	3	196
Lucena Parnella, d. Ezekiel Y. & Lucena, b. Oct. 4, 1806	2	293
Luther Peirson, s. Elisha & Olive, b. June 19, 1788	2	196
Mary Jane, d. [Daniel & Maria], b. Nov. 7, 1835	3	143
Roswell Clark, s. Ezekiel Y. & Lucena, b. June 30, 1815	2	293
Ruth, of Lyme, m. William **CROWELL**, of East Haddam, Aug. 26, 1792	2	255
Samuel, m. Bethia **LOTHROP**, Feb. 7, 1750/51	LR4	468
Theodore Dwight, s. Ezekiel Y. & Lucena, b. Nov. 19, 1817	2	293

	Vol.	Page
PECK, PEEK, PICK, (cont.)		
William Emmons, s. Elisha & Olive, b. Sept. 15, 1786	2	196
Zedekiah, s. Samuel & Bethiah, b. Oct. 15, 1761	LR4	468
PEEK, [see under **PECK**]		
PELHAM, Luman T., of Hartford, m. Lucretia **CAPLES**, of East Haddam, Jan. 20, 1840, by Rev. Nathaniel Miner	3	174
PELLET, Timothy Wheeler, m. Temperance P. **ANDREWS**, Sept. 30, 1832, by Rev. Isaac Parsons	3	125
PEMBERTON, Calvin P., shoe manufacutrer, ae 22, b. in West Bradford, Mass., res. East Haddam, m. Sarah J. **SILLIMAN**, ae 18, of East Haddam, Sept. 16, 1848, by Isaac Parsons	4	9-10
Calvin P., m. Sarah T. **SILLIMAN**, Sept. 17, 1848, by Rev. Isaac Parsons	3	214
Clara C., ae 21, b. in Bradford, Mass., res. E. Haddam, m. Thomas H. **ALLEN**, shoemaker, ae 21, b. in Windham, res. E. Haddam, June 2, 1850, by Isaac Parsons	4	19-20
Clarissa E., of Bradford, Mass., m. Thomas H. **ALLEN**, of Williamantic, June 2, 1850, by Rev. Isaac Parsons	3	225
Elmer E., s. Calvin P., shoe manufacturer, ae 22, & Sarah J., ae 18, b. May 9, 1849	4	13-14
PERCIVAL, PARSEVAL, PARSIVAL, PARSIVEL, PASAVEL, PASEVEL, PASSAUEL, PASSEAUL, PERCIVEL, Abigail, d. James & Elizabeth, b. June 15, 1735	LR2	1126
Ann, d. Ebenezer & Lucy, b. June 17, 1762	LR5	265
Anna, d. James & Elizabeth, b. June 9, 1737	LR2	1126
Anson, s. Dr. Francis & Meriam, b. Jan. 24, 1788	2	86
Azel, s. Ebenezer & Lucy, b. Feb. 11, 1761	LR5	265
Claracy, d. Dr. Francis & Miriam, b. Feb. 17, 1779	2	86
Dorothy, d. John, 2d, & Dorothy, b. Sept. 22, 1788	2	138
Dorothy, w. of James, d. Dec. 21, 1792, in the 49th y. of her age	2	13
Dorothy, w. of John, 2d, d. Mar. 16, 1808	2	139
Dorothy, of East Haddam, m. Nathaniel **PURPLE**, of Chatham, Feb. 5, 1824, by Rev. Isaac Parsons	3	56-57
Ebenezer, s. James & Elizabeth, b. May 30, 1731	LR2	1126
Ebenezer, m. Lucy **KNOWLTON**, Dec. 13, 1749	LR5	265
Ebenezer, s. Ebenezer & Lucy, b. May 15, 1764	LR5	265
Elizabeth, d. John & Hannah, b. Aug. [ ], 1737	LR2	1096
Elizabeth, w. of James, d. Nov. 18, 1739	LR2	1126
Elizabeth, d. John & Hannah, d. May 7, 1748	LR2	1096
Elizabeth, d. Ebenezer & Lucy, b. May 21, 1753	LR5	265
Elizabeth, d. John & Hannah, b. June 19, 1755	LR2	1096
Francis, s. John & Hannah, b. Aug. 7, 1743	LR2	1096
Francis, Dr., m. Meriam **CHAPMAN**, b. of East Haddam, May 24, 1774	2	86
Francis, s. Dr. Frances & Meriam, b. Aug. 1, 1775	2	86
George, s. Dr. Gurdon & Sarah, b. May 27, 1789	2	132

	Vol.	Page
PERCIVAL, PARSEVAL, PARSIVAL, PARSIVEL, PASAVEL, PASEVEL, PASSAUEL, PASSEAUL, PERCIVEL, (cont.)		
Gideon, s. John & Hannah, b. Aug. 10, 1745	LR2	1096
Gideon, s. John & Hannah, d. Aug. last day, 1748	LR2	1096
Gideon, s. John & Hannah, b. June 8, 1749	LR2	1096
Gordon, s. Dr. Gordon & Sarah, b. Apr. 2, 1784	2	132
Hannah, d. John & Hannah, b. Sept. 10, 1738	LR2	1123
Hannah, m. Timothy **GATES**, b. of East Haddam, June 18, 1761	LR6	504
Hannah, wid. of Capt. John, d. May 2, 1803, said to be in the 93rd y. of her age	2	13
Hezekiah W., Jr., m. Harriet M. **WILLIAMS**, Sept. 5, 1825, by Rev. Isaac Parsons	3	79
Jabez Chapman, s. Dr. Gordon & Sarah, b. Jan. 8, 1787	2	132
James, m. Elizabeth **BACKEN**, July 9, 1730	LR2	1126
James, s. John & Hannah, b. July 6, 1736	LR2	1123
James, d. Mar. 19, 1738	LR2	1126
James, s. Ebenezer & Lucy, b. Feb. 14, 1749/50	LR5	265
James, m. Dorothy **GATES**, June 19, 1766	LR7	413
James, s. James & Dorothy, b. Apr. 20, 1767	LR7	413
Jeremiah, s. Ebenezer & Lucy, b. Sept. 1, 1754	LR5	265
John, s. James, b. Oct. 17, 1706	LR1	6
John, m. Hannah **WHITMORE**, Aug. 5, 1731	LR2	1123
John, s. John & Hannah, b. June 1, 1734	LR2	1123
John, Jr., of East Haddam, m. Mary **BRAINERD**, of Middletown, Nov. 7, 1754	LR7	4
John, s. John, Jr. & Mary, b. Jan. 16, 1755	LR7	4
John, s. John, Jr. & Mary, d. Jan. 12, 1756	LR7	4
John, 3rd, m. Dorothy **BURT**, b. of East Haddam, May 24, 1781	2	138
John, s. John, 3rd, & Dorothy, b. Apr. 25, 1782	2	138
John, Capt., d. Sept. 14, 1786, in the 80th y. of his age	2	13
John, d. Jan. 22, 1813, in the 79th y. of his age	2	13
John, hatter, d. Oct. 3, 1848, ae 66	4	17-18
Jordon, s. Dr. Gordon & Sarah, b. Apr. 2, 1784* (*Entry crossed out)	2	129
Jordon, see also Gordon		
Loren, [twin with Warren], s. Dr. Francis & Miriam, b. Apr. 5, 1783	2	86
Lucy, d. Ebenezer & Lucy, b. Feb. 19, 1756	LR5	265
Mary, d. James & Elizabeth, b. Mar. 25, 1733	LR2	1126
Mary, m. Thomas **OLCOTT**, b. of East Haddam, Apr. 7, 1756	LR5	268
Mary, d. Ebenezer & Lucy, b. Oct. 4, 1757	LR5	265
Mary, w. of James, d. May 8, 1759	LR7	2
Mary B., m. William L. **FOWLER**, Jr., b. of East Haddam, Apr. 20, 1853, by Rev. Isaac Parsons	3	238a
Mary B., ae 22, m. William L. **FOWLER**, shoemaker, ae 22, b. of E. Haddam. Apr. 20, 1853, by Rev. Isaac Persons	4	43-4

	Vol.	Page
PERCIVAL, PARSEVAL, PARSIVAL, PARSIVEL, PASAVEL, PASEVEL, PASSAUEL, PASSEAUL, PERCIVEL, (cont.)		
Miriam, d. Dr. Francis & Meriam, b. Mar. 14, 1777	2	86
Olive, d. Ebenezer & Lucy, b. June 17, 1759	LR5	265
Orville B., of East Haddam, m. Emeline **WARD**, of Chatman, Sept. 20, 1838, by Isaac Parsons, V. D. M.	3	166
Paul, s. John & Hannah, b. June 5, 1751 or 1752	LR2	1096
Phebe, d. John & Hannah, b. Mar. 19, 1754	LR2	1096
Phebe, m. Abner **HALL**, b. of East Haddam, Nov. 29, 1772	2	54
Phebe, m. Alvah **LEONARD**, b. of East Haddam, June 23, 1823, by Rev. Isaac Parsons	3	42-43
Rowland, m. Sible **FULLER**, b. of East Haddam, June 30, 1763	LR7	4
Rowlin, s. John & Hannah, b. Aug. 4, 1741	LR2	1123
Samuel, s. Dr. Francis & Miriam, b. May 31, 1781	2	86
Sophia, d. Dr. Gordon & Sarah, b. Apr. 29, 1794	2	132
Stephen, s. Ebenezer & Lucy, b. Mar. 29, 1752	LR5	265
Timothy, s. James & Abbygale, b. Oct. 2, 1712	LR1	8
Timothy, s. John & Hannah, b. Feb. 4, 1733/4	LR2	1123
Warren, [twin with Loren], s. Dr. Francis & Miriam, b. Apr. 5, 1783	2	86
PERKINS, Henry A.,of Hartford, m. Sarah **EMMONS**, of East Haddam, May 24, 1831, by Rev. Nathaniel Miner	3	124
PETERS, William P., of Sheffield, Mass., m. Sarah Ann **JONES**, b. in Glastenbury, resident of East Haddam, Nov. 7, 1830, by Rev. Isaacc Parsons	3	115
PHELPS, Buley, d. David & Temperance, b. Aug. 14, 1787	2	174
Chauncey B., m. Flora **FULLER**, b. of East Haddam, Jan. 22, 1828, by Rev. Isaac Parsons	3	96
Chauncey B., of East Haddam, m. Thirza **HOLMES**, of Campton, N. H., Apr. 4, 1830, by Samuel Griswold	3	105
Chine, d. Samuel & Hannah, b. Mar. 17, 1787	2	217
Chine, d. Samuel & Hannah, d. Sept. 6, 1794	2	218
David, m. Temperance **WILLEY**, b. of East Haddam, Feb. 12, 1784	2	174
Dorothy, m. Samuel **PALMER**, Nov. 27, 1825, by Ozias Holmes, J. P.	3	80-81
Dorothy S., of East Haddam, m. John W. **BEEBE**, of Lebanon, Oct. 22, 1840, by Rev. George Carrington, of Hadlyme	3	184
Edwin, s. Chauncey B. & Thirza, b. Feb. 21, 1836	3	105
Esther Peck, d. Chauncey B. & Thirza, b. Mar. 26, 1833	3	105
Flora, w. of Chauncey B., d. Nov. 21, 1829, ae 28	3	106
George N., of Lyme, m. Sarah F. **PHELPS**, of East Haddam, Nov. 7, 1841, by Charles William Bradley	3	188
Griswold C., m. Lydia **CHADWICK**, b. of East Haddam, Jan. 16, 1825, by Rev. Simeon Shailer, of Haddam	3	70-71
Hannah Brainerd, d. Samuel & Hannah, b. Apr. 16, 1785	2	217
Hannah Brainerd, d. Samuel & Hannah, d. Aug. 11, 1794	2	218
Hiram Fuller, s. Chauncey B. & Flora, b. Nov. 5, 1829	3	105

	Vol.	Page
PHELPS, (cont.)		
Irena, d. David & Temperance, b. Nov. 14, 1784	2	174
Jabez A., m. Dorothy A. **BEEBE**, Aug. 4, 1833, by Rev. Benjamin G. Goff	3	132
John, s. Samuel & Hannah, b. Mar. 3, 1793	2	217
John Manly, s. Aholiab, b. Nov. 29, 1782	2	263
Joseph, s. David & Temperance, b. Mar. 21, 1790	2	174
Livia, m. Joseph **MARTIN**, Oct. 1, 1817	3	161
Marg[a]ret, of Lyme, m. Joshua **BURNHAM**, of East Haddam, Jan. 9, 1755	LR7	3
Maria E., factory operative, ae 33, b. in East Haddam, m. Luther M. **KING**, joiner, ae 35, b. in W. Longmeadow, Mass., res. S. Wilbraham, Mass., Oct. 18, 1849, by Alpheas Geer	4	19-20
Mariah E., of East Haddam, m. Luther M. **KING**, of Mass., Dec. 16, 1849, by Rev. Alpheas Geer	3	221
Martha A., ae 20, res. East Haddam, m. Samuel W. **GATES**, ae 23, b. in East Haddam, res. East Haddam, Aug. 12, 1855, by Rev. Moses Chace. Int. pub. July 9, 1855	4	61
Martha Palmer, d. Chauncey B. & Thirza, b. Dec. 8, 1834	3	105
Niles, m. Betsey **THOMAS**, b. of East Haddam, Aug. 7, 1825, by Rev. Herman L. Vaill	3	78
Ogden N., m. Charlotte **HUNGERFORD**, b. of East Haddam, Sept. 28, 1823, by Rev. Joseph Viell, of Hadlyme	3	44-45
Rebe[c]kah, d. Samuel & Hannah, b. Mar. 20, 1791	2	217
Rebe[c]kah, d. Samuel & Hannah, d. Aug. 13, 1794	2	218
Samuel, m. Hannah **WARNER**, b. of East Haddam, June 17, 1784	2	217
Samuel, s. Samuel & Hannah, b. June 19, 1789	2	217
Samuel Holmes, s. Chauncey B. & Thirza, b. Feb. 3, 1832	3	105
Sarah, m. John **HARVEY**, b. of East Haddam, Mar. 26, 1767	LR7	413
Sarah F., of East Haddam, m. George N. **PHELPS**, of Lyme, Nov. 7, 1841, by Charles William Bradley	3	188
Silence, of Lyme, m. Cha[u]nc[e]y **BECKWITH**, of East Haddam, Nov. 29, 1787	2	198
PIERCE, Ichabod, s. John (who changed his surname to "**WALES**") & Lydia, b. Mar. 10, 1776	2	89
PIKE, Charles, b. in New Jersey, res. East Haddam, d. Dec. 7, 1847, ae 14 m.	4	7-8
David B., m. Susannah S. **CONE**, b. of East Haddam, Apr. 16, 1832, by Rev. Isaac Parsons	3	122
PILGRIM, Adeline, d. Thomas & Dorcas, b. Sept. 17, 1817	2	307
Adeline, d. Thomas & Dorcas, d. July 21, 1818	2	308
Adeline, d. Thomas & Dorcas, b. May 17, 1819	2	307
David, s. Thomas & Dorcas, b. Oct. 15, 1807	2	307
David, s. Thomas & Dorcas, d. Dec. 3, 1807	2	308
Elizabeth Ann, d. Thomas & Dorcas, b. May 25, 1813	2	307
Elizabeth Ann, of East Haddam, m. Joseph F. **MEIGS**, of		

	Vol.	Page
PILGRAM, (cont.)		
Madison, Mar. 24, 1831, by Rev. Simon Shailer, of Haddam	3	116
George Washington, s. Thomas & Dorcas, b. Feb. 25, 1811	2	307
Lydia, m. Moses D. **BECKWITH**, b. of East Haddam, Sept. 2, 1827, by Rev. Simon Shailer, of Haddam	3	94
Mehitable, d. Thomas & Dorcas, b. Nov. 17, 1821	2	307
Richard, s. Thomas & Dorcas, b. Oct. 25, 1808	2	307
Sophia, d. Thomas & Dorcas, b. July 12, 1815	2	307
PLATO, Abraham, m. Abba **MASON**, Apr. 1, 1821, by Josiah Griffin, J. P.	3	6
PLUMB, Eunice, housekeeper, d. June 5, 1850, ae 85	4	29-30
Maragaret, m. Sylvester **HALL**, Jan. 10, 1798	3	105
PORTER, Martha, m. Moses **ROWLEE**, Jr., Sept. 7, 1707	LR3	16
Prudence, wid. of John, late of Farmington, & once the w. of Daniel **BRAINARD**, also mother of Susannah, Prudence and Mary **BRAINARD**, d. June 8, [ ]	2	37
POST, Ackmon, of Saybrook, m. Azubah K. **CHAPMAN**, of East Haddam, Oct. 20, 1830, by Rev. Isaac Parsons	3	108
Ezra. s. Samuel & Huldah, b. Feb. 14, 1784	2	58
Huldah, d. Samuel & Huldah, b. Oct. 31, 1778	2	58
John, s. Samuel & Huldah, b. Feb. 2, 1783	2	58
John, s. Samuel & Huldah, d. Mar. 28, 1783	2	59
Lusanda, d. Sam[ue]ll & Huldah, b. June 2, 1781	2	58
Mary, d. Sam[ue]ll & Huldah, b. Feb. 14, 1787	2	58
Nancy B., of Essex, m. Richard H. **PRATT**, of East Haddam, July 27, 1828, by Benjamin G. Goff	3	99
Samuel, of East Haddam, m. Huldah **BEEBE**, of Lyme, Jan. 6, 1774	2	58
Samuel, s. Sam[ue]ll & Huldah, b. Apr. 30, 1776	2	58
Sarah, d. Samuel & Huldah, b. Feb. 2, 1775	2	58
Sarah, d. Samuel & Huldah, b. Feb. 2, 1775	2	62
Silas A., ae 27, b. at Westbrook, res. Westbrook, m. Abby **MARTIN**, ae 25, b. at East Haddam, res. East Haddam, June 12, 1855, at Gelston Hotel, by Rev. George W. Nichols. Int. pub. June 11, 1855	4	57
Silas H., of Saybrook, m. Betsey **CHURCH**, d. Capt. Jo[seph], of East Haddam, Oct. 27, 1822, by Rev. Isaac Parsons	3	28-29
POTTER, David, m. Phebe A. **ARNOLD**, b. of East Haddam, Sept. 19, 1847, by Rev. Levi H. Wakeman	3	210
David, mechanic, ae 23, of East Haddam, m. Phebe A. **ARNOLD**, of East Haddam, Sept. [ ], 1848, by L. H. Wakeman	4	1-2
Ernest, s. Francis, manufacturer, ae 25, & Jane E., ae 17, b. Apr. 1, 1850	4	25-6
Ernest, d. May 15, 1850, ae 1 1/2 m.	4	29-30
Francis F., d. David, manufacturer, ae 26, & Phebe A.,		

	Vol.	Page
POTTER,(cont.)		
ae 25, b. Dec. 16, 1850	4	31-32
-----. child of Francis, mechanic, b. Oct. 19, 1853	4	47-48
POWERS, Merebeth, of Saybrook, Conn., m. Capt. Nehemiah **HAYDEN**, of Mobile, Ala., Sept. 17, 1829, by Rev. Peter G. Clarke	3	102
PRATT, A----, d. [Richard S. & Mary], b. July 31, 1845	3	157
Eliza, b. in East Haddam, res. East Haddam, married, d. Dec. 22, 1855, ae 47	4	73
Erastus W., of Essex, m. Sarah **BRADLEY**, of Hartford, Oct. 8, 1837, by Rev. Stephen Beach	3	159
Eugene Henry, s. [Nathan, Jr. & Orpha Ann], b. Oct. 19, 1833	3	139
George Spencer, s. [Nathan, Jr. & Orpha Ann], b. Sept. 20, 1835	3	139
George White, s. [Richard S. & Mary], b. May 6, 1837	3	157
George White, s. Richard S. & Mary Bulkley, d. Sept. 28, 1838	3	158
George White, s. [Richard S. & Mary], b. Mar. 23, 1840	3	157
Horace Belden, s. [Nathan, Jr. & Orpha Ann], b. Nov. 2, 1829	3	139
Jennette Hurd, d. [Richard S. & Mary], b. May 18, 1843	3	157
Jen[n]ette Hurd, [d. Richard S. & Mary B.], d. Oct. 6, 1844	3	158
Marshall Green, s. [Nathan, Jr. & Orpha Ann], b. Mar. 15, 1828	3	139
Mary, of Lebanon, m. Samuel **HALL**, of East Haddam, Nov. 15, 1764	LR7	416
Mary Champion, d. [Richard S. & Mary], b. Nov. 12, 1838	3	157
Mary Champion, [d. Richard S. & Mary B.], d. Sept. 14, 1844	3	158
Mary Champion, d. [Richard S. & Mary], b. Mar. 7, 1847	3	157
Nancy, of East Haddam, m. Samuel **CLARKE**, of New York, Sept. 16, 1827, by Rev. Isaac Parsons	3	95
Nathan, Jr., m. Orpha Ann **CARTER**, Nov. [ ], 1827, by Rev. John Marsh, at Haddam	3	139
Richard, m. Eliza Ann **SMITH**, May 5, 1835, by Rev. Isaac Parsons	3	137
Richard, ae 56, b. at Saybrook, Ct., res. Shelbourne Falls, Mass. m. Mary H. **BECKWITH**, ae 38, of East Haddam, Nov. 25, 1856, by Rev. Nath[anie]l Miner. Int. pub. Nov. 21, 1856	4	113
Richard H., of East Haddam, m. Nancy B. **POST**, of Essex, July 27, 1828, by Benjamin G. Goff	3	99
Richard S., s. Sylvester & Sarah, b. Oct. 23, 1805	2	271
Richard S., m. Mary **BULKLEY**, Apr. 25, 1836, by Rev. Isaac Parsons	3	142
Richard S., m. Mary **BULKLEY**, Apr. 25, 1836	3	157
Sarah Louisa, d. [Richard S. & Mary], b. Dec. 17, 1841	3	157
Sarah Louisa,[d. Richard S. & Mary B.], d. Nov. 11, 1844	3	158
Sarah Louisa, d. [Richard S. & Mary], b. Apr. 19, 1851	3	157
Sarah Louisa, d. Richard S., merchant, ae 45, & Mary, ae 36, b. Apr. 19, 1851	4	31-2
Sarah Louisa, [d. Richard S. & Mary B.], d. Dec. 1, 1851	3	158

	Vol.	Page
PRATT, (cont.)		
Sarah W., d. Sylvester & Sarah, b. Dec. 11, 1809	2	271
Sarah W., m. Lester **PASCO**, Aug. 4, 1833, by Rev. Isaac Parsons	3	132
Sarah W., m. Richard W. **HAYDEN**, b. of Saybrook, Oct. 4, 1830, by Rev. Peter G. Clarke	3	115
Sylvester, of Saybrook, m. Sarah **WHITE**, of East Haddam, Oct. 4, 1801	2	271
Wealthy, of East Haddam, m. Asher L. **SMITH**, of Lebanon, Feb. 12, 1826, by Isaac Parsons	3	84-85
William Wyllys, m. Julia **ATTWOOD**, June 12, 1825, by Rev. William Jarvis	3	76-77
-----, d. [Richard S. & Mary B.], d. Jan. 31, 1845	3	158
PRENTICE, Phebe, d. Thaddeus & Almira, b. Dec. 30, 1827	3	9
PRESCOTT, Anson, of Whites Town, N. Y., m. Hannah **PADDOCK**, of East Haddam, Oct. 22, 1820, by Rev. W[illia]m Lyman	2	325
PRICE, Marcy, m. Samuel **FULLER**, Apr. 19, 1733/4	LR2	1125
PURPLE, Abby, m. George E. **McCANN**, b. of East Haddam, June 16, 1844, by W[illia]m Marsh, J. P.	3	199
Amanda, m. Warren **MITCHEL**, b. of East Haddam, Nov. 9, 1820, by Rev. Isaac Parsons	2	323
Caroline E., m. Jeremiah **ACKLEY**, Feb. 16, 1851, by Rev. Jacob Gardner	3	230
Daniel, of East Haddam, m. Almira **JOHNSON**, [of East Haddam], Sept. 12, 1856, at Colchester, by Octavius Emmons, J. P.	4	98
Daniel, ae 35, b. in East Haddam, res. East Haddam, m. Almira **JOHNSON**, ae 18, b. in East Haddam, res. East Haddam, Sept. 12, 1856, at Colchester, by Octavius Emmons, J. P. Int. pub. Sept. 12, 1856	4	97-98
David, s. Richard & Hannah, b. Jan. 17, 1728/9	LR1	578
David, m. Lucy **SCONE**, Sept. 13, 1753	LR7	415
David S., m. Eliza G. **FULLER**, Sept. 11, 1844, by Rev. Isaac Parsons	3	200
Deborah, b. Apr. 25, 1788; m. Whiting **ATWOOD**	2	262
Edmund C., m. Hannah E. **HURD**, b. of East Haddam, Nov. 22, 1846, by Rev. Levi H. Wakeman	3	207
Edward H., m. Caroline A. **GATES**, b. of East Haddam, Sept. 26, 1832, by Nathaniel Miner	3	127
Eli, m. C[h]loe **SPENCER**, b. of East Haddam, Mar. 3, 1793	2	241
Elijah B., m. Alice A. **CHALKER**, b. of East Haddam, Dec. 14, 1834, by Rev. Stephen Beach	3	136
Eliza, m. Erastus **HURD**, b. of East Haddam, June 23, 1850, by Nathaniel Miner. Int. pub.	3	226
Elvira, ae 21, m. Erastus L. **HURD**, farmer, ae 20, b. of E. Haddam, June 25, 1850, by Nathaniel Miner	4	19-20
Esther, d. Richard & Hannah, b. May 30, 1725	LR1	578

	Vol.	Page
PURPLE, (cont.)		
Frances, s. Amanda, b. Dec. [ ], 1849	4	25-6
Hannah, d. Richard & Hannah, b. Mar. 3, 1719	LR1	578
Hannah M., m. Erastus S. **CLARK**, b. of East Haddam, July 5, 1846, by Alpheas Geer	3	206
Harriet A., d. Levi, day laborer, ae 26, & Ellen, ae 25, b. July 5, 1850	4	27-8
Henry, laborer, ae 20, m. Mary E. **FOX**, ae 15, b. of E. Haddam, Oct. 12, 1851, by Rev. W. Alburtson	4	37-8
John, d. Aug. 24, 1745	LR3	19
Lucinda A., m. Alden **SMITH**, b. of East Haddam, May 2, 1849, by Rev. Alpheas Geer	3	217
Lucinda A., ae 23, of East Haddam, m. Alden **SMITH**, farmer, ae 29, of East Haddam, May 2, 1849, by Rev. Alpheas Geer	4	9-10
Lucy, d. David & Lucy, b. July 19, 1760	LR7	415
Nathaniel, of Chatham, m. Dorothy **PERCIVAL**, of East Haddam, Feb. 5, 1824, by Rev. Isaac Parsons	3	56-57
Patience, d. David & Lucy, b. June 10, 1755	LR7	415
Patience, d. David & Lucy, d. June 27, 1758	LR7	415
Richard, m. Hannah **SPENCER**, Sept. 20, 1717	LR1	578
Richard, s. Richard & Hannah, b. Mar. 28, 1721	LR1	578
Sarah, d. Richard & Hannah, b. Apr. 13, 1723	LR1	578
Sarah, d. David & Lucy, b. July 7, 1758	LR7	415
Statira, m. Aaron **WATSON**, b. of East Haddam, Nov. 17, 1814	2	277
William L., m. Abby M. **SPENCER**, Sept. 13, 1837, by Rev. Isaac Parsons	3	159
-----, d. Levi, mechanic, ae 31, & Ellen, ae 26, b. Sept. 23, 1856	4	100
RAMSDELL, Ezra,m. Sarah **SPENCER**, b. of East Haddam, Sept. 24, 1772	2	84
RAMSEY, David S., shoemaker, ae 22, b. in Middle Haddam, res. East Haddam, m. Almira P. **ARNOLD**, ae 22, b. in Saybrook, res. East Haddam, June 2, 1850, by Isaac Parsons	4	19-20
RAND, Jemima, m. Joshua **BLAGNE**, July 26, 1826, by Ozias Holmes, J. P.	3	87
Thomas, m. Mariette **BOGUE**, Nov. 23, 1836, by Rev. George Carrington, of Hadlyme	3	151
RANDALL, RANDAL, Amos, Capt., d. Dec. 21, 1838, ae 83	3	170
Ann, of West Chester, N. Y., m. George **LORD**, of East Haddam, May 9, 1802	2	275
Bethiah, of East Haddam, m. Samuel **TYLER**, of Haddam, Jan. 15, 1823, by Rev. W[illia]m Lyman	3	34-35
Hannah, m. Sidney **MAYNARD**, Jan. 29, 1823, by Russell Dutton, J. P.	3	36-37
Jeneva, w. of Capt. Amos, d. Sept. 20, 1848, in Haddam, ae 87	3	170
RANNEY, RANNY, David S., of Chatham, m. Almira P. **ARNOLD**,		

	Vol.	Page
RANNEY, RANNY, (cont.)		
of East Haddam, June 2, 1850, by Rev. Isaac Parsons	3	225
Sally, of Middletown, m. Joshua **CONE**, of East Haddam, Jan. 18, 1802	2	277
RANSOM, Anna, of Lyme, m. Samuel **BECKWITH**, of East Haddam, June 14, 1774	2	188
Anna F., ae 24, b. in Colchester, res. East Haddam, m. Henry G. **RANSON**, ae 25, of East Haddam, May 31, 1848, by Joel Arnold (Perhaps **RAWSON**?)	4	1-2
Eliza Ann, m. Peter **AUSTIN**, June 9, 1839, by David D. Field, in Millington. Int. pub. in Bozrahville, by H. Mowry	3	172
George, of Lyme, m. Lucy Ann **CONE**, of East Haddam, Feb. 26, 1834, by Rev. Nathaniel Miner	3	133
Hannah, m. Dr. Augustus **MATHER**, May 8, 1811	2	90
Henry C., m. Emeline L. **CHAPMAN**, July 10, 1849, by Rev. Isaac Parsons	3	219
Henry G., ae 25, of East Haddam, m. Anna F. **RANSON**, ae 24, b. in Colchester, res. East Haddam, May 31, 1848, by Joel Arnold (Perhaps "**RAWSON**"?)	4	1-2
Henry G., merchant, b. in Salem, Ct., res. East Haddam, m. Emeline L. **CHAPMAN**, of East Haddam, July 10, 1849, by Isaac Parsons (Henry C.)	4	9-10
Horace, farmer, b. in Salem, res. East Haddam, d. Jan. 18, 1848, ae 52	4	7-8
Lyman C., m. Eunice M. **WATROUS**, b. of East Haddam, Nov. 24, 1833, by Rev. Nathaniel Miner	3	133
Lyman C., m. Eunice M. **WATROUS**, Nov. 24, 1833	3	149
Owin, s. Amos & Jemima, b. Jan. 23, 1789	2	158
Penelope, d. Amos & Penelope, b. Sept. 25, 1784	2	158
Sarah, ae 24, b. in East Haddam, res. Chatham, m. Stephen A. **CARRIER**, tanner, ae 28, of Chatham, June 2, 1850, by Nathaniel Miner	4	19-20
Sarah, of East Haddam, m. Stephen A. **CARRIER**, of Chatham, [June], 5, [1850], by Nathaniel Miner	3	225
Sarah E., ae 20, b. at East Haddam, Res. East Haddam, m. Jason H. **BAKER**, ae 23, b. at Bloomfield, N. Y., res. East Haddam, Oct. 17, 1855, at Salem, by Rev. B. B. Hopkinson. Int. pub. Oct. 16, 1855, at East Haddam	4	64
Sarah Esther, d. Lyman C. & Eunice M., b. Apr. 22, 1835	3	149
Wanton, s. Amos & Jemima, b. Apr. 24, 1787	2	158
-----, st. b. s. Henry G., farmer, ae 26, of Springfield, Mass., & Frances A., ae 24, b. Feb. 17, 1849	4	15-16
RATHBONE, RATHBON, Sarah A., of [Millington], m. Josephus R. **MERRIAM**, of Wallingford, June 6, [1847], by Rev. Nathaniel Miner, of Millington	3	210
----, d. Ransom B., merchant & farmer, ae 45, & Catharine C., ae 27, b. July 12, [1856]	4	109

	Vol.	Page
RAWSON, Anna F., see under Anna F. **RANSOM**	4	1-2
Catharine Chaunc[e]y, d. Edmund G. & Sarah, b. Feb. 4, 1788	2	48
Charles Chauncey, [twin with John Wilson], s. Edmund Grindall & Sarah, b. July 27, 1769	LR8	6
Cha[u]ncey, s. Grindal & Dorothy, b. Oct. 24, 1747; d. Sept. 15, 1752	LR4	473
Dorothy Blackleach, d. Edmund Grindal & Sarah, b. Oct. 17, 1773	2	48
Dorothy Blackleach, d. Edmund Grindal & Sarah, d. Oct. 31, 1774	2	49
Dorothy Nicholas, d. Edmund G. & Sarah, b. July 16, 1780	2	48
Edmond Grindall, m. Sarah **HOLMES**, b. of East Haddam, Nov. 17, 1768	LR8	6
Edmund Grindle, s. Edmund G. & Sarah, b. Jan. 26, 1772	2	48
John Wilson, [twin with Charles Chauncey], s. Edmond Grindall & Sarah, b. July 27, 1769	LR8	6
Joseph Pern, s. Edmund G.& Sarah, b. Dec. 23, 1776	2	48
Ozias Holmes, s. Edmund G. & Sarah, b. Apr. 22, 1775	2	48
Sarah Andrews, d. Edmund G. & Sarah, b. Dec. 31, 1778	2	48
Thomas Hooker, s. Grindal & Dorothy, b. Aug. 15, 1751; d. Aug. 26, 1753	LR4	473
Thomas Hooker, s. Edmund G. & Sarah, b. Sept. 24, 1770	2	48
RAY, Eber, mechanic, of Haddam, m. Flora Lucinda **FULLER**, b. in East Haddam, res. Haddam, [ ], 1848, by Isaac Parsons	4	1-2
Eber R., of Haddam, m. Flora L. **FULLER**, of East Haddam, Nov. 25, 1847, by Rev. Isaac Parsons	3	211
James, of Haddam, m. Mary B. **GATES**, of East Haddam, May 10, 1846, by Rev. Isaac Parsons	3	205
Lydia, m. William **WARNER**, b. of East Haddam, Jan. 21, 1833, by Rev. Isaac Parsons	3	131
Mary, of Haddam, m. Thomas **HURD**, of East Haddam, Feb. 25, 1779	2	122
Warwick, negro, d. June 16, 1826, ae upwards of 70	3	46
RAYMOND, Orlando N., ae 26, of Salem, m. Mary L. **FARGO**, ae 23, of Montville, Mar. 22, 1857, by Rev. Nathaniel Miner. Int. pub. Mar. 22, 1857	4	119
RAYNER, William, m. Eliza **COMSTOCK**, Mar. 27, 1831, by Rev. Isaac Parsons	3	116
REDDING, Nancy A., of Langdon, N. H., m. Alvin **BECKWITH**, of Lyme, May 11, 1851, by Rev. W[illia]m Harris	3	233
REED, Benjamin, m. Hannah **WHITE**, b. of East Haddam, June 10, 1762	LR6	503
Benjamin, s. Benjamin & Hannah, b. Feb. 20, 1765	LR6	503
Joseph, s. Benjamin & Hannah, b. Jan. 2, 1767	LR6	503
Mary, d. Benjamin & Hannah, b. June 11, 1763	LR6	503
REYNOLDS, Elisha, of Martha's Vineyard, m. Phebe **KNIGHT**, of Waterford, Oct. 11, 1829, by Rev. Isaac Parsons	3	102

	Vol.	Page
REYNOLDS. (cont.)		
Frederick B., s. John & Betsey, b. Mar. [ ], 1851	4	31-2
George, m. Mary **MILLER**, b. of Lyme, June 8, 1834, by R. S. Crampton, V. D. M.	3	134
Hiram, of Woodbury, Conn., m. Deborah **SPENCER**, of East Haddam, Mar. 25, 1840, by Nathaniel Miner	3	178
Jane Ann, m. Joseph **BRAMBLE**, b. of Lyme, July 13, 1841, by Ozias Holmes, J. P.	3	186
Joseph N., of Lyme, m. Jane Ann **THOMAS**, Sept. 14, 1834, by Ozias Holmes, J. P.	3	135
Mary E., d. George, mechanic, ae 37, & Mary, ae 38, b. May 27, 1850	4	27-8
Nancy, of New Haven, m. Willam Henry **FOX**, of East Haddam, Feb. 1, 1835, by Rev. Nathaniel Miner	3	136
RICH, Newel, m. Cynthia **SPENCER**, b. of Chatham, Dec. 20, 1832, by Rev. Simeon Dickinson	3	128
Susan, m. Warren A. **WRIGHT**, b. of East Haddam, Jan. 5, 1856, at the house of Mrs. Rich, by W[illia]m Cone	4	80
Wealthy B., m. Charles S. **SPENCER**, b. of East Haddam, June 30, 1850, by Rev. Jacob Gardner, in Moodus	3	227
Wealthy B., ae 27, b. in Middle Haddam, res. E. Haddam, m. Charles T. **SPENCER**, blacksmith, ae 24, of East Haddam, June 30, 1850, by Rev. Jacob Gardner	4	19-20
RICHARDS, Eunice, m. Clark **NILES**, b. of East Haddam, Jan. 25, 1852, by Rev. Nathaniel Miner	3	234
Jehiel, of Waterford, m. Susan A. **MORGAN**, of East Haddam, Feb. 20, 1831, by Rev. Isaac Parsons	3	115
RICHARDSON, Asa, of Middletown, m. Ann **TAYLOR**, of East Haddam, Nov. 20, 1826, by Rev. Isaac Parsons	3	56-57
Jemimah, m. Green **HUNGERFORD**, Mar. 3, 1709	LR1	7
Jemima, alias **HUNGERFORD**, m. Matthias **FULLER**, Apr. 16, 1741	LR2	1099
Lemuell, s. Lemuell & Mahittabell, d. Mar. 9, 1722	LR1	580
Mahittabell, m. John **WARNER**, Mar. 21, 1716	LR1	580
Mehittable, m. Al[l]en **WILLEY**, May 7, 1730	LR2	1122
Prudence, d. Samuel & Sarah, b. July 1, 1744	LR2	1101
Samuel, s. Samuel & Sarah, b. May 1, 1741	LR2	1101
Sarah, d. William & Sarah, b. May 2, 1774	2	82
William, of East Haddam, m. Sarah **TOWNER**, of Haddam, Aug. 19, 1773	2	82
RICHMOND, Frances A., ae 26, b. at Marlborough, res. East Haddam, m. A. S. **SMITH**, ae 30, b. in East Hartford, res. East Haddam, Oct. 9, 1855, by Rev. Isaac Parsons. Int. pub. Oct. 6, 1855	4	63
George S., s. Nelson C., manufacturer, ae 36, & Mary Ann C., ae 32, b. Nov. 16, 1847	4	5-6
George S., Jr., s. George S., mechanic, ae 31, res. East Haddam, b. Jan. 15, 1856	4	82

	Vol.	Page
RICHMOND, (cont.)		
Jane Maria, d. George, manufacturer,ae 26, & Mary, ae 28, b. Nov. 10, 1850	4	31-2
Nelson C., m. Mary Ann C. **CONE**, Sept. 22, 1835, by Rev. Isaac Parsons	3	140-1
William B., b. in Deep River, res. E. Haddam, d. Oct. 10, 1851, ae 1	4	39-40
-----, s. Nelson C., shoemaker, ae 43, & Mary Ann C., ae 40 b. June 19, 1856	4	109
RING, Lucy Graves, of Warner, N. H., m. Jonah G. **SMITH**, of East Haddam, Oct. 4, 1808	2	291
ROBBINS, ROBINS, Clarenda, m. Cooley **MASON**, Oct. 7, 1781	2	34
Laura G., ae 19, b. at Hartford, res. East Haddam, & Charles W. **LORD**, ae 29, b. at Newburyport. Mass., res. Baltimore, Md., had int pub. Nov. 18, 1856; license Nov. 18, 1856	4	117
Margaret S., m. Jeremiah **SMITH**, 3rd, Apr. 27, 1837, in New Jersey	3	179
Mary Ann, m. Abraham **MERCHANT**, Feb. 27, 1833, by Benjamin G. Goff	3	131
Morrison, of East Haddam, m. Martha A. **MUCKET**, of Chatham, July 15, 1848, by Rev. Levi H. Wakeman	3	213
Morrison, blacksmith, ae 22, b. in Lyme, res. East Haddam, m. Martha **MUCKET**, ae 20, b. in Durham, res. East Haddam, July 16, 1848, by Rev. Levi H. Wakeman	4	1-2
Morrison, blacksmith, ae 27, b. in Lyme, res. East Haddam, m. 2nd w. Mary **WARNER**, house maid, ae 21, of East Haddam, Jan. 15, 1854, by [ ]	4	41-2
Morrison, blacksmith, ae 27, b. in Lyme, res. East Haddam, m. 2d w. Mary **WARNER**, house maid, ae 21, of East Haddam, Jan. 15, 1854	4	51-2
Roland A., of Hartford, m. Mary Ann **GOODSPEED**, of East Haddam, Oct. 13, 1836, by Rev. Stephen Beach	3	146
-----, s. Morrison, blacksmith, ae 23, & Martha, ae 22, b. June 29, 1849	4	13-14
ROBERTS, Frederick A., m. Mary S. **EMMONS**, b. of East Haddam, May 6, 1834, by Rev. Nathaniel Miner	3	134
Geo[rge] R., of Chicago, Ill., m. Ann A. **BULKLEY**, of East Haddam, July 30, 1851, by Rev. Alpheas Geer	3	233
George R., merchant, ae 32, b. Bridgewater, N. Y., res. Chicago, Ill., m. Ann A. **BULKELEY**, ae 26, [ ], 1851, by Alpheas Geer	4	37-8
Loren L., of Torrington, m. Mrs. Angeline **MITCHELL**, of East Haddam, Aug. 9, 1835, by Rev. Alfred Gates	3	138
Lucy, m. William **MARTIN**, July 4, 1804, by Rev. W[illia]m Lyman	2	311
Mable, of Middletown, m. Joseph **ANDREWS**, of East Haddam, May 17, 1774	2	78

	Vol.	Page
ROBERTS, (cont.)		
Mary, Mrs., m. Charles C. **CONE**, b. of East Haddam, Feb. 12, 1829, by Alvan Ackley	3	101
ROBINSON, Benj[amin]L., s. of a blacksmith, b. in Portland, res. East Haddam, d. Nov. [ ], 1848, ae 8	4	17-18
Lovisa Jane, m. Charles F. **SISSON**, b. of East Haddam, Feb. 13, 1842, by Rev. Wilson Cogswell. Witnesses: Charles Cone, James Mainard	3	189
Lydiah, alias Lydiah **ACKLY**, m. Jonathan **HINKLEY**, Sept. 6, 1733	LR2	1129
Mary, d. Thomas & Lydia, b. Aug. 23, 1695	LR1	4
Mary, m. Charles **WILLIAMS**, Dec. 17, 1713	LR1	570
ROGERS, Amos, d. Sept. 27, 1846	2	111
Amos, d. Sept. 28, 1846, ae 52	3	123
Anne, d. Thomas & Mary, b. Mar. 12, 1759	LR7	4
Asael, m. Sarah **SCOVEL**, b. of East Haddam, Mar. 15, 1769	2	108
Asenath Simms, d. Thomas & Mary, b. May 21, 1764	LR7	4
Belina, d. John, b. July 28, 1769	LR8	1
Bets[e]y, d. Asael & Sarah, b. Mar. 20, 1776	2	108
Betty, d. Isaiah & Betty, b. Oct. 16, 1769	2	124
Caleb, s. Thomas & Mary, b. Apr. 28, 1772	2	110
Clarney, d. Isaiah & Betty, b. Sept. 12, 1777	2	124
David Leonard, of Lyme, m. Paddis Pamelia **BLY**, of Lebanon, Feb. 14, 1836, by Rev. George Carrington, of Hadlyme	3	142
Dorothy, d. Asael & Sarah, b. Feb. 26, 1774	2	108
Dorothy, d. John, b. Apr. 22, 1762; d. Jan. 21, 1784	LR8	1
Dorothy, d. Gurdon & Ruth, b. Apr. 11, 1785	LR8	1
Elizabeth, [d.] Tho[ma]s & Sarah, b. Mar. 19, 1750	LR4	470
Elisabeth, Mrs., of Boston, m. Rev. Elijah **PARSONS**, of East Haddam, Sept. 16, 1773	2	150
Elliott J., shoemaker, ae 23, of Lyme, m. Mary T. **MUCKET**, ae 19, b. in Durham, Feb. [ ], 1850, by Jacob Gardner	4	37-8
Elliott J., of Lyme, m. Mary T. **MACKET**, of East Haddam, Feb. 9, 1851, by Rev. Jacob Gardner	3	230
Esther, d. Isaiah & Betty, b. Sept. 10, 1773	2	124
George, s. Thomas & Mary, b. May 14, 1770	2	110
Gurdon, s. John, b. July 28, 1760	LR8	1
Gurdon, m. Ruth **BEEBE**, b. of East Haddam, Sept. 11, 1782	LR8	1
Harriet G., of East Haddam, & Alexander **McLEAN**, ae 33, b. at Manchester, Ct., res. East Haddam, had int. pub. Oct. 15, 1856*; license dated Oct. 15, 1856 (* Written 1857)	4	116
Herbert S., s. Sherman B., farmer, ae 30, & Almira M., ae 22, b. Jan. 22, 1850	4	25-6
Isaiah, s. Isaiah & Betty, b. Sept. 17, 1781	2	124
Jane, m. Henry A. **NILES**, b. of Mon[t]ville, Conn., Jan. 8, 1852, by Rev. Nathaniel Miner	3	234
John, s. Thomas & Sarah, b. Feb. 3, 1747/8	LR4	470
John, s. Tho[ma]s & Sarah, d. Aug. 6, 1752	LR4	470

	Vol.	Page
ROGERS, (cont.)		
John, m. [ ], June 1, 1758(?)	LR8	1
John, s. Thomas & Mary, b. Sept. 28, 1761	LR7	4
John Clark, s. Gurdon & Ruth, b. Feb. 27, 1787	LR8	1
Joseph, s. Thomas & Mary, b. Feb. 14, 1768	LR4	470
Joseph, s. Thomas & Mary, b. Feb. 14, 1768	2	110
Joshua, s. Asael & Sarah, b. Oct. 16, 1769	2	108
Lemuel D., of Montville, m. Hannah **STEWART**, of East Haddam, Jan. 15, 1822, by Rufus Dutton, J. P.	3	23
Lucey(?), d. Thomas & Mary, b. Feb. 27, 1766	LR4	470
Lucy, d. Thomas & Mary, b. Feb. 27, 1766	2	110
Lucy, d. Asael & Sarah, b. Nov. 18, 1771	2	108
Mary, d. Tho[ma]s & Sarah, b. July 15, 1752	LR4	470
Mary, d. Isaiah & Betty, b. Oct. 17, 1767	2	124
Mather, s. Isaiah & Betty, b. Sept. 14, 1771	2	124
Mehitable, of Colchester, m. Paul **GATES**, of East Haddam, Jan. 11, 1759	LR6	505
Richard, s. Isaiah & Betty, b. Oct. 24, 1775	2	124
Roswell, s. John, b. Mar. 2, 1764	LR8	1
Roswell, s. Gurdon & Ruth, b. Feb. 3, 1789	LR8	1
Sarah, w. of Thomas, d. Dec. 20, 1754	LR4	470
Sarah, d. John, b. Oct. 23, 1766	LR8	1
Sarah W., ae 26, of East Haddam, m. Theodore **FULLER**, ae 34, of East Haddam, Oct. 12, 1856, by Rev. Nelson Goodrich. Int. Pub. Oct. 11, 1856	4	103-4
Sith, of Lyme, m. Mary Ann **WHITMORE**, of East Haddam, Oct. 28, 1821, by Rev. Isaac Parsons	3	15
Seth Arbut, s. Thomas & Mary, b. Mar. 19, 1774	2	110
Susannah, d. Thomas & Mary, b. Oct. 1, 1763	LR7	4
Thankfull Beckwith, d. Gurdon & Ruth, b. July 14, 1783	LR8	1
Thomas, m. Sarah **SMITH**, Apr. 19, 1746	LR4	470
Thomas, s. Tho[ma]s & Sarah, b. Dec. 15, 1754	LR4	470
Thomas, m. Mary **COOKE**, Feb. 19, 1756	LR7	4
Timothy, s. Thomas & Mary, b. July 24, 1757	LR7	4
ROLLO, ROLO, Alexander, s. William & Patience, b. Apr. 5, 1711	LR1	8
Alexander, m. Elizabeth **WILLIAMS**, Aug. 20, 1752	LR4	464
Alexander, s. Alexander & Elizabeth, b. July 26, 1770	LR4	464
Churchel, s. Alexander & Elizabeth, b. Nov. 8, 1758	LR4	464
Daniel, s. Alexander & Elizabeth, b. June 23, 1761	LR4	464
Daniel, of Burlington, N. Y., m. Elizabeth **BRAINERD**, of East Haddam, May 4, 1829, by Rev. Isaac Parsons	3	102
Ebenezer, s. William & Patience, b. Feb. 26, 1717	LR1	581
Ebenezer, s. Alexander & Elizabeth, b. June 5, 1766	LR4	464
Elizabeth, d. William & Patience, b. Mar. 7, 1709	LR1	8
Elizabeth, d. Alexander & Elizabeth, b. June 13, 1764	LR4	464
Eunice, d. Elexander & Elisabeth, b. Oct. 13, 1772	2	2
Hannah, d. William & Patience, b. Mar. 3, 1713	LR1	9
John, s. William & Patience, b. Feb. 21, 1720	LR1	581

	Vol.	Page
ROLLO, ROLO, (cont.)		
Joseph, s. Alexander & Elizabeth, b. Nov. 5, 1754	LR4	464
Mary, d. William & Patience, b. Apr. 23, 1715	LR1	10
Mary, d. Alexander & Elizabeth, b. July 18, 1768	LR4	464
Samuel, s. Alexander & Elizabeth, b. June 15, 1753	LR4	464
Samuel, s. Alexander & Elizabeth, d. July 1, 1753	LR4	464
William, m. Patience **KNOWLTON**, Mar. 13, 1706	LR1	8
Zechariah, s. Alexander & Elizabeth, b. Jan. 3, 1757	LR4	464
Zerabbabell, s. William & Patience, b. Jan. 11, 1707	LR1	8
ROOD, Starling, m. Olive **HURD**, Oct. 30, 1831, by Thomas C. Bordman, J. P.	3	121
ROOTE, Gustavus, of Portland, m. Catharine E. **WORTHINGTON**, of East Haddam, Mar. 7, 1854, by Rev. Isaac Parsons	3	239
Gustavus, stone cutter, ae 30, b. in Marlborough, res. Portland, m. Catharine E. **WORTHINGTON**, mantua maker, ae 23, of East Haddam, Mar. 7, 1854	4	41-2
Gustavus, stone cutter, ae 30, b. in Marlborough, res. Portland, m. Catharine E. **WORTHINGTON**, mantua maker, ae 23, of East Haddam, Mar. 7, 1854	4	51-2
ROSE, E. A., ae 18, b. in N. Y., res. Williamsburgh, N. Y., m. Silas R. **HOLMES**, teacher, ae 23, of Hadlyme, June 9, 1851, by Thomas K. Beecher	4	37-8
Ebenezer H., of Saybrook, Ct., m. Jennett **CONE**, of East Haddam, Mar. 24, 1857, by Rev. S. W. Robbins	4	119
ROWLEY, ROWLE, ROWLEE, [see also **RYLE**], Abigail, d. Ebenezer & Mary, b. June 6, 1734	LR2	1121
Abigail, d. Eleazer & Abigail, b. Aug. 14, 1773	LR8	2
Anna, m. William **OLMSTEAD**, Nov. 5, 1743	LR3	6
Anne, d. Moses, Jr. & Martha, b. Apr. 5, 1716, in Colchester	LR3	16
Beckle, s. Eleazer & Abigail, b. Sept. 9, 1768	LR8	2
Bethiah, d. Daniel & Bethiah, b. Mar. 9, 1746	LR3	11
Content, d. John & Deborah, b. Mar. 26, 1719	LR1	571
Daniel, s. Moses, Jr. & Martha, b. Mar. 12, 1720, in Colchester	LR3	16
Daniel, m. Bethiah **LANGRELL**, Jan. 24, 1744/5	LR3	11
Deborah, of Colchester, m. Gideon **ACKLY**, of East Haddam, Oct. 27, 1763	LR2	1115
Ebenezer, m. Mary **CHURCH**, June 6, 1719	LR2	1121
Ebenezer, s. Ebenezer & Mary, b. Oct. 20, 1727	LR2	1121
Ebenezer, d. Aug. 24, 1757	LR2	1121
Eleazer, s. Ebenezer & Mary, b. June 14, 1736	LR2	1121
Eleazer, of East Haddam, m. Abigail **SPENCER**, of Chatham, July 21, 1763	LR8	2
Eleazer Dunnam, s. [Eleazer] & Abigail, b. July 10, 1788	LR8	2
Eleazer Dunnam, s. Eleazer & Abigail, b. July 10, 1788	2	40
Gersham, s. Ebenezer & Mary, b. Feb. 1, 1732	LR2	1121
Gursham, s. Eliazer & Abigail, b. Feb. 21, 1771	LR8	2
Gershom, s. Eleazer & Abigail, b. Feb. 22, 1771	2	40
Grisham*, of East Haddam, m. Mary **CIDIS**, of Hebron, Dec.		

	Vol.	Page
ROWLEY, ROWLE, ROWLEE, (cont.)		
14, 1758 (*Probably "Gershom")	LR6	510
Hannah, d. Ebenezer & Mary, b. Dec. 18, 1729	LR2	1121
Jane Maria, of Chatham, m. Reuben **CHAPMAN**, of East Haddam, Nov. 27, 1836, by Rev. Stephen Beach	3	146
John, m. Deborah **FULLER**, Sept. 11, 1716	LR1	571
Joseph, s. John & Deborah, b. May 15, 1722	LR1	571
Kam*, d. Ebenezer & Mary, b. Mar. 21, 1725 (*Nem? See Colchester Probate Files)	LR2	1121
Lucinda C., of Chatham, m. Perry Green **CHIPMAN**, of East Haddam, Jan. 31, 1842, by Rev. Alonzo G. Shears	3	188
Lucy, d. Eleazer & Abigail, b. Oct. 9, 1781	LR8	2
Lucy, d. Eleazer & Abigail, b. Oct. 9, 1781	2	40
Lura, d. Eliazer & Abigail, b. Apr. 25, 1785	LR8	2
Lura, d. Eleazer & Abigail, b. Apr. 25, 1785	2	40
Lidia, d. Moses, Jr. & Martha, b. Sept. 17, 1718, in Colchester	LR3	16
Lydia, m. Ansel **ACKLEY**, Aug. 3, 1818, by Rev. Solomon Blakesley	3	126
Marcy, s. (sic), Moses, Jr., b. Oct. 28, 1729	LR2	1128
Marcy, m. Matthias **SPENCER**, June 23, 1746	LR3	18
Martha, d. Moses, Jr. & Martha, b. Feb. 11, 1710, in Colchester	LR3	16
Martha, m. Thomas **FULLER**, Jr., Sept. 10, 1734	LR2	1113
Mary, m. Samuell **OLMSTEAD**, [ ], 1697	LR1	579
Mary, d. Moses, Jr. & Martha, b. Dec. 5, 1708, in Colchester	LR3	16
Mary, alias Mary **CORNWELL**, m. John **FULLER**, May 10, 1721	LR1	572
Mary, d. Ebenezer & Mary, b. Nov. 4, 1722	LR2	1121
Mary, w. of Moses. d. June 9, 1764, in the 97th y. of her age	LR7	1
Mary, wid. of Ebenezer, d. Dec. 6, 1786	2	41
Mary, d. Eleazer & Abigail, b. Mar. 19, 1779	LR8	2
Mary, d. Eleazer & Abigail, b. Mar. 19, 1779	2	40
Mahittabell, m. Henry **CHAMPEN**, Jan. 16, 1717	LR2	a
Mehitable, d. Moses, Jr. & Martha, b. May 20, 1723, in East Haddam	LR3	16
Mindwell, d. John & Deborah, b. Oct. 9, 1720	LR1	571
Moses, Jr., m. Martha **PORTER**, Sept. 7, 1707	LR3	16
Moses, s. Moses, Jr. & Martha, b. Sept. 5, 1713, in Colchester	LR3	16
Moses, Jr., m. Sarah **CHAPMAN**, Sept. 25, 1729	LR3	16
Moses, d. July 16, 1735	LR3	9
Moses, s. Ebenezer & Mary, b. Nov. 22, 1739	LR2	1121
Moses, s. Ebenezer & Mary, d. Aug. 25, 1757	LR2	1121
Moses, s. Eleazer & Abigail, b. Jan. 30, 1766	LR8	2
Moses, s. Eleazer & Abigail, d. July 18, 1774	2	41
Nathan, s. Moses, Jr., b. July 22, 1726	LR2	1128
Nathaniel, s. Moses, Jr. & Sarah, b. Mar. 3, 1733; d. Nov. [ ], 1741	LR3	16
Nem*, d. Ebenezer & Mary, b. Mar. 21, 1725 (*Arnold copy has "Kam". See Colchester Probate files for correction)	LR2	1121

	Vol.	Page
ROWLEY, ROWLE, ROWLEE, (cont.)		
Olive, d. Eliazer & Abigail, b. Apr. 22, 1764	LR8	2
Patience, d. John & Deborah, b. Aug. 30, 1717	LR1	571
Febe, d. Thomas & Mary, b. July 13, 1719; d. May 8, 1719/20 (sic)	LR1	577
R[e]ubin, s. Moses, Jr. & Martha, b. Sept. 23, 1725	LR3	16
R[e]ubin, s. Moses, Jr. & Martha, d. Aug. 12, 1747	LR3	16
Sarah, d. Moses, Jr. & Sarah, b. June 19, 1730	LR3	16
Sarah, m. Thomas **GATES**, Jr., b. of East Haddam, May 30, 1751	LR7	3
Sarah, m. Asahel **ANDREWS**, b. of East Haddam, Oct. 8, 1764	LR7	415
Sarah, d. Eleazer & Abigail, b. Mar. 5, 1776	LR8	2
Sarah, d. Eleazer & Abigail, b. Mar. 6, 1776	2	40
Susanna, d. Ebenezer & Mary, b. Mar. 30, 1720	LR2	1121
Susannah, m. Francis **CHAPMAN**, Sept. 24, 1741	LR2	1102
Thomas, d. Oct. 24, 1719	LR1	577
RUSS, Cephas B., of Mansfield, m. Mary M. **MARTIN**, of East Haddam, [Oct.] 17, [1839], by Rev. Nathaniel Miner	3	173
RUSSELL, RUSSEL, Alice, d. John & Elizabeth, b. Oct. 10, 1794	2	253
Eunice, of East Haddam, m. Nathan **SCOVEL**, of Lyme, Sept. 27, 1821, by Rev. William Lyman	3	17
John Arnold, s. John & Elizabeth, b. Nov. 26, 1796	2	253
Orinda H., m. Sylvester N. **ELY**, b. of East Haddam, Aug. 27, 1833, by Rev. Isaac Parsons	3	132
Sarah, Mrs., of Essex, m. Gurdon **ELY**, of Lyme, May 7, 1826, by Rev. Joseph Vaill, of Hadlyme	3	86
Stephen, of Haddam, m. Julia Ann F. **ACKLEY**, of East Haddam, Aug. 30, 1840, by Isaac Parsons, V. D. M.	3	182-3
RYLE, [see also **ROWLEY**], Mehitable, m. Ephraim **GRISWOLD**, Dec. 19, 1726	LR2	1120
SAGE, Frederick Russell, s. Russell, laborer, ae 45, & Elizabeth R. **ARNOLD**, ae 39, b. Sept. 3, 1848 (illeg.)	4	13-14
SANDERS, [see also **SAUNDERS**], George A., m. Cynthia **WATROUS**, Aug. 24, 1828, by Ozias Holmes, J. P.	3	100
Sarah, m. John **WILLEY**, Jr., Apr. 5, 1722	LR2	1102
Sarah, of Lyme, m. Nathan **FOX**, of East Haddam, Jan. 11, 1758	2	50
SANDERSON, Abigail, d. John & Tabitha, b. Oct. 28, 1749	LR4	473
Abigail, d. John & Tabitha, d. Aug. 7, 1759	LR4	473
Enoch, s. John & Tabitha, b. Dec. 3, 1752	LR4	473
Hamlin, s. John & Tabitha, b. Dec. 28, 1758	LR4	473
John, s. John & Tabitha, b. Feb. 1, 1751/2	LR4	473
R[e]ubin, s. John & Tabitha, b. Mar. 16, 1754	LR4	473
Tabitha, d. John & Tabitha, b. Mar. 31, 1756	LR4	473
SANFORD, Harriet W., of Wethersfield, m. Joseph W. **BOND**, of Lyme, Aug. 9, 1852, by James Noyes, Hadlyme	3	236
SAUNDERS, [see also **SANDERS**], Luce, [twin with Molle], d. John & Tabitha, b. Mar. 12, 1760; d. May 8, 1760	LR4	473

	Vol.	Page
SAUNDERS, (cont.)		
Molle, [twin with Luce], d. John & Tabitha, b. Mar. 12, 1760	LR4	473
Osmer, of Saybrook, m. Lovisa **MINER**, of Lyme, Jan. 15, 1844, by Rev. Stephen Alonso Loper, of Hadlyme	3	196
SAWYER, SAWER, [see also **SOYER**], Cynthia N., of Lyme, m. Samuel O. **ACKLEY**, of East Haddam, Oct. 13, 1833, by Rev. Joseph Vaill, of Hadlyme	3	47
Eunice, m. Prince **MOBS**, Jan. 27, 1762	LR7	2
Jemima Hill, m. Gideon Spencer **ANDREWS**, May 7, 1812	3	171
John, of East Haddam, m. Lucy **CHANDLER**, of Groton, Aug. 6, 1832, by Ralph S. Crampton, V. D. M.	3	125
Moses, s. Moses & Hannah, b. May 16, 1752	LR4	466
Phebe, of Lyme, m. Lynde **LORD**, of East Haddam, Mar. 27, 1821, by Rev. Joseph Vaill, of Hadlyme	3	4
SAYER, [see under **SOYER**]		
SCHUB, Frederick, ae 24, b. in Prussia, res. East Haddam, m. Mary **McCARTHY**, ae 19, b. in Lismore, Ireland, res. East Haddam, Apr. 8, 1855, by Rev. Isaac Parsons. Int. pub. Apr. 4, 1855	4	56
-----, d. Frederick, mechanic, ae 25, res. East Haddam, & Mary, ae 19, b. Feb. 3, 1856	4	83
SCONE*, Lucy, m. David **PURPLE**, Sept. 13, 1753 (***SCOVEL**?)	LR7	415
SCOVILLE, SCOVEL, SCOVELL, SCOVILL, Alva, s. Salma & Electa, b. June 22, 1801	2	277
Ame, d. Benjamin & Ame, b. Mar. 14, 1708/9	LR1	7
Arter, d. June 1, 1761	LR6	a
Benjamin, s. Salma & Electa, b. Oct. 24, 1793	2	277
Carile, d. Salma & Electa, b. Aug. 27, 1803	2	277
Carisle, of East Haddam, m. Amos **HALLAM**, of New London, Mar. 14, 1852, by Rev. Isaac Parsons	3	235
Daniel, of East Haddam, m. Meriam **CHAMBERLAIN**, of Colchester, July 1, 1756	LR6	507
Daniel, m. Luck* **BECKWITH**, b. of East Haddam, Sept. 24, 1758 (*Lucee?)	LR6	507
Daniel, d. Jan. 18, 1761, in the 44th y. of his age	LR6	507
Edward, s. Benjamin & Ame, b. Apr. 9, 1704	LR1	7
Elizabeth, d. Stephen & Rebeckah, b. Jan. 26, 1744	LR3	506
Emily, m. Enos L. **BRAINERD**, Dec. 27, 1829, by Isaac Parsons	3	104
Ephraim, s. Hezekiah & Mary, b. Oct. 25, 1741	LR5	564
Ephraim, of East Haddam, m. Sarah **SEXTON**, of Colchester, Mar. 15, 1763	LR7	415
Henry, s. Stephen & Rebeckah, b. Mar. 16, 1740	LR3	506
Hezekiah, m. Mary **GATES**, Dec. 24, 1740	LR5	564
Hezekiah, d. July 20, 1753	LR5	564
Irene, d. Stephen & Rebeckah, b. July 20, 1748	LR3	506
James, s. Amory, Jr., b. Oct. 20, 1735	LR2	1128
Jonah, s. Hezekiah & Mary, b. Sept. 1, 1750	LR5	564

	Vol.	Page
SCOVILLE, SCOVEL, SCOVELLE, SCOVILL, (cont.)		
Jonah, m. Sarah **SPENCER**, b. of East Haddam, Feb. 6, 1774	2	94
Jonah, s. Jonah & Sarah, b. Feb. 15, 1777	2	94
Judah, s. Hezekiah & Mary, b. Jan. 12, 1745/6	LR5	564
Lucy, m. David **PURPLE**, Sept. 13, 1753 (Arnold Copy has "Lucy **SCONE**")	LR7	415
Mary, Mrs. m. Joseph **BECKWITH**, b. of East Haddam (or said to be), Mar. 3, 1751	LR8	4
Mary, d. Ephraim & Sarah, b. July 26, 1764	LR7	415
Matilda, d. Salma & Electa, b. July 25, 1797	2	277
Meriam, [w. Daniel], d. July 2, 1757, in the 27th y. of her age	LR6	507
Nathan, of Lyme, m. Eunice **RUSSELL**, of East Haddam, Sept. 27, 1821, by Rev. William Lyman	3	17
Nathan, of East Haddam, m. Abby **FULLER**, of Colchester, Mar. 4, 1832, by Russell Dutton, J. P.	3	122
Rebeckah, d. Stephen & Rebeckah, b. Nov. 25, 1733	LR3	506
Reuben, s. Ephraim & Sarah, b. Apr. 21, 1766	LR7	415
Rhoda A., m. Ephraim R. **ANDREWS**, b. of East Haddam, Jan. 2, 1837, by Rev. Stephen Beach	3	151
Ruth, d. Timothy & Thankfull, b. Dec. 8, 1760	LR6	504
Salma, m. Electa **SPENCER**, Feb. 7, 1793	2	277
Samuel, s. Stephen & Rebeckah, b. Sept. 29, 1731	LR3	506
Sarah, d. Benjamin & Ame, b. Oct. 9, 1706	LR1	7
Sarah, d. Stephen & Rebeckah, b. Mar. 7, 1736	LR3	506
Sarah, d. Stephen & Rebeckah, d. Aug. 15, 1736	LR3	506
Sarah, d. Stephen & Rebeckah, b. May 15, 1742	LR3	506
Sarah, d. Stephen & Rebeckah, d. Aug. 29, 1749	LR3	506
Sarah, m. Asael **ROGERS**, b. of East Haddam, Mar. 15, 1769	2	108
Sarah, d. Jonah & Sarah, b. Dec. 18, 1774	2	94
Sarah, d. Jonah & Sarah, d. Sept. 19, 1776	2	95
Sarah, d. Jonah & Sarah, b. Aug. 5, 1779	2	94
Stephen, m. Rebeckah **MILLARD**, b. of East Haddam, Jan. 16, 1729	LR3	506
Stephen, s. Stephen & Rebeckah, b. Sept. 19, 1729	LR3	506
Stephen, s. Stephen & Rebeckah, b. Jan. 4, 1751	LR3	506
Stephen, s. Stephen & Rebeckah, d. Sept. 29, 1751	LR3	506
Timothy, s. Stephen & Rebeckah, b. Sept. 20, 1737	LR3	506
Timothy, of East Haddam, m. Thankfull **CROCKER**, of Colchester, Sept. 3, 1760	LR6	504
Tryphena, d. Salma & Electa, b. Sept. 25, 1795	2	277
William W., factory operative, ae 21, of East Haddam, m. Mary J. **UFFORD**, factory operative, ae 22, b. in Chatham, res. East Haddam, Feb. 26, 1854	4	41-2
William W., factory operative, ae 21, of E. Haddam, m. Mary J. **UFFORD**, factory operative, ae 21, b. in Chatham, res. East Haddam, Feb. 26, 1854	4	51-2
SCRANTON, Eleazer, m. Eliza **INGRAHAM**, b. of East Haddam, Apr. 5, 1835, by Josiah Griffin, J. P.	3	136

	Vol.	Page
SCRANTON, (cont.)		
Eleazer, m. Eliza **INGRAHAM**, Apr. 5, 1835	3	162-3
Eleazer, of East Haddam, m. Sally **BOGUE**, of Colchester, June 18, 1838, by Rev. Isaac Parsons	3	162-3
Harriet Elizabeth, d. [Eleazer & Eliza], b. July 31, 1837	3	162-3
SEARS, SEYERS, Anne, d. Matthew & Martha, b. Mar. 10, 1763	LR3	510
Ansel, s. Lucynda **MENTOR**, b. Apr. 29, 1799, in Lyme	2	48
Elizabeth, d. Matthew & Martha, b. Feb. 12, 1748/9	LR3	510
Elizabeth, d. Matthew & Martha, d. Mar. 10, 1756	LR3	510
Elizabeth, d. Matthew & Martha, b. Oct. 27, 1757	LR3	510
Jene, d. Matthew & Martha, b. July 11, 1760	LR3	510
Lucy, d. Matthew & Martha, b. Oct. 1, 1752	LR3	510
Martha, d. Matthew & Martha, b. Oct. 13, 1769	LR3	510
Martha, m. Samuel **HUNTINGTON**, Jr., b. of East Haddam, Jan. 24, 1788	2	229
Mary, d. Matthew & Martha, b. July 1, 1747	LR3	510
Mary, Mrs., of East Haddam, m. John **GOULD**, of Lyme, June 15, 1775	2	106
Matthew, m. Martha **WARNER**, Mar. 13, 1746	LR3	510
Matthew, s. Matthew & Martha, b. Nov. 25, 1854	LR3	510
Matthew, only s. Matthew & Martha, d. May 18, 1777, in the 23rd y. of his age	2	83
Matthew, d. Feb. 25, 1796, in the 79th y. of his age	2	83
SELBY, [see also **SOLBY**]. Brainerd, s. William & Dorothy, b. Apr. 29, 1751	LR3	4
Dorothy, d. William & Dorothy, b. Apr. 3, 1757	LR3	4
Dorothy, d. William & Dorothy, d. May 4, 1759	LR3	4
Dorothy, 2d w. of William, d. Apr. 7, 1764	2	21
Dorothy, d. Ephraim & Olive, b. Oct. 22, 1780	2	114
Dyer, s. Jeremiah & Sarah, b. Sept. 14, 1770	2	12
Dyar, s. Jeremiah & Sarah, d. Nov. 22, 1776	2	13
Dyar, s. Jeremiah & Sarah, b. July 4, 1784	2	12
Ephraim, s. William & Dorothy, b. Jan. 13, 1753	LR3	4
Ephraim, m. Olive **SPENCER**, b. of East Haddam, Nov. 18, 1779	2	114
Hannah, w. of William, d. Feb. 1, 1748/9	LR3	4
Hannah, d. William & Dorothy, b. Jan. 22, 1755	LR3	4
Hannah, d. Jeremiah & Sarah, b. Nov. 16, 1781	2	12
Jared Cone, s. Jeremiah & Sarah, b. May 23, 1786	2	12
Jeremiah, s. William & Hannah, b. Dec. 9, 1745	LR3	4
Jeremiah, m. Sarah **CONE**, b. of East Haddam, Mar. 29, 1769	2	12
Jeremiah Brainerd, s. Jeremiah & Sarah, b. Sept. 1, 1788	2	12
Rachel, d. William & Dorothy, b. Apr. 9, 1762	LR3	4
Ruth, d. Jeremiah & Sarah, b. Apr. 29, 1779	2	12
Sarah, d. Jeremiah & Sarah, b. June 24, 1772	2	12
Sarah, 2d, had s. Joseph **CHURCH**, b. Aug. 2, 1793	2	14
Susannah, m. Elisha **BORDEN**, Nov. 6, 1743	LR3	2
Susanna, d. William & Dorothy, b. Feb. 1, 1760	LR3	4

	Vol.	Page
SELBY, (cont.)		
Susannah, m. Josiah **LYON**, b. of East Haddam, Nov. 18, 1779	2	114
Thaddeus, s. Ephraim & Olive, b. Sept. 21, 1782	2	114
Warren, s. Jeremiah & Sarah, b. June 24, 1776	2	12
William, m. Hannah **BRAINERD**, Dec. 26, 1744	LR3	4
William, s. William & Hannah, b. July 23, 1747	LR3	4
William, m. Dorothy **BOOGE**, Feb. 26, 1749/50	LR3	4
William, m. Mrs. Annah **SPARROW**, b. of East Haddam, Feb. 28, 1765	2	20
William, d. Apr. 6, 1804, in the 87th y. of his age, being 86 y. old June 5, 1803, O. S.	2	21
SELDEN, SELDIN, Albert, shoe manufacturer, m. Charlotte **SWAN**, b. of East Haddam, [Sept.] 1848, by Rev. Miner	4	9-10
Ann, d. Joseph & Ann, b. Sept. 5, 1720	LR1	582
Anna, d. Joseph & Jane, b. Nov. 17, 1757	2	168
Anna, m. Israel **COMSTOCK**, b. of East Haddam, Mar. 15, 1775	2	160
Asa, s. Joseph & Abigail, b. Oct. 22, 1786	2	168
Asa, s. Joseph & Abigail, d. Oct. 3, 1788	2	169
Asa Beckwith, s. Joseph & Abigail, b. Sept. 23, 1788	2	168
Azibah, d. Joseph, Jr., b. May 15, 1714	LR1	10
Charlotte G., d. Jan. 22, 1850, ae 18	4	29-30
Eliakim, s. Joseph & Ann, b. Sept. 13, 1718	LR1	582
Elizabeth, d. Joseph & Ann, b. Nov. 27, 1722	LR1	576
Elizabeth, d. Joseph & Ann, b. Nov. 27, 1722	LR1	582
Elizabeth, d. Joseph & Abigail, b. July 25, 1782	2	168
Elizeph, child of Joseph & Jane, b. Oct. 12, 1767	2	168
Elizeph, child of Joseph & Jane, d. Apr. 3, 1773	2	169
Emeline F., m. Cephas C. **BROWN**, of Colchester, Apr. 14, 1835, by Rev. Isaac Parsons	3	138
Fanny D., of East Haddam, m. DeWitt C. **WILLIAMS**, of Chatham, June 23, 1850, by Rev. Isaac Parsons	3	225
Fanny D., ae 26, of E. Haddam, m. Dewitt C. **WILLIAMS**, farmer, ae 25, of Chatham, June 23, 1850, by Isaac Parsons	4	19-20
Hannah, m. Daniell **BRAINARD**, Feb. 2, 1715	LR1	581
Hannah, d. Joseph & Ann, b. Mar. 15, 1727	LR1	576
Hannah, alias **BRAINERD**, m. Jonathan **CHAPMAN**, Dec. 3, 1730	LR2	1120
Hezekiah M., of Chatham, m. Nancy **CHAPMAN**, of East Haddam, Feb. 22, 1826, by Isaac Parsons	3	84-85
Jane, w. of Joseph, d. Feb. 26, 1777	2	169
John, of Middle Haddam, m. Lydia **SPENCER**, of East Haddam, Dec. 6, 1826, by Rev. Isaac Parsons	3	88-89
Joseph, m. Ann **CHAPMAN**, [ ] 19, 1706	LR1	582
Joseph, s. Joseph, Jr., b. Jan. 16, 1710	LR1	8
Joseph, m. Wid. Abigail **BECKWITH**, b. of East Haddam, Nov. 25, 1777	2	168

	Vol.	Page
SELDEN, SELDIN, (cont.)		
Joseph, s. Joseph & Abigail, b. Oct. 5, 1778	2	168
Joseph, s. Joseph & Abigail, d. Dec. 5, 1782	2	169
Joseph, s. Joseph & Abigail, b. Aug. 30, 1784	2	168
Mary, m. Isaac **SPENCER**, Oct. 2, 1707	LR1	6
Phebe, d. Joseph & Jane, b. Aug. 9, 1765	2	168
Phebe, d. Joseph & Jane, d. Aug. 4, 1767	2	169
Phebe Chalker, d. Joseph & Abigail, b. July 25, 1780	2	168
Polly, of Chatham, m. Horatio **CONE**, of East Haddam, Sept. 25, 1803	2	285
Rebec[c]ah, d. Joseph, Jr. & Ann, b. July 19, 1717	LR1	582
William A., m. Charlotte G. **SWAN**, b. of East Haddam, Dec. 31, [1848], by Nathaniel Miner	3	216
William A., shoemaker, ae 30, m. 2d w. Persis J. **SWAN**, ae 29, b. in E. Longmeadow, Mass., Oct. 23, 1851, by Rev. Benedict	4	37-8
SERRALL, William C., of Guilford, m. Abby E. **CHAMPLAIN**, of East Haddam, May 2, 1850, by Rev. Isaac Parsons	3	224
SEXTON, SAXTON, Abigail, of Colchester, m. Nathan **GATES**, of East Haddam, Oct. 11, 1764	LR7	6
Demeris, of Colchester, m. George **CONE**, 2d, of East Haddam, Sept. 5, 1776	2	110
Jedidah, d. Jehiel & Rhoda, b. July 29, 1766	LR7	417
Jehiel, m. Rhoda **ACKLEY**, b. of East Haddam, Jan. 15, 1765	LR7	417
Sarah, of Colchester, m. Ephraim **SCOVEL**, of East Haddam, Mar. 15, 1763	LR7	415
Vianne, of Colchester, m. Russel[l] **WICKHAM**, of East Haddam, [1798?]	2	265
SEYERS, [see under **SEARS**]		
SHAILER, SHALER, SHAYLER, Caroline, of Colchester, m. James S. **SPENCER**, of East Haddam, June 12, 1831, by Rev. Isaac Parsons	3	116
Easther, of Haddam, m. Daniel **CHAPMAN**, of East Haddam, Nov. 18, 1778	2	112
Florilla A., d. Joseph N., ae 17, b. at East Haddam, res. East Haddam, m. Samuel **WETMORE**, ae 21, b. at Haddam, res. East Haddam, Dec. 27, 1855, by Rev. William Cone. Int. pub. Dec. 26, 1855. Consent given by Joseph N. **SHALER**, father of Florilla A.	4	69
Harvey, of Haddam, m. Florinda **STEPHENS**, of East Haddam, Nov. 10, 1844, by Rev. Russell Jennings	3	201
Helen F., ae 25, b. at East Haddam, res. East Haddam, m. Martin L. **DICKINSON**, ae 35, b. at Hadley, Mass., res. West Troy, N. Y., Oct. 17, 1855, by Rev. James M. Phillips. Int. pub. Oct. 17, 1855	4	65-66
Jeduthan, of Haddam, m. Elizabeth **SPENCER**, of East Haddam, Oct. 19, 1822, by Rev. W[illia]m Lyman	3	28-29
Meriam, of East Haddam, m. Courtney **TUCKER**, of Saybrook,		

	Vol.	Page
SHAILER, SHALER, SHAYLER, (cont.)		
Feb. 6, last [1825], by William Gelston, J. P.	3	70-71
Prudence, b. in Colchester, res. East Haddam, d. Dec. 27, 1849, ae 59	4	29-30
SHAW, Henry G., m. Julia **BAILEY**, b. of East Haddam, Nov. 26, 1843, by Rev. Samuel M. Emory, of Portland, in St. Stephen's Church, East Haddam	3	196
SHEFFIELD, -----, d. [ ], minister, ae 35, & Charlotte, ae 31, b. Apr. 16, 1855 [Moodus]	4	78
SHELDON, Martin E., of New Marlborough, Mass., m. Laura S. **SILLIMAN**, of East Haddam, Oct. 26, 1846, by Rev. Isaac Parsons	3	207
SHELTON, Theodore B., of New Haven, m. Harriet N. **EMMONS**, of East Haddam, June 9, 1834, by Rev. Nathaniel Miner	3	134
SHEPARD, Frederic W., of Essex, m. Maria T. **GREEN**, of East Haddam, Oct. 14, 1840, by Isaac Parsons, M. G.	3	182-3
Sarah T., ae 21, b. at Windham, Ct., res. East Haddam, m. Elisha **SHERMAN**, ae 22, b. at Sterling, Ct., res. Oniaga, Ill., Nov. 27, 1856, by Rev. Nath[anie]l Miner. Int. pub. Nov. 27, 1856	4	114a
SHERMAN, Elisha, ae 22, b. at Sterling, Ct., res. Oniaga, Ill., m. Sarah T. **SHEPARD**, ae 21, b. at Windham, Ct., res. East Haddam, Nov. 27, 1856, by Rev. Nath[anie]l Miner. Int. pub. Nov. 27, 1856	4	114a
SHIPMAN, Andrew, s. Beriah N. & Dorcas, b. Aug. 1, 1818	2	317
Cordelia Ann, d. Beriah N. & Dorcas, b. Jan. 1, 1816	2	317
Electa Maria, d. Beriah N. & Dorcas, b. June 11, 1812	2	317
-----, child of W[illia]m D., lawyer, b. Sept. 29, 1853	4	47-8
SILLIMAN, SILLAMON, Alfred G., m. Roxana E. **ELY**, b. of East Haddam, Dec. 21, 1842, by Isaac Parsons, V. D. M.	3	148
Benjamin A., d. Apr. 3, 1850, ae 9	4	29-30
Dorothy, d. William & Dorothy, b. Aug. 9, 1786	2	208
Eliphalet, s. William & Dorothy, b. Aug. 17, 1793	2	208
Eliza G., of East Haddam, m. Samuel **HUNTINGTON**, of Middlefield, N. Y., Mar. 31, 1852, by Rev. Isaac Parsons	3	235
Horace B., of East Haddam, m. Betsey A. W. **MARKHAM**, of Chatham, June 2, 1850, by Rev. Isaac Parsons	3	224
Horace B., shoemaker, ae 20, of East Haddam, m. Betsey A. **MARKHAM**, ae 18, b. in Chatham, res. East Haddam, June 2, 1850, by Isaac Parsons	4	19-20
Huntington, s. W[illia]m & Dorothy, b. June 9, 1795	2	208
Jared B., m. Sarah D. **HIGGINS**, Dec.10, 1848, by Rev. Isaac Parsons	3	216
Jared B., shoemaker, m. Sarah D. **HIGGINS**, b. of East Haddam, Dec. 10, 1848, by Isaac Parsons	4	9-10
Jeremiah, s. William & Dorothy, b. Apr. 21, 1789	2	208
Jeremiah, s. William & Dorothy, d. Dec. 12, 1791	2	209
Joseph, s. William & Dorothy, b. Apr. 25, 1791	2	208

	Vol.	Page
SILLIMAN, SILLAMON, (cont.)		
Joseph, m. Lavinia R. **CHAPMAN**, Oct. 7, 1841, by Isaac Parsons, V. D. M.	3	187
Julia C., ae 20, b. in East Haddam, res. East Haddam, m. Alonzo **WHEELER**, ae 24, b. in East Haddam, res. East Haddam, Apr. 20, 1856, by Rev. Isaac Parsons. Int. pub. Apr. 19, 1856	4	84-85
Laura S., of East Haddam, m. Martin E. **SHELDON**, of New Marlborough, Mass., Oct. 26, 1846, by Rev. Isaac Parsons	3	207
Mason H., m. Lucy P. **WRIGHT**, b. of East Haddam, Feb. 19, 1843, by Rev. Alex[ande]r Burguess	3	193
Olive, of East Haddam, m. John M. **BRAINERD**, of Chatham, Jan. 1, 1829, by Rev. Isaac Parsons	3	101
Oliver S., m. Mary **LESTER**, Nov. 26, 1829, by Isaac Parsons	3	104
Sarah J., ae 18, of East Haddam, m. Calvin P. **PEMBERTON**, shoe manufacturer, ae 22, b. in West Bradford, Mass., res. East Haddam, Sept. 16, 1848, by Isaac Parsons	4	9-10
Sarah T., m. Calvin P. **PEMBERTON**, Sept. 17, 1848, by Rev. Isaac Parsons	3	214
Thomas, m. Cynthia **McINTOSH**, Nov. 30, 1837, by Rev. Stephen Beach	3	159
Thomas F., m. Mary C. **STRANAHAN**, Dec. 10, 1848, by Rev. Isaac Parsons	3	216
Thomas F., shoemaker, m. Mary C. **STRANAHAN**, b. of East Haddam, Dec.10, 1848, by Isaac Parsons	4	9-10
William, m. Dorothy **HUNTINGTON**, b. of East Haddam, Mar. 28, 1782	2	208
William, s. William & Dorothy, b. Aug. 6, 1784	2	208
William, shoemaker, d. Jan. 6, 1851, ae 66	4	39-40
William, shoemaker, ae 20, m. Ellen E. **MOULTON**, ae 18, b. of East Haddam, Jan. 23, 1851, by George W. Brewster	4	37-38
William, m. [ ], June* 27, 1851, by Rev. Geo[rge] W. Brewster (*Probably Jan., as it was recorded Mar. 25, 1851)	3	230
SISSON, Charles F., of East Haddam, m. Lovisa Jane **ROBINSON**, of East Haddam, Feb. 13, 1842, by Rev. Wilson Cogswell. Witnesses: Charles Cone, James Mainard	3	189
Frederick W., s. Charles F., merchant, ae 35, & Louisa J., ae 31, b. Nov. 26, 1849	4	25-6
Jonathan Blivan, s. William & Phebe, b. Oct. 27, 1817	2	301
Mary, m. David **SNOW**, b. of East Haddam, Feb. 28, 1836, by Rev. Andrew M. Smith, of Lyme	3	142
Nathan H., m. Mary Ann **MORGAN**, b. of East Haddam, Oct. 30, 1838, by Rev. Erastus Denison	3	166
Phebe, d. William & Phebe, b. Mar. 7, 1815	2	301
Phebe, m. Daniel **CONE**, Aug. 22, 1841, by Charles William Bradley	3	187
SKINNER, Ebenezer, s. Richard, b. Oct. 22, 1728	LR1	580

	Vol.	Page
SKINNER, (cont.)		
Eliza Ann, of East Haddam, m. Diodate J. **MITCHELL**, of Chatham, July 14, 1828, by Isaac Parsons	3	99
Elizabeth, d. Richard & Hannah, b. Sept. 11, 1722	LR1	580
Emma A., d. John W., shoemaker, ae 25, & Hannah A., ae 22, b. Mar. 2, 1850	4	23-4
Huldah R., of Colchester, m. Capt. Robert **HUNGERFORD**, Jr., of East Haddam, Dec. 28, 1820, by Rev. Jacob Scales, of Colchester	3	6
John M., of Chatham, m. Hannah A. **STRANAHAN**, of East Haddam, Oct. 3, 1847, by Rev. Levi H. Wakeman	3	210
John W., mechanic, ae 23, b. Chatham, res. East Haddam, m. Hannah A. **STRANAHAN**, ae 20, of East Haddam, Oct. 3, 1848, by L. H. Wakeman	4	1-2
Mary, d. Richard & Hannah, b. Aug. 3, 1725	LR1	580
Mary, d. Richard & Hannah, d. Oct. 21, 1728	LR1	580
Richard, s. Richard & Hannah, b. Jan. 16, 1716/17	LR1	580
Richard, s. Richard & Hannah, d. Jan. 31, 1725/6	LR1	580
Thomas, s. Richard & Hannah, d. Jan. 18, 1725/6	LR1	580
SMALL, Edgar C., s. Abner C., ae 25, & Lucinda, ae 25, b. Oct. 3, 1851	4	33-4
Hannah M., of Willimantic, m. Alfred K. **BRAINERD**, of East Haddam, Feb. 20, 1853, by Rev. Isaac Parsons	3	238
Hannah M., worker in cotton mill, ae 20, b. in Willimantic, res. East Haddam, m. Alfred K. **BRAINERD**, shoemaker, ae 24, of East Haddam, Feb. 20, 1853, by Rev. Isaac Parsons	4	43-4
W[illia]m G., s. William J., mechanic, & Abby E., b. Jan. 25, 1851	4	31-2
SMITH, A. S., ae 30, b. East Hartford, res. East Haddam, m. Frances A. **RICHMOND**, ae 26, b. at Marlborough, res. East Haddam, Oct. 9, 1855, by Rev. Isaac Parsons. Int. pub. Oct. 6, 1855	4	63
Abby Ann, d. Jeremiah, Jr. & Dorothy, b. Apr. 28, 1825	2	299
Abby Ann, d. Jeremiah, Jr. & Dorothy, d. Dec. 4, 1828, in the 4th y. of her age	2	300
Abigail S., of Chatham, m. Linus E. **GRIFFING**, of East Haddam, June 23, 1850, by Rev. Jacob Gardiner	3	227
Abigail T., factory operative, ae 21, b. in Chatham, res. East Haddam, m. Linus E. **GRIFFIN**, factory spinner, ae 22, b. in Wallingford, res. East Haddam, June 23, 1850, by Rev. Jacob Gardner	4	19-20
Abner, s. Jeremiah, Jr. & Dorothy, b. Mar. 22, 1822	2	299
Abner Comstock, s. Capt. Jeremiah & Temperance, b. Mar. 29, 1796	2	136
Adaline, d. Asa & Mary, b. Apr. 26, 1817	2	273
Albert, m. Laura J. **MILLER**, b. of East Haddam, Nov. 24, 1845, by Rev. Philo Judson	3	203

	Vol.	Page
SMITH, (cont.)		
Alden, farmer, ae 29, of East Haddam, m. Lucinda A. **PURPLE**, ae 23, of East Haddam, May 2, 1849, by Rev. Alpheas Geer	4	9-10
Alden, m. Lucinda A. **PURPLE**, b. of East Haddam, May 2, 1849, by Rev. Alpheas Geer	3	217
Alden, s. Jeremiah, Jr. & Dorothy, b. July 26, 1819	2	299
Almira, of Clinton, m. William **CLARK**, of Madison, June 16, 1840, by John C. Palmer, J. P.	3	178
Alpha Louisa, [d. Matthew & Fluvia], b. June 17, 1814	3	112-3
Amelia, m. William B. **BINGHAM**, Nov.[ ], 1837, at Portland, Conn.	3	117
Ann, m. Isaac **CROCKER**, Dec. 13, 1718	LR1	575
Anna, w. of Thomas, d. Apr. 16, 1791, in the 76th y. of her age	2	47
Antoinette, d. Asa & Mary, b. May 20, 1824	2	273
Antoinette, d. Asa & Mary, d. Apr. 27, 1826	2	274
Antoinette, d. Asa & Mary, b. Sept. 11, 1826	2	273
Asa, s. Matthew, Jr. & Sarah, b. July 9, 1747	LR3	15
Asa, s. Matthew & Sarah, d. Aug. 6, 1767	LR3	15
Asa, Jr., m. Prudence **WORTHINGTON**, May 7, 1830, by Rev. Joseph Harvey, of Colchester	3	107
Asa, s. Matthew, 2d, & Thankful, b. Mar. 10, 1774	2	46
Asa, s. Matthew, 2d, & Thankful, d. Sept. 6, 1776	2	47
Asa, s. Matthew, 2d, & Thankful, b. Nov. 28, 1781	2	46
Asa, s. Calvin & Anna, b. Mar. 23, 1788	2	204
Asa, m. Mary Brainard **BECKWITH**, b. of East Haddam, Nov. 24, 1802	2	273
Asa, s. Asa & Mary, b. Aug. 22, 1806	2	273
Asher L., of Lebanon, m. Wealthy **PRATT**, of East Haddam, Feb. 12, 1826, by Isaac Parsons	3	84-85
Augustus Stanley, of East Hartford, m. Electa A. **SWAN**, of East Haddam, [Apr.] 12, [1848], by Rev. Nathaniel Miner, of Millington	3	212
Avery, of Waterford, m. Emeline H. **MORGAN**, of East Haddam, Oct. 27, 1824, by Rev. Isaac Parsons	3	66-67
Ezeriah, s. Matthew & Sarah, b. May 16, 1755	LR3	15
Azariah, s. Lieut. Jeremiah & Temperance, b. Nov. 21, 1786	2	136
Azeriah, s. Matthew & Sarah, d. Oct. 10, 1778	LR3	15
Benjamin, s. Thomas, Jr. & Mary, b. Nov. 16, 1761	LR6	503
Betsey, d. Calvin & Anna, b. Jan. 27, 1786	2	204
Betsey A., of East Haddam, m. Hiram **WICKHAM**, of West Stockbridge, Mass., May 19, 1842, by Tho[ma]s G. Salter	3	190
Betsey Ackley, d. [Matthew & Fluvia], b. Sept. 22, 1818	3	112-3
Calvin, s. Matthew & Sarah, b. Nov. 28, 1760	LR3	15
Calvin,m. Anna **AN[N]ABLE**, b. of East Haddam,Jan. 15, 1784	2	204
Calvin, s. Calvin & Anna, b. July 9, 1784	2	204
Ciliab, s. James & Elizabeth, b. Feb. 11, 1705/6	LR1	5
Cordelia M., ae 26, b. in East Haddam, res. Springfield,		

	Vol.	Page
SMITH, (cont.)		
Mass., m. Calvin S. **SPENCER**, mechanic, ae 27, b. in Lyme, res. Springfield, Mass., Oct. [ ], 1848, by Isaac Parsons	4	1-2
Corelia M., of East Haddam, m. Calvin S. **SPENCER**, of East Lynn, Oct. 28, 1847, by Rev. Isaac Parsons	3	211
Corelia Malinda, d. Asa & Mary, b. May 7, 1822	2	273
Cynthia, m. Lewis **MATSON**, Apr. 4, 1824, by Rev. Elijah Parsons	3	58-9
Cynthia, m. Lewis **MATSON**, b. of East Haddam, Nov. 12, 1837, by Roswell Davison, J. P.	3	159
Daniel, m. Ann **ANDREWS**, Dec. 15, 1767	LR7	412
Darius Brainerd, s. Asa & Mary, b. Nov. 19, 1815	2	273
Diodate, [twin with Eliphalet], s. Thomas, Jr. & Mary, b. Sept. 15, 1772	2	52
Diodate, s. Eliphalet & Hannah, b. Apr. 19, 1797	2	257
Dorothy, d. Matthew, 2d, & Thankful, b. Dec. 13, 1778	2	46
Dorothy, d. [Matthew & Fluvia], b. Dec. 2, 1805	3	112-3
Dorothy, m. Jeremiah **SMITH**, Jr., Nov. 27, 1806	2	299
Dorothy, d. Jeremiah, Jr. & Dorothy, b. Dec. 3, 1811	2	299
Dorothy, d. Matthew & Fluvia, d. Nov. 10, 1815	3	114
Dorothy, d. [Matthew & Fluvia], b. Aug. 1, 1816	3	112-3
Dorothy, m. Elijah S. **MACK**, Aug. 23, 1831, by Rev. Benjamin G. Goff	3	119
Dorothy, of East Haddam, m. Henry **HARTSHORN**, of Franklin, June 1, 1843, by Rev. Alex[ande]r Burguess	3	194
Ebenezer, s. James & Elizabeth, b. Feb. 26, 1710	LR1	2
Edmond, s. [Matthew & Fluvia], b. Aug. 4, 1807	3	112-3
Edmund, m. Roxana B. **WILLIAMS**, b. of East Haddam, June 1, 1834, by Rev. Stephen Beach	3	134
Edmund, m. Roxana B. **WILLIAMS**, June 1, 1834	3	162-3
Edward E., s. Alden, farmer, & Lucinda M., b. Feb. 2, 1850	4	23-4
Eliphalet, [twin with Diodate], s. Thomas, Jr. & Mary, b. Sept. 15, 1772	2	52
Eliza Ann, d. Asa & Mary, b. June 4, 1808	2	273
Eliza Ann, m. Richard **PRATT**, May 5, 1835, by Rev. Isaac Parsons	3	137
Elizabeth, d. John & Elizabeth, b. July 15, 1715	LR2	1129
Elizabeth, d. Matthew & Sarah, b. Apr. 20, 1716	LR1	9
Elizabeth, d. Matthew, Jr. & Sarah, b. Nov. 12, 1750	LR3	15
Elizabeth Ann, wid., of East Haddam, m. Octavius **EMMONS**, of Colchester, Feb. 5, 1854, by Rev. Isaac Parsons	3	239
Elizabeth Ann, tailoress, ae 34, of East Haddam, m. 2d h. Octavius **EMMONS**, farmer, ae 48, of Colchester, Feb. 5, 1854	4	41-2
Elizabeth Ann, tailoress, ae 34, of East Haddam, m. 2d h. Octavius **EMMONS**, farmer, ae 48, of Colchester, Feb. 5, 1854	4	51-2

	Vol.	Page
SMITH, (cont.)		
Ella Louisa, d. July 18, 1848, ae 4 m.	4	17-8
Ellen, m. W. **SMITH**, of East Haddam, Apr. [ ], 1851, by Rev. Isaac Parsons	4	37-8
Ellen Louisa, d. Henry, ship carpenter, ae 36, & Elizabeth A., ae 30, b. Mar. 13, 1849	4	11-2
Emily, d. Sept. 20, 1851, ae 45	4	39-40
Erastus, s. Capt. Jeremiah & Temperance, b. Apr. 19, 1799	2	136
Erastus, m. Ann **ALLEN**, June 4, 1818	2	317
Esther, d. Mattthew, 2d, & Thankful, b. Feb. 3, 1770	2	46
Esther, m. Jonah **GATES**, b. of East Haddam, Feb. 25, 1790	2	223
Eveline C., m. William H. **TRACY**, b. of East Haddam, Aug. 9, 1846, by Rev. Levi Wakeman	3	206
Eveline Cornelia, d. Erastus & Ann, b. Jan. 6, 1826	2	317
Ezeriah, see under Azariah		
Fluvia, d. [Matthew & Fluvia], b. Feb. 24, 1812	3	112-3
Frank P., s. Alvin C., mechanic, ae 28, & Lucius, ae 28, b. May 6, 1854	4	53-4
Gad, s. Jeremiah, Jr. & Dorothy, b. Apr. 3, 1817	2	299
Gad, m. Nancy **CONE**, b. of East Haddam, [1838?], in New London	3	180-1
Gad, book-agent, ae 30, b. in East Haddam, m. 2d w. Mary W. **SMITH**, ae 20, b. in Lebanon, Tenn., res. Tenn., Oct. [ ], 1848, by C. C. Correct	4	1-2
George W., m. Adaline A. **PALMER**, Nov. 26, 1835, by Rev. Isaac Parsons	3	140-1
George Washington, s. Asa & Mary, b. Nov. 11, 1813	2	273
Han[n]ah, d. John & Elizabeth, b. Aug. 8, 1708	LR1	7
Hannah, w. Tho[ma]s, d. Jan. 12, 1754	LR2	1107
Hannah, d. Matthew, Jr. & Thankfull, b. Jan. 6, 1764	LR6	505
Hannah, d. Thomas, Jr. & Mary, b. May 12, 1770	2	52
Hannah B., of East Haddam, m. Thomas H. **SPENCER**, of Great Barrington, Sept. 9, 1832, by Rev. Isaac Parsons	3	125
Hannah Brainerd, d. Asa & Mary, b. Jan. 1, 1812	2	273
Harriet Vernon, d. [Jeremiah, 3rd, & Margaret S.], b. Dec. 19, 1839	3	179
Henry, s. Jeremiah, Jr. & Dorothy, b. Sept. 14, 1814	2	299
Henry, m. Emily **WATSON**, Feb. 7, 1828, by Rev. Alvan Ackley. Int. Pub.	3	96
Henry, mechanic, b. in Haddam, res. East Haddam, d. July 27, 1850, ae 37	4	29-30
Henry R., of Portland, m. Cornelia H. **HOLMES**, of East Haddam, Oct. 22, 1854, by Rev. James M. Phillips	3	240
Henry R., butcher, ae 36, b. in East Hartford, res. Portland, m. 3rd w. Cornelia H. **HOLMES**, ae 38, b. in Lyme, res. East Haddam, Oct. 22, 1854, by Rev. James M. Phillips	4	51-2
Henry S., m. Laura Ann **STARK**, May 28, 1850, by Rev. Stephen A. Loper, of Hadlyme	3	222

	Vol.	Page
SMITH, (cont.)		
Horatio, s. Dan & Deborah, b. Oct. 30, 1814	2	257
Jabez, of Chatham, m. Emeline **WHITMORE**, b. of East Haddam, Jan. 18, 1826, by Rev. Isaac Parsons	3	83
James, s. John & Elizabeth, b. Feb. 1, 17[ ]	LR2	1129
James Monroe, s. Asa & Mary, b. Mar. 5, 1821	2	273
Jarvis Ring, s. Jonah G. & Lucy G., b. Nov. 8, 1809	2	291
Jeremiah, s. Matthew & Sarah, b. June 29, 1758	LR3	15
Jeremiah, of East Haddam, m. Temperance **COMSTOCK**, of Lyme, June 17, 1784	2	136
Jeremiah, s. Jeremiah & Temperance, b. May 12, 1785	2	136
Jeremiah, Jr., m. Dorothy **SMITH**, Nov. 27, 1806	2	299
Jeremiah, s. Jeremiah, Jr. & Dorothy, b. July 9, 1809	2	299
Jeremiah, 3rd, m. Margaret S. **ROBBINS**, Apr. 27, 1837, in New Jersey	3	179
John, m. Elizabeth **KINERD**, Aug. 28, 1707	LR2	1129
John, of Lyme, m. Mary M. **TAYLOR**, of East Haddam, May 30, 1854, by Rev. Isaac Parsons	3	239
John, farmer, ae 27, of Lyme, m. Mary M. **TAYLOR**, seamstress, ae 28, of East Haddam, May 30, 1854	4	51-2
John C., m. Ellen C. **FOX**, b. of East Haddam, Nov. 11, 1832, by Nathaniel Miner	3	127
John Cotton, s. Asa & Mary, b. Mar. 12, 1810	2	273
John Howland, s. Ignatius & Susannah, b. Nov. 16, 1762	LR7	5
John Kinner, s. John & Elizabeth, b. Dec. 16, 1710	LR2	1129
Jonah, s. Matthew, Jr. & Thankfull, b. Aug. 13, 1762	LR6	505
Jonah, s. Matthew, Jr. & Thankfull, d. Jan. 5, 1765	LR6	505
Jonah, s. Matthew, 2d, & Thankful, b. Mar. 6, 1772	2	46
Jonah, s. Matthew, 2d, & Thankful, d. Sept. 5, 1776	2	47
Jonah, s. Thomas, Jr. & [Mary], [ ]	LR6	503
Jonah G., of East Haddam, m. Lucy Graves **RING**, of Warner, N. H., Oct. 4, 1808	2	291
Jonah Gates, s. Matthew, 2d, & Thankful, b. Mar. 26, 1785	2	46
Joseph, s. John & Elizabeth, b. Mar. 1, 1720	LR2	1129
Julia, d. [Matthew & Fluvia], b. May 5, 1826	3	112-3
Julia, m. Oliver **MARTIN**, b. of East Haddam, Apr. 1, 1850, by Nathaniel Miner	3	224
Julia Jennings, d. Capt. Jer[emia]h & Temperance, b. July 8, 1801	2	136
Julia Jennings, m. Christopher C. **GATES**, b. of East Haddam, Oct. 15, 1818	2	313
Lydia, d. Matthew & Sarah, b. Feb. 24, 1718	LR1	9
Lydia, m. Josiah **ARNOLD**, Feb. 24, 1742/3	LR2	1197
Lydia, d. Matthew, Jr. & Thankfull, b. Feb. 6, 1766	LR6	505
Lydia, m. Jabez **FULLER**, b. of East Haddam, Apr. 3, 1791	2	247
Maria E., d. Wid. Elizabeth, ae 32, b. Dec. 31, 1850	4	31-2
Marsena LeValley, [d. Matthew & Fluvia], b. Aug. 28, 1828	3	112-3
Martha, d. [Matthew & Fluvia], b. June 4, 1821	3	112-3

	Vol.	Page
SMITH, (cont.)		
Mary, m. Joseph **CONE**, Nov. 28, 1734	LR2	1123
Mary, d. Tho[ma]s. Jr. & Mary, b. Jan. 16, 1767	LR6	503
Mary, m. Diodate **JONES**, b. of East Haddam, July 1, 1789	2	245
Mary, m. Gordon A. **FOWLER**, b. of East Haddam, Mar. 14, 1821, by Rev. Isaac Parsons	3	3
Mary, d. [Matthew & Fluvia], b. July 31, 1823	3	112-3
Mary Ann B., d. Gad, farmer, & Mary, b. Mar. 2, 1850	4	23-4
Mary B., of East Haddam, m. George **BARNARD**, of Hartford, May 25, 1831, by Rev. Isaac Parsons	3	116
Mary B., of East Haddam, m. Henry A. **VENTRES**, of Franklin, N. J., Nov. 29, 1850, by Rev. Alpheas Geer	3	228
Mary Brainard, d. Asa & Mary, b. Feb. 8, 1805	2	273
Mary S., of East Haddam, m. Arnold **CLARK**, of Lyme, Jan. 1, 1822, by Rev. Isaac Parsons	3	21
Mary W., ae 20, b. in Lebanon, Tenn., res. Tenn., m. Gad **SMITH**, book-agent, ae 30, b. in East Haddam, Oct. [ ], 1848, by C. C. Correct	4	1-2
Matthew, m. Sarah **MACK**, Nov. 28, 1706	LR1	9
Matthew, s. Matthew & Sarah, b. Nov. 1, 1722	LR1	571
Matthew, Jr., m. Sarah **CHURCH**, Jan. 16, 1745/6	LR3	15
Matthew, s. Matthew & Sarah, b. May 12, 1753	LR3	15
Matthew, Jr., m. Thankfull **ACKLEY**, b. of East Haddam, May 13, 1761	LR6	505
Matthew, s. Matthew, 2d, & Thankful, b. Jan. 7, 1780	2	46
Matthew, m. Fluvia **ACKLEY**, Jan. 1, 1805	3	112-3
Matthew, s. [Matthew & Fluvia], b. July 31, 1809	3	112-3
Matthew, s. Matthew & Fluvia, d. July 15, 1814	3	114
Matthew, d. July 1, 1824, ae 83 y.	2	47
Matthew, of Middlefield, Mass., m. Mrs. Elizabeth **GATES**, of East Haddam, July 30, 1826, by Rev. Isaac Parsons	3	86
Matthew Edmond, s. [Edmund & Roxana B.], b. Feb. 28, 1839	3	162-3
Mindwell, d, James & Hannah, b. Apr. 22, 1714	LR1	2
Nathan, s. Thomas & Hannah, b. Sept. 11, 1740	LR2	1107
Nathaniel Robbins, s. [Jeremiah, 3rd, & Margaret S.], b. Jan. 13, 1838	3	179
Nehemiah, s. Asa & Mary, b. July 13, 1819	2	273
Olive, d. Matthew, 2d, & Thankful, b. Feb. 12, 1776	2	46
Phebe, alias Phebe **ALMANG**, m. Bazaliel **BRAINARD**, May 19, 1749	LR2	1092
Phebe, of East Haddam, m. Henry C. **HARRIS**, of Middletown, May 26, 1842, by Isaac Parsons, V. D. M.	3	191
Polly, m. Thomas **HALL**, Jr., b. of East Haddam, Jan. 20, 1782	2	30
Rachel, d. Ignatius & Susannah, b. Mar. 16, 1765	LR7	5
Rachel, m. David **BRAINERD**, b. of East Haddam, June 5, 1783	2	164
Rachel, m. Thomas **GATES**, 2d, b. of East Haddam, June 22, 1788	2	152

	Vol.	Page
SMITH, (cont.)		
Ruth, d. Matthew & Sarah, b. Mar. 29, 1720	LR1	571
Ruth, d. John & Elizabeth, b. Feb. 3, 1727/8	LR2	1129
Ruth, m. Jared **CONE**, Dec. [ ], 1738	LR3	11
Samuell, s. John & Elizabeth, b. Aug. 26, 1725	LR2	1129
Samuel, s. Thomas & Anne, b. Dec. 1, 1757	LR2	1107
Sarah, d. Matthew & Sarah, b. Feb. 21, 1711/12	LR1	9
Sarah, d. John & Elizabeth, b. July 15, 1723	LR2	1129
Sarah, m. Thomas **ROGERS**, Apr. 19, 1746	LR4	470
Sarah, w. of Capt. Matthew, d. Jan. 18, 1755	LR3	15
Sarah, d. Matthew & Sarah, b. Aug. 14, 1764	LR3	15
Simon, Jr., of Waterford, m. Mary Ann **MORGAN**, of East Haddam, Mar. 26, 1828, by Rev. Isaac Parsons	3	99
Sophia, d. Capt. Jeremiah & Temperance, b. May 13, 1793	2	136
Sophia, m. Joseph **BRAINERD**, b. of East Haddam, Feb. 13, 1812, by Rev. Elijah Parsons	2	303
Susan[n]ah, d. James & Elizabeth, b. July 3, 1708	LR1	8
Sylvester Williams, s. [Edmund & Roxana B.], b. Sept. 7, 1841	3	162-3
Temperance, d. Jeremiah & Temperance, b. Oct. 27, 1788	2	136
Temperance, m. Joseph Osborn **ACKLEY**, b. of East Haddam, Oct. 31, 1805	2	219
Temperance, d. Jeremiah, Jr. & Dorothy, b. July 15, 1807	2	299
Temperance, d. Jeremiah, Jr. & Dorothy, d. Jan. 26, 1830, in the 23rd y. of her age	2	300
Temperance Abby, d. Jeremiah, Jr. & Dorothy, b. Nov. 29, 1830	2	299
Thankful, d. Matthew, 2d, & Thankful, b. Jan. 28, 1768	2	46
Thankful, w. of Matthew, d. Mar. 20, 1830, ae 90 y.	2	47
Theodore Tolemus, s. Watrous B., manufacturer, ae 47, & Sarah H., ae 41, b. July 15, 1850	4	25-6
Thomas, s. Matthew & Sarah, b. Mar. 26, 1710	LR1	9
Thomas, s. John & Elizabeth, b. Dec. 15, 1717	LR2	1129
Thomas, m. Hannah **GATES**, Feb. 9, 1737/8	LR2	1107
Thomas, s. Thomas & Hannah, b. Jan. 21, 1738/9	LR2	1107
Thomas. of East Haddam, m. Anne **OSBON**, of Middletown, May 27, 1750	LR2	1107
Thomas, Jr., of East Haddam, m. Mary **GREENE**, of Middletown, Dec. 11, 1760	LR6	503
W., of East Haddam, m. Ellen **SMITH**, Apr. [ ], 1851, by Rev. Isaac Parsons	4	37-8
Washington K., of Haddam, m. Almira L. **CHAPMAN**, of East Haddam, Jan. 7, 1840, by Tho[mas] W. Gile	3	174
Watrous B., Jr., m. Ellen **NICHOLS**, b. of East Haddam, Mar. 16, 1851, by Rev. Isaac Parsons	3	230
Watrous Beckwith, s. Asa & Mary, b. May 3, 1803	2	273
Whitby Moore, s. [Edmund & Roxana B.], b. Mar. 12, 1836	3	162-3
William Erastus, s. Erastus & Ann, b. Feb. 18, 1819	2	317
William Gad, s. [Gad & Nancy], b. Feb. 10, 1839	3	180-1

	Vol.	Page
SMITH, (cont.)		
William M., of Lyme, m. Jane S. **CROSBY**, of East Haddam, Apr. 19, 1825, by Rev. Isaac Parsons	3	76-7
-----, child of Gad, book agent, ae 30, of Tenn., & Mary W. ae 20, b. July 17, 1847	4	5-6
-----, st. b. s. Henry, carpenter, ae 48, & Emily, ae 43, b. Jan. 17, 1849	4	15-6
-----, s. Watrous B., manufacturer, ae 46, & Sarah A., ae 40, b. July 15, 1849	4	13-4
-----, child of Watrous B., Jr., mechanic, b. Feb. 9, 1853	4	47-8
-----, s. Augustus S., shoemaker, ae 31, & Frances, ae 27, b. Sept. 17, 1856	4	111
SNOW, Abigail, m. Henry K. **MOULTON**, b. of East Haddam, Aug. 22, 1831, by Rev. Isaac Parsons	3	119
Anne, d. May 30, 1848, ae 72	4	17-8
David, m. Mary **SISSON**, b. of East Haddam, Feb. 28, 1836, by Rev. Andrew M. Smith, of Lyme	3	142
Durinda, m. Salmon F. **WILLEY**, June 3, 1828, by Rev. Isaac Parsons	3	99
Ebenezer, 2d, m. Jerusha Jane **GATES**, Mar. 2, 1842, by Isaac Parsons, D. V. M.	3	189
Ebenezer, m. Julia F. **PALMER**, b. of East Haddam, July 22, 1852, by Rev. W. Emmerson	3	236
Huldah Ann, m. Isaac A. **BEVINS**, b. of East Haddam, Nov. 7, 1830, by Rev. Isaac Parsons	3	115
Julia, of East Haddam, m. William B. **CLARK**, of Norwich, Nov. 29, 1832, by Isaac Parsons	3	127
Lucretia, m. Hiram B. **TUCKER**, June 7, 1829, by Rev. Isaac Parsons	3	102
Mary, of East Haddam, m. Oliver **BRAINERD**, of Greenwich, May 7, 1838, by Rev. Isaac Parsons	3	164-5
Mary E., ae 19, b. in East Haddam, res. East Haddam, m. Alonzo B. **ELY**, ae 21, b. in East Haddam, res. East Haddam, Jan. 21, 1856, by Rev. James M. Phillips. Int. pub. Jan. 19, 1856	4	80-1
Nancy Melinda, of East Haddam, m. Smith **BARTLETT**, of Windham, Mar. 1, 1835, by Rev. Isaac Parsons	3	136
Prudence R., of East Haddam, m. Isaac **FOWLER**, of Vermillion, O., Sept. 6, 1852, by Rev. Warren Emmerson	3	237
Rhoda A., m. Jesse S. **DAVID**, b. of East Haddam, Sept. 7, 1834, by Rev. Stephen Beach	3	136
William A., s. Henry & Anna, b. July 26, 1823	3	92
W[illia]m A., s. W[illia]m A., farmer, ae 26, & Cynthia C., ae 26, b. Jan. 21, 1849	4	11-12
-----, d. David, teamster, ae 35, & Mary, ae 35, b. May 1, 1849	4	13-14
-----, d. William A., farmer, b. July 30, 1851	4	33-4
-----, s. Eben[eze]r, mechanic, ae 45, res. East Haddam, b. June [ ], 1855	4	76

	Vol.	Page
SOLBY, [see also **SELBY**], Jeremiah, m. Susannah **DALTON**, June 12, 1716	LR1	581
Susannah, w. of Jeremiah, d. May 3, 1718	LR1	581
William, s. Jeremiah & Susannah, b. June 5, 1717	LR1	581
SOUTHMAID, Daniel Nichols, s. Dr. Daniel & True, b. Mar. 26, 1778	2	68
Hannah, d. Dr. Daniel & True, b. Feb. 23, 1776	2	68
Hannah, d. Dr. Daniel & True, d. June 14, 1776	2	69
SOUTHWORTH, Ann, m. William **CARTER**, Feb. 23, 1824, by Rev. Simeon Dickinson, at the house of John Southworth	3	56-7
SOYER, [see also **SAWYER**], Hezzediah, of Lyme, m. Isaiah **CHAPMAN**, of East Haddam, Oct. 29, 1764	LR7	4
SPALDING, Lucretia, m. Jeremiah **HUTCHINS**, [ ]	2	329
SPARROW, Alice, see under Ellis		
Annah, d. John & Annah, b. Apr. 19, 1751	LR5	563
Annah, Mrs., m. William **SELBY**, b. of East Haddam, Feb. 28, 1765	2	20
Apphia, d. John & Annah, b. May 2, 1758	LR6	512
Benjamin, s. John & Annah, b. Nov. 9, 1762	LR6	512
Betty, d. Richard & Deborah, b. Aug. 21, 1778	2	58
Deborah, d. Richard & Deborah, b. Dec. 28, 1775	2	58
Elizabeth, d. John & Annah, b. Dec. 13, 1753	LR5	563
Ellis, d. Richard & Deborah, b. Jan. 22, 1767	LR7	415
Hannah, d. Richard & Deborah, b. May 16, 1771	2	58
James, m. Mehitabel* **HOLMES**, b. of East Haddam, Dec. 12, 1770 (*First written "Sarah")	2	90
James, d. Jan. 29, 1774	2	91
John, s. John & Annah, b. Feb. 22, 1756	LR6	512
John, s. Richard & Deborah, b. July 12, 1765	LR7	415
Mary, d. John & Annah, b. Dec. 13, 1749	LR5	563
Mary, m. Ichabod **SPENCER**, 2d, b. of East Haddam, Apr. 26, 1769	2	46
Mehitabel, wid., m. Dr. A[u]gustus **MATHER**, of Lyme, Feb. 28, 1775	2	90
Olive, d. Richard & Deborah, b. July 29, 1782	2	58
Polley, d. Richard & Deborah, b. May 30, 1773	2	58
Polley, d. Richard & Deborah, d. Aug. 13, 1778	2	59
Richard, s. Richard & Deborah, b. Oct. 26, 1768	LR7	415
Richard, d. Oct. 23, 1788, in the 62nd y. of his age	2	59
Sarah, d. James & Mehitabel, b. Sept. 15, 1771	2	90
Stephen, s. John & Annah, b. Nov. 8, 1760	LR6	512
SPENCER, Aaron, s. James & Hannah, b. July 20, 1743	LR4	467
Aaron, s. Thomas & Thankfull, b. Feb. 1, 1761	LR6	508
Abby M., m. William L. **PURPLE**, Sept. 13, 1837, by Rev. Isaac Parsons	3	159
Abby Maria, d. [Warren C. & Anna], b. July 14, 1816	3	109
Abigail, d. James & Hannah, b. Aug. 24, 1728	LR4	467
Abigail, m. David **STOCKING**, b. of East Haddam, June 14,		

	Vol.	Page
SPENCER, (cont.)		
1753	LR4	472
Abigail, d. Jeremiah & Abigail, b. Feb. 23, 1754	LR3	508
Abigail, d. Thomas & Thankfull, b. Oct. 24, 1762	LR6	508
Abigail, of Chatham, m. Eleazer **ROWLEE**, of East Haddam, July 21, 1763	LR8	2
Abigail, d. Fradrick & Hannah, b. Feb. 21, 1766	LR7	2
Abigail, w. of Jonah, d. Mar. 31, 1775	2	15
Abner, s. Peter & Hannah, b. May [ ], 1748; d. Oct. [ ], 1749	LR4	464
Abner, s. Peter & Elizabeth, b. Jan, 4, 1751	LR4	464
Alexander, s. Will[ia]m, Jr. & Sarah, b. July 16, 1694	LR1	3
Almeron Monroe, s. [Warren C. & Anna], b. Dec. 7, 1823	3	109
Alpha, ae 18, b. in East Haddam, m. Henry **SPENCER**, shoe manufacturer, ae 20, b. in East Haddam, res. Colchester, Dec. 24, 1848, by Isaac Parsons	4	9-10
Alpha L., m. Austin K. **SPENCER**, b. of East Haddam, Dec. 24, 1848, by Rev. Isaac Parsons	3	216
Amasa, s. Jonathan & Hannah, b. July 20, 1751	LR3	19
Amaziah, s. Matthias & Marcy, b. Apr. 14, 1753	LR3	18
Amaziah, m. El[e]anor **HARVEY**, b. of East Haddam, July 13, 1780	2	237
Ann, d. Edward & Sarah, b. June 27, 1744	LR4	467
Ann O., of East Haddam, m. Frederic **CURTIS**, Jr., of Hampton, May 29, 1827, by Rev. Isaac Parsons	3	86
Anna, d. Israel & Elizabeth, b. Dec. 5, 1755	LR4	b
Anna, d. Gideon & Elisabeth, b. June 20, 1773	2	54
Anna, d. Gideon & Elisabeth, d. Nov. 16, 1776	2	55
Anna, m. Hezekiah **MACK**, b. of East Haddam, Mar. 20, 1777	2	170
Anna, [twin with Leah], d. Jonah & Elisabeth, b. Aug. 16, 1777	2	14
Anna, d. Samuel & Anna, b. Mar. [ ], 1796	2	287
Anna, d. Samuel & Anna, d. Apr. [ ], 1796	2	288
Anna, w. of Samuel, d. [ ], 1797	2	288
Anna, m. Warren C. **SPENCER**, Sept. 16, 1813, by Rev. William Lyman	3	109
Anna Olmsted, d. Capt. Samuel & Statira, b. Nov. 2, 1802	2	287
Anne, d. Isaac & Mary, b. Nov. 29, 1729	LR2	1127
Anne, d. Stephen & Joannah, b. Feb. 13, 1760	LR6	511
Anne, d. Peter & Elizabeth, b. Mar. 17, 1761	LR4	464
Asa, s. Samuel & Jerusha, b. Jan. 19, 1739	LR2	1126
Asa, s. Samuel & Jerusha, d. Oct. 29, 1743	LR3	15
Asa, s. Peter & Hannah, b. June 14, 1744	LR4	464
Asa, s. Job & Rebeckah, b. Sept. 1, 1747	LR4	466
Austin K., m. Alpha L. **SPENCER**, Dec. 24, 1848, b. of East Haddam, by Rev. Isaac Parsons	3	216
Austin Keeney, s. [Warren C. & Anna], b. Nov. 26, 1828	3	109
Beeman, s. Edward & Sarah, b. Jan. 25, 1747	LR4	467

	Vol.	Page
SPENCER, (cont.)		
Betsey, of East Haddam, m. Griswold **MINER**, of Lyme, Sept. 5, 1831, by Rev. Isaac Parsons	3	120
Betty, d. Jonah & Elisabeth, b. Sept. 11, 1779	2	14
Calvin, s. Samuel & Hannah, b. Sept. 27, 1753	LR4	468
Calvin, s. Stephen & Joannah, b. Oct. 8, 1765	LR6	511
Calvin, m. Mehetabel **BRAINERD**, b. of East Haddam, Nov. 1, 1789	2	210
Calvin S., of East Lynn, m. Corelia M. **SMITH**, of East Haddam, Oct. 28, 1847, by Rev. Isaac Parsons	3	211
Calvin S., mechanic, ae 27, b. in Lyme, res. Springfield, Mass., m. Cordelia M. **SMITH**, ae 26, b. in East Haddam, res. Springfield, Mass., Oct. [ ], 1848, by Isaac Parsons	4	1-2
Caroline Elizabeth, d. Elijah & Mary, b. Feb. 16, 1830	3	87
Charity, [twin with Chloe], d. Judah & Susannah, b. Dec. 12, 1770	2	118
Charity, m. Warren **FOX**, b. of East Haddam, Sept. 15, 1793	2	245
Charles S., m. Wealthy B. **RICH**, b. of East Haddam, June 30, 1850, by Rev. Jacob Gardner, in Moodus	3	227
Charles T., blacksmith, ae 24, of East Haddam, m. Wealthy B. **RICH**, ae 27, b. in Middle Haddam, res. East Haddam, June 30, 1850, by Rev. Jacob Gardner	4	19-20
Charles Thaddeus, s. Elijah & Mary, b. Feb. 23, 1826	3	87
Chloe, [twin with Charity], d. Judah & Susannah, b. Dec. 12, 1770	2	118
C[h]loe, m. Eli **PURPLE**, b. of East Haddam, Mar. 3, 1793	2	241
Clarissa, m. Diodate **FOX**, b. of East Hddam, Aug. 2, 1832, by Oliver Green, J. P.	3	124
Cynthia, m. Newel **RICH**, b. of Chatham, Dec. 20, 1832, by Rev. Simeon Dickinson	3	128
Daniel, s. Ichabod & Susannah, b. Oct. 4, 1734	LR2	1125
Daniel, s. Gideon & Elizabeth, b. Nov. 16, 1757	LR4	470
Daniel, s. Matthias & Mercy, b. Sept. 16, 1770	2	18
Daniel, s. Gideon & Elisabeth, d. Dec. 20, 1776	2	55
Daniel, s. Amaziah & Ele[a]nor, b. July 11, 1787	2	237
David, s. Ebenezer & Hannah, b. Oct. 17, 1748	LR3	8
David B., m. Huldah **BRAINERD**, Feb. 2, 1769	2	38
David B., m. Mary **FULLER**, June 24, 1783	2	38
David B., Col., of East Haddam, m. Mrs. Avis **HYDE**, of Lebanon, Mar. 3, 1792	2	38
David B., Col., d. May 2, 1795	2	39
David Brainerd, s. Samuel & Jerusha, b. Jan. 22, 1744	LR3	15
David Brainerd, m. Huldah **BRAINERD**, Feb. 2, 1769	LR7	410
David Brainerd, s. David B. & Mary, b. Mar. 22, 1787	2	38
Deborah, m. John **HUNGERFORD**, Dec. 3, 1702	LR1	4
Deborah, d. Matthias & Marcy, b. Apr. 8, 1747	LR3	18
Deborah, d. Matthias & Marcy, b. Apr. 11, 1750	LR3	18
Deborah, d. Eliakim & Dorothy, b. Oct. 14, 1763	LR6	503

	Vol.	Page
SPENCER, (cont.)		
Deborah, of East Haddam, m. Hiram **REYNOLDS**, of Woodbury, Conn., Mar. 25, 1840, by Nathaniel Miner	3	178
Dorcas, d. Matthias & Marcy, b. Jan. 2, 1755	LR3	18
Dorothy, d. John & Elizabeth, b. Feb. 14, 1716	LR1	570
Dorothy, m. James **BATE**, Dec. 12, 1734	LR2	1114
Dorothy, d. Samuel & Jerusha, b. Apr. 28, 1735	LR2	1126
Dorothy, m. Daniel **CONE**, Jr., May 15, 1755	LR5	561
Dorothy, d. Jonathan & Hannah, b. Nov. 1, 1756	LR3	19
Dorothy, d. Eliakim & Dorothy, b. Aug. 7, 1761	LR6	503
Dorothy, d. David B. & Huldah, b. Nov. 21, 1772	2	38
Dyar, [twin with Martha], s. Zechariah & Mary, b. July 21, 1777	2	56
Ebenezer, s. John & Elizabeth, b. Feb. 1, 1721	LR1	570
Ebenezer, m. Hannah **GATES**, Mar. 6, 1745/6	LR3	8
Ebenezer, s. Ebenezer & Hannah, b. Mar. 13, 1757	LR3	8
Edwin, s. Isaac, Jr. & Lucretia, b. Nov. 13, 1798	2	132
Eleazer, mechanic, ae 45, b. in Haddam, res. Chatham, m. 2d w. Sarah **BARTMAN**, house wife, ae 42, of East Haddam, Mar. 19, 1854	4	41-2
Eleazer, mechanic, ae 45, b. in Haddam, res. Chatham, m. 2d w. Sarah **BARTMAN**, house work, ae 42, of East Haddam, Mar. 19, 1854	4	51-2
Electa, m. Salma **SCOVEL**, Feb. 7, 1793	2	277
Eliakim, s. Micajah & Sarah, b. Oct. 3, 1734	LR2	1123
Eliakim, m. Dorothy **GATES**, b. of East Haddam, Apr. 16, 1761	LR6	503
Elihu, s. Isaac & Mary, b. Feb. 12, 1721	LR2	1127
Elihu, s. Isaac, Jr.& Lucretia, b. Jan. 26, 1785	2	132
Elijah, s. Stephen & Joannah, b. Apr. 23, 1761	LR6	511
Elijah, of Lyme, m. Mary **BIGELOW**, of Colchester, Sept. 5, 1824, by Simeon Dickinson	3	87
Eliphaz, s. Job & Rebeckah, b. Mar. 23, 1752	LR4	466
Eliza E., m. David S. **CONE**, b. of East Haddam, Dec. 27, 1835, by Rev. Isaac Parsons	3	140-1
Elizabeth, d. John, b. Mar. 15, 1707	LR1	6
Elizabeth, d. Joseph & Hannah, b. Aug. 10, 1711	LR1	2
Elizabeth, w. of John, d. June 15, 1725	LR1	570
Elizabeth, m. Joseph **BATE**, Oct. 12, 1727	LR2	e
Elizabeth, d. Hezekiah & Sarah, b. Jan. 29, 1739	LR2	1124
Elizabeth, d. Peter & Hannah, b. July 20, 1746	LR4	464
Elizabeth, d. Gideon & Elizabeth, b. Nov. 12, 1755	LR3	470
Elizabeth, d. Israel & Elizabeth, b. Feb. 7, 1758	LR5	b
Elizabeth, d. Oliver & Anne, b. May 5, 1761	LR6	505
Elizabeth, d. Gideon & Elisabeth, d. Nov. 9, 1776	2	55
Elisabeth, s. single woman, had s. Charles **BROOKS**, b. Apr. 18, 1779	2	8
Elizabeth, m. Thomas **ACKLEY**, 2d, b. of East Haddam, Nov.		

	Vol.	Page
SPENCER, (cont.)		
2, 1802	2	255
Elizabeth, m. Oren **GATES**, b. of East Haddam, May 2, 1804	2	283
Elizabeth, of East Haddam, m. Jeduthan **SHALER**, of Haddam, Oct. 19, 1822, by Rev. W[illia]m Lyman	3	28-29
Elizabeth, of East Haddam, m. Selden **WARNER**, of Lyme, Jan. 4, 1827, by Rev. Joseph Vaill, of Hadlyme	3	91
Elizabeth H., m. Sylvester M. **CHAPMAN**, Feb. 18, 1838, by Rev. Isaac Parsons	3	160
Ely, s. Eliakim & Dorothy, b. Apr. 20, 1766	LR6	503
Em[m]ons, s. Ebenezer & Hannah, b. July 3, 1761	LR3	8
Ephraim, s. Ebenezer & Hannah, b. Jan. 31, 1759	LR3	8
Esther, d. Isaac & Mary, b. Dec. 16, 1716	LR2	1128
Esther, m. Daniel **BRAINERD**, Jan. 6, 1736/7	LR2	1110
Esther, d. Judah & Susannah, b. Jan. 22, 1777	2	118
Esther Selden, d. Job & Rebeckah, b. Jan. 29, 1764	LR4	466
Eunice, m. Aaron **CLEVELAND**, b. of East Haddam, Sept. 4, 1755	LR4	470
Eunice had s. John **LOVELEY**, b. Sept. 17, 1769; reputed father John **LOVELY**	LR8	1
Eunice, d. Zechariah & Mary, b. July 17, 1779	2	56
Eunice Williams, d. Zacheriah & Mary, b. Oct. 31, 1770	2	56
Eunice Williams, d. Zechariah & Mary, d. Nov. 10, 1776	2	57
Fradrick, s. James & Hannah, b. Feb. 17, 1739/40	LR4	467
Fradrick, m. Hannah **CHAPMAN**, b. of East Haddam, Apr. 1, 1762	LR7	2
Frederick, s. Josiah A., mechanic, ae 33, & Polly M., ae 28, b. Feb.19, 1847	4	3-4
Frederick A., s. Josiah A., ae 34, & Polly M., ae 31, b. Mar. 19, 1848	4	5-6
Gideon, s. Micajah & Sarah, b. Jan. 21, 1729/30	LR1	584
Gideon, m. Elizabeth **HURD**, Nov. 7, 1751	LR4	470
Gideon, s. Gideon & Elizabeth, b. July 25, 1771	LR4	470
Gurdon, m. Dolly **HURD**, b. of East Haddam, May 13, 1832, by Rev. Isaac Parsons	3	122
Gurdon, mechanic, b. in [ ], res. East Haddam, married, d. Mar. 25, 1856, ae 77	4	96
Hannah, d. William, Jr. & Sarah, b. July 16, 1698	LR1	3
Han[n]ah, d. John & Elizabeth, b. Apr. 8, 1705	LR1	3
Hannah, m. Richard **PURPLE**, Sept. 20, 1717	LR1	578
Hannah, d. James & Hannah, b. Dec. 2, 1724	LR1	584
Hannah, d. Peter & Hannah, b. Oct. 10, 1742	LR4	464
Hannah, d. Joseph & Rachel, b. Mar. 26, 1743	LR2	1108
Hannah, m. Jonathan **SPENCER**, Jan. 14, 1746/7	LR3	19
Hannah, d. Ebenezer & Hannah, b. Mar. 27, 1747	LR3	8
Hannah, w. of Peter, d. May [ ], 1749	LR4	464
Hannah, d. Jonathan & Hannah, b. Nov. 5, 1759	LR3	19
Hannah, m. Lemuel **MARSH**, Nov. 17, 1763	LR7	416

	Vol.	Page
SPENCER, (cont.)		
Hannah, d. Fradrick & Hannah, b. Aug. 21, 1764	LR7	2
Hannah, d. Ichabod, 2d, & Mary, b. July 4, 1772	2	46
Hannah, m. Elijah **WILDER**, Nov. 26, 1778	2	10
Hannah, m. Jedediah **HALL**, b. of East Haddam, Dec. 29, 1808	2	307
Hannah, of East Haddam, m. Thomas A. **TILLINGHAST**, of Voluntown, May 3, 1824, by Rev. Isaac Parsons	3	58-9
Hannah, of East Haddam, m. Daniel **JOHNSON**, of Chatham, Dec. 14, 1834, by Rev. Isaac Parsons	3	135
Hannah, d. Feb. 6, 1848, ae 51	4	7-8
Hannah Fuller, d. Jedediah & Mary, b. Oct. 21, 1756	LR4	465
Harriet, of East Haddam, m. Diodate **LEE**, of Lebanon, Nov. 26, 1823, by Rev. Isaac Parsons	3	49
Harriet, d. Elijah & Mary, b. Aug. 2, 1827	3	87
Harvey, s. Amaziah & Ele[a]nor, b. Aug. 14, 1791	2	237
Henry, shoe manufacturer, ae 20, b. in East Haddam, res. Colchester, m. Alpha **SPENCER**, ae 18, b. in East Haddam, Dec. 24, 1848, by Isaac Parsons	4	9-10
Henry C., m. Margaret B. **ELY**, b. of East Haddam, July 9, 1854, by Rev. Isaac Parsons	3	240
Henry C., ae 18, m. Margaret B. **ELY**, ae 17, b. of East Haddam, July 9, 1854, by Rev. Isaac Parsons	4	51-2
Hezekiah, s. Judah & Susannah, b. Feb. 4, 1779	2	118
Hezekaih, s. Judah & Susannah, d. Aug. 20, 1780	2	119
Huldah, d. Judah & Susannah, b. Feb. 25, 1781	2	118
Huldah, w. of David B., d. Jan. 23, 1783* (*Entry crossed out)	2	38
Huldah, w. of David B., d. Jan. 23, 1783	2	39
Huldah, d. Maj. David B. & Mary, b. Mar. 23, 1784	2	38
Huldah, m. Thomas **BOOGE**, b. of East Haddam, Apr. 10 1831, by Rev. Nathaniel Miner	3	127
Ichabod, m. Susannah **VENBRAS***, Dec. 31, 1730 (***VENTRES** corrected in handwritting of margin)	LR2	1125
Ichabod, s. Joseph & Rachel, b. Aug. 22, 1747	LR2	1108
Ichabod, 2d, m. Mary **SPARROW**, b. of East Haddam, Apr. 26, 1769	2	46
Ichabod Stow Selden, s. Samuel & Hannah, b. Sept. 13, 1755	LR4	468
Isaac, m. Mary **SELDIN**, Oct. 2, 1707	LR1	6
Isaac, s. Isaac & Mary, b. May 3, 1723	LR2	1127
Isaac, s. Joseph & Rachel, b. June 10, 1745	LR2	1108
Isaac, Jr., of East Haddam, m. Lucretia **COLT**, of Lyme, Nov. 15, 1781	2	132
Isaac, s. Isaac, Jr. & Lucretia, b. Apr. 26, 1787	2	132
Israel, s. Isaac & Mary, b. Jan. 30, 1731/2	LR2	1127
Israel, m. Elizabeth **MARSH**, Oct. 18, 1753	LR5	b
Israel Selden, s. Israel & Elizabeth, b. Aug. 1, 1762	LR5	b
James, m. Hannah **CRIPPEN**, Jan. 14, 1720	LR1	584
James, s. Jonathan & Hannah, b. May 15, 1754	LR3	19
James, d. Dec. 15, 1758	LR4	467

	Vol.	Page
SPENCER, (cont.)		
James, s. Judah & Susannah, b. May 17, 1783	2	118
James S., of East Haddam, m. Caroline **SHAILER**, of Colchester, June 12, 1831, by Rev. Isaac Parsons	3	116
James T., s. James S., manufacturer, ae 42, & Caroline, ae 38, b. Jan. 3, 1850	4	23-4
Jared, s. Isaac & Mary, b. Nov. 5, 1718	LR2	1128
Jared, m. Nancy **GREEN**, b. of East Haddam, Nov. 29, 1789	2	251
Jared A., ae 40, b. in Westbrook, res. Westbrook, m. Mrs. Jane **CONE**, div. w. of Cyrus W. **CHAPMAN**, ae 32, b. in East Haddam, res. East Haddam, June 30, 1856, by Rev. Nath[aniel] Miner. Int. pub. June 28, 1856	4	91-92
Jared Wilson, s. Israel & Elizabeth, b. Feb. 24, 1760	LR5	b
Jedediah, m. Mary **FULLER**, Jan. 25, 1753	LR4	465
Jeremiah, m. Abigail **BURR**, Jan. 7, 1747/8	LR3	508
Jeremiah, s. Jeremiah & Abigail, b. Feb. 21, 1748/9	LR3	508
Jerusha, d. Samuel & Jerusha, b. Sept. 11, 1741	LR3	15
Jerusha, d. Samuel & Jerusha, d. Nov. 5, 1743	LR3	15
Jerusha, w. of Samuel, d. July 13, 1747	LR3	15
Jerusha, d. Col. David B. & Mary, b. Feb. 13, 1789	2	38
Jerusha, d. Col. David B., b. Feb. 13, 1789; m. William **COOK**, Oct. 1, 1807	2	303
Job, m. Rebeckah **CHAPMAN**, Nov. 13, 1746	LR4	466
Job, s. Job & Rebeckah, b. Oct. 10, 1761	LR4	466
Joel, s. James & Hannah, b. Apr. 13, 1731	LR4	467
John, s. John & Elizabeth, b. Jan. 24, 1708/9	LR1	6
John, Jr., m. Mary **GREEN**, Dec. 27, 1739	LR3	12
John, s. Ebenezer & Hannah, b. June 21, 1750	LR3	8
John, d. Oct. 20, 1770	2	3
John, m. Susannah **WHITE**, b. of East Haddam, Oct. 28, 1772	2	76
John, s. John & Susannah, b. Oct. 17, 1773	2	76
John A., farmer, ae 24, of East Haddam, m. Julia A. **WHITMORE**, ae 15, b. in Foster, R. I., res. East Haddam, Aug. 5, 1848, by David Chapman	4	9-10
John A., m. Julia Ann **WHITMAN**, Aug. 5, 1849, by David A. Chapman	3	219
John Edwin, s. [Warren C. & Anna], b. Aug. 24, 1826	3	109
Jonah, s. Micajah & Sarah, b. Feb. 6, 1744	LR6	510
Jonah, m. Abigail **CALKINS**, Aug. 20, 1767	LR7	410
Jonah, of East Haddam, m. Elisabeth **BAILEY**, of Killingsworth, June 22, 1775	2	14
Jonathan, m. Hannah **SPENCER**, Jan. 14, 1746/7	LR3	19
Jonathan, s. Jedediah & Mary, b. Aug. 15, 1760	LR4	465
Jonathan, Sergt., d. Aug. 16, 1760	LR3	19
Joseph, s. Joseph & Hannah, b. Jan. 6, 1712	LR1	2
Joseph, s. Isaac & Mary, b. Oct. 3, 1714	LR2	1127
Joseph, d. Dec. 19, 1717	LR1	2
Joseph, m. Rachel **HUNGERFORD**, June 24, 1736	LR4	1108

	Vol.	Page
SPENCER, (cont.)		
Joseph, Jr., m. Martha **BRAINERD**, Aug. 2, 1738	LR2	1112
Joseph, s. Joseph & Rachel, b. May 11, 1739	LR2	1108
Joseph, d. Mar. 31, 1747 (Arnold Copy had "Joseph **HADDAM**")	LR2	1108
Joseph, s. Ichabod, 2d, & Mary, b. May 26, 1770	2	46
Joseph, s. Isaac, Jr. & Lucretia, b. Dec. 29, 1789	2	132
Judah, s. James & Hannah, b. Nov. 26, 1734	LR4	467
Judah, m. Susannah **BEEBE**, b. of East Haddam, Mar. 5, 1767	2	118
Judah, s. Judah & Susannah, b. Mar. 26, 1773	2	118
Julia E. Markham, d. Austin K., shoemaker, ae 21, & Alpha, ae 19, b. Feb. 5, 1850	4	23-4
Julia S., m. Amasa B. **CLARK**, b. of East Haddam, Nov. 25, 1840, by Rev. Moses Stoddard	3	184
Julia Salome, d. [Warren C. & Anna], b. May 27, 1818	3	109
Keziah, d, Hezekiah & Sarah, b. May 10, 1739	LR2	1124
Leah, [twin with Anna], d. Jonah & Elisabeth, b. Aug. 16 1777	2	14
Loley, d. Jedediah & Mary, b. Sept. 8, 1762	LR4	465
Lucretia, [twin with Polly], d. Jared & Nancy, b. Sept. 12, 1793	2	251
Lucy, d. Jonah & Abigail, b. Aug. 12, 1768	LR7	410
Lucy, m. Samuel W. **BURKE**, Jan. 8, 1843, by Nathaniel Miner	3	193
Lucy D., d. James B., wheelwright, ae 23, & Lucy A., ae 22, b. Oct. 17, 1849	4	25-6
Luke, s. Samuel & Jerusha, b. Jan. 28, 1746; d. June 30, 1747	LR3	15
Luke Hawley, s. Samuel & Hannah, b. Dec. 15, 1751	LR4	468
Lidiah, w. of James, d. Jan. 2, 1762	LR4	467
Lydia, d. Tho[ma]s & Thankfull, b. July 13, 1764	LR6	508
Lydia, d. Gideon & Elizabeth, b. June 14, 1766	LR4	470
Lydia, of East Haddam, m. John **SELDEN**, of Middle Haddam, Dec. 6, 1826, by Rev. Isaac Parsonss	3	88-9
Marg[a]ret, m. John **STEWARD**, 2d, b. of East Haddam, June 23, 1746	LR5	270
Maria, of Lyme, m. Ira **GODDARD**, of Hillsborough, Ga., Sept. 23, 1824, by Rev. Joseph Vaill, of Hadlyme	3	66-7
Martha, d. Joseph, Jr. & Martha, b. May 8, 1739	LR2	1112
Martha, d. Joseph, Jr. & Martha, d. Feb. 24, 1739/40	LR2	1112
Martha, m. Joseph **CONE**, Jr., b. of East Haddam, June 14, 1759	LR6	507
Martha, d. Zachariah & Mary, b. Oct. 24, 1767	LR7	415
Martha, d. Zechariah & Mary, d. Nov. 10, 1776	2	57
Martha, [twin with Dyar], d. Zechariah & Mary, b. July 21, 1777	2	56
Mary, d. William, Jr. & Sarah, b. Sept. 1, 1687	LR1	3
Mary, d. Isaac & Mary, b. June 24, 1710	LR2	1127
Mary, d. John & Elizabeth, b. Aug. 4, 1716 [sic]	LR1	570
Mary, d. James & Hannah, b. Sept. 10, 1722	LR1	584
Mary, m. Daniel **CONE**, Jr., Mar. 14, 1728	LR2	1119

	Vol.	Page
SPENCER, (cont.)		
Mary, d. William & Lydia, b. Sept. 27, 1736; d. Oct. 3, 1736	LR2	1119
Mary, d. Ichabod & Susannah, b. Mar. 15, 1739	LR2	1125
Mary, d. John, of East Haddam, m. Samuel **BAKER**, s. Joseph, of Tolland, Oct. 28, 1746	LR3	12
Mary, d. Jonathan & Hannah, b. Mar. 8, 1748/9	LR3	19
Mary, d. Jeremiah & Abigail, b. June 6, 1751	LR3	508
Mary, d. Peter & Elizabeth, b. May 19, 1759	LR4	464
Mary, d. Gideon & Elizabeth, b. Oct. 17, 1763	LR4	470
Mary, d. Jedediah & Mary, b. May 21, 1765	LR4	465
Mary, d. Maj. David B. & Mary, b. July 8, 1785	2	38
Mary, m. Turner **MINER**, b. of East Haddam, Sept.18, 1788	2	178
Mary, d. Amaziah & Ele[a]nor, b. Apr. 13, 1789	2	237
Mary Albertine, d. [Warren C. & Anna], b. May 1, 1836	3	109
Mary Ann, of East Haddam, m. Robert C. **DEMAY**, of Lyme, Sept. 9, 1821, by Rev. Isaac Parsons	3	9
Mary E., ae 20, of East Haddam, m. Albert A. **BURDICK**, ae 21, of East Haddam, Aug. 31, 1856, by Rev. Nelson Goodrich. Int. pub. Aug. 26, 1856	4	98
Mary Mehitable, d. Elijah & Mary, b. Sept. 26, 1837	3	87
Mary P., m. Perley D. **WHITMORE**, Jan. 16, 1828, by Rev. Isaac Parsons	3	99
Mary Pratt, d. Samuel & Statira, b. Aug. 15, 1805	2	287
Matthias, m. Marcy **ROWLEE**, June 23, 1746	LR3	18
Matthias, s. Amaziah & Ele[a]nor, b. Nov. 15, 1795	2	237
Mehittabell, d. Isaac & Mary, b. Mar. 29, 1725	LR2	1127
Mehittabell, d. Hezekiah & Sarah, b. Dec. 19, 1736	LR2	1124
Mehetable, d. Samuel & Jerusha, b. June 15, 1738	LR2	1126
Mehitable, d. Matthias & Marcy, b. Feb. 22, 1760	LR3	18
Mehetable, d. Israel & Elizabeth, b. Oct. 10, 1765	LR5	b
Meliscent, m. Rev. Elijah **PARSONS**, b. of East Haddam, Jan, 18, 1813	2	150
Micajah, m. Sarah **BOOGE**, Dec. 27, 1722	LR1	584
Micajah, s. Micajah & Sarah, b. Jan. 30, 1725/6	LR1	584
Molley, d. John & Susannah, b. July 23, 1775	2	76
Nancy, d. Gideon & Elizabeth, b. Jan. 29, 1769	LR4	470
Nancy, d. Gideon & Elisabeth, d. Aug. 27, 1774	2	55
Nancy, d. Jared & Nancy, b. May 29, 1791	2	251
Nancy, b. in East Haddam, res. East Haddam, wid., d. Nov. 11, 1855, ae 88	4	73
Nathan, s. Micajah & Sarah, b. Nov. 4, 1723	LR1	584
Olive, d. Jedediah & Mary, b. Sept. 24, 1758	LR4	465
Olive, m. Ephraim **SELBY**, b. of East Haddam, Nov. 18, 1779	2	114
Oliver, s. Samuel & Jerusha, b. Oct. 6, 1736	LR2	1126
Oliver, of East Haddam, m. Anne **OGDEN**, of Elizabethtown, N.J., Jan. 22, 1758	LR6	505
Oliver, s. John & Susannah, b. Aug. 25, 1777	2	76
Penelope, d. Amaziah & Ele[a]nor, b. Dec. 23, 1784	2	237

	Vol.	Page
SPENCER, (cont.)		
Peter, of East Haddam, m. Hannah **BROWN**, of Colchester, June 4, 1741	LR4	464
Peter, m. Elizabeth **EM[M]ONS**, b. of East Haddam, Feb. 1, 1749/50	LR4	464
Peter, s. Peter & Elizabeth, b. Nov. 30, 1755	LR4	464
Phebe, d. Jedediah & Mary, b. May 9, 1767	LR4	465
Polly, [twin with Lucretia], d. Jared & Nancy, b. Sept. 12, 1793	2	251
Rachel, d. Micajah & Sarah, b. Mar. 6. 1728	LR1	584
Rachel, d. Joseph & Rachel, b. June 28, 1737	LR2	1108
Rachel, d. Gideon & Elizabeth, b. Dec. 27, 1761	LR4	470
Rebeckah, d. Isaac & Mary, b. Aug. 1, 1712	LR1	8
Rebeckah, d. Isaac & Mary, b. Aug. 2, 1712	LR2	1127
Rebeckah, m. Daniel **OLMSTEAD**, Dec. 28, 1738	LR2	1107
Rebeckah, d. Samuel & Jerusha, b. Apr. 6, 1743	LR3	15
Rebeckah, m. William **FULLER**, b. of East Haddam, Mar. 8, 1757	LR6	506
Rebeckah, d. Zacheas & Eunice, b. Feb. 17, 1763	LR7	2
Rebeckah, m. Martin **CONE**, b. of East Haddam, June 5, 1764	LR7	7
R[e]uben, s. Matthias & Marcy, b. Dec. 7, 1748	LR3	18
R[e]uben, s. Gideon & Elizabeth, b. June 8, 1752	LR4	470
Reubin, m. Elisabeth **CONE**, b. of East Haddam, Mar. 17, 1774	2	80
Reuben, s. Amaziah & Ele[a]nor, b. Mar. 7, 1781	2	237
Robert, s. Oliver & Anne, b. Apr. 2, 1759	LR6	505
Robert, s. Col. David B. & Avis, b. Aug. 8, 1793	2	38
Ruth, d. Peter & Elizabeth, b. May 16, 1757	LR4	464
Samuell, d. Aug. 7, 1705	LR1	4
Samuell, s. Isaac & Mary, b. July 10, 1708	LR1	6
Samuell, m. Jerusha **BRAINERD**, Dec. 19, 1732	LR2	1126
Samuel, s. Samuel & Jerusha, b. Jan. 21, 1734	LR2	1126
Samuel, s. Job & Rebeckah, b. Oct. 5, 1749	LR4	466
Samuel, m. Hannah **HAWLEY**, Apr. 9, 1751	LR4	468
Samuel, s. Fradrick & Hannah, b. Feb. 21, 1763	LR7	2
Samuel, s. David B. & Huldah, b. Apr. 29, 1771	2	38
Samuel, m. Anna **OLMSTED**, b. of East Haddam, Sept. 22, 1795	2	287
Samuel, Capt., m. Statira **HALL**, b. of East Haddam, Nov. 15, 1801	2	287
Samuel, m. Hannah **INGRAHAM**, Jan. 9, 1827, by Isaac Parsons	3	91
Samuel White, s. John & Susannah, b. Oct. 8, 1779	2	76
Samuel Wright, s. Zacheriah & Mary, b. Apr. 7, 1769	2	56
Sarah, d. William, Jr. & Sarah, b. Mar. 1, 1696	LR1	3
Sarah, d. John & Elizabeth, b. Mar. 6, 1714	LR1	570
Sarah, d. Hezekiah & Sarah, b. Feb. 10, 1730	LR2	1124
Sarah, d. Joseph & Rachel, b. Jan. 11, 1740/41	LR2	1108
Sarah, d. Hezekiah & Sarah, d. June 18, 1750	LR2	1124

	Vol.	Page
SPENCER, (cont.)		
Sarah, d. Ebenezer & Hannah, b. Aug. 26, 1752	LR3	8
Sarah, d. Gideon & Elizabeth, b. Feb. 4, 1754	LR4	470
Sarah, d. Matthias & Marcy, b. May 5, 1765	LR3	18
Sarah, d. Matthias & Marcy, b. July 23, 1767	LR3	18
Sarah, m. Ezra **RAMSDELL**, b. of East Haddam,Sept. 24, 1772	2	84
Sarah, m. Roswel[l] **CONE**, Nov. 22, 1773	2	66
Sarah, m. Jonah **SCOVEL**, b. of East Haddam, Feb. 6, 1774	2	94
Sarah C., m. Horace **CONE**, b. of Haddam, July 23, 1837, by Roswell Davison, J. P.	3	152
Selden, s. Amaziah & Ele[a]nor, b. Nov. 26, 1794	2	237
Silas, s. Hezekiah & Sarah, b. Jan. 28, 1746	LR2	1124
Simeon, s. Hezekiah & Sarah, b. Apr. 25, 1733	LR2	1124
Solomon, s. Hezekiah & Sarah, b. June 26, 1748	LR2	1124
Solon, s. Ezra & Sarah, b. Dec. 8, 1780	2	84
Statira, d. Jonah & Abigail, b. Aug. 25, 1770	2	14
Statira, m. Isaac **TAYLOR**, Sept. 29, 1833, by Rev. Isaac Parsons	3	132
Stephen, s. Micajah & Sarah, b. May 7, 1732	LR2	1123
Stephen, m. Joannah **CROCKER**, b. of East Haddam, Mar. 8, 1759	LR6	511
Stephen, d. May 15, 1766	LR6	511
Stephen, s. Eliakim & Dorothy, b. Aug. 4, 1769	LR6	503
Susannah, d. Hezekiah & Sarah, b. July 31, 1728	LR2	1124
Susannah, d. Ichabod & Susannah, b. Aug. 14, 1730 [sic]	LR2	1125
Susannah, m. Ebenezer **EM[M]ONS**, Apr. 4, 1754	LR5	562
Susannah, d. Ebenezer & Hannah, b. Sept. 19, 1754	LR3	8
Susannah, d. Judah & Susannah, b. Dec. 20, 1768	2	118
Susannah, m. Ephraim **GATES**, b. of East Haddam, Feb. 19, 1775	2	100
Susannah, d. John & Susannah, b. Sept. 12, 1781	2	76
Temperance C., m. Samuel M. **BROCKWAY**, b. of Lyme, Sept. 27, 1825, by Rev. Joseph Vaill, of Hadlyme	3	78
Thaddeus, s. Jedediah & Mary, b. Sept. 16, 1754	LR4	465
Thankfull, d. Job. & Rebeckah, b. Nov. 28, 1753; d. June 24, 1758	LR4	466
Thankfull, d. Job & Rebeckah, b. Mar. 21, 1759	LR4	466
Thankfull, d. Gideon & Elizabeth, b. Mar. 16, 1760	LR4	470
Tharis, [twin with Zara], s. Judah & Susannah, b. Apr. 14, 1775	2	118
Thedidah, d. Jedediah & Mary, b. July 2, 1769	LR4	465
Theodotia Ann, d. [Warren C. & Anna], b. Aug. 25, 1814	3	109
Thomas, s. James & Hannah, b. Feb. 27, 1725/6	LR4	467
Thomas, m. Thankfull **ACKLEY**, b. of East Haddam, Aug. 27, 1760	LR6	508
Thomas Elijah, s. Elijah & Mary, b. June 18, 1834	3	87
Thomas H., of Great Barrington, m. Hannah B. **SMITH**, of East Haddam, Sept. 9, 1832, by Rev. Isaac Parsons	3	125
Thomas Hall, s. Capt. Samuel & Statira, b. Mar. 15, 1807	2	287

	Vol.	Page
SPENCER, (cont.)		
Timothy, s. Matthias & Marcy, b. Nov. 6, 1756	LR3	18
Tryphenia, d. Job & Rebeckah, b. June 22, 1756	LR4	466
Tryphenia, m. Henry **DINGWELL**, Oct. 3, 1822, by Rev. Elijah Parsons	3	33
Warren, s. Zechariah & Mary, b. Sept. 25, 1775	2	56
Warren C., m. Anna **SPENCER**, Sept. 16, 1813, by Rev. William Lyman	3	109
Warren S., m. Azubah Ann **CONE**, Aug. 4, 1833, by Rev. Stephen Beach	3	132
William, s. William, Jr. & Sarah, b. June 3, 1706	LR1	5
William, s. Matthias & Marcy, b. Dec. 31, 1762	LR3	18
William Booge, s. Zacheriah & Mary, b. July 19, 1772	2	56
William C., m. Mary M. **BROWNELL**, b. of East Haddam, Sept. 27, 1854, by Rev. Isaac Parsons	3	240
William C., merchant, ae 30, b. in Lyme, res. East Haddam, m. Mary U. **BROWNELL**, teacher, ae 23, of East Haddam, Sept. 27, 1854	4	51-2
William Henry, s. Isaac, Jr. & Lucretia, b. Nov. 29, 1782	2	132
Wilson, s. Zacheriah & Mary, b. May 1, 1774	2	56
Zachary, s. James & Hannah, b. Mar. 24, 1738	LR4	467
Zechariah, s. Micajah & Sarah, b. July 1, 1741	LR6	510
Zachariah, m. Mary **WRIGHT**, b. of East Haddam, Nov. 11, 1766	LR7	415
Zacheas, m. Eunice **DIBBLE**, b. of East Haddam, May 9, 1762	LR7	2
Zacheas, d. Nov. 22, 1764	LR7	2
Zara, [twin with Tharis], s. Judah & Susannah, b. Apr. 14, 1775	2	118
Zilpha, d. Jonah & Abigail, b. Aug. 26, 1772	2	14
-----, d. Matthias & Marcy, b. Mar. 2, 1759	LR3	18
-----, child of W[illia]m, farmer, b. Nov. 1, 1852	4	47-8
-----, d. Charles T., blacksmith, ae 30, & Wealthy B., ae 34, b. May 16, 1856	4	108
SQUIRES, SQUIRE, Clarissa, of East Haddam, m. Daniel **BROOKS**, 2d, of East Haddam, Mar. 31, 1839, by Rev. Isaac Parsons	3	168
Content, m. Oliver **GATES**, b. of East Haddam, Jan. 1, 1823, by Rev. Isaac Parsons	3	34-5
E. Amy, d. John, farmer, & M., d. June 20, 1849, ae 10 w.	4	11-2
Jesse, m. Lucinda **MACK**, b. of East Haddam, July 3, 1823, by Rev. Isaac Parsons	3	42-3
John, m. Marilla **CHALKER**, Dec. 13, 1840, by Isaac Parsons, V. D. M.	3	184
Samuel, of East Haddam, m. Sarah M. **LUTHER**, of Lyme, Feb. 25, 1828, by Rev. Peter G. Clarke	3	96
STANELEFT, Martha, of Middletown, m. Fitch John **WHITMORE**, of East Haddam, Sept. 15, 1763	2	102
STANTELY, Rebeckah, of Middletown, m. Timothy **BOOGE**, of		

	Vol.	Page
STANTELY, (cont.)		
East Haddam, May 7, 1766	2	44
STANTON, Isaballa, of the Island of Barbado[e]s, m. Zechariah **CHAPMAN**, of East Haddam, July 19, 1767	2	68
STAPLES, George M., of Colchester, m. Clarissa A. **BASSETT**, of Guilford, Jan. 1, 1839, by Rev. Isaac Parsons	3	167
STARK, Andrew, of Lyme, m. Laura **CHESTER**, of East Haddam, Mar. 28, 1825, by Rev. Simeon Dickinson, at the house of Isaac Chester	3	72-3
Caroline, m. William B. **JONES**, Dec. 24, 1826, by Russell Dutton, J. P.	3	91
Denison, m. Statira **LYON**, Oct. 11, 1821, by Rev. Simeon Dickinson	3	13
Emily A., ae 18, b. in East Haddam, res. East Haddam, m. Charles C. **NEWBURY**, ae 21, b. in East Haddam, res. East Haddam, Oct. 14, 1855, by Rev. Thomas Barbee. Int. pub. Oct. 13, 1855	4	63-4
Harriet Eliza, m. Nicholos **WORTHINGTON**, b. of Colchester, Sept. 15, 1828, by Rev. Peter G. Clarke	3	100
Jeremiah R., of Lebanon, m. Lucy **CHAMPION**, of East Haddam, Nov. 28, 1822, by Rev. W[illia]m Jarvis	3	34-5
John, Jr., m. Hannah S. **JONES**, Dec. 25, 1826, by Russell Dutton, J. P.	3	91
Lauiston M., ae 24, b. at East Haddam, res. East Haddam, m. Mary E. **DICKINSON**, ae 22, b. at East Haddam, res. East Haddam, Oct. 18, 1855, by Rev. James M. Phillips. Int. pub. Oct. 17, 1855	4	66
Laura Ann, m. Henry S. **SMITH**, May 28, 1850, by Rev. Stephen A. Loper, of Hadlyme	3	222
Nathan, 2d, of Lyme, m. Emily **JEWETT**, of East Haddam, Dec. 20, 1831, by Rev. Alvan Ackley	3	121
STARLING, STARLIN, David, s. Simon, b. May 12, 1773	2	130
Eliza, see under Liza		
Jane, of Lyme, m. James **MARKHAM**, of East Haddam, Nov. 17, 1763	2	2
Liza, d. Simon, b. May 7, 1775	2	130
Marvil, s. Simon, b. May 6, 1771	2	130
Phebe, of Lyme, m. Joseph **CHURCH**, of East Haddam, Jan. 24, 1765	LR7	411
Polly, d. Simon, b. Mar. 5, 1777	2	130
Samuel, s. Simon, b. July 3, 1784	2	130
Simon, s. Simon, b. Sept. 21, 1779	2	130
STARR, Mary E., m. Ansel **BEEBE**, Jr., Oct. 31, 1821, by Rev. W[illia]m Lyman	3	36-7
STEPHENS, STEVENS, Alvin, of Providence, m. Louis **STEPHENS**, of East Haddam, July 3, 1825, by Rev. Isaac Parsons	3	78
Florinda, of East Haddam, m. Harvey **SHAILER**, of Haddam,		

	Vol.	Page
STEPHENS, STEVENS, (cont.)		
Nov. 10, 1844, by Rev. Russell Jennings	3	201
Ja[me]s, farmer, ae 24, b. in Colchester, res. East Haddam, m. Betsey A. **ATWELL**, ae 16, of East Haddam, Aug. 5, 1848, by David Chapman	4	9-10
Joseph S., m. Betsey Ann **ATWELL**, Aug. 5, 1849, by David A. Chapman	3	210
Louis, of East Haddam, m. Alvin **STEPHENS**, of Providence, July 3, 1825, by Rev. Isaac Parsons	3	78
Polly Maria, m. Horace **ARNOLD**, b. of East Haddam, Oct. 30, 1836, by W[illia]m Marsh, J. P.	3	145
William H., ae 24, b. in Hebron, res. East Haddam, m. Jenette G. **CHAPMAN**, ae 17, b. in Glastonbury, res. East Haddam, Oct. 5, 1856, by Rev. N. Goodrich. Int. pub. Oct. 4, 1856	4	102
STEVENS, [see under **STEPHENS**]		
STEWART, STEWARD, Elizabeth, m. Green **HUNGERFORD**, Feb. 20, 1746	LR5	269
Elizabeth, d. John & Marg[a]ret, b. Dec. 14, 1747	LR5	270
Esther, m. Rufus **CONE**, b. of East Haddam, Dec. 18, 1761	LR6	508
Hannah, d. William & Hannah, b. June 7, 1735	LR5	559
Hannah, w. of William, d. June 21, 1743	LR5	559
Hannah, d. William & Hannah, d. Aug. 21, 1749	LR5	559
Hannah, of East Haddam, m. Lemuel D. **ROGERS**, of Montville, Jan. 15, 1822, by Rufus Dutton, J. P.	3	23
John, 2d, m. Marg[a]ret **SPENCER**, b. of East Haddam, June 23, 1746	LR5	270
Joseph, s. William & Hannah, b. June 8, 1741	LR5	559
Joseph, s. William & Hannah, d. Aug. 19, 1749	LR5	559
Joseph, s. John & Marg[a]ret, b. June 23, 1755	LR5	270
Joseph, d. Apr. 8, 1823	2	316
Marcus, m. Alette **WHEELOCK**, b. of East Haddam, Nov. 11, 1821, by Josiah Griffin, J. P.	3	17
Nathan, s. William & Hannah, b. June 27, 1739	LR5	559
Samuel, s. William & Hannah, b. June 9, 1737	LR5	559
Samuel, s. William & Hannah, d. Aug. 29, 1749	LR5	559
Sarah, d. William & Sarah, b. Apr. 7, 1745	LR5	559
Sarah, w. of William d. Sept. 6, 1745	LR5	559
Sarah, m. Lemuel **HUNGERFORD**, b. of East Haddam, July 27, 1755	LR5	270
Silas, s. John & Marg[a]ret, b. Nov. 24, 1751	LR5	270
Statira, d. John & Marg[a]ret, b. Mar. 27, 1749	LR5	270
Thankfull, w. of William, d. Sept. [ ], 1746	LR5	559
William, m. Hannah **CAMPBELL**, Feb. 2, 1732	LR5	559
William, s. William & Hannah, b. Dec. 29, 1733	LR5	559
William, m. Sarah **BUCK**, May 8, 1744	LR5	559
William, m. Thankfull **GRAVES**, Apr. 7, 1746	LR5	559
William, s. William & Hannah, d. Aug. 14. 1749	LR4	559

	Vol.	Page
STEWART, STEWARD, (cont.)		
William, m. Mary **McWILLIAMS**, Apr. 8, 1756	LR5	559
STOCKING, STOCKIN, Abigail, d. David & Abigail, b. May 25, 1760	LR4	472
Azubah, d. David & Abigail, b. Aug. 9, 1757	LR4	472
David, m. Abigail **SPENCER**, b. of East Haddam, June 14, 1753	LR4	472
Elizabeth, d. David & Abigail, b. Dec. 21, 1754	LR4	472
Eunice, d. George & Eunice, b. Apr. 30, 1765	LR7	413
Huldah, d. David & Abigail, b. Dec. 27, 1762	LR4	472
Julia A., of New York, m. Wells **MARTIN**, Dec. 26, 1852, by Rev. Nathaniel Miner, of Millington	3	238
Julia A., ae 24, b. in Catskill, N. Y., res. N. Y., m. Wells **MARTIN**, farmer, ae 30, of East Haddam, Dec. 26, 1853, by Rev. Nathaniel Miner	4	43-4
Rachel, d. David & Abigail, b. June 14, 1765	LR4	472
Sabre, s. George & Eunice, b. May 6, 1767	LR7	413
STODDARD, Emily M., m. Willis **McCANN**, Feb. 28, 1847, by W[illia]m Marsh, J. P.	3	208
Horace H., of East Haddam, m. Mary E. **WELLS**, of Chatham, Sept. 21, 1851, by Rev. Alpheas Geer	3	233
Ralph H., of East Haddam, m. Julia Amelia **TOOKER**, of Lyme, Mar. 29, 1847, by Rev. Alpheas Geer	3	209
-----, child of Ralph, farmer, b. Feb. 18, 1853	4	47-8
-----, d. Ralph, laborer, res. East Haddam, b. May 28, 1856	4	95
STRANAHAN, Hannah A., of East Haddam, m. John M. **SKINNER**, of Chatham, Oct. 3, 1847, by Rev. Levi H. Wakeman	3	210
Hannah A., ae 20, of East Haddam, m. John W. **SKINNER**, mechanic, ae 23, b. in Chatham, res. East Haddam, Oct. 3, 1848, by L. H. Wakeman	4	1-2
James, Jr., m. Hannah B. **MINER**, b. of East Haddam, Jan. 18, 1826, by Rev. Isaac Parsons	3	83
Martha, m. Henry **MINER**, Jan. 17, 1827, by Isaac Parsons	3	93
Mary, m. Samuel **GATES**, Apr. 12, 1821, by Rev. Isaac Parsons	3	9
Mary C., m. Thomas F. **SILLIMAN**, Dec. 10, 1848, by Rev. Isaac Parsons	3	216
Mary C., m. Thomas F. **SILLIMAN**, b. of East Haddam, Dec. 10, 1848, by Isaac Parsons	4	9-10
Sarah, m. Nathaniel F. **HOLMES**, Nov. 25, 1830, by Rev. Isaac Parsons	3	115
STRAWBRIDGE, STROBRIDGE, [see also **TROWBRIDGE**], Benjamin, m. Han[n]ah **AC[K]L[E]Y**, July 9, 1705	LR1	3
Mary, m. Clement **BATE**, Jan. 1, 1734/5	LR2	1124
STRICKLAND, Thomas, of Montville, m. Frances E. **GRIFFING**, of East Haddam, Feb. 21, 1842, by Rev. James Hepburn, of Montville	3	189

	Vol.	Page
STROBRIDGE, [see under **STRAWBRIDGE**]		
STRONG, Charles H., s. David, farmer, ae 32, & Sarah, ae 29, b. Jan. 18, 1851	4	35-6
Daniel, of Southampton, L. I., m. Sarah W. **WARNER**, of Hadlyme, June 26, 1846, by Rev. Stephen Alonzo Loper, of Hadlyme	3	202
Orris, of East Haddam, m. George **MASON**, of Lyme, Nov. 28, 1822, by Rev. Isaac Parsons	3	33
Patience, m. Christopher **LORD**, Apr. 15, 1747	LR3	506
STROUT, Mary Augustus, of Auburn, Me., m. William Wallace **JONES**, of LaCross, Wis., Feb. 16, 1859, at Auburn, Me.	3	94
SWADDLE, Esther, of Middletown, m. Dan **CLARK**, of East Haddam, Jan. 3, 1760	LR6	505
SWAN, Charlotte, m. Albert **SELDEN**, shoe manufacturer, b. of East Haddam, [Sept.], 1848, by Rev. Miner	4	9-10
Charlotte G., m. William A. **SELDEN**, b. of East Haddam, Dec. 31, [1848], by Nathaniel Miner	3	216
Cynthia M., m. Oliver C. **CLARK**, Oct. 11, 1831, by Rev. Isaac Parsons	3	120
Cyrus W., m. Eliza S. **MINER**, b. of East Haddam, Feb. 11, 1827, by Rev. Issac Parsons	3	93
Electa A., of East Haddam, m. Augustus Stanley **SMITH**, of East Hartford, [Apr.] 12, [1848], by Rev. Nathaniel Miner, of Millington	3	212
Eliza J., of East Haddam, m. Griswold **BURNHAM**, of Hebron, Mar. 26, 1838, by Rev. Isaac Parsons	3	160
Geo[rge] F., m. Louisa M. **MACK**, Jan. 31, 1841, by Rev. Nathaniel Miner	3	186
Hannah E., m. Lewis B. **OLMSTED**, b. of East Haddam, Oct. 31, 1821, by Rev. W[illia]m Lyman	3	36-7
Harriet M., m. Joseph H. **ARNOLD**, b. of East Haddam, Sept. 25, 1854, by Rev. Natnaniel Miner	3	240
Harriet M.,ae 16, m. Joseph H. **ARNOLD**, cooper, ae 28, b. of East Haaddam, Sept. 25, 1854, by Rev. Nathaniel Miner	4	41-2
Harriet M., ae 16, m. Joseph H. **ARNOLD**, cooper, ae 28, b. of East Haddam, Sept. 25, 1854, by Rev. Nathaniel Miner	4	51-2
Hubbard, m. Manere **CHURCH**, b. of East Haddam, May 23, 1833, by Nathaniel Miner	3	131
Huldah O., m. Josiah A. **CHAPMAN**, b. of East Haddam, May 5, 1825, by Rev. Herman L. Vaill	3	74-5
James E., m. Lydia M. **HARRIS**, b. of East Haddam, Apr. 26, 1836, by Rev. Nathaniel Miner	3	142
John R., d. Sept. 22, 1849, ae 9 m.	4	29-30
John Rogers, s. Thomas S., farmer, ae 32, & C. A. **SWAN**, ae 25, b. Dec. 25, 1848	4	15-6
Louisa M., of East Haddam, m. Jabez D. **PARKER**, of Chester, Nov. 23, 1845, by Rev. Alpheas Geer	3	203
Lucena P., ae 20, of East Haddam, m. David B. **EMMONS**,		

	Vol.	Page
SWAN, (cont.)		
ae 23, of East Haddam, Mar. 25, 1857, by Rev. Nathaniel Miner. Int. pub. Mar. 21, 1857	4	118
Lucy W., of East Haddam. m. Ezekiel S. **CLARKE**, of Haddam, Dec. 9, 1824, by Rev. Isaac Parsons	3	69
Mary M., m. Alfred **GATES**, Mar. 29, 1832, by Rev. Isaac Parsons	3	122
Mary M., m. Eliphalet **EMMONS**, Mar. 26, 1838, by Rev. Nathaniel Miner, of Millington	3	164-5
Persis J., ae 29, b. in E. Longmeadow, Mass., m. William A. **SELDEN**, shoemaker, ae 30, of East Haddam, Oct. 23, 1851, by Rev. Benedict	4	37-8
Rufus W., m. Lucy B. **BEEBE**, of East Haddam, Nov. 21, 1822, by Rev. W[illia]m Lyman, Millington	3	30-1
Rufus W., m. Henrietta M. **CHAPMAN**, Mar. 26, 1828, by Rev. Isaac Parsons	3	99
Rufus W., d. Mar. 4, 1836, ae 42	3	32
Rufus W., d. Mar. 4, 1836, ae 42	3	123
Rufus W., m. Mary **CONE**, Apr. 16, 1840, by Nathaniel Miner	3	178
Sarah Ann, m. George **GATES**, b. of East Haddam, Dec. 7, 1825, by Rev. Herman L. Vaill	3	80-1
Sophia, m. Erastus F. **PECK**, Mar. 13, 1832, by Nathaniel Miner	3	124
Thomas G., ae 23, of East Haddam, m. Susan A. **HEFFLON**, ae 21, b. at Saybrook, res. East Haddam, Oct. 23, 1856, by Rev. N. Goodrich. Int. pub. Oct. 22, 1856	4	105-6
-----, d. James E., farmer, of Millington, & Lydia, b. June [ ], 1851	4	33-4
-----, child of Thomas S., farmer, b. Oct. 14, 1852	4	47-8
SWARTZ, Catharine S., m. Christian **GROSS**, Sept. 12, 1836, by Rev. Isaac Parsons	3	145
SWEET, Albert, merchant, ae 28, of New Hartford, m. Ann M. **PALMER**, ae 20, b. in East Haddam, res. New Hartford, Nov. 26, 1848, by Isaac Parsons	4	9-10
SWEETLAND, Anne, d. Rev. Eleazer & Elisabeth, b. Aug. 3, 1786	2	126
Eleazer, Rev., of East Haddam, m. Mrs. Elizabeth **GOULD**, of Lyme, Dec. 26, 1781	2	126
Eleazer, s. Rev. Eleazer & Elizabeth, b. Sept. 23, 1782	2	126
Eleazer, Rev., d. Mar. 25, 1787	2	127
Elizabeth, d. Rev. Eleazer & Elizabeth, b. Nov. 19, 1784	2	126
Elisabeth, Mrs., m. Charles **OTIS**, b. of East Haddam, Mar. 19, 1788	2	126
SWIFT, S. Everest, M. D., of Colchester, m. Mary M. **PARSONS**, of East Haddam, Mar. 31, 1845, by Isaac Parsons, V. D. M.	3	201
TANNER, Elizabeth, d. Thomas & Martha, b. Apr. 14, 1730	LR2	1131
[M]artha, d. Thomas & Martha, b. Dec. 28, 1727	LR2	1131
Mehittabell, d. Thomas & Martha, b. Dec. 21, 1721	LR2	1131

	Vol.	Page
TANNER, (cont.)		
Rebeckah, d. Thomas & Martha, b. Jan. 6, 1724/5	LR2	1131
Thomas, m. Martha [ ], Jan. 3, 1716/17	LR2	1131
William, s. Thomas & Martha, b. Mar. 15, 1719	LR2	1131
TAYLOR, TAILOR, Ann, d. Isaac & Mary, b. June 10, 1746	LR3	507
Ann, of East Haddam, m. Asa **RICHARDSON**, of Middletown, Nov. 20, 1826, by Rev. Isaac Parsons	3	56-7
Anna, had d. Electa **NEWCOMB**, b. Jan. 30, 1800; reputed father Israel **NEWCOMB**	2	305
Anna, of Colchester, m. John **BOOGE**, of East Haddam, Dec. 5, 1802, by John Isham	2	305
Anne, m. Phineas **GATES**, b. of East Haddam, Dec. 14, 1773	2	94
Charles, of Great Barrington, Mass., m. Adaline S. **HYDE**, of East Haddam, Jan. 2, 1842, by Thomas G. Salter	3	188
Daniel C., of Middletown, m. Rebecca Adaline **WRIGHT**, of East Haddam, May 15, 1842, by Tho[ma]s G. Salter	3	190
Eldad, of Suffield, m. Gertrude M. **PALMER**, of East Haddam, Sept. 19, 1832, by Rev. Isaac Parsons	3	125
Eunice Elizabeth, m. George **HUNTLEY**, Apr. 30, 1855, by Rev. Isaac Parsons	4	55
Eunice Elizabeth, ae 22, b. at Bozrah, res. Colchester, & George **HUNTLEY**, ae 24, b. at Colchester, res. East Haddam, had int. pub. Apr. 30, 1855	4	56
Frederick, of Salem, m. Selinda **INGRAHAM**, of East Haddam, Aug. 3, 1834, by Russell Dutton, J. P.	3	134
Harriet, of East Haddam, m. Austin **FULLER**, of Monson, Mass., Sept. 9, 1822, by Rev. Isaac Parsons	3	26-7
Isaac, s. Isaac & Mary, b. June 2, 1753	LR3	507
Isaac, m. Sarah **FULLER**, b. of East Haddam, Nov. 8, 1781	2	202
Isaac, [twin with Joseph], s. Isaac & Sarah, b. Jan. 24, 1783	2	202
Isaac, s. Isaac & Sarah, d. Aug. 11, 1785	2	203
Isaac, m. Statira **SPENCER**,Sept. 29, 1833,by Rev.Isaac Parson	3	132
Joshua, of Middle Haddam, m. Adosha **JONES**, of East Haddam, Sept. 24, 1837, by Nathaniel Miner	3	159
Josiah, s. Isaac & Mary, b. Aug. 1, 1749	LR3	507
Josiah, [twin with Isaac], s. Isaac & Sarah, b. Jan. 24, 1783	2	202
Josiah, s. Isaac & Sarah, d. Mar. 7, 1783	2	203
Mary, m. John **WARNER**, Feb. 20, 1750/51	LR4	466
Mary M., of East Haddam, m. John **SMITH**, of Lyme, May 30, 1854, by Rev. Isaac Parsons	3	239
Mary M., seamstress, ae 28, of East Haddam, m. John **SMITH**, farmer, ae 27, of Lyme, May 30, 1854	4	51-2
Sarah, d. Isaac & Sarah, b. Sept. 10, 1784	2	202
William, of Lee, Mass., m. Rebecca **HOADLEY**, of East Haddam, May 6, 1846, by Rev. Stephen Geer	3	205
Wilson, s. Isaac & Sarah, b. July 21, 1787	2	202
TEW, John, of Salem, m. Mercy C. **BEEBE**, of East Haddam, Jan. 1, 1830, by Russell Dutton, J. P.	3	104

	Vol.	Page
THOMAS, Albert J., joiner, ae 23, b. in East Haddam, res. Chatham, m. Elizabeth C. **ANDREWS**, ae 18, b. in East Haddam, Oct. 17, 1848, by Henry Forbush	4	9-10
Betsey, m. Niles **PHELPS**, b. of East Haddam, Aug. 7, 1825, by Rev. Herman L. Vaill	3	78
Jane Ann, m. Joseph N. **REYNOLDS**, of Lyme, Sept. 14, 1834, by Ozias Holmes, J. P.	3	135
Mary, m. William H. **JOELS**, Oct. 26, 1831, by Rev. Benjamin G. Goff	3	120
-----, d. Albert J., joiner, ae 25, & Elizabeth C., ae 19, b. Nov. 10, 1849	4	23-4
THOMPSON, THOMSON, Almyra C., m. Samuel P. **COMSTOCK**, Sept. 29, 1844, by Rev. Stephen Alonzo Loper, of Hadlyme	3	200
Charlotte, of East Haddam, m. William **BABCOCK**, of Salem, Nov. 21, 1837, by Nathan Jewett, Jr., J. P.	3	160
Gurdon, of Saybrook, m. Patience **BEEBE**, of East Haddam, Oct. 1, 1830, by Russell Dutton, J. P.	3	108
Jemima J., of Portland, m. John P. **UFFORD**, of East Haddam, Aug. 13, 1848, by Rev. Levi H. Wakeman	3	214
Joseph, of Portland, m. Lucy Ann **UFFORD**, of East Haddam, June 11, 1848, by Rev. Levi H. Wakeman	3	213
-----, s. Joseph, manufacturer, ae 23, & Lucy Ann, ae 22, b. Apr. 18, 1849	4	11-2
TIBBALS, Samuel, of Meriden, m. Abigail **LINDSLEY**, of East Haddam, May 20, 1822, by Reuben Ives. Int. pub. in Meriden	3	25
TIFFANY, Emeline L., of Lyme, m. Wilson **BECKWITH**, of Palmyra, N. Y., Mar. 17, 1841, by Rev. George Carrington, of Hadlyme	3	185
John K., of Lyme, m. Miranda **HUNGERFORD**, of East Haddam, Aug. 18, 1825, by Rev. Joseph Vaill, of Hadlyme	3	78
TIFFT, Anna, d. Samuell & Mary, b. Nov. 19, 1729	LR2	e
TILDEN, Silence, of Haddam, m. Jonathan **HUNTINGTON**, of East Haddam, Sept. 17, 1767	2	6
TILEY, [see also **TYLER**], S. J., of Essex, m. Orphila M. **BATES** of East Haddam, Mar. 5, 1854, by Rev. Isaac Parsons	3	239
S. J., merchant, ae 23, b. in Essex, res. East Haddam, m. Orphelia M. **BATES**, music teacher, ae 19, b. in East Haddam, res. Essex, Mar. 5, 1854	4	41-2
S. J., merchant, ae 23, of Essex, m. Ophelia M. **BATES**, music teacher, ae 19, of East Haddam, Mar. 5, 1854	4	51-2
TILLINGHAST, Thomas A., of Voluntown, m. Hannah **SPENCER**, of East Haddam, May 3, 1824, by Rev. Isaac Parsons	3	58-9
TILLOTSON, Lucinda M., of Lyme, m. Asa A. **FOWLER**, of East Haddam, July 7, 1836, by Rev. Isaac Parsons	3	145
TINKER, Abigael, d. Silvanus & Abigail, b. Mar. 24, 1758	2	4

	Vol.	Page
TINKER, (cont.)		
Abigail, w. of Silvanus, d. Oct. 22, 1773	2	5
Emeline, m. Randall **WATROUS**, b. of Lyme, Jan. 7, 1838, by Rev. David Todd	3	160
Harriot, d. Silvanus & Wealthy, b. July 30, 1784	2	4
Indiana, m. William **GREEN**, b. of East Haddam, Oct. 26, 1791	2	233
Joseph, s. Silvanus & Abagail, b. July 23, 1763	2	4
Lorinah, d. Silvanus & Abigail, b. May 20, 1768	2	4
Lucy S., of Lyme, m. Erastus **CONE**, of East Haddam, Mar. 18, 1833, by Nathaniel Miner	3	131
Olive, d. Silvanus & Abagail, b. Jan. 19, 1761	2	4
Reuben, s. Silvanus & Abagail, b. Dec. 19, 1765	2	4
Reuben, s. Silvanus & Abigail, d. Aug. 11, 1770. Was drowned	2	5
Salley, d. Silvanus & Abigail, b. Sept. 5, 1773	2	4
Silvanus, m. Abagail **OLMSTED**, Sept. 24, 1755	2	4
Silvanus, of East Haddam, m. Mrs. Wealthy **GILBERT**, of Lebanon, May 23, 1781	2	4
Silvanus, d. Oct. 13, 1815, in the 85th y. of her age	2	5
Silvester, s. Silvanus & Abagail, b. Mar. 24, 1756	2	4
Silvester, s. Silvanus & Abigail, d. Jan. 13, 1768. Was drowned	2	5
William Olmsted, s. Silvanus & Abigail, b. Oct. 17, 1770	2	4
TITIATE, ----, child of George, laborer, colored, of Millington, & Jerusha, b. June [ ], 1851	4	33-4
-----. st. b. child of George, colored, b. in East Haddam, res. Millington, June [ ], 1851	4	39-40
TOMPKINS, Daniel, of Middletown, m. Elizabeth J. **CONE**, of East Haddam, Sept. 2, 1837, by Roswell Davison, J. P.	3	152
Elizabeth J., of Lyme, m. Simon P. **BEERS**, of Chatham, Sept. 20, 1840, by Isaac Parsons, D. V. M.	3	182-3
TOOKER, [see under **TUCKER**]		
TOWNER, Sarah, of Haddam, m. William **RICHARDSON**, of East Haddam, Aug. 19, 1773	2	82
TRACY, TRACEY, Abby, m. Samuel **MARTIN**, b. of East Haddam, Jan. 1, 1852, by Rev. Nathaniel Miner	3	234
Abby Ann, d. [Gamaleel R. & Lydia], b. Dec. 13, 1831	3	7
Abigail, m. Nathan **BEEBE**, Oct. 25, 1825, by Russell Dutton, J. P.	3	79
Aliphaz, s. Nehemiah & Susannah, b. May 1, 1772	2	22
Aliphaz, s. Nehemiah & Susannah, d. Aug. 29, 1776	2	23
Arobul, s. Nehemiah & Lucy, b. Feb. 21, 1796 (Date conflicts with birth of Bulkley **TRACY**)	2	212
Benajah Collins, s. Neh[emia]h & Lucy, b. July 14, 1804	2	212
Bulkley, s. Nehemiah & Lucy, b. June 3, 1796 (Date conflicts with birth of Arobul)	2	212
Daniel, s. Nehemiah & Susannah, b. Jan. 9, 1765	LR4	466
Elizabeth, d. Nehemiah & Susannah, b. July 5, 1767	LR4	466
Elizabeth, m. Elisha **CONE**, b. of East Haddam, Sept. 28, 1786* (*Entry crossed out)	2	157

	Vol.	Page
TRACY, TRACEY, (cont.)		
Elizabeth, m. Elisha **CONE**, b. of East Haddam, Sept. 28, 1786	2	239
Gamaleel R., m. Lydia **CLARK**, May 17, 1821, by Rev. Solomon Blakesley	3	7
Gamaleel R., m. Floretta **BINGHAM**, b. of East Haddam, Mar. 20, 1842, by Thomas G. Salter	3	189
Gamaleel R., of New London, m. Henrietta **MARTIN**, of East Haddam, July 26, [1846?], by Nathaniel Miner, at Millington	3	206
Gameleel Ripley, s. Nehemiah & Susannah, b. Feb. 17, 1759	LR4	466
Gamaliel Ripley, s. Gamali R. & Sally, b. Oct. 13, 1795	2	215
Gamaliel Ripley, of East Haddam, m. Sally **LEWIS**, of Colchester, Oct. 15, 1789	2	215
Hannah Smith, d. Nehemiah & Susannah, b. Oct. 20, 1760	LR4	466
James Gorham, s. Nehemiah & Lucy, d. Sept. 10, 1800 (1802?)	2	213
James Gorham, s. Nehemiah & Lucy, b. Feb. 17, 1802	2	212
James Olmsted, s. Nehemiah & Lucy, b. Nov. 22, 1790	2	212
Jedida, d. Nehemiah & Susannah, b. Oct. 16, 1762	LR4	466
Jerusha, d. Nehemiah & Susannah, b. Oct. 23, 1751	LR4	466
Jerusha, d. Gamaliel R. & Sally, b. Oct. 24, 1793	2	215
Nehemiah, s. Nehemiah & Susannah, b. Nov. 8, 1753	LR4	466
Nehemiah, d. Sept. 9, 1776	2	23
Nehemiah, of East Haddam, m. Lucy **OLMSTED**, of Colchester, Oct. 14, 1789	2	212
Nehemiah, s. Gamaliel R. & Sally, b. July 9, 1805, (in Colchester)	2	215
Oliver C., m. Sophronia **McINTOSH**, b. of East Haddam, Dec. 27, 1832, by Rev. Isaac Parsons	3	128
Oramel, s. Nehemiah & Lucy, b. Nov. 25, 1793	2	212
Rachel, d. Nehemiah & Susannah, b. Mar. 18, 1757	LR4	466
Ralph, s. Gamaliel R. & Sally, b. Dec. 26, 1799, in Colchester	2	215
Ralph, m. Harriet E. **LEE**, b. of East Haddam, Aug. 23, 1846, by Rev. Levi Wakeman	3	207
Robbins, s. Gamaliel R. & Sally, b. May 12, 1797	2	215
Sarah, d. Nehemiah & Susannah, b. June 15, 1755	LR4	466
Susan Collins, d. Gamaliel R. & Sally, b. Oct. 20, 1803, in Colchester	2	215
Susannah, d. Nehemiah & Susannah, b. Mar. 14, 1745, at Windham. "Entered here to gratify the parents of said Susannah"	LR4	466
Susannah, of East Haddam, m. Bennajah **COLLINGS**, of Liverpool, Mar. 29, 1770	2	26
Susannah, d. Gamaliel R. & Sally, b. July 4, 1790	2	215
Susannah, d. Gamaliel R. & Sally, d. Jan. 22, 1795	2	216
Tryphena, d. Nehemiah & Susannah, b. Jan. 9, 1746/7; d. Jan. 29, 1746/7	LR4	466
Tryphena, d. Nehemiah & Susannah, b. Apr. 14, 1748	LR4	466
Tryphene, d. Gamaliel R. & Sally, b. Oct. 27, 1791	2	215

	Vol.	Page
TRACY, TRACEY, (cont.)		
William H., m. Eveline C. **SMITH**, b. of East Haddam, Aug. 9, 1846, by Rev. Levi Wakeman	3	206
-----, s. Gamaleel R., farmer, ae 38, res. East Haddam, & [ ], ae 38, b. Oct. 17, 1855	4	77
TREADWAY, Andrew J., of Salem, m. Lucy L. **BEEBE**, of Colchester, Nov. 30, 1854, by Rev. Nathaniel Miner	3	242
Andrew J., merchant, ae 30, of Salem, m. Lucy L. **BEEBE**, ae 20, b. in East Haddam, res. Colchester, Nov. 30, 1854, by Rev. N. Miner	4	51-2
Louisa, ae 21, b. in Salem, res. East Haddam, m. [ ], Apr. 9, 1850, by Rev. Joseph Thompson	4	19-20
TROWBRIDGE, TROBRIDGE, [see also **STRAWBRIDGE**], Anna, m. James **BOOGE**, Nov. 21, 1739	LR3	10
Naomi, m. Charles **BROOKS**, Apr. 9, 1809, by Rev. Ezra Stiles Ely	3	111
TRYON, Adelia H., m. Samuel K. **FOWLER**, Oct. 14, 1829, by Isaac Parsons	3	103
TUBBS, Marcy, of Lyme, m. Zephaniah **ANDREWS**, of East Haddam, Apr. 17, 1759	LR6	510
TUCKER, TOOKER, Courtney, of Saybrook, m. Meriam **SHAYLER**, of East Haddam, Feb. 6, last [1825], by William Gelston, J. P.	3	70-1
Delia, ae 27, of Lyme, m. Franklin **HARVEY**, ae 28, of East Haddam, Jan. 11, 1857, by Israel D. Burnham, J. P. Int. pub. Jan. 7, 1857	4	118
Elizabeth, of East Haddam, m. Hiram H. W. **HEWIT**, of Salem, Apr. 30, 1849, by Rev. Simon Shailer	3	217
Griswold E., of Saybrook, m. Mary E. **GATES**, of East Haddam, Nov. 17, 1845, by Rev. Isaac Parsons	3	203
Hiram B., m. Lucretia **SNOW**, June 7, 1829, by Rev. Isaac Parsons	3	102
Julia Amelia, of Lyme, m. Ralph H. **STODDARD**, of East Haddam, Mar. 29, 1847, by Rev. Alpheas Geer	3	209
Noah, Jr., of Haddam, m. Catherine **MASON**, of New York, Oct. 7, 1849, by Rev. Simon Shailer, of Haddam	3	220
Phebe, of Haddam, m. Curtis S. **ARNOLD**, of East Haddam, Sept. 13, 1840, by Rev. Moses Stoddard	3	182-3
TULLY, TULLEY, [see also **TILLEY**], Betsey, of Saybrook, m. Ozias **HOLMES**, of East Haddam, Jan. 19, 1808, by Rev. Joseph Vail	2	295
Mercy, of Saybrook, m. Dr. Asa M. **HOLT**, of East Haddam, Sept. 18, 1816, by Rev. Fred W[illia]m Hotchkiss, of Saybrook	3	197
TUPPER, Hannah Choate, of Campton, N. H., m. Asa **HOLT**, of East Haddam, Oct. 17, 1841, by Rev. George Carrington, of Hadlyme	3	187
Roswell, of Campton, N. H., m. Ann F. **CHURCH**, of		

	Vol.	Page
TUPPER, (cont.) Millington, Mar. 25, 1838, by Rev. Nathaniel Miner, of Millington	3	164-5
TUTTLE, Daniel, of New York, m. Hannah **GREEN**, of East Haddam, Aug. 28, 1825, by Rev. Isaac Parsons	3	78
TYLER, [see also **TILEY**], Ellen, ae 30, b. in Haddam, res. East Haddam, m. William H. **CHAPMAN**, ae 37, b. in East Haddam, res. New London, Sept. 24, 1856, by Cha[rle]s H. Bullard, of Rockville, Int. pub. Sept. 23, 1856	4	99
Henry S., of Haddam, m. Catharine L. **GREEN**, of East Haddam, June 11, 1845, by Rev. Isaac Parsons	3	202
Henry Whitney, s. Henry S., shipmaster, ae 34, & Catharine L. ae 30, b. Mar. 6, 1850	4	27-8
Josephine Scoville, d. Christopher, ship agent, ae 28, & Hannah, ae 27, b. Feb. 4, 1850	4	27-8
Laura, of Haddam, m. Joseph **GOODSPEED**, of East Haddam, Sept. 26, 1811, by Rev. Solomon Blakesley	3	53
Samuel, of Haddam, m. Bethiah **RANDALL**, of East Haddam, Jan. 15, 1823, by Rev. W[illia]m Lyman	3	34-5
Timothy, of Haddam, m. Mrs. Rachel **GOFF**, of East Haddam, Dec. 1, 1849, by Rev. Levi H. Wakeman	3	220
-----, child of Henry, mariner, ae 33, & Catharine, ae 28, b. May 12, 1848	4	3-4
UFFORD, Andrew Jackson, s. Lucian N., manufacturer, ae 33, & Esther, ae 33, b. Oct. 20, 1848	4	13-14
Ephraim, of Chatham, m. Matilda **CONE**, of East Haddam, Sept. 5, 1824, by David Selden	3	62-63
John P., of East Haddam, m. Jemima J. **THOMPSON**, of Portland, Aug. 13, 1848, by Rev. Levi H. Wakeman	3	214
Lucy Ann, of East Haddam, m. Joseph **THOMSON**, of Portland, June 11, 1848, by Rev. Levi H. Wakeman	3	213
Mary J., factory operative, ae 22, b. in Chatham, res. East Haddam, m. William W. **SCOVILLE**, factory operative, ae 21, of East Haddam, Feb. 26, 1854	4	41-2
Mary J., factory operative, ae 21, b. in Chatham, res. East Haddam, m. William W. **SCOVILLE**, factory operative, ae 21, of East Haddam, Feb. 26, 1854	4	51-2
Russell, of Chatham, m. Charity **CONE**, of East Haddam, Sept. 12, 1824, by Rev. W[illia]m Jarvis	3	64-5
-----, s. John P., fisherman, ae 26, & Jemima, ae 20, b. July 6, 1849	4	11-2
UPHAM, Lyman, of Norwich, m. Ellen **WHITMORE**, of East Haddam, Apr. 23, 1848, by Rev. Isaac Parsons	3	212
Lyman, mechanic, ae 22, b. in Thomson, res. Norwich, m. Ellen J. **WHITMORE**, ae 19, b. in East Haddam, res. Norwich, Apr. 23, 1848, by Isaac Parsons	4	1-2
Nehemiah, of Grafton, Mass., m. Augustua **WHITMORE**, of East Haddam, [Sept.] 20,]1843], by Rev. Isaac Parsons	3	195

	Vol.	Page
USHER, Aaron Cleveland, s. Hezekiah & Lydia, b. Oct. 17, 1770	2	184
Abigail, d. Hez[ekiah] & Lydia, b. Aug. 12, 1764	LR6	512
Charles Lee, s. Hezekiah & Lydia, b. Mar. 13, 1776	2	184
Harris, s. Hez[ekiah] & Lydia, b. Sept. 10, 1762	LR6	512
Harris, s. Hez[ekiah] & Lydia, d. May 17, 1771	LR6	512
Harris, s. Hezekiah & Lydia, b. May 12, 1774	2	184
Hezekiah, of East Haddam, m. Lydia **PARKER**, Nov. 3, 1757	LR6	512
Hezekiah, s. Hezekiah & Lydia, b. Apr. 2, 1767	2	184
James, s. Hezekiah & Abigail, b. July 18, 1747	LR2	1100
Jane, d. Hez[ekiah] & Lydia, b. Aug. 2, 1758	LR6	512
Lidiah, d. Hez[ekiah] & Lydia, b. Feb. 18, 1760	LR6	512
Moses Craft, s. Hezekiah & Lydia, b. Oct. 12, 1782	2	184
Nathaniel, s. Hezekiah & Lydia, b. Oct. 28, 1785	2	184
Olive, d. Hezekiah & Lydia, b. Oct. 17, 1772	2	184
Olive, d. Hezekiah & Lydia, d. Mar. 17, 1775	2	185
Robert, s. Hezekiah & Abigail, b. Jan. 31, 1742/3	LR2	1100
Sarah, d. Hez[ekiah] & Lydia, b. Apr. 1, 1765	LR6	512
Susannah, d. Hezekiah & Lydia, b. Mar. 1, 1769	2	184
Watros, s. Hezekiah & Lydia, b. Feb. 7, 1780	2	184
VAILL, Amanda, of East Haddam, m. David **EVARTS**, of Killingworth, Mar. 2, 1836, by Rev. George Carrington, of Hadlyme	3	142
Charles Benjamin, s. [Rev. Herman L. & Flora G.], b. Sept. 10, 1826	3	100
Elizabeth Sedgwich, d. [Rev. Herman L. & Flora G.], b. Jan. 3, 1828	3	100
Joseph, Rev., m. Sarah **FOWLER**, b. of East Haddam, Oct. 12, 1780	2	150
Joseph, s. Rev. Joseph & Sarah, b. Aug. 29, 1781	2	150
Joseph, s. Rev. Joseph & Sarah, d. Nov. 1, 1785	2	151
Joseph, s. Rev. Joseph & Sarah, b. July 28, 1790	2	150
Sarah, d. Rev. Joseph & Sarah, b. Mar. 29, 1788	2	150
Timothy, s. Rev. Joseph & Sarah, b. June 29, 1785	2	150
William Fowler, s. Rev. Joseph & Sarah, b. June 7, 1783	2	150
VAN HORSEN, VAN HORSON, John, s. John M., mechanic, ae 36, & Mary Ann, ae 34, b. Oct. 21, 1847	4	3-4
----, d. John M., cabinet maker, ae 37, & Mary A., ae 37, b. May 28, 1849	4	11-12
VENTRES, Henry A., of Franklin, N. J., m. Mary B. **SMITH**, of East Haddam, Nov. 29, 1850, by Rev. Alpheas Geer	3	228
VINING, Milton L., of Hartford, m. Catharine M. **HUBBARD**, of East Haddam, July 13, 1843, by Rev. Isaac Parsons	3	194
VONBRAS*, (**VENTRES** corrected in handwritting in margin of original manuscript), Susannah, m. Ichabod **SPENCER**, Dec. 31, 1730	LR2	1125
WAKEMAN, George, ae 29, b. in Wilton, res. East Haddam, m. Virginia **BULKELEY**, ae 25, b. in Colchester, res. East Haddam, June 12, 1856, by Rev. Levi H. Wakeman.		

	Vol.	Page
WAKEMAN, (cont.)		
Int. pub. June 10, 1856	4	89-90
WALES, Ichabod, see under Ichabod **PIERCE**	2	89
John, who changed his surname from "**PIERCE**' to "**WALES**" and Lydia, his w. had s.Ichabod **PIERCE**,b. Mar. 10, 1776	2	89
John, of Hopkenton, Mass., m. Lydia **HURD**, of East Haddam, Oct. 17, 1775, by Rev. Mr. Parsons	2	88
WALKLEY, Elizabeth, m. Sylvester **HALL**, July 5, 1804	3	105
WALTER, Tamson, d. Jacob & Tamson, b. Aug. 28, 1753	LR5	b
WARD, Emeline, of Chatman, m. Orville B. **PERCIVAL**, of East Haddam, Sept. 20, 1838, by Isaac Parsons, V. D. M.	3	166
WARES, Caroline E., of East Haddam, m. William **CORY**, of Colchester, Nov. 24, 1844, by Rev. W[illia]m S. Simmons	3	201
WARNER, Abraham, s. John & Mahittabell, b. Feb. 13, 1725/6	LR1	580
Anna, d. Daniel & Elizabeth, b. Apr. 21, 1774	2	62
Anna, m. Pardon **WINSLOW**, b. of East Haddam, Sept. 6, 1795	2	253
Austin, s. Mehetable, b. June 2, 1800	2	82
Azubah, d. Eli & Azubah, b. Oct. 27, 1755	LR5	560
Betsey A., of East Haddam, m. Guy **DAVENPORT**, of Canterbury, Apr. 8, 1827, by Rev. William Jarvis	3	95
Cephas, reputed s. [ ] **TODD** & Hannah **WARNER**, b. Mar. 25, 1769	2	72
Charity, d. Dan[ie]l & Elizabeth, b. [ ] 26, 1788	2	62
Charles A., ae 23, b. in East Haddam, res. East Haddam, m. Permelia R. **MACK**, ae 20, b. in East Haddam, res. East Haddam, July 20, 1856, at Hadlyme Parish by Rev. E. B. Hillard. Int. pub. July 17, 1856	4	91
Charlotte, d. Eli & Azubah, b. Jan. 25, 1765	LR5	560
Clarice, d. Eli & Azubah, b. Aug. 10, 1766	LR5	560
Daniell, s. John & Mahittabell, b. May 6, 1717	LR1	580
Daniel, s. Jabez & Hannah, b. June 22, 1766	LR4	471
Daniel, m. Elisabeth **CLARK**, b. of East Haddam, July 28, 1774	2	62
Daniel, s. Daniel & Elizabeth, b. July 9, 1776	2	62
Daniel B., m. Mary Ann **GREEN**, Apr. 27, 1835, by Rev. Stephen Beach	3	137
Eli, of East Haddam, m. Azubah **ALLYN**, of Win[d]sor, Dec. 18, 1754	LR5	560
Ely, s. Ely & Azubah, b. Nov. 13, 1758	LR5	560
Elizabeth, d. John & Mahittabell, b. Jan. 25, 1724/5	LR1	580
Elizabeth, m. Bazaliel **BRAINARD**, June 17, 1744	LR2	1092
Elizabeth, d. Jabez & Hannah, b. May 18, 1758	LR4	471
Elisabeth, d. Daniel & Elisabeth, b. Mar. 27, 1772 [or 4]	2	62
Elisabeth, wid. of Daniel, d. Jan. 3, 1778, in the 90th y. of her age	2	83
Ely, see under Eli		

	Vol.	Page
WARNER, (cont.)		
Emeline Eliza, d. [Matthew Griswold & Lucretia Hubbard], b. June 14, 1830	3	94
Ephraim, s. Joseph & Elizabeth, b. Apr. 19, 1767	LR6	505
Eunice, d. Eli & Azubah, b. Jan. 24, 1757	LR5	560
Frederick W., ae 33, of East Haddam, m. Phebe E. **MOSELEY**, ae 23, of East Haddam, Nov. 12, 1856, at Hadlyme, by Rev. E. B. Hillard. Int. pub. Nov. 11, 1856	4	107
Hannah, d. Jabez & Hannah, b. Nov. 21, 1755	LR4	471
Hannah, had s. Cephas **WARNER**, b. Mar. 25, 1769; reputed father ------ **TODD**	2	72
Hannah, m. Samuel **PHELPS**, b. of East Haddam, June 17, 1784	2	217
Hannah, d. Jabez, 2d, & Sarah, b. Apr. 26, 1790	2	162
Henry Allyn, s. Eli & Azubah, b. June 27, 1762	LR5	560
Henry Allyn, s. Eli & Azubah, d. Apr. 28, 1763	LR5	560
Huldah, d. Jabez, 2d, & Sarah, b. Apr. 29, 1788	2	162
Jabez, s. John & Mahittabell, b. Nov. 25, 1720	LR1	580
Jabez, m. Hannah **BRAINERD**, May 9, 1749	LR4	471
Jabez, s. Jabez & Hannah, b. Aug. 19, 1750	LR4	471
Jabez, 2d, m. Sarah **HARVEY**, b. of East Haddam, Dec. 25, 1786	2	162
John, m. Mahittabell **RICHARDSON**, Mar. 21, 1716	LR1	580
John, s. John & Mahittabell, b. Dec. 19, 1716	LR1	580
John, Sergt., d. Mar. 17, 1750	LR2	1116
John, m. Mary **TAILOR**, Feb. 20, 1750/51	LR4	466
John, s. John & Mary, b. June 18, 1754	LR4	466
John, d. May 17, 1827	2	83
John, of Saybrook, m. Lucy **COMSTOCK**, of East Haddam, Sept. 25, 1827, by Rev. Simon Shailer, of Haddam	3	95
Joseph, s. John & Mehittabell, b. Jan. 13, 1731	LR1	579
Joseph, m. Elizabeth **CONE**, b. of East Haddam, Jan. 24, 1760	LR6	505
Joseph, s. Joseph & Elizabeth, b. Feb. 6, 1761	LR6	505
Joseph, Jr., of East Haddam, m. Sarah **OSBORN**, of Long Island, Apr. [ ], 1783	2	212
Joseph, of Lyme, m. Mary Ann **HOLMES**, of East Haddam, Nov. 8, 1829, by Rev. Joseph Vaill	3	103
Joseph Osborn, s. Joseph, Jr. & Sarah, b. July 29, 1788	2	212
Louisa, d. Ely & Azubah, b. June 28, 1760	LR5	560
Lovice, of Lyme, m. Robart **HUNGARFORD**, Jr., of East Haddam, Feb. 14, 1776	2	104
Lucinda, d. Jabez & Hannah, b. Mar. 29, 1773	LR4	471
Lucinda, m. Richard **WYLLIS**, [ ]	2	146
Lucretia, d. Eli & Azubah, b. Oct. 5, 1763	LR5	560
Lucretia Loomis, d. [Matthew Griswold & Lucretia Hubbard], b. July 6, 1828	3	94
Martha, m. Matthew **SEYERS**, Mar. 13, 1746	LR3	510
Mary, d. John & Mary, b. June 15, 1752	LR4	466

	Vol.	Page
WARNER, (cont.)		
Mary, house maid, ae 21, of East Haddam, m. Morrison **ROBBINS**, blacksmith, ae 27, b. in Lyme, res. East Haddam, Jan. 15, 1854	4	41-2
Mary, house maid, ae 21, of East Haddam, m. Morrison **ROBBINS**, blacksmith, ae 27, b. in Lyme, res. East Haddam, Jan. 15, 1854	4	51-2
Matthew Griswold, m. Lucretia Hubbard **LOOMIS**, Nov. 30, 1825, by Rev. Jacob Scales, at Colchester	3	94
Matthew Griswold, s. [Matthew Griswold & Lucretia Hubbard], b. Jan. 1, 1827	3	94
Mehitable, d. Jabez & Hannah, b. Aug. 31, 1763	LR4	471
Mehetable, had s. Austin, b. June 2, 1800	2	82
Nancy C., of East Haddam, m. Sylvester **BLISS**, of Longmeadow, Mass., Sept. 27, 1848, by Rev. Alpheas Geer	3	214
Nancy C., ae 30, b. in East Haddam, res. Longmeadow, Mass., m. Sylvester **BLISS**, farmer, ae 29, b. in Longmeadow, Mass., res. Longmeadow, Mass., Sept. 27, 1848, by Rev. Alpheas Geer	4	9-10
Nathaniell, s. John & Mahittabell, b. Dec. 25, 1718	LR1	580
Noadiah, s. John & Mehittabell, b. Jan. 12, 1728/9	LR1	579
Oliver, s. Joseph & Elizabeth, b. Apr. 13, 1765	LR6	505
Oliver, General, farmer, married, d. Feb. 7, 1853, ae 66* (*or 56, it was struck over and not sure)	4	49-50
Orren, m. Matilda Ann **WILLEY**, b. of East Haddam, Dec. 8, 1830, by Rev. Peter G. Clarke	3	115
Phebe, d. Daniel & Elizabeth, b. July 27, 1782	2	62
Prudence, d. Daniel & Elizabeth, b. Apr. 21, 1785	2	62
Richard, m. Mary M. **GILBERT**, [ ] (The words "brother of Selden" follow this entry)	3	10
Richard, Dr., m. Mary M. **GILBERT**, [ ], at Mansfield	3	10
Richard Selden, s. [Dr. Richard & Mary M.], b. Mar. 27, 1828	3	10
Sarah, d. Jabez & Hannah, b. Mar. 6, 1769	LR4	471
Sarah, d. Jabez, 2d, & Sarah, b. May 29, 1792	2	162
Sarah W., of Hadlyme, m. Daniel **STRONG**, of Southampton, L. I. June 26, 1846, by Rev. Stephen Alonzo Loper, of Hadlyme	3	202
Selden, s. Jabez & Hannah, b. Dec. 8, 1760	LR4	471
Selden, of East Haddam, m. Bette **BROCKWAY**, of Lyme, June 30, 1785	2	164
Selden, s. Selden & Bette, b. Sept. 9, 1787	2	164
Selden, of Lyme, m. Elizabeth **SPENCER**, of East Haddam, Jan. 4, 1827, by Rev. Joseph Vaill, of Hadlyme	3	91
Sidney B., s. Daniel B., machinist, ae 42, & Mary A., ae 32, b. Dec. 5, 1849	4	11-12
Susannah, d. Jabez & Hannah, b. Apr. 9, 1753	LR4	471
Susannah, of East Haddam, m. Joseph **BANNING**, of Lyme,		

	Vol.	Page
WARNER, (cont.)		
Dec. 2, 1773	2	184
William, m. Lydia **RAY**, b. of East Haddam, Jan. 21, 1833, by Rev. Isaac Parsons	3	131
WARREN, Charles, d. Aug. 28, 1854, in Hadlyme	4	53-4
WATERHOUSE, Damaries, m. Eliphalet **HOLMES**, Jan. 25, 1742	LR3	1
WATERS, Lydia, of Hebron, m. Reuben **BEEBE**, of East Haddam, Apr. 21, 1774	2	120
Sorepta A., m. James S. **MITCHELL**, May 29, 1836, by Rev. Isaac Parsons	3	145
WATROUS, Alfred, of Chester, m. Eveline Elvira **MACK**, of East Haddam, Feb. 8, 1843, by Rev. Alex[ande]r Burgess	3	193
Alfred, mechanic, ae 31, b. in Chester, res. Meriden, m. 2d w. Aurelia **MACK**, ae 22, b. in East Haddam, res. Meriden, Apr. 13, 1848, by A. Geer	4	1-2
Alfred, of Mereden, m. Amelia M. **MACK**, of East Haddam, Apr. 30, 1848, by Rev. Alpheas Geer	3	212
Cynthia, m. George A. **SANDERS**, Aug. 24, 1828, by Ozias Holmes, J. P.	3	100
Elijah, ae 38, b. at Colchester, res. Colchester, m. Mrs. Sarah Jane **BAILEY**, ae 35, b. at East Haddam, res. East Haddam, Dec. 6, 1855, at Leesville, by Rev. J. E. Heald. Int. pub. Dec. 3, 1855	4	67-8
Eunice M., m. Lyman C. **RANSOM**, b. of East Haddam, Nov. 24, 1833, by Rev. Nathaniel Miner	3	133
Eunice M., m. Lyman C. **RANSOM**, Nov. 24, 1833	3	149
Henry R., of Lyme, m. Mary **CHADWICK**, of East Haddam, Nov. 22, 1821, by Josiah Griffin, J. P.	3	19
Nancy J., of Colchester, m. Abner **HURD**, of East Haddam, Nov. 12, 1848, by Rev. Isaac Parsons	3	214
Nancy S., b. in Colchester, res. East Haddam, m. Abner **HURD**, shoemaker, of East Haddam, Nov. 12, 1848, by Isaac Parsons	4	9-10
Randall, m. Emeline **TINKER**, b. of Lyme, Jan. 7, 1838, by Rev. David Todd	3	160
Samantha S., of Saybrook, m. David H. **CLARK**, of Columbia, Sept. 25, 1836, by Rev. Isaac Parsons	3	145
William, of Mereden, m. Eveline Addie **ACKLEY**, of East Haddam, Sept. 4, 1842, by Rev. Isaac Parsons	3	191
WATSON, Aaron, m. Statira **PURPLE**, b. of East Haddam, Nov. 17, 1814	2	277
Aaron, s. Aaron & Statira, b. Aug. 27, 1815	2	277
Aaron, d. [ ], "at sea as is supposed with the whole crew of Capt. **BOARDMAN**" ("**BOARDMAN**" written in a different hand)	2	278
Asa, s. John & Sarah, b. Oct. 18, 1761	LR6	504
Emily, m. Henry **SMITH**, Feb. 7, 1828, by Rev. Alvan Ackley. Int. pub.	3	96

	Vol.	Page
WATSON, (cont.)		
Eunice, m. Alvin **ACKLEY**, b. of East Haddam, Apr. 1, 1821, by Rev. Simeon Dickinson, at the house of Asa Watson	3	4
John, of Lebanon, m. Sarah **ARNOLD**, of East Haddam, Feb. 26, 1761	LR6	504
Julia Ann, d. Aaron & Statira, b. Dec. 22, 1818	2	277
Julia Ann, of East Haddam, m. Watsell Strong **HOLDRIDGE**, of Colchester, Feb. 20, 1839, by Rev. Charles William Bradley	3	167
Mary, of East Haddam, m. Asa **CLARK**, of Haddam, Oct. 4, 1829, by Rev. Alvan Ackley	3	102
Orpha, of East Haddam, m. Hubbard **HARRIS**, of Salem, Feb. 9, 1830, by Rev. Alvan Ackley	3	104
Rose, b. in Ireland, res. East Haddam, m. Thomas **EGAN**, b. in Ireland, res. East Haddam, Apr. 8, 1855, in Chester, by Rev. John Lynch, of Chester. Int. pub. Apr. 3, 1855, in East Haddam	4	55
WAY, George, of Colchester, m. Esther W. **CHAPMAN**, of East Haddam, [Aug.] 14, [1820], by Rev. Isaac Parsons	2	321
John G., of Colchester, m. Caroline W. **PALMER**, of East Haddam, Sept. 3, 1834, by R. S. Crampton, V. D. M.	3	135
WEBB, Sally, of Saybrook, m. Richard **GREEN**, of East Haddam, May 1, 1803	3	80-1
WEIRE, Sophia, of Glastenbury, m. Stpehen Mix **MITCHELL**, of East Haddam, Nov. 4, 1832, by Hemon Perry	3	127
WELLS, WELLES, Elizabeth, m. Nathaniel **EM[M]ONS**, Sept. 21, 1727	LR2	1113
Ely P., of Lyme, m. Permelia **LUTHER**, of East Haddam, Oct. 16, 1831, by Rev. Benjamin G. Goff	3	120
Frances, of Lyme, m. George G. **CONE**, of East Haddam, Nov. 8, 1854, by Rev. S. A. Loper, of Higganum	3	241
Frances, ae 25, of Lyme, m. George G. **CONE**, salesman, ae 26, b. in Euclid, Ohio, res. East Haddam, Nov. 8, 1854, by Rev. Stephen A. Loper	4	51-2
John S., m. Maria H. **CHAPMAN**, b. of East Haddam, Mar. 26, 1840, by Isaac Parsons, V. D. M.	3	176-7
Louisa, of Marlborough, m. James S. **MITCHELL**, of East Haddam, Mar. 15, 1846, by Rev. Isaac Parsons	3	204
Martha, m. Jonathan **HUNGERFORD**, Jan. 13, 1736/7	LR3	17
Mary E., of Chatham, m. Horace H. **STODDARD**, of East Haddam, Sept. 21, 1851, by Rev. Alpheas Geer	3	233
WELSH, James M., of Chatham, m. Elisa **HIGGINS**, of East Haddam, Dec. 20, 1843, by Rev. Stephen Alonzo Loper, of Hadlyme	3	196
WEST, Henry E., of New London, m. Abby Ann **GELSTON**, of East Haddam, June 9, 1846, by Rev. Alpheas Geer	3	205
WESTON, Lucy, m Edward Solomon **BLAKESLEY**, Oct. 11,		

	Vol.	Page
WESTON, (cont.)		
1821, by Rev. Russell Wheeler, at Butternuts, N. Y.	3	53
WETHERELL, Emily Augusta, d. Daniel, manufacturer, ae 35, & Mary, ae 32, b. May 21, 1849	4	13-14
George F., single, d. Sept. 27, 1856, & 2 m. 15 d.	4	110
Irene E., d. Ralph T., wagon maker, ae 24, & Clarissa, ae 25, b. Nov. 22, 1849	4	23-4
Ralph P., d. Dec. 2, 1848, ae 1	4	17-8
Ralph T., of Middletown, m. Clarissa **MEECH**, of East Haddam, Oct. 7, 1846, by Rev. S. D. Jewett	3	207
----, s. Daniel, cotton manufacturer, ae 43, & Mary, ae 40, b. June 12, [1856]	4	108
WETMORE, Arnold, ae 23, b. in East Haddam, res. East Haddam, m. Eunice **BROWN**, ae 19, b. in Colchester, res. Colchester, May 24, 1856, by Rev. Henry Torbush. Int. pub. May 20, 1856	4	89
Samuel, ae 21, b. at Haddam, res. East Haddam, m. Florilla A. **SHALER**, d. of Joseph N., ae 17, b. at East Haddam, res. East Haddam, Dec. 27, 1855, by Rev. William Cone. Int. pub. Dec. 26, 1855. Consent given by Joseph N. **SHALER**, father of Florilla A.	4	69
WHEELER, Ahira D., m. Eliza Ann **ATTWOOD**, Mar. 7, 1831, by Rev. Isaac Parsons	3	115
Alonzo, ae 24, b. in East Haddam, res. East Haddam, m. Julia C. **SILLIMAN**, ae 20, b. in East Haddam, res. East Haddam, Apr. 20, 1856, by Rev. Isaac Parsons. Int. pub. Apr. 19, 1856	4	84-5
Amasa, s. Beriah & Lucy, b. Nov. 19, 1808	2	162
Azariah Brainerd, s. Beriah & Lucy, b. Mar. 23, 1816	2	162
David Cicero, s. Beriah & Lucy, b. July 24, 1811	2	162
Edward, s. Almira D., ship carpenter, b. Aug. 4, 1851	3	33-4
Lucretia Jones, d. Beriah & Lucy, b. Feb. 8, 1818	2	162
Seth C., of Hebron, m. Esther **CHAMPLIN**, of East Haddam, Nov. 26, 1835, by Rev. Joseph Harvey, of Colchester	3	140-1
Sophia Amelia, d. Beriah & Lucy, b. Feb. 15, 1821	2	162
Sophia H., of East Haddam, m. Hezekiah **KNOWLES**, of Westbrook, Oct. 20, 1844, by Rev. W[illia]m S. Simmons	3	201
-----, child of Ahira, mechanic, ae 41, & Ann Eliza, ae 37, b. Aug. 3, 1847	4	3-4
-----, s. Ahira D., ship carpenter, & Ann E., b. Aug. 4, 1848	4	13-4
WHEELOCK, Alette, m. Marcus **STEWART**, b. of East Haddam, Nov. 11, 1821, by Josiah Griffin, J. P.	3	17
Ellen Louisa, d. Solomon B. & Ruth, b. May 20, 1844	3	126
WHITE, Abigail, d. Elijah & Abigail, b. Mar. 6, 1752	LR5	269
Abigail, d. Amos & Sarah, b. Oct. 16, 1769	2	225
Abigail, Mrs. m. Dr. Sylvanus **LINDSLEY**, b. of East Haddam, Apr. 28, 1793	2	257
Alice, ae 21, b. at Castle Conner, Ireland, res. East		

	Vol.	Page
WHITE, (cont.)		
Haddam, m. William **ADAMS**, ae 23, b. at Montevella, Ireland, res. East Haddam, Oct. 26, 1856, at Moodus, by John Lynch. Int. pub. Oct. 11, 1856	4	105
Amos, s. Amos White & Mary Gates, b. Feb. 9, 1767	LR7	412
Amos, m. Sarah **GRISWOLD**, Apr. 8, 1767	LR7	412
Amos, m. Sarah **GRISWOLD**, b. of East Haddam, Apr. 8, 1767	2	225
Amos, s. Amos & Sarah, b. Oct. 13, 1772	2	225
Anna, of Colchester, m. Daniel **GATES**, Jr., of East Haddam, Aug. 27, 1770	2	10
Bets[e]y L, ae 37, b. in Chatham, Mass., res. East Haddam, m. 2d h. Griswold **MINER**, carpenter, ae 50, b. in Lyme, res. East Haddam, June 5, 1853, by Jacob Gardner	4	43-4
Carel, s. Dan[ie]l H. & Hannah, b. Feb. 25, 1789, in Granville, N. Y.	2	12
Charles, s. Amos & Sarah, b. Aug. 8, 1785	2	225
Daniel, s. Elijah & Abigail, b. Apr. 13, 1750	LR5	269
Daniel, s. Elijah & Abigail, d. Mar. 6, 1751	LR5	269
Daniel, s. Elijah & Abigail, b. Feb. 26, 1754	LR5	269
Daniel, s. Elijah & Abigail, d. Sept. 27, 1756	LR5	269
Daniel Hulbut, s. Elijah & Abigail, b. July 16, 1757	LR5	269
Daniel Hurlbut, m. Hannah **BRAINERD**, b. of East Haddam, Aug. 31, 1780	2	12
Daniel Hurlbut, d. Feb. 24, 1805, at Granville, N. Y.	2	13
Edward R., of East Haddam, m. Almira **FRANKLIN**, of Killingworth, May 6, 1857, at Killingworth, by Hiram Bell. License issued May 1, 1857	4	121
Elijah, s. Elijah & Abigail, b. Feb. 28, 1748	LR5	269
Elijah, Jr., m. Elizabeth **ARNOLD**, May 9, 1767	LR7	412
Elizabeth, d. Amos & Sarah, b. May 29, 1783	2	225
Fanny, d. D. H. [Daniel H.] & Hannah, b. Sept. 24, 1790, in Granville, N. Y.	2	12
Fanny, d. Dan[ie]l H. & Hannah, d. Jan. 4, 1796, at Granville, N. Y.	2	13
Fanny Fidelia, d. Dan[ie]l H. & Hannah, b. May 27, 1798, in Granville, N. Y.	2	12
Grange, s. Amos & Sarah, b. Feb. 11, 1781	2	225
George, s. Amos & Sarah, d. Apr. 27, 1782	2	226
George, 2d, s. Amos & Sarah, b. Sept. 8, 1787	2	225
Gideon Brainerd, s. Daniel H. & Hannah, b. Feb. 2, 1781, at Guilford	2	12
Gideon Brainerd, s. Dan[iel H. & Hannah, d. Oct. 6, 1795, at Granville, N. Y.	2	13
Hannah, m. Benjamin **REED**, b. of East Haddam, June 10, 1762	LR6	503
Hannah Adela, d. Dan[ie]l H. & Hannah, b. June 24, 1801, in Granville, N. Y.	2	12
Hope Lord, d. Dan[iel]l H. & Hannah, b. Aug. 10, 1786	2	12

	Vol.	Page
WHITE, (cont.)		
Jeremiah Gates Brainerd, s. Dan[ie]l H. & Hannah, b. Dec. 22, 1795, in Granville, N. Y.	2	12
Joseph, of Chatham, m. Hannah **GATES**, of East Haddam, Mar. 29, 1791	2	84
Mary, d. Timothy & Susannah, b. Dec. 15, 1752	LR5	564
Rachel, m. Samuel P. **LORD**, b. of East Haddam, Aug. 30, 1761	LR6	503
Samuel, s. Timothy & Susannah, b. Aug. 16, 1757	LR5	564
Sarah, d. Amos & Sarah, b. May 31, 1776	2	225
Sarah, of East Haddam, m. Sylvester **PRATT**, of Saybrook, Oct. 4, 1801	2	271
Sophia, d. Amos & Sarah, b. July 16, 1790	2	225
Sophia, d. Amos & Sarah, d. Nov. 23, 1790	2	226
Susannah, d. Timothy & Susannah, b. Oct. 5, 1749	LR5	564
Susannah, m. John **SPENCER**, b. of East Haddam, Oct. 28, 1772	2	76
William, s. Amos & Sarah, b. Aug. 16, 1774	2	225
William, s. Amos & Sarah, d. July 27, 1775	2	226
William, 2d, s. Amos & Sarah, b. Oct. 16, 1778	2	225
William, 2d, s. Amos & Sarah, d. Apr. 27, 1782	2	226
William, s. Daniel Hulbert & Hannah, b. Oct. 11, 1783	2	12
WHITLEY, Sarah, d. John & Sarah, b. Mar. 19, 1777, near Ball Town, N. Y.	2	50
WHITMAN,, [see also **WHITMORE**], Albert D., m. Elizabeth A. **CLARK**, May 21, 1844, by Rev. Isaac Parsons	3	199
Clarissa M., m. George W. **LESTER**, b. of East Haddam, Aug. 17, 1842	3	161
Julia Ann, m. John A. **SPENCER**, Aug. 5, 1849, by David A. Chapman	3	219
Martha Philenda, illeg. d. Julia A., ae 15, b. Jan. 2, 1849; father unknown	4	13-4
WHITMORE, [see also **WHITMAN**], Adelia, [d. Joseph & Electa], b. June 10, 1816	3	60-1
Adelia, m. Moses B. **WRIGHT**, b. of East Haddam, Apr. 29, 1832, by Rev. Peter G. Clarke	3	122
Adelia A., of East Haddam, m. James **BULKLEY**, of Waterford, Jan. 1, 1824, by Rev. Isaac Parsons	3	50-1
Almina, [d. Joseph & Electa], b. Feb. 10, 1818	3	60-1
Almina, of East Haddam, m. Martin **CHAPMAN**, of Haddam, Nov. 24, 1835, by Stephen A. Loper	3	140-1
Alvira, [d. Joseph & Electa], b. Apr. 27, 1814	3	60-1
Alvira, m. Dwight A. **LYMAN**, b. of Leesville, Sept. 4, 1831, by Rev. Isaac Parsons	3	119
Augusta, of East Haddam, m. Nehemiah **UPHAM**, of Grafton, Mass., [Sept.] 20, [1843], by Rev. Isaac Parsons	3	195
Carile, [d. Joseph & Electa], b. June 6, 1822	3	60-1
Carile, of East Haddam, m. Tryon A. **HOLMES**, of Norwalk,		

	Vol.	Page
WHITMORE, (cont.)		
May 12, 1839, by Rev. George Carrington, of Hadlyme	3	173
Clarissa M., m. George W. **LESTER**, b. of East Haddam, Aug. 17, 1842, by Isaac Parsons, M. G.	3	191
Ellen, of East Haddam, m. Lyman **UPHAM**, of Norwich, Apr. 23, 1848, by Rev. Isaac Parsons	3	212
Ellen J., ae 19, b. in East Haddam, res. Norwich, m. Lyman **UPHAM**, mechanic, ae 22, b. in Thomson, res. Norwich, Apr. 23, 1848, by Isaac Parsons	4	1-2
Emeline, [d. Joseph & Electa], b. Nov. 21, 1806	3	60-1
Emeline, of East Haddam, m. Jabez **SMITH**, of Chatham, Jan. 18, 1826, by Rev. Isaac Parsons	3	83
Fitch John, reputed s. of [ ]	LR2	1119
Fitch John, of East Haddam, m. Martha **STANELEFT**, of Middletown, Sept. 15, 1763	2	102
Frances E., of East Haddam, m. Charles H. **WITTER**, of Norwich, Aug. 23, 1852, by Rev. Isaac Parsons	3	236
Hannah, m. John **PARSEVAL**, Aug. 5, 1731	LR2	1123
Harriet A., m. Charles D. **WRIGHT**, b. of East Haddam, Mar. 1, 1828, by Rev. Peter G. Clarke	3	96
Harriet Adaline, [d. Joseph & Electa], b. Aug. 31, 1808	3	60-1
Jane E., of East Haddam, m. Seymour **KELLOGG**, of Colchester, Feb. 9, 1840, by Isaac Parsons, V. D. M.	3	176-7
Jane Elizabeth, [d. Joseph & Electa], b. Aug. 15, 1820	3	60-1
John, s. F[itch] John & Martha, b. July 3, 1781	2	102
Joseph, m. Electa **ACKLEY**, June 17, 1804	3	60-1
Joseph, farmer, b. in East Haddam, res. East Haddam, married, d. Oct. 16, 1855, ae 73 y. 10 m. 21 d.	4	69
Julia A., ae 15, b. in Foster, R. I., res. East Haddam, m. John A. **SPENCER**, farmer, ae 24, of East Haddam, Aug. 5, 1848, by David Chapman	4	9-10
Louisa, d. [Joseph & Electa], b. Aug. 7, 1810	3	60-61
Louisa, of East Haddam, m. Halsey **BROWN**, of Chatham, Nov. 24, 1831, by Rev. Isaac Parsons	3	121
Louisa, m. Halsey **BROWN**, Nov. 24, 1831	3	179
Lucy Ann, [d. Joseph & Electa], b. July 4, 1812	3	60-61
Lucy Ann, m. Edwin **BRAINERD**, b. of East Haddam, Nov. 24, 1831, by Rev. Isaac Parsons	3	121
Lydia, d. F[itch] John & Martha, b. Jan. 23, 1773	2	102
Martha, d. F[itch] John & Martha, b. Mar. 22, 1766	2	102
Mary, d. F[itch] John & Martha, b. Oct. 27, 1775	2	102
Mary Ann, [d. Joseph & Electa], b. Aug. 27, 1804	3	60-61
Mary Ann, of East Haddam, m. Sith **ROGERS**, of Lyme, Oct. 28, 1821, by Rev. Isaac Parsons	3	15
Oliver, s. F[itch] John & Martha, b. May 14, 1770	2	102
Perley D., m. Mary P. **SPENCER**, June 16, 1828, by Rev. Isaac Parsons	3	99
Phebe, d. John F. & Martha, b. Oct. 10, 1778	2	18

	Vol.	Page
WHITMORE, (cont.)		
Phebe, d. Fitch John & Martha, b. Oct. 10, 1778	2	102
Timothy, s. Fitch John & Martha, b. Feb. 20, 1764	2	102
Zolva, Rev., of North Guilford, m. Carisle* M. **CONE**, of East Haddam, Oct. 16, 1821, by Rev. Isaac Parsons (*Carrol?)	3	15
WHITTLESEY, John, of Salem, m.Marcia **WILLIAMS**, of East Haddam, Oct. 11, 1829, by Rev. Alvan Ackley	3	103
WICKHAM, WIKHAM, Asenath, d. David & Dimmes, b. May 13, 1767	LR7	4
Calvin B., m. Nancy **BLISH**, Sept. 14, 1830, by Rev. Alvan Ackely	3	108
Calvin B., d. Sept. 29, 1837, ae 36	3	123
Calvin Brooks, s. Russel[l] & Vianne, b. June 30, 1801	2	265
David, m. Dimmes **ACKLEY**, b. of East Haddam, Aug. 23, 1764	LR7	4
David, s. David & Dimmis, b. June 26, 1772	2	64
Dimmis, d. David & Dimmis, b. Mar. 17, 1777	2	64
Harriot, d. Russell & Vianne, b. Mar. 1, 1799, at Haddam	2	265
Hiram, of West Stockbridge, Mass., m. Betsey A. **SMITH**, of East Haddam, May 19, 1842, by Tho[ma]s G. Salter	3	190
Israel Dutton, s. David & Dimmis, b. Oct. 6, 1769	2	64
Lydia, d. David & Dimmis, b. Aug. 17, 1781	2	64
Nancy, [twin with Philo], d. David & Dimmis, b. Apr. 14, 1785	2	64
Oren Olcott, s. Russell & Vianne, d. July 22, 1812	2	265
Phebe, d. David & Dimmes, b. Apr. 27, 1765	LR7	4
Philo, [twin with Nancy], s. David & Dimmis, b. Apr. 14, 1785	2	64
Rensley, s. David & Dimmis, b. Feb. 15, 1778	2	64
Robert U., m. Henrietta **CONE**, b. of East Haddam, Sept. 4, 1831, by Rev. Isaac Parsons	3	120
Robert Usher, s. Russell & Vianne, b. July 3, 1805	2	265
Russel[l], s. David & Dimmis, b. Nov. 2, 1774	2	64
Russel[l], of East Haddam, m. Vianne **SEXTON**, of Colchester, [1798?]	2	265
Russell Sexton, s. Russell & Vianne, b. Sept. 11, 1808	2	265
Ruth, d. David & Dimmis, b. Aug. 6, 1779	2	64
WICKWARE, Benjamin, d. Feb. 25, 1841	3	123
WILBUR, Harriet, of East Haddam, m. Howland **DAWES**, of Windsor, Mass., Apr. 30, 1837, by Nathaniel Miner	3	151
WILCOX, Elizabeth, d. Asa, farmer, & Nancy A., b. May 24, 1850	4	25-6
Thankful, of Killingworth, m. Crippen **HURD**, of East Haddam, June 5, 1798, by Rev. Henry Ely	2	22
WILDER, Elijah, m. Hannah **SPENCER**, Nov. 26, 1778	2	10
Hannah, d. Joseph & Hannah, b. May 24, 1759	LR6	513
Hannah, w. of Joseph, d. Oct. 22, 1762	LR6	513
Sarah, d. Joseph & Hannah, b. Oct. 19, 1762	LR6	513
Thomas, s. Joseph & Hannah, b. Feb. 28, 1756	LR6	513
WILLARD, Mary C., m. Diodate G. **COON**, alias **CALHOUN**, b.		

	Vol.	Page
WILLARD, (cont.)		
of East Haddam, Apr. 23, 1843, by Rev. Charles William Bradley	3	194
Tamzin, of Saybrook, m. Huntington **GILLET**, of Colchester, Dec. 8, 1824, by Rev. Isaac Parson	3	66-7
WILLEY, WILLE, WILLEE, Aaron, s. Joseph & Rebeckah, b. Sept. 1, 1751	LR8	6
Aaron, s. Aaron & Rebec[c]ah, b. Mar. 2, 1776	2	10
Abell, m. Han[n]ah **BRAY**, July 17, 1703	LR1	4
Abigail, m. Elisha **BECKWITH**, b. of East Haddam, Aug. 16, 1759	LR7	5
Abigail, w. of Cyrus, d. June [ ], 1791, ae 21	2	191
Abigail Cone, m. William **MARKHAM**, b. of East Haddam, June 4, 1761	LR6	503
Abraham, s. Al[l]en & Mehitable, b. May 11, 1750	LR2	1117
Abraham, m. Susanna **BECKWITH**, b. of East Haddam, Jan. 12, 1773	2	64
Abraham Wolcott, s. Abraham & Susanna, b. May 7, 1788	2	64
Alfred, m. Clarissa **HAVENS**, [Oct.] 11, [1829], by Josiah Griffin, J. P.	3	103
Alice, b. in East Haddam, res. Millington, d. May 28, 1851, ae 78	4	39-40
Alice, see also Elles		
Allin, s. John & Elizabeth, b. Sept. 29, 1700	LR1	576
Al[l]en, m. Mehittable **RICHARDSON**, May 7, 1730	LR2	1122
Allen, s. Allen & Mehittabell, b. Feb. 11, 1730/31	LR2	1122
Ann, d. Allen & Mehittable, b. June 4, 1734	LR2	1122
Anna, d. Abraham & Susanna, b. Oct. 19, 1773	2	64
Ansel, s. Lemuel & Susannah, b. July 18, 1764	LR7	7
Asa, s. John, Jr. & Sarah, b. Sept. 6, 1740	LR2	1102
Asa, s. John, Jr. & Sarah, d. Oct. 22, 1743	LR2	1102
Azubah, d. Jonathan & Mary, b. May 24, 1767	2	60
Barak Beckwith, s. Abraham & Susannah, b. Mar. 24, 1782	2	64
Barnabus, s. Joseph & Rebeckah, b. Dec. 27, 1747	LR8	6
Benjamin, s. Joseph & Lucretia, b. Sept. 16, 1737	LR2	1100
Benjamin, s. Ephraim, Jr., & Bethier, b. May 12, 1788	2	166
Carolina, d. Joseph & Rebeckah, b. Oct. 22, 1767	LR8	6
Charles, s. Noah, Jr. & Elizabeth, b. Mar. 25, 1777	2	180
Cleament Bates, s. Jonathan & Mary, b. Apr. 19, 1765	2	60
Cyrus, s. Joseph & Rebeckah, b. Mar. 22, 1762	LR8	6
Cyrus, m. Abigail **ACKLEY**, b. of East Haddam, Apr. 6, 1788	2	190
Cyrus, s. Cyrus & Abigail, b. Feb. 20, 1789	2	190
David, s. John, Jr. & Sarah, b. Apr. 19, 1725	LR2	1102
Dimmis, d. Joseph & Rebeckah, b. May 27, 1754	LR8	6
Demis, d. Nov. 9, 1836, in the 83rd y. of her age	3	123
Elizabeth, d. John & Elizabeth, b. Dec. 29, 1701	LR1	576
Elizabeth, d. Joseph & Lucretia, b. Jan. 24, 1728	LR2	1100
Elizabeth, m. Samuel **CONE**, b. of East Haddam, Sept. 23,		

	Vol.	Page
WILLEY, WILLE, WILLEE, (cont.)		
1747	LR7	1
Elizabeth, d. Noah, Jr. & Elizabeth, b. July 3, 1771	2	180
Elizabeth, d. Noah, Jr. & Elizabeth, d. Nov. 25, 1774	2	181
Elizabeth, d. Noah, Jr. & Elizabeth, b. Dec. 22, 1774	2	180
Elizabeth C., m. Edward **WORTHINGTON**, b. of East Haddam, Dec. 9, 1824, by Rev. Isaac Parsons	3	69
Elles, d. Jonathan & Mary, b. Apr. 30, 1769	2	60
Elles, see also Alice		
Ephraim, s. Joseph & Lucretia, b. July 18, 1740	LR2	1100
Ephraim, Jr., m. Bethier **ACKLEY**, Aug. 14, 1781	2	166
Ethan Allen, s. Abraham & Susannah, b. Mar. 6, 1776	2	64
George, s. Noah & Elizabeth, b. Oct. 24, 1786	2	180
Grace, d. Joseph & Lucretia, b. Oct. 6, 1742	LR2	1100
Hannah, d. Jonathan & Mary, b. Apr. 23, 1771	2	60
Harriet, m. Gurden **FULLER**, June 7, 1832, by Nathaniel Miner	3	124
Harriet, m. Gurdon **FULLER**, June 7, 1832	3	139
Hesther, d. Joseph & Lucretia, b. May 1, 1736	LR2	1100
Hesther, d. Joseph & Lucretia, d. Nov. 13, 1736	LR2	1100
Hester, m. John **NEEDHAM**, b. of East Haddam, Aug. 11,1763	LR7	6
Hiram, of New London, m. Charity W. **MOSELEY**, of East Haddam, Sept. 6, 1843, by Rev. Stephen Alonzo Loper, of Hadlyme, in Hadlyme	3	195
Hubbard, s. Ephraim, 2d, & Bethier, b. Sept. 21, 1781	2	166
Huldah, d. Noah, Jr. & Elizabeth, b. Mar. 21, 1773	2	180
Huldah, d. Noah & Elizabeth, d. Dec. 2, 1774	2	181
Jabez, s. Al[l]en & Mehetable, b. May 7, 1741	LR2	1117
Jabez, s. Al[l]en & Mehetable, d. Aug. 23, 1744	LR2	1117
Jabez, s. Al[l]en & Mehitable, b. Nov. 22, 1747; d. July 7, 1751	LR2	1117
Jane, d. Abell & Han[n]ah, b. Mar. 22, 1704/5	LR1	4
Jemima, d. Joseph & Rebeckah, b. Aug. 6, 1758	LR8	6
Jemima, 2d, had d. Rachel **HARVEY**, b. June 24, 1786; reputed father Thomas **HARVEY**	LR8	6
John, m. Elizabeth **HARV[E]Y**, Oct. [ ], 1698	LR1	576
John, s. John & Elizabeth, b. May 24, 1699	LR1	576
John, Jr., m. Sarah **SANDERS**, Apr. 5, 1722	LR2	1102
John, s. Allen & Mehittable, b. Oct. 11, 1732	LR2	1122
John, Jr., d. Nov. 13, 1743	LR2	1102
John, s. Rebeckah, 2d, b. Jan. 9, 1778	LR8	6
Jonathan, s. John, Jr. & Sarah, b. July 10, 1737	LR2	1102
Jonathan, m. Mary **BATES**, b. of East Haddam, May 4, 1758	2	60
Jonathan, s. Jonathan & Mary, b. June 2, 1763	2	60
Joseph, s. John & Elizabeth, b. Apr. 16, 1705	LR1	576
Joseph, m. Lucretia **WILLEY**, May 22, 1727	LR2	1100
Joseph, s. Joseph & Lucretia, b. Mar. 22, 1734	LR2	1100
Joseph, 2d, of East Haddam, m. Irena **BANNING**, of Lyme, Mar. 3. 1764	2	174
Judah. s. Al[l]en & Mehitable, b. Apr. 23, 1743	LR2	1117

	Vol.	Page
WILLEY, WILLE, WILLEE, (cont.)		
Kezia, d. John, Jr. & Sarah, b. Mar. 26, 1723	LR2	1102
Keziah, m. Elihu **MINOR**, Mar. 21, 1745	LR3	10
Keziah, d. Jonathan & Mary, b. Sept. 28, 1773	2	60
Lemuel, s. Allen & Mehittable, b. Mar. 7, 1738/9	LR2	1122
Lemuel,m.Susannah **FULLER**, b. of East Haddam, Jan. 3, 1764	LR7	7
Lucretia, m. Joseph **WILLEY**, May 22, 1727	LR2	1100
Lucretia, d. Joseph & Lucretia, b. July 9, 1732	LR2	1100
Lucretia, m. Nathaniel **ACKLEY**, 3rd, Feb. 16, 1756	LR6	503
Lidea, d. John & Elizabeth, b. Apr. 15, 1707	LR1	576
Lidea, m. Daniell **BOOGE**, Nov. 29, 1722	LR1	571
Lydiah, d. Al[l]en & Mehitable, b. June 3, 1745	LR2	1117
Mary, d. John & Elizabeth, b. Dec. 13, 1703/4	LR1	576
Mary, d. Joseph & Lucretia, b. Oct. 18, 1730	LR2	1100
Mary, d. Jonathan & Mary, b. Mar. 5, 1761	2	60
Mary, d. Ephraim, 2d, & Bethier, b. Sept. 11, 1783	2	166
Mary, m. Alfred **CHAPMAN**, b. of East Haddam, Nov. 14, 1820, by Rev. W[illia]m Lyman	2	327
Mary P., of East Haddam, m. Stephen O. **DAY**, of Colchester, Oct. 6, 1834, by Rev. Joseph Vaill, of Hadlyme	3	135
Matilda Ann, m. Orren **WARNER**, b. of East Haddam, Dec. 8, 1830, by Rev. Peter G. Clarke	3	115
Mehittabell, d. John & Elizabeth, b. Sept. 14, 1711	LR1	576
Mehitable, m. John **MILLARD**, Mar. 18, 1736	LR2	1115
Mehittable, d. Allen & Mehittable, b. Sept. 29, 1736	LR2	1122
Mehetabel Richardson, d. Abraham & Susannah, b. Mar. 28, 1780	2	64
Meriam, of Lyme, m. Daniel **ATWOOD**, of East Haddam, Dec. 4, 1764	LR8	5
Nathan, s. John, Jr. & Sarah, b. Mar. 1, 1734/5	LR2	1102
Noah, Jr., m. Elizabeth **ANDREWES**, b. of East Haddam, Oct. 25, 1770	2	180
Noah, s. Noah & Elizabeth, b. Aug. 15, 1780	2	180
Oris, d. Ephraim, Jr. & Bethier, b. Feb. 12, 1786	2	166
Phebe, d. John & Elizabeth, b. Jan. 6, 1709	LR1	576
Rachel, wid., m. Samuel **GATES**, b. of East Haddam, (or said to be), Apr. 5, 1765	LR8	5
Rebeckah, d. Joseph & Rebeckah, b. Aug. 20, 1749	LR8	6
Rebeckah, 2d, had s. John, b. Jan. 9, 1778	LR8	6
Richard Andrewes, s. Noah & Elizabeth, b. Nov. 19, 1784	2	180
Rufus, m. Selina **CHAPMAN**, b. of East Haddam, Dec. 31, 1821, by Josiah Griffing, J. P.	3	19
Salmon F., m. Durinda **SNOW**, June 3, 1828, by Rev. Isaac Parsons	3	99
Sarah, m. Joseph **BECKWITH**, b. of East Haddam, (or said to be) Oct. 9. 1737	LR8	4
Seth, s. Joseph & Rebeckah, b. Dec. 27. 1756	LR8	6
Sidney B., m. Lucretia B. **GREEN**, June 19, 1831, by Rev.		

	Vol.	Page
WILLEY, WILLE, WILLEE, (cont.)		
Peter G. Clarke	3	119
Susanna, d. Jonathan & Mary, b. Nov. 23, 1758	2	60
Susanna Waddams, d. Abraham & Susanna, b. May 17, 1785	2	64
Temperance, d. Joseph, 2d, & Irena, b. Dec. 15, 1768	2	174
Temperance, m. David **PHELPS**, b. of East Haddam, Feb. 12, 1784	2	174
Titus, s. Joseph & Rebeckah, b. July 3, 1764	LR8	6
Warren S., m. Mattalena C. **WRIGHT**, b. of East Haddam, Sept. 27, 1829, by Rev. Peter G. Clarke	3	102
William M., m. Elizabeth B. **EMMONS**, b. of East Haddam, Oct. 10, 1832, by Nathaniel Miner	3	127
William M., ae 51, b. at East Haddam, res. East Haddam, m. Ellen L. **KIDDER**, ae 26, b. [ ], Mass., res. East Haddam, Nov. 28, 1855, at Hadlyme, by Rev. E. B. Hillard. Int. pub. Nov. 21, 1855	4	67
-----, d. John & Elizabeth, b. June 7, 1713	LR1	576
-----, s. John & Elizabeth, b. Aug. 28, 1716	LR1	576
WILLIAMS, Abigail, w. Robertson, d. Oct. 12, 1741	LR3	7
Abigail, d. Robertson & Elizabeth, b. Sept. 5, 1745	LR3	7
Abigail, d. Robertson & Elizabeth, d. Apr. 21, 1746	LR3	7
Abigail, of Colchester, m. Enoch **ARNOLD**, of East Haddam, Apr. 23, 1755	LR3	12
Abraham, s. Charles, b. Feb. 23, 1721	LR1	570
Abraham, m. Sarah **WILLIAMS**, Feb. 1, 1753	LR4	465
Alice, d. Philip & Hannah, b. Nov. 3, 1747	LR3	4
Asa, s. Charles, Jr. & Elizabeth, b. Jan. 18, 1765	2	84
Caleb, s. Charles, Jr. & Elisabeth, b. Apr. 12, 1767	2	84
Caroline C., of Lyme, m. George G. **CAPLES**, of East Haddam, Sept. 24, 1848, by Nathaniel Miner	3	216
Charles, m. Mary **ROBINSON**, Dec. 17, 1713	LR1	570
Charles, s. Charles & Mary, b. June 10, 1735	LR1	570
Charles, Jr., of East Haddam, m. Elizabeth **HUBBARD**, of Middletown, Mar. 11, 1756	LR6	506
Charles, s. Charles, Jr. & Elizabeth, b. Mar. 3, 1761	LR6	506
Charles, d. Apr. 28, 1769	2	85
Daniell, s. Weeks & Mahittabell, b. Sept. 29, 1719	LR2	b
Datus, m. Clarissa M. **PECK**, Aug. 25, 1824, by Rev. Noah C. Saxton	3	64-5
Deborah, d. Weeks & Mehitable, b. Aug. 13, 1731	LR2	1094
Dewitt C., of Chatham, m. Fanny D. **SELDEN**, of East Haddam, June 23, 1850, by Rev. Isaac Parsons	3	225
Dewitt C., farmer, ae 25, of Chatham, m. Fanny D. **SELDEN**, ae 26, of East Haddam, June 23, 1850, by Isaac Parsons	4	19-20
Electa, of East Haddam, m. Warren **FULLER**, of Salem, Feb. 26, 1832, by Rev. Alvan Ackley	3	121
Elena, d. Charles, b. Mar. 23, 1723	LR1	570
Elener, m. Silas **CLARK**, Mar. 26, 1747	LR5	270

	Vol.	Page
WILLIAMS, (cont.)		
Elijah, s. Weeks & Mahittabell, b. May 21, 1727	LR2	b
Eliza U., m. Albert **HARRIS**, b. of East Haddam, [Feb.] 15, [1842], by Nathaniel Miner. Int. pub.	3	189
Elizabeth, d. Weeks & Meheyable, b. Jan. 11, 1736	LR2	1094
Elizabeth, m. Alexander **ROL[L]O**, Aug. 20, 1752	LR4	464
Elizabeth, w. of Weeks, d. Sept. 19, 1755	LR5	a
Elizabeth, d. Robinson & Elizabeth, b. Aug. 20, 1758	LR3	7
Elsey, of East Haddam, m. Francis O. **BIDWELL**, of Chatham, Oct. 27, 1834, by Rev. Isaac Parsons. Witness: N. L. Foster	3	135
[E]unis, d. Charles, b. Feb. 22, 1719	LR1	570
Eunice, m. William **BOOGE**, Oct. 17, 1745	LR3	3
Eunice, d. Robinson & Elizabeth, b. Dec. 21, 1763	LR3	7
George Gilbert, s. Datus & Clarissa, b. Oct. 9, 1826	3	64-65
Hannah, d. Philip & Hannah, b. Oct. 30, 1749	LR3	4
Hannah, w. of Philip, d. Feb. 11, 1754	LR3	4
Harriet M., m. Hezekiah W. **PERCIVAL**, Jr., Sept. 5, 1825, by Rev. Isaac Parsons	3	79
Harriet Maria, d. Silvester & Mary, b. Dec. 23, 1804	2	289
Henry, s. Jonathan & Abigail, b. Aug. 8, 1765	LR7	4
Henry Egbert, s. Datus & Clarissa, b. June 5, 1825	3	64-65
Hubbard, s. Charles & Elisabeth, b. Sept. 2, 1769	2	84
Huldah, d. Philip & Hannah, b. Dec. 4, 1751	LR3	4
Isaac, s. Charles, Jr. & Elizabeth, b. Apr. 21, 1759	LR6	506
Isaac, s. Charles, Jr. & Elisabeth, d. Dec. 31, 1761	2	85
Isaac, s. Charles, Jr. & Elizabeth, b. Jan. 6, 1763	2	84
Isaac, d. Oct. 19, 1854, ae 54	3	123
John, m. Maria **LOOMIS**, b. colored, May 7, 1835, by Thomas C. Bordman, J. P.	3	137
Jonathan, s. Robertson & Elizabeth, b. Feb. 20, 1743/4	LR3	7
Jonathan, m. Abigail **BURR**, b. of East Haddam, Mar. 29, 1764	LR7	4
Joseph Johnson, s. Charles & Elisabeth, b. Feb. 18, 1772	2	84
Julius C., m. Sarah Ann **GRIFFIN**, Feb. 6, 1839, by Rev. Nathaniel Miner	3	168
Lois, d. Weeks & Mehitable, b. Jan. 2, 1741 (birth-mark)	LR2	1094
Lydia, d. Charles, b. Jan. 30, 1714	LR1	570
Lidia, d. Robertson & Elizabeth, b. Feb. 13, 1750	LR3	7
Marcia, of East Haddam, m. John **WHITTLESEY**, of Salem, Oct. 11, 1829, by Rev. Alvan Ackley	3	103
Martha, ae 16, m. Joseph A., **HURD**, shoemaker, ae 31, b. of East Haddam, Mar. 25, 1850, by S. D. Jewett	4	19-20
Mary, d. Weeks & Mahittabell, b. Jan. 21, 1725	LR2	b
Mary, d. Charles & Mary, b. Nov. 22, 1732	LR1	570
Mary, m. Nathaniel **ACKLY**, b. of East Haddam, Apr. 16, 1734	LR5	560
Mary, d. Robinson & Elizabeth, b. Apr. 4, 1753	LR3	7
Mary, wid. of Charles, d. Feb. 7, 1774	2	85
Mary, m. Asa **CHAPMAN**, b. of East Haddam, Nov. 26, 1778	2	122

	Vol.	Page
WILLIAMS, (cont.)		
Mary, m. Thomas **ACKLEY**, 3rd, Feb. 11, 1830, by Rev. Isaac Parsons	3	104
Mehitable, d. Weeks & Mehitable, b. May 21, 1729	LR2	1094
Mehitable, w. of Weeks, d. Dec. 16, 1742	LR2	1094
Mehitable, d. Weeks & Mehitable, d. Jan. 2, 1757	LR2	1094
Nathan H., s. Francis, ae 34, & Asenath, ae 31, d. Sept. 30, 1855	4	78
Philip, s. Charles, b. Feb. 9, 1717	LR1	570
Philip, m. Hannah **CROCKAH**, Feb. 13, 1745/6	LR3	4
Philip, m. Ruth **ARNOLD**, b. of East Haddam, Feb. 24, 1761	LR3	4
Philip, of East Haddam, m. Mrs. Rachel **BLUSH**, of Colchester, June 11, 1788	2	14
Rachel, d. Robinson & Elizabeth, b. Sept. 27, 1761	LR3	7
Robertson, m. Abigail **ACKL[E]Y**, May 7, 1741	LR3	7
Robertson, m. Elizabeth **HURD**, Apr. 21, 1743	LR3	7
Robinson, s. Charles, b. May 24, 1715	LR1	570
Robinson, s. Robinson & Elizabeth, b. Mar. 15, 1755	LR3	7
Roxana B., m. Edmund **SMITH**, b. of East Haddam, June 1, 1834, by Rev. Stephen Beach	3	134
Roxana b., m. Edmund **SMITH**, June 1, 1834	3	162-3
Russell E., m. Ursula **BRAINERD**, b. of East Haddam, Apr. 26, 1835, by Nathaniel Miner	3	138
Ruth, d. Philip & Ruth, b. June 14, 1763	LR3	4
Ruth, w. of Philip, d. Sept. 18, 1787	LR3	4
Sarah, d. Weeks & Mehitable, b. Jan. 10, 1734	LR2	1094
Sarah, m. Abraham **WILLIAMS**, Feb. 1, 1753	LR4	465
Solomon, s. Robertson & Elizabeth, b. Nov. 20, 1748	LR3	7
Sylvester N., m. Cynthia L. **BRAINERD**, b. of East Haddam. Feb. 25, 1834, by Rev. Isaac Parsons	3	133
Silvester Nelson, s. Silvester & Mary, b. Nov. 26, 1806	2	289
Thomas(?), s. Charles, b. Mar. 12, 1725	LR1	570
Thomas (?), s. Charles, b. Jan. 25, 1728	LR1	570
Weeks, m. Mehitable **CONE**, Dec. 25, 1718	LR2	1094
Weeks, s. Weeks & Mahittabell, b. Apr. 19, 1722	LR2	b
William H., m. Pleiades B. **LAY**, b. of Saybrook, Aug. 8, 1831, by Rev. Isaac Parsons	3	119
Zachariah, s. Weeks & Mehetable, b. Apr. 29, 1738	LR2	1094
Zachariah, m. Sibel **LAMB**, b. of East Haddam, Nov. 21, 1769	LR8	4
Zachariah, d. Oct. 29, 1770	2	27
-------, s. Henry G., mechanic, ae 31, & Joanna, ae 27, b. July 10, 1855	4	79
WINSLOW, Allen, s. Jesse & Kaziah, b. Oct. 15, 1786	2	104
Charles, s. Pardon & Anna, b. Mar. 16, 1796	2	253
Jonathan, s. Jesse & Kazia, b. May 31, 1783	2	104
Mary, d. Jesse & Kazia, b. Feb. 1, 1788	2	104
Pardon, m. Anna **WARNER**, b. of East Haddam, Sept. 6, 1795	2	253
WHITTER, Charles H., of Norwich, m. Frances E. **WHITMORE**,		

	Vol.	Page
WITTER, (cont.)		
of East Haddam, Aug. 23, 1852, by Rev. Isaac Parsons	3	236
WOOD, Carolina, of Lyme, m. Ephraim **BECKWITH**, of East Haddam, Dec. 29, 1783	2	170
WOODRUFF, Hiram, of Middletown, m. Lydia **BURKE**, of East Haddam, Oct. 31, 1821, by Rev. W[illia]m Lyman	3	17
WOODWORTH, Daniel, m. Lucretia **HOLMES**, Aug. 14, 1831, by Rev. Joseph Vaill	3	119
Mary, m. Samuel **BARRY**, Nov. 3, 1823, by Rev. Daniel Austin, at Bozrah	3	117
WORTHINGTON, Catharine E., of East Haddam, m. Gustavus **ROOTE**, of Portland, Mar. 7, 1854, by Rev. Isaac Parsons	3	239
Catharine E., mantua maker, ae 23, of East Haddam, m. Gustavus **ROOTE**, stone cutter, ae 30, b. in Marlborough, res. Portland, Mar. 7, 1854	4	41-2
Catharine E., mantua maker, ae 23, of East Haddam, m. Gustavus **ROOTE**, stone cutter, ae 30, b. in Marlborough, res. Portland, Mar. 7, 1854	4	51-2
Dorothy, w. of Col. Elias, d. Mar. 12, 1791	2	256
Edward, m. Elizabeth C. **WILLEY**, b. of East Haddam, Dec. 9, 1824, by Rev. Isaac Parsons	3	69
Elias, Col., of Colchester, m. Mrs. Dorothy **CONE**, of East Haddam, Jan. 10, 1790	2	265
Nicholos, m. Harriet Eliza **STARK**, b. of Colchester, Sept. 15, 1828, by Rev. Peter G. Clarke	3	100
Prudence, m. Asa **SMITH**, Jr., May 7, 1830, by Rev. Joseph Harvey, of Colchster	3	107
Rebecca R., of East Haddam, m. Alexander **ARTHUR**, of Chatham, Jan. 18, 1832, by Rev. Isaac Parsons	3	121
Sarah Tracy, m. Sylvester **GOFF**, July 11, 1830, by Isaac Parsons	3	107
WRIGHT, RIGHT, Ann T., m. Henry F. **GARDNER**, b. of East Haddam, Mar. 11, 1851, by Rev. Alpheas Geer	3	231
Azubah M., ae 20, b. in Lyme, res. East Haddam, m. Edgar M. **MARTIN**, ae 25, of East Haddam, Oct. 1, 1856, by Rev. W[illia]m Harris. Int. pub. Sept. 26, 1856	4	101
Charles D., m. Harriet A. **WHITMORE**, b. of East Haddam, Mar. 1, 1828, by Rev. Peter G. Clarke	3	96
David, of Saybrook, m. Hannah **ACKLEY**, of East Haddam, June 16, 1825, by Rev. Isaac Parsons	3	76-77
[E]unice, d. Samuel & Rebeckah, b. May 17, 1774	2	86
James W., m. Electa A. **COON**, b. of East Haddam, Apr. 13, 1835, by Nathaniel Miner	3	137
Julia M., ae 21, b. in Winsted, Ms., m. Noadiah B. **GATES**, ae 28, of East Haddam, Aug. 13, 1848, by H. Forbush	4	1-2
Lucy P., m. Mason H. **SILLIMAN**, b. of East Haddam, Feb. 19, 1843, by Rev. Alex[ande]r Burguess	3	193
Mary, m. Zachariah **SPENCER**, b. of East Haddam, Nov. 11,		

	Vol.	Page
WRIGHT, RIGHT, (cont.)		
1766	LR7	415
Mary, d. Samuel & Rebeckah, b. Nov. 19, 1777	2	86
Mary Elizabeth, d. Charles D. & Harriet A., b. Dec. 20, 1828	3	106
Mary S., m. Alphonso M. **HYDE**, b. of East Haddam, Mar. 12, 1829, by Rev. Peter G. Clark	3	101
Matelena, d. Charles C., wheelwright, ae 46, & Harriet, b. Sept. 14, 1849	4	25-6
Mattalena C., m. Warren S. **WILLEY**, b. of East Haddam, Sept. 27, 1829, by Rev. Peter G. Clarke	3	102
Moses B., m. Adelia **WHITMORE**, b. of East Haddam, Apr. 29, 1832, by Rev. Peter G. Clarke	3	122
Prudence C., of East Haddam, m. Roswell **DAVISON**, of Brooklyn, N. Y., May 26, 1831, by Rev. Peter G. Clarke	3	116
Prudence C., m. Roswell **DAVISON**, May 26, 1831	3	157
Rebecca Adaline, of East Haddam, m. Daniel C. **TAYLOR**, of Middletown, May 15, 1842, by Tho[ma]s G. Salter	3	190
Samuel, s. Samuel & Martha, b. June 28, 1753	LR6	a
Samuel, of East Haddam, m. Rebeckah **DIXON***, of Chatham, Dec. 22, 1773 (***DICKINSON**" written in pencil)	2	86
Timothy, m. Matilda **GELSTON**, Jan. 10, 1821, by Rev. Solomon Blakesley	3	1
Warren A., m. Susan **RICH**, b. of East Haddam, Jan. 5, 1856, at the house of Mrs. Rich, by W[illia]m Cone	4	80
William, s. Samuel & Rebeckah, b. Feb. 13, 1776	2	86
-------, child of James W., farmer, ae 38, & Electa A., ae 37, b. Sept. 7, 1848	4	5-6
-------, d. Oct. 5, 1848, ae 1 m.	4	7-8
-------, s. Nathan S., laborer, ae 43, & Harriet D., ae 37, b. Jan. 15, 1850 (Perhaps "June 15")	4	23-4
-------, d. Warren, farmer, ae 19, & Susan E., ae 16, b. Sept. 28, 1856	4	100
WYLLIS, WILLYS, Ann, d. Rich[ar]d & Lucinda, b. May 29, 1805	2	146
Barnabas, s. Rich[ar]d & Lucinda, b. July 24, 1801	2	146
Elizabeth, d. Rich[ar]d & Lucinda, b. July 20, 1803	2	146
Julia, d. Rich[ar]d & Lucinda, b. Oct. 29, 1809	2	146
Lucinda, d. Rich[ar]d & Lucinda, b. Oct. 7, 1799	2	146
Lucina, d. Rich[ar]d & Lucinda, b. Oct. 4, 1811	2	146
Matilda, d. Rich[ar]d & Lucinda, b. June 28, 1807	2	146
Richard, s. Richard & Lucinda, b. Jan. 25, 1798	2	146
Richard, m. Lucinda **WARNER**, [ ]	2	146
YOUNG, Ann, m. Nelson L. **JOHNSON**, Nov. 28, 1839, by Edward P. Brownell, J. P.	3	174
Enos B, m. Julia **COLLINS**, b. of East Haddam, Dec. 7, 1845, by Rev. Stephen A. Loper, of Hadlyme	3	204
Eunice, m. Lemuel C. **DANIELS**, Dec. 13, 1801, by Rev. Daniel Selden, in Chatham	3	97
Hiram, of Chatham, m. Abigail **EMMONS**, of East Haddam,		

	Vol.	Page
YOUNG, (cont.)		
Apr. 12, 1825, by Rev. Isaac Parsons	3	72-3
Josephine Graham, m. Frederick Cornelius **JONES**, b. of New York City, June 15, 1859, at New York City	3	94
William B., of Chatham, m. Ellen A. **BRAINERD**, of East Haddam, Sept. 5, 1852, by Rev. Isaac Parsons	3	237
Zelotes, of Killingly, m. Mary E. **DOAN**, of Essex. Nov. 30, 1837, by Rev. David Todd	3	160
NO SURNAME		
Abigail, m. Samuel **CORBE**, Jan. 21, 1724/5	LR1	571
Cephes, [ ]	2	64
Hannah, d. Lieut, Thomas & Susan[n]ah, b. May 11, [ ]	LR1	580
Martha, m. Thomas **TANNER**, Jan. 3, 1716/17	LR2	1131
Mary Ann, d. [ ]	2	174
Punch, alias John **CAMMEL**, m. Axe **MASON** (negro), b. of East Haddam, Oct. 16, 1803 (People of color but free)	2	289
Sarah, m. Nathaniell **BECKWITH**, Jan, 20, 1703	LR1	6

www.ingramcontent.com/pod-product-compliance
Lightning Source LLC
Chambersburg PA
CBHW070539270326
41926CB00013B/2151

9780806315447